THEORIES OF LEARNING

THEORIES
OF
LEARNING

114881

A Comparative Approach

George M. Gazda, University of Georgia
Raymond J. Corsini, and Contributors

F. E. PEACOCK PUBLISHERS, INC.
ITASCA, ILLINOIS 60143

To Dr. Edward Ignas

Contributors

ROBERT C. BOLLES, Ph.D., Department of Psychology, University of Washington, Washington

CHARLES I. BROOKS, Ph.D., Department of Psychology, Kings College, Pennsylvania

JOHN G. CARLSON, Ph.D., Department of Psychology, University of Hawaii, Hawaii

A. CHARLES CATANIA, Ph.D., Department of Psychology, University of Maryland Baltimore County, Maryland

GEORGE F. FORMAN, Ph.D., School of Education, University of Massachusetts, Massachusetts

CORNELIUS J. HOLLAND, Ph.D., Department of Psychology, University of Windsor, Ontario

BARRY H. KANTOWITZ, Ph.D., Department of Psychological Sciences, Purdue University, Indiana

AKIRA KOBASIGAWA, Ph.D., Department of Psychology, University of Windsor, Ontario

MARY F. MAPLES, Ph.D., College of Education, University of Nevada, Nevada

DAN G. PERKINS, Ph.D., Department of Psychology, Richland College, Texas

E. JERRY PHARES, Ph.D., Department of Psychology, Kansas State University, Kansas

DONALD ROBBINS, Ph.D., Fordham University at Lincoln Center, New York

HENRY L. ROEDIGER, III, Ph.D., Department of Psychological Sciences, Purdue University, Indiana

JOAN M. WEBSTER, Ph.D., Department of Administration, Grand Rapids Public Schools, Michigan

MICHAEL WERTHEIMER, Ph.D., Department of Psychology, University of Colorado, Colorado

Preface

No TOPIC in psychology is more basic to understanding behavior than *learning*. After all, human behavior is either phylogenetically determined, such as maintenance and reflex behavior, or is learned—and thereby modifiable. The enormous variations of the behavior of humans built on essentially similar physiological foundations are all the result of learning, that is to say, *modifications of the physiological potentialities of individuals*. We learn to be humans. We learn how to act social roles; we learn to survive, to cope and to enhance our lives; we learn to interact with others; we learn attitudes and values; and we even learn how to learn.

Nowadays many believe that all forms of life are contiguous, from the most basic, such as viruses and bacteria, through the most complex, such as birds and mammals. The most commonly accepted hierarchy of animal life has to do with relative intelligence—that is to say, the capacity of organisms to learn, the ability of individuals to adjust to their environment and to adjust their environment to them.

In view of the importance of learning, it should come as no surprise to find that this subtopic of psychology is the single most important area of study of professional psychologists. Practically all fields of application in psychology call for understanding of the theory of learning. Psychotherapy, for example, is primarily a form of learning. Indeed, all human development consists of two functions: *maturation* (physiological development) and *learning* (psychological development).

Practically all human misery or happiness depends on a better understanding of the issue of learning. Such eminently practical problems as how to bring up children, how to have happy marriages, how to prevent wars, and how to make a living are essentially issues of learning.

For all these reasons, learning is of extreme importance to professional psychologists, since it serves as the bedrock of other theories, as the ultimate fundamental conceptualization of human nature: what it is, how it evolves, and how it changes.

Theories of Learning seeks to survey the entire field of learning in a comprehensive, authoritative, compact manner. We see it as *comprehensive* for two reasons: First, we have brought together in this book a dozen major theories of learning; and second, each theory is presented in a uniform manner, since each chapter follows an identical outline. The book's chapters are *authoritative,* written by the best available experts in the various theories. And the presentations are *compact,* because strict limitations were put on the various segments of each chapter, and we, as editors, have critically examined each one for clarity and comprehension within the page limits we imposed on the authors.

The format of this book, in which each of the substantive chapters has the same outline permits the critical reader interested in making comparisons among theories to read the book horizontally, as it were, going "across" similar sections in the various chapters. This is a unique feature of this book for texts on learning, and the student interested in making comparisons among theories will find it quite useful. In addition, the reader is provided with annotated bibliographies to facilitate a more comprehensive follow-up of a particular theory.

One of the major purposes of this book is to bring together the major learning theories in the hope that the student of learning, through juxtaposing concepts, examining arguments, and studying the research evidence, can understand and appreciate the unique contribution of each theory and achieve a more complete understanding of this complex subject. Each of the individuals in this field has pursued steadily a search for the truth, each believing that the theory he or she holds has the most promise for obtaining the truth. From the outside we can see the many truths in the various theories.

A number of friends and colleagues have assisted us in a number of ways which they know best, and it is our pleasure to cite them in alphabetical order: W. Scott McDonald, Eli Meyerson, and Eugene Richman. In addition, Dr. Gazda's secretary, Angie Echols, is appreciated for her help in typing correspondence and xeroxing and collating the manuscript. Finally our wives, Barbara and Kleona, assisted in several ways, from typing and critically reading certain portions of the manuscript to doing our chores while we were occupied with this book. We are especially grateful to all these individuals for their unique contributions and support.

However, major credit for the value of *Theories of Learning* must be given to the authors of the chapters, all busy individuals. Many of them found that adapting to the constraints of a preestablished outline was quite difficult, but all of them, upon understanding the value of a common format, graciously acceded in response to our request.

We trust that this book will help build a firm foundation for those students who want to explore the furthest reaches of the human mind.

GEORGE M. GAZDA
RAYMOND J. CORSINI

Table of Contents

1

Thorndike's Connectionism

MARY F. MAPLES and JOAN M. WEBSTER

INTRODUCTION

Overview

Learning is basic to human existence and fundamental to education. It is the base of operations for the study of psychology and essential to understanding the human mind. Indeed, no other topic in psychology has been as thoroughly researched as that of learning. The problem of learning has concerned students of human behavior from the beginning, and it has been a central concern for such thinkers as Aristotle, St. Augustine, and John Locke (Warren, 1916). Concern with the issues and problems of learning reached a peak during the early 20th century.

What *is* learning? Though it is common to all life, the definition and comprehension of this household term remains controversial. There are many definitions of the term, many theories, and few experts on the topic who agree with other experts.

Learning might be simply defined as modification of behavior through experience. Thorndike (1913b, p. 16) called it "a series of changes in human behavior." In defining the term, we must be careful not to confuse it with progress

or with useful advancement. According to Guthrie and Powers (1952), learning, like all other processes, can be progressive or retrogressive. Not all changes can be called learning. Hilgard and Bower (1975) stress that those changes in human activity that result from maturation or that are native responses should not be viewed as learning. Thus, that a child can stand because he or she has matured sufficiently does not mean that he or she has learned to stand. Neither is it learning if a pupil constricts when light is shone on it; this is a reflex. Anderson and Gates (1950) described learning as a process of adaptation of responses to situations. Gagné (1970) called for consideration to be given to factors that are in large part genetically determined (growth) and those that are due primarily to environmental experiences (learning). Thorpe (1956) considered learning as the process which manifests itself by adaptive changes in individual behavior as a result of experience. In summary, learning can be thought of as a process by which behavior changes as a result of experiences.

Horton and Turnage (1976) separate the history of learning into three eras, the *pre-behavioristic,* the *behavioristic,* and the *contemporary.* The pre-behaviorists

1

began with a philosophical period attributed to John Locke, said to have been the founder of British associationism. Taking exception to Locke's position that the mind is a passive tablet upon which experience is written, Immanuel Kant reestablished an earlier conception that the mind has its own *innate* operations, independent of Locke's empiricism. By innate, Kant meant that the mind has unlearned ways in which it organizes incoming information.

A later period of the prebehavioristic era is represented by Wilhelm Wundt, who founded the experimental laboratory at Leipzig. Wundt is credited with the psychology known as *structuralism*. An integral phase of this new psychology was the emphasis on self-introspection which later affected the psychoanalytic work of Sigmund Freud. Wundt's work also influenced the emerging psychological experiments in the United States and contributed to the development of the *functionalist* school of psychology. During this period, the work on memory and list repetition by Hermann Ebbinghaus (1885/1913) was to play a significant role in the later development of the experiments of Edward L. Thorndike, Clark Hull, Edwin Guthrie, and others. Ebbinghaus provided a systematic and objective approach to the study of human learning when experimental psychology was in its infancy.

Behaviorism, the extreme form of connectionism fathered by John B. Watson (1913), was a result of the influence of Ivan Pavlov (1927), who in turn credited Charles Darwin and Thorndike with having influenced his work. The contributions of Pavlov, Thorndike, and Watson led to further influential work by Hull (1934, 1943), Guthrie (1952), and Edward C. Tolman (1917).

In the contemporary era of human learning, there appears a trend toward greater efforts to map the cognitive and affective capacities of the organism (Chomsky, 1965). Less attention is being paid to the discovery of experimentally produced regularities in the chains of behavioral outcomes and more attention to motivation, contiguity, and reinforcement.

Major Issues

Evaluation in Learning. The era of accountability has brought increased attention to measurement in learning. While in the past it has sufficed for learning theorists to submit hypotheses and then to test them, these processes have led to a broader question: What else is being learned? Sophisticated measuring instruments have been developed, to the extent that many practicing educators are becoming increasingly critical of them and fearful of overtesting.

Nevertheless, evaluation continues to grow as an issue in learning. According to Bigge (1964), the learning evaluation program governs a student's study habits, manner of class interaction, and number and quality of learnings. The evaluation program largely determines whether students will pursue learning on the basis of rote memorization or reflection level. This leads the learning theorist to concentrate more strenuously on the evaluation phase of a theory.

Programmed Instruction and Learning. In a sense, the works of the early behaviorists set the stage for the current emphasis on programmed instruction in learning. Smith and Smith (1974) credit the evolution of programmed learning (i.e., the use of cybernetics) to the early works of Ebbinghaus (1885/1913) and his studies on memory; Thorndike (1913a) and his Law of Effect; Guthrie

(1952) and his contiguity theory; Hull's (1943) reinforcement theory; O. Hobart Mowrer (1950) and his extension of Hull's reinforcement to include contiguity conditioning; and Burrhus F. Skinner (1961), who proposed the introduction of teaching machines in applied fields of education as an educational application of basic reinforcement theory. Smith and Smith also analyze the contributions of early learning theorists to programmed instruction in modern education. The apparent successes in programmed instruction will continue to challenge learning theorists.

Labeling such experts as Skinner, Guthrie, and Thorndike as *behavior technologists,* Horton and Turnage (1976) assign much of the credit for progress in programmed learning to them. The practical and applicable methods utilized by Skinner's (1961) teaching machine are cited by Horton and Turnage as a graphic representation in human learning of Skinner's reinforcement technique.

Meaning and Context. The issues of meaning and context also challenge modern learning theorists. Meaning, or the application of semantics through language, is a problem regularly encountered by proponents of various learning theories. The behaviorists were plagued by the difficulty of describing the meaning of stimulus events, and the classical associationists struggled continuously (and often unsuccessfully) with the meaning of ideas. Language is not the only area of research where meaning is important; it is also a considerable problem in the study of memory.

Context is not totally inseparable from meaning. For example, the meaning of an event, no matter how adequately it may be described or defined, depends entirely upon the context in which the event occurs. Future research in human

learning will be influenced significantly by the methods with which the issues of meaning and context are treated.

Basic Concepts

This chapter explores Edward L. Thorndike's position and contributions to learning from the turn of the century to the 1950s. To understand them it is necessary to consider his concepts as he defined them. They may also be explained in the words of other theorists considered in this text, but Thorndike's experiments brought his own meaning to them. The basic concepts are defined here.

Connectionism. The doctrine that all mental processes consist of the functioning of native and acquired connections between situations and responses is called connectionism. It is also referred to as the original *stimulus-response* (S–R) *bond theory.*

Responses. Muscular, glandular, or any other overt reactions (including images and thoughts) to stimuli by an organism are called responses. Thorndike referred only to overt physiological, observable, measurable reactions as they related behavior to environmental surroundings. In present-day terminology, the word *responses* may be considered to refer to physiological (measurable directly) and psychological (measurable indirectly) reactions.

Stimulation. The term *stimulation* has two meanings: (1) Any external agency (a stimulus) applied to an organism, and (2) any change in an organism which is produced by some external agency.

Law of Readiness. The first of Thorndike's primary laws, the Law of Readiness is an accessory principle which characterizes the circumstances under which a learner tends to be satisfied or annoyed (Thorndike, 1913a, p. 128). These characteristics were paraphrased by Hilgard and Bower (1975, p. 32) as follows:

1. Given the arousal of a strong impulse to a particular action sequence, the smooth carrying out of that sequence is *satisfying*.
2. If that action sequence is thwarted or blocked from being completed, that is *annoying*.
3. If a given action is fatigued (tired out) or satiated, then forcing a further repetition of the act is annoying.

Law of Exercise. The second of the primary laws, the Law of Exercise (Thorndike, 1913b, p. 2), states that when a modifiable connection is made between a situation and a response, its strength is (other things being equal) increased (also referred to as the *Law of Use*). When the modifiable connection is discontinued, the strength is weakened (also referred to as the *Law of Disuse*).

Law of Effect. The third of the primary laws is the Law of Effect. When a modifiable connection between a situation and a response is accompanied by a satisfying state of affairs, that connection is increased. When the connection is accompanied or followed by an annoying state of affairs, its strength is decreased. The strengthening effect on a bond of satisfyingness (or the weakening effect of annoyingness) varies with the closeness between the connection and the bond.

Law of Associative Shifting. If a response is kept intact through a series of changes in the stimulating situation, the response may finally be given to a totally new stimulus. The stimulating situation is changed first by addition, then subtraction, until nothing but the original situation remains (Thorndike, 1913b, pp. 10, 15).

Belongingness. A connection is more easily learned if the response belongs to the situation, and an aftereffect does better if it belongs to the connection it strengthens. The belongingness of a reward or punishment depends on its appropriateness in satisfying an aroused motive or want in the learner (Thorndike, 1932, p. 219).

Spread of Effect. The influence of a rewarding state of affairs acts not only on the connection to which it belongs but on adjacent connections both before and after the reward connection. The effect diminishes with each step that the connection is removed from the rewarded one (Thorndike, 1932, p. 17).

HISTORY

Beginnings

Edward L. Thorndike was born in Williamsburg, Massachusetts, on August 31, 1874. The first of his contributions to the world of learning began to have an impact at the beginning of the 20th century.

Since that time there has developed in America a conviction that psychological research is the cornerstone of scientific education (Pax, 1938). From 1860 to 1890, teacher training had been identified with the study of Pestalozzian ideals and methods of instruction which had been determined as a result of a sympathetic attempt to understand the intricate workings of youthful minds. During the latter part of the 19th century the work of Charles DeGarmo (1898) had contributed to the belief that by application of the principles of psychology to education, a scientific pedagogy could ultimately be realized. The work of Joseph H. Herbart first emphasized the dependence of sound educational procedure on a scientific psychology (Boring, 1929).

At the same time that Herbart's ideas were affecting educational research in the United States, the work of Wilhelm Wundt in Germany was beginning to be recognized by Americans. G. Stanley Hall, a student of Wundt's, established the first psychological research laboratory at Johns Hopkins University in 1883. During the same period, the writings of John Dewey (1910), J. M. Baldwin (1889), G. T. Ladd (1887), and William James (1890) were introducing teachers to the "new" psychology fashioned after the physical sciences, in spirit if not entirely yet in method.

The formal groundwork for Thorndike's research into learning was provided in 1913–14 by publication of his three-volume *Educational Psychology,* which specified his precepts regarding the primary laws of connectionism, those of exercise and effect. These precepts were based on his experimental and statistical investigations. His approach was basically observational and problematic: (1) place the person or animal subject in a problem situation, such as seeking to escape from a confining place (particularly with his animal research), (2) rank the subject's attitudes, (3) choose the correct response among several alternatives (to avoid a mild shock, with animals), (4) observe the behavior, and (5) report it in some quantitative form. One of his very first experiments at Harvard was to be the forerunner of the candy reward system later used with children in operant conditioning experiments.

Unlike the theories of psychologist colleagues with whom he shared many beliefs, Thorndike's educational psychology was not viewed as a social one. Thorndike saw learning as primarily a private experience, an organic undertaking, something that happens under one's skin, in the nervous system. The "connections" of interest to the teacher were essentially those between stimulus and response, not the interactions between individual students when viewing a class of children as a social group.

From the publication of his doctoral dissertation, "Animal Intelligence: An Experimental Study of the Associative Processes in Animals" (1898), to his *Human Nature and the Social Order* (1940), Thorndike's writings have claimed the attention of psychologists and educators throughout the world. He reviewed, researched, and revised his theories hundreds of times during his professional life. These revisions may at times seem to be inconsistencies in this chapter on his theories. But Thorndike himself viewed each change in earlier beliefs as further refinements or gains in knowledge regarding a particular theory, the most significant change being made to his Law of Effect in *The Fundamentals of Learning* (1932). An example of this is his Law of Habit, borrowed from James (Thorndike, 1906), and transformed to Law of Frequency (Thorndike, 1910), to Law of Exercise or Use and Disuse (Thorndike, 1912) and finally, to Law of Effect (Thorndike, 1913a), which was modified extensively in the 1932 work.

While this chapter is concerned with the specifics in Thorndike's theory of connectionism, several related factors should play a role in the drama of Thorndike's contribution to learning. They include the following:

1. Thorndike's mentor, William James of Harvard, had a profound influence on him. Thorndike dedicated to James one of his most ambitious works, *Educational Psychology: The Psychology of Learning* (1913b).

2. Thorndike contributed some of the most significant background research to what was later to be referred to as the *reinforcement theory of learning*. He strongly believed that reward is the key to learning, after rejecting his earlier emphasis on punishment as an equally important key (Pax, 1938).

3. In his animal studies, Thorndike (1910) is credited with two research techniques basic to modern psychological studies of animal behavior: the maze and the problem box.

4. Thorndike was an avowed Darwinist and was convinced that, because of evolutionary continuity, the study of animal behavior is instructive for human psychology. Hence, when he had difficulty in securing human subjects, he switched easily to chickens in his Harvard studies (1898).

5. In reading Thorndike's work, it is important to remember that he believed education to be a science. He wrote: "We conquer the facts of nature when we observe and experiment upon them. When we measure them we have made them our servants" (1913a, p. 164).

Major Theorists

In order to appreciate that there are a number of learning theorists indirectly associated with Thorndike's S–R bond theory, or connectionism, we should recognize that Thorndike was an eclectic learning theorist. Throughout his writings he retained certain elements of Herbartian idea associationism in his thinking, while he was also influenced by the new physiological psychology. As a result, he assumed that there are both physical and mental events or units and that in learning the two are joined in various combinations. Further, if we accept a relationship between S–R bond theory, or connectionism, and other aspects of learning such as reinforcement, contiguity, associationism, behaviorism, drive reduction and conditioning, then certain theorists merit discussion: Watson, Hull, and Guthrie.

John B. Watson (1878–1958).

Give me a dozen healthy infants, well-formed, and my own specified world to bring them up in, and I'll guarantee to take any one at random and train him to become any type of specialist I might select—doctor, lawyer, artist, merchant-chief—regardless of his talents, penchants, tendencies, abilities, vocations and race of his ancestors. (Watson, 1930, p. 65)

This proposal immediately identifies Watson as a classical environmentalist, and it helps confirm his reputation for rugged individualism (Bugelski, 1962).

While Watson was not in concert with all of Thorndike's views, particularly his Law of Effect (Bode, 1929), Thorndike's empirical contributions did have some influence on Watson's work (Horton & Turnage, 1976). Watson is included in this section because of (1) his frequency-recency theory, (2) his contributions as a founder of behaviorism, and (3) his criticism of some of Thorndike's work, such as the Law of Effect and his acceptance of other aspects, such as the Law of Associative Shifting (Bigge, 1964).

Watson's frequency-recency theory was influenced by the work of Pavlov (Bigge, 1964; Horton & Turnage, 1976). His principle of *frequency* states that if several responses are made to a stimulus, the response most frequently made will be retained. The individual, according to Watson, will use a trial-and-error method to find the most successful response. Because it is the most strengthened by virtue of frequency, it will become the most normal response to that situation. His principle of *recency* states that if several responses are made to a problem situation, the one most recently made will be selected. He believed frequency to be the most prepotent of the two response modes.

It was in Watson's acceptance as a pure behaviorist that his work came in conflict with Thorndike's. He was critical of Thorndike's concepts of satisfiers and annoyers. However, the Watsonians accepted Thorndike's Law of Associative Shifting as a keystone for the behavioristic movement of the 1920s (Bigge, 1964).

In brief, the Watsonian behaviorist might be described by a conventional morning greeting exchange: "Good morning, how are you?" "I'm fine, and you?" "Just fine." Such an exchange implies self-introspection; each person looks into self to decide his or her shape. To the behaviorist, this is presumably scientifically impossible. Instead, the two would need to inspect each other, and the proper behaviorist would say: "Good morning, you're fine, how am I?" (Bigge, 1964, p. 210).

Clark L. Hull (1884–1952). Hull can be identified, in a sense, as a neobehaviorist (Watson would be seen as a classical behaviorist). While behaviorism in the midtwenties was an impressive movement in the direction of becoming a theory, it really did not accomplish much more than to establish a foundation or a set of attitudes (Koch, Estes, MacCorquodale, Meehl, Muller, Schoenfeld, & Verplanck, 1954). Hull pro-

vided a basis for continuance in the behaviorist tradition, so to speak.

Hull is considered important to this section because of his (1) extension of Thorndike's Law of Effect to his own Law of Primary Reinforcement; (2) commitment to the use of stimulus and response terms (S/R bond) as the basic conceptual units for the designation of the dependent and independent variables of his theory; (3) taking the Darwinism-Thorndikism approach and converting it into a "systematic theory of learning" (Deese & Hulse, 1967); and (4) contribution to the dilemma caused by the concept of drive reduction.

Hull defined his Law of Primary Reinforcement as follows:

> Whenever a reaction (R) takes place in temporal contiguity with an afferent receptor impulse (S) resulting from the impact upon a receptor of stimulus energy (S_e), and this conjunction is followed in the drive (D), and in the drive receptor discharge (S_D), there will result an increment, $\Delta (S \text{——} R)$, in the tendency for that stimulus on subsequent occasions to evoke that reaction. (1943, p. 71)

Hull's approach to the emerging science of psychology was Newtonian. He described the learning process in postulates and corollaries, and the problem of experimentation in psychology was, to him, the testing of hypotheses by a process of logical deduction from these postulates and corollaries. His work on *habit strength* and *reaction potential* contributed significantly to the empirical work of his successors.

Hull introduced the concepts of *drive* (D) and *drive stimulus* (S_D) in his work on food deprivation and hunger. With the hypothetical construct of drive stimulus, Hull handled the concern of reinforcement delay raised by a pure need-reduction approach to reinforcement. In the rat pressing the lever model, he used food pellets as drive stimulus-reducing objects to solve the problem of delays of reinforcement. The food pellets meet needs and produce quick reductions in the intensity of drive stimuli to give them their reinforcement power.

Edwin R. Guthrie (1886–1959). Another of the neobehaviorists, Guthrie, made contributions which center around his theory of contiguity. Through this theory he was credited, more than any other psychologist, with translating the associationism of the British empiricists into a plausible stimulus-response theory of learning (Smith & Smith, 1974). Guthrie's contiguity principle is that "a combination of stimuli which has accompanied a movement will, in its recurrence, be followed by the movement" (Guthrie, 1952, p. 23). According to Melvin Marx (1972) the contiguity theory asserts that the basis for association is *temporal contiguity,* or closeness in time, between the items to be associated.

Guthrie is included in this section because of his relationship to Thorndike's Law of Effect. He presents in a sense a paradoxical approach to Thorndike's theory, because on the one hand he states that rewards have nothing to do with learning, but on the other hand he says that if rewards are employed successfully, it is only because psychologists do not know how to effect similar results without rewards (Guthrie, 1935). Unquestioned support for Guthrie's views on this topic of reward is not ample nor even available (Bugelski, 1962).

With regard to drive stimuli, Guthrie and Hull tend to hold somewhat opposing views, but in the context of the Miller-Dollard category of strong stimulus drives (Miller & Dollard, 1941), the resemblance between Hull and Guthrie is more clear (Bugelski, 1962). Guthrie and Hull do differ, however, on the physiological effect of drive reduction on learning, in that questions often arise as to the conceptualization of what causes rewards to be reinforcing. Guthrie also had nothing positive to contribute on the use of secondary reinforcers, for which Hull had gained considerable acclaim.

Current Status

Thorndike's theoretical system began with the publication of his doctoral dissertation, "Animal Intelligence" (1898), and his direct impact on learning, psychology, and education continued "for over four decades," culminating in publication of *Human Nature and the Social Order* in 1940. While his influence is still being felt whenever learning is the subject for study, the pendulum is swinging away from the behavioristic concept of humans. The current trend is toward an emphasis on cognitive theory, which continues to gain strength, and an interest in the active nature of information processing. The changes seem to be away from involvement with directly solving the great dilemma of what learning is and toward questions about the complex interaction between experience and the biological structure of the organism. Because modern proponents of learning theory do not subscribe to a single or unitary view of the learning process, they are more open to acceptance that there may be specific theories more appropriate for the various components of the learning process.

To discard Thorndike's theories or principles as outmoded or obsolete would be comparable to constructing a skyscraper without a foundation. It cannot be done. Less emphasis, for example, is being placed today on the traditional associative principles of contiguity, frequency, or effect, but they are undeniably important to all learning, past or future. But learning concepts such as associationism have come to play a different role, perhaps an expanded one, in the sense that they are seen as bridges or pathways; they do not appear to be viewed in terms of the strict stimulus-response bond of Thorndike or the habit of Hull. It is likely that the concept of association will certainly survive in psychological thought, but whether it will be more descriptive and theoretically more neutral than in the past is open to question (Horton & Turnage, 1976).

If criticism can be viewed as a high form of flattery, then Thorndike's influence on present-day research can be considered great. In particular, three elements of his research are of value to contemporary theorists: (1) the Law of Effect as applied to human learning, (2) the questions he posed regarding learning without awareness, and (3) the current interpretations of his principle of the spread of effect. Perhaps the most important aspect of the current status of Thorndike's work is that, whether his theories were correct or incorrect, valuable or invaluable, theoretical only or also practical, his research has inspired all of the major learning theorists since his time to question, to hypothesize, to analyze, and to synthesize in extensive attempts to prove or to disprove his beliefs.

Other Theories

Gestaltism. If we accept the neo-behaviorists or associationists as the fore-runners of contemporary learning theories, then the Gestaltists might be viewed as the second major family. The four leaders in this theory are Max Werthei-mer (1880–1943), Wolfgang Köhler (1887–1967), Kurt Koffka (1886–1941), and Kurt Lewin (1890–1947). Although all were born in Germany, where the theory originated, they immigrated to the United States and brought the theory with them.

The Gestaltists view learning phenomena as closely related to perception. Hence, they define learning in terms of reorganization of the learner's perceptual or psychological world—the learner's field. Although there is no formal translation from German to English of the word *Gestalt,* the nearest meaning is *configuration* (Bigge, 1964).

Gathering a large number of exponents in the midtwenties, Gestalt later became the leading rival to S–R associationism. In testing Thorndike's hypothesis of trial-and-error learning, Koffka wrote *Growth of the Mind* (1925). Lewin took the spirit of Gestalt theory, added some new concepts, and coined a new terminology. His cognitive-field psychology is also referred to as vector or topological psychology. His work is considered by many to be the most advanced and systematic approach to field psychology.

One of the number of major differences between Thorndike's connectionism and Lewin's cognitive-field theory is represented by their attitudes toward the *process* of learning. Thorndike believed all learning to be *incremental,* but the field theorists view learning as *insightful.* There is no meeting of the minds on this issue. The principles developed by the Gestalt school in connection with their notion of insight are significant to the psychology of motor learning. A celebrated contribution to the experimental data gathered in this respect was Köhler's work with chimpanzees (Köhler, 1926).

Robert L. Davis (1935) credited the Gestaltists with providing a fresh impetus to the science of psychology. He believed that they reaffirmed the validity of then-current movements in education such as the integrated curriculum, mental hygiene and the emphasis on a socially integrated personality, and the necessity for creative and purposive responses on the part of the learner.

Estes's Statistical Learning Theory. W. K. Estes's theory is included in this section because he is a current learning theorist who has contemporized Thorndike's and Guthrie's works through his stimulus generalization experiments (Estes, 1956), and because of his unorthodox all-or-none experimental work. Estes extended Guthrie's contiguity theory in a paper entitled *Toward a Statistical Theory of Learning* (1950). Before that, Estes had brought sophistication to the world of learning theory by conducting most of his experiments in the statistical mode. Unlike Hull and Skinner, who viewed probability of response as a theoretical dependent variable in their experiments, Estes considered probabilities to exist in a strictly mathematical sense, being related immediately to the experimentally dependent variables such as the proposition of conditioned responses in a classical conditioning experiment or the proportion of right and left turns in a T–maze.

Guthrie stressed the multiplicity of sources of stimulation acting on an organism in conditioning situations, but he was vague on the method by which the sources combined, suggesting or implying that the components act independently. Later he adopted a pattern theory which reduced somewhat the weakness of his method. Estes adopted an independent component view, or, theoretically speaking, a stimulus element theory in his 1950 paper. More recently he has developed some pattern models for learning. His stimulus sampling model and his response model are described in Chapter 9.

Estes (1960) later developed an experimental procedure, reinforcement test–test (RTT), to evaluate the all-or-none hypothesis. He used a situation involving paired-associates (PA) learning by the recall method, with a single presentation of the pairs followed by the two test trials in succession. Consider, for example, the unlikely situation of two subjects learning a single pair by this method, ignoring for the time being the possible individual learning capacity of the subjects. On the first test trial, assume that the proportion of correct responses is 0.50, one subject being correct while the other was not. In the event that the second interpretation is accurate, both subjects are *equally* likely to be correct on the second test. The all-or-none hypothesis states, however, that no learning has occurred prior to the first correct response. Therefore, the probability of a correct response following an incorrect response should be zero, and barring the element of forgetting between test trials, the probability of two correct responses in succession should be 1.0. The experiment can involve the usual PA situation with multiple pairs and several subjects.

The Drive or Motor-Set Theory. In the theories thus far described, the element of drive or set or attitude may have been implied, but it was not directly considered. What makes the learner strive toward a consummatory response, for example, and how does this striving affect selection and elimination?

A major exponent drive theory is Z. Y. Kuo (1922), who emphasized the determination tendency that keeps the individual persistently achieving throughout learning. He distinguishes between habit fixation and error elimination. The major consideration of Kuo's theory is that a principal response or drive, a purposive goal, impels the learner toward a conclusive response. This theory accounts for the persistence of activity in the individual until the consummatory response is effected or until it is rejected as futile or worthless. Kuo does not deal with selection and elimination.

PROPOSITIONS

1. *The Laws of Readiness, Exercise, and Effect govern all processes in learning.*

Although Thorndike varied in his identification of these three laws over the years, he never minimized their importance. According to Thorndike, the Law of Readiness states that when a conduction unit is in readiness to conduct, to do so is satisfying. When any conduction unit is not ready to conduct, to do so would be annoying, and when a conduction unit is in readiness to conduct, for it *not* to do so is also annoying. The Law of Exercise is comprised of the Laws of Use and Disuse. The Law of Use is as follows: When a modifiable connection is made between a situation and a response, that connection's strength is, other things being equal, increased (Thorndike, 1907, p. 12). The strength of the connection appears to mean that the probability exists that the connection will be made when the situation recurs. Logically, then, the Law of Disuse is defined as follows: When a modifiable connection is not made between a situation and a response during a specified length of time, that connection's strength is decreased (Thorndike, 1907, p. 13).

The Law of Effect, then, is the next step following the Law of Exercise and the most important of all Thorndike's principles. When a modifiable connection between a situation and a response is made and is accompanied or followed by a satisfying state of affairs, that connection's strength is increased. When made and accompanied by an annoying state of affairs, the connection's strength is decreased. Thorndike later discarded in toto the second half of this law (Thorndike, 1932).

Thorndike devoted 15 years to formulation of the three laws, and his subsequent contributions to learning depended upon them for their foundation. His significant work *The Psychology of Learning* (1913b) emphasizes and reemphasizes the Law of Effect. In this second volume of *Educational Psychology,* Thorndike states that:

> A person's intellect, character and skill are the sum of that individual's tendencies to respond to situations and elements of situations. The number of different situation-response connections that made up this sum would, in an educated adult, run well up into the millions. (Thorndike, 1913b, p. 4)

Thorndike originally labeled what he believed to be the essence of discussion and experimentation as *tendencies* and later called them *traits* or *functions.* He devoted this empirical research to the connections and their readiness, exercise, and effect. Later scientists would discuss the experiment with more specifics, such as knowledges, powers, attributes, interests, and skills and their ultimate impact on human learning theories. Thorndike recognized, even in his earliest experiments (1913a, 1913b) that he was conducting very basic and primitive research and that more useful and practical opportunities would come later.

Thorndike's Law of Effect was criticized by some (Sheffield & Jenkins, 1952)) who considered his argument to be circular: If a response probability was engendered, for example, it was said to be due to the presence of a satisfying state of affairs; if it was not engendered, it was claimed that satisfaction was absent. Some believed that this did not really allow for a test of the theory, since the same event—that is, increased or decreased probability of a response—was used to detect *both* learning *and* a satisfying state of affairs.

Conversely, Paul E. Meehl (1950), in defending this theory, demonstrated that once something has been used as a satisfier, it can be used in other situations as a behavior modifier. Meehl described the satisfiers as *transituational* in nature and by that definition preserved the Law of Effect from circularity.

Although Thorndike did not abandon these laws after 1930, he found that they were incomplete, particularly the Law of Effect, and he modified them by adding such elements as "belongingness" (Thorndike, 1932). He also stated that "although reward increases the strength of a connection, punishment or the law of reward has no effect on the strength of the connection" (Thorndike, 1931, p. 212). This finding continues to have implications for today's learning theories, as punishment and its effects are debated in teaching institutions throughout the world.

2. *Learning can be categorized by four types: connection-forming, connection-forming with ideas, analysis or abstraction, and selective thinking or reasoning.*

In Thorndike's hierarchy of learning types, connection forming, which occurs in animal learning, is the lowest form.

Thorndike exemplifies this as a 10-month-old baby learning to beat a drum. The next higher form of learning, connection forming with ideas, may be illustrated by a two-year-old girl thinking of her mother after she hears the word *mother,* or a boy saying the word *candy* when a piece is held before him. Analysis or abstraction is the type of learning that occurs when a student of music is attempting to distinguish various tones or to respond to an overtone in a given sound. Selective thinking or reasoning occurs when a person in school learns the meaning of a sentence in a foreign language by using a knowledge of the rules of grammar and syntax and the meanings of the word roots.

The modern student of learning theory may take exception to Thorndike's simplistic approach. It is perhaps difficult to equate his highest form of learning, that of selective thinking or reasoning, with the intricacies of actions or reactions necessary for scientists to perform mental functions in a complex nuclear age. Nevertheless, few contributions have been made which would support a higher plane or additional steps in his hierarchy of learning.

3. *All learning is incremental.*

In most of his experiments, Thorndike noted a slow time decrease in the solution of various and successive trials. He concluded that learning does not happen all of a sudden but arrives by means of small, systematic steps, and never in huge leaps. Herein, of course, lies one of the basic differences between Thorndike and the Gestaltists. Thorndike did not accept insightful learning, because his experiments did not support learning by insight. The graphs upon which he recorded time and trials would have had to indicate a relative stability in time while the animal was not learning or was in the unlearning state. When the animal gained "insight" into the solving of the problem solution, the line would have dropped immediately and would have remained at that stable low point for the duration of the experiment.

4. *In learning there are certain states of affairs which the subject always welcomes and does nothing to avoid: its satisfiers.*

The bonds that the subject's behavior makes between a situation and its responses will grow stronger when accompanied by satisfying states of affairs. Conversely, annoying situations that result in weaker responses eventually will disappear. In other words, exercise strengthens and disuse weakens bonds in animal learning.

Thorndike initially believed this to be the sum and substance of animal learning but was later to reject the effect of annoyers. On the surface, this theory is impressive because it is supported by substantive experimentation and empirical data. B. F. Skinner, however, later disagreed with the acceptance of satisfiers in animal learning (Skinner, 1953). Although Skinner credited Thorndike's Law of Effect as the most important principle in behavioral development, he took exception to Thorndike's use of the term *satisfying consequences* in animal learning. He responded by substituting his own term, *principle of reinforcement* (Skinner, 1938).

5. *The intellect, character, and skill possessed by any person is the product of certain original tendencies and the training those tendencies have received.*

Thorndike proposed that general human nature is the result of (1) the original nature of the person, (2) the laws of learning, and (3) the forces of nature among which the person lives and learns. He listed and described what he considered to be the original tendencies of humans (1913a) and showed that these tendencies constitute an enormous fund of connections or bonds, of varying degrees of directness and strength, between the situation (furnished by physical forces, plants, animals, and other human behavior) and the responses of which each person is capable. Experimentation led Thorndike to believe that many human tendencies are notably modifiable; and some of them—such as vocalization, manipulation, curiosity, doing something to make something happen, and making a variety of responses to an annoying state of affairs which continues in spite of other responses—are "hot-beds for the growth of learned habits" (Thorndike, 1906, p. 1).

Thorndike does not credit these original tendencies to heredity, and he carefully skirts the issue. However, by implication and by his very avoidance of the issue, he does not imply that the original tendencies were created or born in a vacuum.

6. *Learning is extended by spread of effect.*

In the same way that *belongingness* came into Thorndike's work after 1932 (belongingness here means that a connection between two units or ideas is more readily established if the person perceives the two as belonging together, or going together), a new type of experimental evidence was offered in support of the Law of Effect. Thorndike (1933) described it as the *spread of effect.* His experiments purported to indicate that the influence of a rewarding state of affairs appears to act not only on the connection to which it belongs but on temporarily adjacent connections both before and after the connection that has been rewarded. The spread of the effect is, of course, decreased with the distance by which the connection is removed from the one rewarded.

Tilton (1939) experimented with this principle using the words *right* (reward) and *wrong* (punishment) and the spread of effect. He found the spread to be about the same, using both punishment and reward. Later research on the spread of effect has been discussed by Hilgard and Bower (1966) and more sympathetically by Postman (1962).

7. *All mammals learn in the same manner.*

When Thorndike began to reject reason in learning in favor of direct selection and connection, he also began to insist that all learning, both human and animal, followed the same basic laws. Aside from the feedback through language, which does not affect the learning situation directly, Thorndike found no special methods were needed to explain human learning:

> These simple, semi-mechanical phenomena . . . which animal learning discloses, are the fundamentals of human learning also. They are, of course, much complicated in the more advanced states of human learning, such as the acquisition of skill with the violin, or of knowledge of the calculus, or of inventiveness in engineering. But it is impossible to understand the subtler and more planful learning of cultural men without clear ideas of the forces which make learning possible in its first form of directly connecting some gross bodily response with a situation immediately present to the senses. Moreover, no matter how subtle, complicated and advanced a form of learning one has to explain, these simple facts—the selection of connections by use

and satisfaction and their elimination by disuse and annoyance, multiple reaction, the mind's set as a condition, piecemeal activity of a situation, with prepotency of certain elements in determining the response, response by analogy, and shifting of bonds—will, as a matter of fact, still be the main, and perhaps the only, facts needed to explain it. (1913a, p. 16)

RESEARCH

Background

In examining the various components and examples of Thorndike's animal and human studies, it should be noted that the concept of the S–R bond theory, or the "new" connectionism, finds a useful application in describing habitual actions and the lower forms of learning. But when it extended to cover all forms of learning, it is exposed to the very criticism which Thorndike leveled against the Gestalt theory when he observed: "The term configuration must be made so elastic as to be well-nigh useless" (1913b, p. 128). The attempt to encompass all learning within the situation-response formula has resulted in overemphasis on the overt aspects of behavior modification and distortion of the rational features of the learning process.

In Thorndike's system important differences appear occasionally to be disregarded; activities and properties which rightfully belong to mental functions and mental products are attributed to physical structures and physiological processes; and new concepts are invented to vitalize the psychology from which the mind and most of its powers have been excluded. An example of disregard for important differences is his description of reflexes, instincts, and capacities as classes of unlearned tendencies, to be distinguished on the basis of the definiteness of the response and the simplicity of the situation:

> A reflex denotes a tendency to make a very definite and uniform response to a very simple sensory situation; an instinct, a less definite response to a more complex situation; and a capacity, a very indefinite response to a very complex situation. (1913a, p. 5)

Here a tenuous similarity is stressed and important differences are overlooked in order to support the conclusion that it is more "useful and more scientific" to avoid the idea of hard and fast distinctions between reflexes, instincts, and capacities, "since in fact there is a continuous gradation" (1913a, p. 6).

The assumption that it is scientific to make distinctions only among objects which nature presents to us in separate packages has no support in theory or practice. The psychologist studies behavior in order to understand it, not in order to construct a facsimile. The fact that the three forms of reactive behavior depend on anatomical structures of increasing complexity is important for physiology and is of interest to psychology, but it offers little reason to suppose that no other facts need be considered in explaining the observed phenomena and their functional differences. The correlation between complexity of structure and variability of response is evidence of the mind-body relationship, but the correspondence is not of a kind that enables us to explain function in terms of structure.

Another instance of the disregard for obvious differences by reason of incomplete analysis is found in Thorndike's treatment of the various kinds of learning. As stated in Proposition 2 above, he distinguishes four types of learning: (1) connection forming, the common animal type, (2) association of ideas, (3) analysis or abstraction, and (4) selective thinking or reasoning (1913b, p. 17). Throughout his writings there is a tendency to exaggerate the similarities and minimize the differences among these four types of learning. The higher thought processes are simply more elaborate hierarchies of connections, but the forces behind the processes "are very simple, being the elements in the situation and the connections leading from those elements and various combinations thereof which the past experience and present adjustment of the thinker provide" (Thorndike, 1931, pp. 159–160).

It is particularly in the attempted explanations of thought and reasoning that the supplementary principles are pressed into service. "Whatever else it may be, thought is a series of varied reactions" (Thorndike, 1931, p. 145). Thus comprehension in reading and problem solving in arithmetic are simply matters of the piecemeal activity of the situation and the prepotency of certain elements determining the responses. Lack of understanding and errors in reasoning are ascribed to the underpotency of certain connections, to wrong connections, or to right elements being put in wrong relationships. Variations in the difficulty of tasks are accounted for by the principles of identifiability and availability; that is, by "the qualities in a situation which make it easy to connect something with it, and the qualities in a response which make it easy to connect it with something" (Thorndike, 1931, p. 82). As evidence that the same factors operate also at the lower levels, and that in spite of the contrast, the differences are really not essential, we are reminded that after all, all learning is analytic, and all behavior is selection (Thorndike, 1913b). Also, "there is very little mere connection entirely devoid of organization" (Thorndike, 1931, p. 100), and "selection is the rule rather than the exception in learning, even in the learning of the lower animals" (Thorndike, 1931, p. 145). The radical assumptions hidden in these general statements are easily passed over because of the equivocal use of terms. The foregoing illustrations are necessary to understand fully the conduct and results of experiments by Thorndike.

Methodologies

During his early years at Columbia University, Thorndike concentrated his efforts on informing educators of what was already known of human nature and human variation, as in his *Principles of Teaching Based on Psychology* (1906) and *Education: A First Book* (1912). Increasingly, however, he turned away from efforts to convert teachers to scientific attitudes and from deducing educational proofs from scientific thought. He began instead to direct his efforts toward constructing a new educational psychology—one more consistent with the experimental quantified directions being developed in German research centers. He was also impressed by Darwin's observations of animal behavior, by the methodological controls in the memory studies of Ebbinghaus (1913/1885), and by the statistical inventiveness of Sir Francis Galton (1879). After discussions with Jacques Loeb, Thorndike was convinced that his talent lay in "doing science and that he needed to be shut up and kept at research work" (Joncich, 1968, p. 265).

In devising his own methodologies, Thorndike was influenced by a number of precursors. His experiments regarding the Laws of Frequency, Exercise, or Use and Disuse were researched with

the work of Aristotle (cited in Hett, 1935). In his treatise on memory Aristotle wrote of the rapidity with which we recollect what we frequently think about, and he compared the force of habit with reactions that are rooted in nature itself. Although he did not state just what its function is, Aristotle was aware that frequency is not the sole determiner of associative strength, for he noted the fact that, upon seeing some things only once, we sometimes remember them better than others that we see frequently.

The first laboratory evidence in favor of the Law of Frequency was produced by Ebbinghaus (1913/1885) in his experiments with the memorization of nonsense syllables. From the data of his experiments, Ebbinghaus concluded that forgetting is simply a matter of the fading of impressions. He concluded also that the products of learning are subject to the Law of Disuse as well as the Law of Use.

Thorndike believed that repetition has a direct and immediate influence on the modification of behavior. This belief was strengthened by Pavlov's experiments with the conditioned reflex. Following Watson's (1920) experiments with the emotional responses of infants, which showed similar results to Pavlov's, a number of psychologists were willing to accept the conditioned reflex as a basic form of learning. Applied to concrete classroom teaching and learning outcomes, the conditioned reflex proponents implied that methods of teaching should produce devices that provide for a maximum of drill in all school subjects. The effect of drill in the teaching/learning process remains a controversial current issue in educational psychology today.

In broad terms, these are the trends and methods which combined to establish, in Thorndike's belief, the Law of

Use as a primary principle of learning. The emphasis the empiricists gave to frequency as a factor in association gave the principle some force as a well-established tradition. After James, Thorndike's mentor, had reduced habit and association of ideas to one fundamental Law of Neural Habit, the Law of Exercise was accepted by many as a physiological explanation for all forms of learning. The frequency hypothesis had the advantage of a simple explanation capable of wide application. However, in the first 40 experiments reported by Thorndike in his *The Fundamentals of Learning* (1932), he discovered that mere frequency does not promote learning.

The Law of Exercise. The Law of Exercise is an expanded version of the Laws of Use and Disuse. (See definitions on p.11.)

In his experiments, Thorndike equated mental function with any group of connections; so in his research he referred more to mental functions than to connections. Thorndike (1913b) cites the late 19-century Bryan and Harter study as one of the first and best quantitative studies of improvement in a mental function (or group of connections). The study was a forerunner to the pre-post measurement technique and involved the curves of improvement in receiving and sending telegraphic messages on the mechanical equipment provided.

As evidenced by a series of experiments begun in 1926 and reported in *Fundamentals of Learning* (1932), Thorndike began to attach less importance to the Law of Use but did not completely discard it. "We have shown that the repeated occurrence of a connection, in and of itself, does produce learning in the increased strength of that connection, but that this strengthening is rather slow" (Thorndike, 1932, p. 170).

The frequency/use/exercise hypothesis has tended to emphasize the passivity of the organism. The statement, "We learn by doing," directs attention to the fundamental error of mechanistic theories of learning (Pax, 1938). By itself, this does nothing but generate another question, "By doing what?" As Barton (1922, p. 284) says, "We may just as properly reverse it and say 'we do because we have learned.' "

By 1932 Thorndike believed that the Law of Exercise (or Use, or Frequency) had been generally accepted as a part of orthodox psychology. However, he was not so confident about the Law of Effect.

The Law of Effect. Thorndike explains the Law of Effect as follows:

> When a modifiable connection between a situation and a response is made and accompanied by a satisfying state of affairs, that connection is increased: when made and accompanied or followed by an annoying state of affairs, its strength is decreased. The strengthening effect of satisfyingness (or the weakening effect of annoyingness) upon a bond varies with the closeness of the connection between it and the bond. "Strength" means the same as in the Law of Use. (1913b, p. 5)

The incentives of reward (satisfyingness) and punishment (annoyingness) are by no means new. In Thorndike's time they had been used by schoolmasters for years—the latter perhaps more regularly than the former. The nature of pleasure and pain predate even Plato and Aristotle. While these ancient philosophical beliefs helped to clarify the concept, Thorndike's theory of learning was not feasible prior to the 19th-century discoveries regarding the physiology of the sense organs and the histology of the nervous system.

Herbert Spencer (1896) defended the opinion that the tendency to seek the pleasant and avoid the unpleasant is the product of evolution. In accounting for better habits of adaptation, Spencer proposed a physiological theory which was clarified by Cason (1932) as very similar to the explanation that Thorndike gave to the Law of Effect in 1908.

Alexander Bain is credited with the first definite formulation of a Law of Effect by H. L. Hollingworth (1928). In 1877, Bain wrote:

> The Law of the Will, in its side of greatest potency, is that Pleasure sustains the movement that brings it. The whole force of the mind at the moment goes with the pleasure-giving exercise. . . . So it is with the deepening of an impression, the confirming of a bent or bias, the associating of a couple or a sequence of acts; a coinciding burst of joy awakens the attention and thus leads to an enduring stamp on the mental framework. (Hollingworth, 1928, p. 17)

This "engraining efficiency of the pleasurable motive" is said to be "the best foster-mother of our efforts at learning," and this "moderate exhilaration and cheerfulness growing out of the act of learning itself is certainly the most genial, the most effectual means of cementing the unions that we desire to form in the mind" (Hollingworth, 1928, p. 17). Bain's doctrine with respect to the operation of painful aftereffects reads very much like Thorndike's later explanation of the action of annoyers:

> By the Law of the Will, pain repels us from the thing that causes it. . . . The only way that pain can operate is when it is attached to neglect, or to the want of mental concentration in a given subject; . . . It is in every way inferior to the other motives. . . . (Bain cited in Hollingworth, 1928, p. 18)

The Law of Effect had its beginnings for Thorndike in his research on animal learning. In reporting those studies in 1898, Thorndike held that the animal finally comes to associate the successful response with the situation because resulting pleasure has been "stamped in" that one response, and absence of pleasure has been "stamped out" of all the others.

The phrase *Law of Effect* appeared for the first time in *The Elements of Psychology* (Thorndike, 1907). The factors of satisfaction and discomfort were combined with those of frequency, recency, intensity, duration, and readiness to form a general law of habit formation similar to James's theory. Each of these contributing principles was considered from a double point of view, presenting first the physiological and then the dynamic aspects. Physiologically considered, learning is explained by laws of acquired brain connections; dynamically treated, these become the Laws of Association. In Thorndike's 1907 text, the double statement of the Law of Effect is as follows:

> *Physiological:* Connections between neurones are strengthened every time they are used with indifferent or pleasurable results and weakened every time they are used with resulting discomfort. [Or,] The line of least resistance is, other things being equal, that resulting in the greatest satisfaction to the animal. (p. 166)

> *Dynamic:* Any mental state or act which in a given situation does not produce discomfort becomes associated with that situation, so that when the situation recurs, the mental state or act is more likely than before to recur also; the greater the satisfaction produced by it, the stronger the association. Conversely, [a response] . . . which in a given situation does produce discomfort becomes disconnected from that situation . . . the greater the discomfort produced by it, the weaker the association becomes. (p. 205)

Other than the emphasis on the double aspect of the law, the only development since the first formulation was the statement that the effectiveness of satisfaction and discomfort is in direct proportion to their intensity.

Methods Related to Words and Numbers. Many of Thorndike's experiments were concerned with student learning outcomes in reading and arithmetic, particularly with order and sequence of bonds, or connections, and mental functions (1913a). One experiment dealt with the effectiveness of learning to read with two different methods of introducing a story: (1) word by word and phrase by phrase in isolation, or (2) with an entire story, such as "The Three Bears." Thorndike concluded that the order and sequence of "The Three Bears" allowed a stronger bond connection than words and phrases which were isolated and could not be connected by the child.

A more sophisticated experiment reported in *The Fundamentals of Learning* (1932) concerned pairs of words followed by a two-figure number. He called these three experiments the *adopt series,* the *force series,* and the *bacon series* (Thorndike, 1932, p. 148). Thorndike was attempting to measure the influence of various distributions in time upon the formation of a connection. In the adopt series the numbers and words were scattered with no logical sequence. In the force series, the numbers and words were in sequence. In the bacon series, the pairs were both scattered and in sequence. The greatest score was achieved by the groups in the force series, when the distribution of time between experiments was equal.

Thorndike modified many of the experiments concerned with the Law of Effect in *The Fundamentals of Learning* (1932). He also began to accept the qualities of desires, interests, attitudes, and purposes as having some physiological and psychological influence on the Law of Effect. This acceptance led to experimentation by subsequent researchers with these qualities and the Law of Effect.

Animal Studies

Thorndike's behaviorist learnings began with his studies of cats, dogs, turtles, chickens, and later fish and monkeys at Harvard University in the 1890s. From his earlier studies he concluded:

> There are certain states of affairs which the animal welcomes and does nothing to avoid—its satisfiers. There are others which it is tolerant of and rejects, doing one thing or another until relieved from them. Of the bonds which the animal's behavior makes between a situation and responses, those grow stronger which are accompanied by satisfying states of affairs, while those accompanied by annoyance weaken and disappear. Exercise strengthens and disuse weakens bonds. Such is the sum and substance of the bulk of animal learning. (1913a, p. 11)

From these and other studies, Thorndike determined that there are five characteristics of learning which he considered to be secondary in scope only to the Laws of Readiness, Exercise, and Effect. The first of these principles he calls *multiple response to the same external situation.* By this Thorndike meant that the animal has several alternative ways of responding to the situation:

> Its own inner state changes when jumping at the wall at "B" produces a drop back into the pen, so that it will be less likely to jump again—more likely to chirp and run. Running to "C" and being still confronted with the confining walls may produce an inner state which compels it to turn and run back. So one after another of the responses which, by original nature or previous learning, are produced by the confining walls *plus* the failure of the

useless chirping, jumpings, and runnings, are made. (1913a, p. 12)

The second characteristic or principle of animal learning Thorndike calls the *Law of the Learner's Set* (or attitude or determination or adjustment). The chick, for example, may be in a particular attitude toward an external situation, dependent on its age, hunger, vitality, or sleepiness. The sleepier it is, for example, the less likely it will be motivated to get out or care so much about being penned in. In effect, the response is a product of the attitude of the animal.

Thorndike's experiments with cats led to his determination of what he calls the *Law of Partial Activity*. He found that cats could be taught to respond in a particular way in one situation. When removed to another situation which contained some of the physical elements in the first situation, they would tend to look for some feature—a knob, a crack in the box, a handle—that was present in the earlier situation; hence, the partial, or piecemeal, approach by the cat.

The fourth characteristic he calls the *Law of Assimilation* (or analogy). To any situations which have no original or acquired response of their own, the response made will be that which by original or acquired nature is connected with some situation that they resemble. For S_1 to resemble S_2 means for it to arouse more or less of the sensory neurons which S_1 would arouse, and in more or less the same fashion. For example, if a cat is first placed in a box where it receives its milk from a particular door, when placed in a similar box without the door the cat will, for a period of time, seek out that part of the box where the door was placed in the other box.

The last principle Thorndike determined to be common learning in lower forms of animals he labeled *associative shifting*. He cited simple animal tricks

in response to verbal signals as an example. One holds up a bit of fish before a cat and says, "Stand up." The cat, if not trained otherwise and if hungry enough, will stand up in response to the fish. The response, however, forms bonds, not only with the fish but also with the person giving the command, or in other words, with the total situation. After a sufficient number of treatments, by proper experimenting the fish can be omitted and the other elements in the situation will cause the response. Association is later shifted to the oral signal only.

The application of these principles of animal learning to human learning is significantly more complex. They are all, according to Thorndike, as fundamental to human learning as is the selection of connections by exercise or frequency and their elimination by disuse and annoyance. No matter how subtle, complex, or sophisticated a form of learning, these five simple principles: (1) multiple reaction, (2) mind set as a condition, (3) partial activity of a situation, (4) assimilation or analogy, and (5) response by shifting of connections—may ultimately, according to Thorndike, be the main facts necessary to explain learning in general.

His apparently simple approach notwithstanding, Thorndike developed two techniques that are still used in modern psychological experiments: the maze and the problem box. The latter was used extensively with cats and turtles in determining his five principles. He developed these two techniques for use in the classic study of learning, "Animal Intelligence" (1898). As an avowed Darwinist, Thorndike was convinced that, because of evolutionary continuity, the study of animal behavior was indeed applicable to human behavior and even a precursor of human psychology. In "Animal Intelligence," he severely criticized the uncontrolled observations and casually acquired anecdotal reporting prevalent in what little comparative psychology existed in the last decade of the 19th century. These faulty methods, Thorndike declared, contributed spurious data and led to unwarranted interpretations. He believed that the most serious error was attributing to animals a higher form of intelligence than would be justified by scientific observations of animal behavior.

Human Studies

The four general categories of human learning proposed by Thorndike are: (1) connection forming, (2) connection forming involving ideas, (3) analysis or abstraction, and (4) selective thinking or reasoning (see Proposition 2).

Thorndike's early experiments were tied to his belief that all learning is analytic. He stated in 1913 that the bond being formed never involves absolutely the whole state of affairs or the entire situation of the moment, but only parts of it. A point of clarification must be that within any bond formed there are always minor bonds formed from parts of the situation to parts of the response. Each then has a certain degree of independence, so if a part of the response and a part of the situation occur in a new context, that part of the response has a tendency to occur without old accompaniments.

Thorndike symbolizes a bond in the following manner:

$$S_1 \longrightarrow R_1$$

always requires interpretation as

$$(S_{1a} + S_{1b} + S_{1c} + S_{1d} \ldots S_{1n}) \longrightarrow$$
$$(R_{1a} + R_{1b} + R_{1c} + R_{1d} \ldots R_{1n}).$$

Some of the elements of a situation are eliminated and affect the animal or human, while others are left; of those abstracted for efficacy on learning and future behavior, one will be selected by one neuron group, and another by an alternate. Although these neuron groups coact in making connection with further response to the situation, they do not coact indissolubly as an absolute unit but form preferential bonds.

The experiments which led Thorndike to revise his Law of Effect utilized the translation of Spanish words into English. In the responses the experimenter told the subject "Right" (rewarded response) or "Wrong" (punished response). In at least six separate experiments of this nature, Thorndike concluded that the pronouncement of the punished "Wrong" did not contribute to a weakening of the connections enough to counteract the slight increase in strength gained from the stimulus and response occurring (1932, p. 288).

Thorndike's experiments on the spread of effect was perhaps his most significant contribution to the continuance of contemporary studies of connectionism. Thorndike's firm empirical outcomes have withstood the test of time and trial by his critics.

IMPLICATIONS

Theoretical

While much criticism has been leveled at the work of E. L. Thorndike, it is generally agreed that he was one of the most significant innovators in the field of educational psychology that this country has ever known. Thorndike's prolific contributions to human and animal learning laid the foundation upon which theorists like Hull, Guthrie, Skinner, and Kenneth Spence developed their theories.

During the first part of the 20th century, Thorndike's work played a major role in the evolution of intelligence measurement, the teaching of reading and arithmetic, handwriting, career guidance, and the ancient adage that "practice makes perfect." His Law of Effect stamped Thorndike's name on the minds of all educational psychologists who followed. He provided considerable impetus to his successors with his experiments on transfer of learning. When he developed his Law of Identical Elements, he laid the groundwork for further experiments with transfer. Picking up where Thorndike and other behaviorist-associationists left off, Skinner streamlined Thorndike's Law of Effect with his own extensive experiments on reinforcement.

Thorndike laid to rest traditional theories about classical education and discipline of the mind. He used intelligence tests in the 1920s to study the doctrine of formal or mental discipline. Researching over 12,000 students in secondary school, he observed the transfer effect of studying Latin on their IQ gains in comprehending other school subjects. He concluded that there was no significant different academic growth between those who studied Latin and those who did not. As a result of this study (Thorndike, 1924), the theory of formal or mental discipline should have been laid to final rest. Yet many secondary schools throughout the United States in the 1950s still maintained Latin and Greek in their curriculum programs, without sufficient educational rationale for such a practice. It would be of interest to survey the number of schools still offering the ancient languages in their programs of studies, more than 50 years after this study.

Another significant contribution of Thorndike's which continues to influence educational psychology was his research on the use of punishment in learning.

While the pleasure-pain concept in learning can be traced as far back as Aristotle, it was Thorndike who defined and redefined the theory of punishment and its impact on learning. Thorndike's ability to say he was wrong (Thorndike, 1932) was evident in his later denial of the emphasis on punishment. The element of emotional reaction in the conditioning of the behavior being studied was implied but not directly dealt with in Thorndike's work on the punishment theory in learning. Thorndike's experiments made it evident that punishment has a limited value in the learning process.

While considerable research has been conducted to support or reject Thorndike's primary and secondary Laws of Learning, there are many problems yet to be resolved by present and future research. Thorndike, for example, believed that learning takes place without awareness. Greenspoon (1955) conducted experiments in a classroom setting to record the operant rate of certain types of verbal behavior in the use of reinforcing plural nouns. These experimenters were in fact manipulating the persons speaking to isolate the plural nouns from all other words in their verbal demonstrations. In the manipulation the experimenter said "Yes, that's right" after the person pronounced each plural noun. At the conclusion of the experiment, the persons being tested were asked if they were aware of the purpose and method of the experiment, and their response was negative. Saltz (1971) determined that the problem of learning without awareness was yet unresolved.

According to Robert Bolles (1972), Thorndike's foremost accomplishment was to break down the mentalistic-mechanistic, intelligence-instinct, or man-animal dualism that had had such a hold on psychological thought at the turn of the century. He accomplished this primarily by emphasizing that behavior is different from the mechanisms of the nervous system. After Thorndike's work the basic unit for describing behavior was no longer to be an idea or a nerve cell; rather it was to be an S/R connection.

Practical

As one of the most prominent legacies of Thorndike's educational psychology we have a confused and often contradictory attitude toward unstructured practice or drill. On the one hand, theoretically, we tend to minimize the value of drill; yet, practically, many teachers, coaches, and parents not only accept but promulgate the old maxim that practice makes perfect. While Thorndike redefined the Law of Exercise several times during his productive years, his contribution to the use of drill is often overlooked or even ignored. Too often, educators have sought to use drill as an end in itself. Thorndike's approach suggests that repetition, or practice, should be utilized in learning situations as a prime means to an end—the end being mastery of the subject being taught.

Thorndike and Woodworth (1901) stressed the importance of habits and procedures in "learning how to learn" (p. 258). Students today criticize teachers for attempting to cover too much extraneous material in their subject areas. Teachers, conversely, criticize students for their inability to determine the relevant from the irrelevant in their studies. By following Thorndike and Woodworth's practical suggestions regarding methods and process in the art of studying, today's students might avoid unnecessary frustration and grief. In the 1901 study the authors, on the basis of repeated experimentation, emphasized

the importance of methods and procedures in research on transfer. Regarding content, no subject appeared to have any value over others. While routine drill in science is probably futile, if emphasis is placed on a scientific method of problem solution in real-life situations, the subject will not only be more interesting, but the transfer value will be greatly increased. This statement implies the importance of the teaching process in its assumed partnership with learning, in that the amount of material taught (and learned) is less valuable than *how* it is taught (and learned).

Thorndike early recognized that the average teacher might encounter difficulty in using his primary laws in a classroom setting. What he seemed to be implying was that teaching personnel should know a considerable amount about the laws of teaching and learning before trying to utilize the following considerations in a classroom: (1) ease of identification of the bonds that were to be formed or broken, (2) ease of identifying the states of affairs with students that would be either pleasing or annoying, and (3) ease of application of satisfaction and annoyance at the identified states of affairs (1913b, pp. 213-217). The teacher and the student must agree on the characteristics of good performance in order that practice may be appropriately arranged. Errors need diagnosing so that they are not repeated. There is a constant need for clarity about what is being taught and learned, so that practice will strengthen the right connections and, ultimately, the wrong connections can be eliminated. Simultaneously, necessary connections, unknown to teacher or student, may be weakened by disuse.

A limitation, or perhaps an oversight, of Thorndike's theory was the difficulty of teaching such intangibles as imagination, creativity, forcefulness, and beauty in literature. These were later developed as the affective domain in learning by Benjamin Bloom (1977). The most significant implication on the affective, or feeling, level in learning for which Thorndike can be credited was a section in *The Original Nature of Man* (1913a) known as the *interest* series (pp. 217–226). Thorndike listed five aids to learning which would be cited today as motivational tools (though Thorndike did not label them as such). For improvement in learning, there must be: (1) interest in the work, (2) interest in improvement of performance, (3) significance of the lesson for some goal to the student, (4) problem attitude in which the student is made aware of a need which will be satisfied in learning the lesson, and (5) attentiveness to the work. While these five elements may have been expanded by learning theorists since Thorndike, they remain the basic facets of motivation in any learning situation.

Thorndike provided much of the groundwork inherent in modern research. For example, his hypothesis regarding aftereffects gave impetus to the experiments of Buchwald (1967) and Estes (1960). The hypothesis suggests that S–R–O (stimulus, response, outcome) may be remembered simply because they occurred together (while "belonging"), and that the person's memory of the outcome causes him or her, at the next attempt, to produce the same response or to alter it, according to whether or not the person wants that same outcome again. Buchwald (1967) supported that viewpoint. Thorndike explained his formulation as follows:

> The first of these theories declares that [aftereffects influence connections] by calling up ideas of themselves or of some

equivalents for themselves in the mind. For example, in our experiments in learning to choose the right meaning for a word, the person has these experiences: Seeing word A, response 1, hearing "Wrong"; seeing word A, response 2, hearing "Wrong"; seeing Word A, response 3, hearing "Right." When he next sees word A, any tendency to make response 1 or response 2 calls to his mind some image or memory or ideational equivalent of "Right." So this theory would state. It would further state that such memories or ideas of wrong associated with a tendency must *inhibit* the tendency, and that such memories and ideas of right associated with a tendency must *encourage* it to act, and so preserve and strengthen it. (1931, p. 47)

The above paragraph is indicative of the current theory supported by Estes and Buchwald. Thorndike's influence on the work of Spence (1956) is evident in an additional paragraph:

> In the same way this theory . . . would explain the learning of a cat who came to avoid the exit S at which it received a mild shock and to favor the exit F which led to food, by the supposition that the tendency to approach and enter S calls to the cat's mind some image or idea of the painful shock, whereas the tendency to approach and enter F calls to its mind some representation of the food, and that these representations respectively check and favor these tendencies. (1931, pp. 47-48)

Thorndike's impact on modern learning theory has been lasting and significant. His dogged pursuit of the belief that all learning involves the formation of new connections was a breakthrough in the psychological theories of his time. His introduction of the concept of reinforcement in learning provided the mortar for subsequent building in that area. His laboratory studies of animals gave impetus to the work of past, present, and future psychologists, as did his commitment to the belief that education is a science. All these helped earn him the title of "father of American educational psychology" (Biehler, 1974, p. 207).

SUMMARY

Inquiries in the fields of education and psychology continue to be centered around the how's and why's of the learning process. Modern educational objectives and progress in learning achievement reflect the application by educational psychologists to school procedures of now extant, well-formulated, but still controversial learning theories.

One of the earliest and more controversial of the learning theorists who have contributed so much to present-day practice was Edward L. Thorndike. Often referred to as the father of educational psychology, he is the originator of connectionism in learning. Since the learning process is so complex, no one explanation of its function is acceptable or complete. Thorndike's theory has been described in this chapter as an impetus for those that were to follow. In a real sense, Thorndike opened the floodgates that may ultimately wash away the questions which still exist concerning the nature, processes, and products of human learning.

Thorndike's theory began with the concepts of stimulus and response. He was particularly concerned with the *neural bond*—the synaptic connection between the neurons which complete the stimulus-response circuit. Basically, Thorndike was interested in the physiological bases of learning. His earliest experiments dealt with animal learning, but he was convinced that human learning could be explained in an almost identical manner—at least at the lower levels. According to his connectionism theory, learning consists of the completion of neural bonds or circuits.

Thorndike introduced, as outcomes of his experimentation, three primary laws of learning explained earlier in this chapter: the Law of Readiness, the Law of Exercise, and the Law of Effect. He also determined five subsidiary laws of learning: the Law of Multiple Response; the Law of Attitude, Disposition, or Set; the Law of Partial Activity; the Law of Assimilation or Analogy; and the Law of Associative Shifting.

The promulgation of the theory of connectionism heralded considerable experimentation which resulted in several of the other learning theories discussed in this text. Since connectionism seemed only to consider hypotheses regarding the physiological aspect of the learning process, many subsequent studies were directed at the discovery of other aspects. For a time, Thorndike's hypotheses were discredited by some psychologists, and the controversy has been renewed by the current emphasis on developmental, affective, or humanistic education (Bloom, 1977; Gazda, 1976; Krathwohl, Bloom, & Masia, 1964; Read & Simon, 1975). Thorndike's theory can be tolerated best by this group of theorists if they can accept their hypotheses as providing the necessary "missing link" to the work of Thorndike, Hull, Guthrie, Skinner and perhaps also to the theories of the cognitive-field theorists.

There can be no doubt of the contribution made by Thorndike to modern learning. While no teacher in a classroom today might be readily identified as a Thorndikean practitioner, very few would practice the art of teaching without utilizing Thorndike's laws.

ANNOTATED BIBLIOGRAPHY

Bigge, M. L. *Learning theories for teachers.* New York: Harper & Row, 1964.

This text is of value to the practitioner as a brief course in learning theories. Particular attention is paid to comparisons among various contributors to modern learning.

Joncich, G. *The sane positivist: A biography of Edward L. Thorndike.* Middletown, Conn.: Wesleyan University Press, 1968.

This is one of the most sympathetic and humanistic approaches to the life and work of Edward L. "Ned" Thorndike. A serious student would benefit from reading this sensitive treatment of Thorndike as a person before delving into his research and theories.

Pax, W. *A critical study of Thorndike's theory and laws of learning.* Unpublished doctoral dissertation, Catholic University of America, 1938.

This treatise was written during the height of Thorndike's influence and, simultaneously, the height of criticism against his work. It highlights the experimentation which was contemporary and valuable at the time, but which, while still valuable, has lost its impact with the passage of years.

Thorndike, E. L. *Educational psychology* (Vol. 2). *The original nature of man* (Vol. 1) and *The psychology of learning* (Vol. 2). New York: Teachers College Press, 1913.

These two volumes, part of a three-volume publication, contain the sum and substance of all of Thorndike's research during a 20-year period. They are not lightly written and it is easy to lose interest in the unending experiments, but these volumes are testimony to Thorndike's unwavering persistence in arriving at solutions to learning problems.

Thorndike, E. L. *The fundamentals of learning.* New York: Teachers College Press, 1932.

Written approximately 20 years after the three-volume publication *Educational Psychology,* in this text Thorndike "amends" many of his earlier theories and discusses supportive accompanying research.

REFERENCES

Anderson, G. L., & Gates, A. I. The general nature of learning. In *49th Yearbook of the National Society for the Study of Education.* Chicago: University of Chicago Press, 1950.

Bain, A. Education as a science. *Mind,* 1887, *2,* 201–210.

Bain, A. *The emotions and the will.* Boston: Appleton Press, 1888.

Baldwin, J. M. *Handbook of psychology: Senses and intellect.* New York: H. Holt, 1889.

Barton, W. J. Repetition vs. other factors in learning. *Pedagogical Seminar,* 1922, *29,* 216–228.

Biehler, R. F. *Psychology applied to teaching* (2nd ed.). Boston: Houghton Mifflin, 1974.

Bigge, M. L. *Learning theories for teachers.* New York: Harper & Row, 1964.

Bloom, B. A. Affective outcomes of schooling. *Phi Delta Kappan,* 1977, *3,* 59, 193–198.

Bode, B. H. *Conflicting psychologies of learning.* New York: Heath, 1929.

Bolles, R. C. The avoidance learning problem. In G. H. Bower (Ed.), *The psychology of learning and motivation: Advances in research and theory* (Vol. 6). New York: Academic Press, 1972.

Boring, E. G. *A history of experimental psychology.* New York: Century Press, 1929.

Buchwald, A. M. Effects of immediate vs. delayed outcomes in associative learning. *Journal of Verbal Learning and Verbal Behavior,* 1967, *6,* 317–320.

Buchwald, A. M. Effects of "right" and "wrong" on subsequent behavior: A new interpretation. *Psychological Review,* 1969, *76,* 132–143.

Bugelski, T. *The psychology of learning.* New York: Holt, Rinehart & Winston, 1962.

Cason, H. The learning and retention of pleasant and unpleasant activities. *Archives of Psychology,* 1932, *21,* 121–125.

Chomsky, N. *Aspects of the theory of syntax.* Cambridge: M.I.T. Press, 1965.

Davis, R. L. *The integrated curriculum: Innovation for instruction.* Unpublished doctoral dissertation, University of Chicago, 1935.

Deese, J., & Hulse, S. H. *The psychology of learning.* New York: McGraw-Hill, 1967.

DeGarmo, C. Psychology and education by Hugo Munsterberg. *Psychological Review,* 1898, *5,* 179–185.

Dewey, J. *The influence of Darwin on philosophy and other essays.* New York: Henry Holt, 1910.

Dollard, J., & Miller, N. E. *Personality and psychotherapy: An analysis in terms of learning, thinking, and culture.* New York: McGraw-Hill, 1950.

Ebbinghaus, H. [*Memory*] (H. A. Ruger and C. E. Busenius, Eds. and trans.). New York: Teachers College Press, 1913. (Originally published 1885.)

Estes, W. K. Toward a statistical theory of learning. *Psychological Review,* 1950, *57,* 94–107.

Estes, W. K. Learning. *Annual Review of Psychology,* 1956, *1,* 1–38.

Estes, W. K. Research and theory on the learning of probabilities. *Journal of the American Statistical Association,* 1960, *67,* 81–102.

Gagné, Robert. *The conditions of learning* (Rev. ed.). New York: Holt, Rinehart, & Winston, 1970.

Galton, F. Psychometric experiments. *Brain,* 1879, *2,* 18–25.

Gazda, G. M. Developmental education: The conceptual framework for the components of a comprehensive counseling and guidance program. *Guidance Personnel 1984* (CPGA Monograph, No. 3). Fullerton, Cal.: California Personnel and Guidance Association, 1976.

Greenspoon, J. The reinforcing effect of two spoken sounds on the frequency of two responses. *American Journal of Psychology,* 1955, *68,* 409–416.

Guthrie, E. R. *The psychology of learning.* New York: Harper, 1935.

Guthrie, E. R., & Powers, F. F. *Educational psychology.* New York: Ronald Press, 1952.

Hett, J. W. *Memory* (Ed. and trans.). New York: Scribner's, 1935.

Hilgard, E. R., & Bower, G. H. *Theories of learning* (3rd ed.). Englewood Cliffs, N.J.: Prentice-Hall, 1966.

Hilgard, E. R., & Bower, G. H. *Theories of learning* (4th ed.). Englewood Cliffs, N.J.: Prentice-Hall, 1975.

Hollingworth, H. L. *Psychology: Its facts and principles.* Boston: Appleton Press, 1928.

Horton, D. L., & Turnage, T. W. *Human learning.* Englewood Cliffs, N.J.: Prentice-Hall, 1976.

Hull, C. L. *Learning II.* The factor of the conditioned reflex. In C. Murchison (Ed.), *A handbook of general experimental psychology.* Worcester, Mass.: Clark University Press, 1934.

Hull, C. L. *Principles of behavior: An introduction to behavior theory.* New York: Appleton-Century-Crofts, 1943.

James, W. *The principles of psychology* (Vol. 2). New York: Holt & Co., 1890.

Joncich, G. *The sane positivist: A biography of Edward L. Thorndike.* Middletown, Conn.: Wesleyan University Press, 1968.

Koch, S., Estes, W. K., MacCorquodale, K., Meehl, P. E., Muller, C. G., Schoenfeld, W. N., & Verplanck, W. S. *Clark L. Hull in modern learning theory.* New York: Appleton-Century-Crofts, 1954.

Koffka, K. *The growth of the mind.* New York: Harcourt-Brace, 1925.

Kohler, W. *Mentality of apes.* New York: Harcourt-Brace, 1926.

Krathwohl, D. R., Bloom, B. S., & Masia, B. B. *Taxonomy of educational objectives: The classification of educational objectives. Handbook II: Affective domain.* New York: David McKay, 1964.

Kuo, Z. Y. The nature of unsuccessful acts and their order of elimination in learning. *Journal of Comparative Psychology,* 1922, *2,* 1-27.

Ladd, G. T. *Elements of physiological psychology.* Boston: Scribner's, 1887.

Marx, M. H. *Theories in contemporary psychology* (2nd ed.). New York: Macmillan, 1972.

Meehl, P. E. On the circularity of the law of effect. *Psychological Bulletin,* 1950, *47,* 42–47.

Miller, N. E., & Dollard, J. *Social learning and imitation.* New Haven, Conn.: Yale University Press, 1941.

Mowrer, O. H. *Learning theory and personality dynamics.* New York: Ronald Press, 1950.

Pavlov, I. P. Conditional reflexes (G. V.

Anrep, trans.). New York: Oxford University Press, 1927.

Pax, W. *A critical study of Thorndike's theory and laws of learning.* Unpublished doctoral dissertation, Catholic University of America, 1938.

Postman, L. Rewards and punishment in human learning. *Psychology in the making.* New York: Alfred A. Knopf, 1962.

Read, D. A., & Simon, S. B. *Humanistic education sourcebook.* Englewood Cliffs, N.J.: Prentice-Hall, 1975.

Saltz, E. *The cognitive bases of human learning.* Homewood, Ill.: Dorsey Press, 1971.

Sheffield, F. D., & Jenkins, W. L. Level of repetition in the spread of effect. *Journal of Experimental Psychology,* 1952, *44,* 101–107.

Skinner, B. F. *The behavior of organisms: An experimental analysis.* New York: Appleton-Century-Crofts, 1938.

Skinner, B. F. *Science and human behavior.* New York: Macmillan, 1953.

Skinner, B. F. *Cumulative record* (3rd ed.). Englewood Cliffs, N.J.: Prentice-Hall, 1961.

Smith, K. V., & Smith, M. F. *Cybernetic principles of learning and educational design.* New York: Holt, Rinehart & Winston, 1974.

Spence, K. W. *Behavior theory and conditioning.* New Haven, Conn.: Yale University Press, 1956.

Spencer, H. *The principles of psychology.* Boston: Appleton Press, 1896.

Thorndike, E. L. Animal intelligence: An experimental study of the associative processes in animals. *The Psychological Review Monograph Supplements,* 1898, *2,* 4–160.

Thorndike, E. L. *Principles of teaching based on psychology.* New York: A. G. Seiler, 1906.

Thorndike, E. L. *The elements of psychology.* New York: A. G. Seiler, 1907.

Thorndike, E. L. Darwin's contribution to psychology. *University of California Chronicle,* 1910, *12,* 112–116.

Thorndike, E. L. *Education: A first book.* New York: Macmillan, 1912.

Thorndike, E. L. *Educational psychology: The original nature of man* (Vol. 1). New York: Teachers College Press, 1913. (a)

Thorndike, E. L. *Educational psychology: The psychology of learning* (Vol. 2). New York: Teachers College Press, 1913. (b)

Thorndike, E. L. Mental discipline in high school studies. *Journal of Educational Psychology,* 1924, *15,* 1–22; 83–98.

Thorndike, E. L. *Human learning.* New York: Century Press, 1931.

Thorndike, E. L. *The fundamentals of learning.* New York: Teachers College Press, 1932.

Thorndike, E. L. A proof of the law of effect. *Science,* 1933, *77,* 75–79.

Thorndike, E. L. *Human nature and the social order.* New York: Macmillan, 1940.

Thorndike, E. L., & Woodworth, R. S. The influence of improvement in one mental function upon the efficiency of other functions. *Psychological Review,* 1901, *8,* 247–261.

Thorpe, W. H. *Learning and instinct in animals.* London: Methuen, 1956.

Tilton, J. W. The effect of right and wrong upon the learning of nonsense syllables in multiple-choice arrangements. *Journal of Educational Psychology,* 1939, *30,* 95–115.

Tolman, E. C. Retroactive inhibition as affected by conditions of learning. *Psychological Monographs,* 1917, 25–107.

Warren, H. C. Mental association from Plato to Hume. *Psychological Review,* 1916, *23,* 208–238.

Watson, J. B. Psychology as the behaviorist sees it. *Psychological Review,* 1913, *20,* 113–116.

Watson, J. B. Conditional emotional reactions. *Journal of Experimental Psychology,* 1920, *3,* 62–82.

Watson, J. B. *Behaviorism* (Rev. ed.). New York: Norton, 1930.

2

Classical Conditioning: Pavlov

DAN G. PERKINS

I dreamed of finding happiness in intellectual work, in science—and I found it.

Pavlov (cited in Cuny, 1962, p. 160).

INTRODUCTION

Overview

Why are people the way they are? Asked this question, a contemporary social scientist might respond that people are a combination of their genetic endowment and what has happened to that genetic material since conception. Much of what has "happened" to you since conception involves a complex interplay with your environment and is subsumed under the general division of knowledge known as *learning*.

Most human behavior is learned. To fully grasp the extent to which learning has influenced your life, imagine that one morning when you awaken all prior learning has been obliterated, and you have returned to what John Locke called the *tabula rasa* (blank slate).

Assuming a clock radio gives you your usual cue to arise, the radio comes on and the announcer is discussing the news of the day. Though you awaken, you lack comprehension of the sounds. Comprehension requires previous experience with language and storage in memory of language mediational units against which you match incoming sounds. Additionally, the behavior of getting out of bed to the radio cue is unknown to you. Once out of bed you are able to walk (walking is thought to be largely maturational but may also involve imitative aspects in humans) but you have trouble moving around, since certain aspects of perception are learned. You pause for a moment to peer at a picture of yourself, but since a picture depicts a three-dimensional object on a two-dimensional surface and you have not learned to "put in" the third dimension, you are unable to perceive the figure before you. You do not dress yourself, since dressing is a habit learned from the culture, and you find that you do not have bladder and bowel control, since humans are, after all, toilet trained. Additionally, you are unkempt but are not the least bit concerned about it, as good grooming is a learned value and grooming skills are largely learned behaviors.

Certainly much of what constitutes "you" is attributable to learning. You have learned many complex and diverse tasks which range from tying your shoes

29

to operating an automobile. Through the process of learning, you have acquired goals and values as well as your particular life-style of generally being tense or relaxed.

It is hardly possible to mention the subject of learning—especially conditioned reflexes—without thinking of the distinguished Russian physiologist, Ivan Petrovich Pavlov (1849–1936). *Pavlovian conditioning* is also known as *respondent conditioning* and *classical conditioning*. It is worthwhile to remember that these three names are essentially equivalent terms. To further complicate nomenclature, Burrhus F. Skinner (1937) has used the term *Type S Learning* to designate the form of learning studied by Pavlov.

Though Pavlov won the Nobel Prize in 1904 for his work on the digestive system, he is perhaps best known for his later experiments with dogs, in which he rang a bell that had previously been associated with meat powder and eventually conditioned the dogs to salivate to the sound of the bell. Few of us realize how this form of learning operates in our everyday life. Think for a few moments about your favorite food, focusing on the aspects of that dish that you like best. Try to imagine that you are eating your favorite meal and that it tastes as delicious as you have ever known it to be. There is a good chance that saliva has begun to flow before you finished reading the previous sentence—especially if you are hungry—yet you have not tasted a single morsel of your favorite dish. The flow of the saliva must depend on your earlier experience with your favorite dish, and the thought of your favorite food has produced an effect (salivation) very much like the salivary response that occurs in the actual presence of the dish.

Laboratory-type learning is ordinarily divided into two parts: classical (the subject of this chapter) and operant or instrumental learning. Clarifications are called for. In classical learning, the type that Pavlov investigated, an organism has a natural or unconditioned reaction to some stimulus: That is, when a hungry dog is presented with the sight of food (unconditioned stimulus or US) he begins to salivate (unconditioned response or UR). If the sound of a bell is now associated with the presentation of food, after a while the sound of the bell (conditioned stimulus or CS) alone will produce salivation (conditioned response or CR). In short, the dog has learned to respond to a previously neutral stimulus (the bell) as though it were the natural stimulus (the food).

Instrumental or operant learning, on the other hand, operates as follows: The organism, in moving about randomly, does something (such as press a lever) which in turn does something else, such as produce food. After a while the *instrumental* behavior is influenced by its consequences. So, if lever A produces food and lever B does not, the organism learns to operate lever A.

Some people think that all learning can be subsumed under these two headings, classical and operant (instrumental) learning.

Major Issues

A continuing debate has existed over whether classical and instrumental conditioning are governed by different laws of learning (Hearst, 1975). Historical attempts to answer this question have focused on the investigation of conditionable responses thought to be unique to the specific process. For example, instrumental conditioning was thought to explain voluntary responses, while classical conditioning was used to describe reflexive responses. A second distinction sometimes made was that classical conditioning involves autonomic responses, while instrumental conditioning governs skeletal motor behavior. Evidence in support of the forementioned dichotomies is not convincing. Are there two types of learning or one? This question is still unanswered, but a new tack to probe it was taken in Rescorla and Solomon (1967) by examining the interaction of classical and instrumental conditioning.

Another major issue in classical conditioning focuses on specifying the characteristics of the conditioned response. Wickens (1939) showed that the topography of conditioned responses differs from voluntary responses in both persistence and latency. This distinction is especially crucial in experiments such as human eyelid conditioning, since the response can be either voluntary or involuntary. Another confounding factor that can obscure the true conditioned response is *pseudoconditioning*—a response given, at times, in the absence of conditioning procedures.

What relationships between events must take place for learning to occur? Contiguity in time has been the historical answer (Hull, 1943; Pavlov, 1927), but more recent examinations of the problem (Rescorla, 1972) suggest that contiguity alone is insufficient to produce conditioning. Additionally, the conditioned stimulus appears to need to provide relevant information to the organism which lets it know that attention to the conditioned stimulus will eventuate in a worthwhile consequence.

Other major issues that confront the investigator in the field of classical conditioning focus on such variables as the optimal time interval between the conditioned stimulus and the unconditioned stimulus or the effect of different intensities and durations of the unconditioned stimulus to achieve learning. Likewise, the specific effect of different intensities of the conditioned stimulus in producing results is currently an issue (Champion, 1962).

Another major issue in classical conditioning research is understanding what happens during the *inhibition process,* when a conditioned response operates to inhibit or to prevent the occurrence of a response. Also of current interest to learning theorists is the area of *introceptive conditioning,* which has shown that a variety of bodily functions such as heart rate, blood pressure, and urine formation can be influenced by classical conditioning procedures (see, e.g., Fredrikson & Ohman, 1979). Even cortical neurons may be conditionable (O'Brien, Wilder, & Stevens, 1977).

While it was previously believed by some learning theorists that almost any system inside or outside an organism's body that moved, squirted, or secreted could be conditioned according to the laws of learning, this is now a questionable assumption. Research in an area called *constraints of learning* indicates that the biological predisposition of the organism seems to overrule or to negate certain responses. A phenomenon called *bait-shyness* is a conditioned aversion to a substance designed to make the organism temporarily sick. Because an extended period of time elapses between the ingestion of the substance and the experience of being sick, bait-shyness appears to violate the temporal laws of learning as presently understood. Neither of these topics—constraints on learning or bait-shyness—fits neatly into the current models of classical conditioning, which means that the current models may need to be changed to accommodate these concepts.

Pavlov called the ability to use language the *second signal system,* and he believed it was an important factor in human learning. A spin-off of this observation in current Pavlovian research is *semantic generalization,* which examines such things as how language develops (Luria, 1961) and how language generalization occurs. For example, prejudice toward minority groups appears in many individuals who lack personal experience with such groups, indicating that verbal associations transfer from one person to another. Though this is understood on a molar level, the exact mechanisms underlying this generalization process are not understood, and they are currently the topics of research.

A final major issue in classical conditioning research focuses on how abnormal behavior develops and what can be done to eliminate it. It was in Pavlov's laboratory that *experimental neurosis* was produced in a dog; and Pavlov, in his later years, became quite interested in psychiatric problems. Sleep therapy developed by the Russians was based on Pavlovian principles. The idea was that when an individual is flooded by too much stimulation the individual begins to shut out such stimulation through a mechanism called *protective inhibition.* Sleep therapy, then, is a method of reducing the overstimulation and presumably assisting the person to regain equilibrium (Gantt, 1965).

Though sleep therapy as a specific mode of treatment did not catch on in America, many therapeutic procedures based on Pavlovian conditioning are currently in use. These are collectively known as *behavior therapy.* However, because "behavior therapy" has many other procedures, it needs to be said that Pavlovian procedures are only part of behavior therapy.

Basic Concepts

Unconditioned Stimulus. Abbreviated as either US or UCS, this is any potent stimulus which evokes a regular unlearned response. Pavlov used food powder as an unconditioned stimulus which had the predictable effect of reliably producing the reflexive response of salivation, over which the dog had no control.

Unconditioned Response. Abbreviated either UR or UCR, this is a response reliably and naturally elicited by the presentation of the US. The UR is usually viewed as a highly reflexive response which follows the presentation of the US. Common examples of UR's are eyeblinks to a puff of air, knee jerks after receiving a tap to the patellar tendon, and salivation to food.

Conditioned Stimulus. Abbreviated CS, this is the stimulus, initially "neutral," which through its presentation prior to (or at the same time as) the unconditioned stimulus comes to produce the conditioned response, or CR. An important feature of the conditioned stimulus is that it must be an event within the sensory range of the organism being conditioned. Another important feature of the CS is that it should not, prior to conditioning, have any response-producing properties. That is, when this signal occurs there should be no discernible difference in the about-to-be conditioned organism to give evidence that the event is in fact a *neutral stimulus.* Some *neutral stimuli* which are to be used as conditioned stimuli have attention-getting properties for the organism; this has been termed the *orienting reflex* by Robert Hinde (1970). Since they do not produce a response which resembles the about-to-be conditioned response such as salivation, they are still considered neutral.

Conditioned Response. Abbreviated CR, this is the new learned reflex which comes about as the result of pairing of the CS with the US. *An essential feature of Pavlovian conditioning is the pairing of the CS with the US.* The conditioned response (CR) is not exactly the same as the unconditioned response (UR), and this response may vary in terms of its strength or amplitude or duration or latency. More specifically, the time between the onset of the conditioned stimulus and occurrence of the conditioned response may be longer or shorter than the interval between the onset of the unconditioned stimulus and the occurrence of the unconditioned response. Conditioned responses are sometimes described as preparatory, since they prepare the organism for the arrival of the US.

Excitation and Inhibition. In Pavlovian learning, this simply means that when a previously neutral stimulus has been paired with the unconditioned stimulus and has become a conditioned stimulus, it has developed *excitatory* properties, since it is capable of eliciting the conditioned response.

The principle of excitation is contrasted with the principle of inhibition, which occurs after a previously conditioned stimulus fails to be followed by the unconditioned stimulus and extinction occurs. It is generally believed that the previously conditioned stimulus has not been lost or forgotten, but instead the organism comes to inhibit actively the conditioned response when the conditioned stimulus is presented.

Though inhibition is seen externally as inactivity on the part of the organism, many investigators believe it is one of the most interesting aspects of conditioning, since the organism has, in a sense, learned to "shut off" sensory inputs which have not eventuated in reinforcement.

Stimulus Generalization. At the early stages of the conditioning, organisms may respond in essentially the same way to a variety of stimuli. For example, a dog might salivate to tones of several pitches similar to the one to which conditioning is occurring. The dog does not discriminate between tones at the early stages of conditioning; instead, there's a spreading effect in which the dog responds unselectively to many stimuli similar in nature. This is referred to as *stimulus generalization.* A human example of this phenomenon would be that an individual, after having been stung by a bee, views all insects as capable of producing pain.

In laboratory experiments, typically organisms initially respond in similar ways to stimuli that are somewhat like the original conditioned stimulus. In time their responding becomes more and more selective and they respond maximally to the conditioned stimulus and to a lesser degree to stimuli that are similar in nature. Generally, it can be said that the more other stimuli are similar to the conditioned stimulus, the greater the probability that they will produce the conditioned response.

Discrimination. As the conditioning process begins to take place, the organism learns to discriminate between relevant and irrelevant stimuli. Through discrimination the organism selectively responds to specific stimuli and fails to respond or simply inhibits a response to unreinforced stimuli. Conditioning can be conceptualized as a process in which discrimination and inhibition ultimately win out over a more generalized response, and therefore these processes are in direct opposition to a generalized response.

Generally, it has been found that the more distinguishable a specific signal, the more quickly it can be identified and attended to by the organism, and therefore the more quickly it can be learned.

Extinction. Since it is necessary for organisms to learn connections between reinforcing events and their environment and appropriate ways to respond to those events, it is also necessary for them to cease responding to stimuli no longer capable of providing reinforcement. Extinction of a response is the name given to this phenomenon. Extinction simply means that when the conditioned stimulus is presented repeatedly and is not followed by the unconditioned stimulus, responding eventually stops.

HISTORY

Beginnings

Ivan Pavlov, born September 14, 1849, was the son of a Russian priest. He attended church school and later went on to a theological seminary in preparation for the priesthood. A good student, he nevertheless frequently received low marks on "deportment." As he was nearing the end of his work at the theological seminary he became interested in the digestive system and began to wonder how it worked. A drawing of the digestive system in George Henry Lewis's *The Physiology of Common Life* (1860) changed Pavlov's life; he gave up the idea of becoming a priest and began his training in science.

After studying at the University of St. Petersburg he entered the Military Medical Academy to become a surgeon-experimenter. While there he published his first paper, on how cardiac nerves affect cardiac muscles. This important scientific work was instrumental in earning Pavlov the degree of Doctor of Medicine. Later Pavlov developed a process that made it possible to follow digestion in living organisms without causing nerve damage. For this contribution Pavlov was awarded the Nobel Prize in 1904. During the Russian Revolution, Pavlov fell upon hard times but continued to work in his laboratory, even though he sometimes worked without the benefit of heat. In his later life, the brain became the focus of his interests, and much of his effort was devoted to trying to understand its activity.

Pavlov had a wide variety of interests such as literature, science, and philosophy. His library contained hundreds of volumes. He also collected stamps, had a herbarium, loved music and gardening, and was an avid swimmer during the summer months. Pavlov followed a rigid, measured schedule while always remaining active and energetic. Throughout his life he maintained a dedication to research and encouraged dissent from his peers and colleagues. One of the ways that Pavlov promoted feedback on his ideas was to meditate aloud, thinking through what he was currently working on in the presence of his colleagues.

Pavlov was the director of the physiological laboratory at the Institute for Experimental Medicine in St. Petersburg from 1890 until his death in 1936. In the course of his work on the digestive system, he devised an apparatus which allowed him to monitor directly the amount of saliva secreted by dogs when food had been placed in their mouths. Around 1902 Pavlov noticed that the dogs used in the experiments actually began to salivate at the sight of the at-

Figure 2.1
Pavlov's Dog in Apparatus for Experiment

tendant who usually brought food, or even to the sound of his footsteps before the food actually reached their mouths. This important observation was to have tremendous influence on the development of the field of scientific psychology. Pavlov realized that the sight of the attendant was not the natural stimulus for the salivary reflex, but the attendant had come, through experience, to be a cue to the dog that food was coming. He was quick to recognize that he had happened upon a phenomenon that must be of immense importance in assisting the organism in adapting to its environment, and, additionally, he saw in his new-found discovery a method to study the brain while leaving it intact.

Initially, Pavlov named the newly discovered reflexes "psychic secretions" but later changed to the term *conditioned reflex,* to avoid implications about the dogs' mental life. Actually, conditioned reflex represents somewhat of a translation error from Russian to English. A more accurate translation would have been condition*al* reflexes, indicating that

the reflex is found only under certain conditions and is conditional or dependent on its association with the US.

One of the features of the newly discovered conditioned reflexes that interested Pavlov most was that the conditioned responses he was observing are cortical events, unlike true reflexes, which are subcortical. This led to the realization that he had discovered a way to investigate what he called "higher nervous activity."

Pavlov then moved to establish procedures to produce reliably the conditioned salivary response. A hungry dog was placed in the experimental apparatus (Figure 2.1) and allowed to habituate to the surroundings and the apparatus. Once the dog had become acclimated to the experimental conditions, Pavlov activated a metronome and allowed it to tick for half a minute, at which time meat powder was placed in the dog's mouth. This produced saliva. Multiple repetitions of this procedure were carried on at 15-minute intervals until saliva began to flow during the half-minute

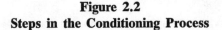

Figure 2.2
Steps in the Conditioning Process

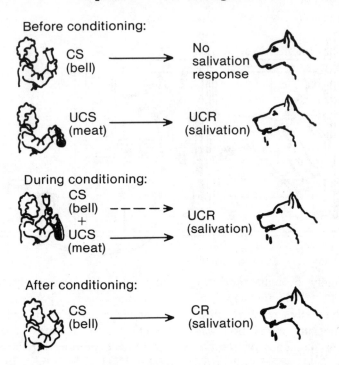

interval prior to the presentation of the unconditioned stimulus, US, or meat powder. The meat powder, in addition to being called the US, was also referred to as the *reinforcement*. Once the dog began to salivate to the sound of the metronome that sound became the conditioned stimulus (CS), and salivation in response to the metronome (CS) was termed the conditioned response (CR). The process is illustrated in Figure 2.2.

With his laboratory procedures reliably established, Pavlov began to experiment with variations on his original experiment. It is worth keeping in mind that Pavlov was dedicated to understanding behavior by trying to understand physiology, and his real interest was not in learning. In fact, Pavlov was less than enthusiastic about the use made of his

ideas by psychologists (Pavlov, 1932b). Pavlov maintained that his experiments were purely physiological studies of brain processes. Here it is interesting to note his conditioning method did not allow any direct measure of what was going on in the brain, as do many contemporary studies which use inner cranial stimulation techniques (Mis, 1977). Pavlov believed that by observing the stimulus and the response a method for examining the intervening brain processes was made available. In Pavlov's cerebral theory the US is thought of as occurring *first,* which arouses activity in the hunger center of the brain. This in turn would "attract" the CS by opening up a new neural pathway. Soon the CS would become a substitute stimulus—an issue of current debate (Estes, 1975)—and arouse the hunger center. As we know, however, Pavlov found it necessary to present the CS before the US, and this temporal relationship appeared to be very important. To reconcile this seeming contradiction, Pavlov proposed a signaling theory which he believed provided a consistent explanation between his conditioning data and his cerebral theory.

The central ideas of Pavlov's physiological theory were two cortical processes which he referred to as *excitation* and *inhibition* (see Basic Concepts above). He suggested several kinds of inhibition which he believed could be accounted for by different variables. *External inhibition* meant that some extraneous environmental variable temporarily distracted the dog and as a result produced a decrement in the CR. *Internal inhibition* occurs as a result of changes in stimulation from the CS. He designated four types of internal inhibition:

1. *Extinction* (see Figure 2.3) results from repeated presentations of the CS without reinforcement.
2. *Differential inhibition* results when a CR has been trained to two different stimuli initially followed by conditioning trials that reinforce responding to one CS and not the other. In present-day learning terminology, discrimination training occurred. Pavlov said that inhibition of the nonreinforced stimuli had taken place.
3. *Conditioned inhibition* takes place when the CS is presented within a complex of other nonreinforced stimuli. Though the lone reinforced stimulus will produce the CR when presented independently, it fails to do so when presented in combination with the nonreinforced stimuli.
4. *Inhibition of delay* results from the delay between the time of onset of

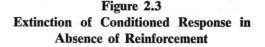

Figure 2.3
Extinction of Conditioned Response in Absence of Reinforcement

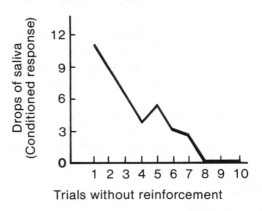

Trials without reinforcement

the CS and reinforcement. Because a longer than optimal time is used between the onset of the CS and the presentation of the reinforcer (US), as in the cases of delayed and trace conditioning (see Methodologies for a description of these procedures), inhibition of the CR occurs early in the time period between the CS and US. As the time for reinforcement nears the inhibition effect is countermanded by excitation, which eventuates in the conditioned response.

Pavlov believed that both inhibition and excitation spread through the cortex. He referred to this process as *irradiation,* the behavioral referent being generalization. He also described an opposing process called *concentration* which results when excitation and inhibition are confined within restricted cortical areas. These localizations of functions in the cortex were referred to by Pavlov as the *mosaic of functions.*

In summary, Pavlov was responsible for having the conditioned reflex accepted as one of the basic units of learning. His experiments and ideas had a tremendous heuristic effect on not only the field of learning but on psychology in general. Gregory Razran (1965) estimates that at the time of his survey there had been approximately 6,000 experiments using Pavlov's specific procedures, and the results from these experiments had been published in 29 different languages.

Finally, Pavlov insisted on rigorous scientific procedures. This led him to be able to quantify many of the significant variables involved in the conditioning process.

Major Theorists

Ivan M. Sechenov (1829-1905) was the father of Russian physiology. Though Pavlov was the most distinguished Russian scientist, he acknowledged that Sechenov's *Reflexes of the Brain* (1935), published in Russia in 1863, was the single most important inspiration for his work. Sechenov had been trained in Germany and France and was responsible for bringing many foreign ideas to Russia. He had been most influenced by the German work but wanted to establish the psychical processes of the Wundtian laboratory on a sounder physiological basis. The main goal of his work was to try to spell out the physiological processes underlying psychical processes. He held that an explanation of psychical activity could be based on the idea of the reflex. *Objective psychology* was the name given to his approach, which held that both conscious and unconscious psychical phenomena are ultimately reducible to muscular movements or reflex activity.

Though Sechenov's objective psychology was influential in Pavlov's thinking, little if any attention was paid to Sechen-

ov's work in America, since his works were not available in English until the middle of the 20th century.

Vladimir Bekhterev (1857–1927), like Sechenov and Pavlov, was a Russian reflexologist who also worked at the Military Medical Academy in St. Petersburg. In 1907 he founded the Psychoneurological Institute, where he worked more in the role of a psychiatrist than a physiologist. Unlike Pavlov, Bekhterev was interested in creating a new psychology based on conditioning principles. His important work *Objective Psychology* (1913) first appeared in Russian in 1907, followed by German and French translations in 1913 and an English translation, under the title of *General Principles of Human Reflexology,* in 1932. His studies of conditioning were at first independent of Pavlov, and he, more than Pavlov, was initially responsible for the wide acceptance of conditioning by psychologists. His position gradually came to be known as *reflexology,* which stresses the concepts of physiology and emphasizes the denial of mentalistic or introspective methods. He was successful in demonstrating conditioning of responses, such as cardiac and respiratory responses, as well as leg and finger flexion. This form of conditioning appealed more to many American psychologists than the idea of salivary conditioning. He also advanced the idea that thinking is simply subvocal speech, a view later to be picked up by John B. Watson and by Skinner.

Using Pavlov's basic procedures, Bekhterev (1913) was able to show an important variation in classical conditioning. He sounded a neutral stimulus in the form of a tone, which he then followed by an electrical shock to the forepaw of a dog. After several pairings of the tone and the shock, the tone alone came to elicit the flexing response. The experiment differed from Pavlov's classical experiment in at least two ways: (1) The stimulus used to elicit the reflex initially was electrical shock, and (2) no reinforcer was consumed, as was the case in Pavlov's appetitive experiment. This form of conditioning is usually referred to as *defense conditioning*. This experiment was particularly important in convincing Watson to integrate conditioned reflex methods into American behaviorism.

Edwin Guthrie, Clark Hull, Kenneth Spence, and Edward C. Tolman—as well as Watson and Skinner—were all influenced by the work of Pavlov and Edward L. Thorndike (see Chapter 1). Of these it was perhaps John B. Watson (1878–1958) who was the most influenced by the work of the Russian reflexologists. Watson had initially been more interested in philosophy than psychology and had gone to the University of Chicago to study philosophy under the tutelage of John Dewey. He found Dewey to be "incomprehensible" and soon became more interested in psychology. He had been trained in functionalism at the University of Chicago but eventually found it, as well as structuralism, lacking, since both used mentalistic methods for understanding behavior. Watson saw in Pavlov's work a way for American psychology to move from the mentalistic approach to a more objective psychology. His behaviorism rejected the use of mentalistic terms such as *mind, consciousness,* and *feeling* in favor of direct study of behavioral acts—notably the stimulus and the response. Watson's aim was to establish laws of action between the stimulus and response. He saw the appropriate subject matter for psychology as an understanding of how a given stimulus results in a particular response. Empha-

sizing the role of the environment in his explanation of behavior, Watson (1929) viewed complex human behavior as a result of prior conditioning and the development of habits. Personality was seen as nothing more than habits and conditioned reflexes (the basic building blocks of behavior) which have become more complex.

Watson and Pavlov prepared the groundwork for current learning approaches to clinical phenomena. Watson was also familiar with the effects of stress. During his graduate work at Chicago he had earned a living by taking care of rats, waiting tables in a fraternity house, and doing janitorial work. In the year his degree was granted, 1903, he experienced debilitating anxiety attacks which resulted in excessive fears and an inability to sleep without the lights on. After a brief period of rest, Watson recovered from his breakdown and was able to return to work. This personal experience was influential in his later investigation of the acquisition of fears and procedures for their removal (Watson & Rayner, 1920).

Current Status

Today the Pavlov Institute of Physiology is a huge establishment with hundreds of scientific workers, located in Pavlovo, a beautiful, well-forested district on the outskirts of Leningrad. Currently Pavlov's apartment in Leningrad is a museum. While Pavlov was alive he received many important visitors from all over the world, among them the noted novelist, sociologist, journalist, and popular historian H. G. Wells. While visiting Pavlov, Wells commented that "In a hundred years Pavlov's work will be appreciated even more than it is now." Such predictions may be coming true.

William K. Estes (1975), in the second volume of his *Handbook of Learning and Cognitive Processes,* points out that "An interesting change of emphasis with regard to individual theorists is the rediscovery of Pavlov" (p. 2).

Currently numerous journals devote a considerable percentage of their space to learning. Among them are *The Journal of Comparative and Physiological Psychology, Journal of Experimental Psychology, Psychological Review, Psychological Bulletin, Journal of the Experimental Analysis of Behavior,* and *Psychonomic Science.* Those with a more applied bent are *The Journal of Behavioral Research and Therapy, Behavior Therapy,* and *The Journal of Experimental Psychiatry and Behavior Therapy.*

Perhaps the hottest issue in classical conditioning research today is the question of exactly what is learned during the conditioning process. The leading investigators in this area are Robert Rescorla and Allan Wagner at Yale University (Rescorla, 1972; Rescorla & Wagner, 1972).

Until recently it had been assumed by many investigators that simple temporal contiguity of the CS and the US were the essential components in effective conditioning. More recent evidence, however, suggests that the CS must contain informational components which reliably allow the organism to predict certain CS–US relationships. These informational components include the extent to which the CS reliably predicts (1) the occurrence of the US, (2) the quality of the US, (3) when the US will be presented temporally, and (4) where the US will occur. Even though these forementioned variables may be optimal, this still does not guarantee that an event will become a viable CS, since the stimulus seems to need to add additional significant information before it becomes "relevant." That is, even though a stimulus provides valuable information, conditioning may not take place if another more potent and historically more reliable stimulus is already providing the same information. Thus mere contiguity does not appear adequate to account for the CS–US relationship. Instead, Rescorla and Wagner (1972) convincingly argue for a more cognitive approach which emphasizes the organism's capacity to learn the predictive value of a stimulus.

Though the foregoing discussion has dealt with excitation, the same ideas appear to support an explanation for conditioning of inhibition. That is, conditioned inhibition occurs in the presence of cues that have reliably been associated with the absence of the US. Other stimulus variables currently under investigation include the optimum CS–US interval (Ross & Ross, 1971), CS intensity (Champion, 1962), and US intensity and duration.

Introceptive conditioning is another current area of interest. Here the conditioned stimulus or the unconditioned stimulus is applied directly to an internal part of the body. Razran (1961) delineated four distinct methods of applying introceptive conditioning procedures. They are (1) intro-introceptive conditioning, where both the CS and the US are applied internally, (2) extero-exteroceptive conditioning, where both the CS and the US are applied externally, (3) extero-introceptive conditioning, where the CS is external and the US is internal, (4) intro-exteroceptive conditioning, where the CS is internal and the US is external.

Research in this area indicates that many responses are conditionable—hypertension, urination, and insulin release, to mention only a few (Brown, 1974).

The following is a representative example of an extero-introceptive procedure to condition the reported need to urinate in humans who have had balloons surgically implanted in their bladder for medical reasons. The patients observed an arrow on a dial move up as the balloon in their bladder was inflated, which created the urge to urinate. Here the dial served as the CS and the inflated balloon was the US, while the need to urinate was the UR. After several trials the balloon was not inflated but the dial was adjusted upward to the place that it would typically be when the balloon was inflated. Now the patients reported a need to urinate even though the balloon had not been inflated. The dial had become a CS for the need to urinate.

Other areas of keen interest and research in classical conditioning include semantic conditioning, taste aversion, constraints on learning, phylogenic comparisons, and the orienting reflex. Most of these issues are considered elsewhere in this chapter.

Other Theories

Prior to 1928 no explicit distinction was made between operant and classical conditioning, and even today many Russian investigators do not make any distinction. Miller and Konorski (1928) suggested that different mechanisms operate in instrumental and classical conditioning, and Skinner, in his classic *The Behavior of Organisms* (1938), extended the distinction by stating that classical or respondent behavior is elicited by a *known* stimulus (called Type S learning), and operant behavior is elicited by learning (called Type R learning) which is emitted spontaneously without being "pulled out" by some specific stimulus event. Skinner (1953) therefore

concluded that the two processes were distinct and required separate analysis.

Two-process learning theories, which began with Harold Schlosberg (1937), attempted to account for the apparent differences between classical and instrumental learning and bring them under one theoretical umbrella. O. Hobart Mowrer (1953), in his extension of the two-factor learning theory, attempted to account for the varying results of such experimenters and theorists as Guthrie, Tolman, Thorndike, Hull, and Pavlov. Latest on the scene of two-factor theorists are R. L. Solomon and his associates, who have proposed a modified version of Mowrer's two-factor model (Rescorla & Solomon, 1967). Gregory Kimble (1971) is of the opinion that because of the complex nature of learning, even the two-factor models of learning are largely oversimplified. In a recent review of the classical-instrumental distinction, Eliot Hearst (1975) points out that a biased belief exists. He admonishes against the tunnel vision which comes from "preconceptions and biases about behavioral categories" and encourages a new look at what may be a pseudo-distinction (p. 218). It is interesting to note that the classical-instrumental distinction is seldom made by contemporary Russian investigators.

PROPOSITIONS

1. *An organism can be conditioned to previously neutral stimuli.*

Kleitman and Crisler (1927), using dogs as subjects, were able to demonstrate nausea as a conditioned response. Dogs were first harnessed into a stock, where they remained for various periods of time. Then an unconditioned stimulus (US) consisting of a morphine injection was administered subcutaneously, which acted on many centers in the nervous system to produce a general nausea in the dogs. The dogs' behaviors exhibited panting, profuse salivation, vomiting, and other signs of distress. After the procedure was repeated for many months the dogs began to exhibit many of the nauseous behaviors shortly after they had been harnessed into the stock and without the injection of morphine. Being placed in the experimental stock had become a conditioned stimulus (CS) for producing the conditioned response (CR) of nausea.

Experiments such as these have laid the groundwork for later human applications. Mount, Payton, Ellis, and Barnes (1976) reported a treatment procedure in which they injected anectine into the arm of alcoholic clients immediately after they drank a jigger of their favorite alcohol. The drug produced a paralyzing effect on the clients' respiratory system and was perceived by the clients as a very frightening experience. Follow-up of the nine clients described in this study indicated only one had begun to drink again.

Attempts to cure habits by aversive means have had a long history. One of the earliest recorded aversion treatments was used by the Romans; live eels were put into a wine cup as a cure for alcoholism (Forness & MacMillan, 1970).

2. *The CR may be weakened and eventually extinguished by presentation of the CS alone.*

Pavlov found that after the dogs had been conditioned to a tone paired with food, if the tone was presented alone over numerous trials, the dogs would eventually cease to salivate. The CR became weaker and eventually nonexistent; at this point, the response was extinguished. The trials or the pairings of the conditioned stimulus plus no US that bring it about are referred to as extinction trials.

Actually, once the response is extinguished it is probably not lost forever; instead, it is probably inhibited. It is known that after extinction has occurred, followed by a rest period, the CS then has the capability of briefly revitalizing the CR. This phenomenon is called *spontaneous recovery*. Though the response occurs in a somewhat weaker form, additional pairings of the CS and the US will cause the previously conditioned stimulus to return to its former strength. However, if further extinction trials are given, the response will become weaker and finally will be permanently extinguished.

Other responses that have been associated with the initial CS will also, when not being reinforced, undergo this extinction process. The spread of this inhibition process is known as the *generalization decrement*.

3. *Stimulus generalization follows specific principles.*

Stimulus generalization can be demonstrated by using as the CS a tone with 1,000 cycles per second (cps). As an example, we can use food as the US for a hungry animal. We begin by pairing the tone with food and eventually the tone alone produces salivation, but this time we do things a little differently. After we have brought about the conditioning, we present the tone to the animal and determine the magnitude of the CR by measuring drops of saliva. The more drops, the greater the CR. In addition to presenting the 1,000-cps tone, we present tones with a higher frequency and tones with a lower frequency: tones, for example, of 250 cps, 2,000 cps, 400 cps, and so on. What we find is that we get a CR not only to the exact CS that we paired with the US, but we also get a CR to other stimuli close to the CS. In other words, we get a CR to the tone of 1,200 cps and 500 cps as well as to other tones, although the 1,000-cps tone was the CS. However, the magnitude as measured by drops of saliva of the CR to these other tones is less, as determined by their similarity to the original CS, which was 1,000 cps. *As similarity goes down, so does the magnitude of the CR.* A graph of the results would show the greatest CR to the 1,000-cps tone, with diminishing magnitude of CR on both sides of that tone. This is referred to as the *stimulus generalization gradient.*

Pavlov's explanation for stimulus generalization in this experiment is that the information would travel from the sense receptors, which he called the analyzers, to some area of the cortex where there was a specific area that was stimulated by the 1,000-cps tone. Other similar tones would have their localization near the 1,000-cps tone area in the brain, and the excitation caused by stimulation in this area would spread or irradiate to neighboring regions of the cortex. *Irradiation* was Pavlov's physiological explanation for generalization.

The opposite of generalization is *discrimination*. Discrimination comes about when an organism learns to respond to one stimulus and not to others, although the others may be similar to the first. This can be demonstrated by introducing two tones during training and differentially rewarding one and not the other. Using our preceding example, we might present a 1,000-cps tone which is always paired with food powder. A 750-cps tone is also used but never paired with food. With these procedures the animal will learn to respond only to the 1,000-cps tone and will inhibit the response to the 750-cps tone.

Pavlov's physiological explanation for discrimination is that activity in the brain area corresponding to the 750-cps tone would be inhibited, while excitation would occur in the area of the brain corresponding to the 1,000-cps tone. Therefore excitation would become specific to the area corresponding to the 1,000-cps tone, and there would be inhibition in the area corresponding to the 750-cps tone. When these two processes have stabilized, *reciprocal induction* is said to have occurred. This was Pavlov's physiological explanation for discrimination. It shows how excitation and inhibition work in oppositional ways.

It is interesting to note that Pavlov's conditioning method did not afford any direct observations of what was going on in the cortex. He observed stimulus and response and offered what seemed to him a reasonable theory of the intervening brain process.

4. *Higher-order conditioning occurs when substitute stimuli produce the conditioned response.*

The process by which other conditioned stimuli may serve as a substitute for the original CS and themselves produce the response is called higher-order conditioning. Once a CS has acquired the power to elicit a strong CR, it can presumably be paired with any other stimulus that the organism can perceive, and soon the second CS will come to elicit the CR in the absence of both the original CS and the US. Higher-order conditioning gives an explanation for why human behavior can be controlled by stimuli very different from those originally present during conditioning. Symbols such as words or gestures exemplify higher-order conditioning.

A traditional Pavlovian animal experiment can be used to illustrate some of the specifics of higher-order conditioning. We begin with a conditioned stimulus, a light, which we designate CS_1. It has already been paired with the US (food powder), and there is a strong CR (salivation). Now we add another neutral stimulus, which we designate CS_2, and we begin to pair it with CS_1 in the same way we paired CS_1 with food powder. At this point, however, food powder is no longer part of the experiment. We are pairing CS_2, which we will say is a bell, with CS_1, which is a light. The pairing proceeds as follows: CS_1 with CS_2, first the bell and then the light. By pairing the bell and the light, the second neutral stimulus now develops the capacity of producing salivation. This phenomenon is referred to as higher-order conditioning. An interesting feature is that the CS_1 acts very much like an unconditioned stimulus. This procedure can sometimes be repeated again and third-order conditioning can be achieved. Few people have been successful in going higher than third-order conditioning.

5. *Classical conditioning may not necessarily require a strong biological unconditioned stimulus.*

What is actually learned during the process of conditioning? In studies of sensory preconditioning, it has been found that by pairing two stimuli an association appears to develop (Coppock, 1958; Thompson, 1972). The experimenter begins by selecting two stimuli such as a light and a tone that do not appear to produce a response. Next the two stimuli are paired or associated with each other by turning on one (tone)

and then the other (light). The third step involves conditioning a response such as galvanic skin response (GSR) to the first of the two stimuli (the tone). After conditioning the GSR to the tone, the other stimulus or substitute stimulus (light) is used. Interestingly, the light now produces the GSR response (Coppock, 1958).

Findings such as these suggest that by simply pairing two stimuli an association takes place. Since the light was not used as the CS in this study, it is argued that the important association is stimulus-stimulus (tone-light) rather than stimulus-response. In this sensory preconditioning study it appears that classical conditioning does not require a CS which has been paired with a biologically significant US. Instead, conditioning involves associations that are subtle and of little biological significance.

6. *Conditional emotional responses can be established through conditioning having motivational components.*

In addition to conditioned salivary responses, sometimes called *appetitive conditioning,* Pavlov also investigated *aversive conditioning.* Here again he used dogs, administering an electric shock to the paw. The shock was the US, while the withdrawal of the dog's leg, the leg flexion, was the UR. He used a variety of sound and visual stimuli for the CS. Since the dog was strapped into the apparatus and could not escape the electric shock, it soon learned to respond to the aversive stimulus with a leg flexion, but it would also exhibit a generalized fear response. Soon all the stimuli that preceded the US regularly, be it a bell, a tone, or the sight of the experimenter, came to be connected with the shock and functioned as a CS to elicit a general fear response in the dog.

7. *Fear is a learned drive.*

Knowledge of conditioning procedures makes more understandable behavior that may otherwise appear somewhat "crazy" and difficult to understand. For example, in the movie *The Diary of Anne Frank* a wailing siren usually preceded the arrival of the Nazi SS troops, who frequently directed some horrifying action against the Jews. The siren became a CS which elicited feelings of fear (CR) in many members of the Jewish community as they anticipated some horror which was about to befall them (US).

Neal Miller (1951) conducted important studies which showed that emotions such as fear could function as a learned drive. Rats were initially shocked in the white compartment of a two-compartment box. During the shock the rat found that it was able to escape through the door to the second compartment, which was painted black. Repetition of this procedure taught the rat the important cues, such as the white compartment, signaled the onset of painful shock, and therefore presumably the fear response was conditioned in the rat while in the white side of the compartment. Additionally, it taught the rat that the black compartment was safe and devoid of shock.

To test the hypothesis that conditioned emotional reactions acquire motivational properties through fear reduction, Miller attempted to discover if the rats would learn a new response of turning an activity wheel. The only reinforcement consisted of presumed reduction of fear when the rats were allowed to escape into the black compartment. These results indicate that conditioned emotional reactions develop drive states, the reduction of which can function as a reinforcer.

8. *Aversive Pavlovian conditioning can be a constraint on later learning.*

Learned helplessness, a phenomenon commanding increasing attention, was first so named by Seligman and Maier (1967). First an experimental group of dogs were given electric shocks while they were strapped in a harness. The control group received no shocks. On the following day the dogs that had received the shock were placed in a shuttlebox, which is a chamber with two compartments separated by a barrier. The floor of the chamber is designed to be electrified. The dogs had to learn the task of responding to a warning signal by jumping over the barrier to the other side of the box within 10 seconds. If they failed to jump, they received a painful electric shock.

About two thirds of these dogs were unable to learn the avoidance behavior quickly, as compared to the control-group dogs. The experimental-group dogs often suffered the shock, even though on a trial or two they may have actually avoided it by jumping the barrier.

When the unshocked control-group dogs were shocked they lost bowel and bladder control and ran about howling, then jumped the barrier to safety. The previously shocked dogs in the experimental group would, after initially demonstrating similar behavior, lie down and passively take repeated shocks. They did not learn the appropriate avoidance behavior and had to be dragged across the barrier as many as 200 times to be taught the response. Physiological functioning also suffered. In this situation there is loss of appetite and weight, and ulcers might develop.

Comparable results were obtained using humans by Hiroto (1974). It appears that at the human level a belief develops that it is useless to continue responding. There seem to be many parallels between learned helplessness in the laboratory and depression in humans in the natural environment.

RESEARCH

Methodologies

Before Pavlov's experiment he made a surgical incision in the cheek of the dog and attached a small glass tube to the salivary gland, in order to have a direct measure of the amount of salivation produced during conditioning. After the dog's recovery from the operation, Pavlov sounded a tuning fork for about seven to eight seconds, and followed this with meat powder placed in the dog's mouth. Pairing of the tone and the meat powder was repeated approximately 10 times, after which the tone was given by itself for a 30-second period. A few seconds later Pavlov noted that salivation was appearing. However, after 30 or so pairings, the dog salivated a great deal in response to the tone, even when it was not accompanied by food.

Measures of the Conditioned Response. Since we cannot measure the strength of the CR directly, we infer it from other kinds of observable measures. Pavlov used amplitude of the response, or the amount of saliva the dogs secreted, as his measure of the response strength. Latency of the response has also been used to measure the strength of conditioning, that is, how much time elapses between the onset of the CS and the CR. Another measure of the strength of the CR is the frequency or rate of making

the response. A fourth measure of the strength of the CR is its resistance to extinction. Essentially, this measure of the strength of conditioning occurs when the CS is presented without the US. Then the number of trials needed before the CR no longer occurs is measured. These trials are referred to as extinction trials.

Classical conditioning experiments have been structured in two basic ways in order to measure the CR. The first system is the *test-trial technique,* which intersperses test trials throughout training. Here the CS is given for a longer period than on the training trials. The main pitfall of this technique is that since the CS is given without the US, the CR may be weakened through extinction. Therefore it is difficult to know if the measure of the CR is accurate or an artifact of the measuring procedure.

A second technique used to evaluate the strength of the CR is referred to as the *anticipation method.* Here the CS is turned off for a long enough period to permit the experimental subject to anticipate the US by responding before it occurs. The problem with this technique is that different response systems differ according to their latency of onset. For example, the amount of time required between the onset of the CS and a galvanic skin response (CR) is about two seconds. Because this response is comparatively slow it creates problems, since the optimum interval between the onset of the CS and the US is only 0.5 seconds (White & Schlosberg, 1952). Here again the measure of the CR may be an artifact of the testing procedure, since the time relationship between the CS and the US is able to predict that the US is not forthcoming.

A third technique of evaluating the strength of the CR allows us to avoid such problems. It is referred to as the *maximum-strength* procedure. Here, the CS and the US are conditioned over several trials for different groups of subjects, and then after conditioning has presumably occurred, the strength of the CR is measured by presenting the CS only one time in the absence of the US. Since this is done at the end of training, it is presumed that the CR is near maximum strength.

Another experimental problem learning theorists face is making sure that the CR they are measuring is really the result of their conditioning procedures and not an artifact of the experiment or some other extraneous voluntary response. Wickens (1939) illustrates this problem. Wickens used the buzzer as the CS, pairing it with a mild shock to the forefingers of one group of persons (US). A second group were threatened with shock but did not actually receive it, while a third group was instructed to make voluntary finger withdrawal responses when a light was flashed on. The findings were that Groups 2 and 3 showed very little conditioning; their responses to the CS were highly variable and rather sluggish. The first group, which had undergone the actual conditioning procedures, made many more responses to the CS than did the other two. The conditioned responses of this group were more stable and reflexive (quick) and continued long after the shock had been terminated. Wickens concluded that the true conditioned response differed in terms of latency and persistence when compared to the voluntary responses.

Temporal Relationships between the CS and the US. As has been mentioned, one of the fundamental distinguishing features of Pavlovian conditioning is the pairing of the CS and the US. There are several ways that the CS and the US can be arranged in relationship to each other. These temporal relationships fall into two general categories: (1) procedures in which the CS and US overlap, and (2) procedures in which the CS and US do not overlap.

1. *Overlapping procedures in simultaneous conditioning.* Both the CS and the US can come on and go off at the same time. In *delayed conditioning* the conditioned stimulus occurs first and is followed by the US after a period of delay.

2. *Nonoverlapping procedures in trace conditioning.* The CS comes on and goes off, and, after a brief period of delay, the US is presented. In *backward conditioning* the conditioned stimulus is presented *after* the US has been turned on and turned off.

These temporal relationships are commonly used to identify and to distinguish different experimental procedures in classical conditioning. The important point concerning the CS–US temporal relationships is that they allow researchers to vary and to study systematically an important dimension of classical conditioning. The temporal relationships described above by no means exhaust all of the possibilities for various combinations of the procedures.

Numerous studies have attempted to understand the optimal CS–US interval, beginning with Pavlov himself, who found that animals could learn to delay a conditioned response, such as salivation, for long periods of time. The dogs seemed able to anticipate accurately when the US (food) was about to appear and would begin their conditioned response of salivation just prior to its appearance. Pavlov experimented with both trace and delayed CS–US intervals and concluded that trace conditioning of the CR is more difficult to establish than delayed conditioning of the CR. However, current research suggests that this finding of Pavlov's may not always hold true with other species. Ross and Ross (1971) found no differences between trace and delayed procedures with human eyelid conditioning, while Schneiderman (1966) found that delayed procedures are superior to trace procedures in eyelid conditioning of the rabbit.

Pavlov believed that backward conditioning, that is conditioning in which the US precedes the CS, could not take place. Some studies have purported to show backward conditioning by administering a noxious stimulus (US) such as an electric shock prior to the CS. These results have generally been interpreted to suggest that instead of actual backward conditioning occurring, a noxious stimulus serves mainly to sensitize the subject to almost any stimulus; therefore what is actually being observed is an increased level of arousal.

CS–US Interval. By increasing the number of pairings of the conditioned and unconditioned stimulus, the strength of the CR increases up to a particular level. It has been shown that a half second between the onset of the CS and the onset of the US is about the most favorable interval to maximize the effects of conditioning. Numerous experiments have dealt with varying the length of the interval between the CS and the US. These findings have generally suggested that shorter time intervals reduce the signaling value of the CS, while longer ones allow time for extraneous stimuli to occur and loss of attention to the specific CS to take place.

The time interval itself can become a CS for the organism. After training, experimental subjects learn to anticipate the US, since the temporal pattern becomes a cue that predicts the US. When the subject learns to respond purely to the interval by making a response just before the US is presented, or is due to appear, *temporal conditioning is said to have occurred.*

Animal Studies

Many early comparative psychologists were inspired by the idea that once the principles of behavior had been teased out in lower animals they could be easily extended up the phylogenetic scale to explain human behavior. As research continued this hope became more and more unrealistic, until in the past decade, with the increased interest in cognitive psychology, lower animal research seemed near its demise. The 1970s saw a renewed interest in animal research, from a less naive perspective. Contemporary comparative psychologists are less interested in trying to generalize their findings to other species. Instead, they tend to examine how a single species is affected when a single element in the learning environment is changed. They are also interested in examining the learning capabilities of organisms at different levels on the phylogenetic scale (Razran, 1971).

Another important recent development in the literature is the research on *constraints on learning.* Previously it had been assumed by many students of learning that almost any response that the organism was capable of making could be conditioned in accordance with the laws of learning. Recently evidence has been accumulating which brings this assumption into question (Seligman, 1970). Because organisms have evolved certain adaptive behavior systems over millions of years, it makes sense that a conditioning procedure is unlikely to countermand these responses. Keller and Marian Breland (Breland & Breland, 1961), who were in the business of training performing animals, called this phenomenon *instinctial drift.* They noted a number of instances in which the organism's innate behavior appears to override the conditioned behavior. For example, pigs were conditioned to pick up a large wooden coin and place it in a bank to obtain a food reward. However, the response seemed to be interrupted by rooting behavior. Also, chickens that had been trained to stand on a platform for a brief period of time before receiving a food reward began scratching the platform.

Research such as this suggests that the current laws of learning must be modified to account for species-specific constraints on learning. In a sense Pavlov hinted at the constraints on learning when he recognized that the capacity to be conditioned depends, in part, on the type of nervous system of the subject.

Another related area is the so-called *bait-shyness* or acquired *taste aversion* research. Bait-shyness could be defined as a conditioned aversion to the taste of a given substance on the basis of a single learning experience which resulted in an animal becoming temporarily sick from having ingested the substance. Once the animal has recovered it refuses to eat the substance that made it sick. This is obviously a survival response.

One problem of trying to fit such research into the traditional classical conditioning paradigm is that the long delay period between the time the noxious substance is eaten and the onset of sickness exceeds "optimal" temporal relationships as they are currently understood; yet the conditioning does occur. Facts dispute theory.

Bait-shyness appears at first glance to be a kind of esoteric academic problem destined for Senator William Proxmire's uncoveted Golden Fleece Award, but closer examination shows some interesting applications for this idea. Gustavson, Garcia, Hankins, and Rusiniak (1974), aware of the controversy between the conservationists and the farmers concerning wild coyotes that roamed the western United States and killed sheep, fed three coyotes some lamb which had previously been treated with lithium chloride—a substance designed to make them sick and produce the bait-shy effect. Three other coyotes ate rabbit also treated with lithium chloride. The results of their experiments indicated that after one or two meals of the treated food the coyotes ceased to attack the prey whose meat had made them sick.

Many therapeutic aversion procedures such as those used for tobacco and alcohol control appear to have elements in common with the bait-shy effect. Animal research on bait-shyness continues to expand into a variety of uncharted areas, for example, learned sexual aversions (Johnston, Zahorik, Immler, & Zakon, 1978).

Another area of animal learning has focused on conditioning visceral and autonomic functions, reviewed in Harris and Brady (1974). Heart rate is typically conditioned by pairing a stimulus with shock. Research indicates that the cardiac response is affected by classical conditioning procedures, though some researchers have found an increase in the cardiac response while others have found a decrease while using essentially the same procedures. Other circulatory functions such as blood pressure and blood flow also appear to be affected by classical conditioning procedures (Dykman, Mack, & Ackerman, 1965; Yehle, Dauth, & Schneiderman, 1967).

Some of the most interesting animal research—known as the cannibal worm studies—has used classically conditioned planaria, or flatworms. In the initial phase of one experiment (McConnell, Shigehista, and Salive, 1970), the planaria, housed in water, were presented with a light (CS-to-be) which was paired with a shock (US), which produces body contractions (UR). After repeated pairings the light became the CS and elicited muscle contractions (CR). Once the flatworms had been trained they were fed to untrained flatworms (planaria are cannibals). The important experimental question is: Will the untrained flatworms that ate the smart (trained) flatworms be able to outperform significantly a group of control flatworms in the conditioning task? James McConnell (1964) found that the untrained worms that ate the "smart" worms outperformed the control group in learning body contractions to the light (CS). His explanation for these results is that memory storage is partially chemical and can be transferred from one organism to another. In other experiments (McConnell, Shigehista, & Salive, 1970) McConnell ground up trained worms and extracted ribonucleic acid (RNA), a complex molecule believed to be an important chemical mediator for memory. He then injected untrained worms with this RNA and compared their ability to learn the conditioning task with a group of worms that had received RNA from untrained worms. Again McConnell found that the worms that had received the RNA from the "smart" worms significantly outperformed the control group.

Another study, Unger (1966), dealt with memory transfer in rats. In the initial phase of the experiment rats were trained to fear the dark. Then their brains were ground up and a protein called scotophobin (from the Greek words meaning to fear the dark) was extracted. After the protein was injected into untrained rats, they became fearful of the dark. This fascinating area of research conjures up fantasies that we may one day be able to go to the corner drugstore and buy a Ph.D. pill. Before you place your order you should know that even though more than 100 different laboratories have successfully replicated RNA transfer studies with rats and flatworms, many other researchers have failed to replicate successfully the studies cited here (Trotter & McConnell, 1978). For nonconforming studies see, for example, Bennett and Calvin (1964) and McConnell's rebuttal (McConnell, 1966).

Human Research

One of Pavlov's assistants observed that some conditioned dogs appeared to have many of the same characteristics as humans with neuroses. The term *experimental neuroses* was given to this phenomenon. For example, to achieve experimental neurosis initially a dog was taught to salivate to a circle but not to an ellipse. As conditioning proceeded both the ellipse and the circle continued to be presented, but the ellipse was slowly altered so that it began to look more like the circle. As the discrimination became more difficult the formerly tranquil dog began squealing and barking and showed signs of fear of the room as well as being drowsy and sleepy. These behaviors have been interpreted as being similar to human neurotic symptoms. A side note is that after the dog had become apparently disorganized by its inability to make the appropriate discrimination, when presented with the original simple discrimination the dog was no longer able to respond appropriately.

This further suggests that a condition analogous to neuroses may have been operating, since one of the characteristics of neurotics is excessive anxiety with debilitating consequences. Similar reactions have been found in other experimental animals such as sheep, cats, and rats.

Watson was impressed with the work of Pavlov because it provided an objective method of evaluating behavior without relying on an introspective or mentalistic analysis. Watson and Rayner (1920) carried out one of the most famous experiments in all psychology with an 11-month-old infant they called Little Albert. They first presented Albert with a series of objects: a white rat, a rabbit, a dog, a fur coat, a cotton ball, and some masks. Albert's reaction to these objects was to reach for them, play with them, and show interest in them. Then the researchers unexpectedly startled the infant by striking a steel bar behind him to make a loud "bong" noise; Albert began to cry. Next they paired the noise with a white rat, and as Albert reached for the rat they again produced the loud noise by striking the bar behind the infant. This procedure was repeated twice, and a week later the rat was reintroduced. Albert had been conditioned to the extent that he showed a strong negative response to the rat; he began to cry and turned and crawled away as fast as possible. A week later his fear was generalized from the white rat to a friendly rabbit he had known, and other white furry objects, such as the dog and a fur coat, frightened him. He also pulled away from a cotton ball and reacted negatively to a Santa Claus mask, though he had shown no such fear of these objects prior to the conditioning.

This experiment by Watson has been used by present-day learning theorists to illustrate how the neurotic conditions called phobias are acquired. Situations and circumstances over which people become anxious to a lesser degree are also generally understood to be acquired in much the same way.

Second Signal System. Pavlov referred to language in humans as the second signal system. He believed this is a feature that distinguishes humans from animals; lack of speech in animals causes their thinking to be limited to what Pavlov called *object thinking* or *concrete thinking*. The second signal system further distinguishes humans' higher nervous activity from that of animals. The conditioned reflexes that he studied in animals make up a *first signaling system,* but because animals do not have speech their intellectual activity is limited. The characteristic of human thinking is the ability not only to learn from experience but especially to generate concepts. Though Washoe[1] would probably take issue with some of Pavlov's statements, classical conditioning procedures have been employed extensively to investigate language acquisition, mediation, and generalization.

A more recent development in the study of language is *semantic generalization,* reviewed in Razran (1961). An example of semantic generalization would begin with experimental procedures that delivered a mild shock when an experimental participant viewed the number *3* on a screen. After several pairings of the number and shock, *3* would become a CS and would elicit the same emotional state that the shock did. The emotional reaction to the shock could be measured by using a psychogalvanometer to measure galvanic skin response. Now an interesting aspect of semantic

[1] Washoe is the first chimpanzee to acquire sign language (see Gardner & Gardner, 1969).

conditioning would occur. Since conditioning has taken place to the number *3*, we might read a list of numbers to the participant, such as 12, 29, 41, but in the list we would also include problems such as 1.5 plus 1.5, the square root of 9, 6 divided by 2, and 30 divided by 10. We would find that a GSR occurs to problems whose answer is 3 but does not when the answer is not 3. Apparently what has been conditioned is "threeness." It appears that the participant asked to work a problem such as 6 divided by 2 experiences the answer, which is 3 (the CR), and this produces the GSR. It is important to recognize that this is a departure from the traditional Pavlovian model, since it deals with meaning and mediational responses as opposed to the specific stimulus involved in training.

Recent evidence in this area suggests that the anxiety level (GSR) demonstrated was done "unconsciously," since the participants were unaware of the word-shock relationships involved. This technique promises to provide tools for investigating unconscious emotional processes.

IMPLICATIONS

Theoretical

The idea of contiguity dominates much of what has been written about classical conditioning. According to the stimulus substitution theory the CS eventually takes the place of the US as a result of their previous contiguous presentation. If this were an accurate description, then once conditioning occurred it would be expected that the CR would be the same as the UR. As mentioned earlier this is not the case, since the CR is usually a somewhat weaker response. Another line of evidence that runs counter to the stimulus substitution hypothesis is that certain reflexes, such as the pupillary reflex, do not seem amenable to conditioning to a stimulus light (proposed CS), though they respond to light (US).

Simple contiguity appears to be in trouble as a predictive variable. Though it appears contiguity must occur between the CS and US, just because they are contiguous in time doesn't necessarily mean that conditioning will result. The CS must form an association with a worthwhile consequence for conditioning to take place (Rescorla, 1967).

Another theoretical revamping taking place in contiguity theory centers around multiple cue learning. Contiguity theory holds that when an organism is presented with multiple cues, each of which is associated with the US, an equal association will develop between and among the different cues. This idea is under attack from researchers like Leon Kamin (1969), who conditioned rats by pairing a noise (CS) with a shock (US). Next he added a redundant light stimulus which was presented along with the noise during continuing shock trials. Kamin found that the light acquired little conditioning, even though it was paired with the shock. His interpretation is that the light failed to be conditioned because it was redundant and did not provide any additional relevant information. Since equal association did not develop between both cues, this suggests that mere contiguity is an insufficient condition for conditioning.

As an extension of this idea, it has been suggested that for a new stimulus to become conditioned in a situation in which a reliable CS already exists, the new stimulus must act as a surprise (predict a new relevant consequence) before learning will occur. This suggests that if one relevant stimulus already exists it blocks conditioning to a second stimulus unless it is a relevant cue. Therefore, stimuli appear to compete for strength, with the most relevant being attended to most. This is a fact observed by every teacher.

Practical Implications

Extinction of Fear. For a conditioned fear response to extinguish, conditions must be arranged so that the individual can experience the conditioned stimulus in a situation which is not followed by the aversive aspects that conditioned the excessive fear or phobia in the first place. Better yet, if the previously fear-evoking stimulus situation is followed by a pleasant event, the elimination of the fear should be enhanced and hastened. In this case, *counterconditioning* takes place.

These phenomena have been demonstrated in the laboratory. In Solomon, Kamin, and Wynne (1953), dogs were placed in a box that had a barrier in the middle over which the dog was able to jump. One side of the box had an electrified grid and the other side was the "safe" side. The dogs were given 10 conditioning trials in which they were shocked on one side of the box, and they learned that they could escape to the safe side by jumping the barrier. After the 10th conditioning trial, shock was never presented again. However, each time the dogs were placed in the compartment that had previously produced the shock they continued to jump to the safe side of the box. This response was so strong that they continued to jump, without evidence of extinction, for 500 trials. The essence of this study is that extinc-

tion never occurred because the dogs never stayed in the side that had been electrified long enough to learn that the shock had been turned off.

This experiment has implications that help explain why phobias may not extinguish in a natural environment. Individuals made fearful by a certain situation may never again spend enough time in that situation to learn that it is not dangerous. For example, an individual who has developed fear of water as a result of almost drowning may never re-enter the water long enough for the fear to extinguish.

Another example of conditioning which helps us make sense out of a behavior that otherwise appears to be "crazy" comes from the work of Dan G. Perkins (1975). A client's generalized fear of telephones made little sense until it was learned that he had had an extramarital affair with a married woman who subsequently told her husband about the encounter. The irate husband then began calling the client and haranguing him on the phone. Fearful that his wife would discover what he had done, the client became quite apprehensive each time his phone rang at home, especially when his wife happened to be there. Subsequently his fear generalized to phones at work and in other people's homes.

Not only physical stimuli, but also words and symbols can become conditioned stimuli. Think, for example, the words *dentist's drill* and examine your own internal reactions, or imagine someone is raking fingernails across a chalk board. These thoughts by themselves often produce internal changes in the absence of any external stimuli. Or think how strong an internal reaction may take place when a flag is raised or a band plays the national anthem, or you hear a song on the radio with special meaning. These examples give firsthand knowledge about how conditioning has impacted your life.

Work is being carried on with appetitive behavior in humans. There is evidence that people who have difficulty in controlling their eating behavior are considerably more amenable to external stimuli than others without this problem. They are more likely to respond to commercials, food signs, or merely the fact that the clock says it is time to eat. The implication is that more extensive conditioning to external cues may have occurred in overweight people, and others who do not have weight problems tend to focus more on internal cues (Schachter, 1971).

Applications of conditioning techniques range from G. Stanley Hall's attempt to use Pavlov's ideas to understand how the mind migrates to the stomach—what he called the "pyloric soul"—to the modification of migraine headaches (Sturgis, Tollison, & Adams, 1978) and public masturbation (Cook, Altman, Shaw, & Blaylock, 1978). Even before Pavlov set forth the principles of conditioning, the basic procedures were known to animal trainers. Stolurow (1973) reported that Gypsies trained bears to dance to music by first chaining the bear to a stone surface, under which a fire was built. As the bear moved about to relieve the pain caused by the hot surface, music was played. After conditioning had occurred, music became a CS which produced dance-like movements, even though the surface was no longer hot.

This chapter has pointed out that the differences between classical and instrumental conditioning are not clear-cut (Estes, 1975). Some even suggest that the distinction is a pseudodichotomy.

Nowhere is the distinction less clear than in the attempt to explain human maladaptive behavior and its treatment from within a learning framework. A case in point is the Watson and Rayner (1920) study of Little Albert. Though the fear response to white furry objects was caused by using Pavlovian procedures, the escape and avoidance behavior which followed is best understood as an instrumental act. Therefore, the topography of the response has elements of both classical and instrumental conditioning. It is no wonder that Hull, in his well-known book *Principles of Behavior* published in 1943, tried to reduce classical conditioning to instrumental conditioning. What is not well known is that Pavlov (1932b) tried to reduce instrumental conditioning to classical conditioning.

Behavior Therapies with Classical Conditioning Components. In addition to his laboratory work, Pavlov also published extensively to show how his findings could be used to explain and to treat abnormal behavior (1932a, 1934, 1941). Bekhterev also published his experimental findings (1932), as well as their applications to maladaptive behavior (1912). In America, early attempts to explain abnormal behavior within a Pavlovian framework were published by Watson (1916) and Mateer (1917). In the 1930s a group of studies showed the successful conditioning of experimental neuroses in such animals as the rat, pig, sheep, and cat (e.g., Masserman, 1943).

Later procedures have built on these early works. Notable among the newer procedures is a counterconditioning technique referred to as *systematic desensitization,* developed by Joseph Wolpe (1958). This procedure is especially helpful for treatment of excessive fears, known as phobias. It is in wide use by *behavior therapists,* mental health personnel who emphasize applied learning principles in their therapeutic approach. To a lesser degree educators have discovered its usefulness in reducing such fears as speech phobias, test phobias, and performance anxieties such as stage fright and fear of failure. The goal of Wolpe's procedures is to weaken the associations between precipitating environmental stimuli and patients' anxiety response. The three central components of systematic desensitization programs are (1) construction of an anxiety hierarchy, (2) training in a relaxation procedure, and (3) presentation of the hierarchy items during relaxation.

Anxiety hierarchy. The anxiety hierarchy consists of a list of anxiety-producing events ordered from most to least anxiety arousing. Each step on the hierarchy is said to be one subjective, just noticeable difference stronger than the preceding item. In other words, the client arranges the items so that each preceding step is one subjective unit stronger than the previous step. Recent investigations (Suinn, Edie, & Spinelli, 1970), however, indicate that item order in the hierarchy may be less important than originally believed.

Here is a sample hierarchy used to desensitize a test-anxious college woman (Wolpe, 1973).

1. On the way to the university on the day of the examination.
2. In the process of answering an examination paper.
3. Before the unopened doors of the examination room.
4. Awaiting the distribution of the examination papers.
5. The examination paper lies face down before her.
6. The night before the exam.
7. One day before an examination.
8. Two days before an examination.
9. Three days before an examination.
10. Four days before an examination.
11. Five days before an examination.
12. A week before an examination.
13. Two weeks before an examination.
14. A month before an examination.

It is interesting to note that the client felt more anxious on the way to school to take the exam than during the actual exam. Similarly, parachutists report experiencing more anxiety just before their jumps than they do once the jumps have been made.

Relaxation training. While the hierarchy is being constructed the client is taught to master a relaxation technique such as the one based on procedures developed by Jacobson (1938). Clients first learn to discriminate between tension and relaxation by tensing their major muscle groups and then releasing the tension and noticing the difference. Clients are instructed to practice tensing and relaxing at home between sessions. The idea is that once relaxation is mastered it can be used to inhibit the excitatory response of anxiety. Wolpe (1958) called this procedure *reciprocal inhibition.* Additional therapeutic variables that are probably operating during the desensitization are extinction and the client's increased ability to view the fear more rationally.

Imagining the anxiety items while relaxed. The final stage requires the client to first achieve deep relaxation and then to imagine the weakest item on the hierarchy for about 10 seconds before reinducing relaxation. If, during that time, the client is imagining a scene and becomes anxious he or she is instructed to stop imagining and reinduce relaxation. Inability to move beyond an item on the hierarchy usually means that the hierarchy steps are too large and should be broken down into smaller steps. Successfully working through hierarchies has been shown to be quite effective in fear reduction.

There is a fourth step in the process— behaving successfully in real-life situations. Recently, desensitization self-help books have appeared on the market which allow clients to work through the desensitization procedure on their own (e.g., Weinrich, Danley, & General, 1976). Also, a computer-assisted systematic desensitization program called DAD (Device for Automated Desensitization) has been used successfully (Lang, 1968; Lang, Melamed, & Hart, 1970). In the first session the phobic client meets with a therapist and the anxiety hierarchy is constructed: the client is also taught relaxation procedures. Then the computer takes over: the client relaxes in a comfortable chair and the computer administers relaxation instructions through earphones. Once the client is relaxed, the computer begins administering the hierarchy items. If the client becomes fearful he or she presses a button, and the item is terminated and relaxation instructions are again given. Once the client has achieved a relaxed state, the computer repeats the procedure until the client has successfully moved through all of the items. An additional feature is that during the session DAD records a variety of physiological data, such as heart rate and galvanic skin response. This provides an objective measure of the physiological concomitants of anxiety.

Lang, Melamed, and Hart (1970) also compared automated desensitization, traditional desensitization using a therapist, and a control group with snake-phobic individuals. The findings were that both the automated procedure and the traditional procedure using a therapist were successful, as compared to the untreated control group.

Therapists using desensitization today borrow heavily from the ideas of Watson, which were first implemented by Mary Cover Jones (1924). Her procedures were actually *in vivo* (meaning that she applied her procedures in a real-life situation). Working with phobic children, she gradually moved the fear-producing object closer and closer to the children while they were eating. In this counterconditioning model it can be seen that the original stimulus-response relationship is being extinguished and a new and less fear-producing connection is being formed, or, in the light of Kamin's (1969) multiple-cue hypothesis, perhaps the food cues are more important to the hungry child and are thus inhibiting the fear-producing cues.

Assertive Training. Like systematic desensitization, assertive training is based on the principle of reciprocal inhibition. One of the first advocates of assertive training was Andrew Salter (1949), author of *Conditioned Reflex Therapy*. The general idea is that if you can learn to be assertive in a situation in which you have been anxious, the assertion will operate to inhibit the anxiety response. Assertive training is conducted both on an individual basis (Wolpe, 1958) and in groups (Lazarus, 1968; Perkins, 1972): Though it is a counterconditioning procedure for anxiety, it also relies heavily on operant conditioning techniques.

One of the key aspects of assertive training is behavioral rehearsal, which calls for rehearsing new behaviors to be used in the future. The behavioral rehearsal technique has several advantages.

First, it allows the client an opportunity to practice the new behavior in a protective environment. Also, the new behavior can undergo a shaping process, since the therapist is there and actively involved in providing feedback as to the adequacy of the new behavior. The client begins with rather simple nonthreatening assertive exercises and works up the assertive training hierarchy to progressively more difficult tasks. This method is comparable to *psychodrama.*

Other assertive training techniques have included instructions and modeling. Salter (1949), the father of assertive training, developed six rules his clients were instructed to practice:

1. Verbally express your feelings by letting people know when you feel happy, bored, or angry.
2. Show your emotions nonverbally by, for example, laughing when you are happy.
3. When you disagree with someone, express your disagreement.
4. Use the pronoun *I* as much as possible.
5. Express agreement when praised. For example, if someone says to you, "That was a very good speech," reply, "Yes, I know it was; I worked very hard on it. Thank you for noticing."
6. Improvise; live for the moment and do not put your life off until retirement or summer vacation.

Two other counterconditioning procedures which rely heavily on extinction are *flooding* and *implosive therapy.* The general idea of these procedures is to get the client to come into contact with the fear-producing stimuli either *in vivo,* as with flooding, or through thoughts and images, as with implosive therapy. It is reasoned that if the client can make contact with the fear-producing agent for a long enough time and learns that no harm will come, then extinction should take place. Though flooding and implosion have worked with some clients, others seem to have a negative side effect after treatment, such as recurring thoughts or dreams about the fear-producing stimuli.

Aversion Procedures. Bekhterev (1913) was one of the earliest investigators to use aversive classical conditioning with a tone which he paired with a shock administered to the forepaw of a dog. As Pavlov also learned, the tone began as a neutral stimulus and soon became associated with the shock, so that the dog's response of flexing the forepaw appeared to the tone alone.

An early therapeutic use of aversive conditioning was developed in Russia for use with alcoholics (Kantorovich, 1930). This technique was also used in the United States during the late thirties and early forties (Lamere & Voegtlin, 1950). Basically, the technique consisted of associating the sight, smell, and taste of liquor with nausea and vomiting. Participants were first injected with the drug emetine in doses too small to induce sickness alone. They then were asked to drink whiskey, which with the drug was enough to produce nausea and vomiting.

Despite the fact that these aversion techniques were effective and are still used, interest dwindled in their application and it was not until the 1960s that studies in aversive conditioning again began to appear in the literature. Currently, aversive conditioning is in vogue as a treatment for smoking and weight control. With smokers, a typical procedure consists of having the persons smoke rapidly while smoke is blown into their faces. This continues until they can no longer tolerate it (Schmahl, Lichtenstein, & Harris, 1972). Electric shock paired with smoke inhalation has also been used with some success (McGuire & Vallance, 1964).

In working with the obese, electric shock has been paired with specific foods to produce aversion (Stollak, 1967). Foreyt and Kennedy (1971) paired the sight and odor of foods with aversive odors such as butyric acid. Such a device (a vial of acid) is more portable than shock and is obviously more closely associated physiologically with food.

Similar techniques have been utilized to treat sexual deviates. Shock is the most common aversion technique utilized in these cases. In a study of transvestites and fetishists, Marks and Gelder (1967) shocked individuals in the presence of their particular objects of sexual arousal. Such conditioning appeared to be rather specific to each object or condition, however.

Aversive techniques can also be employed at a covert level. Instead of actually using a drug to induce vomiting, a nauseating scene can be imagined in the presence of alcohol or food (Cautela, 1967; Janda & Rimm, 1972). For example, while looking at a beer or a piece of cake, a person might imagine all the vivid details of being locked in a portable toilet on a hot summer day. Obviously this technique has some operant properties but also fits into the respondent conditioning paradigm.

Covert Sensitization. An example of how aversive conditioning occurs in the natural environment is given in a case reported by F. M. Perkins (1978). A client who was in therapy for other reasons reported that she had developed an aversion to a popular singer's voice. It seems that in the early months of a pregnancy (US) during which she suffered severe morning sickness (UR), she habitually played a tape by the singer (neutral stimulus) on her way to work. Later in her pregnancy, after the bouts of morning sickness had subsided, the client noticed that whenever she played the tape (CS) she would feel nauseated (CR). Furthermore, she found that she felt somewhat queasy when hearing the songs from the tape sung by other singers (response generalization).

Schizokinesis. Liddell (1934) studied respondent conditioning in sheep by pairing a bell with an electric shock administered to the sheep's leg. Soon the sheep learned to move their legs when they heard the bell. An additional finding was that there were also marked changes in breathing, heart rate, and general activity when the CS was presented. Apparently these other responses had also undergone conditioning. An interesting feature of this research is that the CR appeared to have several additional components that the simple unconditioned response did not have.

Human cardiac responses were conditioned by Zeaman and Smith (1965) by pairing a light and a shock. Their findings were similar to Liddell's work with sheep in that conditioning of the respiratory response also occurred in addition to cardiac conditioning. Further support for the idea that additional conditioning occurs in conjunction with the primary conditioning comes from the work of Neal Miller. When Miller (1969) conditioned a number of autonomic responses, he found that numerous other autonomic functions were conditioned, in addition to the target response he was attempting to train.

The term given to this phenomenon, *schizokinesis,* was coined by William Gantt (1966). It refers to parts of the CR which remain and have effects at a physiological level, even in the absence of any kind of overt response to a CS. Schizokinesis additionally suggests that conditioned reflexes are very difficult to eradicate once they have been achieved. Gantt makes the point that as we grow old we become a museum of antique conditioned responses. Many of these reactions are no longer useful, and some may be actually detrimental. This is especially true for cardiovascular functioning, and it is these conditioned reflexes that are more enduring. Individuals who have undergone cardiovascular conditioning may be reacting to some old situation that no longer exists. Reaction, usually at an unconscious level, causes increases in heart rate or blood pressure which may result in hypertension or cardiac problems.

Research in support of this statement is provided in Edwards and Acker (1962). This study showed that stimuli which have once been conditioned may have long-term effects on the individual. Hospitalized veterans who had been exposed to a repetitive gong sounding (CS) which warned of forthcoming combat, the call to battle stations for U.S. Navy ships during World War II, were compared in 1962 to Army veterans who had not heard the same conditioned stimulus. Edwards and Acker found that the signal continued to elicit a strong autonomic response in the Navy veterans, even though more than 15 years had elapsed since the end of the war.

Unlearning Learned Helplessness. The acquisition of learned helplessness in humans has been discussed earlier in this chapter (Hiroto, 1974). Some individuals have apparently learned that it is useless to continue responding (trying to solve life's problems), and they become depressed.

Philip Zimbardo and Floyd Ruch (1977) have offered several suggestions for combating learned helplessness in humans.

1. *"Immunization" against learned helplessness.* Persons should be made to feel that they can control their environment. Such mastery training should begin in childhood.
2. *Predictability to reduce uncertainty.* When aversion cannot be avoided, its disrupting effects can be minimized by making it as predictable as possible, thus reducing stress and anxiety. Clearly delineated behavioral rules and consequences swiftly applied could assist children where aversive consequences are necessary.
3. *Superstitious control.* Zimbardo and Ruch suggest that superstition provides a psychological function by giving the superstitious person the illusion of control. Belief in self-control is important in the prevention of helplessness.
4. *Retroactive therapy.* For depressed humans, this means relearning or discovering for the first time that responses produce consequences. Such a program should include shaping of appropriate responses through a heavy reinforcement schedule.

SUMMARY

Ivan Pavlov (1849-1936), a Russian physiologist, worked out the basic principles of classical conditioning. Additionally he made significant contributions to physiology and to the understanding of the causes and treatment of abnormal behavior. His influence has been felt worldwide, and his impact on the field of psychology in America has significantly influenced and inspired major learning theorists, past and present. Currently in America there is a rediscovery of Pavlov, while related Russian research has continued unabated.

Many debates are ongoing in the area of classical conditioning. Among them are such issues as the exact nature of the inhibition process, the similarities and differences between instrumental and classical conditioning, the effect of the CS–US interval on conditioning, the effect of varying intensities and durations of the US, and the effect of giving instructions on the conditioning process. Other interests are semantic conditioning, introceptive conditioning, phylogenetic comparisons, constraints on learning, and the bait-shy effect.

Some of the strongest interest is currently being shown in research which challenges the traditional assumption that during the process of conditioning the CS comes to be substituted for the US. Convincing evidence is accumulating to suggest that mere contiguity is a necessary but not sufficient condition for conditioning to occur. Instead, it is argued that stimuli compete for the organism's attention, and for a stimulus to be conditioned it must provide relevant information beyond those stimuli with which it is competing. If it fails to do so by being redundant or weak, conditioning fails to occur.

Practical applications of Pavlovian conditioning procedures are perhaps most evident and widely used in the field of counseling and therapy. Behavioral scientists who employ learning procedures to correct abnormal behavior are referred to as behavior therapists. They have developed a variety of applications based on both instrumental and classical conditioning procedures. The procedures discussed here relate either historically or theoretically to classical conditioning. They include the counterconditioning and extinction procedures of systematic desensitization, assertive training, flooding, impulsive therapy, and aversion techniques. Other applications are for the bait-shy effect and introceptive conditioning, which was discussed as a model for understanding unconscious reactions and feelings as well as psychosomatic illness.

ANNOTATED BIBLIOGRAPHY

Hilgard, E. R., & Bower, G. H. *Theories of learning* (4th ed.). Englewood Cliffs, N.J.: Prentice-Hall, 1975.

A broad survey of current research, theories, and developments in the field of learning is presented in one of the standard texts in the field. It thoroughly covers topics of current importance.

Hulse, S. H., Deese, J., Egeth, H. *The psychology of learning* (4th ed.). New York: McGraw-Hill, 1975.

This introductory-level textbook in the field of learning is organized according to topics or areas rather than by various theorists. It is generally well written and understandable.

Pavlov, I. P. *Conditioned reflexes.* New York: Dover Publications, 1960.

One of the best introductions to Pavlov's work to be found, this book is a translation of a series of lectures by Pavlov in 1924 which summarized his research and theory. It should not be difficult to read after you have mastered the fundamental ideas in this chapter.

Prokasy, W. F. (Ed.) *Classical conditioning I.* New York: Appleton-Century-Crofts, 1965.

Black, A., & Prokasy, W. F. (Eds.). *Classical Conditioning II.* New York: Appleton-Century-Crofts, 1972.

These two volumes deal with specific fine-grain research issues in classical conditioning and are designed for the student with more than a passing interest in the topic.

Razran, G. *Mind in evolution: An East-West synthesis of learned behavior and cognition.* Boston: Houghton Mifflin, 1971.

The author's fluency and background in both Russian and English allow him to synthesize ideas from both cultures.

REFERENCES

Bennett, E. L., & Calvin, M. Failure to train Planarians reliably. *Neurosciences Research Program Bulletin,* 1964, *2,* 3–24.

Bekhterev, V. M. Die Anwendung der Methode der motorischen Assoziationsreflexe zue Aufdeckung der Simulation. *Zeit Ges. Neurological Psychiatry,* 1912, *13,* 183-181.

Bekhterev, V. M. *La psychologic objective.* Paris: Alcan, 1913.

Bekhterev, V. M. *General principles of human reflexology.* New York: International Universities Press, 1932.

Breland, K., & Breland, M. The misbehavior of organisms. *American Psychologist,* 1961, *16,* 681–684.

Brown, B. B. *New mind, new body.* New York: Harper & Row, 1974.

Cautela, J. R. Covert sensitization. *Psychological Record,* 1967, *20,* 459–468.

Champion, R. A. Stimulus-intensity effects in response evocation. *Psychological Review,* 1962, *69,* 428–449.

Cook, J. W., Altman, K., Shaw, J., & Blaylock, M. Use of contingent lemon juice to eliminate public masturbation by a severely retarded boy. *Behavior Research and Therapy,* 1978, *16,* 131–134.

Coppock, W. J. Pre-extinction in sensory preconditioning. *Journal of Experimental Psychology,* 1958, *55,* 213-219.

Cuny, H. *Ivan Pavlov: The man and his theories.* New York: Premier Books, 1962.

Dykman, R. A., Mack, R. L., & Ackerman, P. T. The evaluation of autonomic and motor components of the nonavoidance conditioned response of the dog. *Psychophysiology,* 1965, *1,* 209–230.

Edwards, A. E., & Acker, L. E. A demonstration of the long-term retention of a conditioned galvanic skin response. *Psychosomatic Medicine,* 1962, *24,* 459–463.

Estes, W. K. *Handbook of learning and cognitive processes: Conditioning and behavior theory* (Vol. 2). Hillsdale, N.J.: Lawrence Erlbaum Associates, 1975.

Fearing, F. *Reflex action: A study in the history of physiological psychology.* Baltimore, Md.: Williams & Wilkins, 1930.

Foreyt, J. P., & Kennedy, W. A. Treatment of overweight by aversion therapy. *Behavior Research and Therapy,* 1971, *9,* 29–34.

Forness, S. R., & MacMillan, O. K. The origins of behavior modification with exceptional children. *Exceptional Children,* 1970, *37,* 93–100.

Fredrikson, M., & Ohman, A. Electrodermal responses conditioned to fear-relevant stimuli. *Psychophysiology,* 1979, *16,* 1–7.

Gantt, W. H. Pavlov's system. In B. B. Wolman & E. Nagel (Eds.), *Scientific psychology.* New York: Basic Books, 1965.

Gantt, W. H. Reflexology, schizokinesis, autokinesis. *Conditional Reflex,* 1966, *1,* 57-68.

Gardner, R., & Gardner, B. T. Teaching sign language to a chimpanzee. *Science,* 1969, *165,* 664–672.

Gustavson, C. R., Garcia, J., Hankins, W. G., & Rusiniak, K. W. Coyote predation control by aversive conditioning. *Science,* 1974, *194,* 581–583.

Harris, A. H., & Brady, J. V. Animal learning: Visceral and autonomic conditioning. In M. R. Rosenzweig & L. W. Porter (Eds.), *Annual Review of Psychology* (Vol. 25). Palo Alto, Cal.: Annual Reviews, 1974.

Hearst, E. The classical-instrumental distinction: Reflexes, voluntary behavior and categories of associative learning. In W. K. Estes (Ed.), *Handbook of learning and cognitive processes: Conditioning and behavior theory* (Vol. 2). Hillsdale, N.J.: Lawrence Erlbaum Associates, 1975.

Hinde, R. A. *Animal behavior* (2nd ed.). New York: McGraw-Hill, 1970.

Hiroto, D. S. Laws of control and learned helplessness. *Journal of Experimental Psychology,* 1974, *102,* 187–193.

Hull, C. L. *Principles of behavior.* New York: Appleton-Century-Crofts, 1943.

Jacobson, E. *Progressive relaxation.* Chicago: University of Chicago Press, 1938.

Janda, L. H., & Rimm, D. C. Covert sensitization in treatment of obesity. *Journal of Abnormal Psychology*, 1972, *80*, 37–42.

Johnston, R. E., Zahorik, D. M., Immler, H., & Zakon, H. Alterations of male sexual behavior by learned aversions to hamster vaginal secretions. *Journal of Comparative and Physiological Psychology*, 1978, *92*, 85–93.

Jones, M. C. A laboratory study of fear: The case of Peter. *Journal of Genetic Psychology*, 1924, *31*, 308–315.

Kamin, L. J. Selective association and conditioning. In N. J. Mackintosh & W. K. Honig (Eds.), *Fundamental issues in associative learning*. Halifax, N.S.: Dalhousie University Press, 1969.

Kantorovich, N. V. [An attempt at associative reflex therapy in alcoholism.] *Novoe V. Refleksologii Fiziologii I. Nervnoi Systemy*, 1929, *3*, 436–437. (*Psychological Abstracts*, 1930, No. 4282.)

Kimble, G. A. Cognitive inhibition in classical conditioning. In H. H. Kindler & J. T. Spence (Eds.), *Essays in neobehaviorism*. New York: Appleton-Century-Crofts, 1971.

Kleitman, N., & Crisler, G. A quantitative study of a salivary conditioned reflex. *American Journal of Physiology*, 1927, *79*, 571–614.

Lang, P. J. Fear reduction and fear behavior: Problems in treating a construct. In J. M. Schlien (Ed.), *Research in psychotherapy* (Vol. 3). Washington, D.C.: American Psychological Association, 1968.

Lang, P. J., Melamed, B. G., & Hart, J. A. A psychophysiological analysis of fear modification using automated desensitization procedures. *Journal of Abnormal Psychology*, 1970, *76*, 220–235.

Lamere, F., & Voegtlin, W. An evaluation of the aversive treatment of alcoholism. *Quarterly Journal of Studies on Alcohol*, 1950, *11*, 199–204.

Lazarus, A. A. Behavior therapy in groups. In G. M. Gazda (Ed.), *Basic approaches to group psychotherapy and group counseling*. Springfield, Ill.: Charles C Thomas, 1968.

Lewis, G. H. *The physiology of common life*. New York: D. Appleton, 1860.

Liddell, H. S. The conditioned reflex. In F.

A. Moss (Ed.), *Comparative psychology*. New York: Prentice-Hall, 1934.

Luria, A. R. *The role of speech in the regulation of normal and abnormal behavior*. New York: J. B. Lippincott, 1961.

Marks, I. M., & Gelder, M. G. Transvestism and fetishism: Clinical and psychological changes during faradic aversion. *British Journal of Psychiatry*, 1967, *119*, 711–730.

Masserman, J. H. *Behavior and neurosis*. Chicago: University of Chicago Press, 1943.

Mateer, F. *Child behavior: A critical and experimental study of young children by the method of conditioned reflexes*. Boston: Badger, 1917.

McConnell, J. V. Cannibalism and memory in flatworms. *New Scientist*, 1964, *21*, 465–468.

McConnell, J. V. Comparative physiology: Learning in invertebrates. *Annual Review of Physiology*, 1966, *28*, 107–136.

McConnell, J. V., Shigehista, T., & Salive, J. In K. H. Pribram & D. E. Broadbent (Eds.), *Biology and memory*. New York: Academic Press, 1970.

McGuire, R. J., & Vallance, M. Aversion therapy by electric shock: A simple technique. *British Medical Journal*, 1964, *1*, 151–153.

Miller, N. E. Learnable drives and rewards. In S. S. Stevens (Ed.), *Handbook of experimental psychology*. New York: John Wiley & Sons, 1951.

Miller, N. E. Learning of visceral and glandular responses. *Science*, 1969, *163*, 435–445.

Miller, S., & Konorski, J. Sur une forme particuliers des reflexes conditionnels. *Compte rendu hebdomadaire des seanees et memoires de la Societé de Biologie*, 1928, *99*, 1155–1157.

Mis, F. W. A midbrain-brain stem circuit for conditioned inhibition in the rabbit. *Journal of Comparative and Physiological Psychology*, 1977, *91*, 975–988.

Mount, G. R., Payton, T., Ellis, J., & Barnes, P. A multimodal behavioral approach to the treatment of alcoholism. *Behavioral Engineering*, 1976, *33*, 61–66.

Mowrer, O. H. Neurosis, psychotherapy,

and two-factor learning theory. In O. H. Mowrer (Ed.), *Psychotherapy: Theory and research.* New York: Ronald Press, 1953.

O'Brien, J. H., Wilder, M. B., & Stevens, C. D. Conditioning of cortical neurons in cats with antidromic activation as the unconditioned stimulus. *Journal of Comparative and Physiological Psychology,* 1977, *91,* 918–927.

Pavlov, I. P. *Conditioned reflexes.* London: Clarendon Press, 1927.

Pavlov, I. P. Neurosis in man and animals. *Journal of the American Medical Association,* 1932, *99,* 1012–1013. (a)

Pavlov, I. P. The reply of a physiologist to psychologists. *Psychological Review,* 1932, *39,* 91–127. (b)

Pavlov, I. P. An attempt at physiological interpretations of obsessional neurosis and paranoia. *Journal of Mental Science,* 1934, *80,* 187–197.

Pavlov, I. P. *Conditioned reflexes in psychiatry* (W. H. Gantt, trans.). New York: International Universities Press, 1941.

Perkins, D. G. *The effectiveness of three procedures for increasing assertiveness in low assertive college students.* Unpublished doctoral dissertation, North Texas State University, Denton, 1972.

Perkins, D. G. *Acquisition of excessive fear of telephones.* Unpublished paper, Richland College, Dallas, 1975.

Perkins, F. M. Personal communication, July 12, 1978.

Razran, G. The observable unconscious and the inferable conscious in current Soviet psychophysiology: Interoceptive conditioning, semantic conditioning, and the orienting reflex. *Psychological Review,* 1961, *68,* 81–147.

Razran, G. Russian physiologists' psychology and American experimental psychology. *Psychological Bulletin,* 1965, *63,* 42–64.

Razran, G. *Mind in evolution: An East-West synthesis of learned behavior and cognition.* Boston: Houghton Mifflin, 1971.

Rescorla, R. A. Inhibition of delay in Pavlovian fear conditioning. *Journal of Comparative and Physiological Psychology,* 1967, *64,* 114–120.

Rescorla, R. A. Informational variables in Pavlovian conditioning. In G. Bower (Ed.), *The psychology of learning and motivation* (Vol. 6). New York: Academic Press, 1972.

Rescorla, R. A., & Solomon, R. L. The two-process learning theory: Relationships between Pavlovian conditioning and instrumental learning. *Psychological Review,* 1967, *74,* 151–182.

Rescorla, R. A., & Wagner, A. R. A theory of Pavlovian conditioning: Variations in effectiveness of reinforcement and non-reinforcement. In A. Black & W. F. Prokasy, Jr. (Eds.), *Classical conditioning II.* New York: Appleton-Century-Crofts, 1972.

Ross, S. M., & Ross, L. E. Comparison of trace and delay classical eyelid conditioning as a function of interstimulus interval. *Journal of Experimental Psychology,* 1971, *91,* 165–167.

Salter, A. *Conditioned reflex therapy.* New York: Capricorn Books, 1949.

Schachter, S. *Emotion, obesity and crime.* New York: Academic Press, 1971.

Schlosberg, H. The relationship between success and the laws of conditioning. *Psychological Review,* 1937, *44,* 379–392.

Schmahl, D., Lichtenstein, E., & Harris, D. Successful treatment of habitual smokers with warm, smoky air and rapid smoking. *Journal of Consulting and Clinical Psychology,* 1972, *38,* 105–111.

Schneiderman, N. Interstimulus interval function of the nictitating membrane response of the rabbit under delay versus trace conditioning. *Journal of Comparative and Physiological Psychology,* 1966, *62,* 397–402.

Sechenov, J. M. Reflexes of the brain. In A. A. Subkov (Ed.), *Selected works.* Moscow: State Publishing House, 1935.

Seligman, M. E. P. On the generality of the law of learning. *Psychological Review,* 1970, *77,* 406–418.

Seligman, M. E. P., & Maier, S. F. Failure to escape traumatic shock. *Journal of Experimental Psychology,* 1967, *74,* 1–9.

Skinner, B. F. Two types of conditioned reflex: A reply to Konorski and Miller. *Journal of General Psychology,* 1937, *16,* 272–279.

Skinner, B. F. *The behavior of organisms.* New York: Appleton-Century-Crofts, 1938.

Skinner, B. F. *Science and human behavior.* New York: Macmillan, 1953.

Solomon, R. L., Kamin, L., & Wynne, L. C. Traumatic avoidance learning: The outcome of several extinction procedures with dogs. *Journal of Abnormal and Social Psychology,* 1953, *48, 291–302.*

Stollak, G. E. Weight loss obtained under different experimental procedures. *Psychotherapy: Theory, Research and Practice,* 1967, *4,* 61–64.

Stolurow, L. M. Conditioning. In B. B. Wolman (Ed.), *Handbook of general psychology.* Englewood Cliffs, N.J.: Prentice-Hall, 1973.

Sturgis, E. T., Tollison, C. D., & Adams, H. E. Modification of combined migraine muscle contractions headaches using BVP and EMG feedback. *Journal of Applied Behavior Analysis,* 1978, *11,* 215–223.

Suinn, R., Edie, C., & Spinelli, P. Accelerated massed desensitization: Innovation in short-term treatment. *Behavior Therapy,* 1970, *1,* 303–311.

Thompson, R. F. Sensory preconditioning. In R. F. Thompson & J. S. Voss (Eds.), *Topics in learning and performance.* New York: Academic Press, 1972.

Trotter, R. J., & McConnell, J. V. *Psychology: The human science.* New York: Holt, Rinehart & Winston, 1978.

Unger, G. Chemical transfer of learning; its stimulus specificity. *Proceedings, Federation of American Society for Experimental Biology,* 1966, *25,* 109.

Watson, J. B. Behaviorism and the concept of mental disease. *Journal of Philosophical and Psychological Scientific Methods,* 1916, *13,* 587–597.

Watson, J. B. *Psychology from the standpoint of the behaviorist* (3rd ed.). Philadelphia: Lippincott, 1929.

Watson, J. B., & Rayner, R. Conditioned emotional reactions. *Journal of Experimental Psychology,* 1920, *3,* 1–14.

Weinrich, W. W., Danley, H. H., & General, D. A. *Self-directed systematic desensitization: A guide for the student, client and therapist.* Kalamazoo, Mich.: Behaviordelia, 1976.

White, C. T., & Schlosberg, H. Degree of conditioning of the GSR as a function of the period of delay. *Journal of Experimental Psychology,* 1952, *43,* 357–362.

Wickens, D. D. A study of voluntary and involuntary finger conditioning. *Journal of Experimental Psychology,* 1939, *25,* 127–140.

Wolpe, J. *Psychotherapy by reciprocal inhibition.* Stanford, Cal.: Stanford University Press, 1958.

Wolpe, J. *The practice of behavior therapy* (2nd ed.). New York: Pergamon Press, 1973.

Yehle, A. L., Dauth, G., & Schneiderman, N. Correlates of heart rate classical conditioning in curarized rabbits. *Journal of Comparative Physiological Psychology,* 1967, *64,* 98–104.

Zeaman, D., & Smith, R. W. Review and analysis of some recent findings in human cardiac conditioning. In W. F. Prokasky (Ed.), *Classical conditioning.* New York: Appleton-Century-Crofts, 1965.

Zimbardo, P. G., & Ruch, F. L. *Psychology and life.* Glenview, Ill.: Scott Foresman, 1977.

3

Guthrie's Theory of Learning

JOHN G. CARLSON

INTRODUCTION

Overview

The term *learning* commonly describes a more or less permanent change in behavior which is not attributable to maturational variables or to factors producing relatively temporary or cyclical effects (such as drugs or fatigue). A child who builds houses with blocks learns that certain ways of stacking them are more successful than others. But a child who cries before naptime did not learn to become tired. Moreover, blockbuilding will be an enduring skill, whereas the fatigue will dissipate with sleep. Many theorists have also included practice and some type of reward mechanism in their definitions of learning (Kimble, 1961), despite considerable debate on their respective roles.

In the 1930s Edwin R. Guthrie (1886–1959) developed a theory based on the view that learning is "The ability to . . . respond differently to a situation because of past response to the situation . . . [It] distinguishes those living creatures which common sense endows with minds" (1935, p. 3). Despite the role of mind, however, Guthrie also pointed out that learning is merely behavioral

change, not necessarily improvement. In other words, we may learn maladaptive as well as adaptive responses, a fact that later provided Guthrie (1938) with considerable subject matter for an analysis of human conflict.

Theories of Learning. Theories of learning are attempts to organize, simplify, explain, and predict the facts of learning. No theory so far has done an outstanding job of this, including the one devised by Guthrie. This undoubtedly is due to the enormous breadth of the field and the facts to be dealt with, rather than to a lack of imaginative effort on the part of the theorists. The sheer numbers of attempts to develop viable theories of learning in this century attest to the struggles of psychologists to deal with this important topic.

A convention helpful in placing Guthrie's views into historical and conceptual perspective is a threefold categorization of major theories of learning (Hergenhahn, 1976). One class of theories, labeled *associationistic,* includes the views of Ivan Pavlov, John B. Watson, Edwin Guthrie, and William K. Estes. These theories stress the connections formed between environmental events and behavior. Learning is seen as the process of the formation of associations. The nature of the associations themselves provides the basis for major theoretical differences.

Another class of theories, *functionalistic* views, is represented by the models given to us by Edward L. Thorndike, Clark Hull, and Burrhus F. Skinner. In these theories, emphasis is on the *functions* that behavior serves (though processes of association still play a necessary role). Traditionally, people have been distinguished from the rest of the animal world in terms of the greater intentionality, purpose, or goal-directedness their behavior shows. We respond in accordance with outcomes of our behavior or, in Skinner's and Hull's terminology, the *reinforcers* of our actions. The antecedent stimuli for responses may be less important than their consequences or *effects*.

A third class of theories places a greater emphasis on processes inside the individual—thinking, planning, decision making, and the like—than on the environment outside or overt responses. These predominantly "cognitive" theories include the Gestalt notions of Max Wertheimer, Wolfgang Köhler and Kurt Koffka, the developmental psychology of Jean Piaget, and the early animal "purposivism" of Edward C. Tolman. Recently, there has been a resurgence of interest in cognitively oriented views.

The theories of the associationists and functionalists fit squarely into a period of American psychology dominated by the position that the proper subject matter of the science is *behavior* rather than mental events. Guthrie's theory, which showed little fundamental change from its earliest forms (1930, 1935) through later clarification and development (1940, 1952, 1959), was clearly a behavioral view. His definition of the response as the movement of a muscle or secretion of a gland was in perfect accord with Watson's (1913) admonition that to make the field respectable we must make its data observable and recordable. Similarly, Guthrie held a strict physicalistic view of the "stimulus" that did not undergo serious modification until the end of his career. While by training Guthrie was a philosopher, and by his own account (Guthrie, 1959) he was lastingly impressed by the works of the philosopher E. A. Singer, he was committed to the possibility that a strictly empirical and objective analysis of stimuli and responses is the most fruitful way to go about explaining the activities of humans.

Major Issues

Guthrie's theory has been at the heart of some of the major topics of discussion on learning. Some of the points that follow will be clarified in later discussion of the theory; this section provides an introduction to issues that differentiate Guthrie's position from others.

Maturation and Learning. American learning theorists of Guthrie's time downplayed the importance of genetic and maturational factors in behavior. In part, this was a manifestation of the basic doctrine of empiricism, which stresses the influence of the external world upon our sensory systems. Traditionally, genetic determination implies fixedness or rigidity in behavior; learning connotes flexibility and adaptiveness.

Guthrie was not close-minded, however, on the possible role of maturational and instinct variables in behavior. In 1935, he stated, "We cannot go the whole distance with [E. B.] Holt (1931) and say that all stimulus-response associations are dependent on conditioning. Maturation of the nervous system appears to be the principal determiner of many classes of acts" (p. 38). He went on to cite several studies of infants in accord with this view. However, he maintained that "conditioning remains the principal way in which the behavior of a person is adjusted to the peculiarities of his environment" (Guthrie, 1935, p. 39).

Recently, learning psychologists have come to recognize the significance of genetic variables in behavior (see Bolles, 1975, Chap. 9, and Chap. 6 of this text). Guthrie's view was an enlightened one for its time. A theory that fails to take into account interactions between learning and structures and processes of the organism as determined by its species limitations simply cannot handle all the facts of behavior.

Contiguity vs. Reinforcement. Guthrie's brand of associationism maintained that the predominant mechanism operating in learning is temporal relatedness, the close correlation in time between a stimulus and response. This is now called a "contiguity" position; it stands in direct contrast to theories that stress the importance of motivation or of reinforcement in learning. The latter, functionalistic, views have historical roots in the doctrine of *hedonism,* that a person's actions are largely designed to attain pleasure and to avoid pain. Though there is little formal resemblance between the 18th-century philosophies of hedonism and the contemporary behavioral views of positive and negative reinforcement, functionalist theories have all incorporated the outcomes of behavior into their learning mechanisms. Guthrie was forced to deal with the facts of "reward learning," but he handled the functions of goals in a rather

novel fashion and maintained throughout that rewards are not essential to the learning process.

The issue of whether learning is primarily a contiguity or reinforcement process is no longer a concern to theorists, many of whom now incorporate both mechanisms into their models. Moreover, for the more notable contemporary learning psychologists, such as Skinner, reinforcers are defined as among those events that modify the probability of responding, nothing more. This frees the reinforcement concept from hedonistic implications and also frees learning theorists of arguments that are philosophical rather than empirical in nature.

Continuity vs. All-or-None Learning. The maxim "Practice makes perfect" expresses one of the earliest known features of learned behavior, that repeating an action often seems to improve its effectiveness. In terms of errors made, time to completion of a task, numbers of responses required, and other measures, the course of learning is typically a course of improvement with repetition of an act. Learning theories commonly incorporate mechanisms designed to account for practice effects. A continuity position regards the course of learning as a more or less continuous change in responding over trials. The extreme alternative is to regard the actual process of learning as virtually instantaneous; that is, learning either occurs all at once or not at all.

Guthrie's theory fits into the latter camp. A stimulus response association is either formed at once, or it is not formed. The all-or-none position has received substantial elaboration in recent mathematical learning models and related research, especially that involving learning in verbal association tasks. However, this is not a subject of current debate among learning psychologists. Models of all-or-none learning offer alternatives to more traditional approaches and seem to fit many laboratory situations nicely. Guthrie deserves considerable credit for demonstrating at least the theoretical possibility of this conception of learning.

One or More Learning Factors. Guthrie's is a *single-factor* learning theory. He viewed all learning phenomena as subsumable under one principle: stimulus-response association. With respect to his stress upon one learning mechanism, he did not differ from Pavlov, Watson, or Hull (although the specific form of the learning mechanism differed somewhat among these single-factor theorists). In the development of learning theory, however, the trend has been toward models with more than one factor, usually two, paralleling the two different views of learning set forth by Pavlov and Thorndike (to be cited later in this chapter). Skinner (1938) and O. Hobart Mowrer (1947) were early two-factor theorists. Recently, the field of learning, especially animal learning, has been dominated by two-factor views.

Whether learning involves one or more processes hinges upon a number of arguments (see Rescorla & Solomon, 1967) at the forefront of which is the physiological distinction between two nervous systems, the more primitive involuntary autonomic system, and the higher-order voluntary central nervous system. Guthrie, however, described the learning of Pavlov's dogs in the same terms as learning by Thorndikian reward procedures, since he was intent upon applying his model across all situations. He seems to have been largely unconcerned with possible differences between responses of nervous systems and remained convinced throughout his career

of the viability of his single principle of association.

Basic Concepts

Guthrie introduced relatively few new terms into his theory beyond those employed by many other theorists of his day. The following are some concepts that Guthrie stressed or used in a manner different from his contemporaries.

Association. The basis for learning (or conditioning) in Guthrie's theory is the formation of an associative relationship between a stimulus and a response. The association is understood as a tendency for a response to a stimulus to recur when the response has previously occurred in the presence of that stimulus (therefore the response has become associated to the stimulus).

Associative Inhibition. This is Guthrie's term for the process more commonly referred to as *extinction*. According to Guthrie, associations do *not* undergo a process of progressive deterioration during extinction. Rather, the response in an association is displaced or replaced by an alternative response which is incompatible with the original response (see *Inhibition*). Extinction is thus a process of the formation of new and inhibitory associations.

Inhibition. Emotional responses as well as muscular movements were seen by Guthrie to be sometimes prevented by the occurrence of another activity. He viewed the inhibitory process as fundamentally an event in the central nervous system—that is, the blocking of nerve impulses to one response due to the occurrence of impulses for another (Guthrie, 1942).

Learning. Learning in Guthrie's theory is understood simply as the ability to come to behave differently and permanently because of prior behavior in a given situation. It is the feature that distinguishes creatures with "minds" from those without them. The definition precludes impermanent changes in behavior, such as those due to fatigue and sense organ adaptation.

Maintaining Stimulus. Motivation, in Guthrie's system, is manifested in a set of continuous, internal stimuli that persist until a consummatory response occurs (usually at a goal). These stimuli, along with movement-produced stimuli, are often important in the maintenance of integrated, goal-directed activity.

Movement. Guthrie's interest was primarily in muscular movements rather than in the outcome or goal of an integrated pattern of behavior. The latter could be called an *act,* whereas the movement is the primary response, that is, the portion of the act that enters into associations with stimuli. By the distinction between movements and acts, Guthrie was able to explain gradual improvement in performance in learning, despite the instantaneous manner in which stimulus-response associations are formed.

Movement-Produced Stimuli. Guthrie argues that every movement is a stimulus for receptors in the muscles, tendons, and joints (proprioceptors) as well as potentially a stimulus for the exteroceptors through its effects. This notion aids in the understanding of complex, integrated series of movements.

Punishment. A punisher in Guthrie's theory is viewed simply as a stimulus. By this notion, the punishing stimulus does not suppress or weaken associations, it initiates new action. "Sitting on tacks does not discourage learning. It encourages one in learning to do something else than sit" (Guthrie, 1952, p. 132). Punishment is therefore the process of initiating a new response, one that may

be incompatible with the punished one and that will replace it in association with the related stimuli.

Reward. As with the concept of punishment, there is no unique event in this theory that qualifies as a reward. The latter, too, is merely a form of stimulus or stimulus change, one that most often occurs at the end of a sequence of behavior. Rewards are said to have a preserving or maintaining influence on prior associations simply because they function to remove the organism from a situation and prevent the formation of associations between the stimuli and new responses.

Response. (See *Movement.*)

Stimulus. The concept of the stimulus in this system is very broad. Essentially any physical change that is detected by receptors and to which a response is made qualifies as a stimulus.

HISTORY

Beginnings

Guthrie's learning theory is a theory of the process of association. The concept of association is ancient. Aristotle's analysis of the process of recollection included a reference to the importance of a regular relationship between events in experience: "Acts of recollection, as they occur in experience, are due to the fact that one movement has by nature another that succeeds it in regular order" (cited in Dennis, 1948, p. 5).

Across the Middle Ages, most people probably had more pressing concerns than theories of the workings of the mind —mere survival took precedence. However, as the Western world emerged from this era, the more favorable social climate of Renaissance England allowed for a host of ideas to flourish concerning ways in which humans transform the world around them into experience. The first of the British associationists was John Locke. By contrast with some of the philosophers who preceded him, Locke argued that people's experience was a product of their empirical world—we are not endowed with knowledge at birth, we acquire it. Further, knowledge, or more commonly, ideas that correspond to the world outside the senses may become complex through compounding or "association," he stated. His example was that of the substance, lead. The complex idea of this element consists of combining a number of simpler ideas involving lead's color, hardness, weight, and so forth. The complex idea is the result of the association of simpler ones.

The Mills agreed with the concept of associationism but were more specific on the nature of the process. James Mill defined the principle of association as "The tendency for ideas to group themselves or succeed one another after the manner of their originals" (cited in Warren, 1921, p. 94). Mill developed an elaborate logical or mechanical account of this process. His son, John Stuart Mill, by contrast, viewed the association process as more experiential. Most important, he argued that simple ideas *generate* more complex ones, such that a complex association is more than the total of its individual parts. The idea of *tree* is something more than the combination of trunk, leaves, and branches.

Early forms of the doctrine of associationism can be traced to Alexander Bain. Bain outlined a so-called Law of Contiguity which held that actions or sensations that tend to recur together will "cohere," so that the idea of one will bring up the idea of the other. He also expanded the notion of association to include the possibility that a number of weaker ideas might compound into a stronger one.

That is, several ideas that individually may not relate to another idea might together call up an earlier associate.

Guthrie was explicit on the differences between his associationist theory and those of his philosophical predecessors. Guthrie was a behaviorist and scientist; the early associationists were philosophers.

> What is associated? Aristotle, Hobbes, Locke, and . . . Bain . . . appear to have been vaguely aware that sights and sounds and other forms of sensation can arouse ideas, and that ideas can somehow arouse action and can certainly stimulate other ideas. But it is our desire to apply the principle to material that can be observed and material with which the principle can be verified. Our position is that what is associated is a stimulus and a response. (Guthrie, 1942, p. 23)

Major Theorists

By the turn of the century, a discipline of human study was emerging that was somewhat more experimental than its philosophical antecedents. At the forefront was a Russian physiologist, Ivan Pavlov. While Guthrie was clearly influenced by Pavlov's (1927) restatement of the association principle in explicit and objective terms, he expounded at length (Guthrie, 1935) on the differences between his theory and Pavlov's earlier one (as well as the deficiencies of the latter). Pavlov's was a stimulus-stimulus association theory. According to Pavlov, a tone (substitute stimulus) associated with food (original stimulus) comes to evoke responses originally evoked by the food, such as salivation. In Guthrie's view, Pavlov had erred:

> The essential mistake of this description . . . lies in viewing the two stimuli, the original stimulus and the substitute stimulus, as the associated items. It is the

time relations between these stimuli that are observed and recorded. But . . . *it is the time relations between the substitute siimulus and the response that count.* (Guthrie, 1935, p. 49)

In other words, learning—or more specifically, the process of association—ultimately is not a result of a correlation between a stimulus and a stimulus but rather a correlation between a stimulus and a *response*. Guthrie's theory is therefore a stimulus-response association theory. If a dog salivates to a tone, it is not because the tone and food previously were paired, but because the tone and the response, salivation (elicited by the food), were paired. In many cases, the distinction is purely theoretical, owing to the close proximity in time of stimuli and responses during classical conditioning. But certain of the implications of the differences between the two theories have been experimentally tested, with results not always sympathetic with a stimulus-response contiguity position (e.g., Mowrer & Lamoreaux, 1942).

Guthrie also took on another of the notable early figures in psychology, Edward L. Thorndike, although he had respect for this theorist's experimental approach to the study of learning. In fact, one of Guthrie's own most notable laboratory efforts was basically a modification of Thorndike's early problem-box experiments. In 1911, Thorndike published a series of experiments in which cats and other animals were placed in boxes from which escape was possible by such means as clawing a hanging rope. Outside the box the animals found food as well as freedom. Thorndike observed progressive decreases in the time required for the animals to escape from the box. He attributed this to a "stamping in" process caused by the animal's success in making its escape to food.

Thorndike's view of animal learning based on these studies came to be called an *effect theory,* since it was the effect of the act (reward and escape) that was seen to produce the gradual improvement in performance. To this point, Guthrie took great exception.

Guthrie seems also to have been influenced by a lesser known figure of his time, Edwin B. Holt. Guthrie was quite sympathetic with elements of Holt's *Animal Drive and the Learning Process* (1931), in which Holt clearly articulated a conditioning process, though it was more broadly applied than Guthrie seems to have preferred. For instance, Holt contended that even the child's first walking was a product of learning processes alone, while Guthrie felt that maturation must also be involved. But Holt was committed to behavior as the prime topic of psychology, and he rejected the notion of the Pavlovian reflex as the fundamental component of behavior. Guthrie found great appeal in these positions as well as in Holt's views on the self-sustaining feature of muscle contractions (later embodied in Guthrie's movement-produced stimulus concept), and in certain of Holt's ideas concerning avoidance learning.

Guthrie's contemporaries and successors—Clark Hull, Burrhus F. Skinner, and Edward C. Tolman—also spent considerable time in the analysis of animal behavior, but each with somewhat different emphases. Of the three, Guthrie seems to have been least sympathetic with Tolman. Guthrie found two aspects of Tolman's theory especially objectionable. First Guthrie attacked (with humor) Tolman's concern with goals or outcomes of action:

I must confess at this point a certain awe of the psychologists who, like Tolman, say (1932, p. 10) that "behavior

. . . always seems to have the character of getting-to or getting-from a specific goal object, or goal situation." So much of my own behavior lacks this admirable quality . . . that I am inclined to suspect even the higher animals of at least . . . occasional aimlessness. (Guthrie, 1935, p. 167)

The second feature of Tolman's theorizing with which Guthrie took exception was the stress upon cognitive or "mentalistic" sounding concepts. This prompted Guthrie's famous analysis of the situation of the rat who must cognize, judge, hypothesize, and the like in Tolman's mazes: "So far as [Tolman's] theory is concerned the rat is left buried in thought" at the choice point (Guthrie, 1935, p. 172). In other words, Guthrie felt that Tolman's theory was seriously deficient in that it lacked a mechanism for translating learning processes into behavior.

Despite substantial differences between the views of Hull and Skinner, Guthrie's theory does have a kinship with their concern for the particulars of animal behavior. Hull shared Guthrie's interest in understanding precisely why, for instance, a rat locomotes from a start box to the end of a runway, but his hypothetico-deductive form of theorizing was infinitely more systematic than Guthrie's. His solution, too, differed markedly from Guthrie's. Hull (1943) maintained that the most significant event in runway behavior was the *goal* (typically food). This produces an increment in a bond between the stimuli of the runway and the rat's response of running, a bond referred to as "habit." In short, Hull was an associationist too, but like Thorndike, he stressed outcomes (goals) in the reinforcement of stimulus-response connections. Guthrie disagreed with the view that goals are essential for learning as well as with Hull's notion that associa-

tions (habits) are formed gradually or "continuously" during learning.

Skinner (e.g., 1938) also stressed the importance of reinforcing events in the development of certain learned behaviors, or *operants,* and in this fundamental way his view differed from Guthrie's. However, Skinner's analysis of the operant *is* consistent with Guthrie's theory of behavior in at least one respect. The operant, by contrast with the reflex or *respondent* in Skinner's account, is normally characterized by an absence of obvious, observable, antecedent stimuli. This is why, in Skinner's view, psychology has been burdened with so many theories of behavior. We are tempted to mediate the mysterious gap between the observable environment and observable behavior with a myriad of psychological constructs —will, intention, expectations, and the like. Skinner reserves the term *emitted behavior* for operants to remind us of the elusive nature of their antecedent stimuli, but otherwise his analysis strives generally to downplay their importance. Similarly, Guthrie argued that "for some behavior the stimuli are obscure" (1942, pp. 45–46). However, he proceeded with the assumption that the proper analysis of behavior is still in terms of its stimulus-response components. While the stimuli may be obscure, they still exist, either outside the organism or inside it (in the form of movement-produced stimuli and maintaining stimuli).

A major respect in which Skinner's and Guthrie's theories differ is in their views of the fundamental process of learning itself. Skinner very early adopted his distinction between respondent behaviors, conditionable by the Pavlovian methods of stimulus-stimulus pairing, and operant behaviors, conditionable through response-reinforcement contingencies. Guthrie, by contrast, was a *single-process* theorist. His stimulus-response contiguity model was applied in the analysis of Pavlovian reflexes as well as the more complex and seemingly goal-directed behaviors that American learning theorists found of greater interest. To this day the issue of whether learning involves basically one or more fundamental processes remains of interest to students of learning (cf. Rescorla & Solomon, 1967).

Current Status

Guthrie's major contributions to learning during the 1930s and 1940s came at a time when leading theorists were striving to develop broad-scale, comprehensive theories of learning. Since the 1950s, theorists (with the notable exception of Skinner) have been somewhat less ambitious in the range of phenomena to which they apply their theories or, more appropriately, *models* of learning. One instance of this trend, Estes's mathematical theory, is cited in the next section and is the subject of Chapter 9. The result has been more intensive research and, in some cases, remarkably thorough analyses of traditionally difficult problems in generalization, discrimination, patterns of reinforcement, extinction, and other learning phenomena. This is especially true in animal learning, the area in which Guthrie focused his primary efforts.

Besides the miniaturization of theories in the past two decades, the recent inroads of cognitive views of learning on American psychology have resulted in a dichotomization of the field. On the one side are those who argue that the development of stimulus and response concepts assures the field of a solid foundation in its traditional research paradigms, as well as continuity in the shift from

mentalism to scientific empiricism which took place at the turn of the century. The behavioral terms now familiar to all students of psychology—conditioning, reinforcement, extinction, punishment, and the like—continue to be the language of thousands of psychologists committed to the understanding of learning. Skinner has emerged as the foremost spokesperson for the continuance of the behavioristic approach to learning (e.g., Skinner, 1974). However, the large numbers of notable investigators and theorists of many differing persuasions cited in the animal conditioning portions of introductory learning texts attest to the continued breadth and strength of this view.

There are also those who argue that many of the traditional concepts of learning are outmoded and possibly useless for the understanding of behavior. They advocate the development of cognitive constructs, such as structures, expectancies, information, and imagery. Cognitive psychologists tend largely to work with humans and in the context of memory (see Horton & Turnage, 1976). However, related trends in animal psychology are also notable. Following Tolman's (1932) early lead, in the 1960s some animal investigators began to realize the inadequacies of some of the traditional learning and motivation concepts in dealing with certain complex learning tasks (Rescorla & Solomon, 1967; Trapold & Overmier, 1972). Full-scale learning models have begun to appear (Bindra, 1974; Bolles, 1972) which incorporate many cognitive-sounding constructs in the interpretation of animal behavior.

Where would Guthrie have fit into the contemporary learning scene? If he had continued to champion his stimulus-response association model, it is likely that these concepts would have undergone revision to accommodate the results of increasingly sophisticated animal research paradigms. In particular, Guthrie would have been compelled to deal with data consistent with informational and expectancy analyses of animal behavior. He probably would have been forced to rely increasingly upon his concepts of internal stimuli (explained in Proposition 2) and attentional mechanisms (Guthrie, 1959). It is not at all clear that Guthrie would have adopted more mathematically oriented concepts, since he did not avail himself of the opportunity even in his last writings.

In general, Guthrie's theory was a product of its time, now largely a historical curiosity rather than a viable device for the interpretation of wide varieties of behavior. There are no schools of Guthrian psychology. Tributes to Guthrie are mainly paid to certain of his ideas and not to a current impact on theories of learning.

Other Theories

If we accept B. R. Hergenhahn's (1976) distinction between the more behavioral associationistic theories and the cognitive learning theories, and if the trend of contemporary theorizing is predominantly cognitive rather than behavioral in orientation, it seems to follow that the views of Guthrie would have little relevance for current theories. Considering, however, the ties between some aspects of Guthrie's analysis and mathematical learning theory, Guthrie's views are still not entirely out of date.

William Estes (e.g., 1959) paid Guthrie a compliment through the development of some of the basic tenets of Guthrie's rather loose-knit theory into a tight, formal, and highly mathematical system. At the same time, Estes is quite clear that the scope of his model is somewhat narrower than that of his behavioral predecessors, Guthrie, Hull, or Skinner. The essential basis for Estes's theory is Guthrie's association principle, namely that a stimulus is attached (conditioned) to a response when the two occur simultaneously in time. Like Guthrie, Estes also argued that conditioning is of the all-or-none variety; at any instance of learning, either a stimulus is attached to a response or it is not. There can be no in-between stage or partial degree of stimulus-response association, such as possible in, say, Hull's (1943) habit-strength notion.

On the other hand, Estes's view of the stimulus and response differs from Guthrie's in several respects. Like Guthrie, Estes believes the environment at any moment is composed of many "stimulus elements." However, Estes's concept of the stimulus is largely an abstract, mathematical one, rather than being based on properties of the actual environment or characteristics of the organism's receptor systems. On a given conditioning trial, some proportion (theta) of stimulus elements is sampled, that is, attached to a given response. Across successive trials, different samples of stimuli are selected, much like reaching into a jar filled with marbles and repeatedly taking out handfuls. For this reason, Estes's theory has been called a *stimulus-sampling model* of learning.

Estes's response concept also has somewhat different characteristics than Guthrie's. For Guthrie a response (movement) is a somewhat particularistic (some would say *molecular*) aspect of behavior, typically an action of an individual muscle or gland. Estes's response is a much more molar (and, once again, mathematical) concept, more closely resembling Guthrie's concept of the act. At any given time, according to Estes, the organism is capable of just two kinds of responses, A1 or A2. The one is the logical opposite of the other (say, *not* running as opposed to running). Therefore, putting the concepts of stimulus, response, and conditioning together, on a given learning trial some proportion of the available stimulus elements becomes attached to the response, A1. The remainder is attached to A2. On each successive trial, more and more of the elements become attached to A1, and the response becomes more and more probable.

Others of Estes's concepts have some features in common with Guthrie's. Examples are his views of forgetting and spontaneous recovery, both of which are functions of continual shifts in the available stimuli and/or the replacement of some responses with others. Estes, too, minimized the importance of the reinforcement process, viewing it primarily as a source of stimuli.

The development of mathematical learning theory by Estes and others (e.g., Atkinson & Shiffrin, 1965; Bower, 1972) is probably the foremost link, albeit in many ways tenuous, between more recent theories of learning and some of Guthrie's major contributions. Other theorists' attempts to modify explicitly Guthrie's theory for more limited purposes (Sheffield, 1961; Vocks, 1950) will be discussed later.

PROPOSITIONS

1. *Learning is an association between stimulus and response.*

The appeal of Guthrie's theory lies mainly in his single, simple principle of learning: "A combination of stimuli which has accompanied a movement will on its recurrence tend to be followed by that movement" (Guthrie, 1935, p. 26). Guthrie restated the basic form of the principle nearly a quarter of a century later (1959), attesting to his conviction of the validity of his analysis of learned behavior. The basic statement contains no mention of reinforcement, motivation, punishment, or any of the other variables that Guthrie's contemporaries, such as Hull, Thorndike, and Tolman, included in their theories. Unfortunately, the apparent simplicity of Guthrie's fundamental principle of learning is deceptive because it is only possible with the addition of a number of complicating assumptions. Nevertheless, the major premise is that when a stimulus and response occur together in time, recurrence of the stimulus will likely produce recurrence of the response. For this reason, Guthrie's theory has been referred to as a *contiguity* view of learning.

The terms *stimulus* and *movement* are essential to understanding Guthrie's conditioning principle. In his early work, Guthrie defined a stimulus as any change in the physical world that evokes a response (1935). Therefore, the concept of stimulus is equated with those features of the environment that affect sense receptors, including light, touch, sound, taste, and olfactory cues, alone and in combination. This is a fairly straightforward physicalistic view of the world, characteristic of the behaviorists of the 1930s. Guthrie (1959) was later to modify his stimulus concept by emphasizing attentional mechanisms, to be discussed later.

Guthrie's response concept was somewhat less typical. He distinguished between complex patterns of behavior, *acts,* and the individual muscle *movements* that make up an act. A cat that learns to pull a latch to release a small door and get outside the house has learned the *act* of latch pulling. However, according to Guthrie, the animal must be seen as actually having learned a series of individual *movements* involving muscles in its legs, back, neck, and perhaps other parts of the body as well. Guthrie's conditioning principle asserts a relationship between these muscle movements and stimuli of the animal's environment, *not* between the act of latch pulling and the related cues. That is, the animal learns, for instance, to move particular shoulder and leg muscles when it sees the latch because movements of those muscles are the last responses to occur in the setting in the presence of the latch. Learning any complex behavioral act is the process of forming numerous associations between features of the environment (stimuli) and particular muscle movements (responses).

2. *Movements themselves are a source of stimuli.*

Guthrie maintained that besides the external environment, responses provide another source of stimuli for behavior. Largely, these were the proprioceptive or interoceptive stimuli generated by muscular or other internal events. An association is possible between a movement and the residual stimuli from a preceding movement due to the close temporal association between successive movements. Movement-produced stimuli are thus "stimuli for which movements are directly responsible. . . . What a man is doing is normally the chief determiner of what he will do next, because what he is doing furnishes the bulk of the stimuli that will affect his muscles" (Guthrie, 1942, p. 37).

The importance of movement-produced stimuli is most evident in the case of complex behaviors in a less than complex environment. That is, if the external situation does not undergo many changes but in that situation an integrated series of movements occurs, a theory that depends strictly upon stimulus-response associations as the foundation for behavior requires a source of additional cues for the behavior. If each response produces the stimulus that occasions the next response, a behavioral act may be maintained in the absence of obvious external stimulus changes. In the words of E. R. Hilgard and G. H. Bower (1975), "Such covert movement-produced stimuli provide ever-present explanations for conduct which cannot be inferred from external S–R relationships" (p. 93). Coupled with his notions concerning motivation, discussed below in the section on maintaining stimuli, Guthrie thus had a means for handling even the most lengthy and complex series of behaviors. The concept of the response-produced stimulus forms the basis for present-day analyses of the process of *chaining*.

3. *Learning is an "all-or-none" process.*

Theorists of Guthrie's time incorporated mechanisms in their learning principles to account for the apparent gradualness with which learning takes place. Guthrie, however, maintained that learning occurs all at once. There is no place in his principle of association for a gradual strengthening of a stimulus-movement connection. If a stimulus and a response occur together, an association will be formed—instantaneously. This is a so-called all-or-none concept of learning.

This view seems inconsistent with the obvious nature of learning. It is rare that any pattern of behavior is learned all at once. Practice does make perfect in most cases. Although there have been reports of learning that fit an all-or-none model, such as that in Voeks (1954), discussed in a later section, gradual improvement in performance over trials generally is the most common course of behavior in learning tasks.

Guthrie's theory actually handles practice effects nicely, especially in the case of complex behaviors. Guthrie (1930, 1935) assumes that any stimulus situation is rather complex, consisting of many types of cues varying continuously across time. While at a given moment, or on a given trial, a movement becomes associated with an existing stimulus, there usually must be many opportunities for a large number of cues to become attached to a series of movements before the greater part of the stimulus complex will evoke the response. In addition, a complex act consists of many individual movements, each of which must become attached to the existing cues of the situation as well as to the movement-produced stimuli themselves. Therefore, the development of an integrated sequence of responses making up a complex act or skill may be a gradual process consisting of hundreds or, conceivably, thousands of opportunities for the conditioning of stimulus-response associations.

Another important corollary to Guthrie's basic principle of learning is his recency concept, later to be called the *principle of postremity* (Voeks, 1950). Essentially, this principle states that the last or most recent association between stimulus and response is retained. The best predictor of precisely what response will occur to a given stimulus is the response that last occurred in the presence of the stimulus. If something induces an organism to make a different response from one previously associated with the stimulus, the new response takes the

place of the previous one. This principle is also important to an understanding of the processes of inhibition and forgetting.

4. *Extinction of responding is actually a process of association.*

Guthrie's principle of association provides for the *forming* of stimulus-response relationships, but how are responses "unlearned" or extinguished in this system? Guthrie's analysis of associative inhibition provides an account of the extinction process.

The principle of inhibitory conditioning is actually just a restatement of Guthrie's principle of association by contiguity: "A stimulus may . . . be unconditioned by the very simple means of becoming a conditioner for incompatible movement. Unlearning becomes merely a case of learning something else" (Guthrie, 1935, p. 66). Once any habit has been learned, it may be broken by the formation of a new stimulus-response association containing the stimulus of the earlier association and a different response. The response itself must be incompatible with the earlier response to prevent the latter from recurring to the stimulus. This might be a case as simple as a basic incompatibility in muscle movements. For instance, a baby cannot both cry and swallow food at the same time, due to the opposing muscles involved in these two reflexes. Therefore, any association between a stimulus and crying could presumably be inhibited by an association between the stimulus and eating. Judging by the frequency with which candy is offered to children who cry in public places, this must be a rule that parents, wittingly or unwittingly, learn early. Guthrie (1942) admitted to less simple or obvious cases of response incompatibility too—the level of incompatibility is basically neural: Nerve impulses to one muscle system may be blocked by opposing ones to another system.

Guthrie's (1935) account of the Pavlovian extinction procedure follows directly from this analysis. A dog that has learned to salivate to a stimulus previously paired with food may then not salivate if food is omitted on some occasions. In Guthrie's view, this must be because some other response takes the place of salivation when food is omitted and therefore competes with it. It is easy to see that the absence of food would lessen the likelihood of digestive responses, such as salivation, in the laboratory setting. Then, anything else that a dog might do could substitute for the original salivation, such as turning its head or listening to distracting noises. To the extent that these other responses are incompatible with digestion, the dog may salivate less, that is, show some extinction. In various forms, this "interference" theory of extinction has continued to be one of the major alternatives to the inhibition theories, such as the early ones of Pavlov (1927) or Hull (1943).

The inhibition analysis of extinction applies as well to the phenomenon of forgetting. Across time, new responses may occur in the presence of stimuli that will inhibit old responses. The inability to remember a certain event or person may therefore be due to the many more recent events or people that have taken part in one's associations. The term *retroactive inhibition* has been used to describe this form of forgetting.

Central to Guthrie's view of extinction and forgetting is his notion of the inhibitory response. The occurrence of a given associate once it is established to a stimulus can only be reduced if an alternate response to the stimulus interferes with the original. The new response can be acquired in any of four ways. In each case, the original cue is present but the response is prevented from occurring. In one, the stimulus may be below threshold and therefore not evoke the response. In the second, the response may not occur due to fatigue. Third, responses may be evoked that directly compete with the original response. Fourth, the stimulus may be presented during a refractory period. Examples from these methods will be a topic of a later section in this chapter.

5. Rewards are not necessary for learning.

By the time Guthrie was making formal his principle of association by contiguity, Thorndike's Law of Effect had already had a considerable impact on students of learning. Thorndike had asserted that a connection between a stimulus and a response is strengthened if the response produces a "satisfying" state of affairs (Thorndike, 1932, p. 176). In Skinner's (1938) view, the more theoretically neutral term *reinforcement* was applied to the events that strengthen certain kinds of behavior. Hull (1943), too, was to reaffirm the Law of Effect in his theory of habit-strength formation. For several decades, the psychology of learning was strongly influenced by concepts of reinforcement, especially as formalized by these three "effect" theorists.

Guthrie, by contrast, maintained throughout his career that learning itself was a simpler process, not requiring reinforcement for the formation of stimulus-response connections. Temporal contiguity was sufficient. But what of the laboratory demonstrations by effect theorists of the powerful effects of rewards on cats in puzzle boxes and rats in runways or operant conditioning boxes? A hungry rat who finds food in a goal box will almost invariably run more rapidly, seemingly to get to the food, and will gradually not run if the food is taken away. If providing food does not act to strengthen (or removing food to weaken) the act of running in the setting, how do we account for such powerful effects?

Guthrie's solution was in terms of the prevailing stimuli for the act of running or any other response in the "instrumental" or skill category. As outlined earlier, Guthrie maintained that the most recent response to occur in the presence of a stimulus is the one that remains a part of the association. In the case of a rat running in a runway, the cues of the runway become attached to the locomotor responses because these are the last movements to occur prior to the goal box. Food acts to change abruptly the external stimuli impinging on the animal at the end of the runway sequence and thereby functions to "preserve" or maintain any prior associations. In this case, the most significant association would be runway running, formed just in advance of the goal. Therefore, food itself is not a special kind of event that acts to strengthen behavior; it is just a dramatic change in the animal's world immediately following the occurrence of a response, thereby preventing the undoing of the just-formed association.

John Seward (1942) tested a prediction from this view, the results of which were not promising for Guthrie's model. Rats were placed into a box and allowed to press a bar. One group of animals was given food for pressing a bar, while another group was simply removed from the box after pressing. It would seem that by Guthrie's view, both events qualify as significant stimulus changes, with removal from the box perhaps having the

edge. Not surprisingly, however, Seward found that when the rats were placed on extinction the ones previously given food made more bar presses than the ones previously only removed from the box.

6. *Motivation is simply persistent, internal stimulation.*

Guthrie's theory is able to deal with Seward's results by way of the concept of the *maintaining stimulus.* This is as close as Guthrie ever gets to a notion resembling motivation, in the language of other theorists. Essentially, it was argued that physiological states of an organism consist of internal stimuli that may persist throughout performance of an act until some consummatory response occurs: "Maintaining stimuli are ultimately removed by the responses they themselves provoke" (Guthrie, 1935, p. 164). A state of thirst, for instance, consists of a unique class of stimuli that will "maintain" responding until water is consumed. In these terms, Seward's (1942) results can be understood. Lever pressing in these rats occurred in the presence of both the external cues of the box as well as the maintaining stimuli resulting from a current state of food deprivation. Food for lever pressing may be a more effective stimulus change than removal from the box because of its effects upon these maintaining cues. On the other hand, if a rat is still hungry after pressing a lever, though it is removed from the situation the opportunity exists for a variety of subsequent responses to become attached to the maintaining stimuli. Some of these responses may be incompatible with lever pressing, thus retarding later performance. (Seward attempted to control for the effects of the maintaining stimuli by feeding *all* animals a small amount of food prior to a session. But the effects of prefeeding were probably minimal at best.)

Besides entering into associations, maintaining stimuli may serve a second function. Since a motivational state is simply a source of stimuli, differing states or differing levels of one state (e.g., more or less hunger) are simply to be viewed as differing internal stimuli. Thirst may evoke behaviors different from hunger simply because the cues relevant to each state are unique.

A third way in which maintaining stimuli may enter into associations is in long and complex behavioral sequences. Where there are no obvious moment-to-moment external stimulus changes, the maintenance of a series of movements must be related to other cues. Earlier it was noted that movement-produced stimuli may serve this function; each response may produce the stimulus for the next response. Similarly, a continuing source of internal cues (motives) if present during a series of responses will theoretically become associated with the movements and support the act in future occurrences. Presumably, a hungry rat who has learned to climb a staircase, ascend a ladder, pedal a car, and crawl through a tube, among six other activities on its way to press a lever and receive a food pellet (Pierrel & Sherman, 1963), will have all of the successive movements attached to the cues of its hunger condition. The presence of these cues at other times should support the response chain in the same way as any external stimulus may initiate one or more of the related responses.

Despite these functions, however, the concept of maintaining stimuli does not have the status of motivation or drive in the theories of Guthrie's contemporaries. While a persistent internal stimulus may maintain a behavior or influence its vigor,

it is just another class of stimuli in Guthrie's model. In the words of two interpreters of Guthrie's theory, "If a hungry cat acts differently from a well-fed cat, its movements are different, and so its learning may be different. It learns what it does; what it does is more important than what its motivational state happens to be" (Hilgard & Bower, 1975, p. 97).

7. *The important thing about punishers is the behaviors they evoke.*

At the time of Guthrie's earliest formal statements, psychologists were unclear about the nature and effects of punishers. Thorndike's (1911) initial suggestion was that punishers weaken stimulus-response connections in a manner opposite to the way in which reinforcers strengthen them. By 1932, however, he had changed his mind and concluded that punishers do not act directly to weaken stimulus-response associations that precede them. This was based largely on his own experiments in which, for example, telling individuals "That's wrong" following certain verbal associations had no apparent weakening effects on their responses. A number of other theorists followed suit. Skinner (1938) developed a view of punishment that attributed its apparent weakening effects to its tendency to elicit or allow for negative reinforcement of incompatible responses, a prominent approach right down to the present time (Herrnstein, 1969).

Guthrie's view of punishers was similar but somewhat simpler, at least on the surface. Essentially, he argued that it is not what a punisher does to weaken prior behavior that must be accounted for, but the behavior that it causes. If a punisher such as a spanking is administered following a response such as "misbehaving" at the dinner table, its effectiveness in suppressing the behavior will depend upon two things. First, the punisher must cause a response incompatible with the punished behavior. Second, the incompatible behavior must occur in the context of the original behavior, so as to become attached to the cues and subsequently interfere with the punished response (Guthrie, 1935, p. 160). Effectively, then, punishment is a process by which new associations that interfere with the punished ones are formed in a setting and thereby allow the organism to "escape" the punisher. Spanking a child for misbehavior should only be effective if the result is to induce responses that interfere with misbehaving in the same setting in which the misbehavior occurred. Guthrie's (1935) frequently cited example of the punishment principle in operation is that of a mother who must contend with a child who runs into the street. Guthrie's suggestion is that the mother slap the child in the face to cause movement away from the curb rather than to spank the child from behind, which (while perhaps as painful) would cause forward movement. The results of an experimental analog of the essentials of this procedure (Fowler & Miller, 1963) were favorable to Guthrie's analysis.

Two other implications of Guthrie's view of punishment are noteworthy. One is that a punisher is a form of stimulus change, often at least as potent as a reinforcer. Therefore, it would seem that following a response with punishment would be as effective as following it with reward insofar as preserving prior stimulus-response associations is concerned. Where this is contrary to the facts of punishment, the foregoing account of the role of punishers in the acquisition of incompatible behaviors must be relevant.

On the other hand, there are instances in everyone's life in which punished behavior develops and is maintained (for example, so-called masochistic behaviors). Conceivably, some of these cases may reflect the effects of the stimulus-change aspect of punishment.

Another consideration in Guthrie's handling of punishment is the opposite way in which he refers to its effects when contrasted with those of rewards. In the latter case, the stimulus-response association that is preserved involves the act that occurred just prior to reward, often because the reward alters maintaining stimuli, as discussed earlier. In the case of punishment, it is the response just following the event that is learned. The reason for this difference is explained in terms of the concept of the maintaining stimulus: One function of a reward may be the *removal* of maintaining stimuli and, therefore, a dramatic change in the organism's world. A punisher, on the other hand, is a *source* of maintaining stimuli, escape from which via a response incompatible with the punished one functions to change cues in the animal's world.

8. *Attention involves an active response of the organism.*

Guthrie's last major statements were made in 1959. In this discussion he substantially revised his concept of the stimulus. He now recognized the active role the organism plays in the selection of available stimuli. In Guthrie's words, "What is being noticed becomes a signal for what is being done" (1959, p. 188). Further, since the act of noticing an aspect of the environment is temporally associated with any behavior in progress, "Attention becomes, in the present account, the point at which learning occurs" (1959, p. 187). That is, in order for a stimulus and response to be contiguous and thereby become associated, the response of the organism in stimulus selection is a prerequisite.

In the same discussion, Guthrie attempted to clarify his position by way of a set of eight assumptions about stimulus responses and attention. Four of the more significant of these are Items 1, 2, 3, and 6:

1. Patterning of physical stimuli is effective as such, as distinct from the effects of degrees of intensity or the summation of the effects of stimulus elements.

2. The acceptance by an observer of a given pattern of physical stimuli as a cue for the observed organism will depend on data from the past history of the organism or on present observation of the perceptual response to the cue.

3. In the higher animals, the effectiveness of physical stimuli is governed by a class of responses called attention, which may restrict effect by avoiding the orientation and sense organ adjustment required for effectiveness, or by involving postures allowing or excluding particular responses to the stimuli.

.   .   .   .   .

6. It is, therefore, assumed that rules which do not take into account what the animal is doing when stimulated will not be descriptive of the phenomenon of association. (1959, pp. 187–188)

Guthrie reasserted his stimulus-response contiguity position in this paper, but with a somewhat altered and more sophisticated statement of the nature of the stimulus. It is interesting to consider the possibility that, with additional time, he might also have modified his concept of the response. By the mid 1960s, even Skinner had challenged other behaviorists to broaden vastly the response concept to include behaviors previously considered too "private" for a respectable science of the observable world (Skin-ner, 1963). Would Guthrie, too, have come to radicalize his behaviorism on this dimension as well? It is interesting to speculate that the result would have been a psychology of learning much less distinguishable from the current cognitive views than the somewhat conservative stimulus-response model Guthrie proposed.

RESEARCH

Methodologies

One of the most common criticisms of Guthrie's theory is that it has failed to generate a great deal of research. This may be attributed in part to the setting in which Guthrie taught. Because the psychology program at the University of Washington during the peak of Guthrie's productivity was at the undergraduate level, opportunities for graduate theses and dissertations simply did not exist there. By contrast, students of Clark Hull and Kenneth Spence and other of Guthrie's contemporaries generated many tests of their learning theories. Robert C. Bolles (1975) has suggested also that the paucity of research directly relevant to Guthrie's theory may have been due to his tendency to minimize the importance of motivation and reinforcement in learning. Since the bulk of the theory and research in learning during the 1930s and 1940s was largely directed at motivational and reinforcement issues, this put Guthrie's theory into left field with respect to the predominant efforts in the psychology of learning of his day. Perhaps most important, however, was the fact that Guthrie's theory itself was loosely stated and constructed, so that generating solid predictions from it was a very difficult task.

Guthrie, himself, was candid about deficiencies of his theory: "The writer is well aware of his failure to lay down specifications for the data of learning which are sufficiently precise to meet the requirements of laboratory experiment" (Guthrie, 1959, p. 185). As discussed earlier, his 1959 paper included some attempts to state his position more formally. Similarly, F. D. Sheffield (1961) and V. W. Voeks (1950) attempted to formalize some of Guthrie's concepts in order to make testable predictions.

Voeks (1950, pp. 342-348) set forth four postulates that clearly rephrase Guthrie's views on association by contiguity, recency, and the role of stimuli:

Postulate I: Principle of Association. (a) Any stimulus-pattern which once accompanies a response, and/or immediately precedes it (by ½ second or less), becomes a full-strength direct cue for that response. (b) This is the only way in which stimulus-patterns not now cues for a particular response can become direct cues for that response.
Postulate II: Principle of Postremity. (a) A stimulus which has accompanied or immediately preceded two or more incompatible responses is a conditioned stimulus for only the last response made while that stimulus was present. (b) This is the only way in which a stimulus now a cue for a particular response can cease being a cue for that response.
Postulate III: Principle of Response. Probability. The probability of any particular response's occurring (P_{Ry}) at some specified time is an increasing monotonic function (x) of the proportion (N) of the stimuli present which are at the time cues for that response ($S+$).
Postulate IV: Principle of Dynamic Situations. The stimulus-pattern of a situation is not static but from time to time is modified.

On the basis of this system, some precise experimental predictions can be made. For instance, Voeks (1948) examined whether choices of persons to a finger maze were primarily a function of the frequency with which a given choice had been made or precisely what choice was last made. The principle of postremity predicts, of course, that the last choice made will be the determiner. Overwhelmingly, individuals responded in accordance with the principle. In a later experiment, Voeks (1954) obtained support for the all-or-none feature of the principle of association. However, Voeks's efforts were largely in vain. Even in this form, the theory failed to have much impact on research in the field of learning.

Tests of Guthrie's concepts were done with both animal and human subjects. Rats or guinea pigs were commonly used, though Guthrie himself employed cats in one set of studies discussed below. As was common of animal studies at the time, experiments typically were run using alleys or activity wheels. The human studies cited included various classical conditioning procedures. Therefore, no single class of methods characterizes this research.

Animal Studies

Most of the research directly relevant to Guthrie's theory was conducted with animals as subjects. The following studies provided results related to Guthrie's notions concerning the process of association, the role of reinforcement in conditioning, the function of punishment, and Guthrie's view of extinction.

Perhaps the best known of all of the research to be cited here is the classic Guthrie and Horton (1946) experiment. In this study, a series of observations on a number of cats were designed mainly to show Guthrie's association principle in operation. The apparatus Guthrie and Horton used had features in common with Thorndike's (1911) early problem box. Basically, each animal was placed into a confining box in which there was a pole projecting from the floor. If the pole was tilted from vertical, a small door was opened, allowing the animal to escape and to obtain food. A camera was set to record each of the cat's movements at the moment the pole was pushed. Hundreds of such escapes were photographed.

One of the most notable features of the cats' movement in the box was the stereotyping of positions when the pole was pushed. Series of photographs of successive escapes showed a remarkable repetitiveness of movements when the pole was tilted. Between animals there was wide variation in responding, but individual animals tended to use the same movement to move the pole from one trial to the next.

Guthrie and Horton seized on this repetitiveness as support for Guthrie's principle of associative learning. If the last muscle movement made in a situation is the one that gets associated with related stimuli, it follows that the particular movements that tilted the pole permitting the animal to escape were the ones that would be repeated. It is these movements that caused a sudden change in stimuli. "The reason for the remarkable preservation of the end action leading to escape is that this action removes the cat from the situation and hence allows no new responses to become attached to the puzzle-box situation" (Guthrie & Horton, 1946, p. 39). In short, the cats repeated whatever responses were the last to occur in the setting because no other responses occurred to take their place.

Guthrie and Horton also argued that the experiment lent no support to reward or effect theories of learning. By contrast with Thorndike (1911), who

contended that food reward was a primary reason why his cats learned to escape from puzzle boxes, Guthrie and Horton observed that "food or escape from the box were of dubious effect on the action" (1946, p. 39). They viewed their cats as increasingly "indifferent" to the rewards as the trials proceeded.

Two lines of research that were more directly aimed at Guthrie's notions concerning reinforcement included studies by Seward (1942), cited earlier, and Zeaman and Radner (1953). In Seward's experiments, contrary to expectations from a Guthrian stimulus-change concept of reinforcement, animals previously rewarded with food showed shorter latencies of the bar press and more frequent responses in subsequent extinction sessions than animals previously just removed from the box upon bar pressing. However, in at least partial support of the Guthrie view, a control group that was merely placed into the box made *fewer* bar presses than the other groups during extinction. Therefore, removal from the box alone did seem to "preserve" bar pressing, although food reward was somewhat more effective.

Zeaman and Radner (1953) provided additional results which they viewed as inconsistent with Guthrie's theory. Albino rats were placed into a box in which movement from one side to the other caused a slight change of tilt of the floor. For some of the rats, the box was dark upon entry, and floor-tilting responses turned on a bright light. For the remaining animals, the box was initially lit up, and responses turned off the light. Since in both cases there was a form of dramatic stimulus change following a response, it would seem that a Guthrian account of the function of "reward" would predict no differences between the groups. However, latencies of the animals trained on the light on/light-off procedure improved across trials, while those in the opposite condition did not. It would appear that bright light is an aversive condition for the rat and that escaping it is reinforcing.

More recently, a substantial literature has evolved demonstrating the possibility that various forms of mere stimulus change following responding may strengthen performance (see Kish, 1966), but most of these studies were cast in somewhat different theoretical terms from Guthrie's.

Two studies on the nature of punishment lend some support to Guthrie's views on the subject. Recall Guthrie's essential statement, that the most important feature of a punisher is what it causes the organism to *do* rather than how it suppresses performance. Sheffield (1948) provided one demonstration of this principle in operation. Guinea pigs were allowed to run in an activity wheel that was provided with a means for electrically shocking the animals. Each "trial" consisted of a two-second tone, at the end of which a brief shock was delivered. Following some amount of this unavoidable shock training, the animals were placed on an avoidable shock procedure in which running would allow them to escape and to avoid the shock.

The frequency of conditioned running was lower in the unavoidable shock condition than in the avoidable shock condition. A similar result had earlier induced Brogden, Lipman, and Culler (1938) to view sheer contiguity as a less effective learning procedure than one that allowed for reward through shock avoidance. However, this analysis was extended by Sheffield (1948), who determined whether responding in the un-

avoidable shock condition involved either forward locomotion or incompatible behavior in response to the shock. Sheffield observed that if the response to shock while running was continued running, the frequency of running increased from 40% to 50% on the subsequent trial. If, however, the response to shock was incompatible behavior, running declined from 40% to 20% on the next trial. He concluded that the results in Brogden et al. were in fact compatible with a contiguity position after all. Poor performance with unavoidable shock probably was due to the fact that presenting shock during running to the tone often caused running to stop (that is, elicited freezing). In Sheffield's study, whether an animal ran or stopped running in response to the shock significantly increased or decreased, respectively, the probability of subsequent responding. It is what the shock caused an animal to *do* that was important, precisely as Guthrie had suggested of punishers in general.

While an experiment reported by Fowler and Miller (1963) was not a direct test of Guthrie's theory, the results are relevant to his view of punishers. This study was specifically designed to investigate the effects of presentation of shock to different parts of the bodies of rats. The nature of the shock was controlled by varying the portion of the grid in the goal box to which shock was delivered.

Albino rats were run in a straight alley. In a goal box, a grid floor could be electrically charged in either the first portion or the last portion contacted by an animal as it approached food. At the moment of touching food, different groups of rats received shock either to the hind paws (via the rear portion of the grid) or to the forepaws (via the front portion of the grid). All of the animals showed progressively faster speeds as the experiment proceeded. However, animals shocked on their hind paws at the goal box ran *faster* than animals not shocked at all. Conversely, animals shocked on their forepaws ran more slowly than the no-shock controls. In addition, an approach gradient emerged in which the animals shocked on their hind paws ran *faster* the closer they were to the goal.

These results, like the earlier ones of Sheffield (1948), strongly suggest that whether responding will be facilitated or inhibited by "punishment" depends upon the nature of the response elicited by the punisher. If the response is lurching forward, punishment may facilitate approach; otherwise it may inhibit approach. If we recall Guthrie's advice to the mother who has to teach her child not to run into the street, indeed it seems that a spank on the rear may not be the right solution. There is now an abundant literature on punishment, a substantial portion of which could be interpreted in accordance with Guthrie's notion that a punisher is not fundamentally different in effect from any other stimulus.

To conclude this section on animal research, two studies of extinction may be summarized that bear on Guthrie's concept of associative inhibition. Among the procedures suggested by Guthrie (1935) for the conditioning of inhibitory responses was one that might be called a *toleration* method. In this, a conditioned stimulus is introduced gradually by increasing its intensity on successive presentations. In a second (and more common) *exhaustion* method, a conditioned stimulus is presented at full strength throughout extinction. In Guthrie's view, the toleration type of procedure should be more effective because the to-be-extinguished response may never occur. It

should therefore be more likely for an incompatible response to occur and to be conditioned to the stimulus undergoing extinction. To compare the effectiveness of these two extinction methods, Kimble and Kendall (1953) designed a simple comparison of performance of two groups of rats in the apparatus that combined a box and rotating wheel.

Albino rats were placed in a box containing an electric grid and a light of variable intensity. During training, on each trial that the light was turned on, it was followed shortly by an electric shock. If the animals rotated a wheel at one end of the box, the shock was turned off. During the light which preceded the shock, wheel turning would permit the animal to avoid the shock altogether on that trial. During extinction, the shock was no longer presented, and half of the animals were given eight "toleration" trials in which the intensity of the light was gradually increased. Then, additional trials were given during which the conditioned stimulus (CS) was at full strength. The remaining animals were presented the CS at full strength throughout the entire series of extinction trials.

The findings were favorable to Guthrie's theory of extinction. The toleration group made an average of less than half as many wheel-turning responses, on both the toleration and regular extinction trials, as the exhaustion group, a statistically significant difference. Therefore, it appears that a procedure which precludes the occurrence of responding during extinction results in more rapid extinction than one that allows responding to occur throughout.

More recently, a series of experiments (Marx, 1968) failed to support Guthrie's view of extinction. Basically, rats were trained to bar press in a situation in which each press delivered sucrose and caused the bar to be retracted for a period of time. Then the sucrose was omitted (extinction), and responses were counted on this bar plus, for some animals, a second bar as well. From a Guthrie-like position, Marx reasoned that animals for which a second bar was available during extinction would be more likely to make bar presses incompatible with those on the first bar. Thus, the animals with two bars should "extinguish" faster. In fact, however, there was essentially no effect, due to availability of the incompatible response. The two groups made essentially the same number of total bar presses. In fact, it appeared in one study that rather than replacing responses on the first bar, responses on the second bar also underwent extinction (that is, declined across extinction trials).

Animal research directly relevant to Guthrie's theory has produced mixed results. His view of response stereotyping and punishment have both been upheld (see, however, the critique in Mueller & Schoenfeld, 1954, of the Guthrie & Horton, 1946, interpretation of response stereotyping). On the other hand, the inhibition or interference theory of extinction has been challenged, and Guthrie's insistence on the nonimportance of rewards in learning is inconsistent with the bulk of research in learning, as well as with the theoretical attitudes of nearly all animal psychologists. On the latter point, however, emerging cognitive conceptions of learning in animals are causing some serious rethinking of traditional notions concerning reinforcement. While it seems extremely doubtful that this will result in a rebirth of any form of stimulus-response associationism, it may vindicate Guthrie for his brave challenge to conventional thinking on reinforcement and motivational issues.

Human Studies

Human research directly relevant to Guthrie's views is extremely limited. Three representative studies will be cited here, all focusing on Guthrie's notions concerning the formation of stimulus-response associations.

The best known of these experiments was by Voeks (1954). Her study contrasted Guthrie's view that learning is an all-or-none phenomenon with Hull's (1943) notion that learning is a gradual process. College students were observed in a classical eyelid conditioning procedure in which the response was a conditioned eyeblink; the unconditioned stimulus, an air puff; and the conditioned stimulus, a buzzer. The students were instructed to breathe in a prescribed fashion, then to depress two telegraph keys. (The breathing pattern was designed to minimize variability of stimuli with the depression of the keys.) The conditioned stimulus was then sounded, followed shortly by the unconditioned stimulus.

When conditioned eyeblinks were measured, of 32 students, 16 had learning curves with abrupt transitions, and 14 more had nearly perfect curves of this type. In only about 20% of the cases did a later quarter of the training period contain more conditioned responses than an earlier one. Predictions based on Guthrie's recency or postremity principle, that the last response made in the presence of a stimulus (in this case the eyeblink) will be the next response made, were also highly accurate.

Group learning curves showed gradual changes in amplitude and frequency of occurrence. However, when amplitude and probability of the response were plotted for students who had curves with abrupt changes, the trends of the group curves were somewhat more in the all-or-none form as well.

Voeks contended that gradual learning curves are actually a result of three factors: (1) stimulus variability from trial to trial, with resultant response variability; (2) stimulus similarity between trials and between trial periods, allowing for conditioning of incompatible responses; and (3) grouping of data from students who are learning at different points in practice. She regarded her study as evidence for the all-or-none learning view.

An earlier experiment (Seward, Dill, and Holland, 1944) was explicitly designed to test Guthrie's (1935) recency principle. The study was to determine whether when a response is associated with a stimulus, any prior response to that stimulus will be "dissociated" from it, as required in Guthrie's analysis.

Female students were shown colored cards in a memory drum. The task was to press buttons arranged in a display in response to each color. When the "correct" button was pressed, a light was presented. Students first learned to press one button to a stimulus, then were required to learn to press a second. The test for recency involved presenting a stimulus and then observing whether the response learned first or the one learned second was predominant.

Students tended to select the *first* response they had learned more frequently than the second, although overall there was no statistical difference. Either way, the experiment failed to support Guthrie's view that the most recent response is the one that survives in the process of stimulus-response association.

According to Guthrie's theory, a stimulus becomes attached to a response if the two occur together. The stimulus-response connection will persist unless some conflicting response becomes attached to the stimulus. Usually, the correct response changes the available stimuli so that a competing response will not become attached. It follows that if the available stimuli are not immediately changed, the chances are greater that the original association could be disrupted by the formation of a new stimulus-response connection. Accordingly, Wickens and Platt (1954) compared the rate of learning of a muscle flexion response in groups for which the conditioned stimulus either terminated immediately with the occurrence of a conditioned response or was delayed for some period of time.

College students were seated by a shock apparatus. For classical conditioning groups (other groups were included that will not be discussed here), an electrode was fastened to the hand and a tone (conditioned stimulus) was presented, followed shortly by an electric shock on each conditioning trial. No differences in hand flexion responses were found between a group conditioned with a procedure in which the conditioned stimulus terminated at the appearance of the conditioned flexion response and a group for which the conditioned stimulus terminated about a half second after the shock was presented. Assuming that the tone was the critical conditioned stimulus (and *not* movement-produced cues), these results are not favorable to Guthrie's view of competing responses in the formation of stimulus-response associations. The delayed-shock group should have acquired the response more slowly, due to the greater opportunity for conditioning of inhibitory responses.

Few of the studies reviewed in this section support Guthrie's contiguity theory. However, if space here permitted, in most instances the theory could have been shown to handle even negative results by additional assumptions or changes in interpretation. This is possible because of the rather loose way in which Guthrie set forth his learning principles —the theory in its original form is simply not clearly and precisely testable. On the other hand, despite the failure of the model to stand up well to laboratory tests, it is rich with implications and gains in intuitive appeal the more it is used.

IMPLICATIONS

Theoretical

Guthrie's main impact on the psychology of learning derives from his parsimonious view of the fundamental nature of association: that learning is a contiguity process rather than attributable to reinforcement. Forms of learning through contiguity, though usually not the stimulus-response variety, have persisted in the two-factor learning theories popular today (Rescorla & Solomon, 1967). However, more direct effects of Guthrie's views upon recent theorizing are apparent in other forms.

Sheffield (1961) extended a Guthrie-like view of association to problems of perception. Sheffield discusses at length an aspect of behavior he terms the *sensory response,* a totally neural reaction of the organism. (Contrast this concept with Guthrie's insistence that responses are muscle movements or secretions of glands.) A sensory response is basically the neural representation of incoming stimulation, but like any other response it may also serve as a stimulus. Sheffield, however, was sympathetic with the Guthrian contiguity learning principle: A sensory response (image) could be conditioned to an external stimulus that was temporally contiguous with it. For instance, a tune may evoke the memory of the place in which it was last heard. In addition, since sensory responses themselves generate stimuli (the parallel to Guthrie's movement-produced stimuli), they may be conditioned to other responses in a series. Sheffield thus provides an account of the phenomenon of perception in Guthrian terms:

> The position taken here is that what is usually called "perception" refers to cases in which the immediate sensory stimulation is not only eliciting its innate sensory responses, but is also eliciting other sensory responses which have been conditioned to the immediate stimulation in past experience. Thus a block of ice presented only visually is perceived as cold because in the past it has been sensed cutaneously while being sensed visually. (Sheffield, 1961, p. 15)

Other more recent positions that made use of concepts similar to those in Guthrie's theory are the mathematical learning theories (e.g., Estes, 1959; see Chapter 9 of this text) discussed earlier and a lesser known *elicitation hypothesis* proposed by M. R. Denny and H. M. Adelmann (1955). Essentially these theorists argued that there is nothing unique about reinforcers like food. Reinforcers do not strengthen prior associations but rather they *elicit* behaviors, such as approach. Then, if approach (or any other) responses occur in a situation, they may be conditioned to related cues through contiguity. "The stimulus complex (S) which closely precedes in time any response *elicited* by any stimulus (Se) acquires the property to elicit this response" (Denny & Adelmann, 1955, p. 290). Conditioning itself, however, is *not* considered to be an all-or-none process. "With each elicitation there results an increment to the tendency of the stimulus complex (S) to elicit this response" (p. 290).

The model is applicable to several traditional learning situations. The primary similarity between these notions and Guthrie's contiguity position is in Denny and Adelmann's deemphasis of reinforcement in the conditioning process. A reinforcer is simply an elicitor of behavior—learning itself occurs through association alone.

Spence (1956) suggests a more complex view which takes into account unique effects of reinforcers. At least one of the two learning mechanisms in Spence's theory seems to be essentially a restatement of a Guthrian stimulus-response contiguity notion. Spence argues that a rat actually *learns* a response through the sheer act of performing it. Running becomes associated with runway cues through contiguity alone if a rat locomotes from a start box to a goal box. The rat is said to learn the habit of running in this setting without reinforcement (a major departure from Hull's, 1943, position that reinforcement is necessary in the formation of habits). Spence suggests, however, that the actual *performance* of the response occurs through the incentive influence of the goal object, rendering this a two-factor learning theory and therefore fundamentally different from Guthrie's. It is interesting to note the contiguity hypothesis in Spence's model, since Spence was predominantly influenced by Hullian views of reinforcement and motivation.

Guthrie's views have had implications for more recent theories of learning attributable to his insistence on the importance of incompatible or inhibitory responses. Guthrie's argument that extinction is essentially the learning of new and inhibitory associations, rather than the undoing of old ones, has been a major alternative to other theories of the extinction process (Kimble, 1961). Simi-

larly, the importance of a concept of incompatible responses in the interpretation of punishment effects (Azrin & Holz, 1966) may also reflect the impact on the field of Guthrie's views. To be fair, other major theorists, such as Thorndike and Skinner, have also argued for the significance of incompatible behaviors in punishment. Nevertheless, Guthrie deserves considerable credit for developing this position in detail and for showing us a variety of ways in which inhibitory responses may account for the effects of punishers (cf. Guthrie, 1935, Chap. 12).

Practical

Guthrie provided numerous examples and applications of his theory to everyday situations. He gave practical advice to mothers, educators, clinicians, and animal trainers on the proper rearing of children, solutions to varieties of behavioral problems, and teaching tricks to pets. Guthrie devoted considerably more space to exemplifying his theory than to developing its assumptions, a feature that makes his books a joy to read but his theory difficult to test properly.

The principle of association is put to extensive use in a chapter Guthrie wrote for educators (1942). Since associations are formed only when both stimuli and responses occur together, his advice stresses both aspects of the learning process. If students wish to maximize their chances for remembering material for a test, they should strive to maximize the similarity between the environments in which studying and testing are done. Ideally, the two tasks should be performed in the same room. However, *stimulus generalization,* the transfer of responses from one stimulus situation to the next, would also be at work if the material were rehearsed under a variety of conditions. This would permit more of the potential stimuli to become conditioned to the behavior and help to ensure proper responses irrespective of context.

On the response side, the important thing is to get the student to perform the precise response ultimately required: "It is essential that the student be led to do what is to be learned . . . a student does not learn what was in a lecture or in a book. He learns only what the lecture or book caused him to do" (Guthrie, 1942, p. 55). This principle is, of course, at the heart of practicum courses common in graduate education. Therefore, if the stimulus situation is reproduced and the response has previously been performed, recurrence of the response is probable, due to the contiguity principle.

Once a response is learned, Guthrie suggests several methods for "extinguishing" it or, more precisely, for replacing it with other responses. Recall that Guthrie's associative inhibition principle is at the heart of his views of response extinction. To undo a stimulus-response association, the task is to replace the response with an inhibitory one. One way is to change gradually the impinging stimuli while the original response is not being performed. For instance, to establish acceptance of bitterness in food:

> A bitter taste may be so slight that it fails to cause ejection of food. Such a taste may be introduced into food very gradually and the result be a toleration of a degree of bitterness which would have been at first out of the question. . . . The bitter taste . . . becomes a conditioner of appetite and eating, and may eventually be necessary to the enjoyment of some foods. (Guthrie, 1935, pp. 70–71)

As testimony to Guthrie's insight, the gradual introduction of anxiety-inducing stimuli is involved in a standard clinical treatment method called *systematic desensitization* (Wolpe, 1958). In the laboratory, Terrace (1963) described a method of "errorless discrimination learning" in pigeons that also involved gradual stimulus change for response elimination.

A second way to alter a stimulus-response association is to "exhaust" the response in the presence of its stimuli, allowing for different responses to occur. Speakers on stage, "perhaps the majority, recover from stage fright only through being forced to go through with their performance and to continue after the excitement has passed. . . . The stimulus situation which has caused excitement is present but the excitement has been replaced by other behavior" (Guthrie, 1942, p. 72). Clinically, a procedure called *implosive therapy* (Stampfl & Levis, 1967) employs this method. A patient is exposed to anxiety-arousing stimuli in intense forms from the beginning of treatment. Provided that the client can be induced to continue, advocates of this method attest to its effectiveness in eliminating anxiety responses.

A third way to inhibit a prior association is to present the stimulus when the response is not occurring (inhibited) for some other reason. If a student who attempts to read in a library "begins by noticing what is going on in the room, the open book will eventually be a mere cue for looking about." But "if he begins with an engrossing book he will reach a quick adaptation to the noise around him" (Guthrie, 1935, p. 73). In other words, if the cues are present when the unwanted response, looking about, is inhibited by the inherent interest level of the book, the library will become a place to read rather than one in which to look about. Guthrie, who was not sympathetic with traditional psychoanalytic views, suggests that the high sexual content of psychoanalytic treatment actually represents the therapist's attempts to substitute a topic of high interest for neurotic responses. "In psychoanalytic practice, erotic conversation serves in place of the lollypop [for the crying child] for the distraction and inhibition of the undesired response and furnishes a chance for re-training" (Guthrie, 1935, pp. 75–76).

On the topic of punishment, Guthrie's writings are similarly rich with examples. Recall that his basic view is that, to be effective, a punisher must elicit an incompatible response in the same situation as the old cues. "To train a dog to jump through a hoop, the effectiveness of punishment depends on where it is applied, front or rear. It is what the punishment makes the dog *do* that counts or what it makes a man do, not what it makes him feel" (Guthrie, 1935, p. 159). A punisher is, then, simply another kind of stimulus, albeit one that may be more effective than others and therefore more practical to apply. Guthrie (1935, p. 21) recounts a case in which a number of dogs were mysteriously poisoned with meat in a city in the West. Some dog owners took it upon themselves to train their own pets not to eat stray pieces of meat by placing bits of meat into mousetraps that would snap at the unsuspecting animals. As might be expected, the dogs became wary of free pieces of meat for a time.

Guthrie seems not to have shared the more recent sentiments of psychologists who are generally opposed to the use of punishment. Guthrie argued that punishment is a "moral term," not a psychological one. On the other hand, one instance in which Guthrie suggests that use of a punisher may be counterproductive is when it causes what he terms *emotional excitement,* rather than a specific and effective overt action. In this case, there may result a stereotyping or fixation of the behavior that produces the punisher. A child's temper tantrum is a case in point (Guthrie, 1938, pp. 80–82). Kicking and screaming in response to punishment through withdrawal of, say, the opportunity to play outside may simply result in a spanking, then more kicking and screaming. The emotional response to punishment has no effect upon it and may actually result in more of the same.

Another kind of vicious circle that fits a Guthrian analysis, *experimental masochism,* was described by Brown (1969). In this procedure, a rat is taught to run down an electric grid to safety at the end of the runway. Then it is taught to run to safety by placing it onto the uncharged grid and presenting the shock only if the animal does not run (an avoidance procedure). Finally, the animal is placed into a start box without shock but with the electrically charged portion of the grid some distance away. Since the animal has been taught to run in the absence of shock to avoid receiving shock and also to run to safety once it is shocked, it will continue to run "masochistically" from the safe start box to the shocked portion of the runway, then across to safety. In Guthrie's view, the shock does not suppress behavior but rather acts as a stimulus, directly or indirectly, in this case to evoke a rather maladaptive running *to* shock itself.

Hilgard and Bower (1975) summarize the pragmatics of Guthrie's system:

1. To effectively use reward and punishment, determine what cues control a given behavior. Then, to maintain the behavior, see that it occurs in the presence

of the cues. To suppress the behavior, see that the cues are present when the behavior is not.

2. Associate as many cues as possible with a behavior to lessen the effects of other "distracting" stimuli and incompatible responses.

Guthrie was one of the last "general systematists," who established a set of principles to account for a broad range of behavioral phenomena. His abundant practical suggestions probably encouraged many students to consider seriously the contributions of experimental psychology to their everyday lives. Within the field of learning, however, he will be remembered more as a major spokesperson for the principle of association by contiguity, the only viable alternative to the dominant reinforcement theories of this century. In some form, though probably not Guthrie's strict behavioral one, the basic doctrine of associationism will continue to be with us in any successful account of the phenomena of learning.

SUMMARY

Guthrie's theory of learning was an attempt to reduce all learning to a single principle of association: "A stimulus pattern that is acting at the time of a response will, if it recurs, tend to produce that response" (Guthrie, 1942, p. 23). The chief learning mechanism operating is said to be temporal contiguity between stimulus and movement. Reinforcement plays no part in the actual formation of a connection. Moreover, learning is an all-or-none affair; an association is formed instantaneously upon the pairing of stimulus and response.

For the most part, Guthrie equated stimuli with changes in the physical environment. In his final work, however, he recognized the role of attentional responses in defining the effective stimulus for an organism. His concept of the response was always in terms of muscle movements or glandular secretions, a somewhat more molecular view than that of most learning theorists. Since there is an enormous number of potential stimuli in any situation, and since the organism is capable of a large number of responses, the development of a skillful act may require many trials, although the formation of any single stimulus-response association is a one-trial event. This accounts for the usual practice effects observed in learning.

The terminal event in any sequence of responses, a goal for reinforcer, is typically a sudden stimulus change. The effect of a change in stimulus conditions is to preserve or maintain any prior stimulus-response association; if the earlier cues are removed, there is no opportunity for a new association to be formed.

The undoing or extinction of any association is simply the attachment of a new and inhibitory response to a stimulus. Similarly, forgetting is the formation of new associations that inhibit old ones. Thus learning is an ongoing process in which new associations are continually being formed, some of which may become part of a complex skill or act and others of which may interfere with former associations.

Two internal sources of stimuli may enter into associations and facilitate the integration of a series of responses. Movements themselves generate stimuli that may become attached to other movements in a response chain. Maintaining stimuli are the equivalents of motives in other theories; they provide a continuing source of internal cues that are attached to responses that occur in their presence. Punishment is one source of maintaining stimuli. Escape removes these cues by removing the punisher. The escape response functions to "inhibit" the punished response, resulting in response suppression.

Although Guthrie's theory stands as the prime representative of associationistic views of learning, it failed in its attempt to become the broad-scope view that would integrate the enormous range of phenomena in the field. The influence of contiguity theory is primarily seen in more recent mathematical approaches to learning and development of the concept of the inhibitory response.

ANNOTATED BIBLIOGRAPHY

Guthrie, E. R. *The psychology of learning.* New York: Harper & Row, 1935.

This book, revised with few changes in 1952, provides the principal statement of Guthrie's theory. In it, he applies the stimulus-response contiguity principle to numerous daily and laboratory situations and discusses the inhibitory conditioning (associative inhibition) process, forgetting, generalization, reward, punishment, and other common learning phenomena. Early chapters are partly concerned with a description and critique of Pavlov's view of reflex conditioning. In later chapters, Guthrie's model is extended to complex learning situations, intuition, perception, and thought, showing his interest in developing a system with broad applicability.

Guthrie, E. R. *The psychology of human conflict.* New York: Harper & Row, 1938.

This is Guthrie's attempt to apply his theory to common problems in personality and adjustment; it demonstrates his enthusiasm for the usefulness of the system. Following a philosophical discussion on the nature of humanity and life, the basics of the theory are stated. Then Guthrie plunges into some common concepts of personality —consciousness and unconsciousness, the self, motives, beliefs, and others. The remainder of the book is a discussion of a number of clinical concepts and treatments, including nervous breakdowns, phobias and anxiety, neurasthenia, psychasthenia, and various sources of human conflict in the family and society. The book contains fascinating exercises in the application of basic learning processes to subject matter formerly the exclusive province of psychiatrists and clinicians.

Guthrie, E. R. Association by contiguity. In S. Koch (Ed.), *Psychology: A study of a science* (Vol. 2). New York: McGraw-Hill, 1959.

This is Guthrie's final statement, in which he reflects on some of the origins of his position, attempts a formalization of some of his major points, and revises his notion of the stimulus to include reference to attentional responses.

Guthrie, E. R., & Horton, G. *Cats in a puzzle box.* New York: Holt, 1946.

This short book is essentially a report of the research conducted by Guthrie and his colleague at the University of Washington which was designed to answer the question: Does the behavior of the cat in learning to escape from a puzzle box conform to the general principle of association by contiguity? Not only did Guthrie feel that certain features of the cats' behavior answered this question in the affirmative, he was confident of the relevance of this research for human behavior: "In our opinion this puzzle-box learning is strictly comparable to the learning of human beings" (Guthrie, 1942, p. 44).

Mueller, C. G., Jr., & Schoenfeld, W. N. Edwin R. Guthrie. In W. K. Estes et al. (Eds.), *Modern learning theory.* New York: Appleton-Century-Crofts, 1954.

Mueller and Schoenfeld review Guthrie's theory from a logical and methodological standpoint. They are critical of Guthrie's inadequate definitions, his lack of quantitative precision, and his generally casual mode of theorizing. The reviewers conclude that the simplicity of the theory is in fact deceptive and that its applicability demands additional assumptions and constructs.

REFERENCES

Atkinson, R. C., & Shiffrin, R. M. *Mathematical models for memory and learning* (Tech. Report 79, Psychology Series, Institute for Mathematical Studies in the Social Sciences). Stanford, Cal.: Stanford University Press, 1965.

Azrin, N. H., & Holz, W. C. Punishment. In W. K. Honig (Ed.), *Operant behavior: Areas of research and application.* New York: Appleton-Century-Crofts, 1966.

Bindra, D. A motivational view of learning, performance, and behavior modification. *Psychological Review*, 1974, *81*, 199–213.

Bolles, R. C. Reinforcement, expectancy, and learning. *Psychological Review*, 1972, *79*, 394–409.

Bolles, R. C. *Learning theory.* New York: Holt, Rinehart & Winston, 1975.

Bower, G. H. Stimulus sampling theory of encoding variability. In E. Martin & A. Melton (Eds.), *Coding theory and memory.* Washington, D.C.: V. H. Winston, 1972.

Brogden, W. J., Lipman, E. A., & Culler, E. The role of incentive in conditioning and extinction. *American Journal of Psychology*, 1938, *51*, 109–117.

Brown, J. S. Factors affecting self-punitive locomotor behavior. In B. A. Campbell & R. M. Church (Eds.), *Punishment and aversive behavior.* New York: Appleton-Century-Crofts, 1969.

Dennis, W. *Readings in the history of psychology.* New York: Appleton-Century-Crofts, 1948.

Denny, M. R., & Adelman, H. M. Elicitation theory: I. An analysis of two typical learning situations. *Psychological Review*, 1955, *62*, 290–296.

Estes, W. K. The statistical approach to learning theory. In S. Koch (Ed.), *Psychology: A study of a science* (Vol. 2). New York: McGraw-Hill, 1959.

Fowler, H., & Miller, N. E. Facilitation and inhibition of runway performance by hind- and forepaw shock of various intensities. *Journal of Comparative and Physiological Psychology*, 1963, *56*, 801–805.

Guthrie, E. R. Conditioning as a principle of learning. *Psychological Review*, 1930, *37*, 412–428.

Guthrie, E. R. *The psychology of learning.* New York: Harper & Row, 1935.

Guthrie, E. R. *The psychology of human conflict.* New York: Harper & Row, 1938.

Guthrie, E. R. Association and the law of effect. *Psychological Review*, 1940, *47*, 127–148.

Guthrie, E. R. Conditioning: A theory of learning in terms of stimulus, response, and association. In *The psychology of learning*, 41st Yearbook of the National Society for the Study of Education (Part II). Chicago: University of Chicago Press, 1942.

Guthrie, E. R. *The psychology of learning* (Rev. ed.). New York: Harper & Row, 1952.

Guthrie, E. R. Association by contiguity. In S. Koch (Ed.), *Psychology: A study of a science* (Vol. 2). New York: McGraw-Hill, 1959.

Guthrie, E. R., & Horton, G. *Cats in a puzzle box.* New York: Holt, 1946.

Hergenhahn, B. R. *An introduction to theories of learning.* Englewood Cliffs, N.J.: Prentice-Hall, 1976.

Herrnstein, R. J. Method and theory in the study of avoidance. *Psychological Review*, 1969, *76*, 49–69.

Hilgard, E. R., & Bower, G. H. *Theories of learning.* New York: Appleton-Century-Crofts, 1975.

Holt, E. B. *Animal drive and the learning process.* New York: Holt, 1931.

Horton, D. L., & Turnage, T. W. *Human learning.* Englewood Cliffs, N.J.: Prentice-Hall, 1976.

Hull, C. L. *Principles of behavior.* New York: Appleton-Century-Crofts, 1943.

Kimble, G. A. *Hilgard and Marquis' conditioning and learning.* New York: Appleton-Century-Crofts, 1961.

Kimble, G., & Kimball, J. A comparison of two methods of producing experimental extinction. *Journal of Experimental Psychology*, 1953, *45*, 87–90.

Kish, G. B. Studies of sensory reinforcement. In W. K. Honig (Ed.), *Operant behavior: Areas of research and application.* New York: Appleton-Century-Crofts, 1966.

Marx, M. H. An experimental test of the interfering-response theory of extinction. *Psychonomic Science*, 1968, *10*, 233–234.

Mowrer, O. H. On the dual nature of learning: A reinterpretation of "conditioning" and "problem-solving." *Harvard Educational Review,* 1947, *17,* 102–148.

Mowrer, O. H., & Lamoreaux, R. R. Avoidance conditioning and signal duration: A study of secondary motivation and reward. *Psychological Monographs,* 1942, *54* (Whole No. 269).

Mueller, C. G., Jr., & Schoenfeld, W. N. Edwin R. Guthrie. In W. K. Estes et al. (Eds.), *Modern learning theory.* New York: Appleton-Century-Crofts, 1954.

Pavlov, I. P. *Conditioned reflexes.* London: Clarendon Press, 1927.

Pierrel, R., & Sherman, J. G. Train your pet the Barnabus way. *Brown Alumni Monthly,* February, 1963, 8–14.

Rescorla, R. A., & Solomon, R. L. Two-process learning theory: Relationships between Pavlovian conditioning and instrumental learning. *Psychological Review,* 1967, *74,* 151–182.

Seward, J. An experimental study of Guthrie's theory of reinforcement. *Journal of Experimental Psychology,* 1942, *30,* 247–256.

Seward, J., Dill, J., & Holland, M. Guthrie's theory of learning: A second experiment. *Journal of Experimental Psychology,* 1944, *34,* 227–238.

Sheffield, F. D. Avoidance training and the contiguity principle. *Journal of Comparative and Physiological Psychology,* 1948, *41,* 165–177.

Sheffield, F. D. Theoretical considerations in the learning of complex sequential tasks from demonstration and practice. In A. A. Lumsdaine (Ed.), *Student response in programmed instruction.* Washington, D.C.: National Academy of Sciences, 1961.

Skinner, B. F. *The behavior of organisms.* New York: Appleton-Century-Crofts, 1938.

Skinner, B. F. Behaviorism at fifty. *Science,* 1963, *140,* 951–958.

Skinner, B. F. *About behaviorism.* New York: Alfred A. Knopf, 1974.

Spence, K. W. *Behavior theory and conditioning.* New Haven, Conn.: Yale University Press, 1956.

Stampfl, T. G., & Lewis, D. J. Essentials of implosive therapy: A learning theory–based psychodynamic behavioral therapy. *Journal of Abnormal Psychology,* 1967, *72,* 496–503.

Terrace, H. Discrimination learning with and without errors. *Journal of the Experimental Analysis of Behavior,* 1963, *6,* 1–27.

Thorndike, E. L. *Animal intelligence.* New York: Macmillan, 1911.

Thorndike, E. L. *The fundamentals of learning.* New York: Teachers College Press, 1932.

Tolman, E. C. *Purposive behavior in animals and men.* New York: Appleton-Century-Crofts, 1932.

Trapold, M. A., & Overmier, J. B. The second learning process in instrumental learning. In A. J. Black & W. F. Prokasy (Eds.), *Classical conditioning. II: Current research and theory.* New York: Appleton-Century-Crofts, 1972.

Voeks, V. W. Postremity, recency, and frequency as bases for prediction in the maze situation. *Journal of Experimental Psychology,* 1948, *38,* 495–510.

Voeks, V. W. Formalization and clarification of a theory of learning. *Journal of Psychology,* 1950, *30,* 341–363.

Voeks, V. W. Acquisition of S–R connections: A test of Hull's and Guthrie's theories. *Journal of Experimental Psychology,* 1954, *47,* 137–147.

Warren, H. C. *A history of association psychology.* New York: Charles Scribner, 1921.

Watson, J. B. Psychology as the behaviorist views it. *Psychological Review,* 1913, *20,* 158–177.

Wickens, D., & Platt, C. Response termination of the cue stimulus in classical and instrumental conditioning. *Journal of Experimental Psychology,* 1954, *47,* 183–186.

Wolpe, J. *Psychotherapy by reciprocal inhibition.* Stanford, Cal.: Stanford University Press, 1958.

Zeaman, D., & Radner, L. A test of the mechanisms of learning proposed by Hull and Guthrie. *Journal of Experimental Psychology,* 1953, *45,* 239–244.

4

Hull's Drive Theory

CHARLES I. BROOKS

INTRODUCTION

Overview

Learning is the central concept in psychology. It refers to the process by which behavior undergoes relatively permanent changes in an *intact* organism. (The word *intact* rules out behavior changes that might result from injury, surgical intervention, or bodily damage due to aging or infectious agents.) Theoretical and empirical concern with the learning process began in this country in the early 1900s, when the Darwinian model, stressing survival and adaptation to the environment, was incorporated into American psychology. Learning is important in this context, since it is the process which improves the organism's chances for survival.

Clark L. Hull (1884–1952) was a leader of the new learning psychology in America during the 1930s and 1940s. Hull was born in Akron, New York, on May 24, 1884. His early interest was in engineering, and his efforts to construct a formal and precise learning theory reflected his engineering training. Hull was eventually attracted to psychology through his interests in philosophy and theorizing. He received his bachelor's degree from the University of Michigan and his Ph.D. degree from the University of Wisconsin in 1918.

Hull's early work in psychology dealt with performance testing and hypnosis. He was one of the first investigators to submit the phenomenon of hypnosis to experimentation. The main feature of his work was the use of controlled conditions in which both hypnotized and nonhypnotized persons were exposed to the same stimuli. A variety of published papers preceded his book *Hypnosis and Suggestibility: An Experimental Approach* (1933b).

Hull's work in the area of learning began in the 1930s, and in 1943, *Principles of Behavior,* the first account of his theory of learning, was published. The formulation of the theory considered the basic phenomena of classical and instrumental conditioning and proposed a deductive system to account for them. It showed the influence of Thorndike's (1932) work, relying heavily on the Law of Effect, which Hull interpreted as operating through drive reduction. It was based on the hypothesis that learning is a gradual, incremental process, not a sudden, insightful one.

Hull's theory had several characteristics which made it an integral part of learning psychology during the 1940s and 1950s. First, it was global in scope, designed to develop principles from simple situations which would apply to more complex situations. Second, it was mechanistic and compatible with the S–R models of John B. Watson and Edward L. Thorndike. Third, its concepts were closely tied to empirical findings and operations, thus permitting direct laboratory tests of the propositions of the theory.

Hull's theorizing was influenced by the classical and instrumental conditioning methodologies developed by Ivan P. Pavlov and Thorndike, respectively. The core of Hull's hypotheses and propositions was derived from results obtained using these methodologies. In considering these results Hull relied heavily on mathematical statements, which was evidence of the pure laboratory approach to learning rather than the applied emphasis so evident with Thorndike and Burrhus F. Skinner.

As an S–R mechanistic approach to learning, Hull's theory is similar to Edwin R. Guthrie's, but it is clearly different from the sign-expectancy model of Edward C. Tolman and the Gestalt-based field theory of Kurt Lewin. Hull's theory is also energy oriented in that physiological states are seen as driving ongoing behavior. In certain respects, this approach is like early instinct models. Hull's theory, however, does not stress the notion of species-specific behavior characteristic of modern ethological theory.

Major Issues

Hull was involved in a number of theoretical issues. Although at least one of these issues was relegated to the level of a "pseudo-problem" (Kendler, 1952), they were important for the general development of learning theories, and some

even continue today as areas of controversy.

Both Tolman (1948) and Guthrie (1942) noted that the major issue confronting learning theorists is the question: What is learned? The answer in the 1930s and 1940s seemed to be a choice of either S–S relationships or S–R associative bonds.

Tolman best represents the S–S position. Organisms normally learn the succession of stimuli or *signs* that lead to, predict, or *signify* the goal. What is learned, therefore, is a relationship among stimuli. A key concept for Tolman was that of *expectancy*. The organism learns to expect that one particular stimulus (e.g., a startbox) will lead to another (e.g., food in the goalbox).

The S–R position (Guthrie, 1942; Hull, 1943) stresses learning as a process by which particular responses become associated with particular stimuli. The emphasis is on locomotor or manipulative behavior involving muscle contractions. The S–R theorist viewed the work of Pavlov and Thorndike and saw clearly that response changes occur. In classical conditioning, a light or tone comes to elicit a response not previously elicited. In instrumental conditioning, a restructuring of response patterns occurs where originally weak responses became stronger.

Hull's theory has always been placed in the S–R camp, probably because of his extensive use of the conditioning methodologies and his willingness to engage in neurophysiological speculations. The true nature of Hull's concepts lies in mathematical functions relating the concepts to present and antecedent environmental conditions. Hull was prone, however, to speculate as to the physiological locus of a concept in the nervous system, thus giving the concept "surplus meaning" (Spence, 1956). These meanings are not essential to the structure or predictive power of the theory, but they show Hull's stimulus-response thinking.

A second theoretical issue of concern to Hull was the question: Is reinforcement necessary for learning to occur? Hull's answer was affirmative. He maintained that practice will not produce learning unless the practice is reinforced. The opposing point of view is termed the *contiguity* position, represented by both Guthrie and Tolman. (The respective classifications, therefore, are: Hull, S–R/reinforcement; Guthrie, S–R/contiguity; Tolman, S–S/contiguity.) The necessary and sufficient condition for learning, according to Guthrie, is the simultaneous occurrence of a stimulus and a response. The model for this process is Pavlovian conditioning.

A third issue for Hull concerned the nature of the reinforcement mechanism. Hull felt that rewards function by reducing drives, which correspond to physiological needs. The drive reduction hypothesis became a highly controversial part of Hull's theory, and a great deal of research was conducted on this issue.

A fourth issue concerned the speed of the learning process. Hull decided that the process is incremental, whereas Guthrie held to an *all-or-none* position. Proponents of the incremental model see response strength increasing gradually with practice. There is also assumed to be an upper limit, or asymptote, beyond which response strength cannot increase. Hull specified that response strength approaches this asymptote in a negatively accelerated fashion; early training trials produce large increments in response strength, but as training progresses, the increments become smaller and smaller.

The all-or-none model specifies one-trial learning. Response strength can go

from zero to maximum in a single practice trial. The proponents of this model had to deal with the fact that most empirical curves grow incrementally, and compelling arguments explaining such increases from the all-or-none perspective have been presented (Estes, 1964; Guthrie, 1942).

Basic Concepts

Hull's approach to theory is associated with the term *hypothetico-deductive method*. He wanted to construct a formal theoretical system to explain the learning process. The system would begin with a set of defined terms, followed by a small number of basic postulates. The postulates themselves could be general empirical findings, directly verified through laboratory study or at least subject to verification.

In Hull's system, the basic postulates and definitions were to be designed to relate logically the various constructs of the theory to one another and to their respective antecedent and consequent conditions. This process was to produce deductions or predictions (theorems) which could be experimentally tested. Hull intended that only those features of the theory that survived the rigors of experimental testing would remain in the theory intact. Contrary evidence would require a modification of a postulate to bring its predictions in line with the empirical data. The entire system, therefore, would be self-correcting.

One example of Hull's approach to theorizing is seen in *Mathematico-Deductive Theory of Rote Learning* (Hull, Hovland, Ross, Hall, Perkins, & Fitch, 1940), which used the hypothetico-deductive method to deduce testable postulates in the area of rote memorization (see Hilgard & Bower, 1966). While the book did not achieve wide readership or influence, probably because of its formal structure, it nevertheless illustrates the precision attainable in a rigid, formal approach to a behavioral situation.

Hull's major theoretical work is *Principles of Behavior* (1943). In this work he again sought the rigor and precision of the mathematico-deductive approach, but the theory took on a different form. Rather than beginning with postulates to be coordinated with an empirical system of constructs, the 1943 theory introduced concepts in terms of empirical variables. This method, termed the *intervening-variable approach,* is central to Hull's theory.

The use of intervening variables in learning theory was introduced by Tolman (1932, 1948). The intervening variable is a verbal label which represents an inferred organismic process intervening between a stimulus event and the response of the organism. At an empirical level, the researcher observes or manipulates some stimulus event or antecedent condition and observes the consequences. Analysis of the situation need go no further; as the length of time a rat is deprived of food is increased, the frequency of the barpressing response which results in a food reward also increases. Hull, however, chose to go further by tying observed empirical relationships to inferred organismic states. In the preceding example, for instance, Hull theorized that deprivation raises the drive level of the organism, and this increase in drive is responsible for the increase in barpressing.

The essence of the intervening-variable approach is to (1) tie the intervening variable to a correlative antecedent or environmental variable which can be manipulated, and (2) relate the resulting

assumed value of the intervening variable to behavioral outcomes that can be measured. Hull used mathematics to relate these two processes.

The fundamental concepts of Hull's theory, many in the form of intervening variables, are as follows:

Habit Strength (H). Hull's basic unit of behavior is habit strength, a construct representing a relatively permanent receptor-effector connection in the nervous system. Habits are a function of the number of reinforced trials, the precise function being $H = M(1 - e^{-iN})$, where M equals maximum possible learning, e and i are constants to be determined for specific situations, and N equals the number of reinforced trials.

Drive (D). Biological needs are the basis for all motivation in Hull's theory, and they are represented by the construct drive. The major primary drives are hunger, thirst, air-temperature regulation, defecation, urination, rest, sleep, activity, sexual intercourse, nest building, care of the young, and relief from pain (Hull, 1943, pp. 59–60). Internal receptors sense these deprivation states and energize behavior. The true motivating component of a drive, therefore, is the *drive stimulus* (S_D). The total motivational state of the organism results from both *relevant* (e.g., hunger present when responding is reinforced by food) and *irrelevant* (e.g., thirst present in the food reinforcement situation) drives.

Secondary Drives. Stimuli can acquire drive properties. A stimulus paired with pain, for instance, can arouse fear on subsequent occasions. The resulting fear stimuli are able to motivate behavior (Hull, 1951, p. 21).

Incentive (K). Incentive is a motivational concept based on the amount of reinforcement received. Hull assumed, therefore, that amount of reinforcement does not influence the strength of *H,* but it affects performance by changing the motivational level of the organism.

Stimulus-Intensity Dynamism (V). This construct is tied to the intensity of stimuli in the conditioning situation. A strong external stimulus evokes a strong response. As with *K,* this effect is non-associative and does not affect the strength of *H.*

Reaction Potential (E). Following input from the various antecedent conditions, performance occurs and is represented by the construct of reaction potential. Hull assumed that reaction potential *(E)* results from a multiplicative combination of habit strength *(H),* drive *(D),* incentive *(K),* and stimulus intensity *(V),* in the formula $E = H \times D \times K \times V$. Reaction potential itself is tied to four performance measures: response probability, latency, amplitude, and resistance to extinction.

Generalized Habit Strength ($\overline{H}$). "The reaction involved in the original conditioning becomes connected with a considerable zone of stimuli other than . . . the stimulus conventionally involved in the original conditioning" (Hull, 1943, p. 183). These generalized habits contribute to *E.*

Aggregate Inhibitory Potential ($\dot{I}$). Inhibition represents the negative effects of the work involved in performing a response. Specifically, responding produces a negative drive state called *reactive inhibition* (I_R) which motivates the organism to cease responding. When activity does cease, there is a reduction in $I_R,$ and not responding is thus reinforced and develops as a habit. The construct of *conditioned inhibition* $({}_sI_R)$ represents this habit. I_R and ${}_sI_R$ combine to form aggregate inhibitory potential ($\dot{I}$).

Behavioral Oscillation (O). "Even when the strength of a reaction potential has become stabilized, . . . both the amplitude and the latency of the reaction always oscillate from trial to trial" (Hull, 1943, p. 304). This construct accounts for random fluctuations in behavior.

Reaction Threshold (L). For responding to occur, some minimum amount of reaction potential is required.

Primary Reinforcement. Reinforcement occurs when a drive stimulus is reduced. Habit strength *(H)* occurs only when drive reduction takes place (Hull, 1952, pp. 5–6).

Secondary Reinforcement. If a stimulus is paired with primary reinforcement, the stimulus may acquire reinforcing properties. Specifically, through conditioning, the stimulus can elicit a fractional component of the goal response, which would take the form of an anticipation of the goal response. This *fractional anticipatory goal response* is referred to as $r_G,$ and a stimulus has secondary reinforcing properties to the extent it elicits $r_G.$

HISTORY

Beginnings

Hull's theory belongs in a progression of ideas which began largely with Charles Darwin's theory of evolution and which became transformed in this country into a concern with the functional capacities of behaving organisms. Darwin's ideas of struggle, competition, and survival of the fittest all were incorporated into psychological theorizing about human behavior. This survival model was especially influential for Hull, who viewed behavior in the context of need satisfaction. Conditions of need arise, and the purpose of behavior is to satisfy those needs. For Hull, the learning process comprises the mechanism whereby the organism is able to survive. Those responses that are successful in reducing tissue needs become permanent parts of the organism's behavioral repertoire, thus increasing the probability of successful coping with environmental stresses. Hull's stress on survival gave his theory a distinctive motivational flavor. In fact, the theory is more motivational than associative in nature. For Hull, learning is an instrument which enables the organism to satisfy its needs (Cofer & Appley, 1964).

Another major antecedent of Hull's thinking was *drive theory*. Early approaches to motivation stressed instincts, and a major figure, William McDougall, believed they are the prime movers of behavior. According to McDougall (1908), no action can occur without the involvement of an instinct, and behavior is designed to serve the end or *purpose* of the instinct. Psychological forces, therefore, are not mechanical in their functioning but must be understood in the context of a goal that terminates the behavior initiated by the force itself. This teleological aspect of McDougall's viewpoint was not popular in early 20th-century psychology, and drive theory partly developed as an alternative to this view. While McDougall stressed a *pulling* force from an unspecified future event, drive theory stressed a *pushing* process which energizes the organism into action.

Drive theory was initially developed by Robert Woodworth (1918), who viewed drive as a force analogous to the power source which activates a machine. Hull transformed this machine conception of drive into a physiological one, with the source of activation residing in primary states like hunger and thirst. The change from instinct to drive seemed to

fit well with the environmental emphasis of Watson, and the notion of drive seemed to have more objective, physiological promise than that of instinct.

The most direct influences on Hull's theorizing are found in the works of Pavlov, Watson, and Thorndike. Pavlov's *Conditioned Reflexes* (1927) was a milestone in the area of animal learning. It not only outlined the basic laboratory procedure of classical conditioning, it also systematically considered many phenomena like generalization, discrimination, and inhibition. Watson (1913) took the bold step away from consciousness toward objectivity and mechanism. He maintained that the psychologist, like any natural scientist, should proceed to describe natural occurrences and attempt to formulate the nature of the relationships existing among these occurrences. Consciousness may be taken for granted and need not be assigned a special place in psychology.

Watson also attempted to derive complex learning from more elemental forms of learning, especially those based on conditioned responses. Hull viewed this approach as worthwhile, and he assumed that the basic laws of classical and instrumental conditioning would provide the theoretical foundation for analyzing more complex behavior. Hull saw the conditioning methodologies as highly amenable to experimental control and measurement, thus facilitating the discovery of basic laws of learning.

Hull was also influenced by Thorndike's (1932) work and his formulation of the Law of Effect. Thorndike noted that repetition of behavior appears to depend on the success of the response in producing a reward. He suggested that such success tends to "stamp in" associations between environmental stimuli and the response, a conception which coincides quite nicely with the Darwinian survival model. Hull developed his learning theory around the concept of drive reduction, maintaining that learning occurs only when a response produces or signals a reduction in tissue needs. It is important to note that Hull went beyond a simple empirical law of effect, which would describe the empirical relationship between response strength and reward contingencies. He incorporated a theoretical law of effect into his theory and thus became a true reinforcement theorist in the sense that the occurrence of a reinforcer is a necessary condition for learning to take place.

Major Theorists

Kenneth W. Spence (1907–1967). Spence was an early associate of Hull's who made significant contributions to and modifications of Hull's theory (Spence, 1956, 1960); the term *Hull-Spence formulation* is often used. Whereas many similarities do exist in their positions, there are also many differences:

1. Spence did not engage in the formal, theoretical style of Hull, although he did center his theory around intervening variables.
2. Spence did not give his intervening variables surplus meaning derived from neurophysiological speculations.
3. Spence did not believe that tension reduction is a necessary condition for learning in instrumental reward conditioning. In classical defense conditioning, on the other hand, later studies suggested to him such a strong reinforcement position.
4. Spence was generally more cautious in generalizing from simple to complex situations than was Hull. In fact, Spence was very careful in specifying the precise boundary conditions within which his empirical functions operated.

A major contribution of Spence was his proposal that the fractional anticipatory goal response (r_G) has motivational properties (Spence, 1951). Hull's early treatment of reward was purely associative, and reward variables like size and delay were tied to habit. In Hull's 1952 revision of his theory, however, incentive motivation (K) appeared, representing a major refinement in the theory. Spence's 1956 theoretical statement for instrumental reward conditioning also included K, although, unlike Hull, he assumed an additive relationship between drive (D) and incentive motivation (K). Spence's treatment of K and the r_G mechanism greatly improved stimulus-response theory and also served to stimulate development of a motivational theory of extinction (Amsel, 1962).

During the 1960s, Spence continued to refine and modify his theory as new data appeared. His efforts in classical defense conditioning were especially noteworthy, and in one of his last papers (Spence, 1966), he presented an answer to the question of why animals and humans show different extinction rates of the conditioned eyeblink response.

Neal E. Miller. Like Hull, Miller emphasized the importance of drive in the learning process. To Miller, a drive "is a strong stimulus which impels action" (Miller & Dollard, 1941, p. 18). For learning to occur, there must be a reduction in the intensity of a drive. Miller, therefore, like Hull, maintained a drive reduction position with respect to reinforcement.

Miller's work is important in the development of the concept of acquired drives (Miller, 1959). An emotional response to an aversive stimulus can, through Pavlovian conditioning, become attached to a formerly neutral stimulus. This response has strong stimulus consequences which can function as drives. Hence, the CS in the Pavlovian paradigm can elicit a drive state.

Miller's work was a definite enlargement of the drive concept. Whereas Hull stressed primary physiological states arising from conditions of deprivation, Miller emphasized the drive properties of strong stimuli in general. This emphasis, of course, led to much research in aversive conditioning situations.

O. H. Mowrer. Like Miller, Hobart Mowrer stressed the importance of fear as an acquired drive. Fear, a classically conditioned response, is conceptualized as the anticipation of pain, and it serves to motivate avoidance responding (Mowrer, 1956). Mowrer developed a two-factor theory of learning in which classical conditioning is assumed to require contiguity of the CS and UCS, and instrumental conditioning is assumed to require a reinforcement. This position stresses the importance of both drive motivation and drive reduction and is thus closely associated with Hull's theory.

Mowrer (1960) later moved toward a more incentive-based theory. During conditioning, stimuli acquire meaning and elicit emotional responses (e.g., hope or fear) which guide instrumental behavior. This changed emphasis is typical of revisions already noted in the early Hull position which move in the direction of incentive-based, rather than drive-based, motivation.

Current Status

Direct experimental investigation of Hull's theory continued into the 1960s. It is a credit to the theory that it generated such a large number of experiments for so many years. A great many of the advances in learning theory witnessed over the past 20 years may be traced directly to Hull's theory.

One major concern of the theory has centered around the concept of drive (D). A unique feature of Hull's formulation is the assumption that drive energizes all behavior. Any source of drive is able to energize any sort of consummatory behavior, instrumental responding, and even general activity. Contemporary views of the energizing effects of drive, however, place more stress on the relationship of the particular behavior to the motivational condition of the organism (Bolles, 1975). Thus, deprivation states appear most likely to energize those responses which are important in alleviating the deprivation state.

In general, a much greater role is presently given to associative processes in motivated behavior than was the case in Hull's theory. Drive does not appear to be the unified state conceived by Hull, and different sources of drive are not necessarily motivationally equivalent. Current theorizing emphasizes habit, acquired drives, and incentive factors as being involved in motivated behavior. It is also interesting to note that a general dissatisfaction with the D concept has coincided with a resurgence of S–S approaches to theorizing and a general decline of S–R models. Expectancy, the heart of Tolman's view of learning, is mentioned more and more as the basic unit of learning and performance. The current emphasis also appears to be more on information processing and perceptual utilization of cues rather than on reinforcement and motivation (Mackintosh, 1974).

Recent research has questioned the role of incentive as a general drive. Both

Hull and Spence assumed that incentive, like drive, is a source of motivation that serves to energize response tendencies. In recent years this view has been revised in the direction of a more associative account. That is, the motivational effects of an incentive are more likely to be on responses relevant to obtaining the incentive, and not on all activity (Rescorla & Solomon, 1967). Incentive can still be conceived of as the anticipation of a goal. Rather than serving as a motivator, however, the effect is like that of a secondary reinforcer. The drive behind responding, therefore, is the establishment of associations between responding and reinforcement or stimuli paired with reinforcement. These incentive stimuli become goals for responding, not motivators of responding (Mackintosh, 1974).

The degree to which associative models of drive and incentive will dominate the Hull-Spence motivational model in learning remains to be seen. The new emphasis, however, is certainly consistent with other developments, notably the renewed use of expectancy (Bolles, 1975), the development of stimulus selection and cue-utilization models (Rescorla & Wagner, 1972), and the growing influence of ethologically based models (Hinde, 1970).

The reinforcement and motivational stresses remain quite pervasive, however, especially in theorizing about the partial reinforcement effect (Amsel, 1962; Daly, 1974). The theories of Abram Amsel and others (e.g., Logan, 1960) illustrate a change in recent learning theories compared to those presented by Hull, Tolman, and Guthrie. As the difficulties with such global approaches became apparent, learning theories tended to become more molecular, designed to explain more limited phenomena. Amsel's frustration theory, for instance, deals with the partial reinforcement effect in instrumental learning situations. This theory assigns an active role to motivational processes and stresses their influence in affecting behavior during extinction. It is also based on incentive development during acquisition and thus reflects the later refinements made by Hull (1952), Spence (1956), and Logan (1960). Once incentive develops, says Amsel, nonreward elicits frustration in the organism. During partial reinforcement acquisition, the subject essentially learns to continue approaching the goal in spite of the presence of frustration-produced cues. Under continuous reinforcement, of course, no such learning occurs, since no frustration is present.

Perhaps the most controversial arguments concerning Hull's drive concept have centered around avoidance conditioning and the role of fear. During avoidance learning, fear can be viewed as providing the motivation for the avoidance response, and the reinforcement (fear reduction) following the response. The extensive work of McAllister and McAllister (1971) demonstrates the predictive power of this two-factor analysis of aversive conditioning. Alternative points of view (see Mackintosh, 1974) put more stress on the signaling properties of the CS and the response repertoire of the subject as the important variables.

Hull's view of drive reduction has undergone considerable expansion in recent years. Whereas drive-reducing operations qualify as reinforcing operations, all reinforcers are certainly not limited to such operations. The notion of reinforcement has been expanded to include various types of stimulation (Fowler, 1967), the opportunity to engage in other behavior (Premack, 1971), and associative analyses stressing discrimination processes (Capaldi, 1967).

Other Theories

W. N. Schoenfeld. William Schoenfeld (1950) presented a modification of Mowrer's two-factor account of avoidance learning. Rather than postulating an emotional state of fear being elicited during avoidance learning, he placed emphasis on the aversive properties of the CS itself. In other words, the reward in avoidance learning is CS termination, not fear reduction. This emphasis on the CS stimulated studies focusing on the role of the CS in avoidance conditioning and fostered cognitive analyses of avoidance learning.

Robert C. Bolles. In fundamental agreement with Tolman (1932), Bolles (1975) maintains that the subject in a learning experiment acquires an expectancy. In the avoidance situation, for instance, the various signal-shock and response-shock contingencies lead to expectancies of danger and safety. The expectancy can be of the S–S variety, where some important event like a shock occurs following some other environmental stimulus, or it can be based on an expected consequence of responding, as when an organism expects shock termination following a response.

The key to Bolles's theory is his use of the species-specific defense reaction (SSDR). Specifically, the subject learns to expect certain events and then performs instinctive responses (SSDR's) based on the expectancies. Thus, an organism will withdraw or freeze when confronted with cues signaling danger, yet approach or attempt to maximize cues signaling safety.

The response hierarchy also plays a role in Bolles's analysis. When shocked, for instance, the dominant SSDR may be fleeing, and if this response terminates

the shock, the subject will acquire the appropriate expectancy pertaining to the consequence of fleeing. If fleeing does not achieve safety, the subject will perform the next SSDR in the hierarchy, say, freezing. This formulation predicts that when none of the animal's natural SSDRs lead to safety, avoidance performance will be poor.

Dalbir Bindra. Bindra (1972) uses an S–S approach in analyzing motivation and instrumental learning. The organism develops expectancies as it discriminates predictive cues in its environment. Bindra assumes that these cues arouse a central motivational state which instigates specific response classes. These responses also rely on the presence of other stimuli, called *supporting stimuli.* If cues are present which predict the occurrence of food, a central motive state (designated hunger) is aroused. The motive sensitizes the organism to engage in the response class called *eating.* Only if appropriate supporting stimuli are present, however (e.g., food), will the response class appear.

Bindra does not stress the consequences of a response, nor does he deal with response-strengthening mechanisms as Thorndike and Hull did. A cue arouses a motivational state, and the animal performs a class of behavior according to the supportive function of other cues which are present, according to Bindra.

E. J. Capaldi. John Capaldi (1967) presents a theoretical account of the partial reinforcement effect which stresses cognitive, perceptual and memory processes rather than the reinforcement-motivational forces seen in Amsel's theory. Capaldi assumes that stimulus aftereffects of trial events persist as memories from one trial to the next. These memories can function as cues on subsequent trials. One interesting aspect of Capaldi's formulation is that he takes a strong reinforcement position, in that stimulus aftereffects present on a trial acquire habit potential for the instrumental response only on rewarded trials.

Capaldi's theory generates predictions for manipulations which are simply not within the boundary conditions of a drive-based theory like Amsel's. Such manipulations include the length of a succession of nonrewarded trials and the number of nonreward-reward transitions. The theory has also been successfully applied to more traditional manipulations like amount of reward, delay of reward, and intertrial interval.

PROPOSITIONS

1. *Habit strength increases gradually with number of reinforcements.*

Hull maintained that learning requires contiguity of a stimulus and a response closely associated with a reinforcer. The associative construct, habit (H), is firmly tied to number of reinforcements (N). In formulating the function relating H and N, Hull (1951, p. 32) was characteristically precise:

> If reinforcements follow each other at evenly distributed intervals, everything else constant, the resulting habit will increase in strength as a positive growth function of the number of trials according to the equation
> $$_SH_R = 1 - 10^{-aN}$$

2. *Habit strength decreases with increasing delays in reinforcement.*

Many studies have found that where reinforcement is delayed following completion of a response, performance de-

---

A NOTE ON FORMULA TERMINOLOGY

Since Hull's theory was expressed in mathematical terms, formulas are quite common. For instance, the theory states that $E = H \times D \times K \times V$, which means that reaction potential (E), or behavior, results from a multiplicative combination of habit strength (H), drive (D), incentive (K), and stimulus intensity (V). The special terms and constructs are listed below alphabetically for easy reference.

Designation	Construct
D	Drive
E	Excitatory potential
H	Habit, Habit strength
I_R	Reactive inhibition
$_SI_R$	Conditioned inhibition
J	Delay of reinforcement
K	Incentive motivation
L	Threshold
N	Number of reinforcements
O	Oscillation
R_G	Goal or consummatory response
r_G	Fractional anticipatory goal response
S_D	Drive stimulus
S_D Hunger	Drive stimulus for hunger
S_D Thirst	Drive stimulus for thirst
s_G	Stimulus consequences of r_G
V	Stimulus intensity dynamism

---

clines. From these findings, Hull formulated the *goal-gradient hypothesis.* He maintained that the maximum habit strength attainable "closely approximates a negative growth function of the time separating the reaction from the reinforcing state of affairs" (1943, p. 145). Furthermore, he speculated that this decay function could be influenced by the presence of any secondary reinforcers. The presence of a discrete signal during the delay period, for instance, could attenuate the adverse effect of the delay period on performance.

One deduction from Hull's postulate regarding delay of reinforcement is that organisms should show a preference for shorter delays (since H would be stronger at the short delays). Given a choice between an alley where reward is delayed for 30 seconds and another where it is delayed for 60 seconds, the organism should choose the former. Hull also deduced that responses nearer the goal would be more strongly conditioned than those farther removed.

3. *Habit strength decreases with increases in the CS–UCR interval.*

In instrumental conditioning, delay, for Hull, refers to the time lapse between response completion and the delivery of the reinforcement. As noted above, his considerations in this context led him to the goal-gradient hypothesis. In classical conditioning, however, Hull saw delay as the time period between the CS and the UCR (which is elicited by the UCS). He referred to deviations in this interval as stimulus-response asynchronism. As with delay of reinforcement, Hull postulated an exponential decay function relating H and an increasing CS–UCR interval, showing in both cases his belief that contiguity is a necessary condition for learning. On the basis of some laboratory evidence, Hull felt that the optimal stimulus-response asynchrony would be very short, perhaps about 0.5 seconds.

Hull based conditioning with long CS–UCR intervals on an association of the stimulus and a response *trace*.

> When a brief stimulus impinges upon a suitable receptor there is initiated the recruitment phase of a self-propagating molar afferent trace impulse, the molar stimulus equivalent of which rises as a power function of time (t) since the be-

ginning of the stimulus, reaching its maximum (and termination) when t equals about .450. (1951, p. 11)

The three propositions noted above are summarized in Postulate 4 of Hull's theory as formulated in Hull (1943):

> Whenever an effector activity (S) and a receptor activity (R) occur in close temporal contiguity, and this is closely associated with the diminution of a need or with a stimulus which has been closely and consistently associated with the diminution of a need, there will result an increment to a tendency for that afferent impulse on later occasions to evoke that reaction. The increments from successive reinforcements summate in a manner which yields a combined habit strength which is a simple growth function of the number of reinforcements. The upper limit of this curve of learning is the product of (1) a positive growth function of the magnitude of need reduction which is involved in primary, or which is associated with secondary, reinforcement; (2) a negative function of the delay in reinforcement; and (3) (a) a negative growth function of the degree of asynchronism of S and R when both are of brief durations, or (b), in case the action of S is prolonged so as to overlap the beginning of R, a negative growth function of the duration of the continuous action of S on the receptor when R begins. (pp. 177–178)

The amount of reinforcement was clearly given an associative role and made an antecedent condition for habit (H) in Hull (1943). That is, Hull assumed that amount of reinforcement affects the strength of the association between stimuli in the learning situation and the response of the organism. Hull (1952), however, introduced incentive (K), and tied it to amount of reinforcement. This change meant that Hull no longer saw amount of reinforcement as affecting the strength of the stimulus-response association (i.e., habit). Rather, it was now seen as affecting the strength of incentive motivation (*K*). The change in Hull's thinking is reflected in the next proposition.

4. *The amount of reinforcement affects incentive motivation.*

In Hull's 1952 formulation, amount of reinforcement was assumed to operate through the incentive construct, *K:* "The incentive function (*K*) is a negatively accelerated increasing monotonic function of the weight of food given as reinforcement" (1952, p. 27). Hull changed his thinking about amount of reinforcement because of evidence showing that shifts in reward size produce rapid shifts in performance. Such rapid changes could not take place if the amount directly affected *H,* since *H* is assumed to change gradually. Also, downshifts in reward size produce rapid decrements in performance. Since Hull assumed that habits are relatively permanent, it was difficult to conceive of them weakening. It made better sense, therefore, to tie amount of reward to a nonassociative construct (incentive motivation, *K*) and to use it to account for response decrements resulting from reduction in reward size.

5. *Response probability shows a sigmoid relationship to number of reinforcements.*

Figure 4.1 shows the relationship Hull assumed between response probability and number of reinforcements. This function clearly illustrates the incremental view of learning, which assumes that learning occurs gradually over trials.

It was noted earlier that Hull assumed a negatively accelerated growth function relating *H* and number of reinforcements. Figure 4.1, however, shows an initial period of positive acceleration.

Figure 4.1

Assumed Relationship between Response Probability and Number of Reinforcements

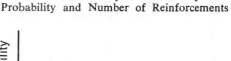
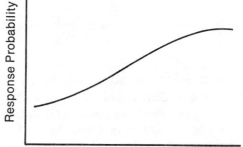

Hull derived this function by assuming that reaction potential had to reach a given level (threshold) before being reflected in performance, and that reaction potential could exhibit random fluctuations (oscillation) from trial to trial. These assumptions are stated in Postulates 10, 11, and 12:

10. Associated with every reaction potential (${}_sE_R$) there exists an inhibitory potentiality (${}_sO_R$) which oscillates in amount from instant to instant according to the normal "law" of chance. (1943, p. 319)
11. The momentary effective reaction potential must exceed the reaction threshold before a stimulus will evoke a given reaction. (1943, p. 344)
12. Other things equal, the probability of striated-muscle reaction evocation is a normal probability (ogival) function of the extent to which the effective reaction potential exceeds the reaction threshold. (1943, p. 344)

When the assumptions concerning the threshold and oscillation were imposed on the negatively accelerated curve relating reaction potential and number of reinforcements, the sigmoid function seen in Figure 4.1 was generated (see Hull, 1943, pp. 326–332). Hull went on to tie reaction potential to the behavioral measures of response latency (Postulate 13), resistance to extinction (Postulate 14), and response amplitude (Postulate 15).

6. *Habits generalize to stimuli other than those involved in original conditioning.*

Hull noted that adaptive behavior requires flexibility. Faced with a new situation, there had to be a mechanism whereby an organism could respond on the basis of previous learning. Generalization provides such a mechanism, and Hull noted three types:

1. The reaction involved in the original conditioning becomes connected with a considerable zone of stimuli other than, but adjacent to, the stimulus conventionally involved in the original conditioning; this is called *stimulus generalization.*
2. The stimulus involved in the original conditioning becomes connected with a considerable zone of reactions other than, but related to, the reaction conventionally involved in the original reinforcement; this may be called *response generalization.*
3. Stimuli not involved in the original reinforcement but lying in a zone related to it become connected with reactions not involved in the original reinforcement but lying in a zone related to it; this may be called *stimulus-response generalization.* (1943, p. 183)

Hull expanded the notion of habit strength to include these processes, and presented the concept of functional or *effective habit strength* in Postulate 5:

The effective habit strength is jointly (1) a negative growth function of the strength of the habit at the point of reinforcement [the original CS] and (2) of the magnitude of the difference on the continuum of the stimulus between the afferent impulses of [the CS and similar stimuli] in units of discrimination thresholds. (1943, p. 199)

In a later formulation, Hull (1952) proposed that changes in the slope of the generalization gradient which occur with practice trials would depend on the degree to which responding becomes associated with irrelevant stimuli in the situation (stimuli like noises, odors, or sounds). Early in training such stimuli could acquire habit potential through chance associations with reinforced responding. Hence, the conditioned response should show a fairly flat generalization gradient early in training. After more extensive training, however, these incidental stimuli should have any habit potential extinguished because they are not consistently paired with reinforced responding. As training proceeds, therefore, responding becomes more restricted to specific stimuli.

Hull used generalization to explain what he called the *stimulus-learning paradox* and the *stimulus-evocation paradox.* The first paradox resulted from Hull's recognition that exactly the same stimuli do not repeat themselves from trial to trial. How, then, could learning take place, since multiple stimulus presentations are obviously required for the growth of habit? The second paradox notes that even if an S–R bond is acquired, since that precise stimulus situation is unlikely to ever reappear, how would the learning ever be made manifest? Hull solved these problems by assuming that all habits, including generalized ones, summate (1943, p. 199). Thus, a single reinforcement produces some habit, yet not enough to produce suprathreshold excitatory potential. The summation of many of these habits, however, produces suprathreshold excitatory potential.

7. Habit, drive, and incentive combine multiplicatively.

Hull maintained that both drive and incentive multiply habit and that their own relationship is multiplicative (i.e., $H \times D \times K$). This assumption is consistent with Hull's view of drive as an energizer and with certain empirical findings.

The equation $H \times D$, for instance, predicts a statistical interaction when levels of a habit factor are varied orthogonally to levels of a drive factor. Consider the design in Figure 4.2. Two levels of H, defined as 10 or 30 reinforced trials, and two levels of D, defined as 24 or 48 hours of food deprivation, are combined. Let us arbitrarily assign a value of 1 to the low levels of D and H, and a value of 3 to the high levels. The multiplicative function gives us the values shown in Figure 4.3.

If we graph these values, we obtain nonparallel lines, a situation signifying a statistical interaction (see Figure 4.4). The $H \times D$ relationship specifies that the effects of D will vary with different levels of H. The same considerations apply for $D \times K$, of course. We will look at that situation in more detail below.

The multiplicative relationship also specifies that some H, some D, and some

Figure 4.2

Experimental Design for Testing the Relation between Habit and Drive

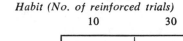

Habit (No. of reinforced trials)

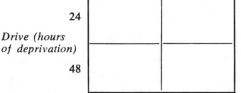

Figure 4.3

Representation of a Multiplicative Relationship between Habit and Drive

Habit

	10	30
24	$1 \times 1 = 1$	$3 \times 1 = 3$
48	$1 \times 3 = 3$	$3 \times 3 = 9$

Drive

A performance value of 1 is assigned to the low levels of habit and drive, and a value of 3 is assigned to the high levels of habit and drive. The multiplicative assumption predicts an interaction between the two variables where the effect of increasing drive is much greater at the higher level of habit. Under low habit, increasing drive increases performance from one to three units, whereas under high habit, performance increases from three to nine units.

K must be present if behavior is to take place. An organism may be full of acquired habits, *potentials* for performing, but if it is unmotivated, these habit potentials will not be translated into performance. By the same token, the motivated organism which has no acquired habits, like barpressing or traversing a maze, will engage in responses like sniffing, grooming, and exploring, which are

Figure 4.4

Interaction of Habit and Drive Factors (where effect of increasing drive is greater for the stronger habit)

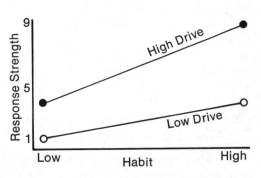

part of the innate equipment of the organism (Hull, 1934a).

In addition to *H, D,* and *K,* in 1951 Hull gave intervening-variable status to stimulus intensity (*V*) and delay of reinforcement (*J*), and he postulated that they also had a multiplicative relationship with *H, D,* and *K* in producing reaction potential.

8. *Drives energize all behavior.*

The fundamental property of Drive (*D*) is that it activates behavior. Drive itself is equated with the total need state of the animal. The most obvious needs are the *relevant* needs, such as hunger for food reinforcement. But *irrelevant* needs might also be present, and they contribute to the total drive level. Such irrelevant needs might be thirst, fear, or sexual tension. Postulate 7 states both the multiplicative relationship of *H* and *D* and the role of relevant and irrelevant drives:

> Any effective habit strength is sensitized into reaction potentiality by all primary drives active within an organism at a given time, the magnitude of this potentiality being a product obtained by multiplying an increasing function of $_sH_R$ by an increasing function of *D*. (1943, p. 253)

Hull clearly saw the effects of *D* as being completely nonspecific. Any ongoing behavior, whether relevant to reinforcement acquisition or not, is activated by *D,* and *D* itself arises from a variety of conditions. Interestingly, Hull saw a similarity between the *D* construct and that of the Freudian libido (1943, p. 252).

9. *Each drive state has a characteristic drive stimulus.*

A physiological need is transformed into a drive state when aspects of the need activate internal receptors. "This receptor activation constitutes the drive stimulus, S_D" (1943, p. 240). The concept of drive stimulus is formally presented in Postulate 6: "Associated with every drive is a characteristic drive stimulus whose intensity is an increasing monotonic function of the drive in question" (1943, p. 253).

Since S_D is a stimulus, it can acquire habit potential and elicit responses. This characteristic, of course, gives a directional influence to motivation. That is, while *D* itself cannot direct behavior, S_D can.

Drive stimuli play an important role in reinforcement in Hull's theory. In the 1951 and 1952 formulations, Hull tied the law of primary reinforcement to S_D reduction. Originally, in the 1943 formulation, the emphasis was on need reduction and thus on reductions in *D*. Later emphasis, however, was on the reduction of the "receptor discharge characteristic of a need (S_D)" (Hull, 1951, p. 15).

The S_D concept greatly complicated a number of empirical situations. Reducing *D,* for instance, would not only take away a source of activation, it would also change S_D (which would bring stimulus generalization into the picture). Even more complex is the situation where an increase in *D* would increase the level of activation yet change the overall stimulus situation by changing S_D. Thus, one effect of increasing *D* should lead to an increase in reaction potential, whereas another effect should lead to a decrease (through stimulus generalization of habit to the new S_D).

10. *Drive properties can be acquired.*

The concept of a learned drive is best illustrated by the example of fear or anxiety. When an animal presses a bar and receives a painful electric shock as a result, Hull saw the proprioceptive stimuli of barpressing as acquiring a habit potential for eliciting a conditioned response, fear. The fear itself is assumed to have drive properties, and it thus contributes to the overall level of *D*. Furthermore, the stimulus consequences of fear (S_Ds) are intense and can serve to arouse and activate behavior. The S_D of fear, therefore, is a learned source of drive. This analysis, of course, endows fear with two qualities: (1) it is a conditioned response in the Pavlovian sense, and (2) it is a drive state. As such, it must be expected to follow all the laws of both the conditioning and drive models.

11. *Reinforcement operates through drive reduction.*

Drive reduction theory was a logical outgrowth of Hull's use of the survival model. Behavior that is adaptive would serve to reduce tissue needs, and thus would be learned. In many conditioning situations, however, it was difficult to conceive of physiological needs being reduced. An animal quickly learns to barpress for a small amount of food, even though the biochemical reduction of hunger occurs long after the response. Also, the evidence showing that neutral stimuli could acquire reinforcing properties presented clear difficulties for a pure need reduction position. Hull recognized these problems and substituted the term *drive reduction* for *need reduction*. The abstraction *drive* could be related to need-producing operations and could also be assumed to be reduced prior to actual need reduction. As noted above, the drive reduction view was only slightly modified in subsequent versions of the theory, when Hull placed more emphasis on drive stimulus reduction rather than need reduction.

12. *Reinforcement properties can be acquired.*

The concept of secondary or learned reinforcement, like that of secondary drive, illustrates the important role Hull assigned to Pavlovian conditioning. Operationally, a secondary reinforcer develops when a neutral stimulus is paired with a primary reinforcer:

> . . . a receptor impulse will acquire the power of acting as a reinforcing agent if it occurs consistently and repeatedly within 20 seconds or so of a functionally potent reinforcing state of affairs, regardless of whether the latter is primary or secondary. (1943, p. 95)

Secondary reinforcers could influence behavior in a variety of situations, notably during extinction and in the maintenance of behavior chains. Secondary reinforcers thus became important elements in the goal gradient.

The mechanism Hull chose as the basis for secondary reinforcement would prove to be a very important one for S–R theories in general. Hull maintained that a secondary reinforcer

> . . . acquires its power of reinforcement by virtue of having conditioned to it some fractional component of the need reduction process of the goal situation whose occurrence, whenever it takes place, has a specific power of reinforcement in a degree proportionate to the intensity of that occurrence. (1943, p. 100)

As we have seen, this fractional goal component is signified by r_G, and the degree to which a stimulus elicits this r_G determines the secondary reinforcing properties of that stimulus. Furthermore, the r_G concept can help in deducing how stimuli early in a behavior chain acquire secondary reinforcing properties. Consider a straight alley divided into a startbox ($S1$), alleyway ($S2$), and goalbox ($S3$). When the organism enters the goalbox and finds food, eating (R_G) occurs. On subsequent trials, there is a Pavlovian situation where the alleyway cues ($S2$) precede the goalbox cues ($S3$) which lead to R_G. Through classical conditioning, $S2$ now comes to elicit a conditioned response, a fractional component of R_G, namely r_G:

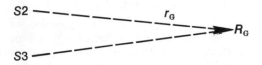

The same process occurs in the startbox, whose cues ($S1$) precede those of the alleyway ($S2$):

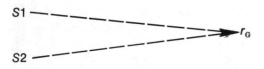

After a number of trials the initial stimulus elements of the situation elicit a component of the goal response and thus serve as secondary reinforcers which begin and which help mediate the behavior chain of traversing the alley. Also, the stimulus consequences of r_G (i.e., s_G), can acquire habit potential for the instrumental response of traversing the alley. The r_G concept, therefore, was clearly an associative mechanism for Hull.

The r_G concept was to become more important as a motivator, however, since it could easily provide the mechanism behind incentive. That is, animals receiving large rewards might have a stronger r_G conditioned to the situational cues than animals receiving a small reward. This stronger r_G can be postulated to represent a stronger expectancy of reward, and thus to motivate behavior (Spence, 1951).

13. *Response effort produces a negative drive state which can be learned.*

Any learning theory must deal with the fact that performance decreases under certain conditions. Not surprisingly, Hull's thinking concerning inhibitory processes counteracting reaction potential revolved around the concept of drive. According to Postulate 8:

> Whenever a reaction is evoked in an organism there is created as a result a primary negative drive (D); (a) this has an innate capacity (I_R) to inhibit the reaction potentiality to that response; (b) the amount of net inhibition generated by a sequence of reaction evocations is a simple linear increasing function of the number of evocations; and (c) it is a positively accelerated increasing function of the work involved in the execution of the response; (d) reactive inhibition (I_R) dissipates as a simple negative growth function of time. (1943, p. 300)

The concept of I_R is clearly tied to response occurrence, response effort, and time. It is also distinctly motivational in nature, but the activation is in the direction of response cessation. It is also important to note that the motivational properties of I_R made it possible to predict a decrease in reaction potential without any corresponding decrease in habit. The performance decrease is the result of the negative drive of I_R. Remove this negative drive (e.g., by allowing a rest period), and performance should once again reflect the amount of habit potential present.

Hull noted that any cessation of activity in the presence of I_R would reduce the drive state and thus provide a reinforcing state of affairs for not responding. Obviously, the conditions for the growth of habit have been met, and Hull saw the need to add a learned component to his inhibition concept. Thus, according to Postulate 9:

> Stimuli closely associated with the cessation of a response (a) become conditioned to the inhibition (I_R) associated with the evocation of that response, thereby generating conditioned inhibition; (b) conditioned inhibitions $(_sI_R)$ summate physiologically with reactive inhibition against the reaction potentiality to a given response as positive habit tendencies summate with each other. (1943, p. 300)

Conditioned inhibition $(_sI_R)$, therefore, is a habit, and as such, it may be expected to show more permanent effects than I_R. For one thing, $_sI_R$ should not dissipate with time, a fact which enabled Hull to account for certain findings associated with extinction. He could use $_sI_R$ to explain cases of permanent extinction. He could explain the incomplete recovery of responding noted in spontaneous recovery. He could explain generalization of extinction $(_sI_R,$ a habit, could generalize), and disinhibition (introduction of a novel stimulus produced generalization decrement of $_sI_R$). The $_sI_R$ concept, therefore, approached the theoretical parsimony Hull sought: incorporating the widest range of phenomena within the smallest possible number of constructs.

RESEARCH

Hull's contributions to learning theory began in 1929 with an article in the *Psychological Review*. The article represents an integration of Pavlov's conditioned response with the Darwinian survival model. Hull was always concerned with the functional utilities and survival value of behavior, and he applied this analysis to a variety of areas: trial-and-error learning (1930b), purposive behavior (1930a), problem solving (1935b), and rote learning (1935a). His work culminated in a system of definitions, postulates, and corollaries designed to bridge the gap between simple and complex forms of learning. The beginnings of the system were outlined in his presidential address before the American Psychological Association at Dartmouth College in 1936 (Hull, 1937), and it was formally presented in *Principles of Behavior* (1943), *Essentials of Behavior* (1951), and *A Behavior System* (1952).

Research played a crucial role in Hull's system. The theory was directly tied to antecedent and consequent events and thus lent itself quite well to empirical testing. There can be no doubt that Hull's theory stimulated an immense quantity of research. Spence (1952) noted that during the 1940s a count of articles appearing in the *Journal of Experimental Psychology* and the *Journal of Comparative and Physiological Psychology* showed that 40% of all experimental studies and 70% of studies concerned with learning and motivation referred to Hull's system.

Methodologies

Hull's theory was based on two methodologies: classical conditioning, as developed by Pavlov (1927), and instrumental conditioning, as developed by Thorndike (1932). The basic paradigm in Pavlov's work is fairly straightforward. A dog is restrained in a harness, and food powder is applied directly into the dog's mouth through tubes. Salivation is measured as it is secreted through the salivary ducts which have been surgically brought to the surface of the cheek. During the actual conditioning procedure, a neutral stimulus such as a light or tone is presented. Shortly after the

Figure 4.5

Acquisition Phases of Classical Conditioning

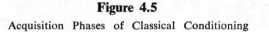

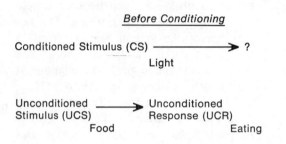

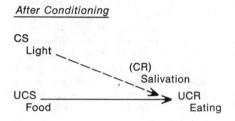

onset of this stimulus, food is delivered into the dog's mouth. This procedure continues over a series of trials (one trial being one contiguous presentation of the two stimuli).

Eventually, a change takes place in that salivation begins to occur *after* the light or tone is turned on, but *prior* to the presentation of the food. This salivation is the *conditioned response* (CR). The response has been conditioned, or learned, because it is now occurring to the light, whereas previously it did not. Classical conditioning may be depicted as shown in Figure 4.5.

In instrumental conditioning, the situation is arranged so that one particular response from the organism produces a reinforcement. In other words, the organism must operate upon the environment in order to receive a reward. In the straight runway, the response is running down the alley. In the Skinner box, the

response is barpressing. In either case, the behavior of the organism is instrumental in producing the reward. Such was clearly not the case in classical conditioning. Pavlov's dogs were basically passive recipients of the stimulus contingencies the experimenter chose to impose upon them. In instrumental conditioning, on the other hand, the organism is a much more active participant.

Let us consider the straight-alley situation and outline in detail the processes assumed to be involved in instrumental conditioning. The response of running down the alley leads to the reinforcement. This response, then, is practiced more than other responses, and an association is thus formed between the cues of the alley and the running response.

This situation is depicted in Figure 4.6. The general environmental cues of the situation function as the CS. These cues come to elicit the running response

Figure 4.6

Processes in Instrumental Conditioning

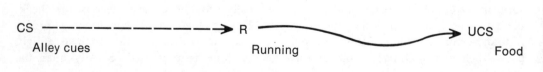

as training progresses, and running thus becomes a conditioned response (CR). Running "leads to" (indicated by the wavy line) food, the reinforcement or (UCS), an event which helps to ensure that running will be likely to occur on subsequent trials.

Animal Studies

The Habit Function. Hull's approach to deriving experimentation from theory is illustrated in a series of studies designed to test the predicted relationship between habit strength and certain antecedent conditions (e.g., number of reinforcements) in an instrumental conditioning situation (Felsinger, Gladstone, Yamaguchi, & Hull, 1947; Gladstone, Yamaguchi, Hull, & Felsinger, 1947; Hull, Felsinger, Gladstone, & Yamaguchi, 1947; Yamaguchi, Hull, Felsinger, & Gladstone, 1948).

The Goal Gradient. Hull noted studies showing that learning decreases as the delay of reward is increased. This fact emerged when rewards were delayed spatially (e.g., increasing the length of an alley) or temporally (e.g., increasing the delay following completion of the response). Hull (1934b) himself found that animals tend to run faster as they near a goal.

Hull clearly saw delay of reinforcement affecting the development of *H,* and he also viewed the situation as comprising a chain of S–R associations. A rat traversing an alley or pressing a bar is actually engaging in a complex series of movements which, when put together, comprise the complete act of approaching or obtaining the reward.

This conception of a chain of responses was very important because it enabled Hull to derive a number of predictions concerning maze learning. Why

does the animal learn the shortest path in a maze? What determines the difficulty of a maze? Why are responses to some blind alleys extinguished before others? The answers to these questions required that the instrumental response be broken down into a chain of smaller S–R units. In its simplest form (Hull, 1930b), the stimulus situation would be broken down into individual parts, such as $S1$, $S2$, $S3$, $S4$, Goal. Each segment would acquire habit strength for a particular reaction, $R1$, $R2$, $R3$, $R4$, R_{Goal}, respectively. The individual associations would be strongest at the goal where delay of reinforcement is brief and would become progressively weaker as the stimuli further and further antedate the goal.

As Figure 4.7 indicates, the chain of responding was also maintained by proprioceptive stimuli from each response which would acquire habit potential for eliciting the next response. The chain involves a response occurring contiguously with both external (S) and internal (s) stimuli, and learning involves a strengthening of both types of S–R bonds. The goal-gradient hypothesis states that those bonds nearer the goal are stronger than those further removed, and that there is an orderly increase in the strength of the S–R bonds as the goal is approached.

One derivation from the goal-gradient hypothesis is that "with training, organisms tend to choose that one of a pair of alternative acts which yields reinforcement with the lesser delay" (Hull, 1943, p. 151). Yoshioka (1929) supported this corollary. Yoshioka trained rats in a maze providing two alternative routes to food. One was 5.63 meters in length, and the other was 11.26 meters from start to goal. The paths could also be adjusted such that varying ratios of long

Figure 4.7
Response Chain

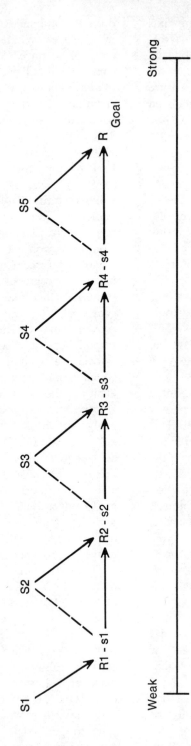

The response chain shows how individual response units are elicited by environmental stimuli (*S*) and internal, proprioceptive stimuli (*s*) from the preceding response.

to short paths could be studied. Yoshi-oka found that rats generally learn to take the shorter path and that the rats took longer to learn the shorter path when the long-to-short ratio was small.

Hull (1932) explained these findings using the goal-gradient hypothesis. The short path, of course, involves a shorter chain of stimuli than the long path. When the rat is placed at the start of the maze, the choice will be made on the basis of the tendency of the initial stimuli of the short and long paths to evoke the first reaction in the response chain. Since the S–R bond beginning the short path will be stronger than the S–R bond beginning the long path, the animal will choose the former.

The goal-gradient hypothesis may also be used to explain the finding that blind alleys near the goal will be eliminated before blind alleys further removed from the goal. Hull assumed that habit strength decreases according to an exponential decay function as delay of reinforcement increases. This function is depicted in Figure 4.8. Clearly, the greatest loss of *H* occurs with the initial increases in delay. The analysis of the backward elimination of blind alleys is described by Gregory Kimble (1961, p. 145):

> Suppose that entering a blind alley adds 5 seconds to the time required to run the maze, and therefore, 5 seconds of delay of reinforcement. . . . Now let us consider the situation as it theoretically exists at choice points three different distances from the goal. . . . Assume that the correct response at the choice point near to the goal is rewarded after only 2 seconds; an error will be reinforced, therefore, after 7 seconds. Assume further that the intermediate and far choice points lead to reinforcement after 80 and 120 seconds for a correct response. This means that errors are reinforced after 85 and 125 seconds, respectively. The delays of reinforcement associated with

Figure 4.8

Habit Strength as a Function of Delay of Reinforcement

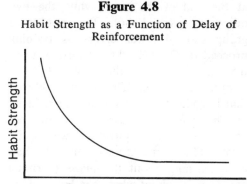

correct and incorrect choices at these three points in the maze are thus 2 and 7 seconds, 80 and 85 seconds, and 120 and 125 seconds.

It is clear from Figure 4.8 that the greatest habit differential exists between the shortest delays, and it becomes progressively smaller as the delays increase. Hull (1949) later used additional concepts to explain the order of elimination of blinds. These concepts included the fractional anticipatory goal response (r_G), stimulus generalization, and stimulus intensity dynamism.

Hull also used the goal gradient to explain the speed-of-locomotion gradient he obtained in an early study (Hull, 1934b). He measured the time rats spent in traversing various segments of a 12.19-meter straight alley and found that running speed increased as measures were taken closer and closer to the goal.

Habit (S–R) vs. Expectancy (S–S). Proponents of Hull's S–R approach to behavior engaged in considerable controversy and argument with proponents of Tolman's S–S approach to behavior. Perhaps the best known attack on the S–R model is seen in studies on *latent learning.* Tolman & Honzik (1930), for example, compared three groups in a maze. For ten days, one group received reward at the end of the maze while the two other groups did not. The reinforced group showed fewer errors as training proceeded. On Day 11, reward was introduced for one of the previously nonreinforced groups. The results showed that introduction of the reward produced an *immediate* decrease in the number of errors. The implication was quite clear. The nonreinforced animals had been learning about the maze (forming expectancies about what area led to what other areas) all along, but this learning was not evident in *performance* because no reinforcement was given. In other words, learning could occur without the presence of a reinforcement.

The S–R reactions to the latent-learning phenomenon took a variety of forms. The end result, however, was that S–R theories moved closer to the S–S position. For instance, Hull (1952) eventually introduced the incentive construct (K) with the assumption that certain aspects of the rewarding event affect performance and not learning. The emphasis was switched from H to E. The r_G concept also became a crucial part of S–R explanations regarding many of the latent-learning findings.

The use of r_G is illustrated in the case where animals are initially trained in a maze with reinforcement present, but under conditions of satiation. When the animal is subsequently placed under the appropriate drive state, performance shows an immediate and abrupt improvement, strongly suggesting that learning occurs without any consumption of the reinforcement. Hull (1952), who had earlier used the r_G mechanism to handle various aspects of generalization and mediation of behavior (Hull, 1930b, 1931), used it in this situation as well. He assumed that even though satiated, the sight of food would be mildly arous-

ing and serve to evoke r_G and its stimulus consequences, s_G. The cues of the maze, then, would acquire some habit potential for eliciting r_G, and s_G would acquire habit potential for eliciting the instrumental response. When drive is subsequently increased, these already developed habits are energized.

The phenomenon of *sensory preconditioning* (Brogden, 1939) also illustrates how the S–R theorist can use the r_G mechanism. Sensory preconditioning involves a three-step procedure: (1) two neutral stimuli, S1 and S2, are presented a number of times together; (2) a response is classically conditioned to S1; (3) S2 is presented alone to see if the response conditioned to S1 occurs. When it does, an S–S analysis is clearly implied.

The S–R analysis of sensory preconditioning (e.g., Coppock, 1958) proceeds as follows: (1) Phase 1 involves classical conditioning to S1 of a covert response (r_G) evoked by S2; (2) proprioceptive stimuli (s_G) acquire habit strength for eliciting the classically conditioned response formed in Phase 2; (3) s_G provides the mediational link for the transfer of the response learned in Phase 2 from one stimulus to the other. This explanation can be depicted as in Figure 4.9.

Note how the S–R theorist is forced toward a more cognitive orientation. The above explanation requires the assumption of covert, implicit responses and a reliance on their sensory consequences. This analysis is considerably different from the classical S–R concentration on environmental stimuli and overt responses, and it began a movement toward a more cognitive/expectation orientation in learning theory.

Another challenge to S–R theory came in studies (e.g., Tolman, Ritchie, & Kalish, 1946) of what became known as *place learning*. In a maze like that shown in Figure 4.10, some rats were required to make a right turn to receive a reward, regardless of whether placed at Start Point A or B. Rats in this condition were designated a *response-learning* group. A second group was required to go to either Goal 1 *or* 2, regardless of where they began (A or B). In this case, the direction of the turn was irrelevant, and the animals had to learn to go to a place. These rats were designated a *place-learning* group.

Tolman et al. found that the place group learned the maze faster than the response group, a finding interpreted in S–S terms. As S–R theorists noted, however, extra/maze cues (ceiling features, room lights, etc.) were present, and these simply acquired habit strength for a general approach response to food-related cues. Thus, maze learning involves both intramaze and extramaze cues.

S_D *Discrimination.* According to Hull, stimuli which arise from peripheral sources (e.g., stomach contractions or a dry mouth) correspond to specific drive states and can acquire ha-

Figure 4.10

Maze Arrangement Used to Demonstrate Place and Response Learning (Tolman, Ritchie, & Kalish, 1946)

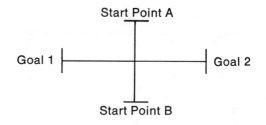

bit potential for evoking instrumental responses. A clear derivation from Hull's theorizing concerning these drive stimuli is that animals should be able to discriminate different drive states. Hull (1933a) trained rats in a simple maze under alternating conditions of hunger and thirst. On hunger days the rats had to make a particular turn in order to obtain reinforcement, whereas on thirst days the opposite turn was required. The task proved very difficult, and even after 1,200 trials most rats were still making a considerable number of errors. Leeper (1935) altered the learning situation such that different turns in the maze led to different goalboxes (an arrangement different from Hull's). After 240 days of training, Leeper found over 80% correct responding, thus supporting the prediction that discrimination learning could occur on the basis of different drive stimuli. Hull's analysis of the situation can be depicted as in Figure 4.11.

Further studies confirmed that the discrimination required different goal areas. This fact immediately suggests the r_a mechanism as the basis for the discrimination (Kendler, Karasik, & Schrier, 1954). During discrimination training, eating becomes conditioned to cues of the goalbox containing the food, and drinking becomes conditioned to cues of

Figure 4.9

Sensory Preconditioning

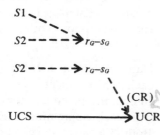

In sensory preconditioning, an assumed response (r_a) common to both $S1$ and $S2$ serves as a mediational link in Phase 3.

Figure 4.11

Hull's Analysis of Drive Discrimination

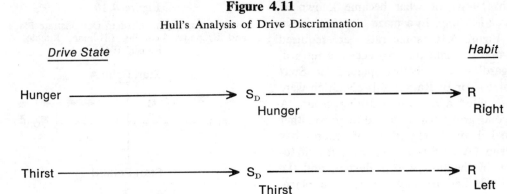

Distinctive internal drive stimuli (S_D) associated with different drives (e.g., hunger and thirst) can acquire habit strength for different responses (e.g., turning right or left).

the goalbox containing the water. During testing, the animal approaches that specific area associated with the current motivational state. If the same area is associated with both hunger and thirst (e.g., Hull, 1933a), the discrimination will be difficult. If separate areas are associated with the motivational states (e.g., Leeper, 1935), the discrimination will be easier.

The Kendler et al. (1954) analysis supported the trend mentioned earlier— away from a drive emphasis and toward an expectancy emphasis, with the r_G mechanism playing a large role. In this respect, it is interesting to compare the comments of two authors, writing at different times, regarding the S_D concept.

It has been demonstrated . . . that different drives can provide distinctive stimuli to which the organism can learn to respond, and that such learning can occur quite quickly under optimal conditions. (Kimble, 1961, pp. 434–435)

It . . . appears that the attempts to demonstrate S_D experimentally have succeeded instead in demonstrating the importance of r_G. . . . The stimulus concomitants of drive have no real existence. (Bolles, 1975, pp. 278–279)

Discrimination Learning. Hull spent a considerable amount of time studying the process of discrimination (Hull, 1939, 1940, 1945, 1950, 1952). His analysis of discrimination learning combines the processes of acquisition and extinction. The reinforced trials to S+ (those stimuli always followed by reinforcement) are conditioning trials, and nonreinforced trials to S− (those stimuli always followed by nonreinforcement) are extinction trials. Hull's thinking along these lines was clearly influenced by Spence's (1936, 1937a, 1937b) pioneering work in the area, and the theory is often referred to as the Hull-Spence conditioning-extinction theory of discrimination (Kimble, 1961).

The assumptions of the theory are quite straightforward:

1. Habit potential for S+ grows with each reinforcement.
2. Inhibition potential for S− grows with each nonreinforcement.
3. Both the excitatory and inhibitory processes generalize to other stimuli.
4. The magnitude of generalized habit is greater than the magnitude of generalized inhibition.

5. The excitatory and inhibitory processes interact algebraically.
6. Responding occurs to stimuli having the highest relative habit potential.

It is interesting to note that the above assumptions are easily derived from the original constructs of the 1943 theory. Hull thus succeeded in integrating discrimination learning into his theory without postulating any additional constructs. Although the discrimination account has weaknesses (Mackintosh, 1974), Hull's approach to the problem is a model of theoretical parsimony. The many predictions from the theory also received much empirical support (Gynther, 1957).

H, D, *and* K *Relationships.* Hull's proposal of a multiplicative relationship between *D* and *H* was influenced by results obtained by Perin (1942) and Williams (1938) which showed the number of responses evoked during extinction following different numbers of reinforcements during acquisition. In similar fashion, he used other studies to relate stimulus intensity (*V*) (Hull, 1951, p. 41), incentive (*K*) (Crespi, 1942), and delay of reinforcement (*J*) (Perin, 1942) to *H* in a multiplicative way. It remained to specify the relationship between *D, V, K,* and *J,* and Hull (1951) decided that "all five of the components probably combine to produce reaction potential by the simple process of multiplication, i.e., that $_sE_R = D \times V \times K \times J \times {_sH_R}$" (pp. 53–54).

The $D \times K$ specification became a theoretical issue when Spence (1956) proposed that the proper combination law is additive: $D + K$. The two laws led to opposing empirical predictions and thus stimulated a good deal of research. Consider Figure 4.12, where *D* and *K* are factorially combined. As before, we have arbitrarily assigned a value of 1 to the low values of *D* and *K* and

Figure 4.12

Representation of Predictions Generated by Multiplicative and Additive Assumptions Concerning *D* and *K*

	Amount of Reinforcement (K)	
	Low	High
Low	$1 + 1 = 2$	$1 + 3 = 4$
	$1 \times 1 = 1$	$1 \times 3 = 3$
High	$3 + 1 = 4$	$3 + 3 = 6$
	$3 \times 1 = 3$	$3 \times 3 = 9$

Deprivation Level (D)

The multiplicative assumption predicts that increasing *D* will have a greater effect on performance when *K* is high. (Performance increases from 1 to 3 under low *K*, but from 3 to 9 under high *K*.) The additive assumption, however, predicts an equal effect of *D* at both levels of *K* (i.e., from 2 to 4 under low *K*, and from 4 to 6 under high *K*).

3 to the high values. Furthermore, in each quadrant of the factorial, we have specified the excitatory potential total specified by the additive law (top line in each quadrant) and the multiplicative law (bottom line in each quadrant). Clearly, the additive function predicts the absence of an interaction between *D* and *K* (where the effect of increasing *D,* for instance, is the same for different levels of *K*), while the multiplicative law predicts an interaction (where the effect of increasing *D* is not constant for all values of *K*). Investigation of the problem provided support for both positions, and Black (1965) proposed a solution where *K* is assumed to be determined by deprivation operations.

Drive Reduction. Hull's drive reduction hypothesis stimulated considerable research. Hull himself (Hull, Livingstone, Rouse, & Barker, 1951) compared real and sham eating in dogs and found both mouth (stimulating) and stomach (reducing) factors important in the reinforcing process. Other studies (e.g., Berkun, Kessen, & Miller, 1952) suggested that drive reduction could occur in the absence of need reduction. On the basis of these considerations, Hull (1952) began to speak of S_D reduction. It is interesting that he even felt S_D reduction could occur when a sweet, nonnutritive substance like saccharine was ingested. Studies have shown (e.g., Sheffield, Roby, & Campbell, 1954) that saccharine has reinforcing properties, and such results were usually viewed as contradictory to Hull's theory.

Other early studies bearing on the drive reduction hypothesis showed the reinforcing effects of exploration and manipulation (e.g., Montgomery, 1954) and brain stimulation (e.g., Olds & Milner, 1954). These studies and others have produced a general abandonment of drive reduction as the only mechanism of reinforcement.

Energizing Effects of Drive. A study by Brown, Kalish, & Farber (1951) is often cited as providing a good example of the energizing effects of *D*. Brown et al. showed that the presence of a fear stimulus increases the intensity of a rat's startle response to a loud noise. Meryman (1952) showed that the startle response was also larger when rats were hungry than when they were satiated. As we noted elsewhere, there is little doubt that certain drive operations can energize ongoing behavior. It would appear, however, that certain classes of behavior are more prone to the energizing effect than others (see Bolles, 1975).

Human Studies

The bulk of the research connected with Hull's theory was done with animals. Hull thought that initial attempts at theorizing should be based on very simple learning situations. Only after extensive work at the animal level would it be time to move to the more complex human level.

Hull's use of human studies was sparing, primarily to illustrate certain basic points. In a GSR conditioning study on college students, Bass and Hull (1934) conditioned the GSR to a vibrotactile stimulus applied to a specific area of the body (using shock as a UCS) and then compared GSR magnitudes elicited by such stimulation at other areas of the body. Their results provided an orderly generalization gradient as test stimuli deviated more and more from the original point of application. Hull also noted human conditioning studies by Hovland (1937) and Shipley (1935) regarding stimulus generalization.

The law of less work, which was derived from the concept of reactive inhibition, led Hull to predict that "distributed-trials learning is more efficient than mass-trials learning" (1952, p. 37). In support of this prediction, Hull noted a study by Kimble (1949) which showed motor performance superior under spaced compared to massed practice.

Hull (1952) applied some of his thinking about complex maze learning and the elimination of blind alleys to serial verbal learning. Specifically, he maintained that "rote learning is a form of heterogeneous serial chaining," and he was able to derive the serial position curve found in verbal learning studies (e.g., Hovland, 1940). Hull's own work in the area of rote learning is represented in the book on the mathematico-deductive theory (Hull et al., 1940).

Hull (1938) used the goal-gradient principle to analyze field-force situations in the behavior of children. This work showed how derivations from the goal-gradient hypothesis, the habit hierarchy, amount of reward, and various field conditions concerning the spatial relationships of the organism to the goal could be used to generate a variety of predictions.

The work of Spence provides two excellent examples of human conditioning approached in the Hullian context. The first of these is eyelid conditioning. In this situation, the CS is usually a light, and the UCS, which follows the CS by about 0.5 seconds, is a puff of air to the cornea. Spence's work eventually led him to a distinction between the influence of cognitive and motivational factors, and in an important article (Spence, 1966), he showed how data from both animal and human eyelid conditioning studies could be approached from a single theoretical system.

The second use of Hullian theory in human conditioning is illustrated in Spence, Farber, and McFann (1956). This study manipulated D on the basis of persons' scores on a test of anxiety. Those scoring high were, by definition, high–D individuals, and those scoring low were low–D individuals. Half of each group was then assigned to a paired-associate verbal learning task of either high or low difficulty. A high difficulty task might be characterized by high intralist stimulus similarity (e.g., using synonyms), whereas a low difficulty list would involve distinctly different stimulus items. These lists are represented as in Figure 4.13.

In the high-difficulty list, because of generalization, there is a strong tendency for any one of the stimulus items to elicit any one of the response items. Put another way, there are many competing habit tendencies. In the low-difficulty list, however, there is no such competition between the individual S–R associations.

Figure 4.13

Representation of Paired-Associates Lists of High and Low Difficulty

High Difficulty		Low Difficulty	
Stimulus Item	*Response Item*	*Stimulus Item*	*Response Item*
A	W	A	W
A'	X	B	X
A"	Y	C	Y
A'''	Z	D	Z

The similarity of stimulus items in the high-difficulty list should produce much response competition. Less competition should occur in the low-difficulty list, where stimulus items are dissimilar.

When the D manipulation is included, on the basis of the $H \times D$ combination law we would predict that high–D persons will be inferior to low–D persons on the high-difficulty task but superior on the low-difficulty task. In the former case, the higher drive serves to energize competing habit tendencies, thus increasing the probability of errors. In the latter case, however, the higher drive energizes S–R associations which are not in competition, thereby energizing the tendency to make a correct response. The Spence et al. (1956) study supported these predictions.

When discussing human behavior from the Hullian context, it is important to remember that Hull's theory is based on nonintentional, goal-oriented behavior of nonarticulate organisms, or with humans operating at a sublanguage level. It is true that Hull hoped to incorporate more complex phenomena into his theory, but the fact remains that the theory as it stands is not designed to deal with information processing and general cognitive skills. Even Hull's ventures into verbal learning were cast in an associationistic framework. Spence's work on verbal learning cited above would appear to be an exception to these comments, but it is not. In the experiments on D and verbal learning, there is really no direct movement toward uncovering the laws of verbal learning. Rather, the attempt is to place a complex learning situation in the framework of Hull-Spence theorizing.

IMPLICATIONS

Theoretical

The fundamental theoretical question for the learning theorist, of course, is, "What is learned?" Hull advocated an S–R position. As we have seen, however, this position required considerable modification in a cognitive direction in order to handle certain experimental findings. The r_G–s_G concept was important in this respect. The mechanism proved valuable in handling expectancies and examples of insightful problem solving. The stimulus consequences of r_G (i.e., s_G) were also important in that they served to guide the behavior of the organism. In this respect, s_G is similar to Guthrie's movement-produced stimuli. Hull's s_G, however, was tied to reinforcement, since s_G accompanies drive reduction as the animal performs the goal response.

The use of the r_G concept within the Hullian context represents a definite convergence of the Watson-Guthrie tradition and the Tolman tradition. That is, ideas and expectations were represented by a response model. Furthermore, r_G allowed a flexibility not easily permitted in Watson's system. Using r_G, Hull could explain learning without responding, learning while satiated, and the fact that animals might take a novel route to obtain a goal object. After the inclusion of r_G, Hull's system was much closer to

Tolman's goal-seeking emphasis than it was to Watson's running-off of habits.

Spence further developed the r_G concept and tied it directly to incentive (K). Spence also viewed both number and amount of reward as independent variables for K. Hull had retained number of rewards as the operation producing habit strength. This reinforcement position, of course, often hindered Hull's ability to handle various latent-learning phenomena. For Spence, however, H depended only on practice, and K depended on reinforcement operations (which elicit r_G). The shift in emphasis brought the Hullian framework closer to Guthrie's contiguity position and to Tolman's expectancy position.

Hull maintained throughout his theorizing that reinforcement requires a reduction in drive. This emphasis was clearly in line with the influence of the Darwinian model in Hull's time. Behaviorism sought to remove concerns with mind and consciousness from American psychology, but the functional emphasis on adaptibility, adjustment, coping, and survival remained. The drive reduction hypothesis was certainly consistent with those emphases.

The overriding assumption of Hull's theory was that any successful account of the learning process required a drive concept. Without basic energy arising out of physiological needs, Hull simply could not see any organismic activity taking place. While Guthrie could conceive of drives in a purely associative context, Hull used drives in a more dynamic, energizing sense. This view led to a deemphasis of innate response patterns and emphasized behavior from the context of a selective strengthening of those responses which successfully reduced the drive state. More recent theories have chosen to deemphasize such drive considerations and concentrate more on the innate response classes of the organism.

Hull clearly saw habit as representing a permanent behavioral change in the organism. This conception produces a problem when behavior during extinction is considered. If habits are permanent, why does performance decline? Hull, of course, postulated a process of inhibition which worked against tendencies to make the learned response. Fundamental to his inhibition concept, however, was the hypothesis that it resulted from making the learned response itself. Whereas this conception enabled Hull to handle a variety of extinction phenomena, its weaknesses were soon apparent. The difficulty was that an overt response had to take place for extinction to occur. Experiments on latent extinction (e.g., Seward & Levy, 1949), however, showed that such responding is not necessary. Just as studies of latent learning showed that habit should not be tied to reinforcement, the latent extinction studies showed that inhibition should not be tied to response occurrence.

Perhaps the most interesting implication of Hull's theory (and Guthrie's and Tolman's as well) is what it says about the benefits of such theorizing. In trying to develop a comprehensive theory to account for all learned behavior, Hull clearly failed. Whereas he stimulated much research and contributed to the building of a system of empirical facts, his theory still showed the futility of trying to encompass all behavior within a single system. Subsequent attempts at theory building, therefore, have proceeded on a much smaller scale, and they are generally restricted to explaining certain kinds of learning in certain situations.

The successes of Hull's theorizing, however, clearly outweigh the shortcomings. Hull inspired more experimental work than any other theorist of his time (and is probably even now exceeded only by Skinner). His positions on acquisition, extinction, delay of reinforcement, drive, reinforcement, generalization, and discrimination are the starting points for any consideration of these topics. Regardless of whether his concepts and derivations withstand the rigors of experimental analysis, whatever level of sophistication and knowledge exists today in the psychology of learning is in large measure a result of Hull's theorizing.

Practical

One of the best known applications of Hull's learning theory is found in the work of John Dollard and Neal Miller, who analyzed psychotherapy as an instrumental reward learning situation and anticipated many aspects of modern behavior therapy. Dollard and Miller (1950) divided the therapeutic situation into four fundamental areas:

1. *Cue.* All behavior in S–R models is tied to some stimulus situation, either internal or external. In maladaptive behavior, such as a neurosis, many of the cues are internal. The symptom itself may be superficially triggered by an external stimulus (e.g., in a phobia), but the essential dynamics of the neurotic conflict are internal, response-produced cues. Therapy must help the patient recognize and label these cues. The patient must be helped to discriminate between the stimuli (perhaps thought-produced) that precede actual behavior, and the responses or deeds elicited by those stimuli.

2. *Response.* The goal of therapy is

new behavior. Response patterns must be reshaped. The old neurotic patterns must be inhibited, and the individual must acquire more successful coping skills. The therapist must help the patient in this process through a shaping regimen. The new and initially tentative responses can be evoked in the relatively safe atmosphere of the therapist's office. Gradually, appropriate behavior can be strengthened through practice and reinforcement from the therapist. Through generalization, the new emerging behavior patterns will increase in frequency outside the therapeutic situation and gradually gain wider applications.

3. *Reward.* New behavior patterns will be strengthened only if they are reinforced. And, since the neurotic patterns have themselves received extensive reinforcement in the individual's past, reinforcements for any new responses must be more satisfying than those that occur for symptoms. This clearly brings secondary reinforcers into the picture, and the therapist must carefully assess any secondary gains derived from neurotic symptoms. Furthermore, reinforcement for adjustive responses should be immediate and must involve drive stimulus reduction.

4. *Drive.* The energy behind responding, be it adjustive or maladjustive, is drive. The patient possesses powerful drives, some representing the neurotic conflict, some arising as effects of the conflict, and even some which push the patient toward therapy. These drives must be reduced, but only contingent upon appropriate responding from the patient. To the extent that neurotic symptoms are "successful," thereby reducing drive to some extent, the task of the therapist is greatly complicated.

The essentials of Dollard and Miller's analysis are clearly compatible with Hull's theorizing. Successful therapy requires a drive-induced response to be reinforced in the presence of an appropriate stimulus. Since many of these stimuli can be internally produced, the therapist can help the patient in developing a chain of responses. Formerly disturbing stimuli, which set off a symptom-based chain of responses, can now evoke adjustive behaviors whose cue consequences produce more appropriate action.

Miller (1959) has also proposed an S–R model of the fundamental problem of a neurosis: conflict. The model makes use of learned drives, number of reinforcements, and the goal gradient. Consider a situation in which a hungry rat traverses an alley and receives both food and an electric shock in the goalbox. On subsequent trials, the animal is said to be in an approach-avoidance conflict. Miller makes the following assumptions regarding the dynamics of the conflict:

1. The tendencies to both approach and avoid the goal are stronger, the closer the subject is to the goal.
2. The avoidance tendency increases faster than the approach tendency as the goal is approached.
3. The strengths of both gradients are influenced by drive.
4. The stronger of the two response tendencies will occur.

These assumptions are illustrated in Figure 4.14. The point of interaction is the point of conflict. The model depicted generates a number of empirical predictions. Either increasing hunger or decreasing fear, for instance, should produce closer approaches to the goal. The opposite operations, on the other hand, should move the point of conflict further away from the goal. The model can also be applied to displacement behavior, rec-

Figure 4.14

Assumed Strengths of Approach and Avoidance
Gradients as a Function of Distance from Goal

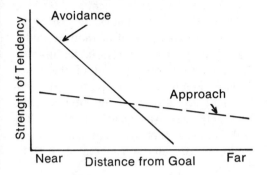

ognized by Freud as a fundamental factor in personality functioning (see Miller & Kraeling, 1952).

Hull's ultimate goal was to show the application of his system to complex behavior. Even though Hull was unable to complete his task, the fact remains that he presented a model to use in analyzing any behavior sequence. The same statement can be made about any theorist in this book. In a general way, each theory spells out a basic conceptual framework to be used in studying behavior. Whether the model is mechanistic, humanistic, cognitive, or mathematical, each one is equally valid as a conceptual approach. Some may have more relevance for certain manipulations and types of behavior than others, but at the conceptual level they are all equally valid.

Hull's model can be reduced to four dimensions or concepts: Habit (H), Drive (D), Incentive (K), and Inhibition (I). The task of the Hullian theorist is to apply these concepts as far as possible to all levels of behavior, to modify them if needed, and perhaps even to add new concepts. But the starting point involves habit, drive, incentive, and inhibition.

Imagine a runway divided into three sections, A, B, and C. Section A is the initial part of the alley, Section B is the middle, and Section C is the goalbox. At the beginning of training, the floors of A and B are electrified, while the floor of C is shock-free. A rat will quickly learn, when placed in A, that traversing the runway will provide escape from shock in C. Over trials, running becomes faster and faster as the habit develops in the situation. Pain and fear motivate the response, and shock termination reinforces the response.

Next, suppose we turn off the shock in Section A but leave it on in Section B. Then, as we did on previous trials, we place the rat in A. Now the smart thing for the rat to do is remain still; since there is no longer shock in A, it can effectively avoid shock by not running. Interestingly enough, however, the rat does not remain still. Rather, it runs from the nonshock section (A) into the shock section (B), and on to the safe area (C) (see, e.g., Brown, Martin, & Morrow, 1964). Why does the rat display this masochistic behavior? Why does it run, thus exposing itself to the pain of B? The question reminds us of those we ask about neurotics and alcoholics: "Why do you continue to behave that way? Can't you see what it's doing to you?" How might the S–R theorist approach these questions?

Considering our rat, we may note, first of all, that even after shock is removed from Section A, the rat should still be afraid when placed in that section. The reason is that fear will be elicited by the cues of Section A as a result of classical conditioning. Thus components (fear) of the original drive state (pain) produced by the shock are still present. Now here is the key question: What has the rat learned to do in this situation when afraid? The answer, of course, is: Run. Practice and habit are the keys here. Afraid, the rat really has no choice but to perform the response he has so thoroughly practiced. And, unfortunately for the rat, running has two consequences: (1) It leads to reinforcement in C, and thus it is likely to occur again; (2) it leads to adverse consequences (pain in B), which ensures that fear of the situation will be maintained, thus maintaining the source of drive behind the running response.

There is, of course, a clear analogy between this masochistic rat and the neurotic or the alcoholic. Anxiety and fear motivate well-practiced, maladaptive response patterns which produce temporary reinforcement but maintain anxiety over the long run. We have, therefore, a fundamental S–R conception of the problem. This is not to say we have *the* conception. The problem can also be approached through cognitive, existential, or humanistic avenues. The Hullian S–R model is only one model, therefore, but it is surely a model which can have great practical relevance. The interested reader should consult Logan (1976) for a number of examples which illustrate at a very fundamental level how some of the concepts developed by Hull can have practical significance.

SUMMARY

At no time did Hull really regard his theory as "final" at even the simplest level. The very nature of his system, formulated as postulates generating experimental predictions, was designed with revisions in mind. Hull stated his postulates and theorems definitively, knowing full well that such precise statements increased the probability of being in error. It is to Hull's credit that he chose

this approach. He developed a theory specific enough that experimental tests were obvious, and contrary evidence could easily be seen as such.

Hull's theory also helped to justify the use of the experimental method in studying learning. The interest in learning in this country developed out of the functionalist emphasis on adaptation and adjustment to a demanding environment. The emphasis was clearly applied. Yet Hull showed that this applied concern could be fruitfully considered in the laboratory.

> Hull did not hesitate to turn away from . . . concrete realities to the study of behavior under controlled and hence obviously artificial conditions. Hull fully realized that, just as the physicist found it necessary to introduce such unworldlike conditions as the vacuum and the biologist such unnatural situations as an isolated piece of tissue "growing" in a test tube, so likewise the psychologist must not hesitate to observe behavior, whether animal or human, under controlled conditions, artificial or otherwise. (Spence, 1952, p. 646)

Laboratory experimentation is often criticized as sacrificing relevance for control, but Hull never wavered in his belief that the behavioral laws uncovered in simple laboratory situations would apply to more complex, real-life situations.

ANNOTATED BIBLIOGRAPHY

Bolles, R. C. *Theory of motivation* (2nd ed.). New York: Harper & Row, 1975.

This is an in-depth survey of empirical studies and theories of the psychology of motivation. Much of the work is presented within the framework of Hullian theory, with the general theme of illustrating the inadequacies of Hull's system.

Hull, C. L. *Principles of behavior*. New York: Appleton-Century-Crofts, 1943.

The first formal presentation of the general system of postulates, theorems, and corollaries, this book serves to introduce and to explain the most basic aspects of the system. In spite of later revisions, it remains the cornerstone of Hull's theoretical efforts.

Hull, C. L. *Essentials of behavior.* New Haven: Yale University Press, 1951.

This brief, formal presentation of revisions in the 1943 system provides only the outlines of the new theory and reasons for the changes. More elaborate treatment is given in the 1952 work described below.

Hull, C. L. *A behavior system.* New Haven: Yale University Press, 1952.

In this formal, detailed presentation of the revised system, much space is given to derivation of theorems and consideration of experimental evidence bearing on the validity of the theorems. The book is much wider in scope than the 1943 work and deals with a broader range of topics.

Kimble, G. A. *Hilgard and Marquis' Conditioning and learning.* New York: Appleton-Century-Crofts, 1961.

Although dated, this book illustrates the state of the art at the beginning of the sixties and the Hullian approach to and analysis of a variety of empirical topics. It captures much of the predictive and explanatory power of Hull's theory.

REFERENCES

Amsel, A. Frustrative nonreward in partial reinforcement and discrimination learning: Some recent history and a theoretical extension. *Psychological Review,* 1962, *69,* 306–328.

Bass, M. J., & Hull, C. L. The irradiation of a tactile conditioned reflex in man. *Journal of Comparative Psychology,* 1934, *17,* 47–65.

Berkun, M., Kessen, M. L., & Miller, N. E. Hunger-reducing effects of food by stomach fistula versus food by mouth measured by a consummatory response. *Journal of Comparative and Physiological Psychology,* 1952, *45,* 550–554.

Bindra, D. A unified account of classical conditioning and operant training. In W. F. Prokasy & A. H. Black (Eds.), *Classical conditioning.* New York: Appleton-Century-Crofts, 1972.

Black, R. W. On the combination of drive and incentive motivation. *Psychological Review,* 1965, *72,* 310–317.

Bolles, R. C. *Theory of motivation* (2nd ed.). New York: Harper & Row, 1975.

Brogden, W. J. Sensory preconditioning. *Journal of Experimental Psychology,* 1939, *25,* 323–332.

Brown, J. S., Kalish, H. I., & Farber, I. E. Conditioned fear as revealed by magnitude of startle response to an auditory stimulus. *Journal of Experimental Psychology,* 1951, *41,* 317–328.

Brown, J. S., Martin, R. C., & Morrow, M. W. Self-punitive behavior in the rat: Facilitative effects of punishment on resistance to extinction. *Journal of Comparative and Physiological Psychology,* 1964, *57,* 127–133.

Capaldi, E. J. A sequential hypothesis of instrumental learning. In K. W. Spence & J. T. Spence (Eds.), *The psychology of learning and motivation* (Vol. 1). New York: Academic Press, 1967.

Cofer, C. N., & Appley, M. H. *Motivation: Theory and research.* New York: Wiley, 1964.

Coppock, W. J. Pre-extinction in sensory preconditioning. *Journal of Experimental Psychology,* 1958, *55,* 213–219.

Crespi, L. P. Quantitative variation of incentive and performance in the white rat. *American Journal of Psychology,* 1942, *55,* 467–517.

Daly, H. B. Reinforcing properties of escape from frustration aroused in various learning situations. In G. H. Bower (Ed.), *The psychology of learning and motivation* (Vol. 8). New York: Academic Press, 1974.

Dollard, J., & Miller, N. E. *Personality and psychotherapy.* New York: McGraw-Hill, 1950.

Estes, W. K. All-or-none processes in learning and retention. *American Psychologist,* 1964, *19,* 16–25.

Felsinger, J. M., Gladstone, A. I., Yamaguchi, H. G., & Hull, C. L. Reaction latency ($_{s}t_{r}$) as a function of the number of reinforcements (*N*). *Journal of Experimental Psychology,* 1947, *37,* 214–228.

Fowler, H. Satiation and curiosity. In K.

W. Spence & J. T. Spence (Eds.), *The psychology of learning and motivation* (Vol. 1). New York: Academic Press, 1967.

Gladstone, A. I., Yamaguchi, H. G., Hull, C. L., & Felsinger, J. M. Some functional relationships of reaction potential ($_sE_R$) and related phenomena. *Journal of Experimental Psychology*, 1947, *37*, 510–526.

Guthrie, E. R. Conditioning: A theory of learning in terms of stimulus, response, and association. In *The psychology of learning*, 41st Yearbook of the National Society for the Study of Education. Bloomington: Public School Publishing, 1942.

Gynther, M. D. Differential eyelid conditioning as a function of stimulus similarity and strength of response to the CS. *Journal of Experimental Psychology*, 1957, *53*, 408–416.

Hilgard, E. R., & Bower, G. H. *Theories of learning*. New York: Appleton-Century-Crofts, 1966.

Hinde, R. A. *Animal behaviour* (2nd ed.). New York: McGraw-Hill, 1970.

Hovland, C. I. The generalization of conditioned responses: II. The sensory generalization of conditioned responses with varying intensities of tone. *Journal of Genetic Psychology*, 1937, *51*, 279–291.

Hovland, C. I. Experimental studies in rote learning theory: VII. Distribution of practice with varying lengths of lists. *Journal of Experimental Psychology*, 1940, *27*, 281–284.

Hull, C. L. A functional interpretation of the conditioned reflex. *Psychological Review*, 1929, *36*, 498–511.

Hull, C. L. Knowledge and purpose as habit mechanisms. *Psychological Review*, 1930, *37*, 511–525. (a)

Hull, C. L. Simple trial-and-error learning: A study in psychological theory. *Psychological Review*, 1930, *37*, 241–256. (b)

Hull, C. L. Goal attraction and directing ideas conceived as habit phenomena. *Psychological Review*, 1931, *38*, 487–506.

Hull, C. L. The goal-gradient hypothesis and maze learning. *Psychological Review*, 1932, *39*, 25–43.

Hull, C. L. Differential habituation to internal stimuli in the albino rat. *Journal of Comparative Psychology*, 1933, *16*, 255–273. (a)

Hull, C. L. *Hypnosis and suggestibility: An experimental approach.* New York: Appleton-Century, 1933. (b)

Hull, C. L. Learning: II. The factor of the conditioned reflex. In C. Murchison (Ed.), *A handbook of general experimental psychology*. Worcester, Mass.: Clark University Press, 1934. (a)

Hull, C. L. The rat's speed-of-locomotion gradient in the approach to food. *Journal of Comparative Psychology*, 1934, *17*, 393–422. (b)

Hull, C. L. The conflicting psychologies of learning: A way out. *Psychological Review*, 1935, *42*, 491–516. (a)

Hull, C. L. The mechanism of the assembly of behavior segments in novel combinations suitable for problem solution. *Psychological Review*, 1935, *42*, 219–245. (b)

Hull, C. L. Mind, mechanism, and adaptive behavior. *Psychological Review*, 1937, *44*, 1–32.

Hull, C. L. The goal-gradient hypothesis applied to some "field-force" problems in the behavior of young children. *Psychological Review*, 1938, *45*, 271–299.

Hull, C. L. The problem of stimulus equivalence in behavior theory. *Psychological Review*, 1939, *46*, 9–30.

Hull, C. L. Explorations in the patterning of stimuli conditioned to the G.S.R. *Journal of Experimental Psychology*, 1940, *27*, 95–110.

Hull, C. L. *Principles of behavior*. New York: Appleton-Century-Crofts, 1943.

Hull, C. L. The discrimination of stimulus configurations and the hypothesis of afferent neural interaction. *Psychological Review*, 1945, *52*, 133–142.

Hull, C. L. Stimulus intensity dynamism (V) and stimulus generalization. *Psychological Review*, 1949, *56*, 67–76.

Hull, C. L. Simple qualitative discrimination learning. *Psychological Review*, 1950, *57*, 303–313.

Hull, C. L. *Essentials of behavior*. New Haven, Conn.: Yale University Press, 1951.

Hull, C. L. *A behavior system*. New Haven, Conn.: Yale University Press, 1952.

Hull, C. L., Felsinger, J. M., Gladstone, A. I., & Yamaguchi, H. G. A proposed quantification of habit strength. *Psychological Review,* 1947, *54,* 237–254.

Hull, C. L., Hovland, C. I., Ross, R. T., Hall, M., Perkins, D. T., & Fitch, F. B. *Mathematico-deductive theory of rote learning: A study in scientific methodology.* New Haven, Conn.: Yale University Press, 1940.

Hull, C. L., Livingstone, J. R., Rouse, R. O., & Barker, A. N. True, sham, and esophageal feeding as reinforcements. *Journal of Comparative and Physiological Psychology,* 1951, *44,* 236–245.

Kendler, H. H. "What is learned?" A theoretical blind alley. *Psychological Review,* 1952, *59,* 269-277.

Kendler, H. H., Karasik, A. D., & Schrier, A. M. Studies of the effect of change in drive: III. Amounts of switching produced by shifting drive from thirst to hunger and from hunger to thirst. *Journal of Experimental Psychology,* 1954, *47,* 149–182.

Kimble, G. A. An experimental test of a two-factor theory of inhibition. *Journal of Experimental Psychology,* 1949, *39,* 15–23.

Kimble, G. A. *Hilgard and Marquis' Conditioning and learning.* New York: Appleton-Century-Crofts, 1961.

Leeper, R. The role of motivation in learning: A study of the phenomenon of differential motivational control of the utilization of habits. *Journal of Genetic Psychology,* 1935, *46,* 3–40.

Logan, F. A. *Incentive.* New Haven, Conn.: Yale University Press, 1960.

Logan, F. A. *Fundamentals of learning and motivation* (2nd ed.). Dubuque, Iowa: William C. Brown, 1976.

Mackintosh, N. J. *The psychology of animal learning.* New York: Academic Press, 1974.

McAllister, W. R., & McAllister, D. E. Behavioral measurement of conditioned fear. In F. R. Brush (Ed.), *Aversive conditioning and learning.* New York: Academic Press, 1971.

McDougall, W. *An introduction to social psychology.* London: Methuen, 1908.

Meryman, J. J. *Magnitude of startle response as a function of hunger and fear.* Unpublished master's thesis, State University of Iowa, 1952.

Miller, N. E. Liberalization of basic S–R concepts: Extensions to conflict behavior, motivation, and social learning. In S. Koch (Ed.), *Psychology, a study of a science* (Vol. 2). New York: McGraw-Hill, 1959.

Miller, N. E., & Dollard, J. C. *Social learning and imitation.* New Haven, Conn.: Yale University Press, 1941.

Miller, N. E., & Kraeling, D. Displacement: Greater generalization of approach than avoidance in generalized approach-avoidance conflict. *Journal of Experimental Psychology,* 1952, *43,* 217–221.

Montgomery, K. C. The role of the exploratory drive in learning. *Journal of Comparative and Physiological Psychology,* 1954, *47,* 60–64.

Mowrer, O. H. Two-factor learning theory reconsidered, with special reference to secondary reinforcement and the concept of habit. *Psychological Review,* 1956, *63,* 114–128.

Mowrer, O. H. *Learning theory and behavior.* New York: John Wiley & Sons, 1960.

Olds, J., & Milner, P. Positive reinforcement produced by electrical stimulation of septal area and other regions of rat brain. *Journal of Comparative and Physiological Psychology,* 1954, *47,* 419–427.

Pavlov, I. P. *Conditioned reflexes* (G. V. Anrep, trans.). London: Oxford University Press, 1927.

Perin, C. T. Behavior potentiality as a joint function of the amount of training and degree of hunger at the time of extinction. *Journal of Experimental Psychology,* 1942, *30,* 93–113.

Premack, D. Catching up with common sense, or two sides of a generalization: Reinforcement and punishment. In R. Glaser (Ed.), *The nature of reinforcement.* New York: Academic Press, 1971.

Rescorla, R. A., & Solomon, R. L. Two-process learning theory: Relationships between Pavlovian conditioning and instrumental learning. *Psychological Review,* 1967, *74,* 151–182.

Rescorla, R. A., & Wagner, A. R. A theory of Pavlovian conditioning: Variations in the effectiveness of reinforcement and nonreinforcement. In A. H. Black & W. F. Prokasy (Eds.), *Classical conditioning II: Current research and theory.* New York: Appleton-Century-Crofts, 1972.

Schoenfeld, W. N. An experimental approach to anxiety, escape, and avoidance behavior. In P. H. Hoch & J. Zubin (Eds.), *Anxiety.* New York: Grune & Stratton, 1950.

Seward, J. P., & Levy, N. Sign learning as a factor in extinction. *Journal of Experimental Psychology,* 1949, *39,* 660–668.

Sheffield, F. D., Roby, T. B., & Campbell, B. A. Drive reduction versus consummatory behavior as determinants of reinforcement. *Journal of Comparative and Physiological Psychology,* 1954, *47,* 349–354.

Shipley, W. C. Indirect conditioning. *Journal of General Psychology,* 1935, *12,* 337–357.

Spence, K. W. The nature of discrimination learning in animals. *Psychological Review,* 1936, *43,* 427–449.

Spence, K. W. Analysis of the formation of visual discrimination habits in chimpanzees. *Journal of Comparative Psychology,* 1937, *23,* 77–100. (a)

Spence, K. W. The differential response in animals to stimuli varying within a single dimension. *Psychological Review,* 1937, *44,* 430–444. (b)

Spence, K. W. Theoretical interpretations of learning. In S. S. Stevens (Ed.), *Handbook of experimental psychology.* New York: John Wiley & Sons, 1951.

Spence, K. W. Clark Leonard Hull: 1884–1952. *American Journal of Psychology,* 1952, *65,* 639–646.

Spence, K. W. *Behavior theory and conditioning.* New Haven, Conn.: Yale University Press, 1956.

Spence, K. W. *Behavior theory and learning.* Englewood Cliffs, N.J.: Prentice-Hall, 1960.

Spence, K. W. Cognitive and drive factors in the extinction of the conditioned eyeblink in human subjects. *Psychological Review,* 1966, *73,* 445–451.

Spence, K. W., Farber, I. E., & McFann, H. H. The relation of anxiety (drive) level to performance in competitional and noncompetitional paired-associates learning. *Journal of Experimental Psychology,* 1956, *52,* 296–305.

Thorndike, E. L. *The fundamentals of learning.* New York: Teachers College Press, 1932.

Tolman, E. C. *Purposive behavior in animals and men.* New York: Appleton-Century, 1932.

Tolman, E. C. Cognitive maps in rats and men. *Psychological Review,* 1948, *55,* 189–208.

Tolman, E. C., & Honzik, C. H. Introduction and removal of reward, and maze performance in rats. *University of California Publications in Psychology,* 1930, *4,* 257–275.

Tolman, E. C., Ritchie, B. F., & Kalish, D. Studies in spatial learning: II. Place learning versus response learning. *Journal of Experimental Psychology,* 1946, *36,* 221–229.

Watson, J. B. Psychology as the behaviorist views it. *Psychological Review,* 1913, *20,* 158–177.

Williams, S. B. Resistance to extinction as a function of the number of reinforcements. *Journal of Experimental Psychology,* 1938, *23,* 506–522.

Woodworth, R. S. *Dynamic psychology.* New York: Columbia University Press, 1918.

Yamaguchi, H. G., Hull, C. L., Felsinger, J. M., & Gladstone, A. I. Characteristics of dispersions based on the pooled momentary reaction potentials ($_s\overline{E}_R$) of a group. *Psychological Review,* 1948, *55,* 216–238.

Yoshioka, J. G. Weber's law in the discrimination of maze distance by the white rat. *University of California Publications in Psychology,* 1929, *4,* 155–184.

5

Operant Theory: Skinner

A. CHARLES CATANIA

INTRODUCTION

Overview

Operant theory is a variety of behaviorism particularly identified with the work of B. F. Skinner.[1] As a systematic context for research in psychology, it is referred to as the *experimental analysis of behavior* (sometimes abbreviated EAB). Its practitioners are called behavior analysts, although they have also gone by such other names as operant conditioners, radical behaviorists, or Skinnerians. In the early years of the field, attention was devoted mainly to basic research questions in the animal laboratory. The concern with basic issues remains, but in recent years many researchers have turned their attention also to ways of applying behavior principles to significant human problems (e.g., the technology of education). Thus, *applied behavior analysis* has emerged as an important specialty within the experimental analysis of behavior.

Operant theory takes behavior as its fundamental subject matter. We study behavior not because it may help us to

resolve problems of physiology, and not because it may open the way to some other cognitive or metaphysical level of reality, but because behavior itself is a basic aspect of human life. It is worth studying for its own sake.

Some types of behavior are produced or elicited by stimuli (e.g., blinking in response to a puff of air to the eye). Others occur or are emitted because of the consequences such behavior has had in the past (e.g., operating a switch that turns a light on or off). The latter type is called *operant behavior:* It operates on the environment. Such behavior makes a difference in the world; it changes the environment in some way. For that reason, it is the behavior of primary interest to the operant theorist. It also corresponds fairly closely to instrumental behavior, or what is colloquially called *voluntary or purposive behavior.* Examples include manipulating objects, talking, and going from one place to another. To the extent that these responses are defined by how they affect the environment, they are all instances of operant behavior. According to this view, the organism is active in its environment; it is not passively pushed and pulled by environmental events.

Not all behavior is operant in nature,

---

[1] Dr. Catania has presented my position with accuracy, and I am glad to have the chapter available—B. F. Skinner.

however. Behavior can be to various degrees innate or learned, and it can depend on what has preceded it (*antecedent* events) as well as on what has followed it (*consequent* events). For example, consider an infant's crying. Pain or discomfort might be sufficient to produce such crying. But perhaps the infant sometimes cries because it has learned that crying usually attracts a parent's attention. To deal appropriately with the infant's crying, we should know its source: whether it was produced by some painful stimulus, or whether it depended instead on the past consequence of attracting attention. In everyday language, we might ask whether the infant is crying because it is hurt or because it wants attention.

Distinguishing among the possible sources of behavior is an essential task of a behavioral analysis. In conducting such an analysis, however, it is not enough simply to observe an instance of behavior. The form of the behavior is not critical. Instead, we must be concerned with its function. A movement produced by some stimulus is different from one that occurs because such movements have had certain consequences in the past. Even though these movements may look alike, they must be treated as different response classes.

Behavior, however, is not simply movement. For example, operant theory does not exclude from its consideration those private events called *mental*. Thinking and imagining are included in what people do and are therefore proper objects for study. What distinguishes this behavioral view is not a rejection of private events but rather the insistence that such events must be treated as kinds of behavior. Behavior is not merely a collection of muscle movements; it must be defined more broadly. This point of view has substantial historical precedent even

outside of operant theory, as illustrated by the following quotation:

> Instead of "memory," we should say "remembering"; instead of "thought" we should say "thinking," instead of "sensation" we should say "seeing, hearing," etc. But, like other learned branches, psychology is prone to transform its verbs into nouns. Then what happens? We forget that our nouns are merely substitutes for verbs, and go hunting for the *things* denoted by the nouns; but there are no such things, there are only the activities that we started with, seeing, remembering, and so on. . . . It is a safe rule, then, on encountering any menacing psychological noun, to strip off its linguistic mask, and see what manner of activity lies behind. (Woodworth, 1929, pp. 5–6)

More than half a century later, the wide-ranging implications of this point of view are yet to be fully appreciated.

Major Issues

Some assumptions about the nature of science were implicit in the development of behavior analysis. Though many researchers agreed that behavior was of interest in its own right, they often regarded their primary task as seeking explanations of behavior in other systems or dimensions, rather than putting the study of behavior itself into good order. In the reductionist view of science, behavior was to be explained in terms of physiology (in particular, the physiology of the nervous system). Physiological processes were then to be understood in terms of biochemical events, which were in turn to be reduced to interactions among elementary physical particles. The problem was that such reductions were premature if the properties of behavior itself were not well understood.

Operant theory started from the view that behavior is to be understood in its own terms and not in terms of concepts imposed by other areas of science. Changes in behavior are undoubtedly related to changes in the nervous system, but it is nevertheless the whole organism that behaves. The organism keeps in contact with the world through its sensory systems, and the organism acts on the world through its muscular systems. A nervous system that had nothing to do with either of these systems would be of little interest. For this reason, behavior has priority over physiology.

This point was made early in Skinner's writings (e.g., 1938, pp. 418–432), but it has often been misunderstood. Behaviorists were later said to be concerned only with the "empty organism," presumably denying that the nervous system is relevant to behavior. Skinner's argument, however, was instead directed mainly against a major trend of those times: the attempt to explain behavior by appealing to properties of a hypothetical nervous system (the CNS not as central nervous system but as *conceptual* nervous system). Skinner put the case as follows:

> . . . there are two independent subject matters (behavior and the nervous system) which must have their own techniques and methods and yield their own respective data. No amount of information about the second will "explain" the first or bring order into it without the direct analytical treatment represented by a science of behavior. The argument applies equally well to other sciences dealing with internal systems related to behavior. No merely endocrinological information will establish the thesis that personality is a matter of glandular secretion or that thought is chemical. What is required in both cases, if the defense of the thesis is to go beyond mere rhetoric, is a formulation of what is meant by personality or thought and the quantitative measurement of their properties. . . . I am asserting, then, not only that a science of behavior is independent of neurology but that it must be established as a separate discipline whether or not a rapprochement with neurology is ever attempted. (Skinner, 1938, pp. 423–424)

Consider an analogy from the study of vision. Human vision in dim light differs qualitatively from vision in bright light, and visual sensitivity and acuity vary with the location of visual stimuli. These differences are attributed to two types of visual receptor in the human retina, rods and cones, which are distinguished on the basis of anatomical structure. The fovea, the central part of the retina which receives light from the point of fixation, consists almost exclusively of cones. The density of cones decreases and the density of rods increases as one moves away from the fovea into the retinal periphery. Compared to rods, cones are relatively insensitive to light, but once light levels are sufficiently high to stimulate the cones, they play a dominant role in the sharpness or acuity of vision and probably also in color vision.

These conclusions about rods and cones are relevant only because of the available behavioral evidence: Humans have different capacities to respond to visual stimuli, depending on where the stimuli are located in the visual field. Without evidence for two qualitatively different varieties of seeing, the anatomical differences between rods and cones might well be ignored. The two different kinds of seeing have to be distinguished before the relevance of the two kinds of receptors can be understood. This is the sense in which behavior with respect to visual stimuli is more fundamental than visual physiology.

In the same sense, an analysis of behavior has priority over an analysis of the nervous system. This is not to say that behavior has no physiological basis. It would be interesting to know what physiological changes accompany behavior. But if we have not determined the properties of behavior, we can hardly know how to study its physiology. Subsequent research in behavior analysis has justified this view by demonstrating properties of behavior in the laboratory that had not been recognized earlier (e.g., the effects of reinforcement schedules).

Another major issue in operant theory is the relation between behavioral analyses and mental or private events. The issue is not the existence of such private events as thinking or imagining, but rather their relation to behavior. Difficulties arise when such events are invoked as explanations of behavior instead of as kinds of behavior in themselves (Skinner, 1963). For example, it can be misleading to say that one behaved in a certain way because of what one thought. Without an independent account of what determines thinking and how thinking may affect other behavior, such a statement is inadequate as an explanation. A particular disadvantage of a mentalistic account is that its superficial appeal may discourage further inquiry. The logic of this argument parallels that for the relation between behavior and physiology. The central issue in both cases is the priority of a behavioral account. The properties of behavior must be dealt with in their own terms.

Basic Concepts

Respondents. Successive responses may be similar, but they are never identical. Thus, it is necessary to deal not with individual responses but rather with classes of responses (Skinner, 1935a). Some classes of responses, *respondents,* are defined by the stimuli that produce or *elicit* them. Such classes are illustrated by the stimulus-response relations called reflexes (Skinner, 1931). For example, cry-

ing produced by freshly sliced onions is a member of a different respondent class (is part of a different reflex) than crying produced by a cold wind in one's face.

Operants. Some classes of responses, *operants,* are defined in terms of their environmental effects rather than in terms of eliciting stimuli. For example, driving to the store, bicycling to the store, and walking to the store all may be members of the same operant class. No eliciting stimuli need be identified for such responses; they are said to be *emitted* rather than elicited. Admitting the possibility that behavior could occur spontaneously was a critical conceptual step in operant theory (Skinner, 1956). Earlier behavioral treatments had assumed that for every response there must be a corresponding eliciting stimulus. In rejecting this assumption, operant theory did not maintain that emitted responses are uncaused; instead, the point was that there are other causes of behavior besides eliciting stimuli. The concept of the operant was based on the finding that past consequences of responding are important determinants of behavior.

Reinforcers and Punishers. When responses have consequences, these consequences may raise or lower subsequent responding. For example, a hungry rat's lever pressing will typically increase if it produces food pellets but decreases if it produces electric shocks. These consequences are respectively called *reinforcers* and *punishers.* In early operant theory, reinforcement was regarded as a principle of behavior. But reinforcement is not an explanation. Instead, it is simply a name that is appropriate for an increase in behavior when the increase is demonstrably caused by the consequences of responding (e.g., the relation between the rat's lever presses and food pellets) rather than by something else. The particular relations that can be established between responses and reinforcers are called *contingencies of reinforcement* (Skinner, 1969).

Discriminated Operants. Some responses have consequences under some circumstances and not under others. If a stimulus signals or *sets the occasion* for different consequences of responding, the stimulus is said to be *discriminative*. If responses then come to depend on the discriminative stimulus, the response class is called a *discriminated operant*. For example, a red traffic light sets the occasion for stepping on the brakes. It would be incorrect to say that the red light elicited this response; the response occurs during red and not during green because the response has different consequences in the presence of each stimulus. Thus, stopping on red and driving on green are discriminated operants. They are *not* respondents. Respondents are distinguished from operants on the basis of whether the consequences of responding play a role. A response is a member of a respondent class if it depends only on the presentation of a stimulus, as in a reflex. But a response is a member of a discriminated operant class if it occurs because of the relation between three terms: the discriminative stimulus, the response, and the consequences of the response in the presence of that stimulus (Skinner, 1935b). Thus, discriminated operants are said to be based on a *three-term contingency*. In setting the occasion for the response, the discriminative stimulus is therefore part of the definition of this operant class.

HISTORY

Beginnings

Operant theory is a variety of behaviorism. But it differs from traditional be-

haviorism in many ways. John B. Watson is usually credited as the founder of behaviorism, perhaps not so much for the originality of his ideas as for the vigor and consistency with which they were presented (Watson, 1913). Early in the 20th century, psychology was marked by substantial disagreements about its methods and its subject matter. Researchers claimed to be able to study the content of consciousness through the method of introspection. Yet they could not agree on fundamental issues, such as whether the basic mental units were sensations or ideas or something else. Quantitative data accumulated, as in experiments on reaction time, but it gradually became clear that disputed issues could not be resolved by such findings. Although psychology was believed to be a potential science, psychologists could not convince each other that any one view of the subject matter was more effective or more defensible than another.

This was the historical context for Watson's introduction of behaviorism. He stressed behavior, as opposed to mind or consciousness, as the only legitimate subject matter of psychology. Later, he buttressed his arguments by incorporating Pavlov's principles of conditioning into his system (Watson, 1925), thereby adding experimental evidence to his case. But on methodological grounds Watson also excluded private events, such as imagining and thinking, as proper areas of inquiry in psychology. Objectivism, the view that science must deal only with measurable public events, was meanwhile gaining strength in various disciplines besides psychology. The preoccupation with the scientific legitimacy of psychology disposed subsequent researchers to look to other sciences for principles of scientific method, and gradually Watsonian behaviorism was merged with the operationism that was newly developing in physics and with the logical positivism that was being introduced as a revolutionary change in the philosophy of science (see Mackenzie, 1977).

During Watson's career in psychology, behaviorism had substantial social impact. His writings appeared in popular magazines, and his recommendations on child-rearing and other practices were taken seriously. The following claim by Watson has often been quoted:

> Give me a dozen healthy infants, well-formed, and my own specified world to bring them up in and I'll guarantee to take any one at random and train him to become any type of specialist I might select—doctor, lawyer, artist, merchant-chief and, yes, even beggar-man and thief, regardless of his talents, penchants, tendencies, abilities, vocations, and race of his ancestors. I am going beyond my facts and I admit it, but so have the advocates of the contrary and they have been doing it for many thousands of years. (Watson, 1925, p. 82)

This was a radical pronouncement, and yet some of its features have become widely accepted. For example, Watson discussed racial and ethnic differences by appealing to differences in the environment rather than to differences in genetic history. Even though we may note the possibly sexist *his* and *him* in Watson's quotation, it is clear that he would have supported many of the current movements of social liberation.

Nevertheless, Watson's views were strongly criticized. The opposition to behaviorism had many sources. Some of its views threatened established institutions. Once the argument had been made for the environmental determination of behavior, it followed that behavior could be controlled. These implications became evident in a variety of ways. In Germany, the playwright Bertholt Brecht read Watson in translation and incorporated a behavioral view into his theory of theater (Rosenbauer, 1970). In Soviet Russia, Ivan Pavlov's psychology gradually became politicized (Joravsky, 1961), and because Watson had made Pavlov's conditioned reflexes a part of his behaviorism, the behaviorist view came to be identified with conditioning and eventually with brainwashing.

The status of behaviorism remains controversial to the present. It is often regarded simply as wrong-headed and misleading. The strong reactions it engenders suggest that it sometimes seems threatening, but it would probably not seem so threatening if many did not see elements of truth in it. The early behaviorists undoubtedly overstated the case for environmentalism in their concern with identifying existing and potential sources of control over human behavior. When such control exists, however, it is exerted not by behaviorists but rather by political, economic, educational, social, and religious institutions. It would be foolhardy to maintain that it is wrong to try to understand such kinds of control; ignorance of the properties of behavior is hardly an effective defense against behavioral control.

In any case, the adherence to objectivism and thereby the rejection of private events as a legitimate subject matter for psychology marked the traditional varieties of behaviorism. Because of their concern with issues of scientific method, such as the operational definition borrowed from physics and the principles of experimental design derived from mathematics and statistics, they were referred to as varieties of *methodological behaviorism*. From these origins came major lines of research and formal theories of behavior, such as those of Clark L. Hull.

Operant theory represents another type

of behaviorism, called *radical behaviorism*. It did not reject private events but rather treated such events as kinds of behavior, and its affinities were more with the biological than with the physical sciences. It was radical not so much because it considered some of the phenomena that methodological behaviorism had rejected, but rather because it had turned its scientific priorities around. Once the science of behavior was taken as fundamental, the behavior of the scientist became part of its subject matter. Scientific methods derived from other disciplines could not dictate methods of behavior analysis, because these methods simply prescribed scientific behavior. In this view, behavior analysis provided a context in terms of which scientific behavior in general could be studied. As behavior analysts refined their understanding of reinforcement contingencies, stimulus control, and verbal behavior, they began also to look explicitly for corresponding processes in their own scientific behavior.

Major Theorists

Burrhus Frederic Skinner is probably better known by his initials, B. F. He found the first name troublesome. Of those on a first-name basis, most call him Fred. To Fred S. Keller, a colleague since his graduate-student days, he remains Burrhus.

Born on March 20, 1904, Skinner grew up in the town of Susquehanna, Pennsylvania. After majoring in English at Hamilton College, he tried a career as a writer but found that he had nothing to say and gave it up. Having some familiarity with the writings of Watson and Pavlov and a long-standing interest in human and animal behavior, Skinner then entered the graduate program in psychology at Harvard University. His account

of his life up to that point (Skinner, 1976) is behaviorally written, in that his presentation of the people and events and settings of those times is basically descriptive; he does not pass judgment on others, or ascribe motives to them, or guess at what they may have been thinking or feeling. The account is nonetheless often moving and insightful; sensitivity and compassion are not precluded by a behavioral approach.

At Harvard, Skinner began a series of experiments on the behavior of rats (Skinner, 1930) that led to more than two dozen journal articles and culminated in a book called *The Behavior of Organisms* (Skinner, 1938). After the style of *The Integrative Action of the Nervous System* (Sherrington, 1906) and *Behavior of the Lower Organisms* (Jennings, 1906), the work not only presented a variety of novel research findings but also provided a systematic context for them. Laws of conditioning and the static and dynamic laws of the reflex were proposed, and two types of conditioning were distinguished: Type S, corresponding to the classical conditioning of Pavlov (1927), and Type R, corresponding to the instrumental learning of Thorndike's Law of Effect (Thorndike, 1911). The concept of the reflex reserve, which argued for a store of responses to be emitted in extinction, was later to be discarded.

Keller (1970) has described Skinner's work as follows:

. . . Burrhus was a solitary worker (*Schedules of Reinforcement* is the principal exception) and a very cautious one. He didn't describe his experiments in advance of their execution; he never responded hastily to a challenging question (sometimes the answer was delayed for years); and he didn't announce a finding until he felt it was secure. . . . In spite of his genius in experimental research, Burrhus Skinner was primarily a systematist, even then, . . . but I saw his contributions as mainly methodological. It was not until the summer of '38, when I began to read my copy of *The Behavior of Organisms,* that I finally saw what had been happening. Then, at last, I had something systematically exciting to give my classes. (pp. 34–35)

The concept of the operant was beginning to emerge. Skinner had already argued for a behavioral rather than a physiological definition of the reflex, as an observed correlation between stimuli and responses (Skinner, 1931). The stimulus-response relation called the reflex had often been abbreviated as S–R, so much so that behavioral approaches were characteristically referred to as S–R or stimulus-response psychologies (even after the concept of the operant made the label inappropriate, at least for operant theory). In *The Behavior of Organisms,* the eliciting stimulus became vestigial; it appeared in notations built around the sequence, $s \cdot R$–S, where S was the reinforcer or consequence produced by response R, and s was simply an obligatory acknowledgment of an eliciting stimulus that was neither identified nor functional in the R–S relation:

The lack of an eliciting stimulus in operant behavior together with the law of the operant reserve throws considerable weight upon the response alone, and this may seem to weaken any attempt to group operants under the general heading of reflexes. It is well to allow for a possible originating event . . . and to provide for the other ways in which a response may be related to a stimulus. Nevertheless, it should be understood that the operant reserve is a reserve of *responses,* not of stimulus-response units. (Skinner, 1938, p. 230)

The term *operant* was probably a relatively late addition to *The Behavior of Organisms,* and the subsequent development of its implications demonstrates that the book should be viewed not as a final system but rather as an extended progress report on Skinner's thinking about the fundamental concepts of behavior theory.

. . . I held doggedly to the term "reflex." Certain characteristics of operant behavior were, however, becoming clear. My first papers were challenged by two Polish physiologists, Konorski and Miller. It was in my answer to them that I first used the term "operant." Its function, then as now, was to identify behavior traceable to reinforcement contingencies rather than to eliciting stimuli. (Skinner, 1967, p. 400)

The exchange with Konorski and Miller (Skinner, 1935b, 1937) set the stage for the elaboration of stimulus control in the three-term contingency. The response of the typical reflex was simply elicited by its stimulus. But the response of what Skinner at first called the "pseudoreflex" occurred because of its consequences in the presence of a stimulus, and thus the pseudoreflex evolved into the discriminated operant.

In 1936, at the end of three years as a Junior Fellow in the Harvard Society of Fellows, Skinner moved to the University of Minnesota. His animal research continued, and his publications also began to reflect his interest in the behavioral analysis of language (e.g., Skinner, 1936). Then, World War II occasioned work on animal applications of behavior principles, including training pigeons to guide missiles (Skinner, 1960). Although that project never got beyond the demonstration stage, its major fringe benefit was the technique of shaping, the development of novel forms of behavior through the differential reinforcement of successive approximations to a response. One other consequence was that pigeons began to replace rats as the dominant organism of the operant laboratory.

Another product of those days was the

Aircrib, which Skinner built for his wife and his second daughter (Skinner, 1945). It was a windowed space with temperature and humidity control that improved on the safety and comfort of the ordinary crib while making the care of the child less burdensome. Rumors to the contrary, it was not used for conditioning the infant; those critics were disappointed who, confusing the Aircrib with the so-called Skinner Box or rat chamber, sought signs of emotional instability in Skinner's daughters. Skinner had pointed out that there was nothing natural about the standard crib, and he simply invented a better one.

In 1945, Skinner assumed the Chair of the Department of Psychology at Indiana University. Then, after giving the 1947 William James Lectures at Harvard University, on the topic of verbal behavior, he returned permanently to the Harvard Department of Psychology. Compared to the growing interest in his experimental work, relatively little notice was given to the publication of his utopian novel *Walden Two* (Skinner, 1948b). Some who later criticized the specifics of that planned society failed to observe that its experimental character was its most important feature; any practice that did not work was to be modified until a more effective substitute was found.

Meanwhile, at Columbia College, Fred S. Keller and W. N. Schoenfeld had created an undergraduate psychology curriculum based on operant theory. It included an innovative textbook and a one-year introductory course with a laboratory (Keller & Schoenfeld, 1949, 1950). Operant theorists were now located at several universities, and meetings of those interested in the experimental analysis of behavior became a series of annual conferences. Eventually a formal division for the Experimental Analysis of Behavior (Division 25) was established within the American Psychological Association. During those years, while the Harvard Pigeon Laboratory provided many students of operant behavior with opportunities to develop their own independent lines of research, Skinner created the subject matter of reinforcement schedules in collaboration with Charles B. Ferster (Ferster & Skinner, 1957); he thoroughly revised and expanded his William James Lectures on language in the book *Verbal Behavior* (Skinner, 1957); and he built the first of his teaching machines (Skinner, 1958). Soon after, Keller began his involvement with the modifications of college teaching that were to become PSI, the Personalized System of Instruction; educational institutions were about to be introduced to self-paced courses and the behavioral definition of teaching objectives (Keller, 1977). The *Journal of the Experimental Analysis of Behavior* began publication in 1958; within a decade, the increased activity in applications of operant theory led to a companion journal, the *Journal of Applied Behavior Analysis*.

Current Status

Behavior analysts are now located in a number of professional organizations, and their research appears in many psychological journals. Experiments on basic processes have been complemented by applications in a variety of settings: schools, clinics, institutes for the retarded, rehabilitation centers, and psychiatric hospitals. The empirical findings of behavior analysis, once surveyed in a single book (Honig, 1966), are now reviewed in three volumes: one devoted to basic research (Honig & Staddon, 1977); one to applications in behavior therapy and behavior pathology (Leitenberg, 1976);

and one to educational and social applications (Catania & Brigham, 1978). In brief compass, it is difficult even merely to list the major advances in basic research, as operant theory was refined through experiments on reinforcement schedules (Schoenfeld, Cumming, & Hearst, 1956), aversive control (Sidman, 1953), psychopharmacology (Dews, 1970), quantitative models of operant behavior (Herrnstein, 1970; Shimp, 1966), the concept of response strength (Nevin, 1974), complex stimulus control (Baer, Peterson, & Sherman, 1967; Sidman, Cresson, & Willson-Morris, 1974), imprinting (Hoffman & Ratner, 1973), and species-specific phenomena (Collier, Hirsch, & Hamlin, 1972; Falk, 1977) to mention only a few.

But those years of rapid advance were not without problems. A highly critical review of Skinner's *Verbal Behavior* (Chomsky, 1959) signaled the beginnings of conflict between behavior analysis and the growing field of cognitive psychology (Neisser, 1967). The conflict may have been inappropriate, because the two approaches were concerned with different psychological problems (Catania, 1973b). But the different empirical interests were also entangled with different vocabularies and with different views on the nature of science.

Another issue was that of biological constraints on learning. Although a strict environmentalism was not essential to operant theory, the role of reinforcement and of environmental determinants of behavior had been so emphasized that some saw novel demonstrations of species-specific phenomena as inconsistent with operant theory. In basic research, studies of species-specific properties of the rat's lever press and the pigeon's key peck, some of which had evolved within behavior analysis itself, led to a period of retrenchment.

As with other major intellectual movements, operant theory had been accepted in some quarters and opposed in others. The enthusiasm of its early students often meant impatience with other points of view, and the increasing specialization of graduate programs in psychology made the problems more serious. Soon there were those taking one or the other side in these controversies who knew the opposing views only superficially, through secondary sources. The consequent misunderstandings were compounded by the competition for academic positions and for research support, as university budgets became more and more constricted during the seventies. While behavior analysis gained ground through its successes in applied settings, it lost ground in academic settings, the source of its future generations of students, teachers, and researchers. Yet some criticism of operant theory was itself behind the times; it was more appropriate to the methodological behaviorism discarded long ago, to the stimulus-response theories of other behavioral systems, and to a strict environmentalism that was irrelevant to its basic concepts. Operant theory is above all an empirical science, and we may expect it to grow as it accommodates new findings.

Other Theories

Skinner's system was included in a midcentury study of five major learning theories (Estes, Koch, MacCorquodale, Meehl, Mueller, Schoenfeld, & Verplanck, 1954). Treated, with Skinner's descriptive behaviorism, were Edward Chase Tolman's purposive behaviorism, Clark Hull's detailed hypothetico-deductive system, Kurt Lewin's mathematical formulation of Gestalt theory, and Edwin Guthrie's ingenious elaboration of the implications of the single principle that, in a given learning situation, the organism simply repeats what it did there the last time. Of the systems surveyed, Tolman's had more in common with Skinner's than did any other. Tolman's experiments on latent learning, which demonstrated that rats learned mazes even when they did not find food in the goalbox, and on cognitive maps, which showed that rats could locate shortcuts and novel paths through mazes when familiar paths were blocked, had challenged existing stimulus-response theories of learning (Tolman, 1948). For Tolman, as for Skinner, behavior was not simply movement and learning was not simply the formation of stimulus-response connections. Perhaps most important, instead of ruling out the traditional cognitive language, such as that of expectancies, both in their different ways dealt explicitly with how such concepts might be incorporated into a behavioral analysis.

Of those systems, Skinner's has most successfully stood the test of time, and has certainly been the source of the widest spectrum of practical applications. More recently, two other developments have been of particular relevance to Skinner's position: Neal E. Miller's research on the operant conditioning of autonomic responses (e.g., Miller & Carmona, 1967), and David Premack's account of reinforcement in terms of relative response probabilities (Premack, 1959, 1971).

Operant conditioning differs from respondent conditioning (e.g., the classical conditioning of Pavlov). The simplest basis for the operant-respondent distinction is procedural: In operant conditioning a response produces a stimulus, whereas in respondent conditioning a stimulus is followed by a stimulus (Schlosberg, 1937; Skinner, 1935b). Early formulations of the distinction also asserted that operant conditioning involves only skeletal responses, whereas respondent conditioning involves only autonomic responses (e.g., salivation). Miller demonstrated operant conditioning of various autonomic responses in an extensive series of experiments, some of which remain controversial (e.g., Black, Osborne, & Ristow, 1977). Combined with concurrent demonstrations of autoshaping, the respondent conditioning of skeletal responses (Brown & Jenkins, 1968), Miller's experiments in effect made the operant-respondent distinction independent of whether responding is skeletal or autonomic. It is perhaps fitting that empirical support was lost with respect to a physiological and not a behavioral criterion for the distinction.

The concept of reinforcement was essentially descriptive: If responding increases because it produces a stimulus, it is appropriate to call the stimulus a reinforcer. Attempts to explain reinforcement in terms of physiological processes such as drive reduction had been unsuccessful. Premack's contribution was to demonstrate that reinforcers must be defined relative to the responses that they reinforce. The critical step was identifying reinforcers as opportunities for responding. Premack showed that when one response was more probable than another, an opportunity to engage in the more probable response could be used to reinforce the less probable response. For example, at times when a rat is more likely to drink than to run in an activity wheel, an opportunity to drink can reinforce running. But when the rat is more likely to run than to drink, the opportunity to run can reinforce drinking.

Statements of this relativity and reversibility of the reinforcement relation have been referred to as the Premack principle. This theoretical contribution not only put to rest long-standing debates about the circularity of the definition of reinforcement (e.g., Meehl, 1950), it did so by providing a behavioral rather than a physiological criterion for predicting the effectiveness of reinforcers.

PROPOSITIONS

1. *Behavior analysis examines relations between experimental operations and changes in responding.*

Behavior analysis is concerned with relations among environmental events, *stimuli,* and the organism's actions, *responses.* These relations can be studied by examining how environmental manipulations, *experimental operations,* produce changes in behavior. We can describe manipulations of the environment in terms of three basic types of experimental operations: stimulus presentations; arrangement of consequences; and the signaling procedures of discriminative control.

Presenting stimuli is the simplest operation. When we present stimuli, we can observe the responses these stimuli produce. The major effect of stimulus presentations is to make particular responses more or less likely. For example, we might make a rat salivate by presenting food, but the rat would stop salivating and instead jump and squeak if we substituted electric shock. The effects of stimuli can also vary over time, as when, in adaptation, elicited responding diminishes with repeated stimulus presentations.

The events in an organism's environment, however, do not always occur by themselves. Sometimes the organism makes them happen. Environments can be arranged in which the organism's responding has effects or consequences. A variety of consequences can be arranged, ranging from those of obvious biological significance, such as food or water or a sexual partner, to relatively minor changes in things seen or heard or touched. Consequences are not restricted merely to the production of stimuli. Responses can remove stimuli, as when operating a switch turns off a light; responses can prevent stimuli from occurring, as when unplugging a lamp before repairing it eliminates the possibility of a shock; and responses can even change the consequences of other responses, as when replacing a burnt-out light bulb makes the previously ineffective response of operating the light switch an effective response again. Each type of consequence may affect later behavior.

Once responses have consequences, some may increase and others may decrease, depending on the particular consequences arranged for each. For example, if we present food to a hungry rat whenever it rears up on its hind legs, the rat may rear up on its hind legs more often. But if we present electric shock whenever it grooms its tail, the rat may groom its tail less often. If the organism responds more often because the response has a consequence, we say that the response has been *reinforced.* If the organism responds less often because the response has a consequence, we say that the response has been *punished.*

Matters are further complicated when either stimulus presentations or consequences are arranged only when some additional stimulus is present. Organisms do not behave indiscriminately: They do some things under some circumstances that they do not do under others. Events may signal what will happen or what consequences responding will have under different circumstances. In such operations, one stimulus is used to warn of the imminent occurrence of another, or to signal whether a response will have a particular consequence. For example, we might present food to a rat only when a buzzer sounds, or deliver electric shock only when a light is flashing; these cases correspond to Pavlovian or respondent conditioning procedures. But signals can also be arranged for response consequences. For example, we might present food when a rat rears up on its hind legs only if a lamp is lit, and the rat may come to rear up on its hind legs when the lamp is on and not when it is off; or we might deliver electric shock to the rat when it grooms its tail only if a tone is sounding, and the rat may come to stop tail-grooming when the tone is on but not when it is off. These cases correspond to the discriminative control of operant behavior generated by a three-term contingency. In combination, the three operations of *presenting stimuli, arranging consequences,* and *signaling events* provide an effective basis for analyzing learning procedures.

2. *Consequences can make responding increase (reinforcement) or decrease (punishment).*

Many different kinds of consequences can increase responding. Some involve stimuli produced by responses, as when a rat's lever pressing produces food or water. Such stimuli are called *positive reinforcers,* because responding increases when it adds these stimuli to the organism's environment. Others involve stimuli prevented or removed by responses,

as when a rat's lever pressing delays the onset of an electric shock or turns off a shock. Such stimuli are called *negative reinforcers,* because responding increases when it subtracts these stimuli from the organism's environment. Those arrangements in which responding removes negative reinforcers are called *escape procedures;* those in which responding prevents or delays the presentation of negative reinforcers are called *avoidance procedures.*

In their technical usage, the verbs *reinforce* and *punish* take responses and not organisms as their objects. Thus, it is appropriate to speak of reinforcing not the pigeon but the pigeon's key peck, and of punishing not the rat but the rat's lever press. This usage, which has only recently been accepted as standard in operant theory, has the advantage of discouraging ambiguous descriptions of procedure. For example, "The monkey's chain pull was reinforced with food" is preferable to "The monkey was reinforced with food," simply because the former version includes the response. Skinner's writings have included both usages, but he has adopted this standard technical usage in his more recent work (e.g., Skinner, 1975).

The concept of reinforcement had substantial precedent, as in E. L. Thorndike's Law of Effect. The major change in its role in behavior analysis was its gradual evolution from a principle that seemed to explain increases in responding to a name appropriate only for those increases in responding produced by the consequences of responding. Another feature of this concept is that it implies extinction, the decrease in responding when reinforcement is discontinued. Extinction procedures show how long the effects of reinforcement last. Other learning theories have treated extinction as the active suppression of responding by inhibitory processes. Operant theory, however, treats extinction not as a separate process from reinforcement but rather as a demonstration that the effects of reinforcement are temporary.

3. *Punishment is an effective but undesirable procedure for changing behavior.*

By the preceding definitions, punishment is simply the inverse of reinforcement, but punishment has had a more controversial history. Punishment had been part of Thorndike's early versions of the Law of Effect, when Thorndike argued that behavior could be stamped out by annoyers as well as stamped in by satisfiers. On the basis of verbal learning experiments in which saying "Wrong" had minimal effects on a human learner's responses, Thorndike withdrew this part of the Law of Effect. The conclusion transmitted to later investigators was not simply that saying "Wrong" could be an ineffective punisher but rather that punishment in general could not be demonstrated.

In later experiments (e.g., Estes, 1944), a rat's lever pressing maintained by food reinforcement was reduced when presses also produced electric shock, but the responding recovered to earlier levels once shock punishment was discontinued. The argument then was offered that punishment is an ineffective behavioral procedure, because it could suppress responding only temporarily. Yet with this criterion, reinforcement would also have to be judged ineffective. For some reason, the criteria for the effectiveness of punishment were different from those for the effectiveness of reinforcement. Investigators tended to concentrate on the recovery of responding after punishment

was discontinued rather than the reduction of responding during punishment.

Skinner (1953) also argued that when responding was reduced in punishment, it did so only indirectly. He suggested that, once a response has produced aversive consequences, the organism is likely to emit other responses that remove it from the situation (e.g., if a rat's lever presses produce electric shock, moving away from the lever may be negatively reinforced). But concern with other behavior that may accompany punishment does not alter its definition. In any case, with more extensive research on the properties of punishment (e.g., Azrin, 1956), treating punishment as a procedure that parallels reinforcement but differs from it in sign has become the predominant view.

The effectiveness of punishment, however, does not recommend it as a procedure for changing behavior. Punishment is usually an undesirable method for eliminating behavior—Thorndike and his successors were probably right for the wrong reasons. A major problem is that aversive stimuli used as punishers also have side effects, such as eliciting aggressive behavior.

The ethical questions raised by aversive control have no easy answers. If a parent often punishes a child's behavior, both the parent and the home may become aversive to the child; to the extent that the child then learns to avoid the home and the parent's company, other contingencies than those available to the parent will begin to influence the child's behavior. This kind of outcome would seem sufficient justification for arguing against punishment. Yet if punishment seemed the only technique available that could reduce the dangerous self-mutilating behavior of an autistic child, punishment might be a lesser evil than the damage the child might self-inflict. Because the ethical issues must inevitably be confronted, it is best to do so with the soundest possible understanding of the properties of punishment. Such understanding can come only from an experimental analysis.

4. *Operant classes are created by differential reinforcement.*

If we watched a rat's lever pressing, maintained by food reinforcement, we might see the rat press the lever with its left paw, its right paw, or both paws. Sometimes we might even see the rat press the lever by pushing it down with its chin, by biting it, or by sitting on it. Each is a different response, and even two presses with the same paw would not be identical. Nevertheless, we call all of these responses lever presses. On the other hand, if the rat made similar movements at the other end of the chamber, far from the lever, we would not call them lever presses, no matter how closely they resembled those that operated the lever.

Individual responses are instances of behavior, and each occurs only once. Though they can have common features, they cannot be the same in all respects. Reinforcing one response produces later responses more or less closely resembling the reinforced response, but the later responses must differ in detail from the reinforced response. Yet to avoid dealing with an infinite number of different responses, we cannot simply group all responses together without distinction, because then we would be left only with behavior in general. We must settle for an intermediate level of analysis, at which we speak neither of individual responses nor of behavior in general, but rather of *classes of responses* having common

properties (Catania, 1973a; Skinner, 1935a).

In experiments on lever pressing in rats, the lever is attached to a switch that operates whenever the lever is moved with sufficient force through a sufficient distance. Thus, the common property of all lever presses is this effect: If it operates the switch, the response qualifies as a lever press. With this criterion, we may record lever presses consistently, and we may also arrange that consequences such as food pellets depend upon presses. It is important that in this treatment responses are not defined by their topography or form; instead they are defined by how they function in the organism's interaction with its environment.

But this response class we have established will have no behavioral significance until we know whether changes occur when we arrange reinforcers. We must ask whether responses in this class are made more or less likely by their consequences. If so, the class is called an *operant class;* an operant class is a class of responses affected by the way in which it operates on the environment. This definition depends on the behavioral properties of responding, and not on its physical or physiological properties. The class depends on *differential reinforcement,* the reinforcement of only those responses that fall within the class. Differential reinforcement makes responding correspond more and more closely to the defining properties of the operant class. Thus, the crucial feature of an operant is that the class is identified by the correspondence between responding defined by an environmental effect and responding generated by those consequences. For example, if we arranged food deliveries for responses defined by the operation of a switch, but the food deliveries did not affect the likelihood of these responses, it would be inappropriate to speak of them as members of an operant class.

Because differential reinforcement can be based on any dimension of responding, any dimension of responding may provide the defining properties of an operant class. We cannot always define such dimensions unambiguously. For example, consider the reinforcement of novel responses in the porpoise (Pryor, Haag, & O'Reilly, 1969). Novel performances were generated by selecting for reinforcement, at the start of each experimental session, a class of responses not reinforced in any previous session. After several sessions of this procedure, the porpoise began to emit responses that the experimenters had never seen before. The novel responses were members of an operant class, in that these responses corresponded to the experimenters' criteria for reinforcement. Response novelty had been differentiated, but how else is this operant class to be specified except by describing the reinforcement criteria? Originality and other complex dimensions of behavior may define operant classes, even though we may sometimes have difficulty measuring such dimensions.

5. *New behavior can be shaped by reinforcing successive approximations.*

If we simply place a pigeon in an experimental chamber, we may or may not observe a key peck. With some pigeons, a peck may occur after a short wait; others may remain so long without pecking that our patience is exceeded. Reinforcement cannot affect responding if the response to be reinforced is never emitted. But an alternative is available. Instead of waiting for a peck, we can generate one through the procedure called *shap-*

ing. In this procedure, a new response is established by successively reinforcing other responses that more and more closely approximate it.

Consider shaping the pigeon's key peck. Once the pigeon has begun to eat from the feeder, we operate the feeder only when the pigeon turns toward the key. After reinforcing two or three movements toward the key, we may then reinforce not just any movement toward the key, but only movements that include a forward motion of the pigeon's beak. By this time, the pigeon is spending most of its time in front of the key, and we can shift our attention from its turning toward and facing the key to its forward beak movements and the extent to which these are directed at the key. The forward beak movements approximate pecking more closely than do turns toward the key, and once their reinforcement has assured us that they will continue to occur, we no longer have to reinforce turns toward the key. By now, the pigeon's beak movements are full-fledged pecks, and soon one of them strikes the key. At this point, we can withdraw, because our apparatus is arranged so that subsequent pecks operate the feeder automatically.

An experimenter experienced in working with pigeons can usually shape a key peck within 10 or 15 reinforcements. Some aspects of that skill can be stated explicitly. For example, reinforcing a movement is more efficient than reinforcing a posture. Other aspects of shaping are not so easily formulated. For example, shaping ordinarily compromises between extremes of frequent and infrequent reinforcement. Frequent reinforcement leads to quicker satiation and may overly strengthen some responses that will not be components of the response to be shaped. On the other hand, infrequent reinforcement may reduce responding in general, and once the organism becomes inactive, the progress made up to that point may be lost. Thus, the experimenter must work within these extremes, but rules do not exist for judging where these limits will be for any particular organism and any particular response to be shaped.

Furthermore, some features of shaping are fairly specific to the particular response and organism under study, whereas others can be generalized to the shaping of varied responses in varied organisms. With pigeons, for example, reinforcing a small beak movement aimed directly at the key will more effectively shape key pecking than reinforcing a large sideways beak movement that stops in front of the key. On the other hand, whatever the response and organism, an opportunity should not be missed to reinforce a response more closely approximating the one to be shaped than any response reinforced before.

Shaping is relevant to such diverse skills as gymnastics, handwriting, playing a musical instrument, and speaking a foreign language. As a procedure, shaping involves *differential reinforcement:* at successive stages, some responses are reinforced and others are not. In addition, as responding changes, the criteria for differential reinforcement change, in *successive approximations* to the response to be shaped. An important factor that contributes to shaping is that behavior is variable. Because no two responses are the same, reinforcement of one response produces a spectrum of responses similar to the reinforced response but differing from it along such dimensions as topography, force, magnitude, and direction. Of these, some are closer than others to the response to be shaped and are therefore selected next for reinforcement. Reinforcing these in turn is followed by still

other responses, some of which come even closer to the response to be shaped. Thus, reinforcement is used to change the spectrum of responses until the one to be shaped occurs.

6. *Discriminated operants are established by differential reinforcement with respect to stimuli.*

When responses are differentially reinforced, the relevant properties can include not only response dimensions but also the stimuli in the presence of which those responses occur. For example, reinforcement of a pigeon's key peck may depend on whether the peck occurs in the presence of a blue light or a yellow light. If reinforcement is correlated only with blue, the pigeon may come to peck in the presence of blue but not yellow. A response class established by such differential reinforcement with respect to stimulus properties is called a *discriminated operant.*

Discriminative stimuli correspond to the stimuli colloquially called *signals* or *cues.* They do not elicit responses. Instead, they set the occasion on which responses may have consequences. We measure their effects by noting how responding differs in their presence and absence. The process is called *discrimination.* When such a class is established, the stimulus in the presence of which a response occurs can be regarded as simply another property of the response, like its force or its duration or its topography. We recognize such classes whenever we include stimuli in our descriptions of operant classes (e.g., as when we speak of stopping on red and driving on green). Discriminated operants are pervasive aspects of behavior. We cannot meaningfully speak of responses independently of the environment, and even if we do not arrange differential reinforcement with respect to stimulus properties, some stimuli will be relevant to the organism's performance. The pigeon's key pecks cannot occur in the absence of keys, and even responses that do not depend on objects or apparatuses in an organism's world (e.g., changes in posture) occur in an environment.

Just as the response properties that define operant classes can be changed gradually by shaping, the stimulus properties that define discriminated operant classes can be changed gradually by an analogous procedure called *fading*. For example, given food-reinforced key pecking in pigeons, it is more difficult to establish a discrimination between vertical and horizontal lines than one between red and green lights. But once a discrimination between red and green is established, the discrimination between vertical and horizontal can be successively approximated by superimposing the lines on the colors and then gradually fading the colors out (Terrace, 1963). Similarly, once a vertical-horizontal discrimination is established, it can be changed gradually to more difficult discriminations of line orientation (e.g., between 40° and 50° lines).

The fading procedure is not solely of theoretical interest. By virtue of its potential for applications in education and other areas, it may have considerable practical significance. But as with shaping, no simple set of rules exists to determine the rate at which stimuli should be faded in or out in particular situations. Some fading procedures may be more successful than others, and sometimes attempts to transfer discrimination from one stimulus dimension to another will fail even with the skillful use of fading.

Relatively simple stimulus dimensions, such as intensity or location, can provide the basis for differential reinforcement. But differential reinforcement may also be arranged with respect to complex properties of stimuli and relations among stimuli. For example, a pigeon may learn to peck the odd color of three colors presented on keys (e.g., green of a red-red-green array). Stimulus control based on stimulus relations and on abstract properties of stimuli involves the complex stimulus classes that we speak of in terms of *concepts*. In fact, concepts are to classes of stimuli as operants are to classes of responses. To speak of relations as properties of stimuli implies that, just as responses are not treated simply as movements in operant theory, stimuli are not treated simply as single objects or events in the environment.

7. *Response sequences can be chains or behavioral units in their own right.*

If we divide a behavior sequence into its components, we may treat the sequence as a succession of different operants, each defined by the reinforcing consequence of producing an opportunity to engage in the next. Such a sequence is called a *response chain*. A relevant example is a rat's lever pressing reinforced by food. Rising up to the lever produces contact with the lever, which sets the occasion for pressing the lever, which produces a seen food pellet, which sets the occasion for moving to the food cup, and so on. Each part of the sequence serves the dual functions of reinforcing the preceding response and producing the conditions that occasion the next one.

Some behavior sequences seem reasonably reducible to smaller units in this way. An analysis into such components can be confirmed experimentally by seeing how independent the components are from each other. For example, if lever pressing no longer produces pellets, pressing decreases, but if a pellet is now delivered independently of pressing, it will still occasion movement to the food cup (Skinner, 1934). In other words, the integrity of one component of the sequence is not altered by changing the reinforcement contingencies for another component.

Analyses in terms of chaining were part of Skinner's early treatments of sequential behavior. Later, however, it became clear that some types of sequential behavior could not be reduced to chained sequences (Lashley, 1951). For example, when a skilled typist types *the,* these letters cannot be discriminative stimuli for the next stroke, first because the next stroke will be executed even before the typed letters on the page can have any stimulus effects, and second because the letters cannot be discriminative stimuli uniquely for each of the many possible continuations (e.g., *these, then, their,* or a space and a new word). But this did not imply that sequential behavior is never based on chaining or that sequential behavior always depends on temporally extended units of behavior that cannot be reduced to chains. Some sequences can be put together so that each response produces stimulus conditions that occasion the next one, whereas others must be integrated so that responses appear in the proper order without depending on the consequences of earlier responses. For any behavior sequence, the issue is the experimental one of deciding which type of a sequence it is.

Skinner recognized these problems, particularly in his analysis of verbal behavior (Skinner, 1957). In that work, the chaining of verbal behavior was recognized in a single verbal response class called the *intraverbal,* but other verbal

response classes were described, and temporally extended verbal responses were also recognized as coherent operant units in their own right. Later, sequential behavior that could not be interpreted in terms of chaining was demonstrated even in pigeons (Dews, 1962). Nevertheless, Skinner's treatment of verbal behavior has often been criticized as if chaining had been the only basis for the analysis of sequential verbal responses (e.g., Chomsky, 1959). The historical problem probably was that many researchers of that time felt that a choice had been forced between chained responding and sequential units integrated in other ways. Because they did not admit the possibility of including both types of sequences in a behavioral analysis, the discovery that chaining was included in Skinner's treatment of verbal behavior apparently provided sufficient grounds for the improper conclusion that other types of sequential behavior were excluded. But some sequences can be fractionated in ways that others cannot, and thus a behavioral account can recognize both chaining and temporal structure as alternative properties of sequential behavior.

8. *Operant analyses must consider both arbitrary and species-specific behavior relations.*

The nature of organisms is such that many responses automatically have particular consequences. For example, to see something below eye level, we look down rather than up. Organisms may learn these consequences of responding. Reinforcement describes but does not explain such learning. One task of an experimental analysis is to distinguish behavior maintained by the consequences of responding from behavior that has other sources (e.g., genetically determined behavior specific to a given species).

Consider the example of imprinting (e.g., Hess, 1973). A duckling, upon hatching, sees a moving stimulus (typically, the mother duck). Even on its first day outside of the egg, the duckling begins to follow this stimulus as it moves about. The stimulus is said to be imprinted. But the stimulus does not simply elicit the following response. The natural consequence of walking toward the stimulus is that it remains close; thus, the critical property of imprinting is that the imprinted stimulus has become a reinforcer. This can be demonstrated by changing the environment so that the imprinted stimulus depends on some response other than following. For example, if the duckling can light up a dark compartment containing an imprinted stimulus by pecking a key, and if the light goes out when the duckling follows the stimulus, the duckling will stand and peck rather than follow (Peterson, 1960).

Like the relation between the duckling's peck and the imprinted stimulus, the relation between the rat's lever press and the delivery of food pellets is arbitrary. Natural environments do not include levers connected to feeders. In fact, operant chambers were designed especially to create such arbitrary contingencies, on the assumption that an analysis of natural arrangements was more likely to be complicated by the organism's prior history of responding and by species-specific behavior patterns. Such limitations were recognized even with respect to the rat's lever press and the pigeon's key peck:

> Such responses are not wholly arbitrary. They are chosen because they can be easily executed, and because they can be repeated quickly and over long periods of time without fatigue. In such a bird

as the pigeon, pecking has a certain genetic unity; it is a characteristic bit of behavior which appears with a well-defined topography. (Ferster & Skinner, 1957, p. 7)

Given that the existence of genetic determinants of behavior was assumed in the specification of operant classes, it is ironic that the discovery of species-specific properties of lever pressing and of key pecking later became the basis for criticisms of operant theory. Apparently these responses were not arbitrary enough.

Autoshaping (Brown & Jenkins, 1968) is of particular interest because it was discovered in the context of operant research and therefore illustrates how operant theory can accommodate such findings. Autoshaping was at first introduced as a convenient alternative to shaping the key peck. In a standard pigeon chamber, the key is lit briefly, and then the feeder is operated independently of the pigeon's behavior. After a few presentations, the pigeon begins to face and then move toward the key whenever it lights. After some trials, perhaps as few as 10, the pigeon begins to peck the key whenever it is lit. The possibility that pecks were somehow maintained by their consequences was eliminated by the demonstration that pecking persisted even when pecks caused food presentations to be omitted (Williams & Williams, 1969); pecking stabilized at levels at which enough trials occurred without pecks (and therefore with food) to maintain pecking in the other trials.

Because eating also involves pecking, autoshaping can be regarded as a respondent conditioning procedure imposed on a skeletal response, and its theoretical implications therefore parallel those of the operant control of autonomic responses. The operant-respondent distinction was maintained with respect to procedures, but the correlation of these procedures with response classes defined physiologically had lost support. One task of an experimental analysis is therefore to determine the extent to which responding depends on its consequences. Control by environmental contingencies is not to be taken for granted; it must be demonstrated experimentally.

Experimental superstition provides another example. Skinner (1948a) had noted that a response accidentally followed by a reinforcer might increase even if the response had not produced the reinforcer. He examined this phenomenon by presenting response-independent food to a food-deprived pigeon at 15-second intervals. Responses that occurred just before one food delivery (e.g., head movements, patterns of pacing) were likely to be repeated and therefore to be followed closely by the next food delivery. Through such accidental successions of responses and reinforcers, stereotyped response patterns developed. These varied from pigeon to pigeon and gradually changed over time (topographical drift).

Superstition remains controversial. For example, other investigators noted that in such procedures pecking eventually dominates as the response that just precedes food deliveries (Staddon & Simmelhag, 1971). Thus, it was argued that some responses will be favored over others for species-specific reasons. In any case, although a given response is not likely to be maintained superstitiously for extended time periods, effects of such accidental correlations must be taken into account in operant research. It is usually difficult to determine whether responses are produced by such accidental contingencies or are generated more directly by the stimuli, but the greatest problem created by the phenomenon of supersti-

tion is that it is too easily invoked to explain behavior that has not been accounted for in other ways.

Skinner recognized the "natural lines of fracture along which behavior and environment actually break" (Skinner, 1935a, p. 40). "We divide behavior into hard and fast classes and are then surprised to find that the organism disregards the boundaries we have set" (Skinner, 1953, p. 94). Operant theory is not embarrassed by demonstrations that some responses are more easily established as operant classes than others, or that some discriminations can be established with some reinforcers but not others. Operant analyses assumed from the outset that boundary conditions on the effects of contingencies would have to be determined. Some responses, like the pigeon's key peck, turned out to have greater species-specific constraints than had at first been suspected, but the demonstration of these limits then became an experimental rather than a theoretical issue (Schwartz, 1974).

9. Behavior is a product of evolution.

The selection or survival of patterns of behavior in an organism's lifetime parallels the selection or survival of individuals in the evolution of a species (Skinner, 1966, 1977). Both involve some variation that provides the source materials on which evolution acts, and both involve some basis for selecting what survives. In each case, we must deal not with particular instances but rather with populations or classes of events. Populations of organisms are species, and behavioral populations are response classes such as operants, discriminated operants, and respondents.

Charles Darwin (1859) rejected the concept of immutable species in favor of classes defined by their descent or evolution rather than by their anatomy. Behavior analysis also uses the origins of behavior to define behavior classes. For example, we distinguish innate behavior from behavior that depends on experience; and we distinguish behavior produced by stimuli from behavior maintained by its consequences. Furthermore, even behavior generated by contingencies has an evolutionary basis; the capacity for behavior to be reinforced by some of its consequences must have been acquired through evolution. The evolutionary contribution to behavior is not restricted simply to the difference between operants and respondents; as we have seen, some aspects of that distinction have become obsolete. Instead, we may assume that behavior has been shaped by evolutionary contingencies as well as by the contingencies that exist in the contemporary environment (for example, patterns of migration may have been established gradually as major land masses slowly separated over geologic time: Skinner, 1975). Operant theory is defined more by the methods of behavior analysis, which allow the components of particular instances of behavior to be separated, than by any assumed priority of some behavioral processes over others.

RESEARCH

Methodologies

Throughout its history, the study of animal learning had used diverse puzzle-boxes, mazes, runways, and other apparatuses. Experimenters believed that the intelligence of different species could be compared in terms of how rapidly learning occurred in particular settings. The design of specialized apparatuses was often dictated by theoretical questions: whether learning occurred on a discrete all-or-none basis or instead occurred gradually and continuously; whether organisms learned movements (response learning) or the properties of their environments (stimulus learning); whether the consequences of responding led directly to learning, or only led the organism to demonstrate what it had learned in other ways.

Changes in responding were measured differently in different experiments, depending on apparatuses and experimental aims, but a common feature running through the varied experimental designs was that responses could be made more probable if they had certain consequences. Graphs that showed how responding changed during an experiment were called learning curves: time taken to respond as a function of trials; percentages of correct responses over successive trials; the proportion of organisms reaching some criterion of responding at different stages of an experiment. But the shapes of these curves depend so heavily on the apparatuses used and the measures taken that the progress of learning could not be described in a consistent way.

One problem was the complicated performances studied in those learning experiments. For example, recording the trials it took a rat to stop entering a particular blind alley as it learned its way through a maze was not necessarily relevant to how learning proceeded at a single choice point of the maze. In addition, the average performance of a group of organisms did not necessarily represent the performance of individuals within the group. For such reasons, the complex mazes of early studies were gradually simplified, until what remained was the single choice point in a T-maze or no choice point at all in a straight alley. But these simplifications were only partial solutions.

Performance could still be affected by such irrelevant factors as the direction the animal was facing when a trial began, odor trials left by other animals, the way the animal was handled by the experimenter when it was returned between trials from the goalbox to the startbox of the apparatus, and even the room available in the goalbox for the animal to slow down without banging its head against the wall.

Skinner (1930, 1938, 1950, 1956) developed two experimental innovations that contributed to the solution of these problems and provided the foundations for the subsequent development of operant theory. These innovations were in part inspired by an interest in reducing the handling of the organism and thereby making the experimenter's work easier. But they also produced data with substantial implications for the analysis of behavior.

The first innovation was the design of an apparatus in which the organism could repeatedly emit an easily specified response. The behavior was called *free-operant responding: free* in the sense that the organism's behavior was not arbitrarily limited to discrete trials as in mazes and runways, and *operant* in the sense that the major interest was in how responses operated on the environment. The apparatus has often been referred to as the *Skinner box,* but this appellation has become uncommon in the recent literature of behavior analysis. Instead, the apparatus is usually called an *experimental chamber* or an *experimental space,* or it is named for the organism for which it is designed (e.g., rat chamber, pigeon chamber). Rats and pigeons have been the most common laboratory organisms in the analysis of operant behavior. Their diet, housing, and susceptibility to disease are reasonably well un-

Figure 5.1

Skinner Box

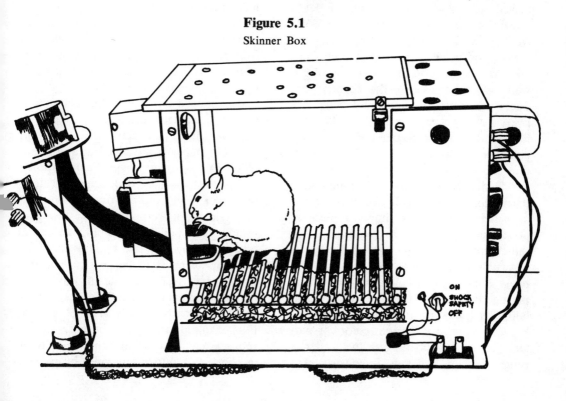

derstood, and their small size, economy, and relatively long life span make them particularly convenient.

The typical chamber includes one or more response devices, mechanisms for delivering reinforcers such as food or water, and stimulus sources such as lamps and loudspeakers. The chamber is remotely controlled by equipment that automatically arranges relations between responses and consequences, presents stimuli, and records behavior. With experiments that require precise temporal specification of the relations between responses and consequences and that generate thousands of responses from individual organisms within single sessions, automation is essential. The relays, counters, timers, and other electromechanical devices that once controlled events in the typical operant laboratory are gradually being superseded by computer control.

In a typical arrangement, a food-deprived rat is placed in a chamber. A lever that the rat can press protrudes from one wall. Near the lever is a food cup into which food pellets can be dispensed from a delivery system on the other side of the wall. Operating the pellet feeder produces a distinctive sound, and pellet deliveries may be accompanied by the brief illumination of the feeder cup. A pigeon chamber differs from a rat chamber in that a key is substituted for the lever and the feeder is designed to accommodate the pigeon's standard diet of mixed grain or pellets. The key is simply a piece of plastic mounted behind a round hole in the chamber wall. One part of the key is a switch that records the pigeon's key pecks if they are of sufficient force. The plastic is usually translucent, so that lamps or miniature projectors behind the key can be used to present colors or patterns on it. The opening to the feeder is centered below the key. It consists of a tray that comes up within the pigeon's reach whenever it is operated. Like the delivery of the rat's pellet, operation of the pigeon feeder produces characteristic sounds, and the feeder is usually lit when operated.

Particular chambers might include a single response device or several response devices in any of a variety of configurations. For example, a pigeon chamber for the study of the interaction of two responses might include two keys placed next to each other on the chamber wall. Typical chambers usually also include other features, such as houselights that provide dim general illumination, a small window for visual observation by the experimenter, sources of noise to mask sound from outside the chamber, provisions for ventilation and temperature control, and so on.

Skinner's second major innovation was the direct measurement of the behavior of individual organisms, in terms of the rate or frequency of responding, rather than indirect measures or measures derived from the behavior of groups of organisms. A derivative of this type of measurement was the *cumulative recorder,* a device that produced a detailed and continuous record of changes in the rate of responding over time. In a cumulative recorder, a roll of paper is advanced at a constant speed past a response pen. Each response moves the pen a fixed distance up along the paper. Thus, the pen draws a line that rises slowly if responding is slow and rapidly if responding is rapid. If there is no responding, the line remains flat. The slope or steepness of the line is then proportional to response rate. More important, momentary changes in responding show up clearly in this type of record. For example, the same number of responses may be emitted either steadily or in short, fast bursts separated by pauses.

The first performance produces a smooth record, whereas the second produces a steplike record in which the rising portions show responding and the flat portions show the pauses. Cumulative records therefore make easily visible the detailed changes in responding that occur from moment to moment over extended experimental sessions.

A distinctive feature of the research that grew out of these methodological innovations was its emphasis on the behavior of the individual organism. Large groups were unnecessary with procedures that generated large and reliable effects, and experiments were often conducted with only three or four organisms. The results of one experiment were then confirmed in later research that extended the original findings. Thus, these experimental analyses were cumulative, in the sense that successive procedures depended on what had gone before. Judgments of reliability were therefore based on consistencies in the performances of individual organisms over systematic replications rather than on statistical tests of significance. If an experiment produced variable results, the solution was sought not by increasing the number of organisms so that several performances could be averaged, but instead by refining the details of procedure to identify the sources of variability. The argument was that a science of behavior that did not apply to the behavior of individual organisms would necessarily be of limited value.

Animal Studies

Studying animal behavior in the laboratory is of particular interest when the outcome is not intuitively obvious. Consider a pigeon in a single-key chamber. The pigeon's pecks have already been shaped. The key is lit white, and the equipment is set so that every 200th peck operates the feeder. This point was reached gradually, first by letting every peck produce food, and then only every fifth peck, and then only every tenth, and so on until the pigeon was pecking 200 times per food delivery.

The requirement of 200 pecks per food delivery is called a *fixed-ratio reinforcement schedule: fixed* because the required number is constant from one reinforcer to the next, and *ratio* because the schedule specifies the ratio of pecks to reinforcers (200 to 1). We do not have to reinforce every peck to keep the pigeon pecking, and the schedule simply determines how we choose the peck that produces food.

Now the feeder has just stopped operating, and the pigeon stands before the white-lit key. Eventually, perhaps only 20 seconds or perhaps several minutes later, the pigeon approaches the key and begins to peck. Within a few pecks, it is pecking at more than five pecks per second, and it does not pause at all as it completes the 200 pecks. The last of these pecks operates the feeder, and the pigeon eats. After the food delivery, time again passes before the pigeon returns to the key and begins its next run of pecks. This is a typical fixed-ratio performance; a pause after reinforcement, followed by rapid and uninterrupted pecking that ends with the next reinforcement.

This is easy to get the pigeon to do. It earns enough food daily to keep itself alive and healthy for an indefinite time. We need not intervene except to provide water, clean the chamber and fill the feeder. Now let us help the pigeon to estimate how many pecks remain in the sequence by presenting different key colors, depending on the number of pecks. After each reinforcement, the key is blue until the pigeon has pecked 50 times. The fiftieth peck turns the key green. After

50 more pecks, the key turns yellow. Then, after 50 more, the key turns red. After 50 pecks with the key now red, the 200 pecks are completed and the last peck operates the feeder. The pigeon eats, and the key is again blue.

The number of pecks required for food remains the same; only the lights on the key have changed. But the surprising effect of adding these stimuli is that the pigeon slows down. The pauses after reinforcement, when the key is blue, become longer. When the key turns green, after 50 pecks, the pigeon may pause before starting the next 50-peck sequence. When the key had been always white, such an interruption of pecking had not occurred. In green, another 50 pecks and the key turns yellow. This time the pigeon is less likely to pause: Fifty more pecks turn the key red. The pigeon quickly emits the last 50 pecks, and food is delivered. But then the key is blue again, and another long pause begins.

The stimuli did not help. The pigeon takes longer between reinforcements than when the key had remained white. In fact, though the pigeon had formerly maintained an adequate daily ration, we would now be wise to watch it carefully to be sure its daily food intake does not decrease substantially. This came about not through changes in the responding required for food, but simply by changes in stimuli. Adding the colors broke down the sequence into four distinct units of 50 pecks each. We call these *chained fixed-ratio schedules;* the colors correspond to the links of the chain. But unlike shorter chains with heterogeneous segments (e.g., lever approach, lever press, feeder approach, ingestion), this chain does not hold together cohesively.

In red, pecking produced food. In blue, however, pecking never produced food. At best, it turned the key green, but

pecking never produced food during this color either. With reduced pecking early in the chain, the time between food deliveries increased. In chained schedules, a stimulus supports less responding the further it is from the end of the sequence (Gollub, 1977). Even severe food deprivation may not counteract this effect. The particular order of colors does not matter as long as it remains constant from one food delivery to the next.

The pigeon's performance can be altered in other ways. For example, increasing the required pecks to 500 will also slow the pigeon down, creating long postreinforcement pauses and frequent interruptions of pecking. This effect is called *ratio strain*. We could also ask about the effects of varying the number of colors or the regularity with which they occur at different locations in the sequence. Our analysis would separate those variables that mattered from those that did not. But the point is that the outcome is not obvious. It arises out of an experimental analysis, and it occurs with other organisms besides the pigeon, with different kinds of responses and response requirements, and with different kinds and orderings of stimuli. Given its substantial generality, the phenomenon may be relevant to human behavior. So much of what we do involves sequential behavior that we may wonder whether we too sometimes operate under the strain of too many links in our chains.

In this example, responding was attenuated by an arrangement of stimuli. But other arrangements can greatly amplify the responding maintained by reinforcers. For example, a chimpanzee's push-button presses were maintained by food pellets according to a fixed-ratio schedule of 4,000 responses (Findley & Brady, 1965). With no other consequences, postreinforcement pauses ranged from many minutes to hours. But when the feeder light that accompanied pellet deliveries was operated briefly after every 400 presses within the ratio, responding increased substantially, and postreinforcement pauses were typically five minutes or less. The effects of reinforcement schedules depend critically on the detailed relations among discriminative stimuli, responses, and consequences.

Reinforcement Schedules. The preceding examples showed that substantial quantities of behavior can be maintained even when only an occasional response produces a reinforcer. Relatively few classes of responses have consistent consequences. Winning is not an invariable consequence of placing a bet, and getting an answer is not an invariable consequence of asking a question. The reinforcement of every response within an operant class is the exception rather than the rule. Reinforcement schedules specify which responses within an operant class will be reinforced. Schedules can arrange reinforcement on the basis of response number, the time at which responses occur, or the rate of responding. Such number, time, and rate requirements can also be combined in diverse ways to produce more complex schedules.

The analysis of schedule effects has become a highly technical area. Unlike other areas of behavior analysis, reinforcement schedules did not even exist as a subject matter until relatively recent times (Ferster & Skinner, 1957). A shortage of food pellets developed one weekend in the mid–1930s during a long-term study of rats' lever pressing (Skinner, 1956). Because Skinner could not obtain the ingredients to make additional pellets, he conserved his supply by delivering pellets for lever presses only at one-minute intervals. The rats did not stop pressing. In later sessions, characteristic performances

emerged, and Skinner began to examine other arrangements, such as reinforcement after a fixed number of responses.

We considered some properties of *fixed-ratio* or FR schedules in earlier examples. The last of a fixed number of responses is reinforced, and performance usually consists of a postreinforcement pause followed by a high and relatively constant rate of responding. A relative of this schedule is the *variable-ratio* or VR schedule, in which the number of responses varies from one reinforcer to the next. Individual ratios may range from a single response to several times the average value. Like the fixed-ratio schedule, the variable-ratio schedule maintains high rates of responding, but because a single response is occasionally reinforced immediately after a preceding reinforcement, this schedule tends not to produce postreinforcement pauses. In both fixed-ratio and variable-ratio schedules, extinction usually consists of abrupt changes from high-rate responding to no responding; gradual changes in rate tend not to be produced by these schedules.

An example of behavior maintained by variable-ratio reinforcement is playing a slot machine. Some proportion of plays will produce the presumably reinforcing jackpot; the player may win twice in a row, but more often many plays occur in succession without a win. The persistence of variable-ratio responding may depend on what other reinforced responses are concurrently available; thus, the properties of this schedule may be relevant to human gambling behavior.

In the *fixed-interval* or FI schedule, a response is reinforced only after some constant time has elapsed since some event; responses occurring before this time have no effect. An example is the response of looking at one's watch during a lecture period. The reinforcer is seeing that the time has arrived when one can leave the classroom. Looking at the watch more often does not make the watch run more rapidly. Fixed-interval performance usually consists of zero or low-rate responding early in the interval, followed by increasing rates later in the interval. We might similarly expect increases in looking at one's watch as the end of the lecture period approached.

The *variable-interval* or VI schedule also arranges that a response is reinforced after a specified time has elapsed, but in this case the time varies from one reinforcer to the next. Again, responses that occur before the scheduled time have no effect. An everyday example is telephoning a friend after having received a busy signal. Reaching the friend will depend on when we call and not on how many times we call. Some variable time will elapse that depends only on the duration of our friend's conversation with someone else; earlier calls will not affect how long the busy signal lasts.

Variable-interval schedules are designated by the average time between successive availabilities of the reinforcer. Because responses may be reinforced soon after as well as long after the last reinforcer, these schedules typically maintain intermediate and roughly constant response rates rather than gradually changing rates. In addition, as long as responding is above some minimal level, the rate at which reinforcers are delivered is determined by the average interreinforcement interval and thus is not appreciably affected by changes in response rate. For these reasons, variable-interval performance is especially useful as a baseline on which other procedures can be superimposed (e.g., drug administration). With both fixed-interval and variable-interval schedules, response rates tend to decrease gradually in extinction.

Another class of schedules is based on the spacing of responses in time. For example, a pigeon's key peck may be reinforced only if preceded by at least 10 seconds of no pecking. Because the reinforced unit of responding is a pause plus a peck, this *differential reinforcement of low rate* or DRL schedule maintains low rates of responding. These and related schedules (e.g., *differential reinforcement of high rate* or DRH schedules) imply that response rate cannot be taken as a simple measure of the effects of reinforcement, because they demonstrate that, like force and topography, response rate is a property of responding that can be differentially reinforced.

Schedules may be arranged in a variety of combinations. Discriminative control may be studied by alternating one schedule in the presence of one stimulus with a second schedule in the presence of another stimulus. Conditioned reinforcers may be studied by making the reinforcer for one schedule a stimulus in the presence of which a second schedule operates. Choice among different reinforcers may be studied by operating two schedules concurrently for two different responses. When two schedules operate concurrently, organisms tend to distribute responses to the schedules in proportion to the reinforcers arranged by each; this phenomenon has been proposed as a general law of behavior, called the *matching law* (Herrnstein, 1970). Thus, the analysis of schedules may be relevant to many long-standing issues in the psychology of learning.

Under some circumstances the effects of schedules seem to override other properties of stimuli, such as whether a stimulus is reinforcing or aversive (Morse & Kelleher, 1977). For example, consider a monkey in a restraining chair with shock electrodes attached to its tail. A 10-

minute fixed-interval schedule of shock presentation has been arranged for lever presses: At the end of successive 10-minute intervals, the next lever press produces a shock. Soon after it has been placed in the chair, the monkey begins to press the lever. Eventually 10 minutes pass, and the monkey's next press produces a shock. The monkey briefly jumps and squeals, and it does not press the lever for a while. Finally it begins lever pressing again, and responds more and more rapidly until it shocks itself once more at the end of the next 10-minute interval. This performance occurs repeatedly in subsequent daily sessions. When shock is discontinued, the monkey's lever pressing ceases; it returns when shock is reinstated. When shock level is raised, the monkey's lever pressing increases; it decreases when shock level is lowered.

The shocks depend completely on the monkey's behavior, and they seem to function as reinforcers rather than as punishers. Behavior like this can be generated in many ways and is easily maintained. Paradoxically, the same shock that maintains responding when delivered according to this fixed-interval schedule suppresses responding when delivered after every lever press. Whether shock is a reinforcer or a punisher seems to depend on its schedule of presentation. (It would not explain anything to call the monkey a masochist; masochism is only a name we apply when a stimulus we believe should be a punisher serves as a reinforcer.)

Shock delivered independently of behavior can elicit manual responses such as lever pressing in monkeys (Hutchinson, Renfrew, & Young, 1971). Perhaps the eliciting effects of shock are so powerful that they override the punishing effects, so that lever presses occur in spite of and not because of the punishment contingency. Some effects of response-produced stimuli may have relatively little to do with whether the organism brought on the stimuli itself (in an analogous human example, the parent who tries to stop a child from crying by punishing the crying with spanking may have trouble because the spanking may elicit the very response the parent is trying to suppress). But the maintenance of the monkey's lever pressing by shock has not been resolved by comparisons of the eliciting and punishing effects of shock. The situation is more complicated, and these performances remain controversial. In fact, such studies would not be defensible if the issues could be resolved so easily and superficially. We cannot yet fully appreciate the implications of these phenomena, but as long as human behavior also includes problems of self-injury and self-abuse, our concern with them is justified.

Multiple Functions. The preceding example not only demonstrates the broad scope of research on schedules but also illustrates the point that stimuli and responses do not ordinarily have single functions. A stimulus that reinforces one response may be in a discriminative relation with another and may elicit a third. The task of an experimental analysis is to disentangle such relations. To analyze something is simply to break it down into its component parts. In the next example, the multiple functions of stimuli are further illustrated by showing how electric shock, ordinarily a punisher, can take on a discriminative function.

In one of two alternating conditions, a pigeon's pecks had no consequences; in the other, every peck produced shock and some pecks produced food (Holz & Azrin, 1961). In the first condition, pecking became relatively infrequent: Pecks that produced no shock produced no food either. But in the second condition, pecking increased: Once pecks began to produce shock, that was the condition under which they also occasionally produced food. This higher rate when pecks produced shock than when they did not persisted for some time, even after food was completely discontinued. An observer who did not know about the prior correlation of shock with food might be puzzled by this outcome. The shock had acquired a discriminative function; shock but not its absence was the occasion for food-reinforced pecking.

Similar relations among reinforcing, discriminative, and punishing effects may be relevant to human behavior. For example, a battered child might provoke a parent to the point of a beating because more attention from the then-remorseful parent follows the beating than ever follows more peaceful parent-child interactions. A parent's attention can be a potent reinforcer and may override consequences that would otherwise be effective punishers.

The analysis of multiple functions must take into account the organism's past history as well as current conditions. For example, assume a rat's baseline lever pressing is maintained by an interval schedule of food reinforcement. If a two-minute tone followed by a brief electric shock is superimposed on this performance, level pressing decreases during the tone. The phenomenon has been called *anxiety* or *conditioned suppression* (Estes & Skinner, 1941). The superimposed stimuli involve a respondent-conditioning procedure: One stimulus, the tone, signals another stimulus, the shock.

This procedure affects many other classes of responses besides lever pressing (e.g., respiration, heart rate). We are likely to invoke the language of emotion when an event has widespread effects across several response classes, and we may be tempted to speak of the rat's fear or anxiety. But it would not do to say that the rat stopped pressing the lever because it was afraid; the effect of the tone on the rat's lever pressing is what led us to speak of the rat's fear in the first place.

The preaversive stimulus, the tone, may be superimposed on other baselines of responding besides food-reinforced lever pressing. If it is superimposed on lever pressing that avoids shock, lever pressing increases rather than decreases during the tone. Furthermore, once the organism has a history of such avoidance responding, increased responding during the preaversive stimulus continues even after a return to a baseline schedule of food reinforcement (Herrnstein & Sidman, 1958). In this instance, an account of responding requires the consideration of several factors, including the current schedule, the superimposed stimuli, and the organism's previous experimental history. Identifying the multiple factors that act on behavior and the multiple functions that stimuli and responses can enter into is an essential component of an experimental analysis of behavior.

Human Studies

Research on the applications of operant theory to human behavior has demonstrated the generality of behavior principles established in the laboratory. The distinction between applied and basic research is therefore usually arbitrary. Nevertheless, many studies of human behavior have been concerned not so much with applications as with determining which properties of human behavior are unique to us and which can be understood in terms of capacities we hold in common with other organisms.

Some experiments have explored the

kinds of responses that can be shaped with humans. One example involved the differential reinforcement of an invisibly small thumb twitch, measured in microvolts of muscle contraction (Hefferline & Keenan, 1963). The reinforcer was the addition to a visual display of counts, each worth a nickel. During unreinforced baseline responding, thumb twitches in the 25 to 30 mv range were infrequent. During reinforcement, responding within this range increased; in extinction, responding returned toward baseline levels. Although the procedure affected behavior, none of the participants was able to report on the thumb twitching or on what had produced the reinforcers. Thus, this experiment has often been cited as a demonstration that the effects of reinforcers do not depend on awareness of the reinforced response or the reinforcement contingency.

Other experiments have examined the role of reinforcement in verbal behavior. For example, verbal responses such as "yes" or "uh-huh" have been used to reinforce particular classes of verbal responses (e.g., plural nouns) or the substantive content of a conversation (Azrin, Holz, Ulrich, & Goldiamond, 1961; Greenspoon, 1955). Some of these experiments have been controversial, but it does not require a laboratory experiment to demonstrate that a listener's response can maintain a speaker's verbal behavior. We tend to stop speaking to people who do not react to what we say. Varied consequences (e.g., an answer to a question, a change in facial expression) can affect verbal behavior, and what keeps a speaker talking may differ from what determines what the speaker says. This is sufficient evidence that the descriptive language of reinforcement is appropriate to verbal behavior. Although reinforcement may contribute to language learning, this does not imply that language is learned solely through reinforcement.

The control of human behavior by reinforcement schedules has been another area of special interest. Vigilance tasks such as monitoring a radar screen provided one context for such studies (Holland, 1958). An observer's button lights up the screen. According to various schedules, a signal is sometimes present and sometimes not. In this instance, the detection and reporting of a signal functions as a reinforcer: Different schedules of signal presentation produce their characteristic rates and patterns of button pressing. The high rate of observing maintained by variable-ratio schedules is of particular interest because the observer detects signals more reliably than one who simply sits in front of a continuously illuminated screen.

In other instances, however, human behavior has been insensitive to differences in reinforcement schedules. For example, when humans are simply told that their presses on a telegraph key will produce points on a counter later exchangeable for money, they tend to press the key at a high and invariant rate without regard to the schedule according to which presses produce points (Weiner, 1969). But the effects of schedules demonstrate that an organism is sensitive to the consequences of its own behavior. Thus, what was puzzling about these results was not that humans were different from pigeons or rats, but that they were inferior to these other organisms in this important respect. The effects of schedules are central to the concept of causality, because they show that it makes a difference whether reinforcers are produced by some number of responses or by a response at a particular time, or whether events are caused by behavior or are accidentally correlated with behavior.

The issue was resolved by the discovery that the insensitivity was produced by instructions (Matthews, Shimoff, Catania, & Sagvolden, 1977). If presses on a telegraph key are reinforced by counts later exchangeable for money, humans whose responding is established without instructions press the key at rates appropriate to the current reinforcement schedule. This showed that humans are sensitive to the consequences of their own behavior after all, but, more important, it illustrated an important property of verbal instructions: Responding generated by instructions is insensitive to its consequences.

Skinner (1969) has distinguished between *contingency-governed behavior,* maintained by its consequences, and *rule-governed behavior,* established by verbal instruction. Following instructions is doing what one is told to do rather than doing what is determined by current contingencies. We ordinarily give instructions when the natural consequences of behavior are not likely to be effective by themselves. A major achievement of human verbal behavior is that it allows behavior to be controlled by descriptions of contingencies, in verbal instructions, rather than by the contingencies themselves. Thus, instructions may be useful in rapidly establishing new behavior, but the insensitivity of instructed behavior to its natural consequences may also create problems. For example, should a behavior therapist tell a client what to do, thereby running the risk that the behavior will not easily adapt to changing circumstances, or should the behavior be established in other but more time-consuming ways? Determining the properties of instructional control is therefore an important aspect of the analysis of human verbal behavior.

An interesting direction for human operant research is the analysis of private events (Skinner, 1953, 1969). A private event is accessible only to the person behaving, but our language of private events must be based at some point on what is accessible to the verbal community, else how could it ever have been learned? Attending and imagining and thinking are not movements, but regarding them as kinds of behavior suggests ways in which we may obtain some experimental access to them. For example, treating imagery as a kind of responding as opposed to something that an observer either has or does not have raises the possibility that visualizing can be taught. An artist presumably learns some of this behavior in progressing from sketching from a live model to sketching from memory without a model. Shaping of visualization might proceed by gradually dimming a scene as an observer describes it or copies it, and by gradually increasing the time between the presentation of the scene and the observer's description. Systematic studies of such phenomena are already feasible and are stimulating prospects for future analyses of human behavior.

IMPLICATIONS

Theoretical

To say that behavior is orderly is simply to say that it can be understood. If human actions were capricious, we could hardly expect to discover general principles in terms of which they could be interpreted. Yet the assumption that our actions are caused or determined or predictable has far-reaching implications for traditional concepts, such as those of freedom and responsibility (Skinner, 1971). To the extent that we look to the environment for causes of behavior, we are that much less likely to hold individuals responsible for their actions. We value freedom, but freedom seems inconsistent with a scientific view of behavior.

The principle of indeterminacy in physics does not resolve the problem. It states that our ability to measure is limited to a known degree by the techniques of measurement themselves. Similarly, the measurement and manipulation of behavior is limited, at least in part because those who measure or manipulate behavior are themselves behaving organisms.

We say we are free when we can make choices. We choose to work or play, to spend time with one person or another, to accept things as they are or try to change them. In each case, the potential consequences of engaging in one alternative or the other influence what we choose. These potential consequences enter into our decisions through our own experience with earlier choices and through what we have learned from the choices of others. We could hardly conceive of a responsible decision in the absence of determining conditions that distinguish responsible from irresponsible actions, and we would probably be unimpressed by a concept of freedom that was limited only to situations in which we were indifferent to the possible outcomes of our choices. Trying to escape from this kind of determinism, as by basing choices on the flip of a coin, does not gain freedom; instead it relinquishes it, allowing consequences to come about by accident rather than by design.

Part of the problem results from confusing two concepts of freedom. The issue of freedom versus determinism is a philosophical question with a long history, but the issue of freedom from coercion is an empirical problem that involves the consequences of various social and political practices. In our daily lives, we are typically concerned not so much

with whether our choices are determined as with how our choices are determined, and by whom. For example, one student may enroll in a course because of its subject matter and another because the course is required; the choice to enroll may be as predictable in one case as in the other, but we would speak only of the former choice as free rather than forced.

Once freedom is defined in terms of the availability of choices, it becomes possible to examine it experimentally. If an organism is said to be free only when choices are available, it can further be said to value freedom only if it prefers the availability of choices to their unavailability. For example, Voss and Homzie (1970) studied food-deprived rats' preferences for two paths leading to food. One path consisted of a single predetermined route; the other allowed the rat to choose between two subpaths. Of 15 rats studied, 14 preferred the path that allowed a choice of subpaths. Analogous preferences have also been demonstrated with pigeons (Catania, 1975).

Whether this preference has phylogenic origins or is somehow acquired during an individual organism's lifetime, it is evident that the concept of freedom has a place in the analysis of behavior; and if a preference for freedom turns out to be part of the phylogenic endowment even of the rat and the pigeon, corresponding human preferences take on a special significance. They need not be attributed merely to the practices of particular human cultures. At this point, behavior analysis may make contact with biological approaches, because it is plausible to assume that organisms with a preference for free choices over forced choices have had an evolutionary advantage over those that did not.

This treatment of the implications of a behavior analysis for the concept of freedom illustrates how such an analysis may be extended to significant human issues. Such approaches often proceed by using an animal experiment to demonstrate some properties of complex human behavior. But the point of producing the animal analogue is not to show what animals can do, or to suggest that there are no important differences between experimental settings and everyday human situations. Instead, the relatively simple animal situation is used to clarify the variables that enter into the more complex human setting. An example is provided by the experimental analysis of self-control (Rachlin & Green, 1972).

Consider a food-deprived pigeon confronted with two keys. The keys can be made available by lighting them, because they only operate when lit. Left-key pecks produce immediate access to food for two seconds; right-key pecks produce access to food for four seconds, but only after a four-second delay. In this situation, pigeons almost invariably peck the left key, producing the immediate two seconds of food rather than the delayed four seconds of food. We may be tempted to say that the pigeon cannot wait, is impatient, or has little self-control. It reliably chooses the immediate small reinforcer over the delayed large one. But now let us make one more response available to the pigeon. Ten seconds before the pigeon has an opportunity to choose between the left key and the right key, we briefly present a third key. If the pigeon pecks that key, then the later left-key presentation is canceled and the right key is presented alone. The pigeon has no choice but to peck the right key, and thus receives the delayed four seconds of food. Under these circumstances, the pigeon comes to peck the third key when it is available, thereby eliminating the left key from its later options.

The pigeon's performance can be analyzed quantitatively in terms of the different delays to the two-second and four-second reinforcers at different times in the procedure. For the present purposes, however, the point is that the pigeon's pecking of the third key can be called a *commitment response*. By pecking this key, the pigeon commits itself to the later delayed but larger reinforcer; at the time of choice, this commitment cannot be overwhelmed by the immediacy of the smaller reinforcer.

Humans too make commitments. For example, putting money in the bank is a way to make cash unavailable for impulse buying (credit cards have reduced the effectiveness of this type of commitment). But an important feature of the experimental analogue is that it makes evident the behavioral dimensions of self-control: Commitment is a kind of response. In humans, commitments do not operate switches; they take a variety of forms, such as spoken promises, written pledges, and even private resolutions. Furthermore, only some kinds of human commitments work by making an option unavailable at a later time of choice. Nevertheless, viewing commitment as a response opens the way to studying its properties. Its topography is less important than the stimulus conditions that occasion it and the consequences it produces. We may come to speak of self-control in terms of detailed relations among discriminative stimuli, responses, and consequences rather than in terms of a generalized trait that someone does or does not possess.

These examples, freedom and self-control, illustrate two important features of operant theory. The first is that of identifying essential properties of behavior, in the functions of stimuli and responses. The second is that of creating an effective behavioral language. In both its vocabulary and its grammar, such a language must allow behavioral phenomena to be coherently described. Among the useful aspects of the contemporary language of operant theory are the distinction between emission and elicitation of responses, the extension of this vocabulary to discriminative control in the usage of responding occasioned by stimuli, and the grammatical constraint on reinforcing or punishing responses rather than organisms. Yet even some of the elementary terms of this language may be troublesome, as when the historical usage of responding as being a response *to* something (i.e., a stimulus) makes it difficult for a student to adopt the usage of responding as emitted. Thus, this behavioral language will undoubtedly evolve in parallel with progress in experimental analyses.

A behavioral language may be particularly effective in extensions to verbal behavior (Skinner, 1957). Speaking and writing are kinds of behavior, but our everyday vocabulary creates difficulties for a behavioral account. For example, we speak of using words. Yet this vocabulary not only fails to distinguish spoken from written verbal behavior but also treats words as manipulable things rather than as kinds of responses. The different circumstances that occasion different words provide a basis for classifying types of verbal behavior. Yet we do not ordinarily say that particular events may occasion particular sentences. Instead, we turn things around by saying that sentences refer to events or are about events. Although such usage is relevant to the effect of verbal behavior on a listener or a reader, it complicates the description of the behavior of a speaker or a writer.

Language. An extended account of the behavioral analysis of language is beyond the scope of the present treatment. Yet it is important to note that such an account is more concerned with the functions of verbal behavior than with its structure. Studies of language in contemporary cognitive psychology and psycholinguistics emphasize grammatical and phonological properties of words and sentences. These are aspects of language structure. But distinctions made on the basis of the various circumstances under which a sentence can occur are distinctions of function. A functional account of verbal behavior is an account based on how verbal responses work: The account attempts to specify the conditions under which they occur and the consequences they may have. For example, we may deal with novel verbal utterances by showing how the various components of a sentence (particular words, phrases, and grammatical structures) have each been occasioned by particular aspects of a current situation. In other words, novelty comes about through novel combinations of existing verbal classes.

We do not have to choose between structural and functional accounts of language, because the two types of accounts complement each other. Unfortunately, verbal behavior has been a controversial topic in the history of psychology (Catania, 1972; Chomsky, 1959; MacCorquodale, 1970; Skinner, 1957), and structural and functional accounts have often been pitted against each other as if they were incompatible instead of complementary (Catania, 1973b, 1978). Some of the controversy has been based on misunderstandings. For example, Skinner's *Verbal Behavior* (1957) has often been treated as if Skinner derived all language from the stimulus-response associations of other varieties of behaviorism. Yet chaining plays a part in Skinner's analysis only in the special class of verbal responses called *intraverbals;* the very fact that such relations were discussed as a specific class of verbal responses indicates that other processes besides the chaining of verbal units were included in the analysis. Important progress in our understanding of language may be waiting upon the integration of the structural analyses of contemporary psycholinguistics and the functional analyses of a behavioral account.

Practical

That human behavior is determined or at least predictable is not, of course, an empirical fact to be confirmed or disproved. It is an assumption with which a scientific account typically proceeds. It does not imply that we should be able to influence or even to interpret every instance of behavior. There are limits to what we can know. It is tempting to ask a psychologist to explain why someone behaved in a particular way, what led up to a particular incident, or how someone came to have particular interests or fears or attachments. But often the psychologist has so little information available that only a plausible interpretation can be provided. The situation, however, is not different from that in other sciences. Just as the principles of aerodynamics are not invalidated if we cannot account for every twist and turn in the path of a falling leaf, the principles of behavior are not invalidated if we cannot account for every detail of an organism's performance on a particular occasion.

Nevertheless, operant theory has provided many applications of its principles to practical human situations. Predicting and controlling human behavior in such settings is a severe test of the adequacy of behavioral principles. An applied behavior analysis begins with the identification of some behavioral problem. For example, some individuals slow down or discontinue their eating to a point at which their inadequate nutrition becomes life-threatening; such individuals are said to be *anorexic*. Anorexics often become institutionalized, and one solution is forced feeding. But techniques for the preferable solution of reestablishing appropriate eating behavior are now available (Bachrach, Erwin, & Mohr, 1965).

Once the behavior to be created or eliminated has been identified, the next step is to determine what consequences might be effective in producing the appropriate change. In the case of the anorexic, the usual consequences of ingesting food have for some reason become inadequate to maintain eating. The kinds of behavior that the individual engages in, however, are likely to indicate what other events might be effective reinforcers. For example, if an anorexic spends substantial periods of time watching television, the availability of a television set might be made contingent on eating. Often, intangible events such as smiles and other simple social interactions between the ward staff and the patient will serve as potent consequences with which to alter behavior.

But in a profound anorexic it may not be sufficient merely to make television watching or other reinforcers depend on eating. If eating does not occur, it cannot be reinforced, and simply telling the anorexic about this arrangement is not likely by itself to be effective. A treatment program must be established with which to shape the appropriate behavior. If the anorexic is ordinarily fed by an attendant, the treatment program might begin with minimal contingencies, such as turning on the television set after a few bites of the meal have been taken. Gradually, perhaps over a period of weeks, television viewing along with other reinforcing consequences may be made to depend on the anorexic's holding the eating utensils, picking up food with them, and eventually ingesting the food.

Even after the anorexic has made the transition from being fed to eating without assistance, the problem is not completely solved. It is important next to establish discriminative control by stimuli correlated with mealtimes, so that meals will not be missed; and if appropriate behavior is to continue after the individual leaves the institution, then a home environment must be arranged that will maintain the behavior that has been established. Thus, the applied methodology includes such components as the specification of a target change in behavior, the identification of important reinforcers, the establishment of stimulus control, and the design of an environment that will maintain behavior once it is established.

Throughout the stages of an applied behavior analysis, behavior must be recorded to document the changes that have occurred, and the design of the procedure must as far as possible allow the behavior analyst to determine which variables have been effective in producing these changes. An application will be of limited value if its important features cannot be communicated to others. But not only is the applied setting more difficult to control than the laboratory; the interests of experimental design must often yield to the interests of the person whose behavior has been changed. For example, if reinforcement has been used to toilet train a retarded child, it would be inappropriate to extinguish this behavior simply to prove that it had occurred because of reinforcement rather than for some other reasons. Such considerations have influenced some aspects of the methodology of applied behavior analysis, but as a result of the similar emphasis on the behavior of the individual, it continues to have much in common with the basic research methods of operant theory.

Other applications that might have been considered here include programmed instruction, the management of elementary school classrooms, the education of retarded children, and the modification of pathological behavior. Such applications range from the shaping of skills in an individual to the organization of systems of contingencies and reinforcers for groups of individuals (e.g., token economies: Ayllon & Azrin, 1968). Perhaps the effectiveness of its applications is an important basis for concern about behavior analysis. For example, some early applications to elementary school classrooms emphasized procedures to keep order in class (e.g., reinforcement of in-seat behavior). Although such procedures were often convenient for the teacher, it was not always clear that students benefited; teaching did not necessarily become more effective (Winett & Winkler, 1972). Who decides on what behavior is to be changed may be an ethical or a legal issue. It is therefore reassuring that the methods of behavior analysis are public and that ethical questions are now explicitly considered in decisions about behavioral interventions in educational and clinical settings. We must guard against the abuse of behavioral technology while seeking its maximum benefit.

SUMMARY

In this treatment of operant theory, we have examined some of its history, its basic concepts, and its controversies. But in such a brief compass we have necessarily omitted its most important feature:

the direct contact with behavior. As recognized in the distinction between contingency-governed and rule-governed behavior, there is no simple verbal substitute for the opportunity to shape a pigeon's key peck or to watch the effects of changing the parameters of a reinforcement schedule.

> In one moment, psychology became converted, for these students, from something read about passively to a practical and powerful activity that influenced large magnitudes of behavior instantly and in orderly ways. For these students, the result of the experiment was more important than what could be said about it. Although a certain level of inarticulateness has been, at times, a badge of honor for those for whom the study of psychology was inseparable from the functional control of the behavior of the individual animal, the real concern was deeper, in the basic motives for working. . . . Perhaps one of the salient features of the work reported in *The Behavior of Organisms* and *Schedules of Reinforcement* was the use of the cumulative record to depict the course of events continuously in time and therefore simulate, for the reader, the direct experience that the experimenter had when the experiment was done. . . . For some, there is a magical sense of playful achievement when a procedure is converted to orderly behavioral control. (Ferster, 1978, p. 348)

We began with a statement about the sufficiency of behavior as a subject matter in its own right. It is appropriate to close with a recapitulation of that point. In an article called "Are Theories of Learning Necessary?" Skinner (1950) contrasted behavioral theories of learning with those that appealed to nonbehavioral dimensions or systems. His conclusion was to reject not theories in general, but only certain types of theories:

> Perhaps to do without theories altogether is a *tour de force* that is too much to expect as a general practice. Theories are fun. But it is possible that the most rapid progress toward an understanding of learning may be made by research that is not designed to test theories. . . . This does not exclude the possibility of theory in another sense. Beyond the collection of uniform relationships lies the need for a formal representation of the data reduced to a minimal number of terms. A theoretical construction may yield greater generality than any assemblage of facts. But such a construction will not refer to another dimensional system and will not, therefore, fall within our present definition. It will not stand in the way of our search for functional relations because it will arise only after relevant variables have been found and studied. Though it may be difficult to understand, it will not be easily misunderstood, and it will have none of the objectionable effects of the theories here considered. (Skinner, 1950, pp. 215–216)

We seem to be ready for theory in this sense.

ANNOTATED BIBLIOGRAPHY

Catania, A. C. (Ed.). *Contemporary research in operant behavior.* Glenview, Ill.: Scott, Foresman, 1968.

This collection of 60 theoretical and experimental articles contains many important contributions to operant theory, ranging from early work by Skinner through pivotal experiments on reinforcement schedules, stimulus control, and operant-respondent interactions. Background for each article is provided by introductory commentary, and a detailed glossary defines and discusses the terminology of operant theory.

Keller, F. S. *Summers and sabbaticals.* Champaign, Ill.: Research Press, 1977.

Subtitled *Selected Papers on Psychology and Education*, this collection of Keller's works ranges from a reminiscence of his graduate student days at Harvard to his recent views on the applications of psychology to instruction. His articles also treat the early development of reinforcement theory, experiments on human learning, an undergraduate psychology curriculum based on operant theory, and the Personalized System of Instruction.

Mackenzie, B. D. *Behaviourism and the limits of scientific method.* Atlantic Highlands, N.J.: Humanities Press, 1977.

This book examines the origins of behaviorism in 19th-century comparative psychology, its later methodological codification in interaction with developments in other sciences and in philosophy, and the current status of the varieties of behaviorism that evolved from Watson's system. Because the account is knowledgeable, well-reasoned, and both sympathetic and highly critical, it is essential reading for those interested in the intellectual (as opposed to experimental) history of behaviorism. It effectively presents arguments against which those who have some commitment to a behavioral position can test their commitment.

Sidman, M. *Tactics of scientific research.* New York: Basic Books, 1960.

An introduction to the research methods of behavior analysis, this book considers problems of data collection and interpretation, advantages and limitations of standard apparatuses, and the distinctive features of experiments designed to study the behavior of an individual organism rather than the behavior of a group. It provides a rich selection of examples from actual experiments to illustrate its points, and it is notable for dealing with these issues concretely, in terms of the psychologist's day-to-day activities in the laboratory rather than an abstracted scientific method. This treatment is consistent with the view that an adequate philosophy of science must be derived from the behavior of scientists, not vice versa.

Skinner, B. F. *The behavior of organisms.* New York: Appleton-Century-Crofts, 1938.

This is Skinner's classic work. Much of the research from his earlier publications as well as many new experiments are presented in the context of a systematic behavioral account. So many of these phenomena have been absorbed into the con-

temporary psychology of learning (e.g., the first records of extinction of an instrumental response) that the present-day reader may have difficulty appreciating how novel these findings were in their time. Although much of the detail of operant theory has since changed, the many anticipations here of later developments in behavior analysis testify to the richness and scope of Skinner's account.

Skinner, B. F. *Science and human behavior.* New York: Macmillan, 1953.

This is intended as an undergraduate text in the analysis of behavior. The parts likely to be of greatest interest to the contemporary reader are not those that examine basic concepts in operant theory but rather the chapters that extend those concepts to important aspects of human behavior. A section on the individual considers thinking, private events, the self, and self-control; later sections discuss social processes and the behavioral features of such cultural institutions as governments and religions.

Skinner, B. F. *Verbal behavior.* New York: Appleton-Century-Crofts, 1957.

Regarded by some as Skinner's most important book, this is probably also the one that has been most often and most seriously misunderstood. More than two decades after its publication, it continues to be described erroneously as a stimulus-response theory of language or as a reinforcement theory of language learning. It is in fact neither of those. It is instead an exploration of a functional vocabulary for the description of language behavior.

Skinner, B. F. *Contingencies of reinforcement.* New York: Appleton-Century-Crofts, 1969.

For this selection of nine of his articles, Skinner has written a set of notes in which many of the issues in the original publications have been refined and elaborated. The articles cover a number of important topics. Of special interest are his treatment of species-specific behavior, in a paper that anticipated much of the subsequent interest in biological aspects of learning; his distinction between contingency-governed and rule-governed behavior, in the context of a behavioral analysis of problem-solving; and his discussion of the nature of private events, in his review of the major assumptions of radical behaviorism. (The articles do not overlap with those in *Cumulative Record*.)

Skinner, B. F. *Cumulative record* (3rd ed.). New York: Appleton-Century-Crofts, 1972.

If one had to choose only a single book from which to learn Skinner's work, this collection of 48 of his articles would have to be it. To say why it is worth reading, little more is necessary than to list some of the topics covered: scientific methods, ESP, ethics, Pavlov, poetry and creativity, teaching machines, Watson, the design of cultures, Ping-Pong playing pigeons, the Aircrib. The variety of topics puts to rest the assumption that the behavioral point of view is necessarily narrow and intellectually confining. Included are many of Skinner's most important theoretical and experimental articles, ranging from his historical treatment of the concept of reflex to various studies of animal learning and of human verbal behavior.

REFERENCES

Ayllon, T., & Azrin, N. H. *The token economy: A motivational system for therapy and rehabilitation.* New York: Appleton-Century-Crofts, 1968.

Azrin, N. H. Some effects of two intermittent schedules of immediate and nonimmediate punishment. *Journal of Psychology*, 1956, *42*, 3–21.

Azrin, N. H., Holz, W., Ulrich, R., & Goldiamond, I. The control of the content of conversation through reinforcement. *Journal of the Experimental Analysis of Behavior*, 1961, *4*, 25–30.

Bachrach, A. J., Erwin, W. J., & Mohr, J. P. The control of eating behavior in an anorexic by operant conditioning techniques. In L. P. Ullman & L. Krasner (Eds.), *Case studies in behavior modification.* New York: Holt, Rinehart & Winston, 1965.

Baer, D. M., Peterson, R. F., & Sherman,

J. A. The development of imitation by reinforcing behavioral similarity to a model. *Journal of the Experimental Analysis of Behavior*, 1967, *10*, 405–416.

Black, A. H., Osborne, B., & Ristow, W. C. A note on the operant conditioning of autonomic responses. In H. Davis & H. M. B. Hurwitz (Eds.), *Operant-Pavlovian interactions.* Hillsdale, N.J.: Lawrence Erlbaum Associates, 1977.

Brown, P. L., & Jenkins, H. M. Autoshaping of the pigeon's key peck. *Journal of the Experimental Analysis of Behavior*, 1968, *11*, 1–8.

Catania, A. C. Chomsky's formal analysis of natural languages: A behavioral translation. *Behaviorism*, 1972, *1*, 1–15.

Catania, A. C. The concept of the operant in the analysis of behavior. *Behaviorism*, 1973, *1*, 103–116. (a)

Catania, A. C. The psychologies of structure, function, and development. *American Psychologist*, 1973, *28*, 434–443. (b)

Catania, A. C. Freedom and knowledge: An experimental analysis of preference in pigeons. *Journal of the Experimental Analysis of Behavior*, 1975, *24*, 89–106.

Catania, A. C. The psychology of learning: Some lessons from the Darwinian revolution. *Annals of the New York Academy of Sciences*, 1978, *309*, 18–28.

Catania, A. C., & Brigham, T. A. (Eds.). *Handbook of applied behavior analysis: Social and instructional processes.* New York: Irvington, 1978.

Chomsky, N. Review of B. F. Skinner's *Verbal behavior. Language*, 1959, *35*, 26–58.

Collier, G., Hirsch, E., & Hamlin, P. E. The ecological determinants of reinforcement in the rat. *Physiology and Behavior*, 1972, *9*, 705–716.

Darwin, C. *On the origin of species.* London: John Murray, 1859.

Dews, P. B. The effect of multiple S^Δ periods on responding on a fixed-interval schedule. *Journal of the Experimental Analysis of Behavior*, 1962, *5*, 369–374.

Dews, P. B. Drugs in psychology. A commentary on Travis Thompson and Charles R. Schuster's *Behavior pharmacology. Journal of the Experimental Analysis of Behavior*, 1970, *13*, 395–406.

Estes, W. K. An experimental study of punishment. *Psychological Monographs,* 1944, *57,* No. 263.

Estes, W. K., Koch, S., MacCorquodale, K., Meehl, P. E., Mueller, C. G., Jr., Schoenfeld, W. N., & Verplanck, W. S. *Modern learning theory.* New York: Appleton-Century-Crofts, 1954.

Estes, W. K., & Skinner, B. F. Some quantitative properties of anxiety. *Journal of Experimental Psychology,* 1941, *29,* 390–400.

Falk, J. L. The origin and functions of adjunctive behavior. *Animal Learning and Behavior,* 1977, *5,* 325–335.

Ferster, C. B. Is operant conditioning getting bored with behavior? *Journal of the Experimental Analysis of Behavior,* 1978, *29,* 347–349.

Ferster, C. B., & Skinner, B. F. *Schedules of reinforcement.* New York: Appleton-Century-Crofts, 1957.

Findley, J. D., & Brady, J. V. Facilitation of large ratio performance by use of conditioned reinforcement. *Journal of the Experimental Analysis of Behavior,* 1965, *8,* 125–129.

Gollub, L. R. Conditioned reinforcement: Schedule effects. In W. K. Honig & J. E. R. Staddon (Eds.), *Handbook of operant behavior.* Englewood Cliffs, N.J.: Prentice-Hall, 1977.

Greenspoon, J. The reinforcing effect of two spoken sounds on the frequency of two responses. *American Journal of Psychology,* 1955, *68,* 409–416.

Hefferline, R. F., & Keenan, B. Amplitude-induction gradient of a smallscale (covert) operant. *Journal of the Experimental Analysis of Behavior,* 1963, *6,* 307–315.

Herrnstein, R. J. On the law of effect. *Journal of the Experimental Analysis of Behavior,* 1970, *13,* 243–266.

Herrnstein, R. J., & Sidman, M. Avoidance conditioning as a factor in the effects of unavoidable shocks on food-reinforced behavior. *Journal of Comparative and Physiological Psychology,* 1958, *51,* 380–385.

Hess, E. H. *Imprinting.* New York: Van Nostrand Reinhold, 1973.

Hoffman, H. S., & Ratner, A. M. A reinforcement model of imprinting: Implications for socialization in monkeys and men. *Psychological Review,* 1973, *80,* 527–544.

Holland, J. G. Human vigilance. *Science,* 1958, *128,* 61–67.

Holz, W. C., & Azrin, N. H. Discriminative properties of punishment. *Journal of the Experimental Analysis of Behavior,* 1961, *4,* 225–232.

Honig, W. K. (Ed.) *Operant behavior: Areas of research and application.* New York: Appleton-Century-Crofts, 1966.

Honig, W. K., & Staddon, J. E. R. (Eds.). *Handbook of operant behavior.* Englewood Cliffs, N.J.: Prentice-Hall, 1977.

Hutchinson, R. R., Renfrew, J. W., & Young, G. A. Effects of long-term shock and associated stimuli on aggressive and manual responses. *Journal of the Experimental Analysis of Behavior,* 1971, *15,* 141–166.

Jennings, H. S. *Behavior of the lower organisms.* New York: Macmillan, 1906.

Joravsky, D. *Soviet Marxism and natural science, 1917–1932.* New York: Columbia University Press, 1961.

Keller, F. S. Psychology at Harvard (1926–1931): A reminiscence. In P. B. Dews (Ed.), *Festschrift for B. F. Skinner.* New York: Appleton-Century-Crofts, 1970.

Keller, F. S. *Summers and sabbaticals.* Champaign, Ill.: Research Press, 1977.

Keller, F. S., & Schoenfeld, W. N. The psychology curriculum at Columbia College. *American Psychologist,* 1949, *4,* 165–172.

Keller, F. S., & Schoenfeld, W. N. *Principles of psychology.* New York: Appleton-Century-Crofts, 1950.

Lashley, K. S. The problem of serial order in behavior. In L. A. Jeffress (Ed.), *Cerebral mechanisms in behavior.* New York: John Wiley & Sons, 1951.

Leitenberg, H. (Ed.). *Handbook of behavior modification and behavior therapy.* Englewood Cliffs, N.J.: Prentice-Hall, 1976.

MacCorquodale, K. On Chomsky's review of Skinner's *Verbal behavior. Journal of the Experimental Analysis of Behavior,* 1970, *13,* 83-99.

Mackenzie, B. D. *Behaviourism and the limits of scientific method.* Atlantic Highlands, N.J.: Humanities Press, 1977.

Matthews, B. A., Shimoff, E., Catania, A. C., & Sagvolden, T. Uninstructed human responding: Sensitivity to ratio and interval contingencies. *Journal of the Experimental Analysis of Behavior,* 1977, *27,* 453-467.

Meehl, P. E. On the circularity of the Law of Effect. *Psychological Bulletin,* 1950, *47,* 52-75.

Miller, N. E., & Carmona, A. Modification of a visceral response, salivation in thirsty dogs, by instrumental training with water reward. *Journal of Comparative and Physiological Psychology,* 1967, *63,* 1-6.

Morse, W. H., & Kelleher, R. T. Determinants of reinforcement and punishment. In W. K. Honig & J. E. R. Staddon (Eds.), *Handbook of operant behavior.* Englewood Cliffs, N.J.: Prentice-Hall, 1977.

Neisser, U. *Cognitive psychology.* New York: Appleton-Century-Crofts, 1967.

Nevin, J. A. Response strength in multiple schedules. *Journal of the Experimental Analysis of Behavior,* 1974, *21,* 389-408.

Pavlov, I. P. *Conditioned reflexes* (G. V. Anrep, trans.). London: Oxford University Press, 1927.

Peterson, N. Control of behavior by presentation of an imprinted stimulus. *Science,* 1960, *132,* 1395-1396.

Premack, D. Toward empirical behavior laws: I. Positive reinforcement. *Psychological Review,* 1959, *66,* 219-233.

Premack, D. Catching up with common sense or two sides of a generalization: Reinforcement and punishment. In R. Glaser (Ed.), *The nature of reinforcement.* New York: Academic Press, 1971.

Pryor, K. W., Haag, R., & O'Reilly, J. The creative porpoise: Training for novel behavior. *Journal of the Experimental Analysis of Behavior,* 1969, *12,* 653-661.

Rachlin, H., & Green, L. Commitment, choice and self-control. *Journal of the Experimental Analysis of Behavior,* 1972, *17,* 15-22.

Rosenbauer, H. *Brecht und der Behaviorismus.* Berlin: Verlag Gehlen, 1970.

Schlosberg, H. The relationship between success and the laws of conditioning. *Psychological Review,* 1937, *44,* 379-394.

Schoenfeld, W. N., Cumming, W. W., & Hearst, E. On the classification of reinforcement schedules. *Proceedings of the National Academy of Sciences,* 1956, *42,* 563-570.

Schwartz, B. On going back to nature: A review of Seligman and Hager's *Biological boundaries of learning. Journal of the Experimental Analysis of Behavior,* 1974, *21,* 183-198.

Sherrington, C. *The integrative action of the nervous system.* New York: Scribner's, 1906.

Shimp, C. P. Probabilistically reinforced choice behavior in pigeons. *Journal of the Experimental Analysis of Behavior,* 1966, *9,* 443-455.

Sidman, M. Two temporal parameters in the maintenance of avoidance behavior by the white rat. *Journal of Comparative and Physiological Psychology,* 1953, *46,* 253-261.

Sidman, M., Cresson, O., Jr., & Willson-Morris, M. Acquisition of matching to sample via mediated transfer. *Journal of the Experimental Analysis of Behavior,* 1974, *22,* 261-273.

Skinner, B. F. On the conditions of elicitation of certain eating reflexes. *Proceedings of the National Academy of Sciences,* 1930, *16,* 433-438.

Skinner, B. F. The concept of the reflex in the description of behavior. *Journal of General Psychology,* 1931, *5,* 427-458.

Skinner, B. F. The extinction of chained reflexes. *Proceedings of the National Academy of Sciences,* 1934, *20,* 234-237.

Skinner, B. F. The generic nature of the concepts of stimulus and response. *Journal of General Psychology,* 1935, *12,* 40-65. (a)

Skinner, B. F. Two types of conditioned reflex and a pseudotype. *Journal of General Psychology,* 1935, *12,* 66-77. (b)

Skinner, B. F. The verbal summator and a method for the study of latent speech. *Journal of Psychology,* 1936, *2,* 71-107.

Skinner, B. F. Two types of conditioned reflex: A reply to Konorski and Miller. *Journal of General Psychology,* 1937, *16,* 272-279.

Skinner, B. F. *The behavior of organisms.* New York: Appleton-Century-Crofts, 1938.

Skinner, B. F. Baby in a box. *Ladies' Home Journal,* October 1945, *62,* 30 ff.

Skinner, B. F. "Superstition" in the pigeon.

Journal of Experimental Psychology, 1948, *38,* 168–172. (a)

Skinner, B. F. *Walden two.* New York: Macmillan, 1948. (b)

Skinner, B. F. Are theories of learning necessary? *Psychological Review,* 1950, *57,* 193–216.

Skinner, B. F. *Science and human behavior.* New York: Macmillan, 1953.

Skinner, B. F. A case history in scientific method. *American Psychologist,* 1956, *11,* 221-233.

Skinner, B. F. *Verbal behavior.* New York: Appleton-Century-Crofts, 1957.

Skinner, B. F. Teaching machines. *Science,* 1958, *128,* 969–977.

Skinner, B. F. Pigeons in a pelican. *American Psychologist,* 1960, *15,* 28–37.

Skinner, B. F. Behaviorism at fifty. *Science,* 1963, *140,* 951–958.

Skinner, B. F. The phylogeny and ontogeny of behavior. *Science,* 1966, *153,* 1205–1213.

Skinner, B. F. Autobiography. In E. G. Boring & G. Lindsley (Eds.), *A history of psychology in autobiography* (Vol. V). New York: Appleton-Century-Crofts, 1967.

Skinner, B. F. *Contingencies of reinforcement.* New York: Appleton-Century-Crofts, 1969.

Skinner, B. F. *Beyond freedom and dignity.* New York: Alfred A. Knopf, 1971.

Skinner, B. F. The shaping of phylogenic behavior. *Journal of the Experimental Analysis of Behavior,* 1975, *24,* 117–120.

Skinner, B. F. *Particulars of my life.* New York: Alfred A. Knopf, 1976.

Skinner, B. F. Herrnstein and the evolution of behaviorism. *American Psychologist,* 1977, *32,* 1006–1012.

Staddon, J. E. R., & Simmelhag, V. L. The "Superstition" experiment: A reexamination of its implications for the principles of adaptive behavior. *Psychological Review,* 1971, *78,* 3–43.

Terrace, H. S. Errorless transfer of a discrimination across two continua. *Journal of the Experimental Analysis of Behavior,* 1963, *6,* 223-232.

Thorndike, E. L. *Animal intelligence.* New York: Macmillan, 1911.

Tolman, E. C. Cognitive maps in rats and men. *Psychological Review,* 1948, *55,* 189–208.

Voss, S. C., & Homzie, M. J. Choice as a value. *Psychological Reports,* 1970, *26,* 912–914.

Watson, J. B. Psychology as the behaviorist views it. *Psychological Review,* 1913, *20,* 158–177.

Watson, J. B. *Behaviorism.* New York: W. W. Norton, 1925.

Weiner, H. Controlling human fixed-interval performance. *Journal of the Experimental Analysis of Behavior,* 1969, *12,* 349–373.

Williams, D. R., & Williams, H. Automaintenance in the pigeon: Sustained pecking despite contingent non-reinforcement. *Journal of the Experimental Analysis of Behavior,* 1969, *12,* 511–520.

Winett, R. A., & Winkler, R. C. Current behavior modification in the classroom: Be still, be quiet, be docile. *Journal of Applied Behavior Analysis,* 1972, *5,* 499–504.

Woodworth, R. S. *Psychology* (Rev. ed.). New York: Holt, 1929.

6

Ethological Learning Theory

ROBERT C. BOLLES

INTRODUCTION

Overview

No one person can be pointed to as the originator or founder of ethological learning theory; there is no Hull, or Guthrie, or Skinner who has presented this type of learning theory in a systematic and comprehensive manner. Those who advocate this theoretical orientation have no leader, nor do they belong to any organized school of thought. They simply share the belief that learning phenomena can be most profitably regarded in evolutionary or ethological terms.

Traditionally, the ethological approach to animal behavior has stood somewhat at cross-purposes to psychological learning theory. Their basic differences in orientation have, on occasion, even led ethologists and learning theorists to open hostility. Ethologists want to observe an animal in the field, in a natural setting. They prefer to observe an animal unobtrusively while it is going about its usual business in its usual environment. By contrast, psychologists are more comfortable observing an animal's behavior in a well-controlled and well-standardized laboratory apparatus, such as the maze or the Skinner box. Ethologists also typically want to study behavior in an animal that is unrestrained, whereas psychologists want to demonstrate that they can control an animal's behavior by imposing various constraints and restrictions on it.

The ethologist is most interested in instinctive behavior patterns, that is, behavior which depends mainly on an animal's genetic inheritance, while the psychologist is much more interested in learning, that is, behavior which depends mostly on an animal's own experience. Consequently, ethologists tend to overemphasize the genetic basis of behavior and the part that natural selection plays in governing behavior, while psychologists are equally inclined to overemphasize the importance of past experience in behavior.

Ethologists are concerned mainly with an animal's major life problems: How does an animal select a mate or defend itself from its predators? Psychologists are more inclined to address themselves to insignificant and rather arbitrary aspects of behavior: How does an animal learn that a red light in the Skinner box signals food and a green light in the Skinner box signals no food? The ethologist is well aware that an animal cannot afford to waste time solving a vital life problem; it must have a ready solution. The psychologist, on the other hand, is willing to give an animal a vast amount of time and training in order to study how it learns some subtle discrimination.

Ethologists are fascinated by the specifics of behavior; nothing seems to be more interesting to them than the discovery that a particular creature solves a particular problem in a unique or unusual way. Psychologists are equally obsessed by the search for generalities. So while the ethologist may study intensively a particular kind of behavior, such as a courting display or an antipredator reaction in a particular species of bird, a psychologist is likely to concentrate efforts on finding learning principles that will, hopefully, apply equally well to all kinds of behavior in all kinds of animals.

For some time it seemed as though there would be no rapprochement between ethology and psychology. The two approaches to behavior embodied such different orientations, asked such different questions, looked at animals so differently, and were even centered on different sides of the Atlantic, that it is indeed remarkable that they were ever able to learn anything from each other. On the other hand, just because of these seemingly inherent differences, there was a great deal that each discipline could possibly contribute to the other. Here we will consider some of the ways in which ethological ways of thinking have recently enriched animal learning theory.

Major Issues

Whenever we see an animal with some unusual physical characteristic we tend to ask why. Why does the giraffe have such a long neck, or the elephant such big ears, or the hawk such keen eyesight? We are told that the long neck permits the giraffe to eat high foliage, the big ears radiate heat, the keen eyes spot prey at a distance. Each of these explanations has the interesting property of providing a how answer to our original why question. In each case the answer describes how a particular animal solves one of its basic life problems, such as obtaining food or regulating its temperature. But the why remains; it has only been postponed. We still want to know why giraffes eat the way they do, or why the elephant cools itself the way it does.

The only ultimate and satisfying answer to such a why question is that a species that solved a particular problem by the gradual evolution of some physical characteristic had some adaptive advantage over animals that did not. If hawks have keen eyesight, we may safely draw three conclusions. One, the eye itself has evolved with a particular structure to maximize acuity, probably with the sacrifice of other capabilities such as accommodation and night vision. In short, the eye has become specialized to perform a certain function unusually well. Two, that part of the nervous system which processes visual information has also evolved a particular structure enabling it to handle the additional information. The scanning mechanisms, the contrast mechanisms, indeed, all parts of the neural machinery have also become specialized to make the eye function with maximum acuity. Three, both the peripheral specialization of the eye and the central specialization of the brain occurred over evolutionary time, because birds that happened to have slightly better acuity than average could live just a little differently and a little more successfully. As this advantage was passed on and multiplied over generations, and as other adaptations occurred in a similar manner, they could live like hawks. That is why hawks have keen eyesight.

There is no reason to think that unusual behavioral characteristics should be explained any differently. If we observe some distinctive courtship display, or some unusual predatory behavior, or some odd food-getting response, we ask why. Again, part of the answer, the how part, lies in an account of the stimuli that elicit the behavior in question and the motivational and other body conditions that regulate it. But another part of the answer, the why part, lies in the evolutionary history of the species. The analysis is exactly the same as before: Behavior that is characteristic of a particular species occurs because over the generations it has conferred some advantage to the species that behaved that way.

Are learned behaviors any different because they depend upon the personal experience of the individual rather than the evolutionary experience of the species? No, not at all, because the capability of learning in the solution of a basic life problem is itself an inherited characteristic. The ability to modify behavior with experience is just as much controlled by an animal's genes as is the ability to respond in a given situation in a fixed, species-characteristic manner. And such a characteristic also arouses why questions. Why does the sparrow learn its song, while many other birds can produce their songs without benefit of prior experience? Why does the rat learn so readily to avoid toxic foods, when many other animals have fixed food preferences? The answer is that these particular learning abilities characterize these particular animals just as much, and for the same reason of adaptation, as do their physical characteristics and their fixed, species-typical behavior patterns.

Basic Concepts

Evolution. It is a mistake to think of evolution as a kind of progress, as a progression of higher forms developing from lower ones. Early thinkers (e.g., Aristotle) could speak of a "scale" of animals with humans at the top (of course), but such a conception is no longer acceptable. It is true that the human is a relatively new mammal, and that there were reptiles before there were mammals, and fishes before there were reptiles, and so on right back to the primitive one-celled forms of life. But the idea of a linear history does not hold together. There were mammals, insignificant ones, at a time when reptiles dominated the earth. There were fishes before there were any insects upon the land. Although mammals are fairly recent, birds are evolving and diversifying much more rapidly today. Many insect species are quite new (and the DDT–resistant strains are avantgarde). The point is that most species of animals are still evolving, still diversifying and adapting to new niches. Those that have been relatively unchanged over millions of years are simply the ones that have established an equilibrium in a relatively unchanging environment and are trapped there.

Evolution is more like a tree than a linear progression (Hodos & Campbell, 1969). The major branches represent the major lines of diversification, where, for example, reptiles diversified and became mammallike and birdlike. The twigs at the top of the tree represent quite recent adaptations. The twigs in different parts of the tree represent the most recent mammals, fishes, insects, or whatever.

Natural Selection. The idea of evolution in one form or another is quite old, as we have seen. The older idea was one of progression or advancement. Darwin's basic contribution was the idea that evolution was a purely passive process. Evolution required no engine to drive it; it had no reason, no purpose, no plan; it just happened. It happened because all living things compete in some way with other living things. The competition may go this way or that. The winner is no more deserving than the loser; the winner is just better able to survive the competition. Typically what happens is that the winner loses, too. It is only the giraffes with the longest necks, or the elephants with the biggest ears, or the hawks with the sharpest eyes that survive. That is how the different species arose.

Fitness. What counts in the competition is the ability to produce offspring like oneself; that is all that winning consists of—producing more offspring than the competitor. We may suppose that the short-neck giraffes could not reproduce as rapidly as their long-necked cousins, or as rapidly as the short-necked zebras. (Competition exists both within a species and between species.) So there are no more short-necked giraffes. Larger horses had some slight survival and reproductive advantage over smaller horses, because horses have gradually become bigger over the past 30 million years. Given sufficient time, the merest edge in reproductive success will make the difference between survival and extinction.

Adaptation. To reproduce, the organism has to survive long enough to mate. With many animals the individual also has to tend the young if it is to reproduce successfully. (If a competing mother can lay a million eggs, she need not worry about caring for all her young; what counts most is that she lay her eggs in a comparatively safe and productive location.) In any case, reproductive success requires the individual to survive long enough to reproduce, and this means

that the individual must feed itself, defend against predators, keep itself healthy, and compete for a mate. It is finding solutions to these problems that constitutes the day-to-day business of the animal.

All animals are adapted to their world in the sense that they do have ways to solve their problems. And it is the manner of solution that defines the animal. Some animals graze, some hunt and kill, some are parasitic, and some are scavengers that eat what no one else will eat. Each of these strategies appears in many variations. Some hunters hunt for ants, others hunt for mice, some hunt for other hunters, the lion hunts for large animals that most other hunters cannot take. Some animals hunt alone, others hunt in packs. And there are just as many strategies for defense or for keeping healthy. Competing for a mate is an enormously varied business. How an animal hunts or goes about its other business depends upon many specific adaptations, its teeth, how big it is, how fast it can go, all sorts of factors. The marvelous diversity of animal life testifies to the great number of different kinds of adaptation that are possible.

Adaptive Strategy. At various points in evolution, where the biggest branches diverge, we may think of alternative strategies being effective. It is as if evolution were making a decision about which way to go. One of the earliest decisions was whether to live quietly, slowly absorbing energy from the sun, like a plant, or to become active and pursue high-energy organic foods, like an animal. Both strategies were successful, and there are now many plants and animals. Another choice was how to reproduce, whether to split up one's own genes and multiply one's own material, or to mix genes with another individual. Both of these strategies proved viable, but the mixers, using sexual reproduction, became far more varied and flexible. Other major strategic decisions were whether to be radially or bilaterally symmetric, whether to stand still or locomote, whether to produce lots of eggs but leave them unprotected or a few eggs that could be better cared for, whether to have fixed or variable behavior patterns. Any decision on such questions as these can be called an adaptive strategy.

Niche. This much-abused word refers to how a species relates to other species in its environment, and not to the environment itself.

HISTORY

Beginnings

Almost everything pertaining to the study of behavior began with Charles Darwin (1809–1882). There were earlier naturalists who observed animals, identified their characteristics, and became wise in their ways. But Darwin had an unusual interest in behavior; when he studied emotion (Darwin, 1872), it was emotion expressed in behavior that concerned him. When he wrote about instinct (Darwin, 1871), it was instinctive behavior. Darwin also gave us a coherent theory of evolution based upon natural selection (Darwin, 1859). One implication of this doctrine had immense importance: The human species is a natural part of the animal kingdom, and not something apart. Only when people began to regard themselves as part of nature could the naturalistic, scientific study of human behavior begin. Only then was psychology possible. Historians of psychology like to trace it back much earlier, but it is only the small area of perception that is very old, and most of psychology, including the study of learn-

ing, springs directly from Darwin. It was his interest in behavior and his concept of continuity between human and animal that started it.

Given the continuity, there are two possible strategies. One is to intellectualize the beast. Darwin's close associate G. J. Romanes (1882) wrote about the marvelous intelligence of animals. But the more popular strategy was the mechanization of the human. Earlier chapters of this book have demonstrated the approach of Edward L. Thorndike, Ivan P. Pavlov, Edwin R. Guthrie—all of the early learning theorists—of reducing all behavior to simple S–R associations. Learning became an automatic, machinelike process. Moreover, learning was homogeneous; all learning was the same. Pavlov only studied salivation in dogs because he assumed that all learning followed the same principles.

The mechanistic bias and the assumption of homogeneity dominated not only psychology but the other life sciences as well. Find out how the kidney or the liver or the eye works in one animal, and we will know how these organs work in general—that was the assumption. The functional approach, the asking of why questions, lagged. So too did the concept of natural selection. Curiously, while biologists all believed in natural selection, it was not seen as having any explanatory value. In the early part of the century everyone was obsessed with mechanical explanations and almost forgot how to ask why questions.

It was R. A. Fisher (1930), the great geneticist and statistician, who rescued natural selection by showing mathematically how slight differences in the adaptiveness of a genetic trait could lead to the success or extinction of the trait. All through the early years of animal behavior there were a number of excellent naturalists: Charles Whitman and Wallace Craig in America, Douglas Spalding and Lloyd Morgan in England, Jacob von Uexkull and Oskar Heinroth in Europe. All of these men not only observed animals, they also did experiments. Spalding did deprivation experiments; Morgan studied learning. These men also asked psychological questions. Von Uexkull wanted to know how the world looks to an animal; Craig wanted to know what motivates different kinds of behavior.

Major Theorists

All of these early trends were brought into focus by Konrad Lorenz, and mainly through his efforts the discipline called ethology started taking shape about 1935. In a most important paper published that year, Lorenz observed that an animal's behavior is innately organized into adaptive patterns, fixed action patterns, he called them. Such a preformed unit of behavior is typically released by certain specific stimuli. Both the releasing stimuli and the fixed action pattern are highly selective and quite specific to a given species. An animal may show considerable flexibility in some aspects of its behavior, especially those appetitive behaviors that lead up to the consummatory response, but the latter is fixed. It is only the last, fixed part of the behavior that is properly considered to be instinctive. The unitary integrity of the fixed action pattern is best demonstrated by the fact that it may occur in the absence of the usual releasing stimuli, in what is called vacuum behavior.

Building on these ideas, Niko Tinbergen began to emphasize the signaling aspects, that is, the communication function, of both the releaser and the fixed action pattern. When the releasing stimulus is some physical characteristic or some behavior of one animal that produces a fixed action pattern in a second animal, and this in turn releases a fixed action pattern in the first, then we have interlocking behaviors, and a form of communication which, if primitive, can be nonetheless extremely important in the regulation of the animals' social system. Complex behavior such as courtship and feeding of young could be seen as a species-specific pattern of instinctive reactions. The task to which the ethologists first set themselves was to demonstrate that the fixed action patterns really were fixed, and to discover what specific stimulus patterns released them. A number of these S–R relationships were described in an influential book by Tinbergen (1951). In addition, the basic S–R principles were overlaid by a motivational theory: Each fixed action pattern has its own motivating energy, but the different energies are arranged in a hierarchical order, and the hierarchy is powered by an animal's physiological condition, including hormone levels, in the case of sexual and reproductive behaviors.

Much of the orientation of the ethologists was antithetical to learning, as has already been noted. But Lorenz, in contrast with many of his followers, has always shown a lively interest in the problem of learning and its relationship to instinctive behavior (Lorenz, 1965, 1969). In his 1935 paper Lorenz presented an analysis of imprinting, which was obviously an instance of learning, since it is a change in behavior due to experience, but which was different from other forms of learning in several respects (see below).

On several counts, the ethological findings presented a clear challenge to the American learning theory establishment. There was imprinting, which had to be accounted for in some way. There was the well-substantiated idea that most motivated behavior has an instinctive, pre-formed character rather than depending mainly on learning. There was the troublesome but inescapable conclusion that a great deal of the learning that occurs in the animal kingdom is highly specialized, and highly specific; learning is not so much a general characteristic by means of which some animals solve all their problems as it is a way in which some animals solve some problems.

Among the first learning theorists to take note of this challenge were Keller and Marion Breland (1966). The Brelands trained animals with operant techniques for advertisements and other commercial ventures. By working with a variety of different birds and mammals, they had discovered the specificity of learning abilities. For example, they reported that while it is easy to train a rat to work diligently in a Skinner box for an occasional piece of food, the cat in the same situation is quite different. The cat knows perfectly well where the food comes from, but instead of pressing the lever the cat is more inclined to sit patiently in front of the food delivery mechanism. When the rat is made more hungry it works more diligently at the lever, but when the cat is made more hungry it only watches and waits more patiently. The success of the rat and the failure of the cat at this task cannot be attributed to differences in motivation or differences in intelligence, the Brelands concluded, but must be understood in terms of how these two kinds of animals normally go about the business of getting food. The rat actively searches for food while the cat hides in ambush and waits for its next meal to appear. The rat is automatically adapted (preadapted) to the Skinner box because the box was designed for the rat, while the cat is not. The Brelands describe a number of comparable cases

where an animal's species membership determines its performance on a simple learning task.

Current Status

At the present time there is not much in the way of systematic theory to direct or to organize ethological learning theory. There is little more than the evolutionary and functional way of thinking about behavior to guide us. The major problem areas are still being mapped out. Some general trends are discernible, however.

With the collapse of the homogeneity assumption, that is, the idea that all learning is the same, there has arisen considerable interest in the various specificities of learning that characterize different animal species. We find differential dependence upon particular stimuli. In some cases, such differences merely reflect different kinds of sensory equipment: Some animals have better eyes or better noses than others. We find differences in motor equipment, too, so that some animals run better or fly better than others. The Brelands (1966) introduced the further idea of behavior cost: Some animals (e.g., porpoises, monkeys, and many birds) are energetic, generate high rates of responding and do not seem to mind making errors, but other animals respond more grudgingly. There are also differences in reinforcers: Rats and primates like sweets, for example, but cats do not (cats do not even assimilate sugars very well if they are force fed).

It is not just the different effectiveness of different stimuli, responses, and reinforcers that interests most psychologists, but the fact that there are important interactions among these different kinds of events. One well-documented interaction is that a rat readily learns to press a lever when food is the reinforcer, but it learns the same response with considerable difficulty when it is reinforced by the avoidance of a negative reinforcer, such as shock. On the other hand, rats readily learn other responses, such as running, to avoid shock. Thus, the ease with which a given species of animal learns a particular response depends not only upon what the response is but also upon what the reinforcer is (or perhaps it is the motivational state that is critical, rather than the reinforcing event per se). Shettleworth (1972) has described many such interactions found both in the laboratory and in more natural settings.

When everyone believed that all learning is alike, it made no difference what learning one studied. But now, learning can be seen as a great multidimensional puzzle. In order to put it together it will be necessary to seek new sources of information. Fortunately, we may turn to nature to gain new insights into how some of the pieces go together. One very useful guiding principle is to look for learning abilities in the laboratory to mirror those found in nature; we may let the animal's natural life-style suggest to us what it can and what it cannot learn. If the rat lives in complex tunnel systems in nature, then we might expect it to excel in learning mazes. If songbirds find their way in the world by means of landmarks, then we might expect them to excel in learning about place cues.

The rapprochement can work both ways. For example, it has long been a mystery how birds navigate in their annual migrations. It was only by the use of laboratory techniques that Emlen (1970) was able to show that at least one species of migrating bird learns a map of the stars as they rotate about the pole star. What Emlen's experiments show is, first, how these birds find their way at night, and second, that there is a special learning skill, which these birds possess and which enables them to live as they do, but which is generally lacking even in the so-called higher and more intelligent animals.

The observation of animals in natural settings has led to the realization that there are a great number of vital problems confronting animals that have been virtually ignored in the laboratory. The laboratory tradition has been so preoccupied with food-getting and shock avoidance that, until recently, little attention was paid to nest-building, temperature regulation, grooming, and many other important behaviors, or to the part learning might play in these activities.

The observation of animals in natural settings has also led to dissatisfaction with the traditional mode of behavior analysis in terms of eliciting stimuli, learned responses, and controlling reinforcers. A more functional approach is to ask how animals spend their time, how they allocate their energies and resources. More modern treatments of reinforcement (e.g., Baum, 1973) have begun to think of it not as a single event localized in time but as a rate of payoff for a particular behavior. Rather than think of a food pellet as a reinforcing event, we should think of obtaining food as a payoff for a particular behavioral strategy, such as pressing a lever at a certain rate. If a rat is hungry, and if food is a reinforcer, then it should spend all of its time pressing a lever. But this does not happen except in a short session. Given appropriate opportunity, the rat provides itself with a specific number of meals per day (Collier, Hirsch, & Hamlin, 1972). What we find, then, is not that food is reinforcing, in the usual sense, but that in this kind of an experimental world the rat quickly adopts a particular feeding "strategy."

The observation of animals in natural settings not only confirms the conviction that there are many specificities in animal learning, it also provides a variety of new discoveries about animal behavior and a number of new ways to think about them.

Other Theories

The emphasis thus far has been upon the specificities of learning. It is also quite possible to regard learning as a very general characteristic, with properties something like the biological traits of mobility. Mobility has so much generality, can occur in such a variety of forms, and can be arrived at by such a multitude of means that we are inclined to think of it more as an abstraction made by the biologist than as a fact of nature. Most animals are mobile, but they may walk, swim, fly, wiggle, or be carried about by the wind. So we are not tempted to seek any common genetic basis for their different means of getting around. Nonetheless, mobility is an important feature of animal behavior which plays a critical role in evolution. Perhaps the ability to learn through individual experience is the same kind of characteristic; perhaps there are many different styles and types of learning, and the only reason for putting them all under the same heading and attaching a common label to them is that learning is an abstraction made by the psychologist.

Animal psychologists have tended to adopt a somewhat more systematic approach to the problem. This approach assumes that there are a few different kinds of learning and that these can be graded. Then it is assumed that the simplest and most primitive grade of learning is to be found widely throughout the animal kingdom, even among the most primitive animals. A somewhat more ad-vanced form of learning, such as classical conditioning, can be found only over a smaller range of species, perhaps just the vertebrates. And so on through the different grades, the highest grade, which might be called abstract or symbolic reasoning, being reserved, of course, just for *Homo sapiens.*

This is a time-honored approach, and there is much to recommend it (Bitterman, 1975). But there are also some difficulties in applying this approach to all animals, one of which is that the concept of the different grades of learning has been developed by studying mostly a particular learning paradigm with a particular animal species. Thus, the theory of classical conditioning was originally developed from the study of salivation in domesticated dogs, and the theory of operant conditioning was developed primarily from the study of food-getting behavior in laboratory-bred rats. In neither case did the theoretical development reflect the possibility that salivation in these dogs or food-getting in these rats might depend upon learning abilities that were relatively specific to these cases, and the learning of other animals doing other things might be quite different. Indeed, the assumption of uniformity that was made so glibly by the early animal psychologists (the assumption that the same basic principles would be revealed no matter in what system learning was studied) can now be seen as premature. One of the main attractions of the ethological approach to learning is the present-day realization that, even within a given grade of learning ability, there is little generality of the basic principles over different species of animals.

So, we are led back to the possibility that learning ability may be rather widespread among animals, and general in that sense, but that it is highly specific in any particular species, endowing its possessor with the ability to solve certain problems in a certain way. Perhaps, then, learning really is like mobility: One animal flies, another wiggles, but we may assume that both modes of movement arose because of the advantage they gave these particular two species in solving their life problems. So, one animal can acquire a glandular anticipation of food while another can learn to manipulate a man-made device to obtain food, and we may assume that both modes of learning arose because of the advantage they gave dogs and rats in adapting to their worlds. The fact that all of these modes of behavior have some generality across species should not lure us into believing that any of them is anything like universal or a necessary part of a species' adaptation. There are perfectly well adapted animals that neither salivate nor manipulate machines, just as there are birds that do not fly and worms that do not wiggle. The ethological approach to learning starts with a respect for the specificity of all adaptations, including the ability to use a flexible nervous system to solve a particular problem.

PROPOSITIONS

1. *Almost all behavior is adaptive.*

The adaptiveness of behavior is easy to see in the case of fixed action patterns, at least once the function of a particular piece of behavior is understood. The moth flying into the light bulb and incinerating itself may not appear adaptive, but the irresistible tendency of moths to orient themselves with regard to a source of light, which is maladaptive in the artificial world of light bulbs, presumably (we are not certain yet) serves the important function of dispersal, since it nor-

mally makes moths fly off in straight lines. The springtime singing of the songbird may appear to be more entertaining than functional and may have the disadvantage of exposing the singer to risk of predation. But the whole reproductive strategy of the male songbird is based upon this singing. It attracts females, defends a territory against other males, and wards off other males. The adaptive significance of the singing is clear, in that it has clear signal value to other members of the species. We may assume that both the ability to produce a species-specific song and the ability of other animals to recognize it have gradually co-evolved over the years, because of the advantage it gave those animals to have such a system. All such behaviors, we may assume, have been gradually molded by selection pressures, so that any existing behavior represents the most successful adaptation of the species to the fixed features of the animal's social and physical environment.

It is also easy to see the adaptive significance of learned behaviors, since, almost by definition, the contingencies that produce learning are those that prevail in the environment, and so they should produce changes in behavior that are optimally suited to dealing with those contingencies. The only difference is that the environment molds the behavior during the life experience of an individual rather than in evolutionary time. Again, however, the adaptive advantage of learning is only apparent when the functional significance of the behavior is understood. It does not appear to be adaptive for a family of young ducklings to follow Lorenz around, when they might be better following their mother, as most ducklings do. But that the imprinting mechanism sometimes misfires in situations contrived by experimenters should not be as important in the long run as the advantage of the duckling being able to learn what its mother looks like, rather than having to rely upon some species-specific, innate recognition of what the mother should look like. It is interesting that imprinting only occurs in, and presumably is only advantageous to, a small range of animals, namely, precocial fowl. Some particular feature of their way of life evidently confers the advantage.

2. *Almost all behavior is functional.*

Very little behavior is wasted. Psychologists are accustomed to thinking of the animals' struggle to find food. Actually, there are several possible strategies. Because it has a particular kind of digestive system and other capabilities, an ungulate such as the horse spends almost no time finding food and a lot of time eating. Is such a creature wasting time eating so much? Not at all; its readily available food supply is so poor in calories that it must eat a great quantity to sustain itself. Alternatively, a carnivore spends a lot of time finding nutritionally rich food and little time eating. But the search time is obviously not wasted either; it is simply part of the strategy. There are animals that, when they find food, do not eat it there but carry it off somewhere else. The chickadee will fly off to an eating place with a seed so small that the food value of the seed hardly seems worth the effort. But it must be remembered that mobility is cheap to the chickadee; because it has such a high metabolism and is so small, it expends little more energy flying than it does just standing around. And flying to a safe eating place gives it the advantage of feeding while hidden.

Behaviors such as play and exploration might seem to lack a function. But quite the contrary, play is very important in establishing a social system among social animals such as primates. And when the carnivore plays he is going about the business of learning to be a carnivore, that is, learning how to run and jump and chase and bite (Eibl-Eibesfeldt, 1970). Time spent exploring the environment may lead to the discovery of food and other commodities, but it may also lead to learning about what is safe and what is dangerous, where things are and how to get to the safety of the nest in the most efficient manner should a danger appear. It is unfortunate that so little is known about the important learning that no doubt occurs during play and exploration. Even grooming behavior is not wasted. Birds groom partly to keep their feathers in order for efficient flying, and grooming helps keep an animal clean and free of parasites.

3. *Almost all behavior solves some problem.*

Animals are confronted with several vital problems, including obtaining food, finding a safe place to rest, minimizing exposure to predators, and reproducing. Many behaviors obviously "belong" to one or another of these problems in the sense that they provide a species-characteristic way of dealing with the problem. It is tempting to think of each life problem in motivational terms, in part because there are handy motivational labels, such as hunger, thirst, and fear, that can be applied to some of them. But there are difficulties with this approach. For one thing, many life problems break down into a series of subproblems. In the case of reproduction in the canary, for example, Hinde (1970) analyzed it into a number of stages, including nest-building, courtship, mating, tending the eggs, feeding the young, and getting the fledglings out of the nest. Each of these stages could be thought of in terms of its own motivational system, and each is dependent upon a particular balance of reproductive hormones in both the male and the female canary. In each stage the birds display a rich variety of fixed action patterns that have been shown experimentally to depend upon hormone levels. It is clear that each stage represents a partial solution to the overall problem of reproduction, but that each stage must be analyzed as a separate kind of functional behavior in which a given species of bird tends to give its own adaptive behavior.

Even hunger is not a single entity, being composed of a number of components, such as hunger for calories or hunger for protein. Moreover, in some animals food-getting behavior, like reproduction, consists of a number of stages, such as searching for food, obtaining the food (chasing and killing it in the case of a carnivore), defending the food against scavengers and conspecifics, and eating. The way of feeding, like the way of reproducing, involves not so much the laboratory model of motivation–response–reinforcement, as it does the adoption of a strategy, the strategy representing a pattern of responding which in the long run solves the problem.

One point to be emphasized is that the strategy for dealing with a problem involves a number of highly specific behaviors, reflexive behaviors, and fixed action patterns, all highly species typical. The strategy is just as much the results of evolutionary selection pressures as are the specific responses. The other side of the coin is that given a particular species-type behavior—a certain form of locomotion, a certain vocalization, a certain display—we may suppose that it is part of the animal's total behavior repertoire because it has evolved for the solution of

a particular problem, such as chasing prey, or signaling the young, or attracting a mate. An interesting question in the study of learning is whether a response that "belongs" to a particular problem can be used in the solution of some other problem. For example, can an animal learn to use a response that evolved in the service of feeding to defend itself? In concrete experimental terms, we might ask if a pigeon can learn to use the pecking response to avoid an electric shock. The experimental evidence indicates that this kind of transproblem or transmotivational learning is very difficult for the pigeon (Hineline & Rachlin, 1969).

4. Almost all behavior is unlearned.

Psychologists are, quite naturally, especially interested in human behavior, in which learning unquestionably plays a large part. But this primary interest in the human, together with a secondary interest in other mammals, has led to a badly distorted picture of the importance of learning in the determination of behavior in general. The fact is that throughout a wide part of the animal kingdom animals live, solve problems, and die without ever learning anything. They do not need to learn anything, and may, in fact, be quite incapable of learning anything.

Learning has been demonstrated experimentally in a variety of arthropods, such as insects, and there is good evidence for some arthropod learning in nature. But most of an arthropod's problems can be solved without benefit of any learning. Among birds and mammals learning is easy to demonstrate both in the laboratory and in the natural setting, but it must be kept in mind that even this learning is merely the surface of a great mass of behavior patterns that are generally quite fixed. A rat eats like a rat, sitting in a particular ratlike manner, holding its food like a rat, gnawing and chewing like a rat. Other animals eat in their own ways. The rat also runs like a rat, not like a horse or cat or lizard, nor can it be trained to run like one of these other animals. The difficulty here lies partly in the physical structure of the legs; its manner of running is a function of its unusually short front legs and feet with toenails. But part of the difficulty lies in the neural control of running. Along with the rat's anatomical features are its neurological features that also make it run like a rat. Averaging across all animals and across all behaviors, the only possible conclusion is that almost all behavior is unlearned.

5. *Learning is an adaptation.*

If so much of an animal's behavior occurs in fixed patterns, then we may suppose that whenever we find some behavior that is learned, it must be for some special reason, and it must have some special adaptive significance. If we find that certain parts of a behavior pattern are fixed but that other parts are modifiable, then we may suppose that the modifiable aspect confers upon the animal some advantage in dealing with some problem. From the ethological point of view, it is not surprising that much of an animal's behavior is not modifiable, or that some part of it is. Nor is it surprising that learning ability is typically rather selective and specialized. All aspects of behavior have these properties, because all aspects of behavior, including modifiability, are the results of evolutionary selection pressures and represent the gradual mutual adjustment that has to develop between an existing species and its environment. We must expect

learning to occur in just those systems, and in the solution of those problems, where uncertain, unpredictable, and rapidly changing aspects of the environment are likely to be encountered. Thus, for example, we must expect an animal with the feeding strategy of an omnivore (such as a rat) to be able to learn what to eat and what not to eat. We should also expect it to learn about different nutritive components, such as carbohydrates and proteins, and to learn about different caloric densities so that it can eat suitable amounts of different foods. Omnivores that are capable of these kinds of modifiability in their feeding behaviors have the capacity to live in different habitats, to live off different foods, and to live, in short, like omnivores. Animals with fixed food habits and set food preferences should not have such learning abilities. Other animals with other feeding strategies should be expected to show other mixtures of fixed and modifiable food-getting behaviors.

There are problems that permit little scope for learning. Whereas an animal may be confronted with some decision about what to eat, there cannot be any question about what to mate with. And while there may be considerable variability in how an animal eats a particular food, there cannot be much variation in how it copulates. Thus, in the variability of the environment we find a reason for learning in connection with eating behavior, but we should expect to find, and we do find, relatively fixed patterns in sexual behavior in most animals. In effect, it is not so much the intelligence of the animal that determines whether a given type of learning can occur as it is the strategic approach, the life-style, of the animal and the character of its physical and social environment.

Interestingly, we might expect to find

life-style to be more important than phylogenetic position in the appearance of learning in different animals. Thus, it might be that octopuses, hawks, and cats share more in their ability to learn about food sources because they are all carnivores than would different species of cephalopods, or different species of birds that had different feeding strategies.

6. *Learning is mostly about stimuli.*

It is, of course, the behavior of an animal that we observe, and it is a change in behavior that we must take as evidence of learning. But it is no longer possible to take for granted the idea that the change in behavior is the learning. It is becoming increasingly common to regard changes in behavior as merely symptomatic of learning, and to think of learning as mainly involving a change in the way stimuli are perceived. According to some theorists (e.g., Bindra, 1974) *all* learning is stimulus learning, and the animal merely responds in fixed, species-typical ways to new stimuli because it has learned something new about those stimuli. Stimuli may become cues, signaling that food is near or that a shock is due. What animals learn, according to this view, is the cue value or signal properties of stimuli around them, and they then respond in highly species-typical ways to those cues, perhaps approaching them, perhaps just watching them carefully.

This recent point of view is quite consistent with an ethological approach, since it permits behavior to change as environmental contingencies change, while still keeping the basic fixity of response patterns. The purpose of learning, from a biological point of view, is to make an animal better adapted in a changing world. What better mechanism could there be for doing this than to have the learning process itself be a direct reflection of the changes that occur in the world?

7. *Animals learn evaluations.*

The study of learning in nature must begin from an analysis of perception, because when an animal perceives a stimulus object it most likely perceives it not in realistic terms but only in terms of its own biased perception. It does not see the stimulus for what it is, but only in relation to its own needs, its current problems, and its characteristic life-style (von Uexkull, 1909/1957). For example, if the animal is hungry it perceives things as being either food related or not food related. In effect, it sees the food-relevant objects and probably does not see much of anything else. Much of this kind of perception must be innately organized, as shown by the release of stereotyped food-getting behaviors by appropriate stimuli. Thus, a hungry frog will strike at any small, dark object that either suddenly appears or that moves slowly across its field of view. Any stimulus with the appropriate size and movement is evaluated as food.

The human perceiver might, depending upon the circumstances, see an insect as something to be killed, or put outdoors, or as a carrier of disease, or as a zoological specimen. The human can evaluate an insect in many ways. By contrast, the frog can only perceive the moving dark spot as food. There is, in effect, only one evaluation the frog can make, and this evaluation is probably innate. The frog cannot learn to see a suitable spot as anything other than food, nor can it learn to see anything else as food. The food-getting system of the frog is quite rigid, and this rigidity is reflected both in the fixity of the kind of stimuli that can release food-getting behavior and in the fixity of the behavior itself (a flick of the tongue at the moving spot).

Other animals have greater flexibility, both in their food-getting responses and in the kinds of stimuli that release these responses. Animals such as the crow display a great variety of foraging behaviors. For example, crows can open clams and can turn over stones to find insects. We may suppose that to the crow doing these tricks the shell on the beach and the stone on the ground are evaluated as food related. They look foody. How is learning involved here? One possibility, which is suggested by conventional approaches, is that the stone-turning behavior is learned through reinforcement, and any statement regarding perceptual learning about the stone is an unwarranted and unnecessary inference on our part. The stone is at most a discriminative stimulus for stone-turning behavior. The other, and more interesting, possibility is that the change in perception is the basic product of learning, and any change in behavior is secondary to and derived from the perceptual learning. Once the stone is evaluated as foody, we may count on the crow manipulating it. Evidence for this second view comes from a variety of findings (discussed below), which suggest that evaluative learning is the essence of classical conditioning. Conditioning makes the conditioned stimulus (CS) in some sense look like the unconditioned stimulus (US), so that the animal reacts to the CS as it does to the US.

8. *Animals learn affordances.*

J. J. Gibson (1977) has introduced into psychology the concept of *affordance* to account for the relationship between stimuli and responses. Some objects look like they could be eaten. Quite apart from the fact that the object may have been eaten before, or that it has a foody look through prior association with food, some objects look like they could be eaten because of their size, shape, and texture. We may say that such objects "afford" eating. Because such an object has the physical properties of eatability, and because such properties as size and texture are directly appreciated by the visual system, the object is immediately perceived as affording eating.

Two ethological aspects of this concept are important. One is that what is eatable to a hippo is not eatable to an ant, and vice versa. Each species must have its own set of affordances for eating, as well as for walking on, for hiding in, for manipulating, and so on. The second point is that during evolution a given species' sensory systems must have adapted to the environment and must have been part of the mutual adjustment of organism and environment, so that important affordances should be perceived automatically, without being dependent upon learning. In short, many affordances must be innately recognized (a point emphasized by Gibson).

We may suppose, however, that for some animals many affordances are learned. Consider again the crow in a world with insects under stones. A distinction can be made between the "foodiness" of the stone resulting from finding insects, and the manipulability of the stone, which either is innate or is learned while the young crow is playing with objects (we cannot be sure which is the case). Manipulability is conceptually different from "foodiness," in this case, and requires us to think about the possibility of a new kind of learning—the learning of affordances. A boy has certain limits on what he can jump over and on what he can lift, and he must learn what these limits are. Then as he grows bigger and stronger, his affordances must change so that an object that did not used to look "pick-upable" now does. Finally, as an old man his affordances must change again so that a space that used to look "jump-overable" now looks like a barrier. Some animals show such changes with development and others do not. But where such changes do occur, they present us with an important category of learning that has been almost totally ignored by conventional learning theory.

The position taken here is that almost all learning is learning about stimuli. We may assume that some of this learning is evaluative: Some stimuli become cues for food, others cues for danger (a predator?), and so on. On the other hand, there is stimulus learning which is related more to the animal's general behavioral systems than to its motivational systems—general-purpose, nonevaluative stimulus learning. The animal learns what is "walk-onable" or "fly-overable" or "crawl-underable," as the case may be.

RESEARCH

Methodologies

The ethological approach to learning does not require a commitment to any particular methodology; the experimeter is free to work with highly controlled laboratory situations or with observational, nonrestrictive, noninterventional methods in the field. As an example of the latter, Orians (1969) reported evidence of predatory learning in pelicans using purely observational methods. Pelicans hunt by diving down to the water and scooping up a fish. Not all dives are successful, by any means, and Orians was able to show that young birds (distin-

guished from mature birds by their plumage) averaged significantly more dives to come up with a fish than did older birds. The greater predatory efficiency of the older animals is presumably due to learning.

With a similar methodology, Kamil (1978) studied the foraging behavior of nectar-feeding birds in Hawaii. He found that when a given bird visits a number of blossoms, it evidently remembers this information when it returns to the trees, because it only rarely revisits a blossom it has visited shortly before. Other birds passing by are much more likely to visit a previously visited blossom, so there is evidently no change in the stimulus properties of the flowers. Such a foraging strategy is not surprising; what is surprising, perhaps, is the ability of these animals to execute it, that is, to remember which flowers they have visited recently. (One advantage of such naturalistic studies is the opportunity to do research while sitting quietly at the seashore or on a Hawaiian mountain!)

It is obvious that the ethological approach encourages, indeed requires, the study of many different animal species. Foraging behavior is expected to depend more on the feeding strategy of a particular animal than on where that animal is located in the phylogenetic tree. Thus, birds and mammals and insects may share more in their foraging behavior if they all obtain food in the same manner, or in the same kind of environment, even though they come from quite different zoological classifications. But evidence for or against this principle can only be obtained by examining the foraging behavior of a number of different species.

The one study which more than any other convinced psychologists that learning is full of specificities was the "bright-noisy water" experiment reported by

John Garcia and R. A. Koelling (1966). These researchers found that rats would quit drinking bright, noisy water if they were punished for doing so by an electric shock to the feet. (Licking the water tube closed a sensing circuit; the current was amplified and used to operate a clicker and a light; thus, drinking was accompanied by bright, noisy stimulation.) They also found that when rats drank bright, noisy water and then were made sick (by drug administration or by radiation) they did not show any aversion to it. When other rats drank tasty water (saccharin added to it) and were punished with the foot shock, they did not quit drinking it, but when they drank the tasty water and were then made sick, they did avoid it.

The four sets of conditions provide an elegant set of controls: We know that electric shock is an effective consequence producing avoidance learning because for one set of conditions it did produce avoidance learning. Similarly, we know that sickness is an effective consequence, and that both kinds of stimulus cues, bright-noisy and tasty, are effective because in some combination each of these stimuli were effective in producing avoidance of drinking. The striking finding here is that only certain combinations of cue and consequence were effective. Evidence of avoidance learning was only found when shock was used in combination with the bright-noisy cue, or when illness was used in combination with taste. Garcia and Koelling suggested that shocks and audio-visual cues are part of the external world of predators and other environmental hazards, whereas taste and illness are part of the internal world of food assimilation. In effect, the different cues and consequences belong together in terms of the animal's normal functioning, and as long as the learning situation takes advantage of this kind of related-

ness, learning is readily obtained, but when there is a crossing of the different systems, there is a failure of learning.

One of the most significant features of this study from the ethological point of view is the demonstration of learning with taste and illness, now generally called the Garcia effect. This learning occurs under conditions that conventionally have been regarded as making learning impossible. It can occur after just a single training trial, and it can occur even when a substantial period of time, up to several hours, intervenes between the taste and the subsequent sickness. Everything we know about learning in rats says that learning under such conditions cannot occur; it would be a waste of time even to test for it. But Garcia knew that in spite of what earlier studies might have shown, such learning had to exist; rats *must* be able to associate tastes with consequences. Because the rat is a generalized eater, it has to be able to learn what is good to eat and what is bad. The learning must occur or there could be no rats, or any other animal with a similar style of feeding. Garcia did the bright-noisy water study to prove the point. Thus, he showed that a sound ethological principle, even though applied rather casually, could be more valid than the rigorously applied principles of conventional learning theory.

Whether we carry out the study of learning in the field or bring the animal into the laboratory—whatever our methodology—we may take how an animal functions in its natural setting as our guide for what it probably can and cannot learn.

Animal Studies

Some of the basic principles of imprinting were known to Spalding (1872). He observed that if domestic chicks were hooded so that they had no opportunity for visual experience until they were three days old, and if then the first thing they saw was Spalding's hand, they would follow his hand as he moved it about. Furthermore, Spalding noted that if he waited until the chicks were four days old to do the experiment, they would flee in fear from his hand. Similar observations were reported by Heinroth (1910) and by Lorenz with other fowl. In summarizing the then-known facts, Lorenz (1935/1957) concluded that imprinting differs from ordinary learning in four respects:

1. It does not depend upon any kind of reinforcement (it was not the association of the imprinted object with food that made the young bird follow it).
2. Imprinting is irreversible (once imprinted upon an inappropriate object, such as Lorenz himself, the young birds would continue to follow him and might later even direct sexual behavior toward him, rather than to members of their own species).
3. Imprinting can occur very rapidly, sometimes in one trial (whereas most learning requires a number of trials).
4. Imprinting only occurs during a "critical period" early in development (whereas most learning can occur at any time).

The enormous amount of research triggered by Lorenz's analysis has gradually led to a softening of all of these distinctions. Thus, for example, the critical period has been shown to be not so critical; imprinting can occur in somewhat older birds, but it may require more trials. There seems to be a time of maximum sensitivity to the effect, rather than a sharply defined stage of development. Similarly, it has now been shown that even though a duckling may imprint on quite unlikely stimulus objects, it imprints most readily on stimuli similar to the natural mother (e.g., Gottlieb, 1965). A number of investigators have demonstrated that while imprinting may not involve positive reinforcement, it probably is related to fear in some manner (which is not yet entirely clear), and it may be reinforced by a reduction in fear. Thus, perhaps, when Spalding moved his hand away from the chick, that event was frightening, and getting closer to his hand was reinforced by the reduction in fear such behavior produced.

The research that followed Lorenz's account of imprinting has revealed a considerably more complicated picture of it than Lorenz originally portrayed. But even if this later work makes it impossible to regard imprinting as totally different from conventional kinds of learning, as Lorenz proposed, the reason is partly that learning itself is now seen as a much more diversified and complex set of processes than it was in 1935. At that time, when ethology was just beginning, it was easy to make a sharp distinction between learned behavior and instinctive behavior—the two were antithetical. Today, in part as a result of the research on imprinting, we can now see the development of behavior as an intricate interweaving of experience factors and genetic factors. Experience by itself means nothing without the genetic constitution to process new information and profit by experience. The genetic predisposition alone means nothing without a suitable opportunity for normal development. Was the effect of the hoods with which Spalding covered his chicks' eyes only to prevent visual experience, or did it disrupt the young animals in some subtle way, perhaps by preventing normal sensory development, or by preventing normal behavioral expression, or by introducing abnormal emotional factors? Lorenz (1969) has noted that there are many interpretive hazards in such "deprivation experiments."

It is still possible to draw some strong conclusions with regard to imprinting. One is that it really is not like other kinds of learning. If not totally different, in accordance with Lorenz's four criteria, it is at least quantitatively different. It mainly occurs just at a particular stage of development. It is stimulus learning of the evaluative variety. The imprinting stimulus is not only followed when it moves, the young bird also directs various nestling and vocal responses to it; it is evaluated as the chick's mother, and this evaluation is learned without the stimulus ever being associated with the mother. Imprinting is thus the particular kind of learning with which particular animals solve a particular problem, namely, becoming attached to and affiliating with members of their species.

Another distinctive form of learning is how some species of birds acquire their characteristic songs. Marler (1970) reported extensive work on the song learning of the white-crowned sparrow. All sparrows sound something alike, but there are subspecies and regional dialects; Male birds in the same region all sing the identical song, which differs in detail from the song of another region. The existence of dialects implies that the local song or dialect is learned in some manner. In Marler's experiments, young birds were caught, brought into the laboratory, and isolated from the sound of other birds. Thus, they could be exposed to different recorded songs at certain ages. Marler found a roughly defined critical period (all critical periods seem to be roughly delimited) between 10 and 50 days of age. If exposed to their own dialect during this period they learned it; if exposed to some other dialect at this time they learned it. If exposed to a quite different, nonsparrow song they did not learn it. If the exposure occurred at some time before 10 days or after 50 days there was little or no learning.

The picture we get, then, is that the young birds must have some sort of pre-experience pattern, a template, some general but inarticulate concept of the sparrow song that does not permit them to sing, but does let them recognize the general form of the sparrow song when they hear it. Then when they hear a particular dialect song, this specific pattern is learned, and remembered, and it can generate the specific dialect song.

One of the further remarkable features of this learning is that it appears to be a variant of latent learning (see Chapter 4). The actual singing of the song requires the presence of sexual hormones, which the young birds will not have until the following spring. It hears its song, "learns" it (perceptual learning again), remembers it, and then produces it after a period of several months when it is sexually mature. If a bird is injected with testosterone at an earlier age, it will produce its learned song at that time. It is also interesting that in other species of birds the development of singing may be quite different. Some species evidently do not need to hear their song being sung; they can be isolated when young, and their song still develops normally at the normal time. In other birds, such as the chickadee, the song is learned, but young birds housed together can teach it to each other. From more or less random chirping, closer and closer approximations to the normal song gradually emerge. It is as if chickadees also have a general template of their song and when they hear sounds close to it they recognize them as "right."

The phenomena of learning are inexorably tied up with memory. Learning does an animal no good unless it can remember what it has learned. It is also true that if an animal's behavior reflects some earlier experience, this provides evidence both of learning and of memory. There are many dramatic examples of such delayed behavior in the ethological literature. Perhaps the best known is the dance of the honeybee, discovered by K. von Frisch. Von Frisch (1953) found that when a bee returns to the hive after a successful foraging trip it dances a curious "waggle dance" in a sort of figure eight pattern. As other bees gather around to watch the performance, they become excited, and soon great numbers of them fly off. The remarkable thing is that these bees fly very close to where the original bee had found food. By studying the dance carefully von Frisch was able to decipher the communication system. The farther the food source is, the flatter and straighter the middle part of the figure eight is, and the slower the dance is performed. In the dance, the figure eight is tilted at the same angle that the food source bears to the rays of the sun.

So all of the information about the bearing and the distance is there. With this information another bee, or an ethologist, can go to the food source, or close to it. The communication process per se, something akin to language, involves the transfer of information from one animal to another, but learning and memory are revealed at two points in the whole exchange. One is that the original bee must remember where it came from at the time it does the dance. The second is that the other bees, having obtained the information, must remember it as they set off to the source of food. In both cases the original stimulus is not present at the time the animal must make the appropriate response to it. It is just this sort of delayed responding that convinces us that the most fruitful approach to animal learning is in terms of stimulus learning and information processing, rather than learning to respond in some immediate specified manner to a stimulus.

The selectivity of perception, that is, the specificity with which an animal responds to one aspect of a stimulus object while ignoring another, is quite impressive. One interesting demonstration of this principle was reported in Kramer (1957). Kramer was interested in navigation in starlings. He had the birds housed in the center of a large enclosure. Once a day the birds would be released to obtain food, different birds being trained to go to different parts of the perimeter of the enclosure. Thus, one bird might be trained to get food to the east, another to the south. The birds quickly learned the problem. But Kramer could not be sure they were actually navigating; it was possible that they were merely orienting with respect to the sun. In the morning, with the sun in the east, the animals that were supposed to be flying east may have been merely flying toward the sun, those flying south may have been merely flying with the sun off the left shoulder, and so on. The critical experiment was to test the birds in the afternoon when the sun had moved to the west. The results left no doubt that the starlings really were navigating to the east, south, or whatever, and not just orienting, that is, moving with a fixed orientation to the sun.

The next question posed by Kramer was whether the starlings could learn to orient. He tried to train them to fly east in the morning and west in the afternoon. He discovered that this problem, simply flying toward the sun wherever it happened to be, could be solved only with great difficulty. In short, these animals are quite adept at learning a complex problem which involved determining the position of the sun and the time of day, and calculating a given learned point of the compass from this information. But they are very poor at ignoring this wealth of information and doing the simple thing of just approaching the sun. For the starling, the sun is an object to determine the time of day from, and to calculate direction from, but not an object to be flown toward or away from.

In 1968 Brown and Jenkins reported what seemed at the time to be a minor, methodological study of what they called *autoshaping*. But the phenomenon of autoshaping was soon to revolutionize thinking about learned behavior, and to point to the value of a more ethological way of regarding it. To understand these developments we should first consider a paper by Breland and Breland (1961) titled "The Misbehavior of Organisms." In training a number of different kinds of animals to do behavioral tricks for commercial purposes, they had obtained considerable success in using operant shaping techniques. But they had also had some notable failures, which were described in their 1961 paper. The trouble was that sometimes when an animal was supposed to manipulate a food token, even when it was consistently reinforced for doing so, instead of behavior becoming stronger with continued training, it would gradually disappear. The reinforced response was replaced by the animal's own characteristic food-getting behavior. Raccoons would dip and rub together the food tokens, pigs would root them, chickens would scratch on the ground, and so on. There was what the Brelands called an *instinctive drift* toward the animals' natural food-getting behavior; there was also a dramatic failure of

the reinforcement contingency to control the new learned behavior.

One of the oldest and most firmly established rituals in the animal laboratory is the initial "shaping" of the desired bar-press or key-peck response. An elaborate rationale for this ritual, based on the gradual shaping of successive approximations to the required response, has also been developed. The whole business is supposed to show the power of reinforcement contingencies in producing the learning of new behaviors. Then came the Brown and Jenkins (1968) report. They found that none of this ritual is necessary. The experimenter does not have to intervene at all; the animal can quickly and efficiently shape itself (hence, "autoshaping"). All that is necessary is to present food to the bird (Brown and Jenkins used pigeons) from time to time without regard to its behavior, and to light the key for a few seconds just before food is presented. It appears that the light on the key becomes a signal or token for food, and the pigeon then directs its natural food-getting pecking response at the key. We might say that the key, when lit, is evaluated as food, so the bird pecks at it. The learning mechanism seems to be exactly the same as in the Brelands' misbehavior phenomenon, the only difference being that rather than competing with the response the experimenter is trying to reinforce, the animal's natural food-getting response is just what the experimenter is looking for.

At first it seemed as though the food-signaling property of the light on the key might merely give the bird another reason to peck it; the reinforcement by the food it produced could still be regarded as the animal's primary reason for pecking. But Williams and Williams (1969) extended the procedure by arranging for key pecks to *prevent* food delivery. With this "omission" procedure, the correlation of key light with food still gave the bird a reason to peck, but the operant contingency gave it a reason not to peck. Thus the relative effectiveness of the two mechanisms could be assessed. The Williams' results were quite clear: The correlation of key light with food was far more important than the reinforcement contingency in controlling pecking.

The next major extension of the procedure was made in Moore (1973), which showed by means of high-speed photographs of the pecking response that the pigeon was actually eating the key. In the pigeon the eating response is characterized by a certain posture, closing of the eyes, and opening of the bill. And the peck always occurs in the same fast, hard manner. All of these characteristics were seen in autoshaped key pecks. Moreover, Moore was able to show that thirsty pigeons, autoshaped with water, were drinking the key, that is, producing pecking responses that agreed in all details with the pigeon's normal drinking response.

The picture that emerges from this work is that key pecking in pigeons, which surely must be the most studied and most characteristic of all operant responses in the Skinnerian tradition, is not an operant after all, and is not even learned because of reinforcement. It is simply another instance of the misbehavior phenomenon; the pigeon pecks the key because, when the discriminative stimulus is on, the key is evaluated as food. It is interesting that other animals may not be as subject to the same kind of learning. Thus, Powell and Kelly (1976) reported that in the crow, an animal characterized by more diverse food-getting behaviors, key pecking is more dependent upon reinforcement and

less dependent upon the food-signaling value of the key. How about the rat; is bar pressing reinforced or autoshaped? The answer is still not clear, but one fact may be noted. Rat levers or bars are always made of steel. The main reason is that if they are made of plastic rats will soon chew them up.

The idea that laboratory studies typically do not involve the learning of arbitrary responses chosen at random by the experimenter, but rather learning where and when to respond with species-specific, preformed, prepackaged chunks of behavior was also advanced by Bolles (1970) to account for a number of anomalies found in avoidance learning. Bolles proposed that avoidance behavior is usually little affected by the reinforcement contingencies that are arranged for it, and that it occurs mainly in the form of species-specific defensive reactions (SSDR's). Part of the argument is that most animals have little or no opportunity to learn about predators and other dangers in the natural setting so they must already have effective ways of responding in dangerous situations. All the animal has to learn is which situations are dangerous.

Another part of the argument is that laboratory rats show great proficiency on some avoidance learning tasks and do very poorly on others. There is a wide spectrum of avoidance learning abilities, the difficulty of the task seeming to depend upon what response the rat is required to perform. Thus, one-way avoidance, where the animal can run consistently from a dangerous part of the apparatus to a safe part, is learned very quickly. Running in a wheel to avoid shock proceeds a little more slowly. Running in a shuttlebox, where the rat must keep returning to a part of the apparatus that was previously dangerous, is slower still. In the Skinner box, most rats do very poorly. The explanation in terms of SSDR's is that in the fast-learning situations the rat is simply misbehaving, trying to run away in the most natural sort of way—but this is just the response the experimenter is trying to train, so the training is trivially easy. In the poor-learning situations the misbehavior is more apparent, as the rat either tries to get away or else just freezes. In both cases the reinforcement contingencies that are supposed to produce learning are quite ineffectual.

The final part of the argument is that most of the avoidance learning that occurs is not response learning; the correct response is not being "shaped." The learning that occurs in avoidance situations is mainly stimulus learning (Bolles, 1978), as the rat comes to evaluate this aspect of the situation as dangerous or that aspect as safe.

Human Studies

In the past few years there has been great interest in what might be called the natural roots of the human race, as opposed to our cultural or social roots. There has been increased enthusiasm for outdoor activities, ranging from camping and farming to athletics and sailboating. There has been a booming interest in natural foods, energy sources, building materials, and more natural (or at least more comfortable) clothing. There has been mounting concern with the creatures of the world, especially those that are endangered. Men and women are now beginning to see themselves as part of nature, rather than as distinct from and opposed to it. And nature is beginning to be seen as something to be related to rather than conquered. There have been

a number of excellent popularizations to introduce the general public to the ethological approach to human behavior, including Ardrey (1966), Montagu (1962), and Morris (1967), as well as Lorenz (1966). A lot of what has been written has been focused on the issue of human aggressiveness. Are we innately aggressive, or have we learned to become that way because of societal influence? A lot of this popular writing has been rather speculative, and, as in most areas of psychology, we are still a long way from any firm answers to such really important and interesting questions.

At the same time, an ever-growing range of ethological questions has been studied experimentally. For about the past 20 years, Robert Sommer and his students have been studying territoriality in humans and demonstrating phenomena such as how to make police less aggressive and how to stake out a chair in a library (e.g., Sommer, 1969). The use of other human-specific social signals (some of them not so specific to the human species) has become a very popular research area (Knapp, 1972). Some social signals—the obvious ones, such as the smile—are well known and have been celebrated in literature since time immemorial, because they can be deliberately used to control others' behavior. How many people have learned to smile their way to success? But other signals are so subtle that most of us are not aware either of giving them or receiving them. Indeed, unless sophisticated observational techniques had been used, hardly anyone would know about some of them.

For example, Eibl-Eibesfeldt (1970) has described an "eyebrow flash," which is commonly given in greeting a friend. Both brows raise and come down again very quickly, within a fifth of a second or so. Most of us are totally unaware of this signal. Signallers are probably only aware that they are glad to see a friend, and signalees are probably only aware that the other parties seem glad to see them. Both parties probably attribute the friendliness of the greeting to the smiles that follow, but experiments have shown that the eyebrow flash can be more important than the smile in creating the impression of friendliness. Eibl-Eibesfeldt (1970) has also demonstrated that this signal occurs in a wide range of different cultures.

The work begun by Darwin (1872) on the expression of human emotions has, 100 years later, been continued by Ekman (1973). Working from an ethological framework, Ekman found, just as Darwin had, that one's emotional expression is largely independent of one's cultural tradition.

The ethological approach has as yet had little influence on the study of human learning per se; most of the emphasis has been on motivational and emotional factors and on social behavior. But there have been a few studies suggesting that the human subject, even though a great learner, has the same sort of specificities and inhomogeneities as other creatures. Watson and Rayner (1920) conditioned fear in Little Albert, the unfortunate infant who had acquired fear of furry animals (see Chapter 2). The study was widely cited, both by Watson and by others, as demonstrating specifically how human fears are learned and more generally how human personality is molded by experience. Not so widely cited, because it did not fit the prevailing empiricistic philosophy, is a study by Bregman (1934). She carried out a careful replication of the earlier study, and again found fear when the CS was a white furry animal. But she also found no fear when the CS was an inanimate object! Is it pos-

sible that humans are innately predisposed to fear animals, or to evaluate animals and certain kinds of situations as dangerous? That is the conclusion of Seligman (1972), based upon an analysis of both experimentally induced fears and clinical phobias. Seligman points out that most fears and phobias are highly specific, almost predictable, and that in very few cases has the individual ever experienced an appropriate US. Those of us who are frightened by snakes or by closed places (two of the most common phobias) have usually never been bitten by snakes or locked in a closet. The learning ability of the human seems to have a genetic basis, too, just like that of any other animal.

The most remarkable learning ability in humans, of course, is language acquisition. Indeed, the learning of language is such a stupendous achievement, in terms of the speed with which the child does it, the subtlety of the cues and the motor skills involved, and the sheer complexity of language, that many theorists believe it must depend upon a special language learning system with its own laws (Chomsky, 1975).

IMPLICATIONS

Theoretical

Learning theorists have been so entrenched in certain traditional assumptions that when new evidence has called these assumptions into question, they are confronted with a crisis, and we can see them struggling either to incorporate the new evidence within the old framework or to dismiss it entirely. Such reactions are a common part of science; they tend to occur whenever revolutionary ideas threaten to take over the establishment (Kuhn, 1962). We may note as reactions

to the ethological revolution the attempt
of Herrnstein and Loveland (1972) to
make autoshaping a reinforcement phenomenon. Bitterman (1976) attempted
to deny that the Garcia effect exists (see
Revusky, 1977, for a spirited rebuttal).
B. F. Skinner himself attempted to reduce all of ethology to the status of an
ineffectual analogy of operant conditioning (Skinner, 1966). More recently, Skinner (1977) has conceded that there may
be "phylogenic intrusions" into operant
behavior, as in autoshaping, but apparently he does not see them as seriously
disturbing the all-important business of
controlling behavior with contingent reinforcement.

What inspires this kind of heated defense of the prevailing systems? There
are some rather fundamental issues involved, but a lot of the resistance to the
ethological approach represents nothing
more principled than the conservativism
one expects to find among those who have
enjoyed a privileged position for some
time, a resistance to anything new. The
operant conditioning approach to learning, the approach of Skinner and his followers, has enjoyed great acceptance
among psychologists, as well as educators, therapists, and other professionals.
Many other learning theorists not aligned
with Skinner, and many comparative psychologists in the tradition of Bitterman
(1975), also have a considerable stake
in preserving the established order.

Apart from these purely political considerations, there are also issues of a more
philosophical nature. These issues relate
to how the organism that learns is best
regarded, and how the study of learning
is best carried out. For a very long time
science has been dominated by a mechanistic philosophy. The machine is the
thing. Certainly animals do not look much
like machines, nor do they behave much

like machines. But that did not deter the
application of mechanistic models to animal behavior. The animal was broken
down into systems—circulatory, respiratory, excretory, different kinds of organ
systems—each of which was described
mechanistically. The heart, the kidney,
and the other organs were viewed as machines. This approach has unquestionably
been extremely valuable in increasing our
understanding of how the different organs
work. But when the same approach was
applied to the behavior of animals, it was
not so successful. The early study of simple animals, those whose behavior was
mainly reflexive, was promising. Put a
stimulus in here and observe the response
coming out there: Afferent connected to
efferent. It did look mechanical.

Other chapters, particularly those on
Pavlov (Chapter 2) and Guthrie (Chapter 3), have described how the S–R formula was applied, at least in principle,
to the highly variable, almost unpredictable, behavior of complex animals, including the human. The basic assumption
in that approach can be seen to be the
idea that any behavior, no matter how
complex, is a reaction to some stimulus,
or some set of complex stimulus conditions. The trouble with this approach
is that in applying it to a phenomenon
as complicated as learned behavior, the
presumed causes of behavior, that is, the
controlling stimulus conditions, are themselves unobserved, or even unobservable.
We are left with no means of testing the
model, no means of determining whether
the behavior really is being controlled
by the stimulus conditions, because the
latter have become purely hypothetical.
We are left in a vacuum.

The ethological approach takes us out
of this dilemma by postulating that the
ultimate causes of behavior are not the
conditions that elicit it, but rather its

adaptive significance. The perspective is totally different. The ethological approach is not antimechanistic. Some ethologists do explore the nervous system, and many ethologists study the effects of hormones on behavior. The ethological theorist is not enslaved by the mechanistic philosophy, however, but can operate and think independently of it. The ethologist is not obliged to explain behavior mechanically, in terms of immediately prior physical events, but is free to explain it in terms of its evolutionary history, or in terms of selection pressures, or in terms of what it means for an animal's adaptation to its environment. By taking a broad biological view of behavior rather than a narrow mechanistic view, and by providing a variety of explanations rather than relying on a single kind of mechanical explanation, the ethological approach is free. But this freedom infringes on the autonomy of the mechanistic philosophy, which in the history of science has been the only acceptable way to think about scientific things. This infringement, this challenge to the mechanistic view, is one of the major achievements of the ethological approach.

There are other doctrines that, historically, have been closely related to the mechanistic philosophy. One of these is the idea that animals are basically passive, inert. An animal will not do anything, according to this doctrine, unless stimulated in some way or unless acted on by some kind of motivating force. A machine, by itself, does not do anything. One of the difficulties with the earliest learning theories was that they made little or no allowance for motivational phenomena. This was a serious limitation of the early theories. Seeing this, Edward Tolman and Clark Hull introduced separate motivational concepts of different kinds to deal with motivation. But the

basically passive view of the organism still prevailed. With no "drive" operating, Hull's rat produced no behavior at all. The ethological perspective is quite different. Animals are not passive or inert; they are always engaged in some kind of activity, always solving some vital problem. Whatever the animal does, even if it be resting, there is going to be some biological payoff for the behavior. So, just as the ethological approach infringes upon the mechanistic philosophy, it also infringes on the related idea that animals are basically passive unless stimulated in some way.

Another doctrine that has always been related to the mechanistic position is associationism. Just as the mechanistic view of the physical world regards it as comprised of a great number of indivisible atoms or elements, each of which obeys simple physical-chemical laws, so the psychological world—the world of behavior —is regarded as comprised of a multitude of indivisible elements—associations, in this case—which also obey simple laws. The task of the learning theorist is to discover what these simple laws of association are. This is an admirable systematic strategy. The trouble with it is (as this book well demonstrates) that it has not worked. The laws of learning are not so simple (as it turned out, the laws of physics and chemistry are not very simple either), and we seem to be as far as we have ever been from discovering them. Perhaps we need only persevere. But perhaps the strategy is not adaptive. Perhaps the parallel with the physical sciences is not valid.

Whatever the truth may ultimately be, it can only be advantageous to entertain alternative possibilities. And the functional viewpoint of the ethological approach is a distinctively different possibility from the atomistic-associationistic doctrine that has dominated learning theory for so long. The ethologist asks what the function of this particular learning is. How does it benefit the animal? Why do we find learning here but not there? The search is not for universal laws of association but for the adaptive significance of particular instances of learning.

A final issue that must be mentioned is that of empiricism versus nativism. Psychologists in general and learning people in particular have always had a strong bias in favor of empiricism. This is the doctrine that all knowledge, everything we know, and all that we are, is a result of our experience. Nothing (or at least as little as possible) is innate. The ontogenic determinants of behavior are all-important. Because the roots of ethology lie in the study of instinctive behavior patterns, it has tended to emphasize the nativistic or phylogenic determinants of behavior. Even learning is put into a nativistic, evolutionary framework, as we have seen. So there is a clear antithesis. And although many writers maintain that it is not profitable to address the issue in an either-or manner, to ask, for example, if some behavior is innate or learned, it is undoubtedly a healthy and productive question for learning theorists to think about. Because the learning theorist has traditionally simply accepted without question the empiricistic view, it may well be illuminating to bring the issue into question and to consider the possibility of an alternative view.

Practical

A practical application, like beauty, is mainly in the eye of the beholder. What one person may see as a promising application, another may regard as of little interest or even as a waste of time. And different people may see quite different implications in the same set of events. In contrast with some of our more well-established learning theories, those that have had ample time to recruit adherents in the more applied areas of psychology, such as clinical, the ethological approach is so new that it cannot be expected to have had much impact in these areas. But psychologists are a vigorous, inventive lot, and it should not be long before the influence of ethological ideas is felt in therapy, in education, and in other areas.

The real problem is the converse one, that is, restraining the enthusiastic extension of ethological ideas to the field of human affairs until such time as they can be properly assimilated and put into a useful perspective. The danger is that it is so easy to address the urgent problems of society—the problems of war, justice, and the quality of life—with a glib reference to an inevitable genetic constitution. It is so easy, for example, to justify violence on the grounds that people are innately aggressive. The truth is, of course, that whatever the genetic basis may be for human aggression, it is expressed in learned ways. It is modified and channeled by society to such a great extent that it is, in effect, a social problem rather than a genetic problem. The major contribution the ethological approach can make at this point is to furnish us with new ways of thinking about our species and how we relate to the rest of nature.

SUMMARY

The ethological approach to learning assumes at the outset that the ability to learn through one's own experience is a marvelous adaptation which has evolved in some animals for the solution of certain life problems. It is as marvelous an adaptation as the wing or the leg or the photosensitive eye. It confers upon those species that have it the ability to adapt individually to their environment, even when the environment changes in unpredictable ways.

As this ability evolved, it appeared here and there in the animal kingdom for the solution of certain specific problems, and so we find remarkable but seemingly anomalous learning abilities, as in the honeybee, which are very finely tuned to the solution of specific problems. Then, just as there are animals that specialized in the development of especially remarkable wings or legs or eyes, there evolved animals that specialized in terms of their flexible and modifiable nervous systems. These animals specialized in the direction of becoming generalists; they are not strongly tied to any given environment because they can learn their way around in and adapt to a range of different environments. But these animals, advantaged though they may be, also have their limits. The better learners are still not perfect learners; they retain many of the specificities of the original learners. They may learn about foods and about places, because the selection pressure still exists for flexibility in the solution of those kinds of problems. But they are not as likely to learn about sex and reproduction, or about their own social signals, because the selection pressures are more conservative for the solution of these kinds of problems.

Moreover, there is, as with any adaptation, a price to pay. Although a bird has the enormous advantage of flight, this advantage has to be balanced off against a high metabolism (and a high demand for fuel), small size, a shortage of legs, and so on. In the same way, the animal that solves a lot of problems through learning has a great advantage, but the advantage has to be balanced off against a low reproductive rate, enormous parental investment in the young, and a long period of vulnerability. All of the benefits and costs are relative; there is no master formula that ensures fitness. Everything depends on the existing selection pressures. Homo sapiens is the animal that is most specialized in terms of learning ability. We solve more problems through the learning approach than any other animal, but this does not make us superior. It only makes us more specialized in our own particular way.

ANNOTATED BIBLIOGRAPHY

Eibl-Eibesfeldt, I. *Ethology, the biology of behavior.* New York: Holt, Rinehart & Winston, 1970.

This is a well-written, relatively up-to-date ethology textbook by one of the pioneers. It contains interesting sections on human ethology and on the place of learning in ethology.

Hinde, R. A. *Animal behavior: A synthesis of ethology and comparative psychology.* New York: McGraw-Hill, 1970.

A wealth of material taken from the areas of animal learning, ethology, and the physiological bases of behavior is presented in this large book. Hinde is unusually knowledgeable in all these areas.

Knapp, M. L. *Nonverbal communication in human interaction.* New York: Holt, Rinehart & Winston, 1972.

This paperback describes in some detail the research on human territoriality, social signals, body language, and emotional expression. Also described are some of the methods for observing and scoring human behaviors.

Schiller, C. H. (Ed. and trans.). *Instinctive behavior.* New York: International Universities Press, 1957.

This collection of early papers, mostly by Lorenz, was translated and edited by Schiller. It includes the marvelous monograph by von Uexkull on the perceptual worlds of different animals.

Seligman, M. E. P., & Hager, J. L. (Eds.). *Biological boundaries of learning.* New York: Appleton-Century-Crofts, 1972.

In this collection of papers, mostly from the animal learning tradition, the gradual emergence of the idea of learning specificities is demonstrated. Seligman and Hager give their own interpretation of specificity. Included are many of the studies cited in this chapter.

REFERENCES

Ardrey, R. *The territorial imperative.* New York: Atheneum, 1966.

Baum, W. M. The correlation-based law of effect. *Journal of the Experimental Analysis of Behavior,* 1973, *20,* 137–153.

Bindra, D. A. motivational view of learning, performance and behavior modification. *Psychological Review,* 1974, *81,* 199–213.

Bitterman, M. E. The comparative analysis of learning. *Science,* 1975, *188,* 699-709.

Bitterman, M. E. Technical comment. Flavor aversion studies. *Science,* 1976, *192,* 266–267.

Bolles, R. C. Species-specific defense reactions and avoidance learning. *Psychological Review,* 1970, *77,* 32–48.

Bolles, R. C. The role of stimulus learning in defensive behavior. In S. Hulse, H. Fowler, & W. Honig (Eds.), *Cognitive processes in animal behavior.* Hillsdale, N.J.: Lawrence Erlbaum Associates, 1978.

Bregman, E. O. An attempt to modify the emotional attitudes of infants by the conditioned response technique. *Journal of Genetic Psychology,* 1934, *45,* 169–178.

Breland, K., & Breland, M. The misbehavior of organisms. *American Psychologist,* 1961, *16,* 681–684.

Breland, K., & Breland, M. *Animal behavior.* New York: Macmillan, 1966.

Brown, P. L., & Jenkins, H. M. Auto-shaping of the pigeon's key-peck. *Journal of the Experimental Analysis of Behavior,* 1968, *11,* 1–8.

Chomsky, N. *Reflections on language.* New York: Pantheon, 1975.

Collier, G. H., Hirsch, E., & Hamlin, P. H. The ecological determinants of reinforcement. *Physiology and Behavior,* 1972, *9,* 705–716.

Darwin, C. *On the origin of species.* London: Murray, 1859.

Darwin, C. *The descent of man and selection in relation to sex.* London: Murray, 1871.

Darwin, C. *The expression of the emotions in man and animals.* London: Murray, 1872.

Eibl-Eibesfeldt, I. *Ethology, the biology of behavior.* New York: Holt, Rinehart & Winston, 1970.

Ekman, P. *Darwin and facial expression.* New York: Academic Press, 1973.

Emlen, S. T. Celestial rotation: Its importance in the development of migratory orientation. *Science,* 1970, *170,* 1198–1201.

Fisher, R. A. *The genetical theory of natural selection.* Oxford: Clarendon, 1930.

Garcia, J., & Koelling, R. A. Relation of cue to consequence in avoidance learning. *Psychonomic Science,* 1966, *4,* 123–124.

Gibson, J. J. The theory of affordances. In R. Shaw & J. Bransford (Eds.), *Perceiving, acting and knowing: Toward an ecological psychology.* Hillsdale, N.J.: Lawrence Erlbaum Associates, 1977.

Gottlieb, G. Imprinting in relation to parental and species identification by avian neonates. *Journal of Comparative and Physiological Psychology,* 1965, *59,* 345–356.

Heinroth, O. Beiträge zur biologie namentlich ethologie und psychologie der amatiden. *Verh. V. Internat. Ornithol. Kongr.* Berlin: 1910, pp. 589–592.

Herrnstein, R. J., & Loveland, D. H. Food-avoidance in hungry pigeons, and other perplexities. *Journal of the Experimental Analysis of Behavior,* 1972, *18,* 369–383.

Hinde, R. A. *Animal behavior: A synthesis of ethology and comparative psychology.* New York: McGraw-Hill, 1970.

Hineline, P. N., & Rachlin, H. Escape and avoidance of shock by pigeons pecking a key. *Journal of the Experimental Analysis of Behavior,* 1969, *12,* 533–538.

Hodos, W., & Campbell, C. B. G. Scala naturae: Why there is no theory in comparative psychology. *Psychological Review,* 1969, *76,* 337–350.

Kamil, A. C. Systematic foraging by a nectar-feeding bird, the amakihi (Loxops virens). *Journal of Comparative and Physiological Psychology,* 1978, *92,* 388–396.

Knapp, M. L. *Nonverbal communication in human interaction.* New York: Holt, Rinehart & Winston, 1972.

Kramer, G. Experiments on bird orientation and their interpretation. *Ibis,* 1957, *99,* 196–227.

Kuhn, T. S. *The structure of scientific revolutions.* Chicago: University of Chicago Press, 1962.

Lorenz, K. [Der Kumpans in der Umwelt des Vogels.] In C. H. Schiller (Ed. and trans.), *Instinctive behavior.* New York: International Universities Press, 1957. (Originally published, 1935.)

Lorenz, K. *Evolution and modification of behavior.* Chicago: University of Chicago Press, 1965.

Lorenz, K. *On aggression.* New York: Harcourt, Brace & World, 1966.

Lorenz, K. Innate bases of learning. In K. Primbram (Ed.), *On the biology of learning.* New York: Harcourt, Brace & World, 1969.

Marler, P. A comparative approach to vocal learning: Song development in white-crowned sparrows. *Journal of Comparative and Physiological Psychology,* 1970, *71,* 1–25.

Montagu, M. F. A. *Culture and the evolution of man.* London: Oxford University Press, 1962.

Moore, B. R. The role of directed Pavlovian reactions in simple instrumental learning in the pigeon. In R. A. Hinde & J. Stevenson-Hinde (Eds.), *Constraints on learning.* New York: Academic Press, 1973.

Morris, D. *The naked ape.* New York: McGraw-Hill, 1967.

Orians, G. H. Age and hunting success in the brown pelican (pelicanus occidentalis). *Animal behavior,* 1969, *17,* 316–319.

Powell, R. W., & Kelly, W. Responding under positive and negative response contingencies in pigeons and crows. *Journal of the Experimental Analysis of Behavior,* 1976, *25,* 219–225.

Revusky, S. Interference with progress by the scientific establishment: Examples from flavor aversion learning. In N. W. Milgram, L. Krames, & T. M. Alloway (Eds.), *Food aversion learning.* New York: Plenum, 1977.

Romanes, G. J. *Animal intelligence.* London: Kegan, Paul & Trench, 1882.

Seligman, M. E. P. Phobias and preparedness. In M. E. P. Seligman & J. L. Hager (Eds.), *Biological boundaries of learning.* New York: Appleton-Century-Crofts, 1972.

Shettleworth, S. J. Constraints on learning. In D. S. Lehrmen, R. A. Hinde, & E. Shaw (Eds.), *Advances in the study of behavior* (Vol. 4). New York: Academic Press, 1972.

Skinner, B. F. The phylogeny and ontogeny of behavior. *Science,* 1966, *153,* 1205–1213.

Skinner, B. F. Herrnstein and the evolution of behaviorism. *American Psychologist,* 1977, *32,* 1006–1012.

Sommer, R. *Personal space.* Englewood Cliffs, N.J.: Prentice-Hall, 1969.

Spalding, D. Instinct with original observations on young animals. *Macmillans Magazine,* 1872, *27,* 282–293.

Tinbergen, N. *The study of instinct.* Oxford: Clarendon, 1951.

Von Frisch, K. *The dancing bees.* New York: Harcourt, Brace & World, 1953.

Von Uexkull, J. V. [Umwelt und Innerwelt de Tiere.] C. H. Schiller (Ed. and trans.), *Instinctive behavior.* New York: International Universities Press, 1957. (Originally published 1909.)

Watson, J. B., & Rayner, R. Conditioned emotional reactions. *Journal of Experimental Psychology,* 1920, *3,* 1–14.

Williams, D. R., & Williams, H. Automaintenance in the pigeon: Sustained pecking despite contingent non-reinforcement. *Journal of the Experimental Analysis of Behavior,* 1969, *12,* 511–529.

7

Gestalt Theory of Learning

MICHAEL WERTHEIMER

INTRODUCTION

Overview

Gestalt theory is one of several rival schools of thought that arose during the first decades of the 20th century in protest against the prevailing mechanistic and associationistic mode of thought. The carefully worked out psychological theory of Wilhelm Wundt, based on a Newtonian conception of the universe, was dominating the intellectual scene about the turn of the century. It conceived of psychology as the science of mental life, a complement to the other natural sciences like physics and chemistry. The contents of the psyche were, by careful introspection (engaged in by sophisticated, trained observers), to be broken down into their constituent elements, and the laws of how such elements combine to form mental wholes were being sought. To understand a mental whole, it was considered necessary to understand its elemental constituents and how these psychic "atoms" get hooked together.

Gestalt theory and its siblings (the school of Gestalt quality, the "wholistic" school, the theory of "layers," etc.) objected to this view of the human psyche as nothing more than the sum total of the elemental bits and pieces (sensations, feelings, etc.) that make it up. Isn't the mind more than just a conglomeration of its contents? Aren't melodies something over and above the successive tones of which they are composed? Is a square nothing but what you get when you add together four equal straight lines plus four right angles? Isn't a symphony something quite different from the sum of the sounds that happen to be made at about the same time by a variety of people playing a variety of musical instruments in the same room? What motivated Gestalt theory and its rivals was the firm conviction that a mechanical, associative, inert image of the psyche does not do justice to the richness, creativity, and intricately organized nature of mental processes and events.

Gestalt theory is the most specific and the most firmly grounded in experimental data among the wholistic schools, and therefore also the most successful and influential one. Its initial concern was with the psychology of thinking (a process which often displays characteristics that are not adequately explained by mere *hookups*) and with problems of cognition in general. It soon spread to the areas of problem solving and perception, aesthetics, personality, and social psychology; it is not primarily a theory of learning as such, but nevertheless has much to say about this topic—and makes substantial, and fervent, recommendations for the process of teaching that follow directly from its main tenets.

To understand why an organism behaves in the way it does, argue the Gestalt theorists, one must understand how the organism perceives itself and the situation in which it finds itself. Perception therefore is a basic issue in all Gestalt analyses; indeed, learning involves seeing—perceiving—things as they really are. Typically, learning is a process of going from a situation in which something is obscure, does not make sense, or is quite unrecognized, to a state in which the previously unknown or incomprehensible now is clear, makes sense, is understood, and can be coped with readily.

The Gestalt approach to learning, therefore, differs radically from earlier views of the field, and, indeed, contrasts sharply as well with most other modern views of learning that concentrate on such questions as how a conditioned stimulus gets attached to an unconditioned stimulus so as to elicit a conditioned response, how a reinforcing stimulus increases the probability of emission of a particular instrumental response in the presence of a given discriminative stimulus, or how nonsense syllables get associated with each other in serial learning. "Genuine" learning has precious little to do with such "and-connections"; at its core is understanding, insight, catching on. Associative hookups, claim the Gestalt theorists, are empty caricatures of "real learning," which, instead, is characterized by getting to the heart of an issue, by being true to the specific nature and structure of the material being learned, and by the satisfying "click" of

understanding something that previously made no sense—the famous "Aha!" experience of genuine insight.

Major Issues

The core issue in Gestalt theory concerns the contrast between what have been called *andsums* and *transsums*. An andsum is a whole that exactly equals the sum total of its constituent parts, like a pile of bricks, a handful of rice kernels, or a sum of money. A transsum (literally, something which transcends a sum) is a whole that is quite different from a sum of a set of mutually indifferent constituent parts—examples include an electrical field, a soap bubble, a magnetic field, or a personality. While a few andsums do exist in reality, contend the Gestalt theorists, the vast majority of natural units and wholes in the real world are transsums. And it does an injustice to them to treat them as though they were in principle no different from such arbitrary synthetic conglomerates. Considering association or conditioning as prototypic of learning, therefore, is substituting an impoverished, passive, and largely artificial process for what is really a lively, active, and naturally rich one. People have to resort to bald memorizing or blind conditioning only when the learning task offered them is by its very nature stupid—which hardly ever occurs in the real world outside the psychological laboratory. While most psychologists theorize as though the world, psychological as well as nonpsychological, were composed of andsums, it actually is composed primarily of transsums.

Consequently, for the Gestalt theorist the issue of primary interest is how organisms develop the kind of understanding of their environment that permits them to cope with it effectively. The core question of the psychology of learning should not be how one thing gets associated with another, how hookups between stimuli and responses get established, or how other connections are formed, but what the conditions are under which genuine understanding of a problem situation, and its solution, is achieved.

The psychological process of insight thus forms the core of the Gestalt theorist's concern with the psychology of learning. Learning has occurred when the learner has understood, has developed an insight into the actual nature of the problem situation, and can act in ways that show that the important features of the task have indeed been grasped. Not association, but insight and understanding are for the Gestalt theorist the central issues in learning.

If understanding and insight have actually occurred, it is only a minor step, and one that presents little difficulty, to transfer the learning to a new situation in which it also applies. Thus one test of whether learning has really happened is to check whether what has been learned will generalize to a related task—if all that has transpired is sheer memorizing or blind associating, the learner will be unable to recognize the similarity between a task that has already been mastered and a new one which, while it may be superficially quite different, requires the same insight to solve it that also worked in the earlier task. Thus the transfer of learning is a central issue for the Gestalt theorist.

A question which is at the core of much contemporary learning theory, the nature of reinforcement and its role in learning, is specifically *not* a major concern for the Gestaltist. Indeed, extrinsic reinforcements like food, gold stars, or a pat on the head are seen by Gestalt theorists as irrelevant distractors, as manipulations that are likely to *interfere* with genuine learning. If you are wrestling with a theorem in geometry or are trying to build a bridge out of blocks, the relevant issue is whether you have understood the proof or whether the bridge actually stands up without falling—not a grade the teacher gives you or a smile from your appreciative parents.

Related to this same issue is the Gestalt theorist's stance on the question, central to many other learning theorists, of the extent to which conditioning (whether classical, instrumental, or both) is fundamental in all learning, i.e., of whether all learning cannot ultimately be reduced to conditioning. The Gestalt position on this question is an unequivocal no. Genuine learning is entirely different from mere conditioning.

Basic Concepts

Gestalt. The most basic concept in Gestalt theory cannot, unfortunately, be readily translated into English. That is, of course, why the German word *Gestalt* has become part of the international technical vocabulary of psychology. The word means roughly the same as form, shape, pattern, structure, or configuration, or as the term *transsum,* used above. A Gestalt is an articulated whole, a system within which the constituent parts are in dynamic interrelation with each other and with the whole, an integrated totality within which each part is in the place, role, and function required for it by the nature of the whole. It is the antithesis of a sum, which is nothing more than a bundle of parts or a concatenation of bits and pieces that happen arbitrarily to be hooked or glued together haphazardly.

Structure. Every Gestalt has an inherent, characteristic structure. Indeed the task of Gestalt theory is the description of natural structures in a manner that does not do violence to their inner root or essence; most Gestalten have their own intrinsic laws. The structure of a typical Gestalt is such that alteration of one part almost inevitably produces changes in other parts; parts in a Gestalt structure are not inert components that are indifferent to each other. A slight displacement of a single playing card in a house of cards will make the entire structure come tumbling down. And a break at one point in a soap bubble produces an instant and dramatic change in the entire structure.

Dynamic Self-Distribution. The parts of a Gestalt are not arbitrarily held together by mechanical forces. Rather, the dynamics of the whole determine where and with what function each part of the whole must occur. Thus a drop of oil in water will take on a spheroid shape, not because the water acts as a rigid mold but because of internal forces, and the parts of the film of a soap bubble distribute themselves so as to produce reasonable uniformity in the thickness of the film throughout the entire bubble. Gestalten strive for optimal form because of forces inherent in the Gestalten themselves, not because of arbitrary forces imposed from without.

Relational Determination. Closely tied to the idea of dynamic self-distribution is that of relational determination: It is the relations of parts to the whole and parts to each other that determine the nature of each part and its function in the whole. The same "element" may play a quite different role, and may be seen quite differently, as part of different wholes: C played on the piano takes on entirely different properties when it functions as a leading tone in a D7 chord (a dominant that requires resolution to a tonic G chord in classical harmony), as the third

in an A minor chord, or as the tonic to which a melody played in the key of C returns.

Insight. Fundamental to the Gestalt view of learning is achieving a veridical impression of a problematic state of affairs: gaining insight into the structure of a problem situation, understanding how it is put together, how it works, and how a solution to the problem is to be gained. Learning has typically not occurred if this kind of insight has not occurred.

Understanding. Insight is a matter of achieving a full understanding of something. Learning has happened if insight has taken place; understanding is the goal of learning.

Organization. The structure of any Gestalt is organized in a particular, characteristic way; understanding that structure means understanding its organization. Formulation of the Gestalt principles of the organization of perception was a major contribution of that school; the principles carried over directly into the psychology of learning. Since seeing into, or having insight into a Gestalt means being cognizant of its structure and how that structure is organized, the principles of Gestalt organization are as fundamental to the psychology of learning as they are to the psychology of perception.

Reorganization. If organisms could correctly perceive and understand every new situation immediately and without any trouble, there would be no need for learning. But many problems are such that the first time you encounter them, you have no idea what to do about them or how to go about solving them, and indeed the problem may initially appear quite incomprehensible, senseless, or opaque. Solution becomes possible only when the central features of the problem are clearly recognized, and paths to a possible approach emerge. Thus, learning frequently involves changing your initial perception of a problem situation, reorganizing that perception until it clicks and you have a way to cope with it. Typically such reorganization means that irrelevant details have been stripped away, that central features have become salient, and that the problem is seen more veridically.

Meaning. Genuine learning does not require arbitrary connections among unrelated elements. Rather, a typical learning sequence involves going from a situation in which things don't make sense, in which arbitrariness seems to be the rule, to a situation in which there *is* meaning, in which relations among parts are understood and make sense. Meaningfulness, rather than sheer, blind association, is the hallmark of genuine learning.

Transfer. The true test of understanding is whether the new insight that has been acquired will transfer to other situations which are structurally similar but which differ in superficial detail. Blind learning by association is unlikely to be generalizable to other relevant settings and problems, but genuine insight will transfer to appropriate related problem areas.

Intrinsic Motivation. The achievement of insight is one of the most inherently rewarding of all experiences. That is, acquisition of understanding or competence serves as its own powerful reward. Hence, use of extrinsic rewards, reinforcements that are not directly and inherently related to the specific task itself about which something is being learned, is to be discouraged. The intrinsic motivation of trying to make sense of something new is fully sufficient to lead to learning and to "stamp it in"; extrinsic motivation is only likely to be distracting and to lead to a concern with something

irrelevant to the immediate learning task itself.

HISTORY

Beginnings

Positions opposed to sheer elementism or mechanical atomism have found their proponents since the golden age of Greek civilization. Heraclitus (ca. 540–475 B.C.) considered energy and change the most basic processes, Anaxagoras (ca. 500–428 B.C.) taught that the most fundamental unit in the universe is a relationship, and Aristotle (384–323 B.C.) claimed that everything can be analyzed into "form" and "matter," with form superordinate to matter. During the 19th century, John Stuart Mill (1806–1873), in opposition to his father James Mill (who formulated an influential mechanistic, associationistic theory of mind), claimed that *mental chemistry* is a better term for the philosophy of mind than *mental mechanics*—mental compounds, he argued, like chemical compounds, can have properties different from those of the "elements" composing them.

Even Wilhelm Wundt recognized that a mental whole may be something different from the mere sum of its constituent parts. He proposed that the mind performs a *creative synthesis* upon the elements provided to it by the processes of sensation and association, yielding integrated wholes that are not identical to the sum of their elemental components. And yet the prevailing orientation in the psychology of the late 19th century was that, to oversimplify a bit, a whole is, in general, and other things being equal, nothing more than the sum of its parts. But a famous paper by Christian von Ehrenfels in 1890 argued that most mental wholes are *more* than the sums of their parts. A triangle is not just the sum of three straight lines plus three appropriate angles, but the sum of these six elements plus a seventh: the "Gestalt quality" or form quality of triangularity. Indeed, he pointed out, you can vary the first six elements substantially without losing the triangularity of the triangle: Triangles come in a great variety of sizes and shapes. Similarly, a melody is not just the sum total of the notes making up that melody, but those notes *plus* the form quality of that particular melody. You can even transpose the melody to a different key, changing all the notes—the "elements"—of the melody, and yet recognize that it is still the same melody. So, argued von Ehrenfels, a whole is *more than* the sum of its parts: It is the sum of the parts plus the Gestalt quality.

That is where matters stood at the beginning of the 20th century. About 1910 Max Wertheimer proposed another radical reorganization of the wholistic view, a reorganization that was to form the core of the Gestalt school of psychology. The entire additive approach, he argued, is wrong. The whole is not equal to the sum of its parts, nor is it merely the sum of its parts plus another element, the Gestalt quality; the whole can be *entirely different from* the sum of its parts. Looking at it in summative terms, as a synthesis of elements, is inadequate; a whole is logically, and epistemologically, *prior to* its parts. Indeed the parts do not become parts, do not function as parts, *until there is a whole of which they are parts.* Gestalt theory claims that a whole is not equal to the sum of its parts, nor is it more than a sum of its parts; rather a whole has a structure, internal dynamics, and an integrated articulation which make it fundamentally different from something conceived of as a mere sum.

This approach was first hinted at in a paper by Wertheimer on primitive music published in an obscure journal in 1910. It was elaborated on in a much longer article by Wertheimer in 1912(b) on the thinking of "primitive" people in the number domain; this paper provides a wealth of examples that show how sensible much primitive numerical thought is, how well structured and appropriate it is to the particular problem situations in which it is employed. The early Gestalt theorists generally tagged another paper by Wertheimer, which was published later in 1912(a) and which dealt with certain phenomena in the perception of apparent motion, as the paper that formally launched the Gestalt school.

Major Theorists

Max Wertheimer (1880–1943) is generally conceded to have founded the Gestalt theory. But he was joined early by Wolfgang Köhler (1887–1967) and Kurt Koffka (1886–1941), and indeed these two published far more about Gestalt psychology than Wertheimer did. Some years later, Kurt Lewin (1890–1947) was associated with the original three and worked in a similar vein, but his approach, while still greatly influenced by the Gestalt mode, was sufficiently different that most psychologists think of him not so much as a Gestalt theorist but as a founder of a closely related school: field theory. Still later, Rudolf Arnheim and Solomon E. Asch became identified with the Gestalt theory.

Gestalt theory was born in Germany; it was introduced to the United States during the 1920s by Koffka and Köhler. In 1924 R. M. Ogden published an English translation of a work by Koffka, *The Growth of the Mind,* and in 1925 appeared the English version of the report of Köhler's famous experiments on problem solving by chimpanzees, *The Mentality of Apes.* The first of all Gestalt publications in English was an article by Koffka in the 1922 *Psychological Bulletin;* its title, "Perception: An Introduction to the Gestalt-Theorie," was to initiate a long history of misunderstanding that identified Gestalt psychology primarily with the field of perception. (While perception was certainly a significant focus for work in the Gestalt tradition, thinking, cognition, problem solving, personality, and social psychology were at least equally as important.) By the mid–1930s all three of the original Gestalt theorists—and Lewin too—had emigrated to the United States, and since that time this country has been the major seat of Gestalt theory, although there have also been many psychologists identified with the Gestalt movement in other countries throughout the world: Japan, Italy, Finland, Germany, India, and others.

Max Wertheimer, the founder, first enunciated the principle that the whole is prior to its parts. His 1912(a) paper on the phi phenomenon reported a series of experiments performed in 1910 and 1911 at the Frankfurt Academy, with Köhler and Koffka as his subjects. The experiments were a series of variations on a prototypic setup in which first one short vertical line (*A*) is briefly exposed just to the left of a fixation point; that line is extinguished; and a moment later, a second short vertical line (*B*) is exposed briefly just to the right of the fixation point. If the time relations are appropriate (specifically, the time between the disappearance of *A* and the appearance of *B*), it looks to the observer not as though first one line, *A,* goes on and then off, and then a second line, *B,* in a slightly different location, goes on and then off, but as though there is only a single line, which first is located in position *A* and then jumps, moves, to position *B.* The apparent motion of a single object does not accord with the stimulus situation viewed in a piecemeal fashion; the perceived whole, the impression of a single item moving from one location to another, is in no sense deducible from the "elements," the physical stimuli, that give rise to it.

And still more convincing as a demonstration of the Gestalt thesis was a particular percept yielded when the time relations were not conducive to this kind of *optimal movement:* If the time interval between the going off of *A* and the going on of *B* is a bit *longer,* observers report a kind of "pure movement," in the sense that *A* does not seem to be displaced to position *B,* but *A* stays where it was and *B* appears in its own location as a separate line, *yet there is a kind of "shadow" of "pure movement," without any object "carrying" that movement,* which appears to flit from *A* to *B.* Wertheimer called this particularly illusory kind of movement *phi* (short for *phenomenon*), and argued that such an experience can certainly not be considered as nothing but the sum of the sensory experiences produced by the stimuli *A* and *B.*

In 1923, Wertheimer published another seminal work in Gestalt psychology, on the principles of organization. The paper addressed the question of how it is that various portions of an experienced environment are articulated and segregated into separate units or wholes. What makes various parts of the "phenomenological field" hang together? The most general principle is the "Law of *Prägnanz*" (another untranslatable German term, roughly equivalent to balance, symmetry, precision, or "filled with significance"; it is a cognate of the English word in phrases such as "a pregnant pause," or "a look pregnant with meaning"), which states that the organization of any whole will be as "good" as the prevailing conditions allow. The paper develops a series of special cases or subcategories of this law, such as the Law of Similarity (similar items will tend to form a group), the Law of Proximity (items close to or near each other will be apprehended as belonging together), the Law of Closure (items which together form a closed, integrated pattern will be seen as a unit), the Law of Good Continuation (items which are natural successors of a series will be seen as belonging to that series), and the Law of Common Fate (objects that are undergoing the same change—e.g., a band marching by a grandstand—are perceived as constituting a whole).

Wertheimer's work that is perhaps most directly related to the area of learning is a short posthumously published book, *Productive Thinking* (1945/1959). In it, he uses examples ranging from the modest insight that the area of a rectangle is equal to the product of its base times its height, through an analysis of the thought processes involved in describing the structure of an office in which a person is employed, to the origins of Albert Einstein's theory of relativity, for the purpose of developing the Gestalt thesis that genuine learning and thinking involve getting to the heart of a problem, understanding the structure of the situation, and achieving insight into the essential features required to make sense of whatever is at issue.

Wolfgang Köhler was to be the most prominent of the Gestalt theorists. He published a series of tightly reasoned books on the theory, including one, simply entitled *Gestalt Psychology,* which has been very popular since it first appeared in 1929 and which has been reissued

several times since in paperback format. He developed Wertheimer's principle of *isomorphism* (that the structure of phenomenological experience has the same fundamental form as the structure of the underlying events in the nervous system) in elaborate technical detail, and he undertook many ingenious experiments to try to demonstrate this principle. In an erudite work published in Germany in 1920 and never fully translated into English, *The Physical Gestalten at Rest and in a Stationary State,* Köhler developed many physical and chemical analogues to the Law of Prägnanz, showing how gravitational and other field phenomena display Gestalt properties. His *The Mentality of Apes* (1925) reported extensive experiments on problem solving in chimpanzees, which can display a striking intelligence in their approach to problem situations—provided that the problem situations themselves make sense and are not artificial or arbitrary.

Kurt Koffka, the first to introduce the Gestalt approach to the English-speaking psychological world, engaged with his students in dozens of experiments inspired by the Gestalt mode. Koffka also compiled the most complete and thorough account of Gestalt theory, *Principles of Gestalt Psychology* (1935), a long, detailed, and scholarly survey of the many experimental and theoretical contributions made by Gestalt theorists and their students during the first two and a half decades of the school's existence.

While Wertheimer, Köhler, and Koffka primarily worked in the traditional realm of general experimental psychology, Kurt Lewin extended the theory to the fields of motivation, personality, and especially social psychology. He evolved a set of symbols for the description of persons in their environments and tried to treat them in a manner consistent with the mathematical specialty of topology, generating what he called a *topological psychology* —a field theory to try to account for behavior in terms of how people view themselves and their own immediate "psychological" environments. His forays into social psychology originated the research area of group dynamics, a flourishing and major subpart of later social psychological work.

Rudolf Arnheim, a younger member of the Gestalt group who also emigrated to the United States, has had a distinguished career, concentrating primarily on the extension of the Gestalt principles to problems in aesthetics. His many books, in particular *Art and Visual Perception* (1954), have been highly influential. Indeed, Arnheim became the incumbent of the first professorship in the psychology of art in the world, at Harvard University.

Solomon E. Asch, of Swarthmore College and Princeton University, was introduced to Gestalt psychology by Wertheimer in the early 1930s—in fact, he helped Wertheimer substantially with his English when Wertheimer first arrived in the United States in 1933. He has made experimental contributions in learning within the Gestalt tradition. But his most significant work was his *Social Psychology* (1952), which developed in detail the Gestalt approach to this field, and which reported Asch's ingenious and influential experiments on the effects of group pressure on individual judgments (initially of the lengths of lines).

Current Status

Gestalt theory flourished in Germany during the 1920s and early 1930s, and then was a major school on the American scene during the late 1930s and early 1940s. Much research inspired by the Gestalt approach was published in a journal edited by the Gestalt psychologists, *Psychologische Forschung* ("Psychological Research"), from the early 1920s through the mid 1930s. Although this journal was temporarily discontinued during World War II, it was resurrected thereafter, with its title changed to the English *Psychological Research* and with its content much less directly related to Gestalt theory than it was during its early years.

Gestalt theory ceased being a specific, strong, and cohesive school after several of its chief proponents, first Koffka, then Wertheimer, then Lewin, died during the 1940s. Köhler continued as champion of the movement until his own death in the late 1960s. Second-generation Gestalt theorists were not as fervent in their identification with the theory as the original triumvirate had been—though they clearly still thought of themselves as Gestalt psychologists. Among this group are Wolfgang Metzger, who was to be very prominent among German-speaking psychologists; Fritz Heider, who joined Wertheimer and Köhler in Berlin in 1921; Köhler's student Mary Henle; Lewin's students Roger Barker and Dorwin Cartwright; and many others. But the school became more diffuse as the years passed. True, there were still Gestalt psychologists in 1980, but most of them thought of themselves more as research psychologists interested in the psychology of cognition, or learning, or social phenomena, or thinking, than primarily as Gestalt theorists.

The influence of Gestalt theory on the current scene is, then, more implicit than explicit (although there also still are studies directly influenced by Gestalt theory, such as the 1977 finding of Pomerantz, Sager, and Stoever that parts of visually presented geometric figures are easier to recognize if they are component segments of larger wholes than if they are presented in isolation). Recent work in problem solving, information processing, and cognitive psychology is probing more deeply into issues raised by Gestalt psychologists a half century earlier—and most current researchers in these areas are aware of the contributions of the Gestalt heritage to the way in which these problem areas are being approached today. Sophisticated computer technology has replaced index cards with India ink drawings, and mathematical formulations have replaced less precise verbal statements in theories about cognitive phenomena. But these modern approaches (e.g., Greeno, 1977, 1978; Kintsch, 1974; Neisser, 1967, 1976; Newell & Simon, 1972; Scandura, 1975) are conceptually not far removed from the original Gestalt notions. The problems of the organization of thinking and memory, of the structure of people's conceptions of the world, of the role of meaning in learning and problem solving have become far more salient in recent years than they were a few decades ago. And the Gestalt instructional precepts have played a major role in educational policy and practice in recent years: The new math and other instructional programs that were developed during the 1950s and 1960s and that were used nationwide within the United States, as well as abroad, were largely based on discovery learning and policies with similar principles that can be traced directly to the Gestalt movement.

Other Theories

As was pointed out in the Introduction, Gestalt psychology was one of several wholistic theories that arose early in the 20th century as objections to the prevailing mechanistic and elementistic spirit of the time in psychology. Two of the rival wholistic schools are the theory of complexes (*Komplextheorie*) of Georg Elias Müller and the wholistic psychology (*Ganzheitspsychologie*) of Fritz Krueger. Müller argued that his concept of the complex is closely related to the core idea of a Gestalt in Gestalt theory; he was concerned with the structure of wholes and with relations both among parts of a whole and among wholes themselves, each of which have their own inherent structure. The chief difference between complex theory and Gestalt theory is that Müller's approach retained the idea that a whole is constituted of parts that are associated, and of the relations among these parts; it remained an and-summative theory that did not acknowledge the primacy of the whole over the parts, as Gestalt theory did. Krueger's wholism is quite similar to Müller's complex theory, differing from the Gestalt approach in the same way. Krueger's wholes are not logically or epistemologically primary relative to their parts; rather, his wholes are analogous to the units produced by Wundtian creative synthesis, which acts upon the parts to consolidate them. Indeed Krueger's theory was a direct descendant of Wundtian theory, and Krueger took over Wundt's professorship at the University of Leipzig when Wundt retired.

Kurt Lewin and Kurt Goldstein were close to the Gestalt school, but never formally privy to its inner sanctum. While Lewin worked for many years at the same institution, the University of Berlin, in which Köhler and Wertheimer were vigorously pursuing the implications of the Gestalt theory, his laboratory was at a different physical location from the rooms being used by Köhler, Wertheimer, and their students. Goldstein, a physician, was primarily interested in neurology, and also was never really close to the founders of the movement. Both Lewin and Goldstein later came to the United States, as did almost all of the early Gestalt theorists, but once in this country they pursued their own interests, largely independently of the work of Wertheimer, Köhler, and Koffka. Lewin went on to develop his topological psychology, his dynamic theory of personality, and his work in group dynamics, extending Gestalt thought into his highly influential field theory—but the original Gestalt psychologists were somewhat uneasy about Lewin's work, suggesting that it to some extent lacked the precision of thought and experiment which they tried always to make an integral part of their own contributions. The original Gestalt theorists had similar qualms about the work of Goldstein, who extended Gestalt ideas broadly to his view of the organism as a whole (he published a book entitled *The Organism* in 1939), largely based on his investigations of the cognitive problems suffered by people with brain damage; his organismic approach became an influential theory in its own right.

Wolfgang Metzger, later at the University of Münster, started out as Wertheimer's assistant at the University of Frankfurt during the early 1930s. He remained closely associated with the Gestalt approach in Germany both during the Hitler years and in the decades following World War II. His widely used introductory text in psychology (1940/1975) and his book on the laws of seeing (*Gesetze des Sehens,* 1940/1975) are direct descendants of the early Gestalt work, and they have kept the Gestalt approach salient among German-speaking psychologists down through the 1970s. Other German psychologists too have continued to work closely within the Gestalt paradigm, like Metzger pursuing the Gestalt mode in ever-greater detail into virtually all major areas of psychology; among these are Edwin Rausch, Wilhelm Witte, and Albert Wellek.

Raymond H. Wheeler, an American, early became inspired by the Gestalt approach and developed his own organismic psychology. It was based largely on Wheeler's interest in the biological and psychological phenomena of human development, and it flourished for a few years during the early 1930s. Generating both animal and human experiments, Wheeler's *configurationism* was, however, largely eclipsed by the Gestalt theorists' own writings after they came to the United States.

Fritz Heider, trained in several of the early wholistic psychologies, is more identified with Gestalt theory than with any other school of psychology. His *Psychology of Interpersonal Relations* (1958) set out to perform a phenomenological analysis of the significant features of social interaction, doing full justice to them in a Gestalt sense, and became the basis for a flourishing new field in social psychology, attribution research. While not a direct Gestalt contribution, his widely influential analysis still is an outgrowth of the Gestalt mode of thought.

Edward C. Tolman, a giant among Americans, identified with the psychology of learning, was locking horns with Clark L. Hull during the 1930s, the 1940s, and the early 1950s. His *Purposive Behavior in Animals and Men* (1932) was one of the first systematic theories of learning to make explicit use of the new Gestalt concepts that were just being discovered by psychologists in the United States. His theory was an ingenious synthesis of ideas from systems as diverse as William McDougall's hormic psychology, John B. Watson's behaviorism, and Gestalt theory. He saw organisms as purposive creatures, striving to achieve particular ends, which learn not simple stimulus-response connections or sequences of reflexes, but "what leads to what." His cognitive behaviorism focused upon *means-end readinesses* (the tendency of an organism to learn what means are likely to lead to what ends), and the learning of what he called *sign-gestalt-expectations* (as organisms learn about specific situations, they come to cognize these situations in their entirety and to develop expectations about what behaviors will lead to what consequences, given the presence of certain critical stimuli—or signs—in that situation). The rivalry between Tolman's and Hull's theories of learning was to generate hundreds of experiments on learning, especially during the 1940s, in the United States.

One other theory that must be mentioned is the psychotherapeutic approach of Fritz Perls and his colleagues, called *gestalt therapy*. A neo-Freudian approach that emphasizes the client's existence in the here and now, this therapy has amassed a large following not only among clinical psychologists but among the lay public as well. While it is true that Perls heard a lecture by Wertheimer once at the University of Berlin and was inspired by it, there is conceptually no relationship whatever between Perls's gestalt psychotherapy and classical Gestalt theory, as documented by Henle (1978), for example. It is a historical accident that Perls's approach was called gestalt therapy, and his practices are in no way related to traditional Gestalt theory:

Evaluations, criticisms, successes, or failures of Gestalt theory have no bearing on the validity of gestalt therapy, nor do evaluations, criticisms, successes, or failures of gestalt therapy have any bearing on the validity of Gestalt theory.

PROPOSITIONS

1. *Learning depends on perception.*

Since learning is a process of discovery about the environment and about the self, the crucial feature of learning is cognitive. Learning means finding out about the nature of reality, realizing what is really so. It is a matter of perceiving what is crucial in a particular situation, of seeing how things are related, of recognizing the inherent structure with which one must cope.

What you learn about a particular task is a direct function of how you see that task. If you can't make sense out of a problem presented to you, if its inherent structure appears opaque, or if it looks to you like a meaningless jumble of arbitrary connections (such as a set of names, battles, and dates to be memorized in a history course taught by a teacher who believes in sheer repetition and memorization), your perception of the material remains disorganized, dull, and undifferentiated, and what you learn therefore also remains disorganized, dull, and undifferentiated. But if you are able to make sense of the details and can see how one thing led to another, how one event precipitated the next, this conception of the material is also what you learn about it.

What is learned is first in perception or cognition, before it goes into memory. Hence to understand what is in memory you must understand the initial input on which it is based. Perception at a particular time produces a trace (cf. Koffka, 1935) that gets laid down in memory; the process of making traces in memory that correspond to perceived or cognized events is what makes remembering possible. If you don't perceive something in the first place, obviously you can't remember anything about it. And *how* you perceive something will directly influence how you encode it in memory. Thus it is almost a truism to say that what is in memory must first have been present in some sensory, perceptual, or cognitive form: Your perceptions determine what you learn.

2. *Learning involves reorganization.*

The usual form of learning is a matter of going from a state in which something does not make sense, in which there is some kind of insurmountable gap, or in which the entire situation appears obscure, to a new state in which things have "clicked" (i.e., made sense), in which the previously puzzling gap is readily overcome, or in which the situation that previously was murky now is crystal clear. Typically a perceptual reorganization occurs, such that the new conception of the problem situation no longer includes the troubling gap, the opacity, or the meaninglessness of the earlier conception.

Consider an example. Rummaging around in a trunk in the attic, you come upon some fragments of an old gold chain. There are five groups of three links each. You take the pieces to the neighborhood jeweler and ask how much it would cost to make a single chain of 15 links out of it. "I'll have to charge you $2 for every link I cut open and resolder," the jeweler says. "I should have it done for you by tomorrow at 3:00

o'clock." "How much will it be?" you ask; "Six dollars" is the answer, and you leave the shop.

When you get home, you do a double take. Six dollars? Shouldn't it be eight dollars? Won't it be necessary to open and resolder four—rather than three—links to repair the chain? You draw yourself a diagram, to try to think the matter through. There are five groups of three links each, like this:

and you want a continuous chain of 15 links, which would look like this:

So what you need to do is open the leftmost link of all of the sets of three (except the one at the left end), and close it over the farthest right link in the adjoining set of three.

Clearly, though, this requires processing of four, not three, links. How can you make the remnants into a single continuous chain of 15 links by opening and reclosing only three of them?

The solution requires reorganization. Initially you see each of the five sets of three links as comparable to all the others. But they need not function in this way. If you perceive the material to be connected not as five identical bits, but as four and one, as in the next diagram, the puzzle can be solved:

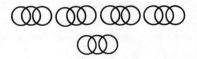

Did this perceptual reorganization do the trick for you? The four sets in the top line now become the items to be joined, and the single set in the bottom line becomes the raw material that can perform the function of connecting the four sets above it. The jeweler can open each one of the links in the lower set, and use these links to fill the *three* gaps in the line above it:

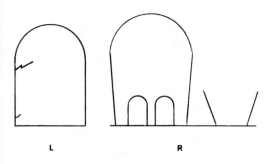

Similar kinds of reorganization play a role in the "droodles" that were such a popular parlor pastime a few years ago. Consider these two sketches. What are they?

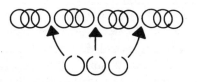

At first, neither one is particularly striking, although they need not appear to be totally senseless. Thus the left-hand one might be a profile of a smiling face with squinting eyes, and the right-hand one could be a strange bald head looking over a fence, with an animal with horns next to it and also behind the fence. But the drawings are sufficiently ambiguous so that they literally can be seen in a different, reorganized way. Thus the left one could be perceived as a soldier and a dog walking past a doorway—now the "eye"

of the profile becomes a fixed bayonet, and the "mouth" becomes the dog's tail. In the right one, imagine that there is a stubborn spot on the floor: A person who is scrubbing the floor is seen from a somewhat compromising perspective—the "eyes" become the soles of the feet, and the "horns" the sides of a bucket.

Or: What does this mean? *Pas de l'y a Rhône que nous.* Even if you know some French, it still doesn't make much sense. "Not there is some . . . Rhône . . . than we. . . ." Now try pronouncing it out loud, as a French phrase—but with an American accent: "Pah dul ear ohn keh noo." The reorganization can be quite striking when you realize that it sounds almost exactly like "Paddle your own canoe."

Much genuine learning has a similar character. There can be a kind of jolt, a "clicking," as things snap into place, as it were; a previously meaningless jumble or incomprehensible collection of things can be reorganized so that it now makes sense. Such perceptual reorganizations are at the core of learning.

3. *Learning does justice to what is learned.*

Learning is not the arbitrary connecting of things that were previously unrelated. Rather, the inherent relationships, structure, and nature of what is to be learned are fully recognized in the reorganization that is the hallmark of insightful learning. What is learned fits the reality, the Gestalt characteristics, of the material being learned. The heart of learning is recognition of the inner laws, the coherent articulation of the material.

In the examples above, realizing that the five sets of three links each need not be seen as all identical, that one can, in effect, serve as the "glue" to hold the other four together, involves a way of looking at the items that the nature of the problem permits and that also solves the problem. The structural features of the two droodles are fully in accord with the more elegant perception of them as soldier and dog, and as janitor, and less so with the more drab conception of them as a profile and as creatures looking over a fence. There is little structure in the meaningless pseudo-French phrase, but it "snaps into place" when recognized as a peculiar way of spelling the aphorism that all of us should work to further our own ends.

Take the modest knowledge that to obtain the area of a rectangle you should multiply the height times the width: $a = h \times w$. This can be nothing more than a memorized formula, which need not be based on understanding, on a recognition of the "nature of what is being learned." It can be quite blind to *why* the area of a rectangle equals its height times its width. But a genuine understanding of the formula does justice to the concepts of area, of height, of width, and of units of measurement.

If you were to teach a child about the area of a rectangle, you might begin with the idea that the area of something means the number of, say, one-centimeter squares it contains. Now if you have a rectangle that is 3 cm high by 4 cm wide, how might the child go about finding out its area? Just drawing the rectangle alone doesn't help much:

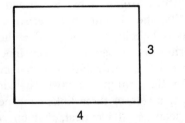

3

4

But breaking it down into the necessary

units, that is, one-centimeter squares, would.

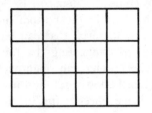

Now the child could try counting the number of 1-cm squares it contains, thereby obtaining its area, by definition. At least this would make the task clear: The child might start at the upper-left square, call it 1, and move to the right, counting the successive squares as 2, 3, 4; then move down one, and continue counting along the middle to the left: 5, 6, 7, 8; then drop down again and count to the right, to the end: 9, 10, 11, 12.

1	2	3	4
8	7	6	5
9	10	11	12

Seeing that the rectangle is three units high and four units wide, the child concludes (already knowing how to do the unit multiplication table) that, sure enough, the total number of counted units does indeed equal 3×4, which the child knows equals 12.

That, according to the Gestalt approach, though, is not enough. It does not do justice to the structure of the rectangle. What is needed is a recognition of *why* the multiplication makes sense. Sheer memorizing that $a = h \times w$, in this case, $12 = 3 \times 4$, does not really suffice. Instead, there must be a recognition of the fact that the 3 and the 4 refer to different—meaningful—subparts of the total structure.

You could look at it this way. The rectangle contains four columns, each of which is composed of three squares:

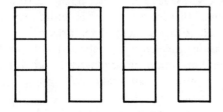

So the product of 3 × 4 means that there are four groups of three each in the rectangle: Since there are four equal columns of three squares each, to get the whole area you have to multiply the number of squares in each column, three, by the number of columns, four. That is why the area is height times width. And it can be an intriguing discovery that there is an entirely different way to break down the rectangle into its component parts. Instead of four columns of three units each, you could also see the rectangle as made up of three *rows,* each of which is composed of four units.

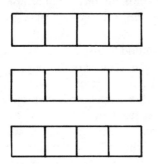

Although your conception of the rectangle now is structurally quite different from before—now the groups form a horizontal pattern, a line of four equal units each, and there are three such rows—the same principle, of course, applies: To find the total area, multiply the number of rows, three, by the number of units in each row, four. The fact that this operation yields the same total, 12, as the other operation (multiplying the number of columns, four, by the number of units in each, three) is not at all self-evident to the child who is thinking about this problem for the first time. Indeed, the fact that under most circumstances, *a* times *b* equals *b* times *a* is an abstract principle of higher mathematics which requires seeing the equivalence of two structurally quite different operations.

4. *Learning is about what leads to what.*

Much of what is learned has to do with the consequences of certain actions. If you lean over too far when you are riding a bicycle, you and the bicycle will fall over. If you insert the correct key in a lock and turn it the right way, the door will be unlocked and you can open it. If you turn right at the corner, walking two blocks farther will get you to the post office. If you are inconsiderate, selfish, and insensitive in the way you act toward other people, they are likely to be mean to you in turn. If you approach a problem with an open mind, determined to get at its root and to solve it in a way that takes all the relevant features into account, you are more likely to succeed in its solution than if you attack it blindly, without regard to its structural characteristics.

This principle is part of Tolman's (1932) concept of sign-Gestalt-expectation. A hungry rat comes to learn that veering to the left at this particular choice point in this maze will bring it to the goalbox that contains food; this particular set of environmental stimuli in this context, based on the rat's past experience with the maze, is associated with the expectation that a right turn here will get it into a blind alley, while a left turn will bring it closer to the goalbox with its coveted food.

Most consequences of behavior make sense and are intrinsically, inherently tied to it. Much learning is a matter of discovering the nature of the real world in the sense of finding out what happens when we do certain things. This holds not only for how to get from here to a desired goal in a maze or in a building or in a city, but also for skill learning—both motor skills and conceptual skills. It applies to improving your tennis stroke (where the ball ends up is a direct consequence of how you hit it) or your skiing style (whether you fall down or not—and how quickly you get through the slalom course—are intimately tied to your bodily movements), to learning to ride a bicycle or skip a rope, to the speed and accuracy of typewriting, indeed to almost any motor skill. And consequences of various strategies used in coping with intellectual challenges are also closely tied to the particular strategies: If you approach your studying tasks with the orientation that studying means memorizing, you are likely to find that the positive results of drill last only a short time, and that you never really do catch on to what you are studying; if you make an effort really to understand what you are studying, you will often have the gratifying experience of developing lasting insights.

5. *Insight avoids stupid errors.*

Such problems as answering a quantitative puzzle with a number that is off by several orders of magnitude—which can happen all too readily when a formula is applied blindly rather than with understanding—are much less likely to occur if the learner approaches the task in a sensible manner that takes the specific structure of the problem into account. Understanding a problem situation with insight into its inherent nature is less likely to lead to such gross errors. If what the learner does is intimately related to the structural features of the situation, the learner's behavior will not be random, blind, unproductive, and fraught with efforts that make no sense in that particular situation.

Mechanical application of rules without regard to relevant features of the situation can lead to stupid behavior. A favorite example of Wertheimer's was the nurse working the late shift on a hospital ward, who goes around waking up one patient after another at 11 P.M. with the message, "It's time for your sleeping pill."

Another instance is related in an appendix to the enlarged edition of Wertheimer's *Productive Thinking* (1959). A school inspector is visiting a classroom in the year 1910 and, attempting to assess the resourcefulness of the pupils, asks, "How many hairs does a horse have?" To his surprise, a boy's hand shoots up almost immediately. "The horse," says the boy, "has 132,468,218 hairs." "How do you know?" asks the somewhat dumbfounded inspector. "If you don't believe me," answers the boy, "you could count them yourself." Everyone laughs, and, as the inspector leaves the room, he tells the teacher, "I'll have to pass that story on to my colleagues when I get back to the office—I'm sure they'll enjoy it." A year later the inspector is back at the same school, and the teacher asks him what his colleagues thought of the story. "I'm afraid I couldn't pass the story on to them," the inspector replies. "I would have loved to, because it certainly is a fine one. But I couldn't. You see, for the life of me I couldn't remember the number of hairs."

What is surprising about this story, of course, is the inspector's blindness—his stupidity in not recognizing that insight into the structure of the story reveals that the particular number the boy said is irrelevant; any (sufficiently large) number would do equally well.

6. *Understanding can be transferred to new situations.*

A general principle, once acquired, can be applied in any situation which it fits —not only in the one in which it was learned in the first place. By contrast, something learned by rote memory is unlikely to be transferred to new situations. The entire purpose of school learning, of course, is to produce acquisition of material for transfer to settings outside the schoolroom—but material that is memorized is typically so specific that it has little transfer value, while something learned with understanding remains part of the learner's repertoire for coping with any similar problems in any setting.

Consider two different ways to learn about a mathematical problem somewhat more difficult than finding the area of a rectangle: computing the area of a parallelogram (Wertheimer, 1945/1959). Many students learn something akin to the following procedure. Given a particular parallelogram, such as this one:

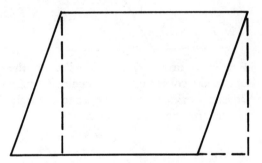

Three auxiliary lines are to be drawn. First you drop a vertical line from the upper-right corner, making it long enough to meet a second line that extends the horizontal line of the base to the right until it in turn meets the line going down from the upper right.

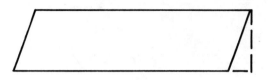

Then you drop another vertical line from the upper-left-hand corner until it meets the base.

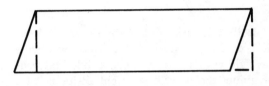

The next task is a geometrical one, namely, to prove the congruence of the two triangles generated in this way. You probably learned how to do this, in terms of the equality of right angles, the equality of two parallel lines bordered by parallel lines, the equality of corresponding angles in the two triangles, and the like. Having memorized all this, you can probably do the same thing with a somewhat different parallelogram:

But many students do not realize what this has to do with the fact that the area of a parallelogram is given by multiplying its base by its height. They dutifully memorize the "proof," without achieving a full understanding of how this does indeed prove that the area of a parallelogram equals the product of its height by its base.

What if they are given a parallelogram like this one,

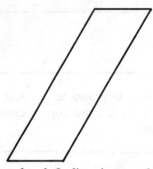

with the task of finding its area? Let's see: Drop a vertical line from the upper-right corner until it meets a line that continues the base to the right. It looks a bit odd, but this operation can be carried out.

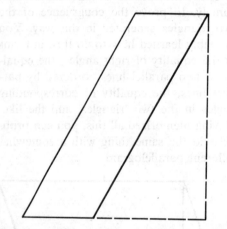

But now, dropping a vertical from the upper-left corner until it reaches the base doesn't work: The line passes to the right of the true base; it never meets it.

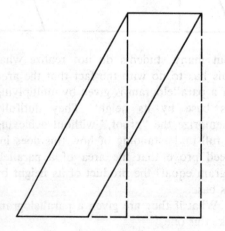

Typically the person who has memorized the "proof" of how to find the area of a parallelogram is stumped at this point and is likely to give up in disgust. Or consider what such a student's reaction is apt to be if given the task of finding the area of a figure like this one:

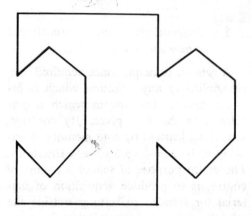

If the proof for the formula, area equals height times base, has just been memorized, the reaction is apt to be something like "We haven't had that yet," or "I don't have the faintest idea."

But if you have learned *why* the formula yields the area of the parallelogram, if you have understood the process, and have achieved insight into how it works, then such tasks hardly present a problem. Let us return to the original proof. Why does it make sense to draw the auxiliary lines in the first place? Why bother to prove the congruence of the two new triangles? Begin with the problem of finding the area of a rectangle: height times width, because one gives you the number of rows (or columns), and the other gives you the number of units in each column (or row). Now this doesn't work with a parallelogram, since it is not the same as a rectangle: There is, in a sense, "too much," an excess, at one end of it (say the left), and "not enough" at the other end (say the right).

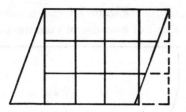

There are two trouble areas, one at each end, as the ovals show.

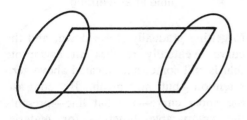

But—and this is the crucial insight—the too much at one end is exactly equal to the too little at the other! If you were to cut off the triangle at the left and move it over to the right, it would exactly fill up the gap on the right—and result in a rectangle, whose height is still the same as that of the parallelogram, and whose width is equal to the base of the parallelogram.

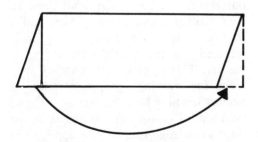

And, of course, it doesn't even matter *where* you cut the parallelogram vertically (as long as the cut is between the top-left corner and the bottom-right corner); simple switching of the right and left pieces generates a rectangle whose height and width are known to you, and therefore whose area is also easy to figure out.

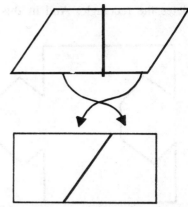

This strategy, of changing the strange shape of a parallelogram into the familiar shape of the rectangle, with known height and width, can be transferred to new patterns with little difficulty. In this one, you have to cut twice:

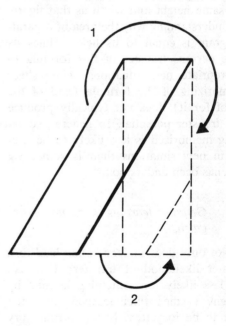

The first cut produces a piece which, when shifted to the right (1), doesn't quite make it; a small triangular chunk sticks out at the bottom left—but there is also an exactly matching small remaining gap in the bottom right; so cutting that bit off and moving it to the bottom right (2)

completes the rectangle. And in this figure,

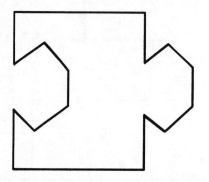

if the "hole" on the left is exactly equal to the "bump" on the right, then cutting the bump off and using it to fill the gap will produce a rectangle of the same area as the original unfamiliar figure, and with the same height and width as that figure.

Understanding why the area of a parallelogram is equal to its height times its base permits transfer of this formula to appropriate new situations, while sheer memorizing of the formula (and of the proof for it) does not typically produce this transfer potential. In general, something memorized is less likely to be useful in new situations than is something that has been understood.

7. *Genuine learning does not extinguish.*

Not only does understanding lead to a greater likelihood of transfer; it is also far less likely for something learned by insight (rather than learned by rote) ever to be forgotten. Every introductory psychology text mentions the famous *curve of retention* or *forgetting function,* first empirically obtained and described by Hermann Ebbinghaus (1885); it is depicted in schematic form in the bottom curve of Figure 7.1. The forgetting of memorized material occurs rapidly right after the time of memorizing; the rate of

Figure 7.1

Curve of Retention of Learning

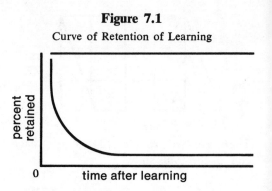

forgetting gradually slows down, and the curve eventually reaches an asymptote that is still somewhat elevated above zero retention—but not much. By contrast, the upper curve—the flat line—presents the comparable function for material learned by insight: Once you have caught on, it is unlikely that you will ever forget what you have learned. Even if several years intervene between now and the next time you encounter the droodles or the pseudo-French discussed a few pages back, chances are that (assuming the examples made sense to you) you will recognize them immediately again as the soldier, the janitor, and the aphorism.

Insights become permanent parts of our repertoire; they enter what some recent writers about memory have called long-term storage, and they are apt to be retained for the whole lifetime of the learner. This is, of course, another argument for learning by understanding as against learning by rote; just as the practical aim of classroom learning is to produce knowledge that can be applied outside the immediate schoolroom setting, so the school teacher hopes to impart learning that will last.

8. *Memorizing is a poor substitute for understanding.*

Both preceding propositions lead to the generalization stated in this one; memorizing produces learning that cannot be transferred as easily, and that is not retained as well, as learning with understanding. But these are not the only advantages of insight over rote memorizing. As another proposition suggested, understanding is less likely to lead to stupid errors or inappropriate actions. While in a way the following instances *do* show how desperately people try to make sense of things, the examples still exhibit a kind of stupidity that would have been impossible if what had been learned had been acquired with full understanding, rather than blindly by rote.

There is the famous instance of the child who believes that the psalm sung so often in church refers to a grizzly bear with crossed eyes, whose name is Gladly: "Gladly, the cross-eyed bear." Or consider the New Yorker who, in intoning the Lord's Prayer, fervently admonishes God, "And lead me not into Penn Station." And there is the version of the Pledge of Allegiance to the United States of America which refers to "one nation, invisible."

The celebrated essayist Michel de Montaigne is said to have been the author of the phrase, "*savoir par coeur n'est pas savoir*"—to know by heart is not to *know*. And Mark Twain is said to have quipped that a schoolboy is someone who can tell you what he knows in the order in which he learned it. There have been many who have recognized the inherent weakness of learning by rote.

The example about finding the area of a parallelogram is, of course, relevant to this proposition as well. Memorizing the proof for the formula for the area of a parallelogram does not necessarily yield the understanding of why the proof actually *is* a proof.

Another example of the advantage of insight over sheer memorizing is provided by Katona (1940). This is an experiment

you can easily try on your friends. Write out the following set of numbers for them on a card; hand it to them, with the instruction that they can study it for 15 seconds, after which you will take the card back and will ask them to write down as many of the digits as they can remember:

1 4 9 1 6 2 5 3 6 4 9 6 4 8 1

This turns out to be a rather difficult task; most people's digit span is much shorter than 15 units. Frustrating though the task is, your friend may well oblige you nevertheless, and perhaps even be able to reproduce at least a small portion of the list correctly. Now ask your friend a week later to reproduce the list once more, without being given the opportunity to look at it again—and you are apt to be met by a blank, somewhat incredulous, stare.

But if you instruct someone else, just before you display the card, to look for some system that makes sense out of the numbers before trying to commit them to memory, you may get an entirely different reaction: "Why, of course, this is the squares of the digits from 1 to 9!" And this person is apt to be able to reproduce the list without any difficulty, even weeks or months later.

9. *Learning by insight is its own reward.*

Genuine learning is often accompanied by a feeling of exhilaration. Seeing meaningful relationships, understanding the inherent structure of a Gestalt, being able to make sense out of things, is a pleasant experience. Perhaps you had such an "Aha!" experience with some of the examples presented earlier in this section, and doubtless you have often felt the joy of understanding in schoolroom situations, real-life settings, or troubleshooting chores, when you were faced with a puzzle that at first did not make sense, seemed incomprehensible, or was somehow recalcitrant and that suddenly became transparent, meaningful, and readily soluble. The satisfaction of achieving insight, as mentioned earlier, is one of the most positive experiences that people can have.

For this reason, incidentally, Gestalt theorists often inveigh against the use of arbitrary external rewards, such as candy, praise, good grades, gold stars, or money, in trying to motivate learning. To be sure, when there is no other incentive, and when it is impossible to learn with understanding (which does occur, although it is rare), some such rewards can be used. But their indiscriminate use is likely to distract the learner from the main task at hand, trying to achieve an insightful understanding of a problem situation. In general, it is advisable to let the achievement of understanding be its own reward.

10. *Similarity plays a crucial role in memory.*

While other learning theories emphasize contiguity and repetition as central to learning, the Gestalt psychologists point to more relational characteristics. In particular, a Gestalt property relating a new instance (of something familiar) to the previous experience of that same stimulus is crucial to the fundamental process of recognition itself.

How does recognition occur? How do you know that you have previously heard a melody that is now playing on the radio? How do you know that someone you see at a party is someone you have met before? How do you recognize your car in a parking lot?

Recall, recognition, indeed any process in which an item is retrieved from memory involves *similarity* in a critical manner. In the way the Gestalt theorists conceive of the matter, begin with, say, the first time you meet someone unfamiliar to you. The experience of this person (call it A) sets up a trace in your long-term memory store (call it a). Now at a later time, you run across the same person again: Call this new experience A'. How is it possible for you to recognize the person as someone you have seen before? In order for this to occur, the perceptual process, A' (seeing the person again), must somehow make contact with the trace, a, that was set down during the first encounter, A. But how can A' achieve this contact with the trace a? Only by virtue of the *similarity* between A' and A (or, more accurately, between A' and a, the memory trace of experience A).

The fact of recognition in this instance is realizing that you have seen the person before. If you conceive of long-term memory storage as consisting of a large set of traces of past events, then the new input must, in effect, be compared with the entire contents of the memory store to determine whether there is anything in it that resembles the new input sufficiently so that the search of the memory trace set can stop—since the new input is similar to that particular trace. The only way the search can stop, and yield recognition, is by a process which specifies that the new input is *similar* to the particular relevant trace of your earlier experience of the person. If you have not seen the person before, the search will continue until your entire set of traces of experiences of people is exhausted, without the new experience finding a trace of a similar one, and you realize that you have never met this person before. But recognition of the person requires similarity between the new experience and the trace. Recognition, the most basic process in memory, is crucially determined by the similarity between a new experience and an earlier one.

RESEARCH

Methodologies

Since the Gestalt approach emphasizes the meaningfulness of most learning, a typical procedure is to set problems for a learner that are not arbitrary, whose inner structure is at least potentially comprehensible to the learner, and whose solution is sensibly related to the conditions of the problem. A different strategy is to pose problems that are not soluble by insight—and show that nonsense tasks lead to blind, random behavior; the nature of the task determines the kinds of approach a learner will use in trying to cope with the problem.

One striking demonstration was used regularly by Wolfgang Köhler in his classes (I was privileged to participate in one of these demonstrations by Köhler at Swarthmore College during the mid–1940s). It was intended to illustrate the arbitrary nature of the typical learning tasks used by theorists who did not understand the Gestalt message. Köhler would designate a particular student as the subject but would encourage the rest of the class to pay close attention, too, and to try to master the learning task presented to the subject.

"I will give you a series of trials," Köhler begins. "On each trial, you are to indicate whether the response should be 'flim' or 'flam.' When you have made your choice, I will tell you whether you were right or not. Ready? Here is the first trial." The bewildered subject makes

a random guess, and Köhler provides feedback: "Yes; good; flim was correct. Now here is Trial 2." Again the subject makes a wild guess: "Flam." "Very good," says Köhler; "flam is correct. Here is Trial 3." Let's say the subject guesses "flim." "No," says Köhler; "I'm sorry, but flim is wrong. The correct response is 'flam.' Now here's Trial 4."

And so the experiment continues, with the subject—and the rest of the class—becoming ever more frustrated. Perhaps several members of the class, who have been observing very closely, do catch on after a while, in which case their hands shoot up, and Köhler, smiling, admonishes them not to share their knowledge with their colleagues and to check their responses on several further trials, to make sure that they have actually learned the solution. The trials continue, with Köhler standing at the front of the classroom, moving about a little between trials, and announcing the beginning of each new trial as well as providing feedback about the correctness of each response. The typical unfortunate subject does not improve much with successive trials, although perhaps gradually more and more of the other students claim they have caught on—especially as Köhler engages in somewhat more exaggerated movements between trials.

Eventually the experiment is stopped, and Köhler asks for solutions. "I tried to check out whether there was systematic alternation, so that if flim was right on one trial, flam would be correct on the next," says one student, "but that didn't work." Another reports, "Whether flim or flam was right was somehow related to how you were standing at the lectern, but I couldn't quite figure it out." And a third did manage to discover the principle: "When your right hand was above your left, flim was the correct response, but when your left hand was higher than your right, we had to say flam."

Spontaneous solutions to this puzzle are not frequent—largely, Köhler claimed, because the relationship between the stimulus configuration and the designated response is entirely arbitrary. There is no logical, meaningful, necessary, or even interpretable relation between "flim" or "flam" and the particular way in which Köhler happened to be holding his hands. No wonder that a learner confronted with such a problem engages in blind, random trial and error. The entire arrangement permits no better strategy. And such tasks, in which the relations among situation, behavior, and consequence are arbitrary, claim the Gestalt theorists, are prototypic of the senseless learning tasks used by other psychologists in most experiments on learning. It is therefore not surprising that they present an impoverished view of learning as dependent upon contiguity, repetition, reinforcement, trial and error, and other similar arbitrary processes.

Problems that at least give the learner the opportunity to act in a sensible manner are much more appropriate for the study of real-life, prototypic learning. One situation to which the Gestalt theorists frequently refer is the detour problem (Köhler, 1925). Place a hungry dog on one side of a chicken-wire fence, and some food on the other side; the dog will go away from the food along the fence, trying to get around it—and will typically succeed in this endeavor. This situation is not very difficult for most dogs. But a chicken placed in this dilemma will not be likely to solve it—it is apt to move at most a few feet back and forth along the fence opposite the location of the food, in sharp contrast to the smooth trajectory of the dog, who may run directly around the end of the fence (after

a few moments of fruitless attempts to get the food directly through the fence).

Problems which involve reorganization are also appropriate for studying learning. N. R. F. Maier (1930, 1945) performed some classical experiments that required subjects to solve some very concrete problems. One of these was to tie together the ends of two pieces of string, each hanging from the ceiling—but far enough apart that it was impossible for the subject to reach the end of the second string while holding on to the end of the first. The strings were tied to wooden crossbars wedged against the ceiling of a large room; the crossbars were held in place by two vertical wooden members each; each of the vertical members was composed of two 2×4 sticks of wood held together by clamps. All that the subject could use for the solution were the materials already mentioned, and anything else in the otherwise sparsely furnished room. The solution required reorganizing a pair of pliers into a pendulum bob: Tie the pliers to the end of one string, set that string swinging back and forth; go over to the other string and, holding its end, move back to as close to the first (swinging) string as you can, and catch the pair of pliers; now you are holding both strings, and can tie them together.

Then Maier posed a second problem. After the apparatus for the pendulum problem had been dismantled, the subject was asked to construct a hatrack. Now the pliers and string are of little use; instead, all the subject needs are two sticks and a clamp—the solution requires clamping two sticks together so that they are wedged against the ceiling, and the clamp itself can be used as a hook to hold a hat. A restructuring is required; initially the sticks clamped together were seen as instrumental to holding the cross-pieces against the ceiling, and the cross-pieces served as anchors for the strings; now the sticks themselves are to be wedged against the ceiling, with the clamp serving the double duty of holding the sticks in place and serving as a hook.

Use of puzzles in which people naturally make unwarranted assumptions (which must be overcome if the solution is to be achieved) is another favorite procedure for the study of "sensible" learning. Consider the task of drawing four continuous straight lines (that is, without lifting your pencil from the paper) such that each of these nine dots has at least one line going through it.

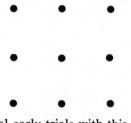

The typical early trials with this task take on a form something like these attempts:

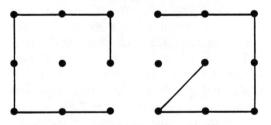

Somehow there is always one dot left that does not have a line through it. The actual solution is quite elegant; it is not a "trick" solution, but it does require giving up a natural assumption (which happens to be an assumption strongly suggested by the perceptual pattern, the Gestalt, of the nine dots itself). After you have made a few trials yourself, see whether this hint helps: *Don't* think of the pattern as a square. That is, there is nothing specified in the conditions of the

task that prohibits your going "outside" the square formed by the nine dots. The solution in a sense requires ignoring the square shape of the pattern, doing violence to the square that you spontaneously see when the pattern is first shown to you. You must extend several critical lines beyond the boundaries of the square.

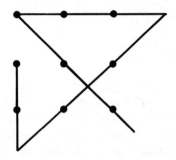

Another methodological suggestion that follows from the Gestalt orientation is to omit traditional rewards, reinforcements, and other contingencies presumed by non-Gestalt psychologists to be essential for learning, and see whether some learning about the situation occurs nevertheless: This is the paradigm for the *latent learning* or *incidental learning* studies by such workers as Tolman and Honzik (1930), discussed below under "Animal Studies." Related strategies include interfering in other ways with processes presumed in other views to be crucial for learning to occur (Rock, 1957; see below under "Human Studies"), or demonstrating that Gestalt organizational principles are stronger than repetition, past experience, or other processes that other views consider to be crucial.

Demonstrations of this last kind are typically not experiments in the usual sense, but rather critical single instances that are purported to be decisive in helping to determine which of several opposing positions is correct. The design in Figure 7.2, for example (after Metzger,

Figure 7.2

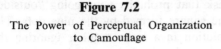

The Power of Perceptual Organization to Camouflage

1975, following earlier versions by Köhler), is typically seen as a rather unfamiliar set of two closed figures with a line across them; in spite of the fact that this pattern is much less familiar than the number 4, you typically have to search in the figure before you even manage to locate the numeral 4 in it—even though it is there in a complete, undistorted form. The principles of perceptual organization are more significant in determining how you see something than are thousands of instances of relevant past experience. This strategy was also used by Gottschaldt (1926, 1929), who camouflaged simple figures by the careful application of Gestalt principles of perceptual organization in such a way that they became difficult to discern, even when the simple figures had been exposed to the subjects hundreds of times before they were shown in their camouflaged form.

Animal Studies

Gestalt psychologists have done most of their experimental work with human subjects, but many studies were also performed on animal species as diverse as rats, ravens, jaybirds, bees, chickens, and chimpanzees. We will consider some representative work with several of these species—and then summarize a few studies by Edward Tolman who, while not a Gestalt theorist as such, did borrow several Gestalt concepts in formulating his own purposive behaviorism.

Before David Krech anglicized his name and began devoting his attention to problems in behavioral genetics, in biopsychology, and in social psychology, he performed some experiments on rats in mazes that produced results very much in line with Gestalt theory (Krechevsky, 1932). A maze is, of course, an arbitrarily constructed edifice, with the correct response at any choice point determined by how the path happens to continue thereafter. So all a rat in a maze can do, at least in the first few times that it is exposed to a new maze, is randomly explore the various parts of the maze, including its blind alleys, to see where they might lead. What Krech found was that the rats' behavior was not blind; they did not, in general, follow a strategy of sheer random trial and error. Instead, each rat behaved as though it were, in effect, trying out various "hypotheses," various "principles" that would make the path through the maze more reasonable. The rat might begin by always turning right (or left) at each choice point, or alternating right and left turns, or always choosing the darker (or the lighter) alley, and so on, and, as each "hypothesis" turned out not to work, try out another— as demonstrated by the pattern of "errors." Even rats, apparently, look for "principles" that help them get along in the world.

Mathilde Hertz (1928) hid bits of food under small upside-down flower pots placed on the ground of a large cage, while two young jaybirds in the cage watched; the birds soon became expert in tipping over the pots to obtain the food. Then she proceeded to study the discriminative learning capacities of the birds, by adding further distracting pots. She found that while the birds could not readily learn to choose the center pot in a row of three upside-down ones, they had no difficulty in discriminating between three pots, two of which were right side up (and empty) and one of which was upside down (and covered the bit of food). They also easily learned to approach a single (correct) pot at some distance from a massed group of several upside-down decoys.

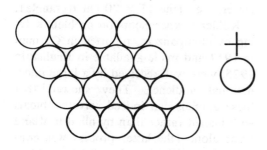

Even a correct pot (with the food hidden under it) adjacent to, and touching, one of a series of incorrect ones was approached immediately and without confusion, as long as the incorrect ones constituted a "good Gestalt," such as a circle or an oval.

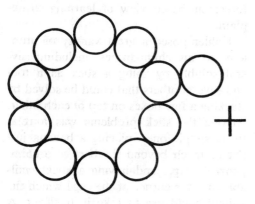

But placing the pot with the lure under it next to the corner of a square com-posed of upside-down pots without food under them resulted in errors that make good sense from a Gestalt point of view; the line in the figure below shows the path taken by one of the birds.

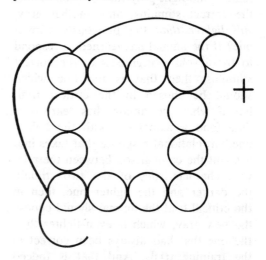

The jay tipped over the bottom-left and upper-left pots before tipping over the one containing the bit of food—the one next to the upper-right corner of the square. Apparently the distinctiveness of the corners of a square is a figural Gestalt characteristic to which such birds are sensitive.

In 1918 Köhler published a series of experiments on transposition phenomena in chimpanzees and domesticated chickens. At issue was the question of what is learned in discrimination experiments: Do animals respond to absolute characteristics of stimuli, or are they sensitive instead to relational characteristics of stimulus attributes? He explicitly refers to work by Pavlov and others, in which, say, dogs are trained to respond to the lighter of two grays and to avoid the darker one. Pavlov also refers to *generalization phenomena,* in which it is demonstrated that the response learned to the positive stimulus, the lighter gray, will also be elicited—though to a slightly decreased extent—by other light grays that are similar to the initial positive training stimulus.

What happens if a *critical trial* is presented: the light gray that previously was the correct stimulus, and another gray, *still lighter than* the previously correct one? If the animal has learned to respond to the absolute brightness of the correct stimulus, then that is the one which should be chosen in the critical trial; but if what the animal has learned is "the food is associated with the lighter one," a relational response that takes into account the comparison between the relevant characteristics of the two stimuli, the darker and the lighter one, then in the critical trial the animal should choose the new gray, which is even lighter than the one that had always been correct in the training trials. And that is indeed what occurs—with children, dogs, chimpanzees, and even the lowly chicken. What is learned in discrimination experiments is not an association between a reward and a particular absolute stimulus, but instead an association between a reward and a relational, Gestalt characteristic of the entire stimulus complex: not choose this (particular) gray, but choose the lighter of the two.

Köhler performed additional experiments which showed that, as could be expected, this same kind of result was obtained with all the species he tested when the training involved choosing the darker of two grays and avoiding the lighter one. He also extended the procedure to train chimpanzees to respond to stimuli of different hues (purples produced by mixtures containing different amounts of red and blue), or to different sizes of stimuli: The consistent finding was transposition of a relationship. That is, if the training consisted of avoiding a stimulus composed of 200° blue and 160° red and choosing one composed of 270° blue and 90° red, and the critical trial presented 270° blue and 90° red pitted against 360° blue, the chimpanzees chose the 360° blue stimulus. Training with one rectangle 9 × 12 cm large (negative) and one whose dimensions are 12 × 16 cm (positive), and presentation of a critical pair composed of a rectangle 12 × 16 cm as against another 15 × 20 cm large resulted in choice not of the one correct in the training trials (the 12 × 16 cm rectangle) but of "the larger one" (the 15 × 20 cm rectangle).

Köhler's experiments on problem solving by chimpanzees, reported in German in 1917 and made available in English in 1925, were well received by a large international audience. They showed that these animals can indeed solve problems with insight rather than by blind trial and error alone (the latter process was considered prototypic of animal problem solving and learning by the leading American psychologists of the time, such as Edward L. Thorndike and John B. Watson). The intelligent behavior of Köhler's chimpanzee subjects remains a difficult set of phenomena for anyone espousing a pure contiguity and reinforcement-based view of learning to explain.

Köhler posed a great variety of problems to his chimpanzees, including several soluble by using a stick as a tool and several others that could be solved by stacking a few boxes on top of each other. Among the stick problems was a relatively simple one—placing a banana just out of reach beyond the bars of a chimpanzee's cage, and having a stick available in a far corner of the cage which the animal could use to rake in the fruit. A more complicated version required the chimp to use a short stick (not quite long enough to reach the distant banana) to rake in a longer stick, which in turn could be used to pull in the banana. Among the more dramatic successful tool-constructing behaviors exhibited by Köhler's chimps was a spontaneous performance by Sultan, one of the brighter animals Köhler worked with: Sultan made a long bamboo stick out of two shorter ones by inserting the end of the narrower one into the hollow end of the wider one.

For the box-stacking problem, Köhler suspended a lure from the top of a cage in which several sturdy boxes were scattered (chimpanzees enjoy using boxes as toys). After several unsuccessful but creative trials (such as placing a box directly beneath the banana, getting up on the box, and trying to reach the banana by jumping up from the top of the box—but not quite being able to reach the fruit), several chimpanzees built modest towers of two or even three boxes right beneath the lure. Their architectural skills were not outstanding (the boxes would be placed precariously on top of each other, and the entire structure stood only long enough for the chimp to climb on top of it, snatch the banana, and jump clear as the tower collapsed) but they sufficed for solving the problem. One chimp (as reported by Köhler during a seminar in 1946), who was a particularly good friend of Köhler's, once took him by the hand (not an infrequent occurrence between Köhler and the chimps) in a cage set up with the box-stacking problem; he walked with Köhler, guiding him to the spot directly beneath the banana— and before Köhler had realized why the chimpanzee had brought him there, Köhler had been used successfully as a ladder by the chimp, who climbed on his shoulders, grabbed the banana, and jumped back down to the ground.

Tolman and Honzik (1930) per- formed an ingenious experiment on *latent learning* which was to generate much controversy and many additional related experiments during the 1930s and 1940s, and which helped to corroborate the Gestalt position that learning concerns the characteristics of the situations in which organisms find themselves. It also showed that learning can occur in the absence of reinforcement and reward (which should not be possible, according to many other theories). They used three groups of rats in a rather complex maze consisting of 14 choice points. Trials began for subjects in all three groups when they were placed in the startbox and ended when they had reached the goalbox; counted for each rat on each trial were the number of errors, defined as entries into blind alleys.

The three groups were treated differently. One found food in the goalbox every time it arrived there; error scores for this regularly rewarded group dropped steadily on successive days. A second group never found a reward in the goalbox; as could be expected, their error scores hardly declined at all over the 17 days of the experiment. The third group obtained no reward in the goalbox during the first 10 days of the experiment but was fed regularly in the goalbox from the 11th day onward; during the first 11 days, their error scores could not be distinguished from those of the second (unrewarded) group, but from the 12th day on, *their scores were as good as those of the regularly rewarded group.* Clearly, during the first 10 days, they had learned something about the layout of the maze and how to get around in it, but their error scores did not reflect this learning— there was, in effect, no reason to rush to the goalbox, since it contained no reward. The learning thus remained "latent." It was only when reward was introduced into the goalbox that getting to that box in a hurry made sense; introduction of the reward made the previously latent learning manifest.

Another contribution by Tolman and his collaborators helped to show that rat maze performance does not involve the mere automatic running off of a sequence of stamped-in movements or the blind performance of habitual responses is a series of *place-learning* studies. Rats appear to develop a kind of cognitive map of the maze, an understanding of its geographical properties. Tolman, Ritchie, and Kalish (1946), for example, used a maze with a floor plan shaped like a plus sign in an effort to assess whether it would be easier to teach a rat to turn left (or right) on each trial or to go to a particular location each time—even if this would involve turning left on some occasions, turning right on others. There were goalboxes at both ends of the horizontal crosspiece, either of which could contain food; and there were startboxes at both ends of the vertical crosspiece.

For the response group, if the response to be taught was to turn right, and the animal was placed into the south startbox, then the east goalbox would be baited but the west one would remain empty; if the rat was placed into the north startbox, the west goalbox would contain food, while the east one would remain empty. Thus a right turn would always lead to food, irrespective of whether the animal started out from the south or the north, and a left turn would lead the rat to an empty goalbox. A comparable "left response" group was, of course, also run; if they were started at the south the west goalbox was baited and the east one remained empty, while if they were started in the north box the east goalbox contained food but the west

one did not. For the place-learning groups, food was always in the same goalbox: For half of these rats it was always the east goalbox (irrespective of whether they were started from the north or the south) that contained the food; for the other half it was the west goalbox. Note that for the place-learning rats, obtaining the food would sometimes require a left turn at the center choice point, sometimes a right one: If the baited goalbox was the west one, a rat starting from the south must make a left turn, while that same rat starting from the north must make a right turn in order to reach the goalbox that contained the food.

According to prevailing theories (e.g., that of Clark Hull) rats learn sequences of *responses*. Accordingly, it should be much easier for rats in the response group to learn the correct behavior than it should be for rats in the place group to learn what is required of them. But it turned out that the place group reached criterion in far fewer trials than the response group: Apparently it is easier for rats to learn *where food is to be found* than to learn to make an arbitrary (right or left) turn in a maze.

Human Studies

Among studies of learning on humans by Gestalt psychologists is a 1935 monograph by Karl Duncker (translated and published in English in 1945), on problem solving. His technique was the commonsense one of giving individuals thought puzzles and asking them to report their thinking about the puzzles out loud. On the basis of his protocols, he concluded that thinking is clearly directed, that insights can be partial (they may go part way toward achieving understanding, without resulting in complete insight in depth), that errors can be useful (they can help avoid related blind alleys), that there often develops a kind of fixity of approach that may be hard to overcome, that subjects recognize the characteristics required of a solution by the specific nature and structure of the problem, and similar observations.

More typical of Gestalt work in the area, since it uses the experimental approach more explicitly, is a monograph describing the research of Abraham Luchins (1942), performed under the guidance of Max Wertheimer. It concentrates on the potentially "blinding" effect of a set which, while it may initially be useful in solving a problem, can become so mechanical and persisting as to interfere with effective further work. The puzzle used for the investigation is the well-known water jar problem, which requires a person to think about how to measure out a specific amount of water, given jars that hold particular numbers of units.

The first problem asks the person to end up with 20 units of water; all that is given are two jars, one of which holds 29 units and the other of which holds 3. The solution is to fill the first jar, then pour off from it into the smaller jar three times; what is left in the first jar will then be exactly 20 units: $29 - (3 \times 3) = 20$. The next problem is to end up with 100 units, using three different jars which hold exactly 21, 127, and 3 units, respectively (call the first [left-hand] jar A, the second [center] B, and the third [right-hand] C). After individuals have worked for a few minutes on this problem, the experimenter explains that exactly 100 units of water will remain in jar B if they fill it first, pour off water from it into jar A (leaving 106), and then fill jar C twice from jar A.

The next few problems are the following: Problem 3 is to obtain 99 units; the three jars, A, B and C, have volumes of

14, 163, and 25 units, respectively. Problem 4 is to obtain 5 units; jars A, B, and C hold 18, 43, and 10 units. Problem 5 asks the person to obtain 21 units, using jars that hold 9, 42, and 6 units. And so it continues. In each case, the same procedure works as in Problem 2: Fill the middle jar (B), pour off once into the left-hand one (A) and twice into the right-hand one (C), and you will have the requested amount of water left in the middle jar (B). Expressed as a formula, the solution is $B - A - 2C$.

The same solution works for the next few problems too. Problem 6 provides jars that hold 20, 59, and 4 units, respectively, and asks for 31. Problem 7 provides jars that hold 23, 49, and 3 units and requests 20. Problem 8 asks for 18 units, given jars that hold 15, 39, and 3 units. Then Problem 9 requests 25 units, using jars that hold 28, 76, and 3 units, respectively—and the $B - A - 2C$ formula no longer yields a solution. At this point the typical person is stumped, at least for a moment. Soon it will dawn on the person that a much simpler procedure will work than before: Simply ignore the middle jar, B; fill A (28 units), pour off once into jar C (3 units), and you will have the requested amount (25 units) left in jar A.

Indeed Problems 7 and 8 were soluble with this easier formula ($A - C$ or $A + C$) too, but most individuals—from grade-school pupils through graduate students—use the more laborious $B - A - 2C$ procedure for these problems; they have been "blinded" to the more direct solution by mechanically following the procedure that had worked so far. Control subjects who go directly from Problem 1 to Problems 7 through 9 immediately use the $A - C$ or $A + C$ solution, of course; they have not been influenced by the set induced in Problems 2 through 6 and are free to use the simpler procedure. Incidentally, instructions such as "don't be blind," introduced just before Problem 7, do not have an appreciable effect; most individuals continue blithely using the elaborate procedure for solving Problems 7 and 8, in spite of the admonition.

Max Wertheimer's book, *Productive Thinking* (1945/1959), was mentioned in the discussion of several of the propositions earlier in this chapter. Insight into why the area of a parallelogram is given by multiplying its height by its base involves recognizing that the "too much" at one end of the parallelogram exactly compensates for the "too little" at the other end; whether or not this has been learned can be checked by use of new figures. If the insight has been achieved, then it should transfer to other situations in which it is appropriate. Wertheimer constructed a series of figures to which it applies (which he called A figures) as well as others, superficially similar to the A figures, to which it does not (B figures). One way to check whether someone has truly understood the principles of finding the area of a parallelogram is to ask that person which of a set of figures like those in Figure 7.3 are A figures and which ones are B figures—that is, for which ones the area is the height times the base. Among these four, of course, the left ones happen to be A figures, and the right ones are B figures.

An experiment carried out by von Restorff (1933) under the direction of Köhler examined the effect of perceptual salience on memorizing. Individuals were asked to memorize series of paired associates. Each series consisted of eight pairs; the entire list was read to the person, after which the stimulus member of each pair was presented, with the person requested to provide the response member. Pairs were made up of different

Figure 7.3

A Test of Insight in Determining What Figures' Area Can Be Determined by the Formula for Area of a Parallelogram

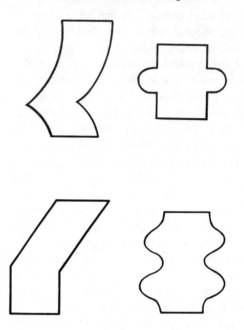

kinds of material: nonsense syllables, geometrical figures, two-digit numbers, letters, and small rectangles of different colors. A given set of eight pairs was composed of four sets of one kind, and one pair of each of the four remaining kinds; one set, for example, had four pairs of nonsense syllables and one pair each of figures, numbers, letters, and colors. Repetition of a particular kind of material, of course, made the pairs of that material rather homogeneous in the trace field of the person, while each of the nonrepeated pairs was, by contrast, more distinctive. That is, the isolated pairs stood out from the repeated pairs in memory. It turned out, as would be expected on the basis of the salience of the nonrepeated pairs, that such pairs were remembered substantially better than repeated pairs. The mean percent correct responses for a given pair when it was a member of a repeated pair was 43, while the percent of correct responses for the same pair when it was isolated was 75.

In a variation of the experiment, von Restorff increased the degree of isolation by using only three kinds of material: syllables, numbers, and figures, with each list composed of six pairs of one kind and one pair of each of the other kinds of material interspersed among them; thus a set to be memorized might contain one pair of syllables, six pairs of two-digit numbers, and one pair of geometric figures. This enhanced salience of the isolated pairs also increased the difference in recall: The average percent correct responses for repeated pairs now was 25, but it was a dramatic 87% for isolated pairs. What is distinctive in the stimulus materials remains distinctive in memory; Gestalt properties of the materials to be learned greatly affect how well they are retained. As Koffka (1935) put it:

> The result of these experiments is this: the difficulty of learning a series of nonsense syllables arises largely from the fact that the sequence of homogeneous terms interferes with the learning effect by robbing the individual traces of their individuality. But this is only possible if the traces of the terms are not independent of each other but form interconnected systems in which each part is influenced by every other part. (p. 484)

A related study by Wulf (1922) examined spontaneous changes in the trace field itself. Individuals were shown a series of geometrical figures (unfamiliar, irregular, asymmetrical ones) with the instruction to memorize them; at various times after initial exposure they were requested to draw them again, reproducing them from memory. The principle of dynamic self-distribution of forces within a Gestalt suggests that, over time, the memory traces of the figures should become more "prägnant," should turn into "bet-

ter" Gestalten. The implication is that the figures should become more unified and more symmetrical and that distinctive parts of them should become more salient—or the figures should become more similar to a familiar shape. Wulf compared the reproductions with the original stimuli and classified them as instances of *leveling* (smoothing out irregularities), *sharpening* (accentuation of salient features) or *assimilation* (becoming more similar to a familiar object). Although many reproductions were substantially correct, Wulf also found a large number of each of the kinds of changes predicted by the dynamic trace theory of memory. This study, incidentally, was to generate many later similar experiments on leveling, sharpening, and assimilation in memory and reproduction, including an influential investigation by Bartlett (1932), who asked for reproduction of stories as well as of figures and found large effects comparable to those Wulf obtained with his irregular drawings.

Yet another Gestalt approach to learning and memory was undertaken by Bluma Zeigarnik (1927), a student of Kurt Lewin. Properties of memory traces other than their sheer salience or irregularity should also affect retention. A memory trace of something that has a gap, is incomplete, or contains unresolved strains should be different from one that is closed, complete, or resolved. This kind of reasoning led Zeigarnik to try a novel experiment on memory. She devised a large number of tasks (such as stringing beads; punching holes in paper; putting together a jigsaw puzzle; drawing a prescribed pattern; or thinking of philosophers, cities, and actors whose names begin with a particular letter) and asked individual subjects to perform them one after the other. Some of the tasks she interrupted before the person was finished;

she permitted the person to complete the others. Which ones could be completed and which ones were interrupted was determined in a random fashion, and each task was completed by some individuals, but interrupted for others.

At the end of the experimental hour with each person, she asked the person to recall as many of the 20 or so tasks that had been engaged in as possible. She reasoned that the setting of a task in the first place produces a kind of tension to engage in and complete the task; once the task is finished, the tension is dissipated. But if the person is interrupted in mid-task, without having been permitted to complete it, then the tension remains unresolved—and becomes part of the trace system of the memory of that task. Such unresolved tensions in the trace system should make memories of the incompleted tasks more vexing and more salient than memories of the completed tasks. Sure enough, she found that incompleted tasks were recalled much better than completed ones; the typical finding was that about twice as many incomplete as completed tasks were recalled by the subjects.

Somewhat related to this experiment is another attributed to Lewin (the writer heard about it from Wolfgang Köhler during the 1940s but has never seen a formal reference to it in print) which can be used as an effective classroom demonstration. A psychology class is divided into experimenter-subject pairs, and each experimenter is given an index card containing, say, 12 nonsense syllables. Within each pair, the experimenter tries to teach the list of syllables to the subject, who tries to learn it. There are several trials, on each of which (after the first) the experimenter reads out the first syllable, whereupon the subject tries to say the next one. The experimenter then reads the correct second syllable off the card

and the subject tries to anticipate the third syllable, whereupon the experimenter reads the correct third syllable out loud and the subject tries to anticipate the fourth one; and so on, through all of the syllables. At a particular moment the teacher asks everyone to stop and to put away the index cards and the response sheets; all students in the entire class—both "subjects" and "experimenters" alike—are then asked to write down all the nonsense syllables from the list that they can remember. Now even though the experimenters were able to read the syllables out loud and to look at them during the whole practice period (while the subjects only heard them), they are able to reproduce far fewer of them than the subjects. The subjects approached the practice period with the intent to learn, while this intent was not present among the experimenters.

Is memorizing paired associates a matter of gradually strengthening the connection between items to be associated, and does the connection between such items slowly get more firm as the items are repeated? Or is the connection an all-or-nothing affair, such that it either is fully present or does not yet exist at all? The idea of gradual strengthening of connections is less consistent with a Gestalt view than is the notion that either a connection is present for a subject or the subject does not yet see the relation—in-between stages make little sense to a Gestalt theorist.

Irving Rock (1957) tried a clever experiment that directly gets at this question. He gave persons lists of paired associates to learn. But in every pair the person got wrong, Rock *substituted a different second item* for that pair in subsequent trials. Thus if, for example, the pair was NUG–XEL, and the person reported XEL when NUG was presented, that pair stayed the same in the next trial;

but if the person got it wrong, in the next trial the second member of the pair was changed, so that the pair might become NUG–VAD. Such substitutions were made in subsequent trials for all wrong responses, until the person had memorized all the pairs. Now if there is partial learning on trials in which the person gives wrong responses, and if the forming of the paired associations is a gradual process of strengthening the connection between the stimulus item and the response item, Rock's substitution procedure should result in many more trials being required for memorizing the whole set of pairs than if such substitutions were not made. But Rock found no significant increase in the number of trials required to reach criterion when he made such substitutions relative to the trials needed when he left all pairs intact from one trial to the next. From this he concluded that even in paired-associate memorizing, learning tends to be an all-or-none affair, rather than a matter of a gradual strengthening of connections with repetition.

IMPLICATIONS

Theoretical

The main point of the Gestalt approach to learning is that learning is a sensible process, a matter of finding out about the real world, a potentially exciting journey of discovery that can yield insight into the intricacies of the natural structures we confront in everyday life. Gestalt theory deplores the blind, mechanical, automatic view of learning; it argues that theories which assume that this view adequately describes the learning process paint an unrealistically drab and stupid picture of what genuine learning is all about. Real learning involves understanding, not conditioning or the

formation of arbitrary associations; the prototype of meaningful learning is insight into inner relations, not the gradual building up of connections among items chosen, as it were, at random.

Blind trial and error characterize learning only when the organism is placed into an artificial situation in which nothing it can do makes sense. Gradual learning curves and continuous, slow increases in the relative frequency of a "correct" response (which typify the findings of conditioning theorists, of Hullian psychologists who run rats in mazes, of followers of Thorndike who use "puzzle boxes" whose mechanical arrangements cannot be understood by the subject, or of psychologists who study "verbal learning" by requiring subjects to memorize long lists of nonsense material) are *products of the method itself* by which learning is being studied, rather than inherent characteristics of learning. Give an organism an arbitrary, stupid, or meaningless task, and of course the organism has no other choice than to act in ways that are arbitrary, stupid, or meaningless. But if the task and the situation can at least potentially make sense, and if an understanding of the task is within the natural capacity of the organism, then learning can emerge as the insightful, often elegant process that it really is.

That learning is not typically the random hooking together of inert, arbitrary parts, but a matter of forming dynamic and veridical impressions of the material at hand provides further support to the Gestalt thesis that wholes are primary and determine the nature of their parts— rather than being "sum-totals" of aggregated parts. Indeed, the Gestalt admonition that analysis should proceed from above down rather than from below up recognizes the primacy of the whole and its decisive role in articulating its parts. Most wholes in nature are dynamic

Gestalten, starting with a set of pre-conceived "parts" which are, as it were, glued together, does not yield a veridical picture of the whole. Most psychological theories, however, do approach phenomena from below, starting with presumed elemental processes such as stimuli and responses, mental images, sensory attributes, or probabilities of responses and try to construct complex behavior out of combinations or connections among such elements. To do justice to the integrated, articulated, and dynamic nature of a whole, though, it is much more appropriate to start at the level of the whole and work down to its constituent parts, rather than to try to go up to the level of the Gestalt nature of the whole by beginning with preconceived elements that are presumed to make it up. Such an endeavor is doomed to failure.

Not only is learning itself a dynamic process, but the traces of learning too, the structures that constitute memory, are not inert stored bits that are indifferent to each other. The store of memory is not static. As shown by several of the experiments discussed in the preceding section, the traces in the memory store are active, in dynamic interaction with each other. Thus the assertion that the long-term memory store is analogous to the inert memory of a modern high-speed computer is incomplete: Real psychological memory is not a large collection of individual items, each conveniently insulated from the rest, and all in a permanent, neat, and purely logical order.

The exclusive emphasis of other learning theories on contiguity, repetition, and reinforcement leaves out the most central feature of real learning: the striving to make sense out of what is being learned, the active working with the material, and the achievement of insight into the nature and structure of problem situations. Sit-

uations in which contiguity, repetition, and reinforcement are significant represent a very special case—an extreme of arbitrary associations which is anything but typical of the real world. True, there may be occasions on which connections that must be learned are strictly arbitrary, or nearly so (such as the relation between names of friends and their telephone numbers, or the location of certain offices, or the letter that happens to be assigned as the code for a particular bus or subway route) but such relationships are the exception rather than the rule, and they are not typical of most real learning tasks. And even when something that is to be learned is arbitrary, sensible factors nevertheless can play a profound role in the learning process—such as the intent to learn, the extent to which the material is salient and stands out in sharp contrast to the undifferentiated background, and its general perceptual organization and structure. Approaches to learning theory that ignore such fundamental aspects of learning can never hope to provide a complete and satisfactory account of learning as it naturally occurs in the real world. Focus on the arbitrary, the meaningless, the random can only yield an impoverished, unrealistic description of learning.

Practical

These theoretical considerations, of course, have immediate—and profound—practical consequences. The practical implications are particularly salient in the areas of educational psychology, schoolroom practices, and training in problem-solving strategies; but they go far beyond these domains as well. Gestalt theory suggests a mode of approach to everyday life, indeed a way of viewing the world—a *Weltanschauung*—that can be applied in a diverse and versatile manner to almost any real-life problem, from the most modest household concern, through social interactions and the solving of puzzles in business transactions, to coping with national and international dilemmas of intergroup tensions, world resource depletion, and the population explosion. While this claim appears immodest, it *is* often possible to approach such issues in a new and more productive way by being sensitive to the inherent nature of the various components of a problem situation, to how the components relate to each other and to the total situation, and to the context within which the problem situation occurs.

Indeed, Wertheimer showed how a Gestalt analysis of such fundamental ideas as freedom (1940), the nature of truth (1934), the theory of ethics (1935), and the concept of democracy (1937) can yield new insights into some of the more perplexing issues facing humanity. There are indeed many realms of human endeavor in which, as Lewin was fond of saying to his students, there is nothing as practical as a good theory. And Gestalt theory can turn out to be a very practical theory in many domains. Consider a not atypical illustration of its practical applicability in an area far removed from the psychological laboratory: Wertheimer's oldest son, the late Valentin Wertheimer (who was a high official in a major American labor union for many years), self-consciously used a Gestalt approach in his challenging, exacting, and far-reaching task of engaging in negotiations between labor and management. By keeping the entire context of the negotiations constantly in mind; by trying to see each issue and proposal from the point of view of the worker, the foreman, the manager, and the stockholder; by trying to develop a clear picture of the heart of a conflict; and by striving always for fairness, he was able to help resolve the problems of many a deadlocked negotiating session.

The practical implications of the Gestalt theory of learning as such are relatively obvious and straightforward. Most of them are elaborations on the admonition to act in ways that are sensible, to remain open to the inherent nature of things, not to impose arbitrary and senseless rules, and to help the learner develop insight into what is being learned. The implications follow almost directly from the propositions discussed earlier in this chapter, and they can be applied by teachers at all levels from kindergarten through graduate school, by students in their efforts to enhance the effectiveness of their own study methods, and by trainers in almost any setting.

Since learning about a situation is intimately related to how that situation is perceived, efforts should be made to present the material to be learned in a way that makes its inherent structure as clear and readily understandable as possible. The teacher can point out salient structural features of the material and can try to help the learner see what is central and what is peripheral; the learner should be encouraged to perceive the crux of the material and how its various component parts are interrelated. Pointing to similarities between the new material and what the learner already knows can also help the learner develop a clear and adequate conception of what the new material is all about. If the learner is able to generate a veridical perception of the material, a perception that does not omit any essential aspects but that also does not place undue emphasis on any ancillary or inessential features, the learning should occur relatively quickly and efficiently.

Since learning often involves reorganization, the teacher should help the learner make the transition from a previously unclear, vague, and underdeveloped impression of the matter to be learned to the new conception that takes all relevant features into account, and lets the learner make sense of the material. If there are still remaining gaps, parts that seem arbitrary or nonsensical, or obscure aspects to the learner's perception of the material, the teacher should undertake efforts to identify them, clarify them, and show the learner how they can "click" into the entire whole once they are looked at in a different, more productive way.

Genuine learning does justice to the nature and structure of what is being learned. Thus arbitrary memorization and rote drill are to be avoided, if some meaningful explanation of *why* something is the way it is can be found—and it usually can. The example of teaching about how to find the area of a rectangle discussed above is a case in point. Rather than asking children just to memorize the formula for how to find the area of a rectangle, it is worthwhile to show them how it makes sense to multiply the number of rows making up the rectangle by the number of units making up each row (or the number of columns composing it times the number of units contained in each column) in order to compute the total number of units the rectangle has in it. While this implication is particularly easy to develop (and to use) in the teaching of arithmetic, geometry, and mathematics in general, it can also be applied in many other areas—including some where it at first may not appear to be useful. In learning vocabulary in a foreign language, for example (especially other Indo-European ones like French, German, Spanish, Russian, or Italian), it is often possible to discern similarities between the foreign word and its counterpart in English which can make learning the foreign word much easier; blind, rote memorization should only be used as a last resort, if at all.

Much learning is about what leads to what. Before children ever begin formal schooling, they have already acquired a great deal of wisdom about the real world. The physical world is a dispassionate, relentless, and effective teacher. Trip over a rock and you might have a painful fall. Do something nice for someone else, and the other person's reaction is likely to make you feel good. Put your hand on a hot stove, and your hand will get hurt. Turn the latch on the door the right way, and the door will open. Much learning of this kind occurs very effectively without a teacher; and teachers should avoid interfering with this kind of natural learning by the use of irrelevant rewards, unnecessary explanations, or superfluous verbiage. To be sure, the teacher can help the child learn how and why one thing led to another, why the outcome was a natural consequence of what the child did, but the focus should always be on the events themselves and how they are interrelated—not on extrinsic, irrelevant material.

Since one of the best ways to avoid stupid errors is to develop clear-cut insights, the teacher's emphasis should be not on the right answer but on the right approach. The goal of classroom activities should be the development of understanding, not the parroting of arbitrarily defined "right answers." If the learner achieves insight, unproductive or blind ways of trying to deal with the relevant material are much less likely to occur.

The aim of education is the acquisition of knowledge that can be used outside the classroom. Teaching should therefore always be directed at the achievement of knowledge that can be transferred to new situations. Since rote memorizing is inevitably viewed by the learner as an arbitrary matter, it is to be avoided if at all possible—and methods of teaching that promote genuine understanding should be used instead. Something that is understood is much more likely to be transferable than something that is only memorized. The example of finding the area of the parallelogram, developed in some detail above, serves to illustrate this point: A genuine understanding of why the area of a parallelogram is provided by multiplying the base times the height can be transferred to finding the area of a wide variety of shapes other than the parallelogram.

Every teacher hopes that what students learn will remain with them for life. Yet learning by rote produces memory traces that dissipate rapidly; most of what is memorized is retained for only a short time. If acquisition occurs by the process of insight, the material is apt to stick with the learner far longer than if rote memorizing is the method of learning. This same implication follows from the general proposition that memorizing is typically a poor substitute for understanding; not only is something that is understood apt to be retained far longer, but also by definition it will make more sense to the learner.

Since learning by insight is a pleasurable process, since coming to understand something is an inherently satisfying experience in its own right, it follows that external goads or rewards for learning are usually inappropriate. There is no need for extrinsic reinforcers like gold stars, gratuitous words of praise, or punishment for mistakes, if the learning process is permitted to follow its natural course. The glow that comes with the achievement of insight is all the "reinforcement" needed for most learning.

Specific further implications can, of course, be drawn from various experiments performed by Gestalt psychologists—such as that the intent to learn will produce far better retention than sheer exposure to the material without such an intent, that solutions to problems are more likely to be found if you keep yourself open to the potential functions of the components of the problem than if each remains locked in a particular way of seeing it, or that you will be able to learn something more readily if you can segregate it perceptually from other potentially interfering material. There are many practical hints about how to study, how to go about effective problem solving, and how to engage in productive thinking that can be derived from the Gestalt approach and that students can apply with profit to their own studying and learning strategies.

SUMMARY

Gestalt psychology is mainly a theory of thinking and problem solving, although other cognitive processes, such as perception and learning, also have been among its major foci. It is concerned primarily with doing justice to the organized, articulated, and systemic nature of reality, including psychological processes, and with combating a view of the human mind and behavior as nothing but the sum total of a series of arbitrary connections. The basic Gestalt thesis is that the whole does not equal the sum of its parts, nor is a whole simply more than a sum of its parts: A whole is fundamentally different from any summative conception—it is an articulated system composed of interacting parts, and is logically and epistemologically prior to its parts.

Among the basic concepts in Gestalt

theory are structure, dynamic self-distribution, relational determination, organization, reorganization, and meaning; central to the area of learning are the ideas of insight and understanding. The theory was first formulated early in the 20th century by Max Wertheimer, who was soon joined by Wolfgang Köhler and Kurt Koffka; the three formed the core of what became a vigorous, influential school of psychology during the first half of this century. Other theorists identified with the Gestalt school, or strongly influenced by it, are Rudolf Arnheim, Solomon Asch, Kurt Lewin, Kurt Goldstein, Wolfgang Metzger, Fritz Heider, and Edward Tolman. While an explicit Gestalt school was no longer active by the 1970s, many concerns raised by the Gestalt theorists remain central in current research in cognition, information processing, perception, problem solving, and learning.

Gestalt theory claims that learning depends intimately upon perception and typically involves reorganization; while the first impression of something new may be vague and chaotic, the perception of it achieved after proper reorganization does justice to the structure of the material. Learning is often a matter of realizing what leads to what. Genuine learning involves insight, can be transferred to new situations, and is retained far longer than is the case for material that is only learned by rote. Learning with understanding is inherently satisfying, so extrinsic rewards and punishments are unnecessary for such learning to occur. Similarity rather than contiguity, repetition, or reinforcement is crucial in memory.

The Gestalt research strategy tries to maximize insight and understanding in problem solving, thinking, and learning, and it typically is designed to demonstrate the superiority of such an approach to what the Gestalt theorists often characterize as "blind" procedures such as conditioning, or paired-associate or serial memorizing. Among the foci of experimental work with animals have been "hypotheses" in rats learning to run through mazes, the Gestalt nature of the discriminations exhibited in the behavior of birds, transposition (rather than responding to absolute characteristics of stimuli) in chickens and chimpanzees, and tool use by chimpanzees (such as using sticks to rake in food or constructing stacks of boxes to climb on in order to be able to reach a lure). Studies of latent learning and place learning in rats have also been carried out in the Gestalt tradition. Research with humans has concentrated largely on productive thinking and problem solving, with investigations of the blinding function of set, the transfer of principles learned about geometric proofs, and the basic nature of "sensible" thought. Other studies have examined the effect of perceptual isolation of items on how easily they are retained, spontaneous changes in the memory of items in the trace field, the influence of interruption of an activity on how well it is remembered, the role of intent to learn in how well something is retained, and whether the bonds formed in paired-associate learning are all-or-nothing in character.

The chief theoretical implication of Gestalt theory consists in the inadequacy of a "blind" or arbitrary approach to learning; Gestalt psychologists inveigh against rote memorizing, association, trial and error, and conditioning as models for "genuine" learning, and point to the much richer and more true-to-life impression of learning provided by their own emphasis on insight. While Gestalt theory has wide practical applications in other areas as well, it has specific recommendations for processes of teaching and learning that are likely to maximize understanding, with the result that learning in the classroom can become more pleasurable and more effective, can be more easily transferred outside the school setting, and will be better retained. Gestalt theorists are against the arbitrary, blind, and senseless, and for the natural, the insightful, and the meaningful.

ANNOTATED BIBLIOGRAPHY

Ellis, W. D. *A source book of Gestalt psychology.* New York: Harcourt, Brace, 1938. Reissued, New York: Humanities Press, 1967.

This anthology of 35 articles, condensed and translated from the German, makes available in English many of the seminal works in Gestalt psychology published between 1915 and 1929. Broken down into sections on general problems, perception, animal experiments, thought, psychical forces, studies in pathological phenomena, and replies, it contains papers by Wertheimer, Köhler, Koffka, and Lewin and their students.

Henle, M. (Ed.). *Documents of Gestalt psychology.* Berkeley, Calif.: University of California Press, 1961.

This collection of essays, all originally written in English, includes items initially published between 1934 and 1959 by Wertheimer, Köhler, Arnheim, Asch, Henle, and Wallach. The five parts are entitled "Essays by Max Wertheimer," "General Theory," "Cognitive Processes," "Social Psychology and Motivation," and "Psychology of Expression and Art."

Katona, G. *Organizing and memorizing.* New York: Columbia University Press, 1940.

Reports are provided in this book on a wide variety of experiments, inspired by Wertheimer, which were designed to contrast the rote memorizing approach with the understanding approach. The experiments deal with a range of materials from nonsense syllables through matchstick puzzles and are intended to demonstrate that learning by understanding results in better retention and in better transfer.

Koffka, K. *Principles of Gestalt psychology.* New York: Harcourt, Brace, 1935.

This is the fullest, most complete account of Gestalt psychology ever published. It reports in detail many of the experiments inspired by the Gestalt approach and endeavors to synthesize these studies into a single, systematic position.

Köhler, W. *The mentality of apes* (E. Winter, trans.). New York: Harcourt, Brace, 1925.

Originally published in 1917 in German, this book provides a detailed account of what Köhler called "intelligence tests" on chimpanzees which he carried out while marooned during World War I on the island of Tenerife. These famous experiments, demonstrating insight in the problem solving of his subjects, helped launch the Gestalt approach to learning and became very influential.

Köhler, W. *Gestalt psychology.* New York: Liveright, 1929, 1947, 1957.

This early, tightly reasoned, systematic statement was reissued in new editions after its initial publication; it is available in a paperback format. Not as lengthy or thorough as Koffka's 1935 work, it nevertheless is widely regarded as the most carefully prepared book-length presentation of Gestalt theory.

Köhler, W. *The task of Gestalt psychology.* Princeton, N.J.: Princeton University Press, 1969.

This brief volume is the last book published by any of the three original Gestalt theorists. Based on four lectures at Princeton in 1966, its chapters are on early developments in Gestalt psychology, Gestalt psychology and natural science, recent developments in Gestalt psychology, and what thinking is.

Tolman, E. C. *Purposive behavior in animals and men.* New York: Appleton-Century, 1932.

Tolman's book, while not directly in the Gestalt tradition, presents his purposive psychology, which was based on a synthesis of behaviorism, Gestalt theory, and the hormic psychology of McDougall. Functioning as the main theory to rival Hull's approach to learning during the 1930s and 1940s, it was one of the most influential early American positions to keep the Gestalt approach in the psychological limelight in the United States.

Wertheimer, Max. *Productive thinking.* New York: Harper, 1945. Enlarged edition, New York: Harper, 1959.

This posthumous work by the founder of the Gestalt school concentrates on the thought processes that occur during learning at its best. Beginning with the modest issue of learning about the area of a parallelogram, it progresses through such topics as the geometry of vertical angles to Einstein's formulation of the theory of relativity; this is the fullest statement of the Gestalt theory of learning.

Wertheimer, Michael. *Max Wertheimer: Gestalt pioneer.* Book in preparation.

A biography of the founder of Gestalt psychology, this work presents an account of the intellectual development of Wertheimer and of how he came to formulate the Gestalt approach. Excerpts from his early works and translations of later contributions document the origins and development of Gestalt theory.

REFERENCES

Arnheim, R. *Art and visual perception.* Berkeley, Cal.: University of California Press, 1954.

Asch, S. E. *Social psychology.* New York: Prentice-Hall, 1952.

Bartlett, F. C. *Remembering.* Cambridge: Cambridge University Press, 1932.

Duncker, K. On problem solving. *Psychological Monographs,* 1945, *58* (Whole No. 270).

Ebbinghaus, H. *Über das Gedächtnis.* Leipzig: Duncker & Humbolt, 1885.

Goldstein, K. *The organism: A holistic approach to biology derived from pathological data in man.* New York: American Book, 1939.

Gottschaldt, K. Über den Einfluss der Erfahrung auf die Wahrnehmung von Figuren, I. *Psychologische Forschung,* 1926, *8,* 261–317.

Gottschaldt, K. Über den Einfluss der Erfahrung auf die Wahrnehmung von Figuren, II. *Psychologische Forschung,* 1929, *12,* 1–87.

Greeno, J. G. Process of understanding in problem solving. In N. J. Castellan, D. B. Pisoni, & G. R. Potts (Eds.), *Cognitive theory* (Vol. 2). Hillsdale, N. J.: Lawrence Erlbaum Associates, 1977.

Greeno, J. G. Natures of problem solving abilities. In W. K. Estes (Ed.), *Handbook of learning and cognitive processes* (Vol. 5). Hillsdale, N. J.: Lawrence Erlbaum Associates, 1978.

Heider, F. *Psychology of interpersonal relations.* New York: John Wiley & Sons, 1958.

Henle, M. Gestalt psychology and gestalt therapy. *Journal of the History of the Behavioral Sciences,* 1978, *14,* 23–32.

Hertz, M. Wahrnehmungspsychologische Untersuchungen am Eichelhäher: I. *Zeitschrift für wissenschaftliche Biologie, Abt. C, Zeitschrift für vergleichende Physiologie,* 1928, *7,* 144-194.

Katona, G. *Organizing and memorizing.* New York: Columbia University Press, 1940.

Kintsch, W. *The representation of meaning in memory.* Hillsdale, N.J.: Lawrence Erlbaum Associates, 1974.

Koffka, K. Perception: An introduction to the Gestalt-Theorie. *Psychological Bulletin,* 1922, *19,* 531-585.

Koffka, K. *The growth of the mind* (R. M. Ogden, trans.). London: Kegan Paul, Trench, Trubner, 1924.

Koffka, K. *Principles of Gestalt psychology.* New York: Harcourt, Brace, 1935.

Köhler, W. Nachweis einfacher Strukturfunktionen beim Schimpansen und beim Haushuhn: Über eine neue Methode zur Untersuchung des bunten Farbensystems. *Abhandlungen der königlichen Akademie der Wissenschaften, Physische-Mathematische Klasse* (Berlin), 1918, *2,* 1–101.

Köhler, W. *Die physischen Gestalten in Ruhe und im stationären Zustand: Eine naturphilosophische Untersuchung.* Braunschweig: Vieweg, 1920.

Köhler, W. *The mentality of apes* (E. Winter, trans.). New York: Harcourt, Brace, 1925.

Köhler, W. *Gestalt psychology.* New York: Liveright, 1929.

Köhler, W. Personal communication, 1946.

Köhler, W. *The task of Gestalt psychology.* Princeton, N.J.: Princeton University Press, 1969.

Krechevsky, I. "Hypotheses" in rats. *Psychological Review*, 1932, *38*, 516–532.

Luchins, A. S. Mechanization in problem solving: The effect of *Einstellung. Psychological Monographs*, 1942, *54* (Whole No. 248).

Maier, N. R. F. Reasoning in humans: I. On direction. *Journal of Comparative Psychology*, 1930, *10*, 115–143.

Maier, N. R. F. Reasoning in humans: III. The mechanisms of equivalent stimuli and of reasoning. *Journal of Experimental Psychology*, 1945, *35*, 349–360.

Metzger, W. *Gesetze des Sehens.* Frankfurt: Kramer, 1975. (Originally published, 1936.)

Metzger, W. *Psychologie.* Darmstadt: Steinkopff, 1975. (Originally published, 1940.)

Neisser, U. *Cognitive psychology.* New York: Appleton-Century-Crofts, 1967.

Neisser, U. *Cognition and reality: Principles and implications of cognitive psychology.* San Francisco: W. H. Freeman, 1976.

Newell, A., & Simon, H. A. *Human problem solving.* Englewood Cliffs, N.J.: Prentice-Hall, 1972.

Pomerantz, J. R., Sager, L. C., & Stoever, R. J. Perception of wholes and their component parts: Some configural superiority effects. *Journal of Experimental Psychology: Human Perception and Performance*, 1977, *3*, 422–435.

Rock, I. The role of repetition in associative learning. *American Journal of Psychology*, 1957, *70*, 186–193.

Scandura, J. M. *Structural learning: II. Issues and approaches.* New York: Gordon & Breach, 1975.

Tolman, E. C. *Purposive behavior in animals and men.* New York: Appleton-Century, 1932.

Tolman, E. C., & Honzik, C. H. Introduction and removal of reward, and maze performance in rats. *University of California Publications in Psychology*, 1930, *4*, 257–275.

Tolman, E. C., Ritchie, B. F., & Kalish, D. Studies in spatial learning: II. Place learning vs. response learning. *Journal of Experimental Psychology*, 1946, *36*, 221–229.

Von Ehrenfels, C. Über Gestaltqualitäten. *Vierteljahrschrift für wissenschaftliche Philosophie*, 1890, *14*, 249–292.

Von Restorff, H. Über die Wirkung von Bereichsbildung im Spurenfeld. *Psychologische Forschung*, 1933, *18*, 299–342.

Wertheimer, M. Musik der Wedda. *Sammelbände der internationalen Musikgesellschaft*, 1910, *11*, 300–309.

Wertheimer, M. Experimentelle Untersuchungen über das Sehen von Bewegung. *Zeitschrift für Psychologie*, 1912, *61*, 161–265. (a)

Wertheimer, M. Über das Denken der Naturvölker: I. Zahlen und Zahlgebilde. *Zeitschrift für Psychologie*, 1912, *60*, 321–378. (b)

Wertheimer, M. Untersuchungen zur Lehre von der Gestalt: II. *Psychologische Forschung*, 1923, *4*, 301–350.

Wertheimer, M. On truth. *Social Research*, 1934, *1*, 135–146.

Wertheimer, M. Some problems in the theory of ethics. *Social Research*, 1935, *2*, 353–367.

Wertheimer, M. On the concept of democracy. In M. Ascoli & F. Lehman (Eds.), *Political and economic democracy.* New York: Norton, 1937.

Wertheimer, M. A story of three days. In R. N. Anshen (Ed.), *Freedom: Its meaning.* New York: Harcourt, Brace, 1940.

Wertheimer, M. *Productive thinking* (enlarged ed.). New York: Harper, 1959. (Originally published, 1945.)

Wulf, F. Über die Veränderung von Vorstellungen (Gedächtnis und Gestalt). *Psychologische Forschung*, 1922, *1*, 333–389.

Zeigarnik, B. Das Behalten erledigter und unerledigter Handlungen. *Psychologische Forschung*, 1927, *9*, 1–85.

8

Constructivism: Piaget

GEORGE E. FORMAN

INTRODUCTION

Overview

When people change, their acquaintances and family have to make adjustments. To do so, the friends and relations need to know what has determined the changes and how long they will last. Learning theory is concerned with such issues and attempts to give explanations for people's behavior.

People want to change because aspects of their lives, such as their jobs or domestic arrangements, are unsatisfactory. To change, people attempt to learn new ways of thinking and new ways of relating to other people.

All changes do not result from learning, however. People also act differently during sleep, after brain damage, after fatigue has set in, or during a bout of heavy drinking. These changes can be distinguished from learning in that they are temporary, irreversible, or do not result from practice. In most cases learning can be defined as a relatively permanent, but not irreversible, change in behavior that has resulted from practice. This means that we must know the origins of a change in behavior before we can say, "Aha, you've learned it."

When a learned response looks a great deal like an event previously observed, we get the impression that the human mind is rather passive and is shaped by external events. When something a person learns cannot be explained by external events, we get a different impression. The mind can rearrange what it experiences from the outside and come away with an understanding broader than the specific experiences. We can call the first impression of the mind the *copy* view; the second we can call the *creative* view. These two views regarding how people learn have been debated from the beginning of general psychology. This chapter will be no exception.

The choice of where to look also sets limits on what one expects to find. In the *mechanistic model* of learning, for example, we measure learning in terms of connections between elements that do not change. The elements are "out there" in the environment, and we have but to learn how to make sense of them by remembering when one element is followed by another. A door slam means that father is home, for example. The perception of the door slam is a given element; we have but to remember what follows the door slam. In the *organic model* of learning we measure learning in terms of a pattern that does not depend on the constancy of particular elements. The elements change, but the system has certain describable patterns of development. To the infant, the door slam is not an element "in" the external environment; a baby boy, for example, does not turn his head toward the door expecting to see some object, as he will later in life. Then he has learned to differentiate things that are part of the "me" and things that are "not me." This process of "me" versus "not-me" differentiation is inadequately accounted for in terms of connections between elements. A more adequate accounting is possible in terms of a developing system of relations.

Major Issues

Certain major issues in learning theory are important to understand before we discuss the theory of Jean Piaget, the subject of this chapter. The first issue is the *definition of learning.* Some argue that learning is a change in behavior that results from reinforced practice (Clark Hull, Burrhus F. Skinner) while others argue that practice alone is sufficient (Edwin R. Guthrie). Piaget insists that meaningful learning results only when the person reflects. So "reinforcement" to Piaget is not something that comes from the environment, like an M&M candy; rather, it comes from the thoughts of the learner.

A second issue concerns the *measurement of learning.* Skinner proposes that change in rate of behavior is the best measure of learning. If the rate changes in the presence of only certain stimuli, then the person has learned something special about those stimuli. Other theorists prefer to measure the form or pattern of learned behavior. Albert Bandura looks closely to see if the form of, say, a child's aggressive response has the same

pattern as exhibited by an adult model. Both measures indicate learning, but each represents a different view of learning.

Does learning occur gradually or abruptly? This concerns the *course of learning,* the shape of the learning curve. If learning to some high level of mastery takes many trials and gets better and better across trials we can conclude either that a single connection is getting stronger and stronger (Edward L. Thorndike), or the many connections involved in mastery are being made—a few more on each trial (William K. Estes). If learning to some high level of mastery occurs abruptly, say between the fourth and the fifth attempt to hit an overhand smash in tennis, we are more likely to conclude that the student has learned some key to the skill, some rule that brings it all together at once. An abrupt shift in the learning curve generally makes us think that the learning is more conscious, more rule governed, than a curve of improvement which gradually increases.

We can use either rate or pattern to measure learning. But what is actually being learned? The answers to this question of *content of learning* have taken two forms. One theory holds that the person learns what responses to make (Hull). Another theory holds that the person learns what stimuli lead to what other stimuli (Edward C. Tolman). In the first view, stimuli are signals for responses. In the second view, stimuli signal other stimuli. In this respect Piaget's theory is more like Tolman's than Hull's. When a child learns to find an object recently hidden under a box, Piaget reasons that the child who can uncover the hidden object has learned a cognitive map of these several objects in space. The child knows more than what response to make in the presence of a specific stimulus.

What do theorists assume to be the *determinants of learning?* Most American theorists emphasize events in the environment, such as a reduction of need through eating (Hull) or some event which increases rate of behavior (Skinner), such as praise. In Piaget's theory, these are external determinants of learning and represent only one source of knowledge. In a well-nourished and maturing brain there is more knowledge than what "goes in," according to Piaget. There are things that the developing child learns that cannot be accounted for by only physical, social, and maturational determinants. Piaget terms this determinant *equilibration.* It will take this entire chapter to explain equilibration completely, but, in brief, it is seen as an inherited process. Through the process of equilibration the child relates information received in ways that serve to reduce contradiction, such as an object being both longer and shorter than a second object. American learning theorists have not identified equilibration as a major issue, since few if any have thought about learning in the same way Piaget does.

One major issue often goes unrecognized. Underlying all theories of learning rests a definition of an *explanation.* When is a thing explained? Behaviorists look to the events that control behavior and can be used to predict behavior to explain it. This mode of explanation, prediction and control, does not satisfy Piaget. He is more interested in the form of a complicated answer than in its frequency, and he wants to know how all children learn to correct certain errors in their thinking. When universal forms of thinking are considered, it is grossly inadequate to resort to attempts to control stimuli and reinforcements. To Piaget, a child's answer to a question is explained by observing its structure and its develop-

ment across a period of several years. A description of the process of change constitutes an explanation.

Basic Concepts

Sources of Knowledge. Piaget acknowledges that what a person knows results, in part, from what is learned from the social and physical environment, the world of people and objects. He also acknowledges that a healthy, intact organism is a prerequisite for learning to occur. To the social, physical, and maturational determinants of learning, however, Piaget adds the process of *equilibration,* which guides learning. Equilibration is how the person organizes pieces of information into a noncontradictory system of knowledge. It does not result from what a person sees, rather, it helps the person *understand* what he or she sees. With this inherited capability called equilibration, the individual gradually constructs inferences about how things in the world *must be.*

The Process of Equilibration. Piaget (1977) has identified several steps of equilibration whose purpose is to eliminate contradictions. The process begins with some disturbance. The person senses that something is not quite right. Consider a young girl who has predicted that the water poured from a short, fat glass will come up to the same level in a tall, skinny glass. When she sees that the level is higher in the skinny glass than it had been in the fat glass, she is perturbed. This is a *disturbance,* a conflict between something expected and something witnessed. The disturbance sets into actions certain *regulations* to reduce the disturbance. In this example the girl may pour the water back into the fat glass, perhaps to check if she had been wrong in her initial judgment of the water's original level. Eventually, through other types of regulations and after many experiences in everyday life, she would begin to understand why the level is higher in the skinny glass.

Adaptation, the overall aim of the equilibration process, involves an interaction between two subprocesses: assimilation and accommodation. These are, themselves, two varieties of regulations. *Assimilation* is a process of changing the new experience into a familiar experience. Assimilation, without accommodation, even distorts the new experience; the girl in the example, upon seeing the water level drop when poured back into the fat glass, might say, "It leaked some." *Accommodation,* on the other hand, is a process of an exclusive attention to the new experience, independent of past experiences. Accommodation, without assimilation, can lead to incorrect conclusions, such as the girl saying, "Well sometimes it's low and sometimes it's high." Here the child only accommodates to what is present without an attempt to assimilate what is present to past experiences. A balance between assimilation and accommodation is necessary for the child to make a more accurate, and a more adaptive, interpretation of the witnessed events.

Types of Knowledge. Piaget distinguishes two types of knowledge. *Figurative knowledge* refers to a knowledge of stimuli in the strict sense. An infant sees a stimulus, a baby bottle nipple, and begins to suck. A boy sees his father's car coming down the street and runs to the door. Figurative knowledge depends on recognition of the configuration of the stimulus, thus the term *figurative.* The knowledge has not resulted from reasoning.

This form of knowledge which results from reasoning Piaget calls *operative*

knowledge. Operative knowledge involves inference making at some level. For example, say I put a golf ball in the middle of some tennis balls. Then, while a young child watches me, I transfer the golf ball to the middle of some marbles. The golf ball appears larger in this second case. But the child can reason that, since it is the same golf ball, and since objects do not change their size only because they change their position, then this golf ball is now not actually larger than before. In general, operative knowledge considers how things have changed from what they were to what they now are, such as the golf ball's change in position. Figurative knowledge considers only the static states of objects at some point in time.

Levels of Knowledge. Over time the child grows in the ability to use operative knowledge, leaving behind the earlier predominance of figurative aspects of knowing. There are four main stages of cognitive development in children, according to Piaget's theory.

During the first two years of life, the *sensorimotor period,* children learn about the permanence of objects and certain regularities in the physical world. Through grasping, sucking, looking, throwing, and generally moving themselves and things around, they construct a rather good understanding of the limits and potentials of small objects. For example, an object hidden under a pillow can be found again, a coin moved in a closed hand is in a new location, a noise to the rear probably comes from something that can be seen upon turning the head. Through sensorimotor regulations children come to know that some changes make a difference and others do not. Rotating a toy does not make it a new toy, even though it now looks different.

During the next period, the *preoperational period,* ages two to seven, children begin to know things symbolically, and not only through actual actions. They are becoming more conscious of those things they already knew in the sensorimotor period. For example, they can explain why the rotated toy is not a new toy: "You just turned it around, silly." Their words are symbols that represent the action and help them understand, more consciously, why some changes do not make a difference. During the preoperational period children are gaining more fluency with a wide variety of symbols, body gestures, voice noises, and words that help them go beyond knowledge based on the immediate present. Yet, even with the increased fluency with symbols, the preoperational child can not make deductive inferences, i.e., conclusions that are true by logical necessity— thus the term pre*operational*.

During the *concrete operational period,* found from ages 7 to about 12, children develop the ability to think deductively. These deductions are limited to witnessed events, thus the word *concrete*. This term is unfortunate, because students often misunderstand Piaget to mean that the thinking is concrete rather than abstract. In reality, the thinking in this period is deductive (a type of abstract thinking). For example, children in the concrete operational period can deduce that it is logically necessary for stick A to be larger than stick C, even if they only saw that A was larger than B and that B was larger than C. Since they never saw A and C together, we cannot say that their thinking depends on the concrete presence of these objects. But the content of deductions is real objects rather than other deductions.

The fourth period, called the *formal operational period,* begins about age 13. In this stage children can perform deductions on other deductions. The problem

of the ratio is a good example. Give a student three circles and six squares. Then tell the student that you want a total of 12 objects with the same ratio of circles to squares. To solve this problem the student needs to divide 3 by 6 and then multiply the resulting numbers by 12. In the concrete operational stage children can do one mathematical operation or the other, but they do not understand how the two must be related to solve the problem. Older children, in the formal operational stage, understand how the operation of division relates to the operation of multiplication. In essence, they can perform an operation (multiplication) on the results of another operation (division). In this sense their thinking has transcended the limits of using objects as the sole content of thinking. They are actually using operations as the content of thinking.

HISTORY

Beginnings

Piaget was influenced by the work of a number of great men. He read Immanual Kant's works intensively and shared the philosopher's concern for determining the source of human ability to know reality, that is, epistemology. Kant concluded that to learn anything about the world, certain basic concepts of time and space are prerequisite. Concepts such as duration and depth, he said, are not learned but are innate. Piaget agrees that these concepts are fundamental but concludes that they are gradually constructed by the infant through the process of equilibration.

As a biologist Piaget was influenced by Charles Darwin and Jean Baptiste Lamarck. Darwin maintained that offspring who are born with the genetic traits best suited for their environment survive, breed, and pass these traits on to their own offspring. Lamarck maintained that the genetic traits are changed as a direct consequence of effort, and these new traits are automatically transmitted to the offspring. Piaget's theory of equilibration sounds more like Lamarck than Darwin, but there are important differences from Lamarck. Unlike Lamarck, Piaget does not believe that just any sort of effort can cause a change in the genetic code; only certain types of efforts will do this. Certain efforts are followed by an internal regulation which reduces disturbances to the survival of the organism. The activation of these regulatory mechanisms leads to certain changes in the genetic code.

Piaget was first a biologist, but his broad interests also included a study of individual psychological development. He found in James Mark Baldwin a combination of these interests. Baldwin was one of the first psychologists to study child development as a means to answer Kantian questions regarding fundamental notions of reality. Baldwin understood the significance of a child being able to find a hidden object. It meant that the Kantian notion of space had been constructed. Baldwin influenced Piaget in terms of the questions Baldwin asked and the methods he used to answer them.

Gestalt psychology served as a type of counterpoint to Piaget's ideas. The Gestalt psychologists (such as Max Wertheimer, Kurt Koffka and Wolfgang Köhler) studied laws of how humans organize what they see. These laws were all variations on a common theme: The mind perceives things as an organized whole, as when scattered dots are seen as a single figure. Piaget's dispute with Gestalt psychology is the same dispute he has with Kant. The whole are not innate givens;

they are constructed through interaction with the environment.

Jean Piaget was born in 1896 in Neuchatel, Switzerland. At an early age he acquired an interest in the workings of the natural environment, writing his first article at 13 and at 22 receiving his doctorate in biology at the University of Neuchatel. Shortly thereafter he wrote a novel, *Recherche (Search),* in which he laid out questions that have since occupied his life: *What is the relation between chance events in the external world and the absolute conclusions derived through human logic? What is the relation between physics, biology, and epistemology* (theories of knowledge)? While still young Piaget had defined his life's work. What is remarkable is not that this sense of mission was inspired in a young person, but that Piaget stuck to it.

In 1921, at the age of 25, he became Director of Studies at the Jean-Jacques Rousseau Institute in Geneva. Three years later he had published two books: *The Language and Thought of the Child* (1923) and *Judgment and Reasoning in the Child* (1924). These not only identified the qualitative differences between child and adult thinking, they also portrayed the development of thinking toward a more adult form.

Two of Piaget's books were based on observations of his own three children: *The Origins of Intelligence in Children* (1963) and *The Construction of Reality in the Child* (1954). These established Piaget's genius for painstaking observation of the developing infant, combined with his sense of the profound implications of what he observed. For example, Piaget noticed that infants first imitate actions that they can see themselves do, such as waving their hands, and later they stick out their tongues in response to an adult doing the same. To Piaget this development indicated a growing awareness of self, consciousness, if you will, and an increasing ability to reflect on self as an entity in space. Who would think that sticking one's tongue out could be so important? From 1939 to 1951 he wrote other books on the child's conceptions of number, geometry, time, speed, and space. Each served to confirm his belief that these notions of science and math are first understood only in a qualitative fashion and later become objectified and quantified.

In 1955 Piaget founded the International Center for Genetic Epistemology at the University of Geneva. Later he retired as its director, but he remains a professor emeritus at the university. His works since founding the Institute have been prodigious, but two stand out as magnum opuses. *Biology and Knowledge,* published in 1967, had been outlined in 1918 as the mission of his life's work. Almost 50 years later he felt confident enough that he could commit himself to some definitive statements on the relation between biological evolution and individual development. Piaget compares the process by which organisms adapt to changes in their environment and the process by which children construct a more intelligent understanding of their world. He maintains that the growth of intelligence is regulated by the same processes that determine the growth of morphology and changes in the physiology of all living systems.

The Development of Thought: Equilibration of Cognitive Structures (1975) deals with learning, more than any other book Piaget wrote. Most of his emphasis heretofore had been on a precise description of levels of understanding, the four periods of cognitive development identified in the preceding section. In *The De-*

velopment of Thought Piaget traces how the person gets from one cognitive developmental period to the next. Through the principles of equilibration, the person constructs a more accurate understanding of the world. These are principles of learning, from Piaget's perspective.

Major Theorists

Some Piagetian theorists work directly with Piaget in Geneva and others have extended his work in North America. In Geneva, Bärbel Inhelder is the current director of the International Center for Genetic Epistemology. Her co-authorship with Piaget goes as far back as 1941 (French edition of *The Child's Construction of Physical Quantities*). Inhelder has done much to apply Piaget's work to developing an understanding of the learning process. Her work has typically emphasized the child struggling, for many minutes, with a complex problem. She is somewhat more of a psychologist than Piaget, who gives more writing space to the final products of learning and their epistemological significance. Inhelder's current work in Geneva deals with problem-solving strategies, such as what guesses and tests of these guesses a child makes to discover the center of gravity of a board containing a concealed weight in one end (Karmiloff-Smith & Inhelder, 1974). With Hermine Sinclair and Magali Bovet she wrote *Learning and the Development of Cognition* (1974), a landmark contribution in the application of Piaget's theory of equilibration to individual learning. It demonstrates how an adult, by carefully chosen questions, can lead students to challenge their own thinking, without telling the students the answers.

Sinclair, also on the faculty at the University of Geneva, mainly works in psycholinguistics. Her work has helped to substantiate Piaget's belief that the "grammar of action" in the sensorimotor period lays the foundations for linguistic rules later. In perhaps her best known work, *Developmental Psycho-Linguistics* (1969), Sinclair trained children to describe what happens when a ball of clay is changed in both height and width. With some difficulty, but with eventual success, six-year-olds had the relevant vocabulary to say, "The clay is now shorter and longer than it was before," when a ball of clay had been rolled into a sausage shape. However, these same children still thought that the sausage shape had a larger amount of clay than the original ball shape.

Several psychologists from the United States have studied with Piaget, including Hans Furth at Catholic University in Washington, D.C., and David Elkind, now director of the Eliot Pearson Child Study Institute at Tufts University, near Boston. John Flavell, now at Stanford, was instrumental in making Piaget's work known to the American public. His *The Developmental Psychology of Jean Piaget,* written in 1963, is a comprehensive summary of Piaget's stage theory and of the research completed to that date. Elkind shares responsibility with Flavell for creating interest in Piaget in the United States. Elkind responded to the criticism that Piaget's research methods were too clinical and impressionistic. In a series of articles in the *Journal of Genetic Psychology,* beginning in 1961, Elkind replicated basic Piagetian findings using more rigorously controlled laboratory procedures. Furth's *Thinking without Language* (1966) gave support to Piaget's theory that the spoken word cannot account completely for the higher levels of human intelligence. His *Piaget and Knowledge,* published in 1969,

clears away many misunderstandings, particularly about Piaget's theory of the active rather than the passive learner. He also introduced, to those who had not read Piaget's *Biologie et Connaissance* (1967), the biological processes common to intelligence and any other system that exhibits adaptive changes. Where Piaget's writing is turgid and oblique, Furth's is lean and direct.

Current Status

Each year Piaget selects a broad question to be researched at the International Center for Genetic Epistemology. At the end of the year, after numerous seminars and sessions with visiting researchers and scholars from a wide range of disciplines, he writes a monograph that summarizes the year's work. For example, in 1978 the theme at Geneva was dialectics.

The work in Geneva continues to address broad epistemological questions but has also expanded into other areas. Inhelder's work can be described as an interest in the psychological subject rather than the epistemic subject (learning rather than knowing). The range of applications has increased from areas such as reading to areas such as psychopathology. The center seems to be moving from an interdisciplinary approach on a few questions to an interdisciplinary approach to a great diversity of questions.

Almost every issue of every journal on developmental psychology carries articles on some aspect of Piaget's theory. Sohan and Celia Modgil have edited an eight-volume series (1976) abstracting more than 35,000 pieces of research inspired by Piaget. There is a Jean Piaget Society, founded by the Education Department at Temple University, now in its ninth year. This society publishes a quarterly newsletter called *The Genetic Epistemologist* which contains selected bibliographies on topics such as dissertation titles on Piagetian research, articles on theory and method, announcements of concern to educators and researchers interested in Piaget, and the program for the annual symposium of the society held in May, usually in Philadelphia. There is no American journal devoted exclusively to genetic epistemology. The International Center for Genetic Epistemology publishes, in French, *Etudes d'Epistemologie Genetique*.

Piaget's work was expanded greatly through the efforts of Jerome Bruner, who founded the Center for Cognitive Studies at Harvard University. In a major publication of this center, *Studies in Cognitive Growth,* Bruner, Olver and Greenfield (1966) outlined Bruner's explanation of the conservation task. To Bruner, learning to conserve quantity is a matter of learning to ignore irrelevant changes in the stimulus. The child learns, for example, to ignore that the clay is pushed into a new shape, because changing the shape of the clay does not change the amount of clay. This theory of conservation differs from Piaget's in that Piaget defines conservation as the ability to understand these misleading stimuli, rather than to simply ignore them. Elizabeth Peill's *Invention and the Discovery of Reality* (1975), on models of the conservation task, presents a reconciliation of Bruner's and Piaget's models.

A number of psychologists have criticized Piaget's theory or his method. These criticisms range from accusing Piaget of overinterpreting children's thoughts to underinterpreting them. Peter Bryant, at Oxford University in England, falls in the second category. Bryant (1974) presented data which suggest that children younger than the age of the concrete operations level (younger than seven) can make deductive inferences. By eliminating from the transitivity task those components that place a load on memory, Bryant found five-year-olds can reason A is greater than C, using an inference from the givens that A is greater than B and B is greater than C. He also challenges Piaget's theory that children under eight months have no concept of the permanent object. His data show that children around eight months are at least aware that the object seen but not heard is the same object as that object which, a few moments earlier, was heard but not seen. While the challenges to Piaget may be a matter of how one chooses to define these concepts, Bryant's work does extend our understanding of early cognitive development. T. G. R. Bower (1974, 1977) of the University of Edinburgh also employed ingenious methods to extend this understanding.

Charles Brainerd, of the University of Western Ontario, challenges Piaget for overinterpreting children's thoughts. He maintains that there is no need to identify stages of development, since the concept of stage is trivial (Brainerd, 1978). Since there is little empirical evidence that children can solve problems of the same structure in a wide variety of content areas, he asks what the purpose is in referring to a stage. Is Piaget's assumption that children in the preoperational stage are incapable of solving concrete operational tasks as trivial as the assumption that children cannot solve algebraic problems before they learn arithmetic? Algebra is arithmetic plus an additional set of rules. The counterargument against Brainerd comes as a restatement of what Piaget is doing. Piaget finds the stage concept useful as an explanation for cognitive development, as a means to understand that the capability of the child in one stage is qualitatively different from one in the preceding stage. Given this use of the stage concept, there is no need to find that a child is clearly in only one stage. A child who makes one authentic, uncoached deductive inference has done something, from a structural point of view, that cannot be explained by previous experience alone. Piaget is interested in how these categories of cognitive abilities emerge and is less interested in their frequency and range of application.

Several researchers have complained that Piaget's method of plotting cognitive development is not sufficiently precise. Reliance on words rather than a more precise notational system like numbers, they say, makes it extremely difficult to assess both the structure of a given task and the structure of a person's thought processes. Michael Cunningham (1972) has developed a graphic portrayal of sensorimotor development using the feedback circuit motif throughout. Kurt Fischer (in press) has simplified the description of all four stages of cognitive development in describing the transitions between stages. David Klahr and J. G. Wallace (1976) have applied the language of computer programming to stage development. Juan Pasqual-Leone (1976) has used a mathematical notation to improve the predictive power of Piaget's theory. His model of cognitive development includes factors such as memory and attention which are given short shrift in Piaget's work. And Robert Ennis (1978) has improved the logical consistency of how to describe formal operations.

Other Theories

To compare Piaget's developmental theory of learning with the other theories considered in this text, a common example is useful. A child at the age of six and later at the age of eight is given a conservation-of-quantity task. The experimenter presents the child with two identical glass cylinders, each 8″ tall and 2″ wide, both filled with water. The experimenter pours all of the water from one of these, A, into B, a short cylinder 5″ tall and 4″ wide. The other original container, C, is left full of water. Now, not only is the water level in B lower than the water level in C, but also the water does not come full to the brim. The child at the age of six, when asked if C and B have the same amount of water, says no, "Because that one (B) has less, you can see that it does." This same child two years later answers the same question yes, they have the same amount of water, because "you didn't spill or add any, and besides it just looks like (B) has less, but that's just because it's wider." What has happened during these two years? Different learning theorists might account for this change differently.

Ivan Pavlov would probably say that the child has learned what stimuli signal reward. The stimuli would be such things as pouring water, or no spills. But it is not clear what "unconditioned stimulus" reflexively elicited the correct response the first time or the "unconditioned response" that was the first correct response. B. F. Skinner, however, might say that the child had learned to make the second answer as an instrumental response leading to social reinforcements such as praise. This verbal response was gradually shaped by social reinforcement given in the presence of the discriminative stimuli, such as pouring water or no spills. But this too sounds rather forced, since in many instances the eight-year-old will begin the session puzzled, contradict himself or herself for some minutes, and then, with great joy and satisfaction, figure out why the amount does stay the same in spite of the change in appearances. In this case the notion of reinforcement must be changed. There was no external reinforcement; the child, so to speak, is self-taught. While Skinner's theory can account for internal sources of reinforcement, one must step outside of Skinner's theory to account for the degree of self-reinforcement (what Piaget calls self-regulation of thoughts) that leads to an answer that the child feels is based on logical necessity. Skinner probably cannot account for the fact that once this child has understood the conservation problem the experimenter cannot reshape the child's response by giving him or her trick bottles with hidden chambers. The child who understands the structure of the problem can resist such tricks to extinguish correct verbal responses. The child who understands is more likely to assume, without actually seeing the trick, that the experimenter must have done something devious.

Proponents of E. L. Thorndike's connectionism would search for a network of associations between stimuli and responses. This approach would probably not capture the integrity of the cognitive scheme which functions as a whole, thereby making the answer deductive (necessary) rather than probabilistic (based on the most frequently reinforced response). This shift from responses based on reinforcement frequency to responses derived from a scheme of logic also eliminates William Estes's theory of stimulus sampling, since Piaget now prefers a more "active organism" view of perception. Estes's theory relies heavily on the random fluxuations in the stimulus array and a receptive organism. Perhaps Estes would say that the child learns to conserve because those stimulus elements associated with "same amount" occur

more frequently than those associated with "less" or "more." Yet this may be begging Piaget's question of how the child learns the concept "same amount" first, rather than the simpler question of how a child learns *when* to say something already known. Both Skinner and Estes would do better than Piaget in predicting when a child might exhibit what he or she knows, but this is not Piaget's question.

Kurt Lewin would probably look at the water-pouring example in terms of the child's motivation. Certain aspects of the social field would either motivate or fail to motivate the child to persist at this task. Piaget says very little about why a child might quit or persist. He more often assumes that the child is motivated, and any failures result from deficiencies in thinking. A combination of Lewin's field theory and Piaget's cognitive theory could be useful for teachers, parents, and school psychologists.

Albert Bandura no doubt would be interested in the role played by adult models in teaching the child how to conserve. Perhaps the child in our example had observed older children talking about the amount of liquid after pouring in a new vessel. These older children may have argued among themselves until they concluded that quantity was conserved. The young child may have heard this, including the reasons given by the older children. The younger child assimilated what was witnessed and then was able to reapply this learning during the second testing.

This scenario presents several difficulties from a Piagetian perspective. The question remains: How did the older children learn conservation? Did they learn through observing still older children? This infinite regress begs the question of conservation learning. Another question concerns the observing child: What was he "doing" while watching? To be consistent with Piaget's theory of learning, the younger child must have been making predictions in silence and having them confirmed or not confirmed by the actions of the older children. If this type of personal conflict and conflict resolution was going on inside the observing child, in parallel with the older group's struggle, there is really nothing incompatible between Bandura's theory of observational learning and Piaget's theory of equilibration. One might presume, however, that passive watching, while sometimes effective, is not the best way for children to learn complicated concepts. The child who personally enters a debate with the older children probably learns more completely why the amount remains the same.

The information-processing theories would look at the demands that this conservation task makes on memory and attention. Indeed, this is exactly the approach taken by Klahr and Wallace (1976). The six-year-old might fail the task for many reasons, such as forgetting that A and B were initially equal or failing to attend to the width of C and only noticing the height of C, or perhaps forgetting that the question referred to total quantity and not water level. Piaget, in his book on perception (1969) and in his book on memory (Piaget & Inhelder, 1973), acknowledges the importance of attention and memory. But these information processes are insufficient to account for what the child who conserves understands. Even though a child may remember perfectly and attend to all the relevant stimuli, the child still must interrelate these separate pieces of information. This interrelation is an exclusively mental act of coordination. Klahr and Wallace (1976) come fairly close to cap-

turing these mental coordinations in their description of the different types of transformations that the child can consider. For example, spilling water is one type of transformation that changes quantity, while exchanging all of an amount of water from vessel to vessel does not. The advantage and disadvantage of the information-processing approach is its specificity. Information-processing models can account for how a child solves a particular problem, but Piaget's theory is more likely to see parallels between more general systems, such as between self-regulated learning and biological adaptation across species and generations.

Piaget acknowledges the importance of all of these concepts of learning, but he insists that none of them accounts for what has been learned when the child reasons deductively, and few of them can comfortably account for self-regulated learning.

PROPOSITIONS

Learning, in the sense that Piaget prefers to define it, is a process of self-regulation that leads to an understanding of the relations among the elements of a specific concept and an understanding of how that specific concept relates to previously learned concepts.

1. *Learning is a specific case of development.*

Piaget (1970a, 1977) states that not everything that the child can see serves as a stimulus. Very young children may see that one of two equal and parallel sticks is pushed forward slightly, but this transformation does not serve as a stimulus to the response of conservation of length. Later, when they reach a developmental stage where they can compare the forward motion of one stick with its (imaginary) return to the original position, they can reason that since this return demonstrates that the two sticks are the same length, the sliding forward did not really change the length of the stick that protrudes beyond its mate. Before they can understand why the protruding stick misleads them, they must have a mental operation that Piaget calls *reversibility.* Reversibility is the child's ability to understand the implication behind the fact that a given transformation can be undone.

The child who does not yet have the reversibility concept cannot solve this specific task, or better put, cannot understand it even if told the answer. Before children can profit from such raw experiences they must have the requisite mental operations, such as reversibility, to interpret the stimuli. In this sense, development constrains what can be learned. This proposition is not so simple as saying that learning one concept depends on learning more elementary concepts that are constituents of the difficult one. The development of reversibility does not result from experience alone. It requires a form of internal regulation guided by purely mental events, what Piaget terms *reflective abstraction.* Reflective abstraction refers to the manner by which the brain yields a coherent system of information by reflecting on mental activity itself, as opposed to reflecting on events known to occur external to the self.

This proposition involves the following reasoning. A specific concept (say, conservation) can be learned only if the child has the requisite mental competence to interrelate the relevant pieces of information (reversibility, in this case), and this competence results from a process of reflective abstraction that depends on the development of intelligence above and beyond experience with similar concepts. The development of intelligence as a functioning system sets limits on what can be learned.

2. *Development is a process of becoming increasingly conscious of the knower-known relation.*

Before we get into a discussion of the process by which a child learns a specific concept, it is important to maintain the context of the first proposition by discussing development in general. Consider the time span of the first 15 to 16 years of life. The infant less than eight months old does not yet realize that he or she, the *knower,* occupies a position in something that we call space, the *known.* By 12 or 14 months a baby girl, for example, can find hidden objects, remove her own foot from the top of a cloth she wishes to grasp, and perform many other actions that indicate she has become more conscious of her own body, as distinct from objects that are not part of her person.

By age two or three, children can use words to describe how they feel, where they hurt, and what they want. They have become more conscious of their subjective states as well as their physical position in space. For a child to say to an adult, "I am hungry," means that the child is aware of a relation between a subjective state, the known, and who it is who has that subjective state, the knower. For reasons we will discuss later, for the child to say, "I am hungry," is an even greater indication of consciousness.

By the age of four or five, children can appreciate that your view of a stimulus array is different from theirs. Suppose that you and a young girl are sitting opposite a table of toys. You can see a spinning top, but her view of the top is obstructed by a large toy sailboat. Immediately after you say to her, "Oh what a pretty spinning top," she says, "I can't see it from my side." She has, in that statement, indicated her awareness of the difference between her view (the knower) and other possible views (the known). She may even be able to pick out a picture of the array of toys that portrays your perspective. In other words the child is becoming conscious of something called *personal perspective,* which can be known only to the extent that one can differentiate personal perspective from other perspectives. This is not different in kind from discovering the self as an object in space (during the first two years of life) and discovering the self as something with subjective states. The difference is one of the means of expression, acts versus words.

By age 9 or 10 the child begins to use inferences to figure out knower-known relations. For example, take three matches, all the same length. Match A, perpendicular to B, bisects B. Match B, at the same time, is perpendicular to C and bisects C. This arrangement creates the illusion that B is shorter than A and longer than C! But the 9- or 10-year-old reasons that this cannot be possible. These three matches came from the same box, were originally aligned side by side to confirm their equivalence, and have not been snipped or stretched in the meantime. These facts are the known. So how does the child explain the appearance that B is shorter than A and longer than C? The child infers that there must be something wrong with the observation (the knower). "Well, it just looks that way, I'm seeing it funny, but the matches are all the same length." The child is more conscious of the relation between the knower (the appearance) and the known (the objective facts).

By age 14 or 15 the child can use propositional logic to understand the knower-known relation. For example, if the adolescent's country attacks another country to prevent future penetration of its native soil, then other nations probably use the same rationale for their wars. Here the adolescent has reasoned that his or her view (the knower) is one and the same as a person's in another country (the known), even though the other person's view appears sinister and malicious and his or her own view appears righteous and humane. The reasoning involves the ability to separate variables, such as fear of attack or geographical borders, and then systematically to consider all possible combinations of these dimensions as possible social realities. Through the combination of dimensions the adolescent considers the logic of the different propositions and concludes that people in other countries might have the same rationale and justification. Through this process the adolescent becomes more conscious of how one's own ethnocentric view (the knower) colors perceptions of a more objective understanding of people's in other countries (the known).

To Piaget, development across the life span implies a growth of consciousness (or what he calls awareness). But this is not a simple process of gaining more and more information about some external and absolute reality. If this were Piaget's position he would be no more than another empiricist, interested in how the child learns what is absolute in the environment, perhaps by becoming more sensitive to subtleties in the stimulus complex. The consciousness Piaget defines, however, is a growth in sensitivity to *how one's own actions and thoughts* contribute to a positive, more flexible and adaptive construction of the world, regardless of whether it has anything to do with some absolute reality (see Gruber & Vonèche, 1977, pp. xix–xxiii). We do not truly know whether the bisected match in the example above is shorter. It might be, but it is more useful to insist that the match is not shorter and to be conscious of the source of our certainty (i.e., our own actions and thoughts).

This second proposition maintains the context that *what the child learns, across the life span, are more and more things about the procedures by which he or she comes to know anything.* When the Genevans research learning they often ask the child, "How do you know?" which is a step beyond the more usual question, "Do you know?" In fact, they even define learning by this stringent criterion, that if the child cannot explain how he or she knows, for example, that the length of the matchstick has been conserved, then the child has really not learned the concept.

3. *Perception is guided by mental operations that are themselves not the result of previous perceptions.*

This proposition indicates Piaget's dislike for a learning theory based on associations between stimuli perceived directly. Stimuli are no simple matter. They are not elements of sensation. Nor is perception a simple matter of selectively attending to those elements previously associated with reward. To Piaget, a stimulus is known, not just experienced. Even the most simple stimulus, such as the color red, is known as red because of a mental action of comparison. A patch of light could be "seen" as dark, wet, or red, depending on what one chooses to compare it with. If "seen" as red it is because the viewer *knows* that it is not blue (or any other color). The ability to think about what something is *not* is necessary

for meaningful perception. This ability to give meaning to a stimulus by considering what it is *not* involves more than simply recalling previous events. This ability is part of our biological heritage activated by our interaction with our physical environment, but too complicated to be copied from events that occur in the physical environment.

Perception, then, is an active search rather than a wide-angle lens with an open shutter. This too can be easily misinterpreted to mean that the perceiver actively scans the stimulus array. Piaget is referring to mental activity, the *inference*. The perceiver often already *knows* what he or she is looking for, by the mental activity of making inferences. The visual scanning is then only the overt manifestations of the mental activity, the inference. For example, consider two equal sticks, lined up to show their equivalence. After an eight-year-old boy sees the top stick being slid forward and notices its apparent increase in length, he immediately looks to the trailing end of this stick, with the expectation that it will appear shorter than the bottom stick. Because of his inference that the top stick has really not changed in length, he is looking for something, rather than making an uncommitted scanning of the stimulus array. Piaget would point out that if the boy makes this latter type of uncommitted scanning, he will not understand what he sees even when he sees it. That is, the trailing end of the top stick will not be a meaningful stimulus.

4. *Learning is an organic process of creation rather than a mechanical process of accumulation.*

When a child passes from not understanding a concept to understanding that concept, what has happened? Most of the work in American psychology in the 1950s and 1960s assumed that the child, through trial and error, has learned to associate all the defining attributes of a concept to the name of the concept (see Bourne, 1966; Bruner, Goodnow, & Austin, 1956). The defining attributes, say, for the concept *democracy* are those dimensions that define it, such as representative government, open elections, and bipartisanship. The concept is not completely understood until all of the essential dimensions have been associated with the name of the concept. For example, a child who equates democracy with bipartisanship alone has not truly understood the concept.

This view of concept formation gives the impression that learning is a simple mechanical process of accumulating the relevant attributes. Not surprisingly, these researchers use trials-to-mastery as a dependent variable and number of relevant or irrelevant dimensions as an independent variable. The formula that accounts for the rate of learning the tasks designed by these researchers, also not surprisingly, looks a great deal like formulae from physics. An example is Bourne and Restle, 1959, who state that the probability of making a correct response on any trial, $P(n)$, is a ratio of conditioned cues to total number of cues.

These learning models have been helpful in defining the environmental parameters that make certain concepts more difficult to learn. But these models assume that the learner remains the same; only the tasks change. Piaget wants to know how the learner changes in the approach to a problem. For example, Inhelder and Piaget (1958) gave persons a pendulum and asked them to figure out what determined the period of its swing. They were told to consider the length of the string, the weight of the bob, and the height at which the bob was released. Only the age of the subjects was varied. Individuals younger than age 12 had difficulty testing their hypotheses without confounding their tests. They would change the weight of the bob and the length of the string, say, at the same time. Persons older than 12 knew how to organize their tests into a matrix of all possible combinations, taken both singly and in pairs. Assume that Inhelder and Piaget observe a person change from not understanding to a complete understanding of the task. What has this person learned? Of course, the person has learned the critical attribute of the concept, but that was not the purpose of the study. The person has learned a useful approach to the problem, a process or procedure.

When learning is defined as learning new procedures it becomes difficult to account for learning in terms of a mechanical process of accumulating more knowledge. The individual literally invents the procedure. The new procedure is not just a continuation of old procedures. The new procedure is creative; it has a structure qualitatively different from the random trial and error of the earlier procedure, and it results from the person reflecting, not so much on the pendulum, but on the method of asking questions. Both the content and structure of the new procedure are different. In this sense, learning new procedures emerges from old procedures through an organic process of reflection and creation.

5. *Every acquired concept involves an inference.*

This proposition challenges the notion of stimulus generalization, which is the transfer of a response to a new stimulus because the new stimulus looks like, or is otherwise similar to, the original stimulus that elicited the response. Consider, for example, a girl who has already learned that "force" makes ball B roll forward when it has been hit by ball A; say ball A has struck ball B in a row of three balls, B, C, and D. We later hear the girl explain, "Force passes through the middle balls," when she sees ball D roll forward alone. We might conclude that she has used the same response, "force," in this new setup because it looks so similar to the old setup.

Piaget (1977, p. 45) studied carefully how children learn such new setups and concluded that the notion of stimulus generalization cannot account for such learning. First, children think that ball A "sneaks" around balls B and C and hits D directly. Then they think that each ball, B and C, moves "just a little" from left to right, thereby bumping D. Only later do they understand that force must pass through the intermediate balls. Children reason that since D cannot move from an internal energy supply, and since the intermediate balls are not displaced (having confirmed this by placing marks on the table), therefore there *must* have been some force which passed through the intermediate balls. They invent their responses based on deductions; they do not emit an old response to a new, but similar, stimulus. This invention requires an inference, a deduction, every bit as complex as transitivity. If A applies force to B (observed motion), and if D is moved by C (observed movement), then that *same* force must have passed from B to C.

Why don't the children think that D is moved by a force *different* from the one that moves A to B? No one told them to abandon this earlier hypothesis. In fact the hypothesis of the same force "passing through" the intermediate balls is absurd

on the face of it, because the passing through has no observables, no visible movement. The fact that not only do the children invent this notion of passing through but also that they insist it must be true in spite of the lack of visible referents indicates the following: They have not learned to make a response to a new stimulus that looks like a more familiar one. They have gone beyond the domain of observables, because to do less would contradict premises that they know to be inviolate: (1) balls are inert, and (2) the intermediate balls do not move laterally.

6. *Errors often are not the result of carelessness but result from an elementary form of reasoning.*

When the children in the above example invented the answer about ball A "sneaking behind" the intermediate balls, they were trying to make sense of these events. They knew that ball D could not take off by itself. Balls are inert and require external force to make them move. Likewise, when the children said that the intermediate balls moved "just a little bit forward," they were trying not to contradict the rule that balls are inert. Both of these errors came from reasoning, not from carelessness.

The second error seems more advanced than the first. The first did not take into account two facts: (1) Ball A remained stationary after hitting B, and (2) ball C would prevent A from entering behind D to knock it forward, even if A had moved behind the others. The second error accounted for these two facts, but it contradicted the fact that all of the intermediate balls remained in one position. Yet this error was closer to the truth and even took some account of the lack of visible motion. The children said, that they guide by reflecting on these thoughts. Children may not be able to understand the relation among several events, even though each of the events can be clearly seen. But if they are allowed to invent the relation through self-regulation they will more likely understand what they see.

It is important for learners to generate their own questions. A teacher may present a general problem, such as what determines the period of a pendulum's swing, but the sequence of tests used to discover the answer is best left to the student. If the student can come up with a reasonable question, such as the weight of the pendulum bob, then this means that the question is partially related to things that the student already knows. That is, if students construct their own questions, then the questions evidently are constructed from some knowledge base which the students understand. In like manner, since the students understand their own questions, they are more "Well, they move just a little, you can't see it, but they bump each other in turn." Learning, then, is a gradual process of eliminating errors by rethinking the reasons that lead to these errors. Yet to eliminate the final errors requires the cognitive ability to make inferences. These inferences occur through a process of self-regulation, rather than through memorizing answers someone gives to the child.

7. *Meaningful learning requires active self-regulation.*

Self-regulation is the essence of equilibration. Learners do not memorize the constancies of their environment; they construct these constancies (such as the permanent object or conservation of quantity) by a long series of thoughts

prepared to understand the answers they receive by testing out their questions. The answers can be assimilated into the knowledge base the students used to construct the questions.

Look at these two different types of learning, the first case where the question is given to the student, the second case where the student constructs his or her own question. In the first case the teacher says, "What happens when we add more weight to the pendulum?" The student adds more weight and discovers that the period of the swing does not change. But what has the student learned? At the most, an isolated fact about the additional weight and the period of the pendulum.

Now consider the same task, but this time the student independently thinks, "Maybe additional weight will make it swing faster." The student tries this and discovers that the additional weight does not change the period of the swing. Has the student in this second case learned anything more than the student who was given the suggestions by the teacher? Probably. Let's return to the student's implicit thoughts and see why he or she thought about weight in the first place: "Perhaps weight will make it swing faster; heavier weights fall faster (incorrect assumption), the swing is a type of falling, so the pendulum should swing faster." The idea of weight making the pendulum swing faster came from a knowledge base (albeit incorrect) about free-falling objects. Now when this student tests the question, the negative results should call into doubt both the specific task of the pendulum's swing and the more general knowledge base about free-falling objects. If the pendulum really is a special case of falling bodies, the student might well reconsider the relation between weight and speed of falling. Such a reworking of more general principles is not likely when the teacher presents a series of ready-made questions to the student.

Piaget's emphasis on self-regulation is quite different from an S–R approach, which gives the questions as stimuli, and it is also quite different from the Socratic method, which leads the students to the right answer through a series of questions (see Forman & Kuschner, 1977, p. 110). In both of these procedures it is assumed that questions are easily assimilated into previous knowledge bases. Piaget (1970b) believes that such assimilation of questions to earlier knowledge bases can be better assured if the students construct their own questions.

8. *Meaningful learning occurs when the person resolves a discrepancy between predictions and outcomes.*

This proposition states that errors are necessary for meaningful learning. The necessity of errors contradicts the principles of behavior modification (see Ferster & Perrott, 1968). According to behavior modification, meaningful learning results from programming instruction so that the student, by slow and gradual shaping, learns new concepts without ever guessing incorrectly. Piaget thinks it better to have students generate their own questions. This means that they will, and should, commit errors. Why the "should"?

For the self-regulation to occur that characterizes the equilibration, the learner needs to experience some type of disturbance. This disturbance most commonly results from a discrepancy between a prediction and an outcome. The error causes students to both accommodate their own knowledge base and to assimilate the observed outcome into the modified old knowledge base. For example, the student in the previous example, due to an error, might accommodate his or her notions about free-falling bodies and then assimilate to that modified old knowledge base the new experience with pendulums.

Of course, all new learning is not so complicated and therefore does not require self-regulation caused by some disturbance. For a young woman to learn that her friend has been married is a good example. She already knows the friend and already knows what marriage is, so the learning here is no more than an association between two things already known. She need not guess incorrectly about her friend's marital status in order to truly learn that this friend has exchanged wedding vows. This is not what most learning theorists would call "learning a concept"; it is a case of concept utilization rather than concept attainment (see Bruner, Goodnow, & Austin, 1956). The young woman used a concept she already knew (marriage) to identify a new instance of that concept (her friend). The meaning of the concept of marriage and its initial learning (concept attainment) would, in Piaget's theory, require errors to assure more complete understanding.

9. *Meaningful learning occurs by negating earlier, incomplete levels of understanding.*

A contradiction is removed by an act of negation. A discrepancy is resolved, an obstacle is removed, or a gap is filled. These are all forms of negation, the undoing of a problem. As children mature they use more advanced forms of negation. This is a difference of *type*. As children learn a specific concept, they apply negation to different levels of understanding that concept. This is a difference of *level*.

In the sensorimotor period the child can negate the presence of a barrier by knocking it over. Say a one-year-old girl wants to get to her toybox, but a small chair is in her way. She negates the barrier in a direct manner by moving it. This form of negation Piaget calls the *inverse*. The child could have used a more indirect method of walking around the chair. Piaget would call this form of negation the *reciprocal*. Moving the self is reciprocal to moving the chair that was in the way. Both forms of these negations are sensorimotor negations.

The four-year-old child can use preoperational types of negations. A boy who has added so much water to his powder that the resultant paint is too runny, for example, may think about taking out some of the water (inverse negation). When he discovers that the inverse negation is not feasible, he may consider the reciprocal negation, adding more powder. This task is beyond sensorimotor schemes alone because the child must anticipate the consequences of an *interaction* of two objects (water and powder), which is more than a simple anticipation of the position of a single object.

The child continues to develop new types of negations at the concrete operational and formal operational periods. Addition of numbers is a concrete operation that negates subtraction. The proposition, "*Q* sometimes occurs without *P*" can be used by the formal operational child to negate the proposition that *P* is a necessary cause of *Q*. Piaget's (1977) point here is that these advanced types of negation are direct descendants from those negations learned in the sensori-

motor period, preoperational period, and so forth; each type is an outgrowth of its immediate predecessor.

Within each of the developmental types of negation the child will exhibit different levels of understanding, based on how negations are used. There are three levels of understanding. First, the child denies the disturbance or contradiction; second, the child acknowledges the disturbance but will not be able to completely compensate for it; and third, the child both acknowledges and compensates completely.

A child is shown seven circles. The first circle in the row is 10 mms. in diameter and the seventh one is 17 mms. The child can easily see that the first and the last are different sizes. But the adjacent circles are so similar that the child cannot discern that the diameter of each circle increases by 1 mm. Call the first circle A, the second B, and the last G. The experimenter puts this question to the child, "Is A smaller than G?" The child answers "Yes" with no difficulty. "Is A smaller than B?" The child cannot discern any difference and says "No." The questioning proceeds until the child has replied enough to make the answers contradictory, to wit, none of the adjacent circles are different, but the two end circles are different. What does the child do to account for the contradiction between saying all circles are alike and saying the two end ones are different?

At first, the child denies that these two facts, all alike and the end ones different, are contradictory. Piaget (1977, p. 73) calls this *Alpha behavior*. In our example, the child might simply say, "Well, all of these (A through F) are alike, but this one (G) is bigger." In other words the child negates the relevance of G to the perceived similarity among the other six circles. By treating G as a special case, the child removes the source of the disturbance.

Later, the child begins to feel uneasy with these answers and no longer finds it so easy to treat G as irrelevant. The child reasons that the AG comparison is a *variation* of the AB comparison. Once the child senses that the AG comparison is an extension of the AB comparison, the contradiction between AB's similarity and AG's difference is heightened. The child is no longer satisfied with an Alpha compensation for this disturbance. So he or she at least works within these two variations: one, the circles are different, and two, the circles are similar. The child says, "You see, sometimes they are bigger, sometimes they are the same. I guess some of them change sizes." The child understands that whatever he or she says must apply to all of the comparisons as a group, but he or she has not integrated the differences with the similarities. This is called *Beta behavior,* where the child understands each state as a variation on the other states but cannot handle two variations simultaneously. The child handles each variation (comparison, in this case) separately. Now they are all the same; now they are all different. To do this the child has to invent some additional factor like "I guess some of them change sizes."

Nevertheless, Beta behavior represents an advance over Alpha. Beta negates Alpha. Alpha negated the relevance of circle G. Beta negates this negation. That is, the negation of the irrelevance of G makes G relevant once again.

The most advanced form of compensation, called *Gamma behavior,* integrates the two variations. The judgment that AG is different is not seen as a temporary relation that changes when adjacent circles are compared. The AG relationship and AB relationship are treated simultaneously rather than successively. The child reasons, for three adjacent circles, if A equals B (in appearance) and if B equals C (in appearance), then A must be equal to C (by the logic of transitivity). Yet the child can see that C is greater than A, which makes the equalities between AB and BC impossible. This last conclusion can occur only if the child can understand the implication that a series of repeated similarities between adjacent pairs has for the perceived differences between end points. The child must coordinate these two variations at the same time. So in this case the Gamma compensation for the contradiction leads the child to conclude that the similarities are really imperceptible differences. Thus the whole series of adjacent and nonadjacent pairs is understood to be always different, not sometimes similar and sometimes different. The Gamma compensation restores the integrity of the whole at all times.

These three forms of negation build on each other until the child comes up with the most parsimonious way to negate the contradictions and preserve the integrity of the whole. Alpha denies the exception as an exception to rule of the whole. Beta negates Alpha, accepts the exception, but constructs a compensation which changes the whole, now according to one variation, now according to another. Gamma negates Beta by coordination of the two variations so that the whole is preserved at all times.

10. *All negations are constructed by the individual and are not the automatic result of feedback from the environment.*

With this proposition Piaget distinguishes himself from even the new versions of S–R psychology. S–R psychology first described learning in terms of one-way associations between stimulus and response: first, the stimulus, and then, the resultant response. Later this model gave way to feedback models, wherein it is reasoned that the response also modifies the stimulus. The very act of making the response modulates the nature of the stimulus leading to the next response. This model has grown into a science called *cybernetics*.

Piaget is interested in feedback mechanisms, and he has done the most of any psychologist to further understanding of the values of infant reflexes with feedback circuits. Sucking a nipple actually increases the stimulus that leads to sucking, therefore more sucking occurs. These reflexes are the origins of intelligence because their feedback circuitry can include more and more of the external world. For example, the child reaches, grasps, brings bottle to mouth, and sucks, all of which lead to a greater likelihood that these sequences will be repeated.

Piaget (1963) differs with the mechanical concepts of feedback that assume the organism is automatically sensitive to the feedback from its own responses. Piaget (1970a, 1975) says that the organism must construct the relevance of the feedback to the ongoing behavior. This is not some automatic process, as would be true in an electrical circuit where what happens and where impulses are sent are determined by the prearranged wires. Feedback is, after all, another stimulus; and everything that was said earlier about the stimulus being no automatic affair also pertains to feedback.

How does this relate to the concept of negation introduced in Proposition 9? Feedback is negation. Feedback is not the stimulus that results from the re-

sponse but rather is a person's interpretation of that stimulus. A ball landing out of bounds causes you to negate certain aspects of your tennis stroke. These modifications then stabilize because you negate a continuation of these modifications when the ball consistently hits within bounds.

The same view can be taken of any form of reinforcement. First there is some gap; then the organism constructs some negation to eliminate the gap. Eating negates hunger. Good manners negates certain aspects of eating. An intensely strong moral ethic could even negate eating altogether. The relevance of eating is determined by what it is the person seeks to negate: hunger, poor opinion, or social injustice. The "gap" is not automatic. The person must feel the gap and then, once felt, construct the negation. This is the same thing as saying, "If the child does not sense the contradiction, then being told the answer will have no meaning because the answer does not negate the contradiction." If there is no gap, there is no meaningful information. If there are no cognitive structures to sense the gap, there is no gap. People create the gap, gap is great, gap is good. It leads us into the path of understanding through negations.

RESEARCH

Methodologies

Several aspects of Piaget's research have raised controversy from the standpoint of scientific method. For example, Piaget feels no compunction that experimental subjects should get the same set of questions, yet he compares them in terms of their intelligence. Read Tuddenham (1970) comments that the psychologist faced with the task of diagnosing an individual needs a standardized procedure to compare the individual to others in the same age group. Piaget's *methode clinique,* which changes the questions to fit the individual's last answer, does not allow for an assessment of individual differences within an identical test environment.

Tuddenham (1971) and others, such as Peter M. Bentler (1971), have taken Piaget's tasks and have standardized the test procedures so that psychologists can use these tasks to make diagnoses on an individual's standing relative to peer groups. Their work by and large has confirmed Piaget's stage theory and extended the usefulness of Piaget's theory to the practicing psychologist. The work of Monique Laurendeau and Adrien Pinard (1962, 1970) is also notable in regard to standardizing Piaget's test procedures of spatial and causal concepts.

Other aspects of Piaget's methodology have also been controversial. Piaget uses a stringent criterion of mastery to assess conservation. Not only must individuals answer the questions correctly, they must also be able to justify why the quantity changes or remains the same. Charles Brainerd (1977) argues that such a stringent criterion of judgment plus explanation increases the probability that the experimenter will fail persons who should have passed (*a false negative*). When two different criteria, judgment only versus judgment plus explanation, are used, Brainerd's data show that the judgment-only criterion seems to result in fewer false negatives. Assume that a student takes five tests. By the judgment-only criterion (a yes-no response) the student might pass on the first two tests and fail on the last three. By the judgment-plus explanation, the student could fail on all five tests. It appears that the judgment-

plus-explanation criterion falsely rejects the student's mastery of the first two tests.

G. Y. Larsen (1977) challenges the logic of Brainerd's conclusions. In the example above, we could just as well reason that the judgment-only criterion falsely *accepted* mastery on the first two tests. This type of diagnostic error is called a *false positive*. Larsen says that in spite of these arguments over which criterion is best, a choice based only on data is misguided. Criteria should be chosen on the basis of theory. Brainerd prefers the judgment-only criterion, so Larsen says, because he views development as a gradual learning of component skills that accumulate in a stepwise fashion. Therefore, he prefers a mastery criterion that portrays developmental sequences of a refined nature. Piaget, on the other hand, sees development as a series of qualitatively different stages, each defined by rather general mental operations. Therefore he prefers a mastery criterion that measures the pattern of thought so that he can match the individual's performance to the general mental operations that define the stages. This debate between Brainerd and Larsen relates to the measurement of learning, discussed in the first part of this chapter.

Research also has been conducted on the methods of presenting tasks. False negatives can easily occur if a child fails for some trivial reason, such as not knowing a particular word. Vago and Siegler (1977) identified several reasons why children misunderstand instructions in ways trivial to the purpose of the study. Then each possibility was systematically tested using a task of judging the fullness of two different water jars. To solve the task, children, at a minimum, have to relate the amount of water in a glass to the amount of vacant space, do this for both glasses, and make a decision on the basis of the *proportionate* amount of water in each glass. This is a proportionality task which requires them to compare two fractions and not, more simply, two absolute levels of water. Of course children can fail this task, even though they understand proportionality, if the instructions are ambiguous or misleading.

To test the notion that children fail because of not knowing the word *fullness,* Vago and Siegler directly assessed the children's vocabulary by means of an eight-item identification task. Children were given three glasses, each with a different level of water, and were asked to pick the glass that was full, and the one half full, and finally the empty one. Children from six to ten years understood perfectly the term *full.* Next, they tested the possibility that children simply did not look at the relevant features, the filled and the vacant space. This possibility might mean that, had the children known to look at both, they would have the mental competence to interrelate this information to solve the task. Vago and Siegler gave the children 15 trials, on each of which they were told, "There are two very important things you should look at. You should look at both the amount of water in each glass and the amount of empty space in each glass." None of the 20 children who received these explicit directions figured out the proportionality rule required to make an accurate judgment of fullness between the two glasses.

Animal Studies

Piaget began his research career with animals, testing his equilibration theory with the common pond snail, *Limnaea stagnalis.* Given Piaget's theory on the continuity between biological adaptation and cognitive development, these studies of the snail are relevant to human learning.

The *Limnaea* are elongated in tranquil waters but globular in turbulent waters. This well-known fact caused Piaget to test the mutability of these characteristics. He found that when he transferred the globular forms from mildly turbulent waters to tranquil waters, the offspring of these snails were born elongated. This indicated that the globular form was not part of an inherited genetic code. But when he transferred the globular snails from extremely turbulent waters to tranquil waters, the offspring did not resume an elongated shape. This indicated that the time the parent snails had spent in the very turbulent waters had caused an irreversible change in the genetic code. Piaget concluded that, after a certain amount of activity in a particular environment, the resulting changes in the organism are passed on to the offspring automatically. The key to this phrase is the word *activity.* The genetic code of the parent snail is not changed unless the parent snail actively reacts to the turbulence, such as contracting its body to get a better grip on the rocks. Studies in which an organism was a passive recipient of environmental factors showed no genetic changes in the organism. Thus, biologists have not succeeded in getting a single offspring of laboratory rats to be born with a short tail, even after cutting off the tail of both parents for many preceding generations.

These studies show that transmission of traits from parents to offspring is a matter of degree. If the activity of the parents was slight, the offspring might acquire only a heightened sensitivity to certain environmental factors (e.g., a reaction to turbulent waters). If the activity of the parents was more protracted, the offspring might inherit the trait even without the presence of the provocation from the environment (e.g., the offspring are globular at birth, even in tranquil waters). It is Piaget's recognition of the continuity between traits acquired after birth and traits inherited at birth that makes his research in biology relevant to a theory of human learning.

Some research studies show cognitive development in animals such as the cat and squirrel monkeys (Gruber, Girgus, & Banuazizi, 1971; Vaughter, Smotherman, & Ordy, 1972). These studies show that animals of this level can attain object permanence but do not develop as far as humans. Gruber et al. found that kittens could find hidden objects by the age of 24 weeks as well as human infants could only after 12 months. However, the kittens never developed the ability to follow invisible displacements, which is something the average 19-month-old human infant can do. An invisible displacement requires an inference that the object hidden in a container moves when the container moves. The data on monkeys indicate that monkeys can go almost as far in solving complicated forms of the object permanence tasks as can a two-year-old human infant.

The sensorimotor intelligence of monkeys was a common research topic for Gestalt psychologists such as Köhler (1925). While this research was not formulated in Piagetian terms, there is nevertheless a great deal of information on how the chimpanzee can combine schemata (patterns of behavior) to solve complicated problems. In fact, Köhler's book on the mentality of apes (1925) reads very much like Piaget's book on his own children. Both Köhler and Piaget used ingenious techniques to probe the intelligence of nonverbal subjects. By putting desired objects out of reach, both were able to witness the strategies their respective subjects used to gain access to these objects. For Piaget, however, the research purpose was to study development of intelligence over the first three or four years of life. Köhler's research on apes was more a study of primate intelligence per se, without a developmental focus.

Human Studies

Within the limits of this chapter, any summary of the research dealing with Piaget's theory would be presumptuous; Modgil and Modgil (1976) require eight volumes to abstract no fewer than 35,000 articles on Piagetian research. The research reviewed here deals specifically with human learning, but other studies could have been cited. In the areas chosen for review, theorists from a variety of orientations have tried to explain the same thing. These two research areas are object permanence and conservation.

Object permanence. Two main issues are of concern to researchers in this area: When does the child learn that objects have an existence independent of immediate visual contact? What is actually learned when the child performs correctly on various forms of the object permanence tasks? It will be seen that the age of onset for concept mastery depends a great deal on how the concept is measured.

Nelson (1974) had seven-month-old infants watch a man walk to and fro behind a screen. Each time the man disappeared on one side of the screen, he reappeared regularly on the other side. After about 16 trials of watching the man walk to and fro, the infants began to anticipate where the man would reappear.

They would quickly shift their gaze to the other side of the screen, in apparent expectation that the man would reappear there shortly. Nelson reasoned that these seven-month-old children understood that during the time the man was shielded from view, he still existed, or they would never gaze to the other side with such fixed expectations.

Bower, Broughton, and Moore (1971) wanted to know more specifically why infants make anticipatory glances to the other side of the screen. If anticipatory looking was an index that the infants understood that the same object would reappear, then the emergence of a different object from behind the screen should reduce the amount of anticipatory looking. When the experimenters made the switch behind the screen, it made no difference to infants from 7 to 20 weeks of age. What did make a difference was the timing of the reappearance. If the object reappeared virtually instantly after its identical (or different) mate disappeared, the infants did not show much anticipatory looking. If the object reappeared after a period of time equal to the time it would take the slow-moving mate to travel the distance behind the screen, then anticipatory looking did occur. It seems up to the age of seven months the infant conserves the identity of an object based on the assumed continuity of its motion rather than based on the physical shape of the object. That is, if a circle disappears and instantly a triangle emerges on the other side of the shield, the infant does not treat the triangle as the same object that disappeared. However, if the triangle emerges after a delay, the infant does treat it as if it were the same object.

The most interesting finding is that infants treated the triangle as a continuation of the moving circle even when the

circle stopped short of the shield, in full view of the infant. Bower et al. concluded that the infant younger than seven months failed to understand that an object that stops is the same as the object which was moving some seconds prior. Stopping the circle, even in view, led to a search for the object as if it needed to be found, as if the stationary object were not what was desired. Motion is a very primitive source of information about the continued *sameness* of an object.

Bower (1974) presented his data as unaccountable by strict S–R theory. When the infant learns to infer the path of a hidden motion, it is not clear what stimulus has been reinforced. He cites additional research on infants 12 weeks of age looking back and forth between two portholes, horizontally spaced, in which an object alternately appears. When the timing is brief between appearances, the infants use a flat trajectory to shift their gaze across the space of the two portholes. When the timing between appearances is delayed, they use an arching trajectory, as if the motion of the hidden object were like a slow rise and fall. Bower says, "Certainly no reinforcement theory could explain why the useless trajectory is interpolated in this situation" (1974, p. 216). The infant is more likely inferring that the long delay between appearances in the portholes means that the object has been "lobbed" rather than thrown straight. It is not clear just what level of consciousness Bower assumes the infant has regarding these hidden trajectories. Nevertheless, the infant seems to be making an assumption about the physical world, and this assumption cannot be accounted for by an appeal to observable features in the stimulus array somehow selectively reinforced.

When infants get older, say around 12 months, they have no difficulty finding an object even if it is hidden in a new place. At 10 months they might get confused if their favorite toy is hidden under pillow B shortly after they have recently found it under pillow A. They are likely to look for it under pillow A, the last place they found it. They do this even though they see their father hide the toy under B. This is called the *Stage IV error*. There is a growing body of research that tries to explain why infants make such an obviously incorrect response.

Harris (1974) found that 10-month-old infants, after finding an object under A several times, would return to A on a third trial even when the object was placed *in front* of B in full view. Harris concludes that the memory of having searched at A interfered with the infant's attention to the object, even when the object was still in full view. To search successfully, the infant must learn to eliminate these interfering memories (search at A). This interpretation fits nicely with Piaget's emphasis on learning as an act of negation.

Cornell (1978, p. 19) disagrees with Harris. Cornell contends that infants could have been adequately attending to the placement of the toy at position B, but when they began their movement to obtain the toy, that movement was then guided by cues from the previous, successful motion toward A. The problem with the Stage IV error is guidance of the motion, not a failure to properly attend to the toy's placement.

Webb, Massar, and Nadolny (1972) present data that support Cornell's interpretation. They used three hiding places instead of the usual two. Infants 14 and 16 months old (slightly older than Harris's infants) did make the Stage IV error, but then they immediately corrected themselves, with great accuracy. That is, if the toy was hidden under C after hav-

ing been found twice previously under A, these infants would look under A and then immediately look under C. They did not often go to B after failing to find the toy under A! Webb et al. concluded that the children had adequately attended to the placement of the object under C, but they were temporarily sidetracked during their movement to grasp because of motion cues associated with the last successful trial. When that response was executed and led to failure, children then retrieved from memory the appropriate cues associated with the toy hiding under C. Had they remembered nothing about C they would have chosen either B or C randomly, which they did not do.

The research studies cited above use either memory or attention to account for their results. Another study (Gratch, Appel, Evans, LeCompte, & Wright, 1974) used both memory and attention. When nine-month-old children could begin their movements immediately after the toy was hidden under B, they did not approach A; they approached B. When they had to wait three or seven seconds they would approach A, the site of the previous hiding. This study suggests that the Stage IV error (approach the previous site) results from the gradual decay of memory for B. Without the three-second delay, infants demonstrated that they adequately registered the information at B. Piaget (1954) accounts for the Stage IV error as a failure to coordinate the movements of an object. After two hidings of the toy at site A, the object and its site become confused. The location of an object is not yet understood as independent from the object itself. So children return to A when they miss the object (sense its absence). Children see an object placed under B but do not conclude that it is the same object they were playing with some seconds before. Therefore, if Piaget is correct, the infants should not search under B even in the zero-second delay. Gratch et al. found that Piaget's predictions were confirmed for infants under nine months. These younger infants would search under A immediately upon seeing the toy disappear under B. Evidently the difference of a few months during the infancy period can account for the variation in experimental findings.

Conservation. The research on conservation runs to several hundred studies, some of which seek to discover which conservation concepts are learned first (quantity, weight, volume); what is the youngest age at which each type of conservation can be learned; and what cognitive demands each type of conservation task places on the learner. For this chapter, studies will be selected from another category: research on training effects, or what can be done to teach the conservation concepts.

Almost every procedure imaginable has been tried to teach the nonconserver how to conserve. Brainerd (1978) and Modgil and Modgil (1976, Vol. 7) provide good reviews of this research. Four rather different approaches have been used: (1) teaching by presenting the child with models who can conserve (Botvin & Murray, 1975), (2) teaching by directing the child's attention to relevant stimuli (Gelman, 1969), (3) teaching by reinforcing correct answers (Brainerd, 1977), and (4) teaching by inducing conflict between predictions and outcomes (Inhelder, Sinclair, & Bovet, 1974).

Botvin and Murray (1975) asked nonconservers, ages six to nine, to watch a conserver model answer questions about the conservation of number, amount, mass, and weight. These models would demonstrate conservation by explaining to the experimenter that spreading out a row of objects did not change the number in the row because, "You can push them back together and see." Watching the models helped the nonconservers to answer similar questions correctly at a later time. The researchers could not say exactly what the children have learned by watching, but it was evidently not rote learning. The observers gave slightly different justifications, such as "Well, you still have the same objects," rather than a parrotlike repetition of exactly what they had heard. Botvin and Murray concluded that watching another person give an answer different from the one the observer predicted could have provoked enough cognitive conflict to cause the observer to work the problem through successfully in his or her own way.

Gelman (1969) presented nonconservers with three rows of objects. The children were instructed to select either the two rows with the same number or the two rows with a different number. If they pointed correctly, they received a token as a reward. Sometimes the three rows were spread out the same distance between their respective endmost objects but had a different number of objects in each row. Sometimes a row with the fewest number was spread out more than the row with the most. The children, to get reinforcement consistently, had to learn to ignore the spread-out distance and the density among the objects and attend only to the number of objects. After a certain amount of this training, the children were tested on conservation of number. Whereas they had not conserved on the pretests, they showed improvement on the posttests. This improvement even generalized to slightly different tasks and lasted for at least three weeks. Gelman concluded that training a child to discriminate the relevant attributes (number) from the irrelevant attributes (length and density of the row) was an effective procedure to improve conservation of number.

There remains an alternative interpretation of Gelman's study. The children were not trained to conserve, they were trained to count. When the children faced the conservation task, saw the two rows in one-to-one correspondence, and saw the experimenter spread out the top row, they simply counted both rows once again before answering. However, children who truly understood the conservation concept would realize that a second counting, after the spreading out, was absolutely unnecessary. Since no objects were added or subtracted in the spreading out, the numbers are conserved. Gelman may have accepted a less stringent criterion to decide when a child can conserve. As Piaget would say, learning to ignore the irrelevant attributes does not constitute conservation of number. The child must understand the illusion, that is, a gain in a row's length means a commensurate loss in the density between objects. The child, by Piaget's standards, must also know that counting again is unnecessary. This alternative interpretation of Gelman's study does not apply with equal power to her data on transfer of training to different tasks.

Brainerd (1977) gave very explicit feedback to six-year-olds who could not conserve. For example, if a child said that the ball of clay weighed more rolled out than that same ball initially, Brainerd would say, "No, that is not the right answer. The right answer is same weight." The child who answered correctly received an M&M in addition to the statement, "Yes, that is the right answer." The children were not trained to conserve inequality; for example, if two balls of clay are unequal to begin with, rolling

out one does not make them equal, in spite of appearances to the contrary. Then these children were tested for conservation by asking them the relevant questions without any reinforcement. Brainerd did not require the children to explain their answers. All children showed marked improvement on the posttest.

To counter the criticism that these children only learned what to say without understanding, Brainerd gave them posttests on conservation of inequality. On these tests the children would have to say just the reverse ("They are not the same") from what they had been trained to say. And the children did not know in advance which type of test, conservation of equality or inequality, would be presented next. The data revealed that the children also improved on conservation of inequality. This suggests that they had learned, via the training procedure, a true concept and not just a tendency to say "same" on every occasion. Yet the criticism regarding the rather loose criterion Brainerd used remains. Brainerd did not have the children justify their answers, so it is not clear, by Piaget's standards, if these children were giving the right answers for the right reasons.

Inhelder, Sinclair, and Bovet (1974) deliberately staged conservation tasks in a manner that caused the nonconservers to contradict themselves frequently. Their basic strategy was to present the tasks so that a lower form of thinking would lead to predictions that would not be confirmed by observable outcomes. The resulting conflict would then cause the child to rework the way the child thought about the task. In one series of studies, Inhelder et al. used water jars arranged vertically so that the jars could drain into each other with the turn of a valve (see Figure 8.1). A child participating in the

Figure 8.1
Jars Used in Conservation of Quantity Task (Inhelder, Sinclair, & Bovet, 1974)

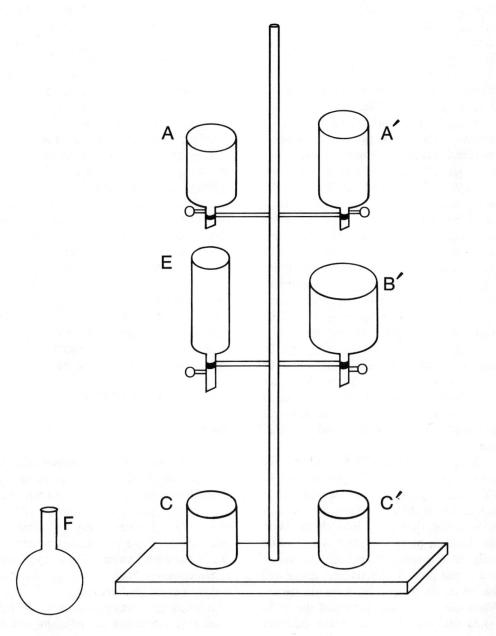

study would first be given an opportunity to pour water into the jars and watch how the water drained from jar to jar. Then the experimenter instructed the child to fill jar F just to the level of the base of its neck. That quantity of water was poured into jar A. Jar F was refilled to the same level and poured into Jar A'. Using this procedure the child could agree that the quantity of water in Jar A was the same as that in jar A'. Then the experimenter asked the child to release enough water from A and A', respectively, to make sure that jars E and B' (nonidentical jars) had the same quantity, "the same amount to drink." Frequently the child would let less water out of jar A than jar A' so that the levels in jars E and B' would be the same. Of course this meant that the quantity in E would be less than the quantity in B'. Once the child stated that the quantities in E and B' were the same, the child was asked to test his or her answer by draining the contents of E and B' into identical jars C and C'. If the quantities were indeed the same, the levels in C and C' should be the same. If the child had made the levels the same in E and B' then, of course, the levels in C and C' would not be the same. When the water was then drained into C and C' the child was thereby confronted with an observation that contradicted the child's prediction.

On other occasions the experimenter would have the child fill jars A and A' with equal quantities but would shield jars E and B' before asking the child to drain equal quantities into them. With the shield in place the child would often drain all the water from both A and A' and would predict that the quantities and the levels in E and B' were the same. When the shield was removed the child would see that the levels were different

and conclude (incorrectly) that the quantities in E and B' were also different. The child would then face yet another conflict when he or she predicted that the levels in C and C' would not be the same after the water in E and B' were released. After several sessions of experiencing conflict between predictions and observations of the outcome, the child eventually learned to conserve quantity independent of changes in water level. The lower form of thinking, that is, that water level is a good indicator of quantity, is replaced with a higher form of thinking, that water levels can be different and quantity remain the same if width also changes.

The importance of this research rests in the self-regulated nature of problem solving. The experimenters never corrected the children and never made them feel that their predictions were wrong. The children had to observe the outcomes themselves and infer for themselves why things did not turn out as they had predicted. The children could have easily assumed, "Well, that is just how water works" and let it go at that. But they did not; they were conflicted and struggled until they reconciled in some logical way the outcomes they observed.

IMPLICATIONS

Theoretical

Piaget's approach to human learning, called *constructivism,* investigates the spontaneous, self-regulated learning found in natural, untutored concept formation. The learner actively constructs relations that are not, indeed could not be, in the environment. There are several implications of Piaget's constructivism for a theory of human learning.

Assimilation-Accommodation. Piaget's choice of the terms *assimilation* and *ac-*

commodation is a deliberate alternative to the more familiar terms *stimulus* and *response*. Theories of learning that begin with the stimulus as the fundamental unit bypass the epistemological questions of how the learner knows the stimulus. Piaget's theory of assimilation-accommodation does not take the stimulus for granted but endeavors to explain its evolution. To Piaget, even a single stimulus is a concept that has to be explained.

Does this mean that the non-Piagetian theories of concept formation can explain the stimulus by inventing a type of microconcept formation theory? The problem here derives from different opinions on when a thing is explained. Even a microanalysis of a single stimulus, such as the shape *square,* could miss the basic assumptions of constructivism. To say that the square is a microconcept, comprised of a set of features such as right angles and straight lines, does not answer the constructivist's question of how the person *knows* the square. To the constructivist, *recognition* of the square (say, pointing and saying "square") is not a criterion for knowing the square and thus cannot be useful in explaining the formation of a stimulus.

Knowing the square involves an attribution of meaning to the stimulus. Is this the same square as seen some minutes before? Can I lift this square? Can this square be converted into a straight line by pressing down on it? Can I convert this square to a circle without, at any point, opening any gaps? Will this square roll or slide if I push it? Can I grab the square at any point with equal comfort to my palm?

Since Piaget is interested in *knowing* rather than *recognizing,* the term *stimulus* does not meet his needs. He prefers to begin his analysis with the *assimilatory scheme,* instead of the stimulus, as the basic unit. He does this to avoid making the naive assumption that the stimulus is ever a pure and raw sensation. It is an inherent function of all biological systems to attribute meaning to sensations, even immediately after birth. Piaget also prefers to talk about the assimilation-accommodation interaction, instead of independent stimuli that can be infinitely permutated with independent responses. This view of independent stimuli and independent responses is too open ended, allows for too much variability in behavior, and completely ignores the schemes of organization inherent in our biological processes. Certain stimuli will coalesce with other stimuli, due to what Piaget calls endogenous processes, themselves patterned by human evolution. These coalesced structures then set constraints on what responses the organism thinks to make, and these responses in turn set constraints on what future events mean and what future events become stimuli.

The implications for learning theory are to look more closely at microprocesses that the organism uses, rather than at microstimuli. The tiny hand movements, eye movements, changes in posture, anticipatory sucking, modifications of the grip—all of these can yield a host of insights regarding the assimilation-accommodation process. Detailed clinical analysis of verbatim transcripts of how one student solves a problem—for example, thinking through how inertia works in outer space—would also provide information on how the student assimilates information to current knowledge and then accommodates that knowledge to new facts that he/she discovers while struggling with the problem.

Some work which used this notion of making a microanalysis of process was done by Forman, Kuschner, and Dempsey (1975), who filmed children from the ages of 9 months to 24 months spontaneously playing with small geometric blocks. The films were coded for every action (lifts, releases, placements, rotations, rolls, drops, constructions) that these children made. Each child was seen once every four months for three testings. From this detailed analysis the experimenters were able to discover, among other things, that a child's use of symmetry in building block structures originates in early infancy when the child takes two identical objects and bangs them together at the midline. The bilateral banging is accommodated over time to bilateral placement of two objects side by side, then a symmetry which results from bisecting a large block with a smaller one, and finally a symmetrical relation between three blocks aligned, such as little circle, large triangle, little circle. The progression from bilateral banging to a stable symmetrical construction passes through an almost logical process of assimilation and accommodation. Through this microanalysis of self-regulated play the experimenters were able to improve their understanding of the *meaning* of the symmetrical construction. They concluded that the symmetrical construction represented the actions used to create it, *frozen motion*. They did not conclude that the children were trying to recreate a representation of static forms of familiar objects seen around them. By understanding the origins of a stimulus (assimilation scheme), as Piaget has endeavored to do, one can discover the child's point of view.

Dialectical Processes in Learning. Piaget emphasizes conflict, which is seen as essential for growth. The old conflicts with the new until, through the dialectical process of equilibration, old and new combine into a new system of understanding. A view of learning as a dialectical process has implications for which theoretical questions should be researched.

The question of whether learning requires conflict brings to fore a whole host of methodological problems of how to measure conflict and semantic problems of how to define learning. Many of these have been mentioned. But more attention needs to be given to an independent assessment of conflict. Too often conflict is assumed rather than measured. If the child learns, the child, according to Piaget, has resolved conflict. If the child fails, the child has not known enough to experience conflict. There is an obvious and regrettable circularity here.

This circle could be broken by establishing independent measures of "experienced conflict." Pauses, smiles, abbreviated alternations between two choices of objects prior to selection, comments, and exclamations are all possible observable, behavioral indications of experienced conflict. These measures could be taken independently of measures of learning. Then an authentic test of the necessity of conflict could be made.

There is a rub. Learning might occur even when these indications for conflict show no measurable presence. Does that mean that conflict was not present or was present in some form not measured? Perhaps the question, "Is conflict necessary for learning?" is a bad question. It might be untestable. Perhaps this question should be reworded, "Under what circumstances is it obvious that conflict facilitates learning?" Research could then tell us definitely when conflict helps, but it would not try to speculate about cases where conflict shows no measurable trace. This more conservative approach to scientific questions should satisfy the needs of most psychologists and educators. But it would not satisfy the broad epistemological interest of Piaget. Piaget's interest in epistemological universals seems to generate questions which are extremely difficult, if not impossible, to test. Yet it is just those epistemological interests that have made testing what can be tested worthwhile.

Testing what creates conflict and how conflict facilitates learning is worthwhile because we can eventually understand how learning is a system not unlike other biological systems. This brings us to the next set of implications of Piaget's work for modern theories of learning.

Biology and Learning. To survive, a biological system must function as an integrated whole. As a disturbance shakes the system, the system either eliminates the disturbance altogether or adjusts. If the adjustments are too severe, the system loses its integrity and does not survive as an intact system. We can view learning in the same way. The learner has some body of knowledge that functions as an integrated whole. As some new fact shakes the assumptions of this body of knowledge, the learner can either reject the disturbance altogether or adjust. If the adjustments are too severe, the old assumptions are rejected and do not "survive" as an integrated whole. Thus the new knowledge becomes rote and ad hoc, isolated from previous assumptions. Alternatively, the adjustments could be better tuned, not so severe, and allow for conservation of the prior assumptions reworked and included in an even higher form of integration.

Does this parallel between general systems of biology and learning imply that learning theorists should become biologists? Perhaps it does, in a sense. Piaget's International Center for Genetic Epistemology is an interdisciplinary center. Not only biologists study there, but also logicians, anthropologists, economists, soci-

ologists, psychologists, and others interested in the function and growth of organic systems. Learning theorists should become biologists at least to the extent that it helps them to improve their questions, their methods, and the way they answer questions. The interdisciplinary atmosphere at Geneva has led to rich discoveries and exciting research projects. There is a pervasive feeling of optimism that comes from a group of scientists working on a common problem with a wide range of expertise. The entire function of the center at Geneva can be seen as the attempt of a system to grow without rejecting the knowledge base of other subsystems, the scientific disciplines as they now exist. It is a massive project for the integration of existing knowledge.

Perhaps this is the greatest implication of Piaget's work. Research should proceed as a system, a whole that functions to assimilate and to accommodate facts from all the disciplines dealing with human development. Learning theorists might elect to continue research on the memory drum or salivary response, but it behooves all of them to know how their part relates to the whole called the organic system, a system that must change to survive, a system in constant motion and development. To research the "adult mind" as some static object probably will not yield the insights that a more developmental theory of learning can provide.

Practical

The implications of Piaget's work in practical applications pertain to almost all areas of human services, from preschool education to help for the aged. All service agencies are interested in the stages and processes of human development, and many have turned to Piaget for help. Piaget's theories have been applied primarily to the diagnosis and development of normal and exceptional children.

Education. It makes eminent sense that Piaget's research on cognitive development has applicational value to education. Piaget has written books on how elementary school and high school students learn number concepts; concepts of time, movement, and speed; geometry, chance and probability, logic, and causality. These concepts have been content areas in school curricula for decades. Piaget's publications have been widely used by science and math teachers in a variety of ways.

Piaget has helped teachers decide what to teach. For example, in geometry Piaget's research indicates that children learn concepts of inside versus outside before they learn concepts of equidistant versus nonequidistant. The new curricula in geometry reflect an understanding of what content should be taught first.

Piaget has helped teachers understand that errors are not always a matter of poor attention or failure to do homework. Children sometimes cannot understand lessons because the concepts make cognitive demands that exceed the child's stage of development. Piaget's stage theory manifests itself in teachers' guides to curricula which utilize curricular levels. For example, the Science 5/13 curriculum (Ennever & Harlen, 1972) divides all science units into three levels which correspond to the preoperational period, the concrete operational period, and the formal operational period. In Renner, Stafford, Lawson, McKinnon, Friot, and Kellogg (1976), college teachers get help in understanding when a student will have difficulty with formal operational tasks.

More recently, Piaget's equilibration theory has helped teachers understand the learning process itself. Education axioms

such as "learning by doing" have taken on new meaning and a detail that goes beyond the rather glib acceptance of principles that seem self-evident. As Gallagher (1978) notes, we are now in a third phase of educational applications of Piaget. The first was the naive application of Piaget's tasks directly to the classroom. The second was a preoccupation with stage differences to the neglect of individual processes of learning. The third is an application of equilibration theory to the process of teaching, where the teacher has a useful framework from which to observe and to understand individual students solving problems. With Piaget's help, teachers are understanding more completely why their intuitions regarding the value of discovery methods of teaching are correct.

Preschool education has been particularly prime for Piaget's theory. Many books have been written on how to teach children from two years to seven years of age using a Piagetian perspective (Almy, 1966; Elkind, 1976; Forman & Kuschner, 1977; Furth, 1970; Kamii & DeVries, 1978; Lavatelli, 1970). However, there is not a great deal of agreement regarding what is the essence of a Piagetian perspective. For Almy it seems to be the nature of the transition from preoperational to concrete operational intelligence. For Lavatelli it is the content, such as seriation and classification tasks. For Furth the emphasis is on the difference between figurative and operative knowing. For Elkind it is the framework one uses to observe the children. For Forman and Kuschner, a Piagetian perspective must deliberately use Piaget's emphasis on transformations, how things change. For Kamii and DeVries, the emphasis is placed on the style of teacher-child interaction in open-ended activities. Perhaps all have their value; but surely not all are logically consistent with Piaget's research. It seems that the essentials of a Piagetian perspective for preschool education would include (1) high regard for self-regulated learning, (2) little attempt to "push" a child to the next higher stage, (3) an awareness and judicious use of conflict to promote the consolidation of concepts, (4) confidence to spend many hours observing children, and (5) activities that provoke thought about change and the relative nature of any "fact" rather than activities that teach the child to see discrete, static stimuli or absolute facts. This last essential item is no less than Piaget's life work on conservation, that is, an understanding of what changes make a difference.

It would be remiss to omit acknowledgment of Piaget's contribution to moral education. Through the research of Lawrence Kohlberg (1970), Piaget's stage theory has been applied to improving young children's ability to solve moral dilemmas. While at first children cannot "de-center" from their own egocentric perspective, they eventually learn, through confrontations with these dilemmas, that other people have motives. They learn to consider a person's motives before judging an act immoral. Kohlberg's objective is not to teach children a "bag of virtues" to be memorized, but rather a process of thinking about moral issues.

Psychopathology. At least since the work of Inhelder (1968), Piaget's theories have been applied to the diagnosis and treatment of psychopathology. Cases of mental retardation, senile dementia, learning disabilities, infantile psychoses, and schizophrenia have been studied from a Piagetian perspective, in hopes of understanding their symptoms and improving their treatment (see Schmid-Kitsikis, 1973).

The early work made the same use of stage theory as was done in the early Piagetian applications to education. For example, this purpose in Inhelder (1968) was to show whether the stages of cognitive development in the mentally retarded follow an order identical (but delayed) to that found in people of normal intelligence. Currently, work is being done in Geneva to apply equilibration theory to psychopathology, which has the advantage of looking for how psychopathology forms rather than a mere description of its static state.

Using the language of equilibration, Schmid-Kitsikis (1973) defined the problems exhibited by adults with "constructive apraxia," an inability to reconstruct spatial relations such as a mosaic design. Adults showed avid concern to perform the spatial construction task but had a characteristic tendency to repeat their errors over and over. These repetitions were not true regulations, even though they were responses to the disturbance created by failure to solve the task. For reasons too complicated for this brief discussion, these apraxic adults were unable to anticipate which responses were closer or further from the solution. Over time the repetition of the errors became so automatic that the disturbance of their incorrectness was annulled, that is, the adults reached a false sense of equilibrium. Schmid-Kitsikis then compared the apraxic adult's successful performance on games of logic with their unsuccessful performance on these spatial construction games. Piaget's distinction between figurative and operative knowledge helped her understand why these adults have such an unusual scattering of abilities and disabilities.

Other researchers have identified cognitive mechanisms that characterize other clinical groups. Voyat (cited in Reid,

1978) found abnormally high levels of egocentric thinking in psychotic children. They seem to resist accommodation of their existing schemes, that is, they over-assimilate. This means that they do not sense disturbance where normal children do, so they are not prompted to regulate their existing impressions of what they see. Reid found that children with learning disabilities concentrated on events that confirmed their guesses. They did not appear to be able to construct a good test to eliminate possibilities; that is, they could not construct negations and use them effectively.

It is not clear how this research will be applied to the treatment of psychopathology. For certain, one good step toward treatment is a better understanding of how the pathological person thinks. Equilibration theory helps the psychologist understand general principles of how different clinical groups think. Treatment design should not be far behind. For example, the knowledge that schizophrenics overassimilate might suggest treatments that zero in on that particular deficit. What researchers have learned about reducing the assimilation process in normals might be tried in concentrated form with schizophrenics. The theoretical framework helps the practicing clinician identify relevant research literature to solve specific problems.

SUMMARY

Piaget gives more attention to the development of learning than the learning of concepts. To Piaget, learning itself takes on different forms at different stages of development. First, children in the sensorimotor period learn through direct action on objects in their environment. Then, in the preoperational period, they learn by representing the static shapes and the movement of objects, but they cannot use the relations between shapes and movement to make inferences about such matters or the conservation of quantity. Children in the concrete operational period can make these inferences, but only in reference to things that they can witness. They cannot yet make inferences on an inferred event (a proposition). This last form of learning is an accomplishment of the formal operational period.

All four of these periods occur in the same order for all children. This is true because each period is a logical prerequisite for the period following. The learning skills of one period are included and expanded in each following period. Thus Piaget's theory can be viewed as a hierarchy of learning skills if we accept the word *skill* as designating a general form of learning not specific to any particular content.

It bears repeating that Piaget is a biologist. He has not arbitrarily chosen organic models of equilibrium to define learning. Learning, to Piaget, is an organic system that functions as a whole to preserve the system. Learning involves an interaction between assimilating new facts to old knowledge and accommodating old knowledge to new facts. When the person learns in only one of these ways, the integrity of the system of knowledge is jeopardized. The person who only accommodates to the new facts loses continuity with past learning. In an extreme form too much assimilation causes the person to be rigid, dogmatic, cautious, and stale. Adaptive learning, on the other hand, involves a good balance between assimilation and accommodation.

Adaptive learning, at any period of development, passes through a definite series of events. First some response, presumed to be adaptive, meets with failure. This creates a disturbance. Without this disturbance the child would continue with the initial response, since he or she would have no reason to change that response. With the disturbance the child makes countermoves to remove that disturbance. Piaget calls these countermoves *regulations*. Regulations usually lead to a compensation for the disturbance, thereby establishing an equilibrium. This equilibrium occurs only because the child has developed to a higher level of understanding. This equilibrium is not a return to the original state prior to the disturbance; at least it does not usually return to the same state.

Sometimes the disturbance is canceled by a return to the same state as before. This happens when the child denies the importance of the disturbance. For example, the child sees that the clay looks like more when long and less when short but denies that these events are in any sense contradictory. But eventually this return to the same form of thinking creates sufficient counterdisturbance so that the child constructs a new equilibrium through a synthesis of the conflicting facts. In this manner Piaget's theory of equilibration describes a process of creative emergence through synthesis, in the same way that Hegel's dialectics describes qualitatively different stages that emerge from their predecessors.

The regulations activated to counter the disturbance are themselves constructed by the learner. Piaget was intrigued with the mystery of regulations. How does the organism know what to do to counter a disturbance? How does the organism know when an attempted regulation is getting closer to synthesizing a new equilibrium? Piaget considered it absurd to think that someone was always there to tell the learner. And, after careful consideration, he considered it equally

absurd to think that the environment could tell the learner. Environments don't talk, they only exist. The learner has to construct that one environmental feedback is an affirmation of a guess, while another environmental feedback is a negation of a guess. Piaget has dispelled simplistic notions that learners automatically know when they are wrong. While there may be many cases of reflex actions to avoid pain or to approach comfort, can these automatic reflexes also account for an avoidance of contradiction or an approach to logical consistency? The environment does not prick children who contradict themselves or supply morsels of food when they do not.

The avoidance of contradiction is constructed, over the years of a child's life, by a process built into what we are as biological systems, with certain inherited forms of functioning. Now this might sound as if our tendency to avoid contradictions is innate. But Piaget differs with Kant on the point that knowledge is present in a complete form at birth. Only the *process* of constructing an avoidance of contradiction is inherited.

The relevance of environmental feedback, therefore, must be constructed (invented) by the learner. To do this the learner must both attend to the observable consequences of his or her response (or prediction) and then compare what he or she observes to the opposite (the negation) of what he or she sees. For example, say a girl predicts that the level of water in a fat glass will be the same when that water is poured into a tall, skinny glass, and then she observes where the level is in the tall, skinny glass. It would be a mistake to say that she "sees" that it is *higher*. She does not automatically see that level as higher, but she might *understand* that it is higher if she compares the vertical distance of the water in the skinny glass to the vertical distance of the water previously in the fat glass. What she understands thereby is that the level now is not-short (the opposite of short), that is, higher. She also could have thought the water is more porous or a lesser amount or not level. The point is, a learner has to decide what aspect of these multiple consequences is relevant to the prediction and how that aspect either confirms or refutes the prediction.

This discussion leads to perhaps the most important assumption in Piaget's theory: The stimulus is never free from enrichments made by active mental comparison of the observer; it is never copied as it exists in some objective reality independent of the observer. Now no one believes that a stimulus can exist independent of an observer, but we may fail to appreciate the degree of transformations the observer makes on the stimulus before it becomes useful. Piaget, as an epistemologist, has been primarily interested in these mental transformations that the observer makes in order to know the stimulus. While many learning theories assume that the learner *sees* the stimulus, Piaget has spent his life studying how the learner comes to *know* the stimulus.

ANNOTATED BIBLIOGRAPHY

Primary Sources

Piaget, J. *Biology and knowledge: An essay on the relationships between organic regulations and cognitive processes.* Chicago: University of Chicago Press, 1971.

In this book Piaget summarizes the research he has done over the past 50 years. He begins with the premise that the usual good fit between mathematics and the objective world should not be passed off lightly as a coincidence: Our systems of mathematics and logic work so well to pre-dict objective events because of a "logic" preexisting in organic regulations. This logic is externalized through our cognitive processes, an externalization of the inherent logic of all biological systems, until the methods of science and math are created. Piaget makes an appeal for a return to the study of organic systems in order to understand our own cognitive processes, warning that we have taken for granted what we know as givens, and we fail to study how they are constructed.

Piaget, J., & Garcia, R. *Understanding causality.* New York: W. W. Norton, 1974.

Piaget, in collaboration with R. Garcia, discusses research projects on children's understanding of how things happen which clearly show that understanding results from assumptions that are logically necessary. The final section, by Garcia, deals with the relationship between development of physics and geometry and the cognitive processes involved to make these advancements possible.

Piaget, J. *The grasp of consciousness: Action and concept in the young child.* Cambridge, Mass.: Harvard University Press, 1976.

Piaget discusses research on the child's consciousness of his or her own actions, demonstrating that knowing how to do something is not the same as knowing what one does. Even a simple task like spinning a ping pong ball with a backspin to make it return to the hand can be done without knowing where the hand was placed and what sort of pressure was applied. The book traces the stages and the mechanisms by which practical knowledge is made explicit and points out that the process of making knowledge conscious involves inferences. It is of interest to learning theorists because Piaget carefully demonstrates how and when the student profits from mistakes and incorrect predictions.

Piaget, J. *The development of thought: Equilibration of cognitive structures.* New York: Viking Press, 1977.

This book was the main source for the present chapter. In it Piaget is more precise about the mechanisms by which a child progresses from one level of understanding to another, through the construction of negations that compensate for disturbances. The book draws heavily on *Biology and Knowledge, Understanding Causality,* and *The Grasp of Consciousness* without giving too much attention to description of the research tasks. The student new to Piaget should read these three books (with *Biology and Knowledge* third), before reading *The Development of Thought,* in which Piaget moves away from a purely structural analysis of the stages of thought and takes a more functional view of the process of equilibration.

Secondary Sources

Furth, H. *Piaget and knowledge: Theoretical foundations.* Englewood Cliffs, N.J.: Prentice-Hall, 1969.

Furth has done much in this book to distinguish Piaget from his contemporaries. He includes essays on the more controversial and misunderstood aspects of Piaget's theory, such as operative knowing, figurative knowing, the difference between learning and development, and the relation between language and intelligence. To shore up the message, Furth has also included short pieces written by Piaget.

Gallager, J., & Reid, K. *The learning theory of Piaget and Inhelder.* Monterey, Cal.: Brooks/Cole, 1979.

This book brings together a readable explanation of equilibration, using examples from biology and psychology. Articulate definitions of concepts such as reflexive abstraction, scheme, and structure are given, and final sections cite applications of Piaget and Inhelder to special education.

Gruber, H. E., & Vonèche, J. J. (Eds.). *The essential Piaget: An interpretive reference and guide.* New York: Basic Books, 1977.

This is the finest single resource on Piaget. The articles, written by Piaget, are arranged, edited, and laced with interpretive comments by the editors. From front to back, it clearly presents the evolution of Piaget's thought, from study of the mollusk

as a biologist, to early political views, and on to a philosophy seasoned with some 50 years of research. In it Piaget proves his remarkable power to ask and to research profound questions.

Inhelder, B., Sinclair, H., & Bovet, M. *Learning and the development of cognition.* Cambridge, Mass.: Harvard University Press, 1974.

In this book it is clear that the Geneva researchers have become more interested in the mechanisms by which children progress from stage to stage. Most of the research discussed deals with ingenious techniques to place in conflict a preoperational scheme of thought with a concrete operation. The book offers clear examples of how experimenters can provoke children to rethink the basis for their answers, without external reinforcement, and to reconstruct their own premises. Research topics include number conservation, class inclusion training, cross-cultural studies, and conservation of length and matter.

Siegel, L. S., & Brainerd, C. J. (Eds.). *Alternatives to Piaget, critical essays on the theory.* New York: Academic Press, 1978.

Despite some misunderstandings of Piaget by several of the authors, this book presents a valid comparison of Piaget to North American learning theory. Topics include object permanence, transfer of training, language, early education, and formal operations. The essays describe alternative interpretations of Piaget's research and challenge notions such as logico-mathematical, operative, and inferential thinking.

REFERENCES

Almy, M. *Young children's thinking: Studies of some aspects of Piaget's theory.* New York: Teachers College Press, 1966.

Bentler, P. M. Monotonicity analysis: An alternative to linear factor and test analysis. In D. R. Green, M. P. Ford, & G. B. Flamer (Eds.), *Measurement and Piaget.* New York: McGraw-Hill, 1971, pp. 220–244.

Botvin, G. J., & Murray, F. B. The efficacy

of peer modeling and social conflict in the acquisition of conservation. *Child Development*, 1975, *46*, 796–799.

Bourne, L. E., Jr. *Human conceptual behavior*. Boston: Allyn & Bacon, 1966.

Bourne, L. E., Jr., & Restle, F. Mathematical theory of concept identification. *Psychological Review*, 1959, *66*, 278–296.

Bower, T. G. R. *Development in infancy*. San Francisco: W. H. Freeman, 1974.

Bower, T. G. R. *A primer of infant development*. San Francisco: W. H. Freeman, 1977.

Bower, T. G. R., Broughton, J. M., & Moore, M. K. Development of the object concept as manifested in changes in the tracking behavior of infants between 7 and 20 weeks of age. *Journal of Experimental Child Psychology*, 1971, *11*, 182–193.

Brainerd, C. J. Feedback, rule knowledge, and conservation learning. *Child Development*, 1977, *48*, 404–411.

Brainerd, C. J. Learning research and Piagetian theory. In L. S. Siegel & C. J. Brainerd (Eds.), *Alternative to Piaget: Critical essays on the theory*. New York: Academic Press, 1978.

Bruner, J. S., Goodnow, J. J., & Austin, G. A. *A study of thinking*. New York: John Wiley & Sons, 1956.

Bruner, J. S., Olver, R. R., & Greenfield, P. M. *Studies in cognitive growth*. New York: John Wiley & Sons, 1966.

Bryant, P. *Perception and understanding in young children: An experimental approach*. New York: Basic Books, 1974.

Cornell, E. H. Learning to find things: A reinterpretation of object permanence studies. In L. S. Siegel & C. J. Brainerd (Eds.), *Alternatives to Piaget: Critical essays on the theory*. New York: Academic Press, 1978.

Cunningham, M. *Intelligence: Its organization and development*. New York: Academic Press, 1972.

Elkind, D. The development of quantitative thinking: A systematic replication of Piaget's studies. *Journal of Genetic Psychology*, 1961, *98*, 37–46.

Elkind, D. Children's discovery of the conservation of mass, weight, and volume: Piaget replication Study II. *Journal of Genetic Psychology*, 1961, *98*, 219–227.

Elkind, D. *Child development and education: A Piagetian perspective*. New York: Oxford University Press, 1976.

Ennever, L., & Harlen, W. *Science 5/13*. London: Macdonald Educational, 1972.

Ennis, R. H. Conceptualization of children's logical competence: Piaget's propositional logic and an alternative proposal. In L. Siegel & C. J. Brainerd (Eds.), *Alternatives to Piaget: Critical essays on the theory*. New York: Academic Press, 1978.

Ferster, C. B., & Perrott, M. C. *Behavior principles*. New York: Meredith, 1968.

Fischer, K. W. A theory of cognitive development: The control and construction of hierarchies of skills. *Psychological Review*, in press.

Flavell, J. H. *The developmental psychology of Jean Piaget*. Princeton, N.J.: D. Van Nostrand, 1963.

Forman, G., & Kuschner, D. *The child's construction of knowledge: Piaget for teaching children*. Monterey, Cal.: Brooks/Cole, 1977.

Forman, G. E., Kuschner, D. S., & Dempsey, J. *Transformations in the manipulations and productions performed with geometric objects: An early system of logic in young children* (Final Rep., Grant NE-G-00-3-0051). Washington, D.C.: National Institute of Education, 1975.

Furth, H. S. *Thinking without language: Psychological implications of deafness*. New York: Free Press, 1966.

Furth, H. S. *Piaget and knowledge: Theoretical foundations*. Englewood Cliffs, N.J.: Prentice-Hall, 1969.

Furth, H. *Piaget for teachers*. Englewood Cliffs, N.J.: Prentice-Hall, 1970.

Gallagher, J. *Knowing how a child knows: Phase three of Piaget and the learning process*. Paper presented at the Eighth Annual Symposium of the Jean Piaget Society, Philadelphia, May 1978.

Gelman, R. Conservation acquisition: A problem of learning to attend to relevant attributes. *Journal of Experimental Child Psychology*, 1969, *7*, 167–187.

Gratch, G., Appel, K. J., Evans, W. F., LeCompte, G. K., & Wright, N. A. Piaget's stage IV object concept error: Evidence of forgetting or object conception? *Child Development*, 1974, *45*, 71–77.

Gruber, H. E., Girgus, J. S. & Banuazizi, A. The development of object permanence in the cat. *Developmental Psychology,* 1971, *4*, 9–15.

Gruber, H. E., & Vonèche, J. J. (Eds.). *The essential Piaget: An interpretive reference and guide.* New York: Basic Books, 1977.

Harris, P. L. Perseverative search at a visibly empty place by young infants. *Journal of Experimental Child Psychology,* 1974, *18*, 535–542.

Inhelder, B. *The diagnosis of reasoning in the mentally retarded.* New York: John Day, 1968.

Inhelder, B., & Piaget, J. *The growth of logical thinking from childhood to adolescence.* London: Routledge & Kegan Paul, 1958.

Inhelder, B., Sinclair, H., & Bovet, M. *Learning and the development of cognition.* Cambridge, Mass.: Harvard University Press, 1974.

Kamii, C., & DeVries, R. *Physical knowledge in preschool education.* Englewood Cliffs, N.J.: Prentice-Hall, 1978.

Karmiloff-Smith, A., & Inhelder, B. If you want to get ahead, get a theory. *Cognition,* 1974, *3*, 195–212.

Klahr, D., & Wallace, J. G. *Cognitive development: An information-processing view.* Hillsdale, N.J.: Lawrence Erlbaum Associates, 1976.

Kohlberg, L. Education for justice: A modern statement of the Platonic view. In N. F. Sizer & T. R. Sizer, *Moral education: Five lectures.* Cambridge, Mass.: Harvard University Press, 1970.

Köhler, W. *The mentality of apes.* New York: Harcourt, Brace & World, 1925.

Larsen, G. Y. Methodology in developmental psychology: An examination of research on Piagetian theory. *Child Development,* 1977, *48*, 1160–1166.

Laurendeau, M., & Pinard, A. *Causal thinking in the child.* New York: International Universities Press, 1962.

Laurendeau, M., & Pinard, A. *The development of the concept of space in the child.* New York: International Universities Press, 1970.

Lavatelli, C. *Piaget's theory applied to an early childhood curriculum.* Boston: American Science of Engineering, 1970.

Modgil, S., & Modgil, C. *Piagetian research: Compilation and commentary* (8 vols.). Windsor, Berkshire: NFER, 1976.

Nelson, K. E. Infants' short-term progress toward one component of object permanence. *Merrill-Palmer Quarterly of Behavior and Development,* 1974, *20*, 3–8.

Pascual-Leone, J. Metasubjective problems of constructive cognition: Forms of knowing and their psychological mechanism. *Canadian Psychological Review,* 1976, *17*, 110–125.

Peill, E. J. *Invention and the discovery of reality.* New York: John Wiley & Sons, 1975.

Piaget, J. *The language and thought of the child.* London: Routledge & Kegan Paul, 1952. (French edition published in 1923.)

Piaget, J. *Judgment and reasoning in the child.* Totowa, N.J.: Littlefield, Adams, 1966. (French edition published in 1924.)

Piaget, J. *The construction of reality in the child.* New York: Basic Books, 1954.

Piaget, J. *The origins of intelligence in children.* New York: W. W. Norton, 1963.

Piaget, J. *Biology and knowledge.* Chicago: University of Chicago Press, 1971. (French edition published in 1967.)

Piaget, J. *The mechanisms of perception.* New York: Basic Books, 1969.

Piaget, J. Piaget's theory. In P. H. Mussen (Ed.), *Carmichael's manual of child psychology* (3rd ed.; Vol. 1). New York: John Wiley & Sons, 1970. (a)

Piaget, J. *The science of education and the psychology of the child.* New York: Viking Press, 1970. (b)

Piaget, J. *The development of thought: Equilibration of cognitive structures.* New York: Viking Press, 1977. (French edition published in 1975.)

Piaget, J., & Inhelder, B. *Le developpement des quantites chez l'enfant.* Neuchatel: Delachaux et Niestle, 1941.

Piaget, J., & Inhelder, B. *Memory and intelligence.* New York: Basic Books, 1973.

Reid, K. *Learning and development from a Piagetian perspective: The exceptional child.* Paper presented at the Eighth Annual Symposium of the Jean Piaget Society, Philadelphia, May 1978.

Renner, J. W., Stafford, D. C., Lawson, A. E., McKinnon, J. W., Friot, F. E., & Kellogg, D. H. *Research, teaching, and learning with the Piaget model.* Norman: University of Oklahoma Press, 1976.

Schmid-Kitsikis, E. Piagetian theory and its approach to psychopathology. *American Journal of Mental Deficiency,* 1973, *77,* 694–705.

Sinclair, H. Developmental psycholinguistics. In D. Elkind & J. H. Flavell, *Studies in cognitive development.* New York: Oxford University Press, 1969.

Tuddenham, R. D. A "Piagetian" test of cognitive development. In B. Dockrell (Ed.), *On Intelligence.* London: Methuen, 1970.

Vago, S., & Siegler, R. S. *The misunderstanding of instructions explanation in developmental psychology.* Paper presented at the biennial meeting of the Society for Research in Child Development, New Orleans, March 1977.

Vaughter, R. M., Smotherman, W., & Ordy, J. M. Development of object permanence in the infant squirrel monkey. *Developmental Psychology,* 1972, *7,* 34–38.

Webb, R. A., Massar, B., & Nadolny, T. Information and strategy in the young child's search for hidden objects. *Child Development,* 1972, *43,* 91–104.

9

Mathematical Learning Theory: W. K. Estes and Stimulus Sampling

DONALD ROBBINS

INTRODUCTION

Overview

Although many learning theories assume that the basic unit of learning is an association between events, theories often differ as to what these events are. Edwin Guthrie, Clark Hull, and Edward Thorndike essentially assumed that these events are *environmental stimuli* and *overt behavior;* responses or *habits* are acquired. On the other hand, Edward Tolman (1932) assumed some sort of *cognitive structure* is acquired. This difference led to one of the major controversies in learning theory in the 1930s and 1940s.

Another issue in learning theory is whether cortical or central mechanisms must be invoked to account for the formation of associations. Alternatively, only peripheral receptors and mechanisms relative to associative bonding could be considered, as many of the so-called S–R theorists believed. Other major issues, such as gradual versus all-or-none learning, and trial-and-error in contrast to insightful learning, as well as questions about the necessary and sufficient conditions for an event to be a re-

inforcing event, have led to a voluminous literature. These issues are also discussed in some of the other chapters in this text.

All of these issues share a common and important characteristic: They are content questions, substantive issues answerable by empirical confirmation or disconfirmation. Another difference that exists between theories of learning cuts across issues, approaches, and theoretical predispositions: the question of whether the theory is qualitative or quantitative. This distinction is not merely whether or not a theory deals with numbers; rather, it concerns the basic epistemological issue of theory testing in science.

Before discussing quantitative theory, we should first make explicit what is meant by *theory*. The purposes of theorizing are myriad. A major purpose of a theory is to pull together a number of experimental results under one umbrella and to place specific information in a more general context. Consequently, theories make assumptions about some aspects of behavior. When these assumptions are put together, predictions or deductive consequences should result. Theories also can tell us where to look and what to look for; they often serve as guiding lights in research. Theories are not set in concrete. Given proper data, theoretical assumptions change—they are slightly or radically altered, depending on circumstances. The situation is similar to a feedback system—a theory predicts specific results, and experimental tests follow. If some results do not support the theory, the theory is changed. Subsequent tests may confirm certain parts of the theory. The process goes on continuously. More disconfirmation leads to yet more changes. Eventually, the theory may be so laden with additional assumptions to account for results that people may begin to abandon it. Theories rarely die, but rather, as the song says of old soldiers, "they fade away."

Thus, all theories, whether qualitative or quantitative, have assumptions (axioms) and deductive consequences. As a result, one should be able to make explicit and specific predictions from the particular theory.

What Is Mathematical Learning Theory? The term *mathematical learning theory* is in some sense erroneous. We should not think of mathematical learning theory as representing a particular theoretical position, in opposition to other theories of learning. Rather, mathematical learning theory reflects an increased use of mathematics, regardless of the psychological orientation of the theory. Issues that have created controversies in the past may either disappear or coexist when formulated in precise, mathematical form.

Although there is an easily identified subgroup of experimental psychologists who may be called *quantitative theorists,* they do not necessarily share the same theoretical orientation. Rather, they share a particular methodology of theorizing, namely a quantitative one. It is logically

possible to have a theory of behavior that leads only to qualitative predictions, but it is difficult to see how such theories could have continued empirical significance. A theory based only on qualitative distinctions often has difficulty in generating even a small number of testable predictions. The absence of explicit axioms in qualitative theories usually leads the theorist to make additional assumptions which are not part of the original theory. This is done to account for new phenomena and to have explicit predictions derived from the theory.

This chapter will focus on the work of William K. Estes, generally considered to be the single most important person in establishing what is often termed *mathematical learning theory*. The specific form of Estes's approach is known as *stimulus sampling theory*.

We must distinguish between issues that arise due to the quantitative nature of the theory and those that deal with the psychological content of the theory. We will turn first to its quantitative aspects.

Major Issues

Advantages of Quantitative Theory. Mathematical learning theory has a number of advantages over its qualitative counterparts (Weinstock, 1970). It allows a finer division of the set of possible outcomes of an experiment into those that support and those that contradict the theoretical predictions. Thus, explicit, unequivocal predictions can be made, since deductive consequences exist. The theorist is forced to coordinate explicitly theoretical and observable dependent variables. Often the measure of behavior according to the theory and the measure in a specific experiment differ, and the theorist needs to relate the two and bring them together. For example, if a theory makes predictions in terms of an entity referred to as *response strength,* the theorist needs to have a specific relationship between, for example, response strength and speed or frequency of responding, or whatever the measure of behavior is in a given experiment.

In evaluating quantitative theory some specific aspects must be considered. An equation will tell how to calculate the probability of a given response for any specific trial number. The equation will have constants, or *free parameters.* For example, in the equation for a straight line, $y = mx + b$, the letters m and b are the constants or free parameters. Given m and b, we can predict values of y for any value of x. Thus if x were trial number and y some measure of behavior, we could predict behavior (as measured by y) for every trial number (x) if we knew m and b. The more of these free parameters there are, the easier it is to predict the values of y, since the task reduces to a curve-fitting exercise. As a result, in quantitative theory, we like to estimate free parameters from one situation and use them in another. However, this is very difficult, if not impossible, in behavioral work. Consequently in this field the number of free parameters is generally kept as small as possible, ideally not more than two.

It is necessary to be able to identify parameters, that is, to know what psychological process or mechanism or variable is represented by the parameters of the theory. It is also necessary to specify the range of application of the theory, or to know the situations to which the theory applies. Otherwise a seemingly disconfirming result may be outside the range of application of the theory, so that it is not disconfirming at all. For example, in applying a quantitative theory to a

choice situation from a no-choice situation, Solomon Weinstock (1970) pointed out that both choices must be rewarded some of the time. Situations in which one choice was rewarded either all of the time or none of the time were outside the range of the theory. Results presented by others which were claimed to be disconfirmations of a particular quantitative view were thus not really disconfirming. Rather, in this experimental situation the theory was inapplicable.

Stimulus Sampling Theory. To appreciate most fully the contributions of W. K. Estes it helps to first explore issues that were not concerns of his theories and then concentrate on his particular view, stimulus sampling theory.

Learning is often defined as a relatively permanent change in behavior due to reinforced practice (Kimble, 1961). *Change* indicates that in its most general sense learning is viewed as behavioral change. As a result, learning encompasses not only traditional areas, such as the acquisition and modification of verbal skills, cognitive skills, and motor skills; it also includes aspects of attitude change, personality change, and the like. Learning is *relatively permanent* rather than permanent and unchangeable, since in theory it is always modifiable. *Reinforced practice* refers to the so-called *empirical law of effect,* which states that any event that maintains or increases behavior is a reinforcer.

The history of psychology is replete with controversy regarding this law which asks: What are the conditions necessary for an event to be reinforcing? During the controversies of the 1940s, the 1950s, and to a lesser extent the 1960s, Estes was never directly involved with this issue. His psychological model contains an assumption of *contiguity theory* (Estes, 1950). Specifically, he made Guthrie's

(1952) assumption that all that is necessary for learning to occur is a contiguous occurrence of stimulus and response. *Contiguous occurrence* means that the stimulus and response occur within a "reasonable time" of one another. This interval has never been given much attention, although most theorists probably have had in mind seconds or minutes. However, recent research on the taste aversion phenomenon (e.g., Revusky & Garcia, 1971) suggests that events that occur hours apart can become associated. In this research an animal is given a novel substance, such as saccharin. A few hours later it is made sick—through X-radiation, injection of a chemical substance, or whatever. After recovery, which sometimes takes a few days, the animal is given a choice between tap water and water sweetened with saccharin. Prior to the poisoning experience it would almost always have chosen the sweet-tasting water that contained saccharin. Now, however, it avoids the sweetener, and the avoidance sometimes lasts for months. Thus in this situation the apparent stimulus (saccharin) and the response (getting sick) are separated by hours, yet they appear to be associated. A number of theories have been proposed to account for this phenomenon. For our purposes, an important point to bear in mind is the looseness of the concept of *contiguity*.

Although in his later work Estes (1969) made assumptions similar to notions of *drive*, he did not perform research directed at the reinforcement controversy. Instead he made assumptions that appeared to be consistent with existing data. Similarly, with regard to the issue of what is learned, Estes again did not perform specific experiments aimed at an aspect of the controversy but rather

always assumed that the basic unit of learning is an association. However, in the development of his theories, the form of the association has changed from an early stimulus-response form, to a later stimulus-stimulus form, to a yet more general association among environmental events, and most recently to a hierarchical association view.

In the development of Estes's theory the events presumed to become associated have been elaborated and expanded as new data, phenomena, and thoughts have emerged. The early form of Estes's formulation was an S–R theory, in which environmental events called *stimuli* become associated with external peripheral behaviors called *responses*. Reward or reinforcement works backwards in time in that it forms (in an all-or-none manner) an associative connection between a stimulus and a response. This concept was subsequently expanded to include associations between stimuli (S–S), between a stimulus and reinforcement (S–Rf), and perhaps even between a response and reinforcement (R–Rf). More recently the concept of reinforcement has been considered by Estes to be more akin to a feedback system. Reward or reinforcement following a situation is thought to provide information to the organism regarding what to expect in the future when a similar situation is encountered. Reinforcement is sometimes thought to *modulate* the flow of information so that, if anything, its action works forward in time, rather than backward.

Recently, hierarchical associations have been proposed by Estes. Events become associated with the general contextual situation within which something occurs. The association is thought to be hierarchical so that a *control element*, assumed to be evoked by the contextual cues, is the apex of a pyramid. The control element has associative connections to both the stimulus and the response, although no direct connection between them exists. Thus, associations between environmental events are connected through these control elements in a hierarchical fashion.

The years preceding Estes's classic 1950 paper, "Toward a Statistical Theory of Learning," were filled with controversy involving all-encompassing general learning theories proposed by theorists such as Clark Hull, Edwin R. Guthrie, Edward C. Tolman, and B. F. Skinner. Estes's theoretical approach was a marked departure in that it was quantitative in form (explicitly so in contrast to Hull's) and was applied to limited areas of learning. Thus, he was heralding the era of "miniature" theories with explicit boundary conditions and constraints.

The period from the 1930s through the 1950s was an era of general, all-encompassing theories of learning as typified by the work of these theorists. Perhaps some of these theories were unsuccessful because they attempted to be too broad, too general in scope. Although they were tested within a fairly restrictive, narrow framework, the range of applications was enormous. Quantitative theory, on the other hand, demands more precision. This leads to fewer and more refined testing situations. In the extreme, quantitative theory can be thought of as a theory or a model of an *experiment,* sometimes referred to as a *miniature* theory or test.

In part, the development of miniature theories was a reaction to the general, global theories of the past, in which precise tests were extremely difficult. Estes is a leader in defining specific situations in which to initially test theory. From these tests emerge systematic expansions and subsequent tests. In contrast to broad generalities, there is a search for specific principles or rules that work in clearly defined situations. The emphasis is on *processing*—that is, how is the information processed in the situation? Experimental answers lead to further expansion and elaboration. Thus, in the era of miniature theories the theorist builds outward from specifics to more general formulations. This is in marked contrast to the older approach, which attempted to predict specific situations from an often nonempirical, general conceptual framework.

Basic Concepts

Probability of Response. Behavior is seen as a probabilistic phenomenon. The major theoretical dependent variable is probability of response. Almost all theoretical equations are expressed in terms of response probability. The empirical measure is simply the relative frequency of a given behavior (response). Thus, a direct correspondence exists between theoretical and empirical behavioral measures. In this manner, Estes avoids the problems some other theorists have in relating a theoretical measure of response strength to a behavioral measure in a specific experiment. By using response probability as his basic measure, Estes was able to utilize a host of mathematical techniques previously developed for totally different purposes. As a result, the famous "urn" model of probability theory or "jar of marbles" analogy could be utilized in applying these concepts to behavioral phenomena.

The Stimulus as a Population of Individual Elements. Estes (1950) assumed contiguity is all that is necessary to form an associative connection. Following B. F. Skinner (1938), he divided the world into mutually exclusive response classes, so that in the case of a T-maze, the probability of a left turn equals 1 minus the probability of a right turn, and in an operant box the probability of a bar press equals 1 minus the probability of anything but a bar press. This greatly simplified response definitions.

A clever innovation was Estes's view of the stimulus or stimulus situation. He assumed that the stimulus can be conceived of as a hypothetical population of entities, called stimulus elements. A given element is associated with only one response at any one time. Further, the associative connection between a stimulus element and a response occurs on an all-or-none basis. How then, one might ask, does his theory generate the typical gradual learning curves and not step functions, which are rarely found? Since the stimulus is a population of stimulus elements, he assumed that on any one trial a random sample of these elements is presented. Only those elements present in the sample are conditioned to whatever event occurs on that trial. The conditioning status of those not sampled is left unchanged. As a result, a learning curve may be viewed as a function reflecting the cumulative number (or proportion) of elements conditioned to some response, as a function of trials. Over the years these axioms have been tested, modified, and extended, while the basic approach, that of stimulus sampling theory, has remained intact.

Emphasis on the Processing of Information. Stimulus sampling theory may be viewed as an attempt to develop relatively simple schemes to describe and to predict the results of specific experiments. It is concerned with developing rules or principles that predict various learning phenomena, with an eye towards emphasizing the events and processes going on in an organism while learning. The explanations are on a behavioral rather than a physiological level. For example, Donald O. Hebb (1949) developed a fairly elaborate theoretical scheme that emphasizes neural events which occur during learning. Estes, on the other hand, concentrates on the processing of information on a behavioral level and does not invoke physiological mechanisms or explanations to account for experimental data.

Responses as Classes of Behaviors. Estes considered responses not as specific sequences of behaviors but rather as a class of activities. For example, any and all behaviors that lead to an organism pressing a bar or pecking a key or pushing a button would all be members of the same response class, despite the fact that they may involve totally different movements and peripheral organs. Furthermore, these classes of behavior are all related to response probability and thus, in turn, may be related to one another.

Association as the Basic Unit of Learning. Learning means that events (or more precisely, stimulus elements) become "connected to" other events (typically responses) so that upon being presented with the same stimulus in the future, the previously connected or conditioned response occurs. Changes in information or reinforcement can change the response with which the stimulus is connected or associated. However, since Estes is an associationist, it must be remembered that events are related in the brain (presumably), and these associative connections form the building blocks of learning or behavioral change.

HISTORY

Beginnings

William Kaye Estes was born in Minneapolis, Minnesota, on June 17, 1919. He began studying the effects of punishment as an undergraduate, working with B. F. Skinner, and continued this work in graduate school. He received his B.A. degree in 1940 and his Ph.D. in 1943 from the University of Minnesota. After service in the armed forces he joined the faculty of Indiana University in 1946, attaining the rank of professor in 1955 and research professor of psychology in 1960. He became a professor of psychology at Stanford University in 1962 and in 1969 moved to Rockefeller University. In 1979, he became professor of psychology at Harvard University. In 1976 he became editor of the leading theoretical psychology journal, *The Psychological Review*.

The Basic Unit of Learning: The Association. An excellent history of associationism can be found in a book by John Anderson and Gordon Bower entitled *Human Associative Memory* (1973). Some of the ancient Greeks were associationists. However, the early behavioral science of the 1800s was largely tied to philosophy, and, as a result, "behavioral theories" were rarely confronted with data. During the latter part of the 19th century, psychology came into being as an empirical science. Nevertheless, associationism has historically been a popular conception.

Be they ideas, sensory information, memory nodes, or similar mental events, these events are associated or connected (presumably in the brain) as a result of experience. Experience then can be reduced to a basic unit—the association.

Rules exist that can lead to complex events from the underlying simple events. The views of Estes are consistent with these historical predecessors.

Major Theorists

The ideas of the early associationists most certainly influenced Edwin R. Guthrie, who was, in turn, an important influence on Estes. Estes's early theorizing, based on stimulus elements, may be viewed as a quantitative version and extension of Guthrie's early work. Although Guthrie was vague as to how components combined, Estes assumed that they combined independently. Furthermore, Estes's pattern model is similar to Guthrie's later view on patterns of stimulation; in both their models, it is the overall pattern of stimulation that matters and not individual elements or components. Estes's theories also show the influence of B. F. Skinner, with whom he studied. As Skinner had done, Estes defined his variables operationally in terms of classes, and he employed a methodical analysis of behavioral events, taking care to establish a strong empirical base for his theoretical position. Estes, however, broke with Skinner's strictly descriptive, atheoretical approach when he published his classic 1950 paper.

The difference may best be understood by referring to an analogy offered by Anderson and Bower (1973, p. 414). Consider a physicist walking through a forest, trying to explain the events about him. He can provide descriptions of the principal forces governing the descent of a leaf to the ground, but would never try to simulate in the laboratory the descent of a specific leaf and would never consider simulating the entire forest. Rather, the physicist would try to abstract from the real world significant components of the phenomena at hand. Similarly, Estes would probably argue, as any theorist might, that a theory can provide quantitative descriptions of the major variables affecting the behavior of organisms. However, one would not attempt in the laboratory to duplicate every aspect of behavior of a specific individual. The theoretical psychologist would try to capture from the real world the significant aspects of the phenomena being studied.

Estes's theory is deeply grounded in psychological phenomena. This is in marked contrast to the approach of Robert Bush and Frederich Mosteller (1955), for example. They begin from mathematical considerations and as a result appear to have a theory in search of a psychological rationale (see Weinstock, 1970). Estes instead uses data as a base for the formulation of assumptions and postulates. He views the learning process as a formation of associations on a probabilistic basis. Learning for Estes may be viewed as connections between operationally defined response classes and operationally defined classes of stimulating situations.

Estes's approach made its first public appearance in 1950, when "Toward a Statistical Theory of Learning" was published in the *Psychological Review*. Although the theory was applied only to an operant conditioning situation, the theory delineated essential aspects which were not modified substantially until the appearance of the pattern model in a 1959 paper.

Estes's influence can be seen not only in his own work, but also in that of others. One of his most prominent students is Richard C. Atkinson, whose early work generalized Estes's approach to complex discriminative situations.

Eventually Atkinson became involved in computer-assisted instruction and second-language acquisition, representing major generalizations of Estes's approach to practical problems. Various current approaches to choice behavior and discriminative behavior may be seen as offshoots, modifications, and variations of views originally proposed by Estes. Bower's work on paired-associate learning represented a generalization of one of Estes's submodels in his system. The area of probability learning, basically on a theoretical level, contains various Estes-type approaches to the phenomena observed. Thus, many of the theories variously referred to as stochastic models, Markov models, or probabilistic models and the like can trace their origins to Estes's formulations.

Current Status

Most recently for Estes (in press), conditioning refers to a process or collection of processes, operative in many if not all forms of learning. Processes of memory and perception are presumed to occur at all phylogenetic and developmental levels, although there are important differences in their overt manifestation related to differences in information-processing capacity. It may be that conditioning processes do not disappear at the higher levels of the phylogenetic scale but rather become subordinate to other processes. In particular, for *Homo sapiens* such processes would include the verbal. Estes suggests that perhaps conditioning can be observed in relatively pure form only within restricted subsystems and in tasks for which the demonstrated experimental restraints do not bring into play the additional capacities and more elaborate processing capabilities of higher organisms. Estes (in press) has noted that J. Konorski (1967) seems to have been the first to see clearly that it is not necessary to look beyond conditioning for evidence of higher processes such as perception and memory, if we define perception as the processing of stimulation that results in an encoded representation. Memory refers to information retrieved by an organism as a result of experience. It is the encoded representation of retained perception.

From these considerations, Estes builds his latest theory. This theory has not taken the formal mathematical form of his prior theories but rather consists largely of flow diagrams. This suggests the considerable influence recent work on computer simulation has had for Estes. It also reveals that as the theories have become more complex, mathematical niceties have gone astray. Often the only way to generate expectations from these more complex views is to simulate the "ideal organism" on the computer. This represents not a movement away from the use of mathematical tools in theorizing but, rather, a movement outward, as new techniques and methods were brought to bear on the issues of the 1970s. One of these is the expanded use of the computer as a simulator of behavior. This use of the computer should be distinguished from its use to study artificial intelligence. Now the mathematical theorists are using computers to reveal whether in a given situation organisms behave in accord with theory.

Other Theories

Previous Attempts at Mathematical Learning Theory. Prior to the 1950s the most significant attempt at quantitative learning theory was that of Clark L.

Hull (1943), subsequently extended and elaborated by Kenneth W. Spence (1956, 1960). Their approach was based on a set of unobservable variables related to observable dependent and independent variables by functions to be empirically determined. Behavior was considered a largely deterministic process, although a probabilistic variable was added.

One of the major problems with Hull's quantitative theory and that of his colleagues (Hull, 1943; Spence, 1956, 1960) was the lack of a clear relationship between the theoretical dependent variable, momentary effective excitatory potential, and observable dependent variables. A disconfirming result may mean that something is wrong with the theory or that something is wrong with the response model relating the theoretical and observable dependent variables. Estes (1950) avoids this problem by using probability of response as his major theoretical dependent variable, measured by the relative frequency of occurrence of a given response. Weinstock (1970) suggests that this may represent a major theoretical contribution of Estes.

In considering the major aspects of the Hull-Spence approach, the ideas of the two theorists can be combined and simplified. Although some distortion results, all major points are valid. The Hull-Spence approach was modeled after theories in physics. The task was to: (1) identify relevant independent variables; (2) figure out how they combine; and (3) relate the result to a theoretical dependent variable, which in turn is to be related to the various experimental measures of behavior. For example, to account for the speed with which a rat runs a straightaway at the end of which is food, we should know how hungry the rat is (its drive state, D); how quickly it will receive the reward when it gets to the end of the straightaway (the delay of reward factor, *L*); how much food it will receive at the end of the runway (the magnitude of reward factor, *M*), and how often the animal has been in this situation (*N*, for number of trials). Assume that the latter three factors affect the strength of an association that is formed as a result of the experience, that is, *habit strength,* denoted *H*. Combine these factors additively so that $H = L + M + N$. The factors *L, M* and *N* are each in turn represented by a formula, a mathematical rule for calculating this number. Finally, the associative factor, *H,* combines with the drive factor, *D,* in a multiplicative manner, so that $E = D \times H$. Note that *E* represents the theoretical dependent variable, which we will call *excitation.* Thus, we need to know values *L, M,* and *N* to obtain *H;* then in turn we need to know *D* to get *E*. Once we have *E* we still cannot compare this to a real organism's behavior because we need to relate *E* to whatever measure of behavior was taken in a particular experiment.

The student should, at this point, realize the difficulties this approach must encounter. If we could get a value for each of these constants or parameters, independent of the situation in which we are measuring them, we would indeed have a situation similar to physics. However, in the behavioral sciences much behavior is strongly affected by the specific situation at that moment. As a result, we cannot come up with parameter values independent of the situation we are presently in; rather, other methods and techniques are required to satisfy observers that indeed we are generating predictions and quantitative descriptions of the behavior of organisms.   ·

PROPOSITIONS

1. *Behavior is a probabilistic phenomenon.*

Estes's formulation assumes that behavior is essentially probabilistic. The major theoretical and empirical measure of behavior is the probability of occurrence of a member of some response class. Behavioral phenomena are interpreted, not by reference to molecular processes, but by specifying the rules of operation. These rules are simple mathematical laws that describe the overt response character of a behavioral system. To Estes the environment, or stimulus, is represented by a large population of discrete conceptual entities called stimulus elements.

2. *Elements are conditioned on an all-or-none basis.*

Each element can be connected to or conditioned on an all-or-none basis to only one response class at any one time. On any trial the organism is conceived to be taking a random sample of stimulus elements from the entire population of stimulus elements. The probability of occurrence of any response class is simply the proportion of elements in the sample conditioned to that class. These aspects of Estes's views are shown in the first two circles in Figure 9.1. A reinforcing event acts on the conditioning relations of the sample of elements in some specified fashion; for example, all elements in the sample become conditioned to the response class denoted by the experimenter as the correct one. The sample is then returned to the population for resampling for the next trial. The function describing changes in response probability turns out to be a linear function

Figure 9.1

Basic Stimulus Sampling Scheme

Assume that we have a jar of marbles. Half of them are painted red (closed circles) and the other half are painted white (open circles). Being painted red is equivalent to conditioning an element to an A_1 response. Being painted white is equivalent to conditioning an element to an A_2 response.

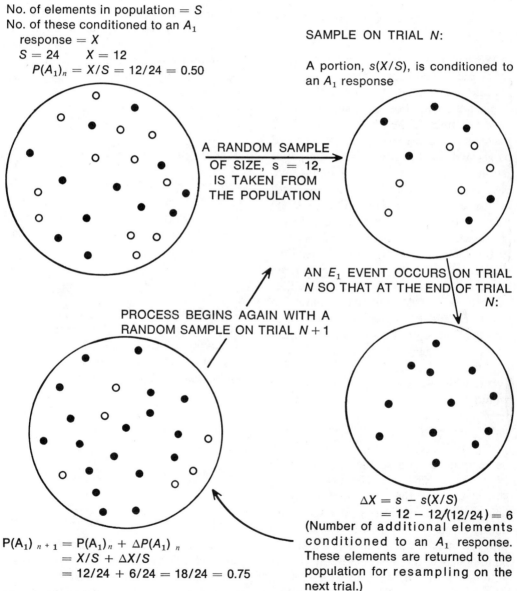

POPULATION AT BEGINNING OF TRIAL N:

No. of elements in population $= S$
No. of these conditioned to an A_1
   response $= X$
$S = 24$ $X = 12$
   $P(A_1)_n = X/S = 12/24 = 0.50$

SAMPLE ON TRIAL N:

A portion, $s(X/S)$, is conditioned to an A_1 response

A RANDOM SAMPLE OF SIZE, s = 12, IS TAKEN FROM THE POPULATION

AN E_1 EVENT OCCURS ON TRIAL N SO THAT AT THE END OF TRIAL N:

PROCESS BEGINS AGAIN WITH A RANDOM SAMPLE ON TRIAL $N + 1$

$\Delta X = s - s(X/S)$
$\quad = 12 - 12/(12/24) = 6$
(Number of additional elements conditioned to an A_1 response. These elements are returned to the population for resampling on the next trial.)

$P(A_1)_{n+1} = P(A_1)_n + \Delta P(A_1)_n$
$\quad = X/S + \Delta X/S$
$\quad = 12/24 + 6/24 = 18/24 = 0.75$

(Proportion of elements in the population conditioned to an A_1 response at the end of trial n and the beginning of trial $n + 1$)

of trials as in the Bush and Mosteller (1955) formulation. Although the same quantitative function is derived by Estes and by Bush and Mosteller, however, the two derivations have very different psychological orientations.

3. *The stimulus situation is viewed as a population of stimulus elements.*

We will use a two-choice situation as the basic experimental procedure to illustrate the theory. For example, in a T-maze the two choices would be a right or a left turn at the choice point of the maze. Let the two responses be denoted as A_1 and A_2. Let S represent the population of elements; X is the number of elements conditioned to an A_1 response at the beginning of trial n, and $S - X$ the number of elements conditioned to an A_2 response. Thus X plus $S - X$ add up to the total population of elements. Further, let s equal the size of the random sample (of fixed size) that the subject samples on a trial. Finally, assume that events E_1 and E_2 represent "reinforcing" events of an A_1 and A_2 response, respectively. For example, food in the left-hand goalbox would be an E_1 reinforcing event, while food in the right-hand side would be an E_2 event. For the present let $E_1 = 1$, and therefore $E_2 = 0$; that is, only A_1 responses are reinforced.

This task may be seen, for example, to be learning to choose the left-hand side of a maze. Since all elements are assumed to have the same probability of being sampled, we can specify the probability of an A_1 response as equal to the proportion of elements in the population conditioned to an A_1 response at the beginning of trial n, denoted as $P(A_1)_n$, which equals X/S. We also assume that the proportion of elements in the *sample*

conditioned to an A_1 response equals the proportion of elements in the *population* conditioned to an A_1 response. The conditioning assumption is all-or-none, so that all elements present on any one trial get conditioned to the reinforced response class.

This can be seen by reference to Figure 9.1. The number of additional elements (ΔX) conditioned to an A_1 response after an E_1 event on the trial is the number in the sample less the number previously conditioned to an A_1; that is,

$$\Delta X = s - s\left(\frac{X}{S}\right).$$

We now divide by S and get

$$\Delta P(A_1)_n = \left(\frac{X}{S}\right)$$

where $\Delta P(A_1)_n$ is the change in probability of an A_1 response on the nth trial. We then get

$$P(A_1)_{n+1} = P(A_1)_n + \frac{X}{S} + \frac{s}{S}\left(1 - \frac{X}{S}\right).$$

Here $P(A_1)_{n+1}$ is the probability of an A_1 response at the end of trial n and at the beginning of trial $n + 1$. Let us now define Θ as s/S, the proportion of elements in the sample. We then get

$$P(A_1)_{n+1} = P(A_1)_n + \Delta P(A_1)_n =$$

$$\frac{X}{S} + \Theta\left(1 - \frac{X}{S}\right),$$

and then,

$$P(A_1)_{n+1} = P(A_1)_n +$$

$$\Theta(1) - P(A_1)_n = P(A_1)_n (1 - \Theta) + \Theta.$$

The basic scheme as depicted in Figure 9.1 illustrates the equation, which is sometimes called the *linear learning operator*. Notice that the probability changes as a linear function of trials. This equation is a difference equation (Goldberg, 1958), the solution of which is

$$P(A_1)_n = 1 - (1 - P_1)(1 - \Theta)^{n-1},$$

where P_1 is the probability of an A_1 response at the beginning of the study.

For illustrative purposes Figure 9.1 represents a jar of marbles in which, at the beginning of trial *n*, there are 12 marbles painted red and 12 painted white. Consider that being painted red is the same as being conditioned, connected, or associated with an A_1 response, while A_2 response associations are painted white. As the first row of Table 9.1 shows, we are assuming for purposes of this example that a random half of the elements in the population are sampled on any one trial; ½ of 24 = 12. Furthermore, since we also assume that the proportion of red and white marbles in the sample is roughly the same as the respective proportions in the population, half of the 12 marbles are red and the other half are white. If an E_1 rewarding event occurs on Trial *n*, the six white marbles are painted red, and the second row of Table 1 illustrates this happening on Trial *n*. The third row shows what happens when the marbles in the sample are returned to the jar. The next row shows how the random sample of 12 marbles is distributed: 9 red and 3 white, which is 0.75 red, the same proportion of red marbles in the population. An E_1 event occurs again on Trial $n + 1$, and the effects are shown on the next row.

Thus you can see how the probability of being conditioned to an A_1 response (being painted red) reflects the proportions of elements in the population conditioned to an A_1 response. Further, you can see how the learning or conditioning function can be viewed as a curve representing the cumulative proportion of red marbles (conditioned to an A_1 response) as a function of trial number.

4. A population of homogenous stimulus elements viewed as a single element.

Another way of deriving the basic learning operator is to ask: What is the fate of a single element? (Weinstock, 1970.) On a given trial an individual element is either sampled (with probability Θ) or not sampled (with prob-

Table 9.1

Basic Stimulus Sampling Scheme

	Population				Sample				
	No. of Red Marbles	No. of White Marbles	Total No.	Proportion of Red Marbles	No. of Red Marbles	No. of White Marbles	Total No.	Proportion of Red Marbles	Reward Event E_1 or E_2
1. Beginning of Trial *n*	12	12	24	0.50	6	6	12	0.50	
2. Trial *n*					+6	−6	12	1.00	E_1
3. End of Trial *n* ...	18	6	24	0.75	12	0	12	1.00	
4. Beginning of Trial $n + 1$	18	6	24	0.75	9	3	12	0.75	
5. Trial $n + 1$					+3	−3	12	1.00	E_1
6. End of Trial $n + 1$	21	3	24	0.88	12	0	12	1.00	
7. Beginning of Trial $n + 2$	21	3	24	0.88	10+	2−	12	0.88	

ability $1 - \Theta$). In the latter case, the probability does not change, that is

$$P(A_1)_{n+1} = P(A_1)_n.$$

However, in the former case, since an E_1 event always occurs in this experimental situation, the conditioning status of the element changes with probability 1 (if it is not already conditioned to an A_1). Thus,

$$P(A_1)_{n+1} = \Theta \cdot 1 + (1 - \Theta) \cdot P(A_1)_n,$$

which is the same learning operator as above. This is illustrated in Figure 9.2.

Estes and Burke (1953) extended this basic notion to the case where some stimulus elements were more likely to be sampled than others. Specifically, they assumed that the thetas for all of the elements were not the same. This is more like what might be encountered in discriminative or attentional situations and the like. Elements with a higher sampling probability tend to get sampled first and, as a result, to be conditioned earliest. For example, in a situation where some elements are sampled with probability Θ_1 while others are sampled with probability Θ_2, where $\Theta_1 > \Theta_2$, on the average the Θ_1 elements would be conditioned before the Θ_2 elements. In contrast to a situation where all the sampling probabilities (Θ's) are equal, the unequal case will lead to an initially faster rising learning curve, although it is overtaken by the equal Θ case, since low sampling probability elements are now being sampled and conditioned. In the limit both functions terminate at the same point.

Figure 9.2

The Single-Element Approach

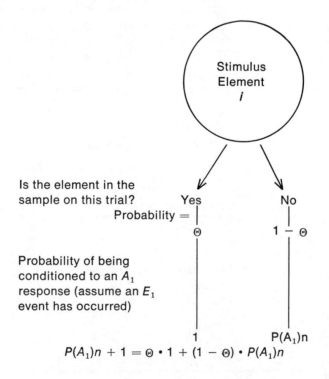

Is the element in the sample on this trial? Yes   No
Probability =

Θ $1 - \Theta$

Probability of being conditioned to an A_1 response (assume an E_1 event has occurred)

1        $P(A_1)n$

$$P(A_1)n + 1 = \Theta \cdot 1 + (1 - \Theta) \cdot P(A_1)n$$

The equal Θ case makes an important assumption, that of *path independence*. Path independence refers to the notion that the probability of response A_1 on trial $n + 1$ is only a function of the experimental outcome on trial n. That is, the prior history of how one got there is unimportant. Consider the meaning of this statement. Assume we have two organisms with the same probability of a given response. One may be in the early stages of learning, while the other may be undergoing extinction or forgetting of what was learned some time ago. Path independence means that these very different histories would have no effect in the situation. Whether such a strong assumption is warranted can be assessed by experimental manipulations. Surprisingly, a number of situations exist that tend to support this assumption.

5. *The passage of time is viewed as the fluctuation of stimulus elements.*

In 1955 two theoretical papers by Estes were published in the *Psychological Review*. One (1955b) dealt with what happens between sessions, usually days, of a conditioning study. The population was redefined in terms of the set available for sampling during the session and those not available during the session. All other axioms remained intact. Between days, elements were assumed to fluctuate between the available and unavailable set until some equilibrium point was reached. During acquisition this permits perfect performance at the end of a session, with regression to a lower value at the beginning of the next session, thus it was called *spontaneous regression*. Similar considerations lead to spontaneous recovery during extinction. If you were not feeling well on one day of an

experiment but on subsequent days felt better, those elements representing your "not feeling well" would now be "unavailable."

Estes's other theoretical paper that year (1955a) dealt with time-dependent phenomena in general. At the time the most obvious implication was with regard to the effects of intertrial interval, as depicted in Figure 9.3. Thus, random fluctuations of elements from an available and unavailable set occurred within a session, as well as between sessions. This may reflect variability in motivation, attention, or perception that the person may undergo during the course of an experimental session. During a trial the sets, both those available and those unavailable, were assumed to remain constant. This was assumed to keep the mathematics tractable, rather than for any psychological rationale. This version, often called *stimulus fluctuation theory,* later reappears as a major theoretical approach to human memory.

6. *Discrimination learning is learning to distinguish between common and unique elements of two stimulus populations.*

What happens when there are two stimulus situations? This question was considered in Burke and Estes (1957). For example, let us put a rat in the following T-maze situation: When the maze is gray (a T_1 trial) an A_1 response is correct, and when the maze is white (a T_2 trial) an A_2 response is correct, thus defining a successive discrimination situation. Conceptually we now have two stimulus populations, representing T_1 and T_2 trials. If the populations are totally distinct, concurrent learning of the two should occur. However, it becomes theoretically interesting when the populations

Figure 9.3

Random Fluctuation of Elements with Time-Dependent Phenomena

Available set is above the line, bisecting the circle, and the unavailable set is below the line. The ratios to the right equal the proportion conditioned to an A_1 response in each set, and X/S is the proportion in the population.

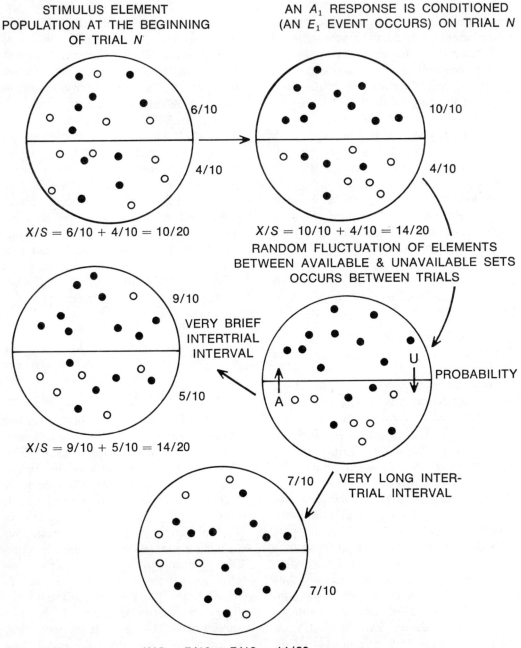

STIMULUS ELEMENT
POPULATION AT THE BEGINNING
OF TRIAL N

AN A_1 RESPONSE IS CONDITIONED
(AN E_1 EVENT OCCURS) ON TRIAL N

6/10

4/10

10/10

4/10

$X/S = 6/10 + 4/10 = 10/20$

$X/S = 10/10 + 4/10 = 14/20$

RANDOM FLUCTUATION OF ELEMENTS
BETWEEN AVAILABLE & UNAVAILABLE SETS
OCCURS BETWEEN TRIALS

9/10

VERY BRIEF
INTERTRIAL
INTERVAL

5/10

U

PROBABILITY

A

$X/S = 9/10 + 5/10 = 14/20$

7/10

VERY LONG INTER-
TRIAL INTERVAL

7/10

$X/S = 7/10 + 7/10 = 14/20$

share elements in common. Thus, the populations, as shown in Figure 9.4, can be viewed as those elements unique to T_1, a proportion $1 - w_1$, those unique to T_2 trials, a proportion $1 - w_2$, and those common to both T_1 and T_2 trial types, w_1 and w_2, respectively (Burke & Estes, 1957). Assuming (again for purposes of simplifying the mathematics) that the unique population sizes are equal, and thus $w_1 = w_2 = w$, leads to the following expectation:

$$P(A_1/T_1)_n = wP\ (A_1/C)_n +$$

$$(1 - w)p(A_1/U_1)_n$$

and

$$P(A_1/T_2)_n = wP(A_1/C)_n +$$

$$(1 - w)\ P(A_1/U_2)_n.$$

The first equation simply tells us that $P(A_1/T_1)n$, the probability of an A_1 response on, for example, gray-maze trials (T_1 trials)—which, by the way, is a correct response to gray—consists of two components: those elements shared in common with T_2 trials, a proportion, w, of them; and those elements that only occur on T_1 trials, that is, are unique to T_1 trials, a proportion, $1 - w$. The common and unique elements may have different probabilities of being conditioned to an A_1 response denoted as $P(A_1/C)_n$ and $P(A_1/U_1)_n$, respectively. Note that for common elements there is no such thing as a correct response, since the correct response depends upon whether it is a T_1 or T_2 trial, and common elements occur on both types of trials. Similarly, $P(A_1/T_2)_n$, the probability of an A_1 response on, for example, white-maze trials (T_2 trials)—which, by the way, is an error: A_2 responses are correct on T_2 trials—also consists of two components: elements occurring on both T_1 and T_2 trials,

the common elements, a proportion, w; and elements occurring only on T_2 type trials, a proportion, $1 - w$.

Note that as long as there are common elements an organism can never achieve a 100% discrimination. In a clever procedure called *probabilistic discrimination learning*, Estes obtained supportive evidence (Estes, Burke, Atkinson, & Frankmann, 1957). Nevertheless one major problem is how to account for situations where common elements exist *and* subjects achieve 100% correct responding. Despite this initial shortcoming, stimulus sampling theory is readily extended to stimulus generalization by assuming decreasing proportions of common elements or overlap as a function of decreasing stimulus similarity. That is, the way the theory deals with differences in stimulation is to assume that there is a positive relationship between how similar stimuli are to one another and the number (and proportion) of common or overlap elements.

7. *An alternative formulation: The stimulus situation is a unique pattern of stimulus elements.*

The problem of how to account for perfect discrimination performance while still having identical elements or components, the *similarity problem*, was resolved in 1959 with the *pattern model* (Estes, 1959). This model, which essentially incorporates Guthrie's stimulus pattern assumptions, is depicted in Figure 9.5. As can be seen, although identical elements in different stimulus patterns may exist, since the subject responds at the level of a stimulus pattern, 100% responding can be achieved. The cost, however, is a failure to have an explicit prediction with regard to stimulus generalization and transfer. This has resulted in the so-called *mixed model,* in which stimulus patterns govern the acquisition of the discrimination task but do not determine transfer or stimulus generalization. Rather, when new patterns are experienced during transfer or stimulus generalizations, the status of individual elements or components becomes decisive.

Various approaches to the similarity problem have been evaluated, based on component-tied-to-pattern rules, independent-component rules and the like. Generally though, theoreticians went on to other problems in the 1960s, and the problem rested without resolution. In its most general form the similarity problem pervades much of cognitive psychology:

Figure 9.4

Schema of a Successive Discrimination Task

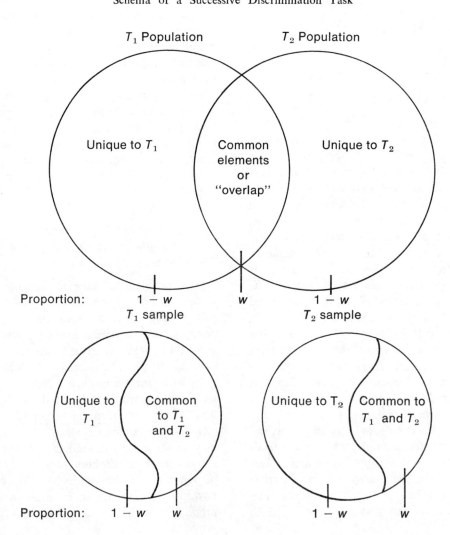

How organisms deal with similar situations is a major issue today. For example, nonpattern attempts at resolution have included notions such as adapting "out" common cues (Restle, 1955) and the reduction of the "attention" value of common cues (Bush & Mosteller, 1951). Although these approaches may solve the acquisition of the discrimination problem, they fail to predict transfer or stimulus generalization without additional mechanisms. More recent attempts have incorporated an "attentional" mechanism at the element or component level which retains the essence of stimulus sampling theory and also accounts for stimulus generalization or transfer (Robbins, 1972).

Figure 9.5

The Pattern Model (each letter represents a stimulus element)

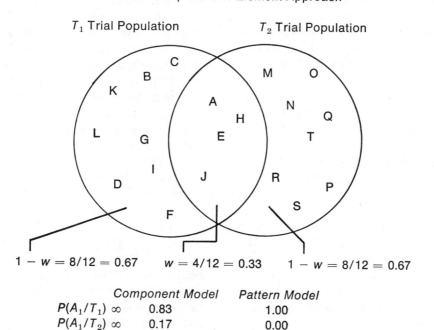

Stimulus patterns presented
on T_1 trials during
acquisition

ABC
DEF
GHI
JKL

Stimulus patterns presented
on T_2 trials during
acquisition

MNA
OPE
QRH
STJ

Stimulus Component or Element Approach

T_1 Trial Population T_2 Trial Population

$1 - w = 8/12 = 0.67$ $w = 4/12 = 0.33$ $1 - w = 8/12 = 0.67$

	Component Model	Pattern Model
$P(A_1/T_1) \infty$	0.83	1.00
$P(A_1/T_2) \infty$	0.17	0.00

8. *Associations are formed on an all-or-none basis.*

The pattern model, which was suggested as a solution to the similarity problem, has other significant applications. In this model, Θ represents the proportion of elements in the sample from the population, denoted as s/S, and s is the number in the sample, while S is the number in the total population. Assume that $s = S$, that is, the entire population is presented on a single trial, or $S = 1$, so that $s = S = 1$, and that a single pattern represents the entire stimulating situation. What should occur in these instances? It should, according to the theory, provide evidence of, or at least a test for the existence of, *all-or-none learning*. All-or-none learning in this case should be not only on the element level, but, since the element equals the entire population, it should represent evidence of all-or-none learning (Estes, 1960) on the macro (i.e., performance) level as well.

Estes (1964) developed the *RTT* procedure (where R represents a reinforced or information feedback trial and the T's represent test trials without feedback) to investigate these questions and to stimulate research efforts in the verbal learning and memory areas that are still ongoing. Bower's (1962) model is an explicit one-element model and a generalization of Estes's view. Extensions readily followed where the stimulus situation was depicted as two patterns and, eventually, a general form as N patterns. Extensions to paired-associate learning, concept learning and identification, and avoidance learning followed. The initial work on all-or-none paired associate learning eventually led to classes of Markov models dealing with various phenomena associated with paired-associate learning and memory.

Fluctuation theory reemerged at this time, as interest in memory phenomena and theory increased. The Estes (1955a) paper dealing with time-dependent phenomena can be readily interpreted as what happens between events in a memory situation. In Figure 9.3, if we substitute retention interval for intertrial interval, a theory of memory begins to emerge. These considerations led to various expectations; one of the predictions is of the so-called *spacing effect*. This effect has to do with how best to distribute the time when studying material more than once. More complex versions of the theory emerged as information about the phenomena became more detailed and complicated.

Although simple conditioning phenomena, namely Pavlovian and operant conditioning, served as the basis for the initial theory, they have largely been ignored in quantitative formulations. The free-operant situation has generally been avoided because of theoretical complexity regarding stimulus specification. Specifically, internal-movement-produced stimulation and other subject-generated stimulation appear to be important in the free-operant context (Weinstock, 1970). Although Burke (1966) presented the outlines of a theory of Pavlovian conditioning in stimulus sampling terms, no other serious work had been done. Further, aside from applications of variants of the pattern model to avoidance and escape procedures (Theios, 1963), little application to aversive conditions has been made.

Recent Modifications: Complex, Hierarchical Associations. In 1969 Estes's "Outline of a Theory of Punishment" was published. This paper is significant for a number of reasons. First, it represented a return to considerations of simple conditioning phenomena. Second, it was the first major quantitative attempt to deal with punishment and the conditioned emotional response. Third, it represented a major change in Estes's position. Along with the stimulus sampling assumptions, he assumed that drive elements needed to be present for behavior to occur. These elements, called *amplifier elements,* were seen to combine multiplicatively with *stimulus situation elements.* Also, he spoke of *active inhibition* and *inhibitory connections,* thus proposing a two-process theory similar in spirit to the Hull-Spence theories. The paper also represented a marked departure from his original concept (Estes, 1958) in which drive elements were seen as merely another source of stimulation. Papers describing a hierarchical association theory, concentrating, in part, on structural aspects of memory (Estes, in press), have followed.

Essentially, this latest scheme attempts to represent what is going on inside the organism's "mind"—how information or events are structured in the memory system. Estes has dealt specifically with conditioning situations. General contextual cues give rise to internal representations called *control elements.* Local contextual cues, such as those available on a specific trial, give rise to another control element, which has associated with it the stimuli the experimenter is manipulating as well as responses of the organism. A subsequent event on a trial, for example a reward, also has its own local context, which along with itself and behavior evoked by the reward became associated with yet another control element. The latter two control elements become associated with one another in a hierarchical fashion via the general contextual cues that all presumably share in common. Inhibitory associations between these two lower level control elements may also occur. Thus, memory and learning conceptions are brought together by Estes by

relating environmental events to hypothesized resulting memory structures. The theory is presently in its early developmental stage, so detailed quantitative versions are not yet available. It is mentioned here, in part, because it might be considered as illustrating the developmental nature of theory construction.

RESEARCH

Methodologies

Researchers engaged in research in mathematical learning theory are not tied to any particular methodology. As pointed out earlier, what is shared by this subgroup of researchers is reliance on a particular tool—mathematics and, more recently, the computer. Keep in mind that the quantitative form of theorizing does not necessarily reflect a conceptual difference with regard to psychological concepts. As a result, experimenters using quantitative theory are free to work in almost any laboratory situation concerning whatever phenomena they are interested in. Typically the research situation is in the laboratory, although there have been mathematical approaches to the study of some behaviors in the real world.

Although specific methodologies are not required, the studies reported here reveal a trend of moving from one kind of experimental design to another. These changes are always dictated by a combination of theoretical considerations and experimental findings. For example, the early studies of probability learning were almost all single-stimuli, two-choice, light-guessing studies in which the subjects were usually given hundreds of button-pressing trials. Various considerations led to the observational learning technique and the multiple-cue technique. These new designs were occasioned by changes in the nature of the questions being raised, sometimes a change in orientation but often a change toward more precision.

Animal Studies

Probability Learning. Although Estes's theory was initially derived from considerations of animal conditioning studies, particularly operant conditioning, few studies using animals have been generated for the mathematical method. This may in part be due to the changing nature of the study of learning, particularly its intertwining with concepts of memory. The last 10–15 years have seen a revolution of sorts in that cognitive concepts have come to the fore and conditioning concepts have slipped to the background. One of the reasons for this is the idea that if we are studying cognition, we should work directly with organisms that we "know" have cognition, namely, *Homo sapiens.* We could, of course, maintain an animal-model approach, generalizing to human behavior from animal studies. However, if we do this we will wonder if infra-human organisms are capable of cognition, awareness, and the like. Nevertheless there is some literature on studies with animal subjects.

Estes (1957a) reported a study with rats in which probability matching was observed. In a two-choice situation, the terminal level of responding under a 70/30 reward schedule showed a group mean proportion of choices of the 70% side of 0.71. The rats were run in a maze that had a left and a right turn at the choice point, a T-maze. On any one trial, a reward was placed in either the right- or left-hand goalbox. A random schedule was used to determine in which side the reward was placed, with one restriction—70% of the time the reward was to be in

the right goalbox, and for the remaining 30% of the trials it was to be in the left goalbox.

In this study a correction procedure was used. If the subject chose the incorrect side on a particular trial (the side that did not contain reward for the trial), it was allowed to retrace its steps and respond to the side that had reward. Probability matching means that the terminal level of responding closely matched the reward schedule. In this study the reward schedule was 0.70 and 0.30 for the right and left sides, respectively, while the group mean proportion of right and left turns was 0.71 and 0.29, respectively. However, a subsequent detailed analysis revealed that, unlike humans, some rats responded 100% of the time to the 70% side, while others responded 100% of the time to the 30% side. However, the average across all animals was approximately 70%. Responding all of the time to one side is called *absorption.* In this study it would appear that probability matching in rats may have been an artifact due to group averaging.

Another popular procedure with the T-maze is a *noncorrection* method. In this technique the rats are not permitted to correct their initial errors. (Remember, an error is defined here simply as choosing the side of the maze that does *not* contain reward for that trial.) Subjects are removed from the incorrect goalbox after spending usually between 10–30 seconds in the unbaited box. Using this method, one study (Weinstock, Brody, & LoGuido, 1965) found that all rats eventually responded 100% of the time to one or the other side of the maze; again, this is a result of absorption rather than probability matching.

This result in the noncorrection situation prompted Weinstock et al. to propose the following: Assume that error trials (that is, trials on which the rat chose the side that did not contain reward) left the probability of the turning response unchanged, often called an *identity operator* model; further assume that only rewarded trials had a direct strengthening effect on the response rewarded (and correspondingly weakened the probability of choosing the other side). In the noncorrection method there is no control over the actual rewards obtained by the rat, since the reward schedule is determined by the experimenter and subject. The experimenter, by using a randomly generated schedule, determines the side on which reward is placed. Whether the subject receives the reward is then dependent on the subject's choice. Weinstock et al. reasoned that if a method was used to guarantee the exact proportion of rewards to one and the other side of the maze, and assuming that error trials have no effect on the probability of the turning response, then under these conditions individual subject matching should be found.

In a series of studies (Robbins, Cohen, Levine, & Olsen, n.d.; Robbins & Warner, 1973; Weinstock, Robbins, & Chen, n.d.) precisely this result was found. The procedure is as follows: A reward schedule is randomly generated, with a stipulation, for example, that 70% of the time reward is available on one side of the maze and 30% of the time on the other side. If the side that contains reward is chosen, the subject receives the reward. The side of reward for the next trial is determined by the randomly generated schedule. However, if the rat makes an error, choosing the side that did not contain reward, the trial is *rerun,* which means the side containing the reward is not changed until the rat responds to that side. The measure of interest to the experimenter is the proportion of choices

to the 70% side on first-choice trials. A *first-choice trial* is one immediately following a reward. These trials should show the effects of reward according to Weinstock's analysis: Only rewarded trials affected choice behavior, while error trials were totally ineffective with regard to choice behavior. The results indicated very stable individual subject probability matching in all the studies cited above.

These data reveal that procedural differences may be critical in accounting for very different behaviors exhibited by an organism. Quantitative theory helped narrow the range of explanations for the various phenomena observed and helped yield a relatively straightforward account of superficially contradictory data.

Human Studies

Probability Learning. One of the earliest applications of stimulus sampling theory involved a simple binary prediction study originally conceived by Lloyd Humphreys (1939) for totally different reasons. Humphreys had individuals guess whether a light in the center of a board would or would not go on during any one trial. The subjects made their predictions by either pressing a button, which indicated their prediction that the light would go on, or not pressing the button, indicating a prediction that the light would not go on. Unknown to the subjects, the sequence of whether the light would go on or not was randomly programmed. As a result there were no cues as to which response would be the correct one on any specific trial. The random programming was such that, on the average, the light would go on on 30%, 50%, or 70% of the trials. (This situation is similar to the T-maze studies with rats mentioned earlier. In fact, early probability learning studies with human subjects were attempts to simulate an animal conditioning situation with human subjects. In this manner, it was argued, the same concepts could apply, and similar results would be expected.) Humphreys found after 100 trials subjects pressed the button an average of 32%, 51%, and 73% of the time for the 30%, 50%, and 70% conditions, respectively.

This procedure was modified by Grant, Hake, and Hornseth (1951) and by Estes and Straughan (1954). A detailed analysis of an extensive study can be found in Friedman, Burke, Cole, Keller, Millward, and Estes (1963). In the Estes studies the two responses, instead of being press or do not press (sometimes referred to as go/no-go), were made explicit. Individuals were told to guess which of two lights would go on and showed their prediction by pressing either the left- or right-hand button, or, in general, made an A_1 or an A_2 response (note the similarity to the T-maze studies now!). After the subject's choice response was made, one of the two lights would go on, in general an E_1 or E_2 event, so that they were always told the correct response after their responses were made. Notice that this is a correction situation. The sequence of lights (correct responses) was randomly programmed such that the proportion of E_1 events, in general was π, and the proportion of E_2 events was $1 - \pi$. Theoretically, this situation will eventually lead to a proportion, π, of stimulus elements being connected or conditioned to an A_1 response, and a proportion, $1 - \pi$, of the elements being associated with an A_2 response.

This result, called *probability matching,* is at odds with what the theory of a "rational" person might predict. This is because if individuals do in fact proba-

bility match they will be correct much less often than if they responded all of the time to the higher π side. For example, let $\pi = 0.7$ and therefore $1 - \pi = 0.3$. This means that a randomly programmed 70% of the trials will terminate with an E_1 event and 30% will terminate with an E_2 event. In accordance with a rational theory, we would expect subjects to maximize the number of times they are correct. Since the sequence of correct lights is randomly programmed, there is no way for the subjects to determine which side is correct for a specific trial. However, it is possible to determine what would occur on the average over a large number of trials.

In the proposed 70/30 example, an individual who "maximized" to the high probability side, that is, responded 100% to this side, would be correct 70% of the time. This is because the reward schedule is such that 70% of the time that side is correct. Thus a rational theory predicts that subjects should eventually respond 100% of the time to the 70% side, to yield the highest probability of being correct. An individual who probability matches would be correct much less frequently. Since probability matching means that on the average the subject would respond to the high π side 70% of the time, and since 70% of the time reward is placed on this side, the subject would, on the average, be correct 70% times 70%, or 49% of the time on the high π side. The lower proportion side is correct $1 - \pi$ of the time—30%, in the present example. Probability matching would mean that 30% of the time the subject pressed this side's button. Again, since the subject's behavior and the reward schedule are independent, on the average the subject will choose this side, and it will be correct 30% times 30%, or 9% of the time. Thus, an individual who probability matches will be correct 49% + 9%, or 58% of the time, which is considerably less than the 70% figure that would occur according to a rational theory.

The significance of the effect of probability matching in contrast to maximizing may be seen by drawing the following analogy: Instead of a light being a cue to signal a prediction, let the signal be various symptoms of diseases. Let the π values represent the probability of a given disease being associated with a specific symptom. If the diagnostician probability matched rather than maximized, more errors in diagnosing diseases would occur!

The Estes and Straughan Study. Estes and Straughan (1954) used a two-phase design so that in Phase I, π, or the probability of reinforcement of one of the sides, was = 0.3, 0.5 or 0.85 for three different groups for 120 trials. In Phase II, all groups were switched to $\pi = 0.3$ for an additional 120 trials. For example, an individual may have seen the left-hand side be the correct side on 85% of the trials during Phase I, and the right-hand side be correct 15% of the time. During Phase II the left-hand side would be correct 30% of the time and the right-hand side would be correct the remaining 70%. In Phase I, the terminal response proportions were 0.37, 0.48 and 0.87 for Groups $\pi = 0.3$, 0.5, and 0.85, respectively. For Phase II the terminal proportions were 0.28, 0.37 and 0.30 for the three groups (when $\pi = 0.30$, of course). That is, the data indicated that human subjects' probability of responding approximately matched the probability of reinforcement; this is the probability matching hypothesis. Thus, some general support was found for the theoretical predictions, although a relationship between the learning rate and the difference between the initial response probability and

π was found, counter to that expected by the theory.

In a subsequent paper, Estes (1959) reported the findings of a detailed study of two individuals who were given a total of 2,000 trials. Every 25 trials the probability of the reinforcing events (E_1 and E_2 events) was changed: Ten different probabilities were used eight times each during the course of the study. The average proportion of A_1 responses closely matched and followed the reinforcement proportion as it changed over blocks of trials. This result confirmed extensions of simple probability learning made by Estes (1957b). In the 1957 theoretical paper Estes extended this model to cases where the reinforcement probability was not constant over trials but changed over blocks of trials (in a steplike fashion) or linearly as a function of trials. Confirmatory evidence has been found in some unpublished studies in the laboratory by Donald Robbins (Robbins et al., n.d.).

Further, Estes (1957a) found that the probability matching phenomenon occurs with individual human subjects as well as with group data. Other research has shown that individuals will deviate from matching when the conditions are appropriately changed. Thus, if correct responses yield reward and errors yield punishments, a subject's response proportion will deviate from matching in the direction of maximizing (Suppes & Atkinson, 1960). To make subjects deviate from matching is not very difficult. What is significant, as noted by Estes (1972b), is that subjects can be found to probability match at all. The conditions leading to matching appear to require an appropriately simplified situation, in which the subject is instructed to indicate predictions on each trial, and no indication of the randomness of the reward schedule is made.

This indicates, according to Estes (1972b), that an individual gains extremely accurate information about event frequencies. It suggests that we may store tremendous amounts of information in our brain, some of this information indicating how frequently various events occur in the world. In addition, we seem to be able to obtain this information about how often things occur by simply observing a set of outcomes over a series of trials, rather than by making choices and observing the outcome of these choices.

The Observational Learning Technique. Experimental evidence for observational learning can be found in studies by Arima (1965) and Reber and Millward (1968). These results indicate that individuals can match event probabilities after simply observing a series of trials during which time one of a few lights go on. In this method the first phase of the study involves observational learning—that is, the subjects simply observe a series of trials during which time one of the two lights terminates a trial. In a subsequent transfer phase, subjects are to respond and are not told if their predictions are correct or not. This method assumes that these no-information trials leave the probability of the choice response unchanged. Subjects are told to respond, based on what they have just observed.

Estes (1976a, 1976b) has extended this relatively new methodology to investigate how information on environmental probabilities is represented in the memory system. He has also used this procedure to reveal the representation of the frequency of event categories in memory, separating probability and frequency.

Multiple-Cue Probability Learning. Another method used to investigate choice behavior is multiple-cue probability learning. In these studies the first phase of the study uses either an observational method or the more conventional method in which individuals are required to respond. A number of specific cues (individual symbols, letters, and the like) are presented alone or with a second cue, and each cue has a given probability of being correct. During the second ("transfer") phase, subjects are tested on old and new cue combinations to evaluate various predictions of their choice behavior. Estes's approach has been consistently successful in accounting for these data (Estes, 1976b; Robbins & Medin, 1971).

Extension to Discriminative Situations. The probability learning situation is conceived of (theoretically) as a single population of stimulus elements (see Proposition 3). When a second population is introduced which shares elements with the first population, a discriminative situation results. According to stimulus sampling theory, as long as common elements exist, subjects should never perfectly discriminate. That is, they will always make some errors, even after thousands of trials.

Although an early study (Schoeffler, 1954) provided supportive evidence for these predictions, a study by Uhl (1964) revealed an important theoretical problem. Uhl used a 6 by 6 matrix of lights as a stimulus source in a two-choice successive discrimination situation. He varied the proportion of common elements (lights) and found close to 100% correct responding across overlap conditions (or common element proportions) of 0–75%. He also obtained probability matching when only common elements (one population) were presented. The finding of near-perfect or perfect choice behavior in the face of common elements is sometimes referred to as the *overlap* or *similarity problem* (see Proposition 7). The attempts to resolve this problem have led to a substantial literature.

The problem is twofold. First, as long as similarity (overlap) exists, the original Burke and Estes model predicts imperfect performance. Mechanisms were sought to yield 100% correct performance. However, in solving this first problem a second problem occurred. Many of the mechanisms suggested to yield perfect performance did so at the price of then being unable to predict stimulus generalization or transfer.

Numerous studies have shown that after training an organism by rewarding responses to one stimulus (an $S+$), which represents a specific value on some stimulus dimension, and nonrewarding responses to a second stimulus (an $S-$), which represents another value on the same stimulus dimension as the $S+$, the organism will respond to stimuli other than the rewarded stimulus, in a manner related to stimulus similarity. Thus, two things are required—100% discrimination and stimulus generalization. To accomplish this, Bush and Mosteller (1951) assumed that the overlap or common elements "shrunk," that is, the organism no longer processed this information. Similarly Restle (1955) assumed that these common cues became "adapted out" of the organism's perceptual system. Both can lead to perfect discrimination performance but cannot, without additional machinery, deal with stimulus generalization or transfer tests with stimulus displays consisting solely of common elements.

Recently Robbins (1972) suggested a model in which it is assumed that an organism goes through an explicit stimulus selection process; specifically, the organism selects an element as the basis for responding that is most highly correlated with reward. In this model, information is acquired about common elements, but as training progresses the common elements are used less and less as a basis for responding. During transfer or stimulus generalization tests, the stored information about common elements can be utilized if required. The Robbins model is essentially an extension of the Burke and Estes (1957) model, with the additional selection process.

Estes, however, took a different route. He suggested the pattern model as a mechanism for being able to predict 100% discrimination performance. In the pattern model, patterns of stimulation become associated with responses, on an all-or-none basis, regardless of whether they share components in common or not. How then are stimulus generalization and transfer accounted for? The answer for Atkinson and Estes (1963, 1967) was the proposal of the *mixed model*. In this model, patterns of stimulation control the organism's behavior. However, if the pattern is not associated with a particular response, such as a new pattern given during transfer or stimulus generalization, the conditioned status of individual components (elements) then controls behavior. In this manner, perfect discrimination performance and stimulus generalization phenomena can be accounted for.

Further Extensions of the Pattern Model. In a general sense a stimulus discrimination situation may be viewed as a classification task where the stimuli are represented on one physical dimension. That is, the subjects' task is to categorize or to classify the stimuli into mutually exclusive response categories where, typically, the stimuli are two values on some identifiable physical dimension. The organism is rewarded for responding to, for example, the right-hand side of a maze on one value of the dimension, and rewarded for responding to the left-hand side of the maze for a second value on the dimension.

For example, assume that the dimension is shape, and triangles require a right turn, and squares a left turn. During the acquisition phase of the discrimination, subjects are presented with a triangle on some trials and a square on the remaining trials. The task is to turn right on "triangle" trials and turn left on "square" trials. On a stimulus generalization test, additional shapes are presented one at a time, and the probability of a right-hand turn is, in general, a function of the similarity between triangles and this new shape. Assume further that two values on the color dimension, blue and red, are also used. When these two colors are combined with the two values of shape there are four distinct stimuli. During training, color is the so-called relevant dimension; red objects require right-hand turns and blue objects require left-hand turns for rewards to be given. Specifically, the red triangle and the red square are rewarded for right-hand turns, while the blue triangle and blue square are rewarded for left-hand turns. This describes an oversimplified but nevertheless classic *concept identification task*.

This task may also be viewed as a *classification task*, that is, it categorizes red "things" to the right and blue "things" to the left. Studies involving the analysis of reversal shifts (red objects now require left-hand turns and blue objects now require right-hand turns for reward to occur), extra-dimensional shifts (triangles signal right-hand turns and squares, left-hand turns) and acquisition

in a concept identification task (Suppes & Ginsberg, 1963) have been undertaken. Various extensions, elaborations, and modifications of the pattern model have been applied with favorable results to these phenomena (e.g., Bower & Theios, 1963; Bower & Trabasso, 1963; Neimark & Estes, 1967).

In these applications the analysis of what the organism is doing changed somewhat. Rather than concentrate solely on the stimulus situation, as in the early versions of stimulus sampling theory, the emphasis shifted to viewing the organism as going through a number of discrete states or stages. These stages were seen to represent a continuum from "no knowledge" to "complete knowledge" of the situation, although the continuum was represented as a series of discrete steps. The number of patterns that represented the situation typically would be one less than the number of states. Mathematically, these models are families of Markov chains and are often referred to as *Markov models*.

For illustrative purposes let us consider a simple paired-associate experiment. The subjects' task is to remember word-number combinations presented to them. For example, individuals are shown items like COW–2 or HOUSE–1, for two seconds each until an entire list of these types of pairs has been shown. A single presentation of all of the pairs is known as a *study trial*. A *test trial* follows during which time only the stimuli (the words) are presented, one at a time, and the subject must give the appropriate response (number) to each word. The subject is not told whether responses are correct on these trials. After going through the entire list (a test trial), another study trial follows. Study and test trials are alternated until subjects can complete some predetermined number of test trials without error. Conceptually, each pair is thought initially to be in an "unlearned" or "no knowledge" state. Each time the pair is presented on a study trial, it provides an opportunity for an all-or-none associative connection to be formed between the pattern representing that stimulus configuration and the appropriate response. This probability is typically less than 1, so that all-or-none learning can be obtained at the level of an individual pair but not with regard to the learning of the entire list.

This one-element model has been extensively investigated by Bower (1962). Note that this methodology is essentially an extension and modification of Estes's *RTT* procedure referred to earlier. Studies in the concept identification area are typically accounted for by two states. As the situation is made more complex, more states or stages, and therefore more patterns, are assumed. Thus a general theoretical approach has evolved in which psychologically meaningful stages are associated with each stage or state in the Markov model and evaluations proceed from this point.

Extensions to Memory. As our knowledge of performance on paired-associate memory studies has increased, the models have become fairly elaborate. Discovery of phenomena such as the *spacing effect* led to revision of the Markov models. The spacing effect refers to the following phenomenon. If an item is repeated, as the interval (the lag or spacing) separating the first and second presentation increases, performance on a subsequent recall test increases. This occurs when the interval between the second presentation and the test (the *retention interval*) is relatively long (15 seconds or more). This spacing or lag ef-

fect reveals the relative benefit of distributed in contrast to massed practice. A version of the model proposed to account for these phenomena incorporates the notions of short-term and long-term memory. A dichotomous memory system has been proposed in which the short-term system retains information for a relatively brief time. Information may be transferred from this short-term system to a relatively permanent storage system, or the long-term memory. Figure 9.6 illustrates this kind of system.

The Fluctuation Model Revisited. The fluctuation model was originally proposed to account for time-dependent phenomena in a conditioning situation, such as the effects of intertrial intervals and changes in performance over days of an experiment, when the organism is not in the stimulus situation during this interval. This view can readily be applied to memory situations, particularly when the range of time is a critical factor. Thus, the fluctuation model has reemerged as a theoretical device for accounting for time-dependent phenomena in the memory literature. The relative success of the fluctuation model points out another successful area of application of stimulus sampling theory.

IMPLICATIONS

Theoretical

The gradual shifting emphasis of the various models and different processes assumed to be occurring reflect basic changes in some of the ways W. K. Estes has considered behavioral phenomena.

Estes (1972a) has presented a series of studies and has pointed to other research which questions the assumption that rewards and punishments have di-

Figure 9.6

Illustrative Dual Storage Markov System

The lower case letters refer to probabilities of transferring from one state to another (transition probabilities). Note that the system does not permit transitions from the initial, no-knowledge state to the long-term memory state, nor from the forget state back to the no-knowledge state.

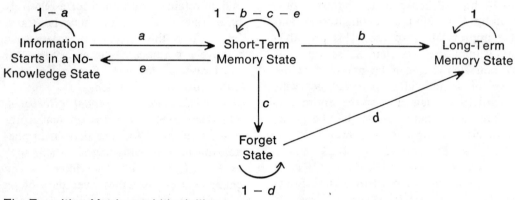

The Transition Matrix would look like:

		In State at the End of Trial n			
		Long term	Forget	Short term	No knowledge
Given in State at Beginning of Trial n	Long term	1	0	0	0
	Forget	d	1-d	0	0
	Short term	b	c	1-b-c	e
	No knowledge	0	0	a	1-a

rect strengthening or weakening effects on the organism's actions. Instead, he proposes an *informational* and *cybernetic* approach. He argues that the effects of rewards and punishments depend on not only the relationship between the stimulus display and the so-called *reinforcing event,* but also on any other information available at that time that will affect the subjects' perception of this relationship on future occasions. He asserts that an individual, in any choice situation, actively scans the available choices and is guided by feedback from anticipated rewards. Typically, choices

that lead to the greatest expectancy of reward are made. Estes doubts Thorndike's classical Law of Effect, which is a statement of the direct strengthening (or weakening) hypothesis. His view emphasizes the *context* of occurrences of the event as being an important part of what the individual expects to occur.

The significance of contextual stimuli as elements is further elaborated by Estes (1973) relative to the relationship between memory and conditioning. He suggests that events are represented in the memory system along with the context in which they occur, in the form of a control element. Control elements become associated with one another in a hierarchical fashion. In this Estes relates conditioning to the area of information processing in a significant way.

The points reflect Estes's recent views and also illustrate the ever-changing face of theory. As more and more information is accumulated, theories become more and more refined, are elaborated, and are made more precise. We have viewed the major aspects of the theoretical enterprise of Estes, spanning three decades. We have seen how and why theoretical changes have taken place. A combination of experimental findings, intuition, and brilliant insight has led to the present formulation, which will undoubtedly undergo further refinement and change.

In some sense we can argue that Estes helped to deliver mathematical learning theory to the world. He has legitimized the use of mathematics as an important tool in the theoretical enterprise in the behavioral sciences. More specifically, in terms of learning and memory theory, he has revealed a number of quantitative formulations which others have modified, refined, and revamped to further our understanding of the behavioral world.

Stimulus sampling theory provides a device with which to tie seemingly disparate research areas together—an emphasis on the analysis of the stimulus situation into patterns, components, and features. In addition, a functional analysis of responses occurs because of the emphasis on response classes in contrast to specific movements. The research encouraged by the theory has revealed that the human brain can apparently keep track of an incredible amount of information. The specific theoretical formulation has indicated and shown some of the

details of the interrelationships of learning and conditioning, memory and perception. Most recently, what might be termed *neoassociation theory* has been shown to be consistent with the theoretical enterprise elaborated by Estes.

The theory also stands as a demonstration of how to go about the theoretical enterprise in the psychological world. The Hull-Spence view failed in part because it followed the form of physical theories. However, situational or contextual variables appear to be critical to much psychological phenomena. Thus, an approach sensitive to such a fact was required. The seeming illusiveness and vagueness of the human mind have been shown to be amenable to experimental investigation; thus painstaking, careful methodology combined with insights can be made to yield real increments in our understanding of the human animal. Further, in his more recent writings, Estes has shown how sensitivities to biological and evolutionary conditions are accommodated. Systems of behaviors are proposed to develop—thus, they are amenable to the continued development of a theory that continually reflects increased knowledge and awareness of behavioral systems within and across species, rather than a sterile, mechanistic theory based on associations.

Most certainly the theoretical oasis that exists today in learning theory would be a virtual desert without the contributions of W. K. Estes.

Practical

In response to the question, "What has psychology done for the world?" psychologists often search for cover. However, it should be borne in mind that psychology as an empirical science is not even

100 years old. In many areas, we are just learning what kinds of questions to ask. In others, we are largely at a pretheoretical level, or our empirical knowledge is expanding along with our theories. Viewed in this context, requiring effects in the marketplace, so to speak, is premature in much of psychology—particularly in terms of the application of knowledge acquired in the laboratory to the real world. There are, however, some natural applications of the theoretical endeavors we have been considering.

The Educational Process. Applications of learning theory to education, in terms of teaching reading, arithmetic, and thinking, are an obviously important and natural endeavor. Estes (1975b) points out that we need to direct our efforts at a deeper understanding of what has been learned in the teaching enterprise. Only after we understand reading skills, for example, can we begin to develop programs directed at discovering and correcting observed deficits in reading.

One of Estes's major points is that processes rather than capacities should be emphasized. Thus he argues against a long tradition which tends to assess capacities and categorize individuals in terms of how they perform on the basis of one type of ability in contrast to others. Rather than devote our efforts to asking "How much of X does individual Y have?" we should be asking what is being learned when an individual is reading. We need to understand the *processes* underlying these skills. Then we could begin to deal with discovering and correcting deficiencies.

On Intelligence. Closely related to the educational process is the concept of intelligence, which plays a large role in today's educational enterprise. The tra-

ditional approach has been to relate performance on a variety of subtests (some measuring "thinking," while others measure associative abilities) to various psychological categories or functions. The concept of intelligence usually carries the notion that it is a *trait* of an individual. Estes (1974) has analyzed a number of subtests of intelligence tests and has concluded that, in terms of what we know about learning theory, it is not clear precisely what abilities lead to high scores on these subtests. He argues that we should not be developing theories of intelligence that look for differences in some trait to account for the difference observed in test results. Rather than look for a better method of categorizing people in terms of intellectual functioning, he argues that we should direct our efforts toward understanding what leads to specific kinds of "competence and incompetence in intellectual activity."

Further, he argues that we should not be searching for better instruments with which to measure intelligence. Instead we should direct our energies to attempts to understand the processes involved in test behavior in terms of the concepts from learning theory. Then we could use these interpretations as a theoretical basis for developing methods to determine the sources of deficits in performance revealed by these tests.

Social Interactions. An unexpected application of stimulus sampling theory has been to social interactions. Surprisingly, these extensions have been shown to be fruitful. For example, Estes (1975a) has applied his theory to a simple two-person game in which the participants exchange messages for or against an issue on a given trial. Assuming that each participant is as likely as the other to affect a change in attitude in a positive direction yields explicit expressions indicating the probability of a positive attitude as a function of trial number for each participant. This model can serve as a basis for understanding how individuals interact in arguments or negotiations and sheds light on what to expect in an exchange-of-information situation similar to the one outlined. Admittedly this is a very simple decision-making system, but the indications of the processes that occur can be readily seen in such oversimplified situations. Then the principles derived from such relatively simple situations can be used to try to understand how elemental processes may combine or interact in more complex situations.

Perhaps 100 years from now, many of the applications in psychology will represent practical implications of our theoretical knowledge rather than artistic renderings based on untested concepts.

SUMMARY

W. K. Estes is probably the single most important individual in developing mathematical learning theory. The emphasis in quantitative theorizing is not on any particular theoretical position but rather on the use of mathematics in the formulation of theory, regardless of the psychological positions taken in the theory.

Mathematical theories often force the theoretician to make explicit what is often implicit in qualitative theories. It directs the theorist to make unequivocal predictions which will make clear whether the experimental results confirm or disconfirm the theory. Such theories are not without problems, as exemplified by the quantitative theoretical attempts of Hull and Spence. Basically their theoretical position related a set of unobservable variables to observable dependent and independent variables by functions to be empirically determined. One of the major problems that arose was that a response model had to be incorporated which related the theoretical and observable dependent variables. Thus disconfirming results may indicate problems with the response model or with a major theoretical postulate. Estes avoids this difficulty by using probability of response as the major theoretical dependent variable and relative frequency of occurrence as the major observable dependent variable.

Estes's specific formulation is called stimulus sampling theory. A major aspect of his view is to conceptualize the stimulus as consisting of a hypothetical population of individual entities called stimulus elements. In an early version of the theory these individual elements were seen as combining independently from the point of view of the perceiver, while in a later version it is assumed that the patterns composed of these individual elements came to control behavior rather than the individual elements themselves. On the response side, Estes simply divided the world into mutually exclusive response categories, so that individual elements or patterns are associated with only one response class at any one time. Further, these associations occur on an all-or-none basis.

Estes's stimulus sampling theory may be viewed as an attempt to develop rules or principles that predict various learning phenomena, with an emphasis on the events and processes going on in an organism on a behavioral rather than physiological level. Given these relatively simple assumptions, stimulus sampling theory has been applied, with relative success, to time-dependent phenomena in animals, choice behavior, and discriminative learning and generalization in animals.

The major applications of the theory have been in the area of human learning and memory. Applications and extensions to probability learning, discrimination, generalization, concept identification, abstraction, paired-associate learning, and various memory phenomena have met with varying degrees of success.

Over the years Estes's approach has undergone changes, so that rewards and punishments are no longer seen to directly strengthen or to weaken associative connections but rather are seen as modulating the flow of information, that is, what an organism learns in any given situation. The significance of contextual stimulation has led Estes to the notion of a control element which begins to attack the problem of the structure of a memory system.

Applications to work on intelligence, the educational process, and even social interactions flow from his most recent conceptions. Perhaps, if as Estes suggests, we emphasize processes rather than capacities, we will begin to see breakthroughs that will indeed lead to increments in our knowledge of intelligence. As a result, contributions to the educational process should readily follow.

ANNOTATED BIBLIOGRAPHY

Atkinson, R. C., Bower, G. H., & Crothers, E. J. *An introduction to mathematical learning theory*. New York: John Wiley & Sons, 1965.

This basic introduction to the fundamental aspects of mathematical learning theory requires only minor familiarity with learning theory and some mathematics and statistics, most of which are presented in the book. It emphasizes the development of various quantitative techniques and demonstrates applications to concept identification, paired-associate learning, choice behavior, avoidance conditioning, and social and economic interaction.

Greeno, J. G. *Elementary theoretical psychology*. Reading, Mass.: Addison-Wesley, 1968.

An excellent introduction to quantitative applications in the areas of judgment, perception, choice, conditioning, motivation, memory, and thinking is provided in this book.

Levine, G., & Burke, C. J. *Mathematical model techniques for learning theories*. New York: Academic Press, 1972.

This text covers the basic techniques required for use in mathematical model construction. Only some elementary college algebra is required, since it gives detailed explications of the necessary mathematical techniques. Examples from learning theory are found throughout. The serious student should find the basic tools to develop mathematical models.

Luce, R. D., Bush, R. R., & Galanter, E. (Eds.). *Handbook of mathematical psychology*. New York: John Wiley & Sons, 1963 (Vol. 1), 1963 (Vol. 2), 1965 (Vol. 3).

These three volumes represent a detailed coverage for the specialist of traditional psychological topics viewed from a mathematical perspective. Volume 1 covers measurement and psychophysics. Volume 2 contains the basic theoretical developments and applications to natural languages, grammars, and social interaction. Volume 3 covers applications to sensory mechanisms, learning, preference, and some mathematical techniques.

Neimark, E. D., & Estes, W. K. *Stimulus sampling theory*. San Francisco: Holden-Day, 1967.

This is an excellent collection of readings which contains many of the important papers published during the period 1950–1965. Topics covered are: general development and theory, associate learning, probability learning, and single and multiprocess models for generalization and discrimination.

Norman, M. F. *Markov processes and learning models.* New York: Academic Press, 1972.

This advanced text provides a thorough exposition of developments in probability theory on a mathematical basis. Applications to aspects of learning are incorporated. To most fully appreciate this monograph, knowledge of graduate-level mathematics is required.

REFERENCES

Anderson, J. R., & Bower, G. H. *Human associative memory.* Washington, D.C.: V. H. Winston & Sons, 1973.

Arima, J. K. Human probability learning with forced training trials and certain and uncertain outcome choice trials. *Journal of Experimental Psychology,* 1965, *70,* 43–50.

Atkinson, R. C., & Estes, W. K. Stimulus sampling theory. In R. D. Luce, R. R. Bush, & E. Galanter (Eds.), *Handbook of mathematical psychology* (Vol. 2). New York: John Wiley & Sons, 1963.

Atkinson, R. C., & Estes, W. K. Interpretation of stimulus generalization. In E. D. Neimark & W. K. Estes (Eds.), *Stimulus sampling theory.* San Francisco: Holden-Day, 1967.

Bower, G. H. A model for response and training variables in paired associate learning. *Psychological Review,* 1962, *69,* 34–53.

Bower, G. H., & Theios, J. A learning model for discrete performance levels. In R. C. Atkinson (Ed.), *Studies in mathematical psychology.* Stanford, Cal.: Stanford University Press, 1963.

Bower, G. H., & Trabasso, T. Concept identification. In R. C. Atkinson (Ed.), *Studies in mathematical psychology.* Stanford, Cal.: Stanford University Press, 1963.

Burke, C. J. Linear model for Pavlovian conditioning. In M. R. Jones (Ed.), *Nebraska Symposium on Motivation* (Vol. 14). Lincoln: University of Nebraska Press, 1966.

Burke, C. J., & Estes, W. K. A component model for stimulus variables in discrimination learning. *Psychometrika,* 1957, *22,* 133–145.

Bush, R. R., & Mosteller, F. A model for stimulus generalization and discrimination. *Psychological Review,* 1951, *58,* 413–423.

Bush, R. R., & Mosteller, F. *Stochastic models for learning.* New York: John Wiley & Sons, 1955.

Estes, W. K. Toward a statistical theory of learning. *Psychological Review,* 1950, *57,* 94–109.

Estes, W. K. Statistical theory of distributional phenomena in learning. *Psychological Review,* 1955, *62,* 369–377. (a)

Estes, W. K. Statistical theory of spontaneous recovery and regression. *Psychological Review,* 1955, *62,* 145–154. (b)

Estes, W. K. Of models and men. *American Psychologist,* 1957, *12,* 609–617. (a)

Estes, W. K. Theory of learning with constant variable or contingent probabilities of reinforcement. *Psychometrika,* 1957, *22,* 113–132. (b)

Estes, W. K. Stimulus-response theory of drive. In M. R. Jones (Ed.), *Nebraska Symposium on Motivation.* Lincoln: University of Nebraska Press, 1958.

Estes, W. K. Component and pattern models with Markovian interpretations. In R. R. Bush & W. K. Estes (Eds.), *Studies in mathematical learning theory.* Stanford, Cal.: Stanford University Press, 1959.

Estes, W. K. Learning theory and the new mental chemistry. *Psychological Review,* 1960, *67,* 207–223.

Estes, W. K. All-or-none processes in learning and retention. *American Psychologist,* 1964, *19,* 16–25.

Estes, W. K. Outline of a theory of punishment. In B. A. Campbell & R. M. Church (Eds.), *Punishment and aversive behavior.* New York: Appleton-Century-Crofts, 1969.

Estes, W. K. Reinforcement in human behavior. *American Scientist,* 1972, *60,* 723–729. (a)

Estes, W. K. Research and theory on the learning of probabilities. *Journal of the American Statistical Association,* 1972, *67,* 81–102. (b)

Estes, W. K. Memory and conditioning. In F. J. McGuigan (Ed.), *Contemporary approaches to conditioning and learning.* Washington, D.C.: V. H. Winston & Sons, 1973.

Estes, W. K. Learning theory and intelligence. *American Psychologist,* 1974, *29,* 740–749.

Estes, W. K. Human behavior in mathematical perspective. *American Scientist,* 1975, *63,* 649–655. (a)

Estes, W. K. The state of the field: General problems and issues of theory and metatheory. In W. K. Estes (Ed.), *Handbook of learning and cognitive processes* (Vol. 1). Hillsdale, N.J.: Lawrence Erlbaum Associates, 1975. (b)

Estes, W. K. The cognitive side of probability learning. *Psychological Review,* 1976, *83,* 37–64. (a)

Estes, W. K. Some functions of memory in probability learning and choice behavior. In G. H. Bower (Ed.), *The psychology of learning and motivation* (Vol. 10). New York: Academic Press, 1976. (b)

Estes, W. K. *Cognitive processes in conditioning.* In press.

Estes, W. K., & Burke, C. J. A theory of stimulus variability. *Psychological Review,* 1953, *60,* 276–286.

Estes, W. K., Burke, C. T., Atkinson, R. C., & Frankmann, T. P. Probabilistic discrimination learning. *Journal of Experimental Psychology,* 1957, *54,* 233–239.

Estes, W. K., & Straughan, J. H. Analysis of a verbal conditioning situation in terms of statistical learning theory. *Journal of Experimental Psychology,* 1954, *47,* 225–234.

Friedman, M. P., Burke, C. J., Cole, M., Keller, L., Millward, R. B., & Estes, W. K. Two-choice behavior under extended training with shifting probabilities of reinforcement. In R. C. Atkinson (Ed.), *Studies in mathematical psychology.* Stanford, Cal.: Stanford University Press, 1963.

Goldberg, S. *Introduction to difference equations.* Englewood Cliffs, N.J.: Prentice-Hall, 1958.

Grant, D. A., Hake, H. W., & Hornseth, J. P. Acquisition and extinction of a verbal conditioned response with differing percentages of reinforcement. *Journal of Experimental Psychology,* 1951, *42,* 1–5.

Guthrie, E. R. *The psychology of learning* (2nd ed.). New York: Harper, 1952.

Hebb, D. O. *The organization of behavior.* New York: John Wiley & Sons, 1949.

Hull, C. L. *Principles of behavior: An introduction to behavior theory.* New York: Appleton-Century-Crofts, 1943.

Humphreys, L. G. Acquisition and extinction of verbal expectations in a situation analogous to conditioning. *Journal of Experimental Psychology,* 1939, *25,* 294–301.

Kimble, G. A. *Hilgard and Marquis' conditioning and learning* (2nd ed.). New York: Appleton-Century-Crofts, 1961.

Kornorski, J. *Integrative activity of the brain.* Chicago: University of Chicago Press, 1967.

Neimark, E. D., & Estes, W. K. *Stimulus sampling theory.* San Francisco: Holden-Day, 1967.

Reber, A. S., & Millward, R. B. Event observations in probability learning. *Journal of Experimental Psychology,* 1968, *77,* 317–327.

Restle, F. A theory of discrimination learning. *Psychological Review,* 1955, *62,* 11–19.

Revusky, S., & Garcia, J. Learned associations over long delays. In G. H. Bower, *The psychology of learning & motivation* (Vol. 4). New York: Academic Press, 1971.

Robbins, D. Some models for successive discrimination. *British Journal of Mathematical and Statistical Psychology,* 1972, *25,* 151–167.

Robbins, D., Cohen, S., Levine, M. E., & Olsen, A. Probability learning in the T-maze with an error rerun procedure. Unpublished study available from senior author, n.d.

Robbins, D., & Medin, D. L. Cue selection offers multiple-cue probability training. *Journal of Experimental Psychology,* 1971, *91,* 333–335.

Robbins, D., & Warner, P. L. Individual organism probability matching with rats in a two-choice task. *Bulletin of the Psychonomic Society,* 1973, *2,* 405–407.

Schoeffler, M. S. Probability of response to compounds of discriminated stimuli. *Journal of Experimental Psychology,* 1954, *48,* 323–329.

Skinner, B. F. *The behavior of organisms.* New York: Appleton-Century-Crofts, 1938.

Spence, K. W. *Behavior theory and condi-*

tioning. New Haven, Conn.: Yale University Press, 1956.

Spence, K. W. *Behavior theory and learning: Selected papers.* Englewood Cliffs, N.J.: Prentice-Hall, 1960.

Suppes, P., & Atkinson, R. C. *Markov learning models for multiperson interactions.* Stanford, Cal.: Stanford University Press, 1960.

Suppes, P., & Ginsberg, R. A fundamental property of all-or-none models, binomial distribution of responses prior to conditioning, with application to concept formation in children. *Psychological Review,* 1963, *70,* 139–161.

Theios, J. Simple conditioning as two-stage all-or-none learning. *Psychological Review,* 1963, *70,* 403–417.

Tolman, E. *Purposive behavior in animals and men.* New York: Appleton-Century-Crofts, 1932.

Uhl, C. N. Effect of overlapping cues upon discrimination learning. *Journal of Experimental Psychology,* 1964, *61,* 322–328.

Weinstock, S. Contiguity theory: An appraisal. In M. H. Marx (Ed.), *Learning: Theories.* New York: Masmallow, 1970.

Weinstock, S., North, A. I., Brody, A. L., & LoGuido, J. Probability learning in the T-maze with noncorrection. *Journal of Comparative and Physiological Psychology,* 1965, *60,* 76–81.

Weinstock, S., Robbins, D., & Chen, W. *Successive knightness discrimination and stimulus generalization in the T-maze.* Unpublished study available from Dr. Donald Robbins, n.d.

10

Memory and Information Processing

BARRY H. KANTOWITZ AND HENRY L. ROEDIGER, III

INTRODUCTION

Overview

This chapter is an introduction to an old approach to the study of behavior which has once again become popular after over a century of obscurity. This approach is called *information processing,* and while it certainly has strong implications for the study of memory, it has also been applied to areas such as perception that are beyond the scope of this text. Since there is no single theorist whose work would be completely typical and representative of the information-processing approach to memory, we take a slightly different tack in this chapter and discuss the theoretical efforts of several researchers, instead of highlighting the work of one theorist or one approach.

We will focus on two problem areas of learning which are currently the subject of intense experimental investigation: *memory* and *attention.* According to an information-processing view, which regards the organism as a system composed of several interacting subsystems, these two topics are virtually the opposite sides of the same coin. We cannot study memory without being aware of attention, and vice versa. The theoretical treatments of both topics frequently share the same terminology and concepts.

We have two main goals in writing this chapter. The first is to acquaint you with the history and some of the models, experiments, and implications associated with the information-processing approach. But we can sample only a tiny fraction of these research efforts, exposing just the tip of the iceberg. Thus, our second goal is more important: to illustrate the logic and unique conceptual framework that underlies current research effort in this area. We shall try to give you the flavor of the approach and some insight into the way information-processing researchers formulate and attack psychological problems related to memory and attention. While we have been careful to refrain from overtly stating that the information-processing approach is necessarily better than the traditional and neotraditional learning theories discussed in other chapters, we certainly hope that after reading this chapter you can see how it is markedly different from them.

Major Issues

Human information processing is not a theory of behavior comparable to some particular theory of learning. It is a general approach based upon a set of pretheoretical assumptions accepted by researchers who adopt this viewpoint. The most important assumption is that behavior is determined by the internal flow of information within the organism. Since this flow is never directly observable, the specific techniques and methodologies used to infer the details of this postulated information flow are complex. But this methodological complexity should not be permitted to obscure the goal of this research: to map internal information pathways.

Information-processing models of any process, be it memory or attention, will differ according to how the theorist wishes to specify a hypothetical internal-flow diagram. Many alternate flow diagrams are tenable, with each theorist trying to show how his or her diagram can better explain behavior. Thus a major issue which distinguishes competing models is the number of tiny internal "black boxes" or processing stages assumed in any theoretical treatment.

In memory research, there is currently considerable debate over how many different types of memory subsystems are present within the human. Some researchers believe there are separate sensory storage registers for each input modality (vision, audition, etc.) characterized by a very rapid loss of information. These sensory registers are thought to feed into a short-term memory system that can hold a small amount of information only if an active effort is made to retain its contents. This short-term memory in turn feeds into a long-term memory system with a huge storage capacity where items need not be actively maintained. However, other researchers believe that there is basically only one kind of memory system. According to this al-

ternate view, what has been interpreted as the operation of different memory systems is really only the influence of different kinds of encoding operations.

Even more important than the number of internal stages is the kind of information transformation effected by a stage. The human is regarded as an active processor of information with great flexibility as to how information can be transformed inside the organism. For example, visually presented information is often transformed into a code that is basically acoustic or articulatory in nature; that is, one based on how the information sounds or is produced. Such transformations of information are common in physical systems. A computer transforms small holes in punched cards into electrical impulses. A loudspeaker transforms electrical impulses into air vibrations. The study of information processing can be viewed as the search for the coding and transformation rules used to modify information as it flows through the organism.

Basic Concepts

The basic concept in information processing is the stage or isolable subsystem (Posner, 1978). A precise definition of a stage of processing requires considerable mathematical sophistication (Taylor, 1976; Townsend, 1974) and so is beyond the scope of this chapter. However, we can offer a fuzzy definition: A stage corresponds roughly to one transformation of information. In general, the output of an internal processing stage differs from the input.

Stages can be arranged in many patterns. The simplest pattern occurs when we have a chain of stages, with the output of one stage feeding directly into the input of the next stage. This is called *serial processing* because any particular stage must wait to do its own transformation until it has received the output from the immediately preceding stage. If several stages can simultaneously have access to the same output, this is called *parallel processing.* Now a stage need not wait for other stages, because all parallel stages can operate on the same information together. Finally, if some processing is serial and some parallel, the resulting model is called *hybrid processing.* While hybrid models are often more general and powerful than either serial or parallel models, they are also far more difficult to analyze and to understand. Most current models are serial or parallel, with serial models having an edge in frequency because most people find them intuitively easier to understand.

However, the division of an information-processing structure into serial and/or parallel processing stages is not enough to specify the behavior of the system. We must also know or assume the "price" each stage charges the system for its operation. This is called allocation of resources or capacity. Most models assume some kind of limitation on the resources available to the organism for processing information; this is another way of stating that the organism cannot process an infinite amount of information in a finite time. So the operation of some particular stage may make it impossible for another stage to fulfill its transformation efficiently, or even at all. Many models assume that stages compete for a limited pool of power, energy, capacity (pick the analogy you prefer), so that every stage cannot always work as quickly or as efficiently as if it were the only processing stage in the system. It is even possible to make serial systems look like parallel systems, and vice versa, by cleverly choosing the right assumptions about capacity.

In summary, to predict the behavior of an organism that is attending or memorizing we must have a model that (1) gives the number and configuration of internal processing stages, and (2) gives the capacity requirements of each stage as well as the total availability of capacity.

HISTORY

The fields of information processing and memory are among the oldest in experimental psychology. Decades before E. L. Thorndike observed cats escaping from puzzleboxes or Pavlov studied the "psychic secretions" produced by dogs, careful studies of information processing and memory were carried out in European laboratories. The work of two men in particular stands out as precursors of those studying cognitive psychology today: Frans Cornelis Donders and Hermann Ebbinghaus.

Beginnings

Frans C. Donders, a Dutch physiologist, was already well known for his research on vision when he turned to the problem of the speed of reaction and what it could tell about how information is processed. Donders (1868/1969) developed three different reaction tasks, which he referred to as A, B, and C reactions. (They are still known by these names.) The Donders A reaction, also called the *simple reaction,* involves a person responding as fast as possible to a single stimulus. In a common experimental situation, a person sits at a table with an electric bulb on it. The person's task is simply to respond as rapidly as possible by pressing a button whenever the light goes on. A naturally occurring case of a simple reaction is stepping on your brake pedal in response to the sudden flash of the brake lights of the car in front of you. Donders believed that the simple or A reaction time reflects such basic factors as the speed of conduction of the nervous impulse, and thus it can be used as a baseline component in analyzing the more complex reaction tasks.

The more complicated B and C reaction tasks involve persons perceiving more than one stimulus. In the B or *choice reaction* task there is more than one stimulus and more than one response; for example, there may be two bulbs and two buttons. Each stimulus governs one response, so that if the left light comes on the person is to press one button, while if the right light is illuminated the other button is to be pressed. Thus the B reaction involves a choice between two responses based on proper identification of the stimulus. It is similar to the decision to be made at a stoplight where one must decide whether to stop or go, depending on the color of the light.

Donders thought the choice reaction involved two mental operations, identification of the stimulus (which light came on?) and selection or choice of the response (which response do I make?). To estimate the time taken by each of these mental operations, it is also necessary to study a third kind of reaction, the C reaction. The C reaction also involves more than one stimulus, but in this case there is only one response and it is to be performed to only one of the two stimuli. A person seated before two lights who is supposed to press a button only when the left light comes on represents an example of a C reaction. Illumination of the other light would not require a response and should be ignored. An example of a C reaction would be waiting for your number to be called at a takeout restaurant; you are not supposed to respond until your number is called. Donders believed that the C reaction involves *stimulus identification,* since one has to determine which stimulus is appropriate, but not response selection (choice), since there is only one response.

Once we have measured the times required to perform the A, B, and C reactions, we can compute the amount of time needed for the mental operations of stimulus identification and choice (response selection). The C reaction involves stimulus identification and the baseline time for other processes such as nervous conduction and response execution, while the A reaction simply involves the baseline time. Thus the time required for stimulus identification can be estimated by subtracting the A reaction time from the C reaction time. Similarly, the amount of time required for choice or response selection can be calculated by subtracting the C time from the B (choice) reaction time. This is because the B reaction is considered to have the components of choice (or response selection), stimulus identification, and the baseline, while the C reaction has only the latter two components.

This *subtraction method* devised by Donders (see Figure 10.1) was an ingenious attack on the problem of measuring the stages in information processing. His method was used widely in the late 1800s to study "mental chronometry," as it is called, of other psychological processes. The method fell into disfavor because the estimated times for the mental processes were often quite variable, but also because the structural psychologists who used introspection did not feel as though the simple reaction tasks really contained these separate stages. It was not until the 1960s that reaction-time experiments were reintroduced to the study of infor-

Figure 10.1

Example of the Logic of the Subtraction Method

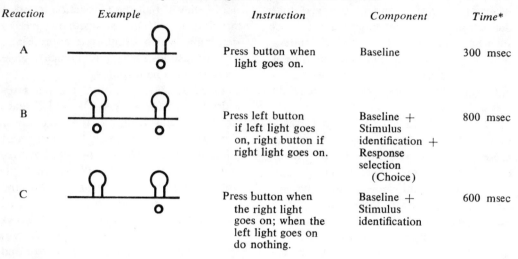

Reaction	Example	Instruction	Component	Time*
A		Press button when light goes on.	Baseline	300 msec
B		Press left button if left light goes on, right button if right light goes on.	Baseline + Stimulus identification + Response selection (Choice)	800 msec
C		Press button when the right light goes on; when the left light goes on do nothing.	Baseline + Stimulus identification	600 msec

To determine time for stimulus identification:

$$C - A = 600 - 300 = 300 \text{ msec}$$

To determine time for response selection or choice:

$$B - C = 800 - 600 = 200 \text{ msec}$$

* Numbers are hypothetical.

mation processing by Saul Sternberg (1969), Michael Posner (1969) and others.

The first person to study human learning and memory scientifically was Hermann Ebbinghaus. He pioneered new methods of study that have been tremendously influential. His work was published in a brief volume translated as *Memory: A Contribution to Experimental Psychology* (1913/1964). Ebbinghaus served as the only subject in all his experiments, and the materials he devised for memorization are referred to as *nonsense syllables*. He made up 2,300 meaningless syllables that contained a vowel surrounded by two consonants, like DAL and BEP. Ebbinghaus used these rather unnatural materials because he hoped to minimize the influence of prior linguistic associations in his experiments that would have been present if he had used words, phrases, sentences, or (as he sometimes did) passages of poetry.

Ebbinghaus selected these syllables at random and placed them into lists of varied length. He would read the nonsense syllables in a list to the beat of a metronome until he thought they were almost learned. Then he would attempt to recite the list after looking away. The measure of learning was the amount of time (or the number of recitations) it took to repeat the list perfectly. When the number of recitations (or trials) to mastery of the list is used, the measure of learning is referred to as a *trials to criterion* measure. In attempting later to recall a list, we could measure simply the number of syllables not recalled. But suppose we attempt to recall a list learned weeks ago, and we cannot produce even a single syllable from the list? Does this mean that there is no memory trace left of that experience? Ebbinghaus did not measure memory or forgetting by the number of syllables that could be recalled at a later time; instead he measured the number of trials (or amount of time) it took for him to *relearn* the list. The memory for the list at the time of relearning could be measured by the *savings* in terms of the fewer number of trials or less time needed to relearn the list than to learn it originally. Thus even if not a single syllable could be recalled from the list, memory for the list could be indirectly measured by the amount of time saved during relearning the list. One of the many interesting things Ebbinghaus discovered was that forgetting is a negatively accelerated function of the time past since learning (i.e., there is great forgetting at first and then the rate slows down). Ebbinghaus applied one of psychology's first mathematical models to account for this forgetting function.

Ebbinghaus pioneered a number of other techniques in the study of memory (see Crowder, 1976, pp. 413–417), and his influence was considerable. Unlike Donders, Ebbinghaus's influence did not wane and remains strong even to the present day, though a number of the specific techniques he invented have been replaced.

Major Theorists

In a field as large as that of information processing and memory it is difficult to name only a handful of major theorists. This section focuses on only some of the people who have influenced cognitive psychology in recent years.

One of the psychologists most respon-

sible for the surge of interest in information processing in the 1950s was Donald E. Broadbent. In 1958 he published *Perception and Communication,* an important book which has inspired much further work. It contained the first information flow diagram, a graph intended to indicate how information passes through an organism in the performance of some task. Broadbent proposed a mechanical model of attention in humans called *filter theory.* Information is believed to be held briefly in a sensory system, and if it is not attended to by the perceptual system it is filtered out or lost (see Figure 10.2). Filter theory has served as a reference point in the study of attention and information processing over the years. Broadbent's views on many of the issues in information processing were updated in *Decision and Stress* (1971).

Saul Sternberg's work in information processing and memory has had great impact in recent years. Sternberg is one of the psychologists most responsible for the rejuvenation of interest in the reaction task and the logic used by Donders in delineating stages in information processing. Sternberg (1969) modified the reaction task to study how information is retrieved from short-term memory. He presented people with a small number of letters or digits to be memorized (e.g., 5, 3, 9, 7). This *positive set* of information was kept small so that individuals could hold it in short-term memory and would not forget it. Then Sternberg presented a test digit that half the time was a member of the positive set (the items presented) and half the time was a member of the *negative set* (the items not presented). The person's task was to respond as rapidly as possible to indicate whether the test item was or was not in the positive set. Since people hardly ever made errors, the interest was in the reaction time to the

Figure 10.2

Information Flow Diagram for Broadbent's Filter Theory of Attention

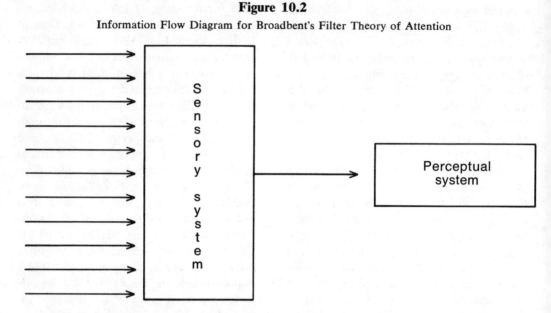

The information flow diagram represents Broadbent's filter theory of attention. All incoming information is held briefly in a sensory (S) system in parallel (simultaneously) before certain information is selected for further processing by the perceptual (P) system. The perceptual system operates on information serially. Information not processed by the perceptual system is thought to be "filtered out," or not processed beyond the sensory system. (Adapted from Broadbent, 1958, p. 216, Figure S.)

test item. Sternberg discovered that as the size of the positive set increased from two to six items, the time for the person to respond increased at about 40 milliseconds per additional item. Sternberg argued from this and other evidence that people retrieve information in short-term memory by successively scanning or examining each item. Many other findings have been produced by investigators using this paradigm, which has come to be called the *Sternberg paradigm*. Sternberg (1975) has recently reviewed the issues involved in this line of research.

Wendell R. Garner also has made important contributions to the study of information processing. He borrowed concepts from information theory as developed by engineers and applied them successfully to perception and memory. Part of his work has been concerned with pattern goodness: Good patterns (as measured in several different ways) have great effects on different information-processing tasks. For example, simple patterns are better remembered than more complex ones. Much of Garner's work is summarized in *The Processing of Information and Structure* (1974).

One idea that has attracted much attention over the past 10 years is that there is not a single memory store, but rather two different memory stores with distinct properties (*short-term store* and *long-term store*). This idea was proposed by a number of researchers, but the most complete proposal was that of Richard C. Atkinson and Richard M. Shiffrin (1968). They developed an extended information flow diagram of the kind first introduced by Broadbent which was meant to model a number of aspects of humans' abilities to process information.

Two psychologists who have greatly influenced the study of memory are Leo Postman and Benton J. Underwood. One of their primary contributions has been the development of the *interference theory of forgetting*. This will be discussed later, but basically the hypothesis is that forgetting of an experience can often be attributed to interference from preceding experiences (*proactive interference*) or succeeding experiences (*retroactive interference*). The interference theory of forgetting is one of the most durable theories of memory, and much of the evidence concerning it has been contributed by Underwood and Postman (for a review, see Postman and Underwood, 1973). Both have also made numerous other contributions.

Endel Tulving has also had a strong influence on the way psychologists think about memory by emphasizing the importance of retrieval processes. Forgetting is not necessarily attributable to a loss or weakening of information as it is stored in memory; instead the difficulty may be in using or retrieving the information. Tulving argues that any experience of remembering must be considered as the product of information from two sources: Information from the memory trace left by the experience and information in the retrieval environment at the time of recall (Tulving, 1974). This point will be explicated later in the chapter.

Allan Paivio has pointed out another important aspect of human memory, the effectiveness of mental imagery as an aid to remembering. There has been a great emphasis in cognitive psychology on the processing of verbal information. This is quite natural, since language is so impor-

tant in human cognition. Paivio's work has served to reintroduce the concept of mental imagery as an important one in understanding human memory and thought. He argues that humans use two primary mental codes to store experience, a spatial/imaginal code and a linguistic code. This idea is referred to as the *dual coding hypothesis*. Much of the work on mental imagery is reviewed in Paivio's *Imagery and Verbal Processes* (1971).

One final theorist (of many possible) to be discussed is W. K. Estes, whose work on mathematical theories is the subject of the preceding chapter. Estes's work has spanned many of the problems in experimental psychology, but in recent years he has turned more to the study of information processing, in particular the problems of perception of letters and words briefly presented (Estes, 1975), the recall of information in the order in which it was presented (serial recall), and probability learning.

Current Status

The study of information processing and memory is one of the most active fields of experimental psychology. After the early and influential work of Donders, Ebbinghaus, and others, the study of information processing and memory for years took a back seat to the study of animal learning and behavior. At about the turn of the century the careful experimental methods of Donders and Ebbinghaus had largely been supplanted by introspective methods. Rather than perform experiments in which behavior was measured, these introspectionists carefully observed their inner mental processes while performing some task and tried to analyze the task into its components on the basis of these reflections. The introspectionists could not agree among themselves as to what components occurred in performing even the simplest of tasks, and this unreliability did much to discredit the introspectionist approach.

When John B. Watson introduced the behaviorist arguments against the introspective approach to psychology, the weak tools and results of the introspectionists were no match. The emphasis of psychologists in studying behavior began with the study of processes that could be observed in species other than humans, and thus topics such as information processing and memory were neglected. Watson (1913) argued strongly that psychology did not need mental constructs, and for a long time topics such as imagery, attention, memory, and so forth were not studied. The exciting issues in experimental psychology for the next 40 years revolved mostly around learning in animals.

In the 1950s and 1960s the study of mental processes was reintroduced into psychology. Rather than using introspective techniques, though, psychologists now studied observable behavior. Mental constructs were reintroduced into psychology, but only with several different lines of firm behavioral evidence to back them up (Garner, Hake, & Ericksen, 1956). This new approach to studying the higher mental processes has been termed *neomentalism* by Paivio (1975). Today the study of the higher mental processes forms the field of cognitive psychology, and it has captured the excitement and fervor that was reserved for other issues only a few decades ago.

Other Theories

The study of information processing and memory is not a theory in any real sense. Rather, these are topic areas about which there are many theories. Thus it makes little sense to contrast this approach with that of the other theories discussed in this book. These other theories actually are distinct theories that address the same content problems from different viewpoints. The approaches discussed in this chapter by and large address different problems from those of the other chapters. Most of the theories reviewed in the other chapters have not been developed to account for the kinds of problems and situations involved in the study of information processing and memory. Similarly, the theoretical viewpoints of this chapter have not usually been extended to cover the kinds of experimental situations considered elsewhere in this book.

PROPOSITIONS

1. *Information flow is the basis for behavior.*

The essence of the information-processing approach is a dominant concern for the flow of information inside the organism. According to this viewpoint, psychology must not only be able to duplicate and control behavior but must also duplicate the detailed processing of information that is hidden. We think of the human as a very complex machine and try to discover what happens inside this "black box." It is not enough to duplicate behavior: A woman singing and a tape recording with a certain brand of tape might both be able to shatter a slender wineglass, but no one would claim that this duplication of behavior demonstrates that the woman and the tape recorder both operate the same way.

Information-processing theorists sometimes represent the human cognitive system as a series of boxes representing information stores and processes that send information back and forth. Each box may represent one kind of information transformation that goes on inside your head. As we discover more about psychology, the level of detail represented in each box becomes finer. These smaller boxes are often called *stages* of information processing. A typical box or stage would be the one that represents the encoding of signals. When you see a printed word, you may transform this visual information into an acoustic or articulatory code based upon the sound of the word or how it is pronounced. Subsequent processing is based upon this code and not upon the visual shape of the original stimulus; indeed, you may be unable to report about the original stimulus—was it in upper or lower case, how tall were the letters, was it script or block lettered, and so on? It is possible to take even this small unit of information processing— that is, the stage that transforms visual input—and break it down into yet smaller stages that process individual letters or even individual strokes within letters. But no matter how many stages are discussed, the logic of the analysis is the same. The attempt is to break down a complex process into its components and to show how these components interact.

Cognitive psychologists often attempt to map the internal information flow by using technologies borrowed from disciplines like engineering and computer science. However, engineers can often get inside their black boxes to insert meters. Psychologists are far less fortunate in this regard. While psychophysiological techniques may offer hope for the distant future, right now we cannot gain direct entry into the processing flow within the organism. So we are forced to infer alternate flows and then to determine which postulated flows are most consistent with observed behavior. There are times when

we discover that two alternate flowcharts are equivalent in terms of predicted behavior, even though they may look quite different at first glance. Thus information-processing psychologists usually concentrate on testing classes of models rather than specific details of one model (Broadbent, 1971, Chap. 1). We may decide, for example, that the class of models postulating some filter mechanism early in the flow of information is not as good as the class that puts the filter nearer the end of the flow of information. Or we may compare the class of models which state that stages can work only one at a time (*serial models*) to the class which allows several stages to operate on the same information simultaneously (*parallel models*). This approach may get a lot more mileage out of an experiment than does the hypothetico-deductive method, in which only one specific theory is tested.

In the traditional approach, in which postulates of one theory were tested, theories and experiments got so complicated they were hard to validate. As more and more postulates were added to a theory, it became awkward to test. And simple tests, while consistent with many hypothetico-deductive theories, were often also consistent with simpler explanations that were not considered. Comparing classes of models, rather than testing one theory at a time, makes better use of experimental effort.

2. *Stimuli that did not occur can exert control over behavior.*

Traditional learning theories, such as Clark Hull's, maintain that behavior is controlled on any given trial by the stimulus present on that trial. This seems obvious, and it is hard to imagine how a stimulus not present can alter behavior.

But information-processing theorists have shown that the set of possible stimuli—that is, all those stimuli that might have occurred—is at least as important as the particular stimulus that did occur.

This can be demonstrated rather easily in a choice reaction-time experiment. It is well known that reaction time increases as a function of the amount of *information* in a stimulus set. The unit of information is the bit: One bit is the amount of information gained by tossing a fair coin that can come up either heads or tails. Tossing two coins has four possible outcomes (HH, HT, TH, TT) and two bits of information. Each time we double the number of equiprobable possible outcomes we gain one bit of information. Choice reaction time is a linear function of information; that is, every time the number of alternatives that must be examined is doubled, reaction time is increased by a constant amount. Let us illustrate this finding. If we have two lights and two response keys we can easily measure choice reaction time: the time between the onset of one of the lights and the depression of the appropriate response key. Now let us add two more lights and keys to the set and again turn on the very same light as before. Now reaction time will be increased. Even though the physical stimulus is the same —say the light on the left end of the row of lights—behavior has changed, as indicated by a change in reaction time. Adding two more S–R alternatives has increased reaction time, even though those alternatives did not occur on this particular trial. However, they could have occurred. Choice reaction time is controlled by the set of possible alternatives rather than the particular stimulus that occurred.

The concept of expectancy has been resisted by many traditional learning theorists. Yet it provides a relatively simple explanation of these choice reaction-time data. Behavior is influenced by the person expecting more alternatives. Expectancy can be manipulated by priming—that is, presenting an initial stimulus that tells the probability of a following stimulus. For example, the following stimulus might be the letter A or the letter B. The priming stimulus could tell the individual that there is an 80% chance that B will be the next stimulus. If a B actually occurs, reaction time is faster than a control condition in which no priming stimulus was given. Of course, if an A occurs, reaction time is slowed down. Expecting a stimulus speeds up reaction time (Posner, 1978).

It would be unfair to claim that these data could not be explained at all by learning theorists. If complicated assumptions about generalization gradients are made, it might be possible to generate accurate predictions. However, this would be cumbersome at best, and the same predictions can be more readily generated from information-processing assumptions.

3. *The human has a limited capacity for processing information.*

This has been the most fruitful proposition of information-processing approaches to behavior. It was originally derived from a model of a telephone communication system devised by Claude Shannon and Warren Weaver (1949), mathematicians at Bell Telephone Laboratories who invented information theory. A telephone cable can only carry so many conversations at a single time; this limit is its capacity to transmit information. Important new insights about human behavior have been gained by thinking of the human as a limited-capacity channel, similar in principle to a telephone line.

The research areas of memory and attention have benefited most from this view of the human's limited capabilities. The important distinction between short- and long-term memory systems is based in part upon differences of capacity. Long-term memory has an almost unlimited capacity for information, whereas short-term memory can only hold from three to six items at one time. Attention is a broad topic which covers both humans' ability to focus on one subset of stimuli while ignoring others and their inability to do several things simultaneously.

Although the idea of a limited-capacity human was the work of many psychologists, the man who was its most articulate advocate was Donald Broadbent (see the History section). His information-flow conception of the human (Broadbent, 1958, 1971) stresses two important mechanisms relevant to attention. The most important, of course, is the limited-capacity channel itself. This has occasionally been misinterpreted to mean that the human can do only one thing at a time. This is false. The model states that the human can process a limited amount of information per unit of time; that is, humans are limited by their *rate* of information processing. This limit is called their channel capacity and is measured in bits/sec. If the total demands of a set of tasks are less than channel capacity, all the component tasks will be performed without impairment. If the total exceeds available capacity, performance on some task(s) will suffer. In the limiting case the set of tasks reduces to only one, but the prediction of the limited-capacity model remains the same. If a single task exceeds channel capacity it will be performed imperfectly; if channel capacity exceeds the demands of a single task no performance decrement will be observed.

The second most important mechanism proposed by Broadbent is a filter that protects the limited-capacity channel from excessive stimulation. Only information that successfully passes the filter is allowed to enter the limited-capacity channel. So the filter can be regarded as an early stage of perceptual processing. While there has been some controversy about the specifics of filter operation (Broadbent, 1971), the basic conclusion about human selectivity is still correct. However, this selectivity may be accomplished at other stages in addition to, or in place of, an early-selection filter.

The great amount of research engendered by the limited-capacity model has resulted in the discovery of a few situations where the human can do more things simultaneously than the model predicts. Although the limited-channel model remains an excellent first approximation, there is now some doubt about many of its specific details. Other models stressing parallel channels and variable capacity mechanisms are challenging Broadbent's views. This in no way diminishes the importance of his model, since it was responsible for getting many learning theorists and experimentalists to think in terms of information flow in the first place. But it is clear that the notion of the human as a limited-capacity processor, while correct in an overall sense, marks the start of a new problem area for psychology rather than the solution.

4. *Mental events can be inferred from chronometric analysis.*

This proposition is often taken as evidence that psychology today is asking the same questions it did over a century ago. The notion of a mental event was the basis for an entire school of psychology based upon introspection. The structural psychologists (such as Edward Titchener) tried to break down mental events into component parts on the basis of analysis of sensations. The information-processing analysis of mental events is quite different, since it is based on analyzing the event in terms of behavioral effects. It is historically interesting that one major tool used for this analysis, measurement of reaction time, was available over 100 years ago but was then rejected, since it could not be corroborated by introspective reports. (See discussion of Donders in the History section.)

Modern chronometric analysis takes up where F. C. Donders left off, although he deserves the credit for demonstrating the utility of reaction time as a dependent variable. Chronometric analysis is defined as the use of reaction-time data to measure mental events; indeed, some researchers go even further and claim that if used properly, accuracy measures also meet the demands of chronometric logic (Posner, 1978). While Donders tried to determine the duration of mental events such as selection and identification, current chronometric analysis is satisfied to identify subunits or stages of mental activity without specifying their duration. The mathematics and details of this technology cannot be covered here (see Sternberg, 1969; Taylor, 1976), but the logic can be sketched.

The method of *additive factors* takes a total reaction time and decomposes it into successive stages of internal information flow. Independent variables or factors are manipulated to alter durations of mental events. The relationships between factors and stages are inferred from analysis of variance and related statistics. Factors which interact influence the same stage, while factors which are additive—that is, fail to interact—influence different processing stages. So, the additive-factors methods allows us to discover the number of processing stages associated with some set of independent variables. This is how measurements of reaction time allow us to infer the existence of mental events.

5. *Memory for a stimulus depends on the complexity of the mental operations applied to it when it was initially processed.*

It has been proposed (Craik & Lockhart, 1972) that memory for an experience is a byproduct of the processing the stimulus receives as it is perceived. Perception is believed to proceed through a series of processing stages from relatively "shallow" sensory analyses through more complex, "deeper" analyses which involve higher cognitive structures, such as long-term memory. Craik and Lockhart proposed that information can be processed to different *levels* and that the greater the depth of initial perceptual processing, the more likely is later recall of the experience. This general viewpoint is referred to as the *levels* (or *depth*) *of processing framework,* and it has proved a popular and useful view in interpreting memory phenomena.

Later in this chapter we consider specific experiments that can be interpreted within the levels-of-processing framework, but let us now consider a common example. Suppose you have had two years of Spanish in high school, and one day while riding around in your car you tune to a Spanish language radio station on which an announcer is talking. You decide to try your best to understand what is being said. However, you soon discover that for many words and passages you cannot make out what is being said, or even where the words begin and end, because the announcer is speaking rapidly and using words to which you are not accustomed. These words and passages are, of course, receiving some obligatory perceptual analysis as you try to understand them, simply because they are being processed by your auditory system. However, this analysis qualifies only as shallow processing, since you are not able to derive the segmentation between the words or their meaning. For other words and phrases you can probably make out the different words and can sound out and repeat them, but you still are not able to understand what they mean. You have thus processed the information beyond a sensory level of coding to the way the words sound, but more complex semantic processing involving the meaning of the message is still lacking. Finally, for some words and phrases you are able to recognize the words and understand what they mean, thus achieving deeper levels of processing of the material.

Now suppose you were asked to recall what you had heard an hour after you listened to the Spanish radio broadcast. What would you be able to recall? You would probably recall almost nothing about those parts that you did not understand (processed only to a shallow level), perhaps a few of the words that you could sound out but did not know the meaning of, and probably a great deal of those parts that you were able to understand (that were processed to a deep level). Many experiments interpreted in the levels-of-processing framework follow the same logic as this example: Individuals given the same stimuli are required to perform different tasks on the material that force processing to different levels, and the effect of this variable on later recall or recognition is observed.

The levels-of-processing framework has undergone considerable modification from the ideas just presented (e.g., Craik & Tulving, 1975), and it has also attracted critics (e.g., Baddeley, 1978; Nelson, 1977). It may be better to formulate the important variable determining recall as "complexity of mental operations performed on the stimulus" rather than the level of processing. Kolers (1973) found that people who had read sentences presented upside down recognized them better later than people who had read the same sentences presented in normal typography! Reading inverted text certainly involves more complicated mental operations than reading normal text, but it probably does not involve a deeper level of processing. Thus complexity of mental operations is emphasized in this proposition, rather than level of processing. Another complex mental operation that improves memory is dealt with in the next proposition.

6. *Forming images of material to be remembered greatly aids later recall.*

People have been aware of the validity of this proposition to a greater or lesser degree for thousands of years. Greek and Roman rhetoricians admonished their students to remember the points in a speech they were to make by forming images of the points and locating them at different places along a familiar path. When they were to give the speech they could retrieve the successive points they wished to make by mentally walking down the path and "looking" to see images of the different points. This technique is known as the *method of loci* and is only one of numerous *mnemonic devices,* or aids to memory, that have been devised (see Yates, 1966). Almost all these memory aids are based on use of mental imagery, as are memory systems suggested in modern books such as *The Memory Book,* by Harry Lorayne and Jerry Lucas (1974).

The experimental methods of modern

psychology have confirmed this belief that imagery aids memory. For example, Bower (1972) found much better recall of word pairs for persons told to form images of the referents of the pairs than for persons simply told to repeat or rehearse the pairs. Paivio (1971) reported similar results and also showed that words rated high in image-evoking value (e.g., blood, table, rhinocerous) are better recalled and recognized than low-imagery words (e.g., truth, beauty, democracy), even when the words are matched on other qualities such as their length or frequency of occurrence in English.

The formation of images to aid recall may be seen as a corollary of the preceding proposition, that complex mental processing applied to an event improves memory for it. However, it has been argued on numerous grounds by Paivio and others that the imaginal system represents a different code for representing experience than linguistic codes. Thus image formation may not simply represent a more complex mental operation but rather a code in a qualitatively different cognitive system. The debate on this issue continues (e.g., Anderson, 1978; Kosslyn & Pomerantz, 1977; Pylyshyn, 1973). The usefulness of mnemonic devices is considered further below in the Implications section.

7. *Memory for an event is a product of information from two sources: the memory trace laid down by the event and the cues in the retrieval environment when recall is attempted.*

The two preceding propositions have focused on how information is stored, with the assumption being that so long as information is stored well, it will be recalled. But adequate storage of information is only half the story; without appropriate retrieval information to complement the information in storage, one will not be able to recall an event. The importance of retrieval for a theory of memory can be illustrated in a number of ways. You have probably often had the experience of trying to recall something, failing in your initial attempt, and then putting the matter aside for a time. Later you may try again, with seemingly no new information at hand, and succeed. Obviously the information was stored in memory and your initial failure to recall it was due to a retrieval failure, since you were able to retrieve it on the second try. Psychologists studying simple events such as the recall of a collection of pictures or words in a list have observed the same phenomenon. Often when people are given repeated tests for the same information or are given one test over a prolonged period of time, information that people could not recall immediately is eventually recalled (Erdelyi & Becker, 1974; Roediger & Thorpe, 1978).

A more direct way to demonstrate the importance of retrieval in the memory process is to manipulate the nature of the retrieval environment by providing the rememberer with different sorts of retrieval cues. In one well-known experiment, Tulving and Pearlstone (1966) presented high school students with lists of words to remember. The words were members of common categories and were presented in appropriate groups, for example: Birds—*Dove, Sparrow;* Furniture —*Couch, Bed;* Colors—*Yellow, Blue,* and so forth. The participants were told that they need remember only the words, not the category names, for later recall. We will consider only two conditions, in both of which people heard 48 words, two words in each of 24 categories. Individuals in the two conditions heard the words under exactly the same conditions of presentation, so we can assume that they stored roughly the same amount and kind of information about the words. The only difference between the two conditions was at recall. Individuals in one condition were simply asked to recall the words in any order they wished (free recall). Those in the other condition were also told to recall the words in any order, but in addition they were given the category names as retrieval cues.

The free-recall students recalled an average of 18.8 words; without further information, we might assume that information about the other 30 or so words was not stored well enough for later recall. However, students given the category names as retrieval cues recalled 35.9 words, or almost twice as many. Since both groups of students stored the information under the same conditions, it is apparent that the difference between the two was due to the different conditions operating at retrieval. The retrieval cues allowed people to recall many words that they could not recall unaided. To use Tulving and Pearlstone's terms, there is more information *available* in the memory store than is *accessible* under conditions of free recall.

It is obvious from the comparison of conditions in the Tulving and Pearlstone (1966) experiment that retrieval cues can be powerful aids in determining recall. But what determines whether or not a retrieval cue will be effective?

8. *The effectiveness of retrieval cues depends on their relation to the nature of the stored information.*

The effectiveness of a retrieval cue depends on the degree to which the cue reinstates the original encoding or interpretation of the to-be-remembered experience. Suppose you were asked to recall as many experiences as possible that happened to you while you were in elementary school. You could probably recall a good number, but after a while you might feel as though you had recalled as many as possible. Suppose you were then taken to the school and allowed to wander the halls freely for a time. You would probably discover that you could now recall many more of your grade school experiences. Presumably the school environment served to remind you of additional experiences, since it helped recreate the original context in which they occurred.

The idea that the effectiveness of retrieval cues depends on their reinstating the original interpretation (or encoding) of the experience has been called the *encoding specificity hypothesis* or *principle* (Tulving & Thomson, 1973). It bears a close formal resemblance to the idea of stimulus generalization (discussed in Chapter 4 in this book), but demonstrating encoding specificity effects is tricky, since it is assumed that the same overt or nominal stimulus can be encoded in different ways. The visible or public characteristics of an event that may seem important to the experimenter may not be the aspects that the subject encodes. Thus the experimenter cannot simply assume that manipulations of the environment along the dimensions that he or she regards as important will determine performance, because individuals may have encoded the information along some other, less obvious, dimension.

Let us consider an example. Suppose you study a long list of words, one of which is *Violet*. If *violet* follows the words *daisy, tulip,* and *zinnia* in the list, you are likely to encode it as a flower. Later on when you are tested you will be more likely to recall *violet* if you are given the retrieval cue *flowers* than if you are simply left on your own to try to recall the words with no cues, in any order (a free-recall memory test). Suppose at the time you were tested you were given the retrieval cues *girls' names.* Would this aid recall of *violet?* Probably not, since *violet* was encoded originally in the context of other flowers rather than in the context of girls' names. If *violet* had been presented along with *Linda, Susan,* and *Barbara* at the time the list was studied, then *girls' names* would serve as an effective retrieval cue, but *flowers* (or *colors*) would not. The basic point is that the "same" word (at least in its overt stimulus properties) can be encoded in different ways, and how the word is encoded determines what kinds of cues will be effective in later allowing the rememberer access to the trace of the word.

The encoding specificity principle generalizes to many other memory situations than those employing words that have more than one meaning. There are a great number of variations that reveal the same type of effect we have just illustrated. The same nominal event can often be embedded in two different contexts, and then two different sorts of cues can be shown to be differentially effective, depending on the original encoding context. One of the more interesting cases of such a mechanism is called *state-dependent retrieval* (Eich, 1977). People who study material while under the influence of a drug that acts on the central nervous system (e.g., alcohol or marijuana) can later recall more information learned during that time if they are given the drug again than if they are sober. The cognitive state at the time of study determines how the information is encoded, and how the information is encoded de-

termines the effectiveness of retrieval routes to the information.

9. *Events occurring prior to or after events that are to be remembered interfere with recall of the to-be-remembered events.*

Two types of interference may be delineated: proactive and retroactive interference. Both can be illustrated by reference to a simple experiment that has an experimental group and a control group. In the case of *proactive interference,* the experimental group first learns some material (call it List A), then learns another set of material (List B), and finally is tested for recall of List B. The control group performs some unrelated activity for a time equivalent to that in which the experimental group learned List A, then they learn List B and are tested on it later. The typical finding is that B is recalled less well by the experimental group than the control. The list learned by the experimental group prior to B is said to interfere proactively with retention of B. Proactive interference is thus the inhibiting effect that the learning of some prior events exerts on retention of events learned later.

In a *retroactive interference* paradigm the experimental group again learns List A and then List B. However, in this case the experimental group is asked to recall A. The control group learns A and then performs some relatively neutral interpolated activity until tested for A. Again the typical finding is that recall of A is worse when B has been learned after A (the experimental condition) than when there has been no learning of similar material afterward (the control condition). The second list is said to provide retroactive interference for the first list.

It should be noted that the terms *proactive* and *retroactive interference* are descriptive terms, not theoretical ones. That is, they merely describe the outcome of typical experimental arrangements, they do not explain why it occurs. The facts of retroactive and proactive interference are basic ones, and any theory of memory that pretends to be at all general must explain the facts associated with these phenomena. Most of the early explanatory attempts dealt more with the phenomenon of retroactive interference, to the relative neglect of proactive interference. J. A. McGeoch (1942) argued that retroactive interference occurs because of *response competition* at retrieval. That is, one set of responses (those in List B) compete at retrieval with those from the appropriate list (List A), so that the rememberer fails to recall the desired items because of an unwanted intrusion in recall of the items from the other list. Thus the basic idea is that forgetting is not a loss in the availability of information from memory but is a blockage at retrieval caused by competing responses. This response competition interpretation also accounts for the effects of proactive interference, which is important; Benton Underwood showed in a classic paper (1957) that a great deal of forgetting can be attributed to proactive interference.

Arthur Melton and Jeffrey Irwin (1940) reported results that they interpreted as indicating another factor besides response competition is necessary to account for retroactive interference. They speculated that this factor is *unlearning,* which has been likened to the extinction of a conditioned response. While individuals learned the second list, first-list responses were thought to be unlearned and were therefore not well recalled after second-list learning. Later first-list responses were thought to recover in strength, just as extinguished responses in other organisms exhibit spontaneous recovery after a delay. Evidence provided in numerous experiments over the course of some 20 years following Melton and Irwin's paper seems to bear out, by and large, their interpretation. Thus in what came to be the accepted interpretation of interference phenomena, called *two-factor theory* or simply the *interference theory of forgetting,* both the factors of response competition and unlearning-recovery were thought to play a role. In more recent years other ideas have been put forward to account for interference phenomena and to challenge two-factor theory, but as yet none has gained general acceptance (see Postman & Underwood, 1973).

RESEARCH

Methodologies

Attention. The basic methodology in studies of attention requires imposing some information overload on the human. This technique is borrowed from engineering, where it is quite common: For example, metal alloys are placed in large hydraulic presses and then placed under great pressure until they fail. Of course, a gentler method of imposing overload is mandated when humans are the objects of study.

Since channel capacity is based upon rate of information flow, there are two ways to impose excess information load. First, we can increase the rate at which successive stimuli impinge on the organism. As the time between successive stimuli decreases it becomes progressively more difficult for the organism to keep up with the incoming information flow. Second, we can increase the number of things the organism is required to do at the same time. Even though the component tasks may be well within available channel capacity, the combination of tasks can easily exceed it.

These two general categories of overload can be broken down into many more specific techniques called *paradigms*. While each paradigm has been originated in hopes of answering some general question about attention, there has been an unfortunate tendency in both memory and information-processing research for these paradigms to become autonomous. Thus, we become so concerned with the paradigm itself that we sometimes forget why it was devised in the first place—a clear case of not seeing the forest because the trees are in the way. In this section we will explain some typical paradigms: how they got started, what we know now, and some representative experiments.

Memory. Contemporary studies of memory usually employ experimental techniques that, as in the study of information processing, overload the cognitive system. However, rather than overload parts of the system responsible for the initial perception of information in the first few hundred milliseconds after it is presented, stimuli in memory experiments are typically presented under fairly leisurely conditions, to ensure that the perception of the stimuli is accurate. The memory system is overloaded by presenting more information than can be perfectly recalled or recognized so that the experimenter can examine the effect of independent variables on the number (or proportion) of items correctly recalled or recognized. It is less common for time measures to be used in memory than information processing, but some recent studies have measured recognition

speed (Sternberg, 1966) and speed of recall (Roediger, Stellon, & Tulving, 1977).

There are numerous ways to measure memory, but all involve some form of recall or recognition. In tests of recall, people are required to reproduce material to which they have been exposed; while in recognition tests, material is presented to people and they are required to judge whether or not they have seen it previously. It is common to distinguish among three types of recall tests: serial recall, free recall, and paired-associate recall. In a *serial recall* task people are required to recall information in the same order as presented to them, while in *free recall* the order of information is irrelevant. People are free to recall the information in any order they want. In *paired-associate recall* individuals are presented with pairs of items, such as *cracker-balloon,* and at recall they are usually given the left-hand member of the pair (*cracker,* called the stimulus) and asked to recall the right-hand member, the response. There are other types of cued recall tests besides paired-associate recall where people are given cues for material they are to remember. For example, following presentation of sentences, people may be given the subjects of the sentences and asked to recall the objects. In other cases they may be given associative cues that were not in the set of study material to determine whether or not the cue will aid recall (e.g., *table* may be provided as a cue for *chair,* which appeared in the list).

Recognition tests are generally of two types. *Forced-choice* recognition tests are multiple-choice tests. Several alternatives are presented, and the person's task is to select the correct one. In yes/no tests people are given the original material they studied mixed in with a number of new but generally similar alternatives. They examine each alternative and decide *yes* or *no* as to whether or not it was a member of the set they were to remember. Forced-choice recognition tests are generally preferred to yes/no tests because the problem of guessing is more easily taken into account.

Recall and recognition tests are usually seen as tapping quite different aspects of performance. However, recently some researchers have viewed the recognition situation as essentially a cued recall situation where the "cues" are very strong. (They are called *copy cues,* since they are copies of the original material that was experienced.) In this section we will illustrate some of the methods that have been briefly outlined here with experimental examples on several different topics.

Animal Studies

Studies of information processing in organisms other than humans are rare, although many of the concepts applied in the study of animal learning resemble those applied to information processing in humans (see Sutherland & Mackintosch, 1971). The parallels between the study of animal and human memory are more direct, although a good part of the research with lower organisms is concerned with discovering the neurophysiological underpinnings of memory.

One issue that has been hotly investigated is the nature of a consolidation process that is thought to be necessary for learning. Consolidation generally refers to perseverating neural activity or time-dependent biochemical changes of some other sort that promote learning after some experience. If some abrupt physiological insult occurs to the organism shortly after some experience, the neural trace may not consolidate, and thus the experience will be forgotten. The forgetting exhibited by people who have had concussions from an accident for events that occurred just prior to the accident may be attributed to a failure of consolidation. Forgetting of prior events in such situations is referred to as *retrograde amnesia.*

Consolidation processes have been studied in animal memory for some years. A typical procedure is to train mice or some other animals on a passive avoidance task. A mouse is placed on a platform, and if it steps off it receives a shock from an electrified grid. Thus the animal learns to avoid the shock by not making a response and by remaining on the platform. In experiments investigating consolidation, animals are given a single trial in a passive avoidance situation and then are given electroconvulsive shock (ECS) from electrodes attached to their ears, at varying intervals after stepping down off the platform. If the shock were to disrupt the consolidation process, the animals should show poor retention of the response when tested later, relative to controls who were not given the electroconvulsive shock. Further, the forgetting should be greater the sooner the ECS occurs after the animal steps down. These are exactly the findings that have been reported (see McGaugh & Dawson, 1971, for a review).

It is also possible to produce such retrograde amnesia by giving an animal certain drugs soon after learning some experience. In fact, if a learning trial is simply followed by a relatively innocuous but unexpected or surprising event, animals will show forgetting of the preceding experience (Wagner, Rudy, & Whitlow, 1973). Thus, as with humans (e.g., Tulving, 1969), retrograde amnesia can be produced in animals by following an event to be learned with an unusual or surprising stimulus.

It was originally thought that the retrograde amnesia produced by ECS indicates a failure of learning or storage on the part of the organism. However, some more recent work has indicated that the memories which seem "lost" after ECS can sometimes be recovered with the passage of time or by providing a reminder stimulus, such as the foot shock that animals received when stepping down from the platform (Miller & Springer, 1973). Similarly, following concussions people often gradually recover their forgotten memories. What this recovery may indicate is that the amnesia produced by ECS may not be due to a disruption in the process of storing information through consolidation, but may rather be due to a disruption in retrieval of stored information. This general viewpoint represents a convergence between researchers studying human and animal memory; forgetting appears to be attributable in many situations to retrieval failures rather than failures in learning and storage (see Spear, 1978, for a detailed review of these issues in studies of both animal and human memory).

Human Studies

Dichotic Listening. In this paradigm, two different messages are presented, one to each ear. This is similar to listening to stereophonic high fidelity, with the important exception that the two messages in dichotic listening are independent, whereas they are closely related in stereophonic listening. The messages themselves can be almost anything: words, sentences, digits, musical tones, and so on. This task requires the listener to follow the information presented in one ear,

despite the simultaneous input of different information in the other ear.

At first, this may seem a strange task that has but little relationship to anything outside the laboratory. After all, people seldom go about with earphones on their heads tuned to two different stations. But this task was originally developed because of observations outside the laboratory and before formal models of attention were well advanced. Broadbent (1954) started his research on dichotic listening because he was concerned with a very practical problem: How could air traffic controllers monitor conversations with several pilots at the same time? When all the messages came over the same loudspeaker it was quite difficult for the controller to hear only one pilot without confusion. If you have never been an air traffic controller you may find it hard to appreciate this difficulty. However, all of us have been at noisy parties where the same attentional effect occurs. Imagine yourself at a party, engrossed in conversation with an attractive member of the opposite sex. Despite the loud background noises—record players, people talking, ice rattling in glasses—you can still focus in on your own conversation, at least enough for successful communication. You have been able to select a single message out of the set of all messages that could be heard at the party. This is precisely the same task faced by an air traffic controller: selecting one message from an ensemble.

Broadbent (1958) solved this practical problem by using more than one loudspeaker, so that each pilot was associated with a specific location. This made it much easier for the air traffic controller who had to attend to a specific pilot, because he could locate the pilot's voice in a particular location. But Broadbent did not stop there. Instead, he went on to ask why that solution proved to be helpful. Broadbent postulated a hypothetical filter device that removes unwanted messages. How did the filter work? Basically, it selected some incoming channel on the basis of a physical characteristic of the stimuli, like its location in space or the frequency characteristics of the voice. Several predictions of this model have been made and tested.

First, the more similar the characteristics or channels of two or more messages, the harder it should be to filter out the unwanted ones. So, for example, if one voice is male (with low auditory frequencies) and the other is female (with high frequencies) it should be easier to follow one and reject the other, compared with the same voice (with a different message of course) in each ear. This prediction was supported by experimental results.

Other predictions fared less well. In the most common variant of the dichotic listening paradigm, listeners must repeat aloud or *shadow* one message: This assures the experimenter that the listener is following instructions and attending to the designated message. According to the filter model, then, information about the other channel should be filtered out and lost. But some experiments (Gray & Wedderburn, 1960) found that the filter "leaked" because unattended information could be retained if it was important; for example, if your name occurred in the unattended channel you would notice it at least part of the time. The filter model predicts you would never notice it. There were some attempts to explain this within the filter model by allowing the filter to switch rapidly back and forth between two channels, but these efforts ultimately were unsuccessful.

A series of dichotic listening studies carried out by Treisman (1960, 1969;

Treisman & Fearnley, 1971; Treisman & Geffen, 1967) did much to convince researchers that the filter was really an attenuator: that is, instead of completely eliminating rejected channels all it did was to weaken them. We shall examine one typical study. In a shadowing experiment, Treisman (1960) presented a passage from ordinary text to one ear and word sequences based upon statistical approximations to English on the other. These sequences were meaningless combinations of words. Individuals were instructed to shadow the ear containing prose. However, during the experiment the two messages would switch so that individuals were then shadowing the approximations to English. At the time of switching, intrusions from the unattended ear occurred. This indicates that the content of the unattended ear was available and that contextual cues such as the constraints of English language could override the filter mechanism. So the filter was better regarded as an attenuator rather than a switch.

Treisman's model, like Broadbent's, is part of a class of *early-selection models,* so called because the attenuator operates on an internal representation of the stimulus before making contact with memory. Unattended or weakened aspects of incoming stimuli are dropped early in the processing chain, so that selectivity begins immediately. The early-selection models compete with a class of models that assume all incoming information makes contact with memory. These *late-selection models* (Norman, 1968) easily explain the retention of information from unattended channels on the grounds that all information, attended and unattended, receives the same initial processing. In a shadowing task, the auditory repetition of the attended message is assumed to interfere with retention of other information, in much the same manner as interference causes memory decrements in learning tasks. It is too early to state which view of attention is correct; indeed, recent research has tended to blend aspects of both early- and late-selection models.

Time-sharing. Like the dichotic listening task, the time-sharing paradigm overloads the human by demanding simultaneous performance of two tasks. However, the overload is even greater than in dichotic listening because both component tasks must be performed, whereas in dichotic listening one channel usually can be ignored. Early studies of time-sharing aimed at testing the limited-capacity model generally were in agreement with its predictions. A typical study —which incidentally won an award for the best doctoral dissertation in experimental psychology that year—was conducted by Louis Herman (1965), who combined a tracking task with an auditory discrimination task. In a tracking task the subject is required to follow (or track) a moving target. Each component task had two levels of difficulty. When two difficult tasks were combined, thus exceeding channel capacity, performance suffered far more than with a combination of two easy tasks.

Quite recently, experimenters have been able to find some task combinations where difficult tasks can be performed together without the decrement predicted by the limited-capacity model. While the first of these findings was greeted with astonishment, if not outright disbelief—much like the finding in chemistry that the noble inert elements could sustain chemical reactions—there is now enough evidence to show clearly that in certain time-sharing situations the limited-capacity model is incorrect. Allport, Antonis, and Reynolds (1972) used component tasks of shadowing and sight-reading music. Sight-reading performance

was unchanged when shadowing was not required versus concurrently required. One might be tempted to dismiss this result as due to insufficient difficulty of the component tasks—that is, the capacity requirements of shadowing and sight-reading together were still within the capacity of the channel. However, Allport et al. were careful to use two levels of difficulty for sight-reading as well as for shadowing, so that this explanation of their results is unlikely. They proposed a multiple-channel model to explain their findings. Several independent processors work side by side in this model. This is an important change because it permits parallel processing. The limited-capacity channel of Broadbent was a strictly serial device, with one operation having to be completed before the next could begin.

While it is not yet clear that the whole of the channel can be duplicated in parallel, at least some parallel processing is required to explain human time-sharing behavior. Indeed, a compromise hybrid model which permits some information flow at early stages to proceed in parallel until a serial bottleneck is reached later in response-processing stages has recently been proposed (Kantowitz & Knight, 1976b).

Psychological Refractory Period. In the psychological refractory period (PRP) paradigm, the human is overloaded by presenting two stimuli in close temporal succession, that is, less than 500 msec apart. The dependent variable is reaction time, defined as the time between the onset of a stimulus and the onset of a response associated with it. The time between the two stimuli is called the *interstimulus interval* (ISI). The rationale behind the PRP paradigm is simple: Try to reduce complicated events to their basic format. Two stimuli are the absolute minimum for inducing attentional overload. It is far easier to make inferences based upon a simple task with only two stimuli than upon a more complicated paradigm like time-sharing, where many aspects of the component tasks can be confounded (Kantowitz & Knight, 1976a). Yet even with this relatively simple paradigm there is a plethora of possible explanations, as we shall see.

The basic finding in the PRP paradigm is an increase in reaction time to the second signal (RT_2) when ISI decreases. This is easily explained by the limited-capacity model. Since the channel is busy processing the first stimulus, processing of any subsequent stimulus information must be delayed because the channel is basically a serial device. Of course, if the combined load of both first and second stimuli was low and within channel capacity, no RT delay would occur, but this outcome is largely restricted to sets of Donders A reactions (see Kantowitz, 1974 for a review). The shorter the ISI, the less time is available for the channel to process the first stimulus before occurrence of the second stimulus; thus, the second stimulus must wait longer to enter the channel at shorter ISIs. This waiting inflates RT_2, which is measured from stimulus onset and not from the time the stimulus enters the channel.

It is easy to test the limited-capacity model because it makes strong predictions about the PRP paradigm. One such prediction concerns the effect of increasing the information load of the first S–R pair (by increasing the number of S–R alternatives from say, one to two to four, etc.). This should increase RT_2 by a constant amount at each increment, resulting in parallel RT_2 functions, one for each S_1–R_1 load. (See Kantowitz, 1974, Table 2 for a numerical example of this.) But when this was tested (e.g., Karlin & Kestenbaum, 1968) the difference in RT_2 as a function of member of S–R alternatives

decreased as ISI decreased, instead of remaining constant.

Other strong predictions have also fared poorly. The limited-channel model predicts that reaction time to the first stimulus (RT_1) should remain unaffected by either ISI or difficulty of the second S–R pair because the first stimulus has already entered the channel by the time the second stimulus has occurred. But a review of RT_1 effects (Herman & Kantowitz, 1970) finds that RT_1 is influenced by ISI. Indeed, if error rates are constant, RT_1 declines over ISI in a manner roughly similar to RT_2. Similarly, increasing the informational load of the second S–R pair causes increases in RT_1 (Kantowitz, 1974).

It is clear that in a PRP paradigm where the limited-channel model makes very precise predictions, the model fails. However, it should be noted that other models (to be discussed later) may appear to do better only because they are more ambiguous and do not make precise predictions. And models that do make equally precise predictions as the limited-channel model are difficult to apply to other types of overload paradigms.

Probe RT. The probe task is becoming more and more popular in the study of attention (Kerr, 1973). A reaction-time task, called the probe, is inserted at various times in relation to a primary task. This overloads the human, but only momentarily. The logic behind the probe task is simple. It is assumed that the primary task occupies some proportion of available channel capacity. Any excess capacity is thus available for probe processing. So reaction time to the probe signal is interpreted as an indicant of available processing capacity. Note that this logic assumes that capacity is not suddenly diverted to the probe task, at the expense of the primary task. An assortment of single-task-only control conditions is necessary to check on the validity of this assumption. The advantage of the probe paradigm is that it can sweep out the temporal changes in capacity demands of the primary task, since the probe stimulus can be presented during any phase of the primary task.

Posner's and Keele's study (1969) is typical of this paradigm. These researchers were interested in the attention demands of a motor response: moving to a target. They found greater probe RT for a narrow target than for a wide target and concluded that the aiming requirements of smaller targets demanded more attention. Taking advantage of the probe paradigm to sweep out attentional demands, they found a U–shaped function with elevated probe RT at the start and end of a wrist rotation. A more detailed follow-up study, Ells (1973), agreed that narrow targets gave greater probe RT but found RT to decrease continuously as the target was approached. This apparent contradiction—all the more puzzling because the two studies were conducted at the same university—was resolved by Salmoni, Sullivan, and Starkes (1976), who realized that the probability of occurrence of the probe signal was two-thirds in the Posner-Keele study and 1.0 in the Ells study. They were able to replicate both findings by varying probe probability. (However, Salmoni et al. had some other problems with their procedure; see Kantowitz & Knight, 1978, for details.)

The point of this discussion is to emphasize the dangers of the probe paradigm. It offers great potential, but investigators must be extremely careful to avoid conclusions based upon limitations of the methodology.

Modality Effects in Serial and Free Recall. Is information better if it is presented visually or auditorily? If you were required to remember in order a short list of digits presented to you, would it be better if you read them (visual presentation) or if someone else read them to you (auditory presentation) at the same rate? Would recall be better if you both saw them and heard them than if you only saw or heard them? These fundamental questions have led to much research on the effect of presentation modality on memory.

A representative study is Murdock and Walker (1969, Experiment 1). Individuals were given lists of 20 words that were to be recalled in any order (free recall). The words were presented at either a one-second or two-second rate (that is, one word presented every one or two seconds), and for some lists the words were presented visually over a slide projector while for other lists presentation was auditory via a tape recorder. After individuals studied and recalled five practice lists, they were tested on 20 more lists, with 5 lists given at each of the four combinations of modality and presentation rate. The effects of varying modality were generally the same at both presentation rates: For the first 15 of the 20 words there was not much difference in recall between having heard the lists and having seen them, but for the last 5 items recall was much better if the words had been presented auditorily than if they had been presented visually. This last finding is referred to as the *modality effect:* Immediate recall of the last few items in a series is better if the items are presented auditorily than if they are presented visually.

The same outcome is obtained when persons are given shorter lists and asked to recall the items in the order in which they were presented (a serial-recall task). Again, recall is better for the last couple of items presented auditorily, with there being little or no difference between visual and auditory presentation for the initial and middle items in the list (e.g., Crowder, 1970). The modality effect is believed to occur because auditory information lingers in the nervous system a bit longer than visual information in a relatively raw, unprocessed form. Thus, when persons recall a list after it is presented auditorily they can rely on this little "echo" to recall better the last few items in the list (Crowder & Morton, 1969). The advantage of this echoic storage, as it is called, only affects the last few items of the list because the echo of the earlier items has either faded away or been displaced by later items by the end of the list.

Thus we cannot generally conclude that "listening is better than reading," because it is only under special conditions that this is so. It is only the last few items of an auditorily presented list that are better recalled, and only when the recall test is given soon after presentation. There appear to be few long-term effects of modality of presentation. For example, when Kintsch and Kozminsky (1977) had people summarize stories after either reading them or listening to them, they found little difference in performance.

Effects of Orienting Tasks on Recall. Under Proposition 5 we discussed the levels-of-processing approach to memory, by which retention is considered to be a function of the level of processing that a stimulus receives when it is initially processed. The example of listening to words in a language one does not know very well was used to illustrate how information could be processed to different depths. One laboratory task that has been used in an attempt to capture the processing of information to different depths is referred to as the use of different orienting tasks in incidental learning (Hyde &

Jenkins, 1969). This takes a bit of explaining. In most memory experiments individuals are explicitly told that they will later be tested on the information with which they are presented (intentional learning). This condition is relatively rare in real life outside the setting of schools. We rarely "study" our experience for an explicit memory test later. Unlike the intentional learning situations that are commonly explored in memory experiments, in incidental learning paradigms people are exposed to information without being told that they will be tested on it later. Instead the material is presented under the guise of performing other tasks with it, and then the later memory test for the material comes as a surprise. The tasks used to present material to the individuals are referred to as *orienting tasks* and different orienting tasks can be chosen that are supposed to determine the level or depth of processing of the material.

An example of an experiment illustrating this logic is Craik and Tulving (1975, Experiment 2). People were told that the experiment was concerned with their speed of reaction in answering simple questions. They were shown a list of 60 words about which they were supposed to answer yes/no questions by pressing one of two buttons. The word was presented for 200 msec (1/5 of a second), and the people were required to answer the question about each word as rapidly as possible by pressing the *yes* or *no* response keys.

There were three types of questions designed to provide for different levels of processing of the words. For some words the question was simply, "Is the word in capital letters?" This defined a structural level of processing where all the participants had to do to answer the question was examine the type in which the word appeared. There was no need to process the word to deeper levels, such as ascertaining its meaning, in order to answer the question. Half the time the word would be printed in upper-case letters, the other half in lower-case letters, so that people responded yes and no equally often. For other words, participants were asked whether or not the word rhymed with a second word. They might be given the question, "Does it rhyme with weight?" and the word presented might be *crate* (a yes response) or *market* (a no response). These questions were meant to induce a phonological level of processing where participants had to at least process the sound of the words. Finally, the questions preceding other words were meant to induce people to determine their meaning. They were asked if the words would fit in a sentence such as "He met a _____ in the street." For yes responses the presented word might be *friend,* for no responses it might be *cloud.*

Each person was given 20 words in each of the three question conditions (structural, phonological, and sentence), and for 10 questions in each condition the answer was yes, while for the other 10 conditions the answer was no. One other important aspect of the procedure was that across all participants in the experiment all the words were used equally often in all six conditions (three questions with yes or no answers to each question). Thus the effects of condition were not due to there being different words in the conditions.

The effects of these different encoding manipulations were measured by a yes/no recognition test. Participants were given a sheet with 180 words on it, and their task was to go through it and circle the 60 words they had seen earlier in the experiment. The 60 target words were randomly mixed in with the 120 "lures," or distractor words. (It should be remembered that this recognition test was unexpected.) For words that participants responded yes to, the proportion correctly recognized was 0.15 in the structural condition, 0.47 in the phonemic condition, and 0.83 in the sentence condition (numbers estimated from Craik & Tulving, 1975, Figure 1). The results were similar for the conditions in which people responded no, but the differences were not as large (0.19, 0.25, and 0.49 recognized in the structural, phonemic, and sentence conditions, respectively). These results indicate that the use of different orienting tasks has a dramatic effect on the recognition of words. If people are given *table,* having just been asked "Is the word in capital letters?" they will recognize it on a later test only 15% of the time. Yet if they were presented the same word but asked if it fit in an appropriate sentence, later recognition would be 81%. While many theories of memory have little to say about the very large difference in memorability under these conditions, according to the levels-of-processing framework the words differ so greatly in their memorability because of the different depths of processing they received when they were initially studied.

State-Dependent Retrieval in Cued and Free Recall. One common tale often told about alcoholics is that they will do something while intoxicated, such as hide some money, and then not be able to recall where they hid it when they have sobered up. This is referred to as *alcoholic amnesia,* as is the more common experience of not being able to recall very well what happens while drunk. However, when alcoholics again become intoxicated, they may recall where they hid their money. This appears then to be a case of state-dependent retrieval. Experiences are better recalled when retrieval is attempted in the same state as when they were originally learned rather than in a different state. This process has been studied experimentally in both animals and humans.

An interesting representative study of state-dependent retrieval with marijuana has been reported in Eich, Weingartner, Stillman, and Gillin (1975). Participants were told that the study was concerned with the effects of marijuana on memory. They were given a cigarette to smoke prior to having their memories tested. For half the participants the cigarettes contained marijuana, while for the other half the cigarette tasted like marijuana but did not have its active ingredient (a placebo condition). After smoking, participants heard a list of 48 words, with instructions to try to remember them for a later test. The lists contained four words from each of 12 semantic categories (e.g., type of vehicle—*streetcar, bus, helicopter, train*). Participants recalled each list some four hours after it had been presented. Half the individuals who learned the words under marijuana were tested again under marijuana, while half were tested after smoking a placebo cigarette. Similarly, for placebo participants half were tested after smoking another placebo and half were tested under marijuana.

The results showed that people who studied words after smoking marijuana tended to recall fewer than those who studied them after smoking the placebo cigarette. Thus marijuana reduced recall. However, the more interesting effect is that people who both studied and recalled the list while under the influence of marijuana recalled more words than others who studied the list after smoking marijuana but who then were tested after smoking the placebo cigarette. Thus, if the list were learned while under the influence of marijuana, it was recalled better when tested under marijuana than when not. This outcome is referred to as *state-dependent retrieval.*

Other participants were treated identically to those just described, except that at recall they were tested under conditions of cued recall rather than free recall. These cued-recall participants were given the category names and asked to recall as many items as possible from the categories. Under conditions of category-name cued recall, the state-dependent retrieval effect was not found. That is, participants who studied and were tested under the influence of marijuana recalled no more words than those who studied while under its influence but who then were tested while sober. This outcome shows that powerful retrieval cues can override the state-dependent retrieval effect (see Eich, 1977, for further discussion).

IMPLICATIONS

Theoretical

It should be clear that the information-processing research described above has called into question many details about the limited-capacity channel model. The model has been the "victim" of the great amount of research it has engendered; this is a happy outcome for any psychological theory. But the most important basic assumption of the model—that behavior can be explained in terms of internal information flow—has been very strongly supported. Any arguments concern the details of the postulated flow of information within the organism.

The major change in the model has been to allow selectivity to occur at stages other than the filter (Broadbent, 1971). In particular, the major bottleneck in attention has been moved away from the stimulus or input end of the chain of processing stages towards the response or output end (Kantowitz, 1974). Some models have been offered that completely relax input restrictions by stating that early in the processing chain information can be handled in parallel (Keele, 1973). This class of model has no bottleneck in early processing stages.

Another important advance has been the realization that the postulated capacity demands of a processing stage are not independent of the configuration of the set of stages (Townsend, 1974). While it was once believed that the serial nature of the original limited-capacity model was a natural consequence of processing a finite rate of information through the channel, we now know that parallel models with limited capacity are quite feasible. Indeed, we can in certain situations create parallel models that make exactly the same predictions as other serial models. So two major items are required in any model that attempts to chart information flow through the organism. First, the arrangement of stages must be specified. This can be serial, parallel or a mixture of both (hybrid). Then the capacity demands of different stages must be defined. It will not always prove possible to distinguish particular models within a given class, and this is why information-processing research tries to limit and to compare *classes* of models. By manipulating information flow and capacity requirements, very powerful and flexible information-processing models can be obtained. This is quite appropriate, since the capabilities of the human information processor cannot easily be captured by simple theories based only upon reflexes and S–R associations.

Several important theoretical implications can also be drawn from the memory research that has been reviewed in this chapter. For many years students of memory and verbal learning have examined the effects of overt stimulus characteristics on memory. Thus, for example, numerous studies have been carried out in which such variables as word length, frequency of occurrence in English, rated meaningfulness of words, and the degree to which the word is associated with others were examined. All these stimulus characteristics and several others can be shown to affect later recall of stimuli to a greater or lesser (usually lesser) extent. One of the conclusions to be drawn from experiments such as that of Craik and Tulving (1975) is that even when all these overt stimulus characteristics are held constant by giving individuals the same words, memory can be varied quite dramatically by having persons perform different mental operations when they are presented with the stimuli. This points up the need to consider internal mental events as crucial parts of any memory theory and not just overt stimulus characteristics of the material to be learned.

Another broad theoretical message that can be presented on the basis of the research is that it is not enough simply to describe memory in terms of characteristics of memory traces. Memory traces may be strong, deep, or what have you, but recall will not occur unless there are appropriate cues in the retrieval environment to allow access to the traces of past experience. Memory is always a product of information from two sources, the memory trace and the cues in the retrieval environment.

To summarize, the research reviewed in this chapter supports three broad theoretical conclusions: First, the single-channel model of information processing has been found faulty in some respects, but the characterization of mental events in terms of information flow has proved extremely useful. Second, the nature of the mental operations used in processing information greatly affects how well it will later be remembered. Third, not just the nature of the information encoded but also the nature of the retrieval cues determine how well some fact or experience will be remembered.

Practical

A number of practical implications may be drawn from current research on information processing and memory. Understanding the nature of information processing and memory through basic research is often useful in attempts to facilitate these matters in human affairs. In today's world there is an information glut. We are being exposed to a tremendous amount of information and are expected to know more and more about complicated aspects of our world. How can we most efficiently arrange this information so that it can be best processed? What steps can be taken to remember the great quantities of information that we are expected to know? How can we design machines so that they will better mesh with the information-processing capacities of humans? This last area of applied information-processing psychology is called human factors (McCormick, 1976). In this section we illustrate some ways to improve memory and also some instances of improved human factors design derived from models of information processing.

Improving Memory. Research reviewed in this chapter has revealed two major factors that influence recall: mental operations performed when a stimulus is being learned, and the nature of retrieval cues provided at the time of test. If both these factors could be included in some way in one memory technique,

this technique should greatly aid memory. In fact, this is exactly the case in the most successful mnemonic devices or memory techniques. They encourage people to perform a useful mental operation when studying the material, and they also supply a person with a powerful set of retrieval cues for later recall. The mnemonic devices reviewed here were developed long ago on a trial-and-error basis, but they can be profitably considered in light of modern memory research. Three of the most common mnemonic devices are: the link method, the method of loci, and the peg method.

The *link method* is quite simple. Suppose you have a 20-item shopping list to remember. What you would do is take the first two items on the shopping list, say bread and milk, and form vivid visual images of them. Then you would link the images of these two objects together in some way, preferably so that the objects are interacting. For example, you might imagine a giant carton of milk standing on a large loaf of bread. (It is often advised that images will be better remembered if they are bizarre rather than mundane, but recent evidence indicates that what is important is that the images be interacting, not bizarre; see Wollen, Weber, & Lowry, 1972.) Then you would take the third object and link an image of it to the second. If the third object is eggs, you might imagine the milk carton rolling off the loaf of bread and smashing down on the eggs. You would proceed through the entire list using the same principle; each successive object should be linked to its predecessor through an interacting image. This method is known as the link method because the items are linked together in this way.

When you get to the store and want to recall the objects, you would recall the first one and then examine the mental image to see what it is linked to. (If you think you would not be able to remember even the first object, you might link it to your wristwatch or some other object that will be at the store.) Thus when you recall bread, it will be quite easy to recall that milk was next on the list, since in your image the large milk carton is sitting on the bread. When the milk topples off onto the eggs, it will serve as a cue for the next item on the list, and so on. The formation of visual images serves as a very potent mental operation for securing appropriate memory traces, while the linking of these items together through interactive images allows each to serve as a retrieval cue for the next.

The link mnemonic is a simple and effective technique that requires little practice. However, there are two drawbacks that make it somewhat less efficient than the two other techniques to be discussed. If one item in the list is forgotten, then the chain is broken and that item cannot serve as a cue for the next item. The rememberer must then be able to break back into the chain of images at some other point. Thus the link method depends on recall of past items to guarantee good cues for recall of additional items. Another difficulty with the link method is that people are required to recall the items in order. If you wanted to know the 15th item on the list, you would have to go through the first 14 to get to it. The case would be similar if you wanted to recall items 10 through 20; you would first have to recall items 1 through 10.

The other two mnemonic devices, the method of loci and the peg method, do not suffer from both these drawbacks, but they do involve a greater initial investment in terms of learning the method. Both these methods, like the link method, are founded on the use of mental imagery

and effective retrieval cues. The *method of loci* has already been briefly discussed in the Propositions section. In order to use this device you must first choose a path that is known very well and that has a number of discrete locations. For example, you might select the path used in walking to school and attending classes every day, or a path in your neighborhood, or a set of locations in a house or some other familiar building. The important points are that the path chosen be one that will not be forgotten, and that it has a number of discrete, easily identifiable, locations.

The trick to the method of loci is that when learning some material, such as the 20-item shopping list, each item should be converted into an image and deposited in the discrete location as you mentally walk down the path. Thus if you wanted to remember bread, milk, and eggs as the first three items, you would mentally imagine yourself walking down the path and, in the first three locations that you came to, depositing an image of the appropriate object. You would continue in this fashion until you had deposited all the objects. Then when you got to the store and wanted to recall the objects, you would again mentally imagine yourself walking down the path and looking in each location for the appropriate object. This technique may sound farfetched, but it is really quite effective. If you practiced it you would see how easy and efficient it really is (Bower, 1970). Notice that in this case if you forget one item in the list (you cannot "see it" at the proper location) this would not prevent you from recalling the next item, as in the link method. However, it would still be difficult to call out the 15th item without mentally walking along the path to recall the first 14. The method of loci is quite effective since the locations on the path that serve as the retrieval cues are not in danger of being forgotten, thus supplying more or less permanent cues, while the traces of items in the locations are made retrievable by the operation of mental imagery.

The *peg method* is quite similar to the method of loci and operates on the same principles. One must invest an initial amount of time in learning a series of pegs that will later serve as retrieval cues in the same way that locations do in the method of loci. There are a great number of peg systems, with a range of up to 1,000 pegs that can serve as retrieval cues. One of the simplest peg systems is based on rhymes for the numbers 1 to 20. The first few are "one is a gun," "two is a shoe," "three is a tree," "four is a door" and so on. You can make up your own, or see Bower and Reitman (1972) for a list of 20. After this list has been learned perfectly, then you can use it for remembering additional information. Again consider the hypothetical grocery list. If the first item is bread, you would form an interacting image between a loaf of bread and the referent of the word that rhymes with one, that is gun. Thus you might imagine a gun shooting a loaf of bread. Similarly, for milk you might image a shoe stuffed into a milk carton. This would continue until every item in the shopping list had been associated to an image of the object that rhymed with a number. When it is necessary to recall the list, there is a set of retrieval cues in the form of the numbers 1 to 20 that are in no danger of being forgotten, and the rhymes to those numbers which have been learned to perfection. Thus to recall the first item, you need to recall that "one is a gun" and then "look at" the image of gun to see what the gun is shooting. The process is the same for recalling the other items in the list.

Once again, the effectiveness of the mnemonic device depends on the use of interactive imagery and the provision of excellent and relatively permanent retrieval cues. The peg method does not depend for its success on recall of previous items, as does the link method, and also with the peg method it is possible to recall a particular item out of order. If the 15th item were desired, one could find the rhyme for 15, then look up the appropriate image.

Mnemonic devices are quite effective for remembering large amounts of information, especially if the information is concrete and one can easily form images of the material (see Paivio, 1971, Chap. 6 for further discussion). These devices can also be made to work for abstract material, but with this sort of material it will take longer to create the appropriate images (Paivio, 1969). Other types of mnemonic systems, many of which are simply variations on the methods already discussed, have been devised to aid recall of faces and names, dates, playing cards and other useful stimuli. One of the better practical books on these methods is Lorayne and Lucas (1974).

Human Factors. We have briefly referred to one important human factors area that has greatly benefited from information-processing research: air traffic control. Broadbent's original discovery that traffic controllers could perform much better when the voice of each pilot came from a separate loudspeaker was only the start of a great deal of applied research. The basic principle of human factors is that it is far more efficient and economic to redesign machines to interface smoothly with people than to train people to deal with poorly designed machines. In order to optimize the person-machine interface we must know enough about human information processing to tell the equipment designer what forms of information input and control or response output are most convenient for the operator. Then systems can be designed to meet these criteria. Even though the machine may be slightly more complicated as a result of human factors analysis, the entire person-machine system will operate better and more reliably.

A simple example shows how the memory capability of the aircraft controller was artificially improved by human factors. In early air traffic control systems the operator had a radar screen on which each airplane was represented only by a dot. In order to match dots to aircraft in the sky, the controller would order sharp maneuvers—such as a 90° turn—that would show up clearly on the radarscope. Sometimes this sharp maneuver would place two aircraft in potential conflict. In modern systems every commercial aircraft has a beacon that sends out a coded signal. The radar screen identifies planes by the label sent from the beacon. This greatly reduces the memory load imposed on the controller, allowing the safe control of more aircraft.

Another problem area in air traffic control concerns the approach to the landing runway. While it is the pilot's responsibility to keep the plane at the proper altitude during descent, it is nevertheless standard procedure for the controller to warn the pilot if it descends below the glide path. In order to do this, the radar screens also display the planes' altitude. However, research on attention has indicated that the more things we make the controller keep track of, the more likely is channel capacity to be exceeded. In the past, accidents have occurred because pilots have literally flown planes into the ground—this is called a "controlled descent into terrain" in pilot jargon, to distinguish it from a crash

where the pilot could not control the plane—without being warned by controllers. The usual response to criticism of the controller is a reply that altitude is the pilot's responsibility. A more helpful approach has been to augment the radar display so that whenever a plane descends below a critical altitude it automatically starts to flash on the radar screen. This immediately gets the controller's attention so that the pilot can be quickly warned.

Human factors research extends into more prosaic areas of life, such as the design of a bathroom fixture. We know from information-processing research that people find it difficult to combine different sources of information. Yet when you take a shower you often must do this. To obtain a desired temperature you must adjust the volume of hot and cold water sources separately. Newer shower controls have a single dial that rotates to control temperature and shifts up and down to control volume. Instead of having to integrate two separate sources of water (and information), this control permits simple decisions about temperature and volume to be made independently.

SUMMARY

Inferring the flow of information and the transformations effected during this flow within the organism is difficult. Yet the richness of behavior and in particular the adaptability of the human information processor demand no less than this kind of effort. The search for mental events in psychology goes back a long way. Its rejection by early behaviorists was appropriate because the tools for such a mentalistic adventure were poorly formed and improperly used. Now our technology and theory have matured to the point where the pursuit of mental events is a proper scientific topic.

We have seen that the life of an information-processing model is relatively short. Such sturdy models as the limited-capacity channel are already under major attack. This is a tribute to the vigor and amount of research such models have engendered. Once the more obvious aspects of behavior have been tested and confirmed, it is only natural to proceed to finer and finer details that eventually modify or even reject the model that started all the research. Thus, the logic and basic conceptual framework of the information-processing approach is more important than any one single model. Efforts to characterize the information flow inside the organism have greatly expanded our ability to understand and to predict human behavior in complex situations that are not easily analyzed within either traditional or neo-behavioristic learning theories. The refinements of chronometric analysis, levels of processing, and other endeavors have just begun.

ANNOTATED BIBLIOGRAPHY

Anderson, J. R., & Bower, G. H. *Human associative memory.* Hillsdale, N.J.: Lawrence Erlbaum Associates, 1973.

In this thorough presentation of the associative theory of memory, the history of associationism is traced and a new computer simulation model (HAM, for Human Associative Memory) is developed. It is applied to a number of experimental situations, from memory for word lists to more complex processes such as sentence memory and question answering.

Broadbent, D. E. *Decision and stress.* New York: Academic Press, 1971.

This is an advanced graduate treatise which traces the development of Broadbent's 1958 limited-capacity model. Each chapter starts with a concise statement of the position in 1958 and then reviews recent research efforts. The implications of this research for the model are discussed in detail, and the model is thereby substantially revised and updated.

While the book is valuable for the theoretical framework erected to house these new data, it is even more useful as an exercise in scientific logic. It shows how information-processing approaches utilize data to modify models and mechanisms. The interaction between data and model is made clear. The reader comes to appreciate that any static picture of the current state of information-processing research is incomplete; what is important is the method of attacking problems.

Crowder, R. G. *Principles of learning and memory.* Hillsdale, N.J.: Lawrence Erlbaum Associates, 1976.

This is one of the more comprehensive textbooks in the field, appropriate for advanced undergraduates or graduate students. A variety of topics is considered in some depth, including sensory memory systems, short-term memory systems, and different aspects of long-term memory and forgetting. One chapter is devoted to nonverbal memory, but most are concerned with verbal memory. A number of distinct theoretical approaches are considered; separate chapters consider the interference theory of forgetting, organization of memory as reflected in free recall, serial organization in memory, and retrieval processes.

Kantowitz, B. H. (Ed.). *Human information processing: Tutorials in performance and cognition.* Hillsdale, N.J.: Lawrence Erlbaum Associates, 1974.

This text is designed to serve beginning graduate students. Each chapter is carefully developed, with minimal assumptions about the reader's background. There is heavy emphasis on methodology. The topics are arranged in a continuum starting with human performance and progressively becoming more cognitive; the final chapter is on computer simulation of thought. Intervening chapters discuss the interpretation of reaction-time data within an information-processing framework, double stimulation and attention, mathematical models of capacity and serial versus parallel processing, cognitive representations of serial patterns, and the perception of printed English.

Kintsch, W. *The representation of meaning in memory*. Hillsdale, N.J.: Lawrence Erlbaum Associates, 1974.

This is an advanced treatment of a number of topics concerned with the processing and remembering of information from prose texts. Basically it contains a statement of Kintsch's influential work and the experimental work that has been done to test and to evaluate his theory. Parts of the book were written in conjunction with students who aided in the research. Although by design it presents a rather partisan approach, it does survey a generous number of interesting problems and presents a good deal of experimental work.

Melton, A. W., & Martin, E. D. *Coding processes in human memory*. Washington, D.C.: V. H. Winston, 1972.

This collection of chapters considers many different aspects of human memory. The contributors are all well known for their work in cognitive psychology, and several of the chapters serve as surveys of their work. Authors of other chapters have chosen to present a statement of some theoretical position or viewpoint. One theme of the book, as the title implies, is how information that is to be remembered is coded in memory. The chapters are uniformly well written, and this book allows the interested student to examine a variety of topics concerned with memory as approached by some of the most influential theorists in the field.

Posner, M. I. *Chronometric explorations of mind*. Hillsdale, N.J.: Lawrence Erlbaum Associates, 1978.

This book describes the author's research program over many years in which the mind is studied by analyzing the time course of internal information flow. Attempts are made to relate human performance and physiological techniques. The book starts with an interesting review of the history of mental chronometry. Later topics are processing systems, coordination of codes, psychological pathways, alertness, conscious attention, and orienting. It concludes with a discussion of implications of this style of research for practical areas like reading, development of intelligence, and personality.

REFERENCES

Allport, D. A., Antonis, B., & Reynolds, P. On the division of attention: A disproof of the single channel hypothesis. *Quarterly Journal of Experimental Psychology*, 1972, *24*, 225–235.

Anderson, J. R. Arguments concerning representations for mental imagery. *Psychological Review*, 1978, *85*, 249–277.

Atkinson, R. C., & Shiffrin, R. M. Human memory: A proposed system and its control processes. In K. W. Spence & J. T. Spence (Eds.), *The psychology of learning and motivation: Advances in research and theory* (Vol. 2). New York: Academic Press, 1968.

Baddeley, A. D. The trouble with levels: A reexamination of Craik and Lockhart's framework for memory research. *Psychological Review*, 1978, *85*, 139–152.

Bower, G. H. Analysis of a mnemonic device. *American Scientist*, 1970, *58*, 496–510.

Bower, G. H. Mental imagery and associative learning. In L. W. Gregg (Ed.), *Cognition in learning and memory*. New York: John Wiley & Sons, 1972.

Bower, G. H., & Reitman, J. S. Mnemonic elaboration in multilist learning. *Journal of Verbal Learning and Verbal Behavior*, 1972, *11*, 478–485.

Broadbent, D. E. The role of auditory localization in attention and memory span. *Journal of Experimental Psychology*, 1954, *47*, 191–196.

Broadbent, D. E. *Perception and communication*. New York: Pergamon Press, 1958.

Broadbent, D. E. *Decision and stress*. New York: Academic Press, 1971.

Craik, F. I. M., & Lockhart, R. S. Levels of processing. A framework for memory research. *Journal of Verbal Learning and Verbal Behavior*, 1972, *11*, 671–684.

Craik, F. I. M., & Tulving, E. Depth of processing and retention of words in episodic memory. *Journal of Experimental Psychology: General*, 1975, *104*, 268–294.

Crowder, R. G. The role of one's own voice in immediate memory. *Cognitive Psychology*, 1970, *1*, 157–178.

Crowder, R. G. *Principles of learning and memory*. Hillsdale, N.J.: Lawrence Erlbaum Associates, 1976.

Crowder, R. G., & Morton, J. Precategorical acoustic storage (PAS). *Perception & Psychophysics*, 1960, *5*, 365–373.

Donders, F. C. Over de nelheid van psychische processen. *Tweede Reeks*, 92–120. Trans. W. G. Koster in Koster (ed.), Attention and performance, II, *Acta Psychologica*, 1969, *30*, 412–431.

Ebbinghaus, H. *Memory: A contribution to experimental psychology*. New York: Dover Publications, 1964. (Originally published, 1913.)

Eich, J. E. State-dependent retrieval of information in episodic memory. In I. M. Birnbaum & E. S. Parker (Eds.), *Alcohol and human memory*. Hillsdale, N.J.: Lawrence Erlbaum Associates, 1977.

Eich, J. E., Weingartner, H., Stillman, R. C., & Gillin, J. C. State dependent accessibility of retrieval cues in the retention of a categorized list. *Journal of Verbal Learning and Verbal Behavior*, 1975, *14*, 408–417.

Ells, J. G. Analysis of temporal and attentional aspects of movement. *Journal of Experimental Psychology*, 1973, *99*, 10–21.

Erdelyi, M. H., & Becker, J. Hypermnesia for pictures: Incremental memory for pictures but not words in multiple recall trials. *Cognitive Psychology*, 1974, *6*, 159–171.

Estes, W. K. Memory, perception, and decision in letter identification. In R. L. Solso (Ed.), *Information processing and cognition: The Loyola Symposium*. Hillsdale, N.J.: Lawrence Erlbaum Associates, 1975.

Garner, W. *The processing of information and structure*. Potomac, Md.: Lawrence Erlbaum Associates, 1974.

Garner, W. R., Hake, H. N., & Ericksen, C. N. Operationism and the concept of perception. *Psychological Review*, 1956, *63*, 149–159.

Gray, J. A., & Wedderburn, A. A. Grouping strategies with simultaneous stimuli. *Quarterly Journal of Experimental Psychology*, 1960, *12*, 180–184.

Herman, L. M. Study of the single-channel hypothesis and input regulation within a continuous task. *Quarterly Journal of Experimental Psychology*, 1965, *57*, 37–46.

Herman, L. M., & Kantowitz, B. H. The psychological refractory period effect: Only half the double-stimulation story? *Psychological Bulletin*, 1970, *73*, 74–88.

Hyde, T. S., & Jenkins, J. J. Differential effects of incidental tasks on the organization of recall of a list of highly associated words. *Journal of Experimental Psychology*, 1969, *82*, 472–481.

Kantowitz, B. H. Double stimulation. In B. H. Kantowitz (Ed.), *Human information processing*. Hillsdale, N.J.: Lawrence Erlbaum Associates, 1974.

Kantowitz, B. H., & Knight, J. L. On experimenter-limited processes. *Psychological Review*, 1976, *83*, 502–507. (a)

Kantowitz, B. H., & Knight, J. L. Testing tapping timesharing, II: Auditory secondary task. *Acta Psychologica*, 1976, *40*, 343–362. (b)

Kantowitz, B. H., & Knight, J. L. Testing tapping timesharing: Attention demands of movement amplitude and target width. In G. E. Stelmach (Ed.), *Information processing and motor control*. New York: Academic Press, 1978.

Karlin, L., & Kestenbaum, R. Effects of number of alternatives on the psychological refractory period. *Quarterly Journal of Experimental Psychology*, 1968, *20*, 167–178.

Keele, S. W. *Attention and human performance*. Pacific Palisades, Cal.: Goodyear, 1973.

Kerr, B. Processing demands during mental operations. *Memory & Cognition*, 1973, *1*, 401–412.

Kintsch, W., & Kozminsky, E. Summarizing stories after reading and listening. *Journal of Educational Psychology*, 1977, *69*, 491–499.

Kolers, P. A. Remembering operations. *Memory & Cognition*, 1973, *1*, 347–355.

Kosslyn, S. M., & Pomerantz, J. R. Imagery, propositions, and the form of internal representations. *Cognitive Psychology*, 1977, *9*, 52–76.

Lorayne, H., & Lucas, J. *The memory book.* New York: Stein & Day, 1974.

McCormick, E. J. *Human factors in engineering and design* (4th ed.). New York: McGraw-Hill, 1976.

McGaugh, J. L., & Dawson, R. G. Modification of memory storage processes. In W. K. Honig & P. H. R. James (Eds.), *Animal memory.* New York: Academic Press, 1971.

McGeoch, J. A. *The psychology of human learning.* New York: Longmans, Green, 1942.

Melton, A. W., & Irwin, J. M. The influence of degree of interpolated learning on retroactive inhibition and the overt transfer of specific responses. *American Journal of Psychology,* 1940, *53,* 173–203.

Miller, R. R., & Springer, A. D. Amnesia, consolidation, and retrieval. *Psychological Review,* 1973, *80,* 69–79.

Murdock, B. B., & Walker, K. D. Modality effects in free recall. *Journal of Verbal Learning and Verbal Behavior,* 1969, *8,* 665–676.

Nelson, T. O. Repetition and depth of processing. *Journal of Verbal Learning and Verbal Behavior,* 1977, *16,* 151–172.

Norman, D. A. Toward a theory of memory and attention. *Psychological Review,* 1968, *75,* 522–536.

Paivio, A. Mental imagery in associative learning and memory. *Psychological Review,* 1969, *76,* 241–263.

Paivio, A. *Imagery and verbal processes.* New York: Holt, Rinehart & Winston, 1971.

Paivio, A. Neomentalism. *Canadian Journal of Psychology,* 1975, *29,* 263–291.

Posner, M. I. Abstraction and the process of recognition. In G. H. Bower & J. T. Spence (Eds.), *The psychology of learning and motivation* (Vol. 3). New York: Academic Press, 1969.

Posner, M. I. *Chronometric explorations of mind.* Hillsdale, N.J.: Lawrence Erlbaum Associates, 1978.

Posner, M. I., & Keele, S. W. Attention demands of movements. *Proceedings of the XVII Congress of Applied Psychology.* Amsterdam: Zeitlinger, 1969.

Postman, L., & Underwood, B. J. Critical issues in interference theory. *Memory & Cognition,* 1973, *1,* 19–40.

Pylyshyn, L. N. What the mind's eye tells the mind's brain: A critique of mental imagery. *Psychological Bulletin,* 1973, *80,* 1–24.

Roediger, H. L., Stellon, C., & Tulving, E. Inhibition from part-list cues and rate of recall. *Journal of Experimental Psychology: Human Learning and Memory,* 1977, *3,* 174–188.

Roediger, H. L., & Thorpe, L. A. The role of recall time in producing hypermnesia. *Memory & Cognition,* 1978, *6,* 296–305.

Salmoni, A. W., Sullivan, S. J., & Starkes, J. L. The attention demands of movements: A critique of the probe technique. *Journal of Motor Behavior,* 1976, *8,* 161–169.

Shannon, C. E., & Weaver, W. *The Mathematical theory of communication.* Urbana: University of Illinois Press, 1949.

Spear, N. W. *The processing of memories: Retention and forgetting.* Hillsdale, N.J.: Lawrence Erlbaum Associates, 1978.

Sternberg, S. High-speed scanning in human memory. *Science,* 1966, *153,* 652–654.

Sternberg, S. Memory scanning: Mental processes revealed by reaction time experiments. *American Scientist,* 1969, *57,* 421–457.

Sternberg, S. Memory scanning: New findings and current controversies. *Quarterly Journal of Experimental Psychology,* 1975, *27,* 1–32.

Sutherland, N. S., & Mackintosh, N. J. *Mechanisms of animal discrimination learning.* New York: Academic Press, 1971.

Taylor, D. A. Stage analysis of reaction time. *Psychological Bulletin,* 1976, *83,* 161–191.

Townsend, J. T. Issues and models concerning the processing of a finite number of inputs. In B. H. Kantowitz (Ed.), *Human information processing.* Hillsdale, N.J.: Lawrence Erlbaum Associates, 1974.

Treisman, A. M. Contextual cues in selective listening. *Quarterly Journal of Experimental Psychology,* 1960, *12,* 242–248.

Treisman, A. M. Strategies and models of selective attention. *Psychological Review,* 1969, *76,* 282–299.

Treisman, A. M., & Fearnley, S. Can simultaneous speech be classified in parallel? *Perception and Psychophysics,* 1971, *10,* 1–7.

Treisman, A. M., & Geffen, G. Selective attention: Perception or response. *Quarterly Journal of Experimental Psychology,* 1967, *19,* 1–17.

Tulving, E. Retrograde amnesia in free recall. *Science,* 1969, *164,* 88–90.

Tulving, E. Cue-dependent forgetting. *American Scientist,* 1974, *62,* 74–82.

Tulving, E., & Pearlstone, Z. Availability versus accessibility of information in memory for words. *Journal of Verbal Learning and Verbal Behavior,* 1966, *5,* 381–391.

Tulving, E., & Thomson, D. Encoding specificity and retrieval processes in epi-sodic memory. *Psychological Review,* 1973, *80,* 352–373.

Underwood, B. J. Interference and forgetting. *Psychological Review,* 1957, *64,* 49–60.

Wagner, A. R., Rudy, J. W., & Whilow, T. W. Rehearsal in animal conditioning. *Journal of Experimental Psychology Monograph,* 1973, *97,* 407–426.

Watson, J. B. Psychology as the behaviorist views it. *Psychological Review,* 1913, *20,* 158–177.

Wollen, K. A., Weber, A., & Lowry, D. Bizarreness versus interaction of mental images as determinants of learning. *Cognitive Psychology,* 1972, *3,* 518–523.

Yates, F. A. *The art of memory.* Chicago: University of Chicago Press, 1966.

11

Observational Learning: Bandura

CORNELIUS J. HOLLAND AND AKIRA KOBASIGAWA

INTRODUCTION

Overview

The central enterprise of contemporary psychology has been the search for the causes of human behavior. Much of the effort toward this end has been directed to the investigation of what and how stimuli from the external environment are connected to response capacities of the organism, or to investigation of the essential internal impelling forces which cause animals and humans to behave the way they do. The former approach has commanded the attention of much of learning theory, while the latter has preoccupied those who search for instincts, traits, and so on as the major explanatory factors. Both of these positions are limited in scope, according to Albert Bandura (1977a, 1978), and can be characterized as unidirectional determinisms, in that the major determining forces act in a single direction only. Environmental determinists such as B. F. Skinner (see Chapter 5 of this text) maintain that behavior is controlled by outside forces impinging upon an organism which has a capacity to react and be formed by external events. Personal determinists, in contrast, hold that in-

ternal events in the form of instincts, drives, traits, and so on impel the organism to behave in fixed ways which constitute the formed personality. Although the formation takes place in an environment, it merely serves to modify the impelling forces without developing them or transforming them in any essential way.

An alternative traditional position is *interactionism,* a position which recognizes the importance of internal *and* external influences, of personality factors as well as the environment as contributing determinants. However, within the interactionistic position are wide differences of opinion as to how the interaction of the inner and the outer takes place, and this contact has been conceptualized in three fundamentally different ways. One way is to construe the person and the environment as independent entities which combine in various manners to effect the behavior product. This can be schematically represented by the familiar

$$B = f (P, E).$$

This represents the idea that behavior is a function of independent personal variables and independent environmental variables.

A second way of conceptualizing the

interactionist position is to view the person and environment as interdependent rather than independent causes of the behavior effect. This is schematized as:

$$B = f\,(P \rightleftharpoons E).$$

This underlies the assumption of much factorial design research in which behavioral measures are analyzed to determine how much of the variance in behavior is due to personal characteristics, how much to situational variations, and how much to the effect of the interaction of both jointly. This conceptualization is criticized by Bandura because it reduces behavior to a by-product of the interaction but does not recognize that the behavior itself enters as an integral part of the causal process.

The third way of construing interactionism is to conceptualize behavior, personal determinants, and the environment as an interlocking system of mutual or reciprocating influences. In considering these three major sources of determinants no single one is given a preeminent status over the other two, although in specific situations any one may emerge as the dominant influence. Bandura calls this, his own position, *reciprocal determinism,* and conceives of the determining influences as probabilistic in nature, rather than inducing inevitability. It is schematically represented by:

$$(B \underset{\longleftrightarrow}{\overset{P}{\longleftrightarrow}} E).$$

In reciprocal determinism, human behavior is a function of learned antecedent and consequent determinants. Each set of determinants contains variables which are largely, but not exclusively, cognitive in nature. These cognitions come about through the observation of the consequences of the person's own behavior and/or the observation of others. Thus two major sources of learning are response consequences (learning by doing), and what has been traditionally studied under the various labels of imitation, vicarious processes, modeling, or observational learning (learning by observing).

Cognitions are central in Bandura's theory of human functioning. They are considered symbolic representational systems, usually taking the form of thoughts and images. Cognitions are both controlling of and controllable by the person's behavior and the environment.

Antecedent determinants of behavior are those complex influences which occur before the behavior takes place; they include physiological and emotional variables, cognitive events such as expectations and anticipations, and inborn mechanisms of learning. Consequent determinants include reinforcements or punishments which can be external in nature, internal, or self-induced.

Reciprocal determinism therefore is a complex and comprehensive empirically derived theory of human behavior which concerns itself with both broad and narrow issues of human functioning, gives due recognition to the mutuality of internal as well as external events, and attempts to provide testable hypotheses about the complex interdependence of inner states, outer conditions, and the person's own behavior. The major issues to which such a theory addresses itself have important implications for understanding human nature and human learning.

Although Bandura's theory in its most recent form touches upon a wide range of psychological and philosophical problems, the narrower focus of this chapter will be a discussion of his theory of observational learning and a review of pertinent studies. In this section we will present four major issues that must be dealt with by any comprehensive theory of observational learning, and definitions of basic concepts in the area.

Major Issues

According to Bandura (Bandura, 1971; Bandura & Walters, 1963), one of the major issues for any adequate theory of learning is to answer the question: How does a person learn a new response in social situations? One answer is that a person is rewarded whenever approximations to the final response are made. While there is evidence suggesting that virtually all forms of social behavior may be acquired through this operant shaping procedure, research reports also show that people can learn new responses by merely observing other people's behaviors. These other people are technically known as *models,* and the acquisition of responses through such observation is called *modeling.* The major issue for a theory of observational learning, then, is to explain the acquisition of new responses as a result of observing another person.

A second issue for any theory of observational learning is to explicate the person's capacity that mediates the observation of a model's responses and the subsequent performance of these behaviors by the observer. In social learning, an individual does not have to perform overtly the model's responses during the acquisition phase, nor do rewards have to be given either to the model or to the observing person. Furthermore, overt evidence that an observed response has been acquired may not appear for days, weeks, or even months (Bandura, 1971). Therefore, the issue addresses the question of whether a response-reinforcement analysis is sufficient to account for the phenomena described above or whether

the observer's capacity to encode, store, and retrieve information about modeled responses must be included in a theory of observational learning.

A third issue is related to the selective aspect of observational learning. For example, even though children are exposed to the same model, some children will learn different features of the model's behavior. A comprehensive theory of observational learning must explain not only how patterns of responses are acquired, but also why some aspects of the model's responses are attended to and retained by an observer, while other aspects are not (Bandura, 1971).

This selective aspect is also seen during the actual performance of what has been learned observationally. As will be illustrated later (see Methodologies), children know what the model has performed, but they may not always show that knowledge by their behavior (Bandura, 1965). Under what conditions does a person reproduce modeled responses? Which one of the observationally learned responses does an individual want to perform? A comprehensive theory of observational learning must deal with the question of what motivational factors regulate selective performance of observationally acquired behaviors (Bandura, 1971). In summary, there are four major issues in the area of observational learning: *novelty, capacity, selectivity,* and *motivation.* (See also Kuhn, 1973.)

Basic Concepts

Three basic interrelated mechanisms underly much of Bandura's position: (1) vicarious, (2) cognitive, and (3) self-regulatory processes. The significance of vicarious processes can best be illustrated with Bandura's own words: "Virtually all learning phenomena resulting from direct experiences can occur on a vicarious basis through observation of other people's behavior and its consequences for the observer" (Bandura, 1976, p. 392). This means observational learning may explain, for example, irrational fears of objects about which the person has no direct experiences. Further, this type of learning may be an indispensable necessity for learning complex skills, large components of which cannot be acquired through trial-and-error learning, such as driving a car or performing a surgical operation. Finally, many behaviors which society considers important areas of concern, such as altruism or violence, can best be understood by incorporating the observational learning process as an explanation of the presence or absence of these qualities.

The second mechanism is the cognitive process. Inferred symbolic representations of external events are necessary to explain observational learning phenomena and to explain the great versatility found in human functioning. These cognitive processes are important in human learning generally. According to Bandura (1976), research demonstrates that "behavioral changes produced through instrumental conditioning, classical conditioning, extinction and punishment are largely cognitively mediated" (p. 392).

The third mechanism is the self-regulatory process. In Bandura's words, "Persons can regulate their own behavior to some extent by visualizing self-generated consequences, with the many changes accompanying conditioning operations explained in terms of self-control processes rather than direct S–R linkages" (Bandura, 1976, p. 392). This notion of self-direction is a natural and necessary extension of the manner in which Bandura conceptualizes the nature and function of cognitive processes as they trans-

form and are transformed by experiences which arise as the person behaves in the external environment.

Much of Bandura's research career has been spent in elucidating the role of these three processes, especially vicarious or observational learning, to explain human behavior. The major focus of this chapter will be on observational learning with tangential reference to symbolic and self-regulatory processes.

HISTORY

Beginnings

People have always known that many behaviors, social and otherwise, are acquired through imitation and observational learning. As Aristotle long ago said, "imitation is implanted in man from childhood, one difference between him and other animals being that he is the most imitative of living creatures, and through imitation learns his earliest lessons" (Butcher, 1922, p. 15). The main developments in the conceptualization of imitation, briefly summarized here, provide a contemporary context for Bandura's work on observational learning. More extensive and critical reviews of theories or hypotheses pertaining to imitation may be found elsewhere (Bandura, 1971; McLaughlin, 1971; Miller & Dollard, 1941; Parton, 1976).

Instinct. During the latter half of the 19th century and the beginning of the present one, *instinct* was an important concept used by psychologists to explain many social behaviors. In reflecting this importance, theorists of this period (e.g., Bagehot, 1873; McDougall, 1908; Tarde, 1903) regarded imitative behavior as an innate tendency to copy the behaviors of others. Walter Bagehot, for instance, called children "born mimics" (1873,

p. 101). In time, however, instinct theory came under increasing challenge as psychologists became dissatisfied with its value as an explanation capable of experimental verification.

Classical Conditioning. In rejecting the instinct theory, attention then turned to the issue of how the first imitative response occurs, a problem of *learning to imitate.* E. B. Holt (1931), as an example, attempted to explain how imitative behavior begins. An infant's vocalizations stimulate his or her own ears, which send a distinctive excitation along the auditory nerves to the central nervous system. After some repetitions of this process, the specific impulses the sound elicits will acquire a synaptic connection with the motor nerves going out to the same muscles used in producing the sound. A reflex-circle is established, and, subsequently, the infant begins to repeat some of the sounds he or she makes and hears. When this process is well established, the infant then repeats some of the sounds that other people utter. Imitation is thus a copying response based on the reflex circle.

The purpose of Holt's theory is to explain how the human infant acquires the ability to imitate a model's behavior through the principle of classical conditioning, as interpreted by Edwin Guthrie's (1952) contiguity theory (see Chapter 3 of this text). The classical conditioning theory of imitation, however, is limited by its failure to explain why people sometimes do not imitate behavior (i.e., the issue of selectivity; see Miller & Dollard, 1941) and its failure to account for the acquisition of responses not already in the observer's repertoire (i.e., the issue of novel responses; see Bandura, 1971).

Instrumental Conditioning. It appears that the first systematic attempt to investigate imitation occurred with the publication of *Social Learning Theory* by Neal Miller and John Dollard (1941). This work offered a Hullian interpretation of the development of imitative tendencies (see Chapter 4 of this text). Miller and Dollard studied a form of imitation called *matched-dependent behavior.* In their typical experiments, children watched a model choose one of two boxes containing candy (reward) and then made their own choice. Half of the children were rewarded whenever they matched the choice of the model, while the remaining children were rewarded when they did not imitate. Through this procedure, they established that the children could be selectively trained to imitate or not imitate a model's behavior. Furthermore, they showed that this acquired tendency could generalize to other models and new tasks. Learning is viewed in this analysis, just as in the associationistic analysis (i.e., Holt), in terms of the formation of links between social stimuli and matched responses. Unlike the associationistic position, however, reinforcement is emphasized as the factor determining which of the model's behaviors will be imitated.

Miller and Dollard's concern was not restricted to the problem of learning to imitate. They note, "It is certain that in both child and adult life, imitation is a means to many important types of learning. Athletes pick up new points on form, new tricks of play, by watching other athletes. Experimentalists pick up apparatus hints by watching mechanics at work" (1941, p. 210). Thus, these two theorists recognized the likelihood that a person may acquire, through imitation, responses not already in the behavior repertoire. They did not, however, specify *how* imitation might become a mechanism for the acquisition of the new responses.

Although Miller and Dollard's book

contains many thought-provoking hypotheses, it stimulated only a few studies (e.g., McDavid, 1959; Wilson, 1958). It took 20 years longer before imitation became an important theoretical and research problem. A major theme of the investigation of imitation shifted from the analysis of learning to imitate to that of *learning by observation,* which addresses itself centrally to the issue of the acquisition of novel responses.

Major Theorists

Albert Bandura has contributed most to the current resurgence of interest in imitative learning. Bandura's early experiments are summarized in his Nebraska Symposium paper entitled "Social Learning through Imitation" (1962). He also collaborated with Richard Walters (Bandura's first Ph.D. student) on *Social Learning and Personality Development* (1963). These two publications became a major impetus for the considerable production of theoretical and research papers on imitation during the next decade.

The treatment of imitative processes in Bandura and Walters (1963) was fresh and unique in several ways. First, they identified three different consequences of exposure to a model. An observer may (1) acquire a new pattern of responses (observational learning effect), (2) strengthen or weaken the inhibition of responses (inhibitory and disinhibitory effect), or (3) display previously learned responses by using the model's behavior as a cue (social facilitation effect). Bandura and Walters argued that theories of imitation based solely on reinforcement principles (e.g., Miller & Dollard, 1941) are inadequate to account for these diverse modeling effects. Further, they demonstrated that imitative processes play a significant role in the development

of a wide variety of social behaviors, including aggression, sex-typed behaviors, and standards for self-evaluation. Finally, Bandura and Walters broadened the scope of imitative learning. Traditionally, imitative behavior was equated with mere "mimicry." Contrary to this common assumption, they showed that the observer child abstracted general rules underlying the model's specific responses and was able to solve entirely new problems by applying observationally acquired rules to new situations. They also demonstrated that the observer exhibited novel and innovative behaviors on the basis of imitative processes by selecting and combining different aspects of different models.

Bandura and Walters made a distinction between *acquisition* and *performance* of imitative responses. During the early 1960s, these investigators were mainly concerned with identifying important determinants of imitative *performance.* These determinants included characteristics of models (nurturance vs. nonnurturance), types of modeled behaviors (task-oriented vs. incidental behaviors), and consequences of model's responses (vicarious reward vs. vicarious punishment). The mechanisms required for observational learning (i.e., acquisitions) were not analyzed systematically at this time. Bandura (1962) pointed out, however, that two representational processes, *imaginal* and *verbal,* are important for observational learning to occur. This proposition resembles one made by F. E. Sheffield (1961; see also Lumsdain, 1961).

Unfortunately, Walters died in 1968 in the midst of his highly productive career. Bandura, however, continued to broaden and refine his theory and specified the mechanisms underlying observational learning in three subsequent publications: *Principles of Behavior Modification*

(1969), *Psychological Modeling: Conflicting Theories* (1971), and *Aggression: A Social Learning Analysis* (1973). According to this expansion of the theory, observational learning involves four interrelated subprocesses, each with its own determinants. For observational learning to be properly assessed, a person must: (1) attend to relevant features of a model's actions (*attention process*), (2) then retain the observed events in some symbolic forms for future retrieval (*retention process*), (3) have the physical capabilities to reproduce the retained information (*motoric reproduction process*), and finally (4) be motivated to perform the modeled behavior (*motivational process*).[1]

Current Status

Bandura's conceptualization of observational learning is only one of the components of his social learning theory. Currently, he is articulating a comprehensive and unified theory of human behavior. He is attempting to effect a major reinterpretation of broad areas of psychology, especially learning theory, by encouraging psychologists, through tight reasoning and empirical evidence, to appreciate the central and pervasive influences of observational learning, cognition, and self-regulating activities. Re-

[1] About the time Bandura analyzed observational learning in terms of these four subprocesses, Aronfreed (1969) proposed a similar theory of imitation. Aronfreed also emphasized the role of cognitive representational processes in observational learning. In this theory, the observer's representation of modeled responses is called a *cognitive template*. Aronfreed's theory differs from Bandura's with respect to the following assumption: During observation, Aronfreed holds, pleasurable and aversive affective states are conditioned to cognitive templates. Overt performance of observationally acquired behavior is assumed to be controlled by this affective component.

cently major statements of a theoretical nature (e.g., self-efficacy and reciprocal determinism) are being made at an accelerated pace, each presenting a demonstration of the power of the observational learning model to synthesize and predict behavior (Bandura, 1977a, 1977b, 1978). These statements are the fruition of ideas cultivated through many years of thought and carefully programmed research, and many of the matured ideas can be found implicitly in earlier works on observational learning phenomena (e.g., Bandura & Walters, 1963).

On a more practical level, Bandura is making efforts to apply his model to the areas of clinical, developmental, and social psychology. Applications of principles of social learning theory to psychotherapy have already been made (Bandura, 1969, 1977a). Applications to social psychology and cultural anthropology are in incipient stages (Bandura, 1977b). The theory as presented to date is congruous with current aspects of psychology, both naturalistic and experimental, and so compatible with current developments that it must be considered a preeminent resource for research possibilities. It is likely that in the not too distant future, this theory will receive even more recognition from students undertaking theses and dissertations as well as research psychologists.

Other Theories

While for the past 15 years Bandura's theory of social learning has been most influential in the area of observational learning, alternative approaches (as Miller & Dollard, 1941) specify reinforcement as a necessary condition for imitative learning to occur. One difficulty confronting a reinforcement theory of imitation is its need to explain why people perform imitative responses that have not been explicitly reinforced (Bandura, 1971).

In attempting to resolve this difficulty, Donald Baer and his associates proposed a hypothesis that appeared to favor the response-reinforcement analysis of imitation (Baer, Peterson, & Sherman, 1967; Baer & Sherman, 1964). If a child receives extrinsic reinforcement for imitating a model's behavior, the similarity between the behavior of the model and the behavior of the child will eventually acquire secondary reinforcing properties. Because the similarity has become reinforcing in its own right, other imitative behaviors will become prevalent, even though they are not reinforced explicitly. These investigators have demonstrated through research that children produce nonrewarded imitative behavior as long as other imitative responses are extrinsically rewarded. Their studies ostensibly provide a clear demonstration of the role of reinforcement in controlling and maintaining children's generalized imitation.

Other research findings are available, however, which cast doubt on this conclusion (e.g., Bandura & Barab, 1971; Steinman, 1976). Explanations of nonreinforced imitation in terms of secondary reinforcement present at least one difficulty, according to Bandura (1971). If behavior similarity is inherently rewarding, as Baer maintains, then people should imitate all types of behaviors. In reality, however, people seem to imitate other people selectively.

A second explanation also consistent, at least in part, with the operant model was advanced by Milton Rosenbaum (Rosenbaum & Arenson, 1968). According to this view, the analysis of how a child learns to imitate in the first place is a necessary prerequisite for our understanding of how that person later becomes able to learn by using imitative skills (i.e., observational learning). The child will become, Rosenbaum holds, a selective "imitative organism" through the imitation-reinforcement process. A child who becomes this imitative organism may then show instances of apparently nonrewarded imitation. Thus, occurrences of nonrewarded imitation are dependent on past extrinsic reinforcements. Rosenbaum recognizes that there are occasions in which an imitative organism cannot overtly perform modeled responses immediately. Under such situations the person performs "covert imitations," mainly verbal representations, that guide subsequent overt imitative performance (a similar hypothesis was advanced in Maccoby, 1959).

This hypothesis is similar to Bandura's in that Rosenbaum introduces the notion of mediational processes to account for the occurrence of observational learning in the absence of external practice. Rosenbaum differs from Bandura, however, with respect to one of the major issues of observational learning, namely, how people acquire novel responses. According to Rosenbaum, a person cannot acquire a novel behavior solely through covert imitation or observational learning, as Bandura maintains. Instead, novel skilled acts like golfing must first be performed overtly, then followed by extrinsic reinforcement. They can never be acquired through observation alone.

Bandura's theory has not gone without direct challenge. Perhaps the most detailed critique has been presented by Jacob Gewirtz (Gewirtz, 1971; Gewirtz & Stingle, 1968). Bandura rejects contemporary S–R reinforcement positions because they overlook the fact that people can learn a great deal, in the absence of overt practice and extrinsic reinforcement, merely by observing sequences of behavior displayed by other people. Gewirtz feels uncomfortable in concluding that this really demonstrates the learning of new responses. He says this conclusion is not possible because the entire past learning history of persons is not known in typical experiments purporting to demonstrate the acquisition of a novel response. Instead, learning through observation can be considered more appropriately a special case of instrumental conditioning in which the presence of a model and the model's action facilitates the observer's previously learned response, rather than occasioning new ones. It is also possible, Gewirtz holds, that the observer may have acquired a response class of imitative behavior across various modeling situations. Within the response class of imitation, behaviors are functionally equivalent because they have resulted in extrinsic reinforcement in the past and because they have been matched to the model's responses. Since the response class as a whole is maintained by extrinsic reinforcement on an intermittent schedule (i.e., only a portion of the responses is reinforced), some of the imitative behaviors are performed even though they themselves do not receive reinforcement. The use of a concept of a response class in this manner accounts for the occurrence of nonreinforced imitation.

In answer to Gewirtz's statements, Bandura argues that we can certainly bring about an observer's previously learned instrumental responses by using a model. But bringing about a previously acquired behavior by this means is called *social facilitation* (see Propositions 9 and 11), and this is not the same as the issue of novelty (Bandura, 1971).[2] The im-

portant issue for a theory of observational learning, according to Bandura, is to examine how a person acquires new responses observationally, not to examine how already learned responses are facilitated. Instead of controlling for all possible past imitative learning experiences, Bandura typically uses such novel verbal stimuli as "estosmacko," which his subjects have never heard prior to his experiments. Not only is it unnecessary to control for all possible past learning, but Bandura (1971) even questions whether knowledge about conditions associated with early imitation is useful for explaining later observational learning. Children may want to learn different models and different behaviors at different developmental stages. Therefore, the determinants of early imitations may provide an insufficient or even a misleading explanation of how modeled responses are later acquired.

PROPOSITIONS

1. *Much of human learning is cognitive.*

Humans, like other animals, learn motor responses to environmental situations. But humans also have the capacity to acquire symbolic representations of

---

[2] Both Gewirtz's and Holt's theories have been criticized by Bandura on the grounds that they are mainly concerned with social facilitation. These theories, however, address themselves to an important developmental problem, the origin of imitation. The available empirical data strongly suggest that imitation during the first six months of life is virtually social facilitation. That is, infants can imitate only well-practiced actions available in their own response repertoires (e.g., McCall, Parke, & Kavanaugh, 1977). As a result, if we are interested in the problem of the origin of imitation, we must deal with the question of how infants come to aquire the capacity to copy the model's responses that are within their response repertoires (social facilitation). A scholarly review of imitation theories concerning this problem is available (Parton, 1976).

external events, and this allows the vastly superior variability and flexibility of human behavior compared with the behavior of infrahuman species.

These symbolic representations, or cognitions, include language systems, images, and musical and numerical notions. Their value to the behaving person depends on the close correspondence of the symbol system with the external events to which they refer. If the correspondence is close or exact, the symbol arrangements provide close or exact approximations to the physical operations to be performed in the environment. For example, covert operations of numerical notations give the same result as arranging the objects in space. Two objects that are arranged four different times will give the same outcome as the symbolic codes which represent the number 2, the number 4, and the arithmetic rule for multiplications.

Once cognitions are developed, they become major factors in areas of functioning, such as perception, problem solving, and motivation. They enter into the process of determining which external events will be observed and which will be ignored, how external events will be perceived, and whether or not any lasting impressions of these events are made. They enter into the problem-solving behavior of humans and the construction of novel solutions. And finally, they enter into the motivational process by providing incentives and sanctions not immediately present in the physical environment.

2. *One major source of human learning is response consequences.*

When a response occurs it leads to some consequence, either positive, negative, or neutral, which exerts influences on the behavioral repertoire of the person. The influences can be threefold: Consequences occasion (1) information, (2) motivation, and (3) reinforcement.

Information. The informational nature of response consequences provides the person with the opportunity to construct hypotheses concerning which behaviors will result in successful outcomes under specific conditions. This hypothesis-constructing function which information provides serves as a guide to future action based on the probabilities developed for different behaviors. The child, for example, perceives a parent smiling and laughing. Past behaviors of requesting a cookie under these conditions often met with success. The hypothesis developed by the child, even though perhaps not able to be articulated, is that under these circumstances a successful outcome is highly probable. The request is made and the cookie is refused, let us say, because the time is too close to dinner. This additional information is incorporated into the hypothesis concerning the request, and so forth. The environment, therefore, is continually supplying information through response consequences under different conditions which modify hypotheses concerning probabilities of success or failure.

Motivation. A second function of response consequences is motivational in nature. Information already acquired can become an incentive condition for behavior in the present through anticipations and expectations, even though an incentive condition is not immediately present in the physical environment. For example, some response in the past has led to an unsuccessful outcome, a punishment of some type. The symbolic representation of this outcome by anticipation can exert a negative sanction and control the response, even though the punishing agent or situation is not immediately present in the physical environment.

Reinforcement. The third function of response consequences is to increase or decrease the frequency of the prior response. This is an area of major controversy which Bandura has with many adherents of instrumental (operant) conditioning. Psychologists unanimously agree that consequences strengthen or weaken responses. It is the nature of the strengthening and weakening process which generates dispute. One of the working assumptions generally made in instrumental conditioning in human as well as animal studies is that consequences exert their influence or control automatically and mechanically. Awareness of the response-consequence connection, although perhaps present, does not contribute intrinsically to the strengthening or weakening operation, appearing instead as epiphenomenon. Bandura believes that at least with humans, the effects of consequences are mediated so much by cognitive structures that any instances of an automatic effect can be better understood within a framework that recognizes mental activities rather than within one that eschews them.

For example, in one experiment (Kaufman, Baron, & Kopp, 1966) three groups of persons were placed on identical variable-interval schedules of reinforcement (a reinforcement occurring on an average of one a minute) for a manual response. Each group, however, was given different information about performance-reward contingencies. One group was given correct information about the schedule, while one of the remaining groups was misinformed that behavior would be reinforced exactly every minute (a fixed-interval schedule) and the other that reinforcement would occur after 150 responses on the average (a variable-ratio schedule). Differences in response rates show that performance was influenced more by beliefs about the schedule than by direct experience. It is Bandura's contention that the cognitive mediators (in this case belief about reward) exert major influences in most reinforcement situations.

3. *A second major source of learning is through observation.*

A great deal of human behavior has been acquired by watching what other people do and what happens to them when they do it. Many of the most important acquisitions, such as language, cultural rules, attitudes, and many emotions, can be better explained by the process of observational learning than by successive approximations to these acquisitions by trial and error or by direct experience. Bandura does not deny the effects of trial and error or direct experience learning, but many complex acquisitions such as surgery do not permit a trial-and-error procedure, and many fears and attitudes are acquired not through direct contact with the object but rather vicariously. Indeed, social learning theory maintains that at least for humans, observation is the major source of learning in contemporary culture, in which the environment is preeminently symbolic.

In studying observational learning, Bandura has identified four processes to explain the completed learning event: (1) attention, (2) retention, (3) motor reproduction, and (4) motivation. A failure in observational learning lies in a deficiency in one or more of these components, each governed by different principles.

The first process is *attention*. The mere

presence of a model will not influence the observer unless the observer attends to it in some manner. There must be some degree of input of the modeling stimuli for observational learning to occur.

The second process is *retention*. The material to be observationally learned must be symbolically coded and stored, at least for the length of time it takes for the observed response to occur.

The third process is *motor reproduction*. A person may attend sufficiently to a model's behavior and adequately retain the coded stimuli, but if the motor capacity is not adequate, the behavior cannot be reproduced.

The fourth process is *motivation*. Proper incentive conditions must be present for the acquired response to be performed. This merely means that attention, retention, and motor reproduction may be quite sufficient; a response may be acquired, retained, and able to be performed, but unless there is reason for doing so, it will not become overt.

A distinction between acquisition of a response and the performance of it is necessary because responses can be learned through observation, but they may never be made manifest unless performance conditions are sufficient. Of the four processes, attention and retention are mainly concerned with acquisition, while motor reproduction and motivation are mainly concerned with performance. Each of these four components is influenced by many factors, to be discussed more fully in Propositions 4-7 below.

4. *The attention process is influenced by the model, the observer, and incentive conditions.*

Attention to a model is controlled by many factors. Whether an observer will perceive the model's behavior accurately, attend to the model closely, or select properly the relevant cues will depend on characteristics of the model, characteristics of the observer, and motivational states.

A major influence of the model on the attention of an observer is interpersonal attractiveness, such as warmth, nurturance, or acceptance. Another important factor is the model's perceived competence and the related variables of perceived status or social power. Other factors which seem to exert an influence are similarities in age, sex, and socioeconomic levels.

However, under virtually the same conditions of modeling stimulation (e.g., the same degree of model competence or social power), some observers display higher levels of learning than others. This variation seems to be due to observer characteristics such as dependency, level of competence, socioeconomic status, race, and sex, as well as previous social learning experiences such as being rewarded for imitating.

Incentive conditions have also been found to have influences on the attentional process in that they can enhance, impede, or channel looking or observing responses. Some forms of observational learning such as television are so intrinsically rewarding that attention may be controlled for many hours at a time.

5. *The retentional process is aided by coding and rehearsal.*

For sensory registration to be retained, it must be symbolically coded. Once coding has occurred, retention can be enhanced by various rehearsal strategies.

Symbolic coding can be either imaginal or verbal, but the latter seems to account more for explaining the speed in acquisition and the long-lasting retention found in observational learning among humans. Visual information transformed into verbal codes allows for a great deal of information to be readily stored and made accessible for retrieval.

Rehearsal operations are also important factors facilitating retention. They serve to strengthen and to stabilize the acquisitions and can be either overt or covert. The facilitation effects of rehearsal on retention, however, seem to be due more to an *active* process than to mechanical repetition. Indeed the benefits of rehearsal often seem to be due more to an active reorganization of the events of the response to be learned, an active self-induced symbolic transformational process, than to a mere associative strengthening due to repetition of the elements acquired.

6. *The motor reproductive process involves images and thoughts to guide overt performance.*

The images and thoughts acquired through observational learning can act as internal stimuli analogous to the external stimuli which the model provides. These internal cues provide the basis upon which responses are selected and organized at the cognitive level. Any manifestation of actual behavior guided by the acquired codes is dependent on motor skills being available to the person. If the motor requirements are not fully available, as in the case of multicomponent skill development, the deficient components must first be developed by observation and practice. Furthermore, even if all the components of the skill are available, corrective adjustment of initial efforts usually must be carried out.

7. *The motivational process is influenced by (1) external reinforcement, (2) vicarious reinforcement, and/or (3) self-reinforcement.*

Learning that has taken place through observation will manifest itself in overt behavior, depending on the presence of necessary incentive conditions. Observation of others is an extensive human enterprise, with countless instances in which the behavior of others is coded and retained. Those learned responses that are likely to result in some direct external positive consequence will be manifested overtly, whereas those that lead to neutral consequences or that are negatively sanctioned may not be translated in behavior.

Another condition favorable to the acquisition's being performed is the observation of another person being reinforced for the behavior; conversely, the observation of another person's being punished leads to behavioral suppression. Thus major motivational factors are occasioned by vicarious reward or punishment.

Finally, modeled behavior may become manifest or inhibited in the absence of external sources of influence. In these self-regulating processes, the person experiences covert reinforcement or punishment based on evaluations of his or her own behavior, compared to standards that have been assimilated through observation (Bandura & Kupers, 1964).

8. *Response information in observational learning is conveyed through physical demonstration, words, or pictures.*

Acquisition of responses can result from observation of a model performing live actions in the environment. Physical demonstrations most commonly account for children's imitation of their parents' behavior and adoption of like-sex characteristics, peculiarities, skills, and so on. With the acquisition of verbal skills, words often become the most important way of transmitting information about responses to be modeled. Pictorial representation of a model's behavior is another important source of information, especially through the media of television and films. Attitudes, emotional responses, and new patterns of behavior have been conveyed through electronic media; this form of model transmission promises to become increasingly influential, and it is increasingly a matter of concern.

Alhough the basic modeling process is the same whatever the means of transmission, the different forms are not equally effective in conveying information for all response acquisition requirements. Physical or pictorial demonstration can convey far more information than verbal descriptions. For other tasks, verbal codes may contain more information than live action or media demonstration, depending on the level of verbal development and the cognitive prerequisites of the task. Further research is required to determine the optimum mode of transmission of response information for different types of tasks and different developmental levels.

9.   *Exposure to a model may produce different effects.*

Exposure to models can produce at least three different effects on observers' behaviors. Although all phenomena to be discussed here are frequently subsumed under the term *imitation,* it is important to distinguish among the three different effects because each involves a different process.

First, the observer may acquire novel responses by watching others' behavior.

A novel response is one not available to the observer prior to the modeling situation; thus it has a zero probability of occurrence under ordinary stimulus conditions. Most novel responses used in typical experimental situations are composed of elements already available to the observer due to previous learning. These elements are, however, recombined to bring about the novel patterns of response. This is called the *observational learning effect.*

The second effect of modeling stimuli is to strengthen or weaken the inhibition of responses already available to the observer. *Inhibitory effects* result in situations in which the observer reduces a response tendency as a result of watching punishing consequences to the model. In one of Bandura's studies (Bandura, Ross, & Ross, 1963), for example, preschool children who initially watched an aggressive model being punished showed relatively few aggressive behaviors. *Disinhibitory effects* may be seen when the observer increases performance of generally inhibited behavior following the observation of rewarding consequences to the model. Bandura and his associates (e.g., Bandura, Grusec, & Menlove, 1967) have shown that a well-established fear of dogs (inhibition of approach response) can be eliminated by exposing fearful children to peer models who show positive interactions with a dog. Many of the children in the 1967 study reduced their fear through this procedure and consequently were willing to stay alone in a room with the formerly feared object.

The third effect of observation of a model is to bring forth a response already available in an observer's repertoire. This *social facilitation effect* is distinguished from observational learning in that no new response is acquired. It is also distinguished from disinhibition in that it does not involve elimination of fear or inhibition.

10. *Observational learning is a major source of rules or principles.*

One of the most important roles of observational learning is the acquisition of rules or principles which go beyond the specific responses observed. What occurs is an abstraction of common elements of the model's behavior which can be applied appropriately to situations in which the observer has never seen the model behave. Specific features of a model's behavior are observed, coded, and applied in ways which show more than what would occur if the process were mere mimicry. This ability to extract and apply features which are not limited to the specific modeling stimuli is the basis for the tremendous versatility and flexibility of human behavior. The process, called *abstract modeling* or *higher-order forms of observational learning,* is central to the development of the grammatical rules of language.

Some of the factors affecting the acquisition of rule behavior are the complexity of the rule being acquired, differential feedback which occurs when the rule is applied appropriately or inappropriately, and referents which concretely illustrate the rule.

11. *Observational learning is a major source of creative behavior.*

Creative expression is influenced when the observer is exposed to different models. Most often modeled behavior is not restricted to what has been observed; instead it is the result of a combination of features from various models which leads to responses that differ from any of the original individual sources. The more di-

verse and the more numerous the models, the more likely is the response product to be innovative. For example, children exposed to the same parental models acquire different features from both parents which are then combined in different ways, leading to personality characteristics which are dissimilar from those of either parent. Children exposed to extended family members, especially if these members are not part of a homogeneous subculture, will likely exhibit even more innovative patterns of responses.

Creative endeavors such as literature or painting can be seen as a developmental progression of the artist combining, recombining, and discarding features from various models, achieving some measure of synthesis, incorporating new features from a more recent model, and continuing until at the highest levels of accomplishment the artist approaches a seeming uniqueness.

RESEARCH

Methodologies

Typical observational learning experiments can be illustrated by summarizing the classic investigation (Bandura, 1965). This study asked two major questions:

1. Do children learn aggressive behavior from a model regardless of whether the model receives reward or punishment?
2. Do children spontaneously imitate or reproduce observed aggressive acts more frequently when the model is rewarded than when the model is punished?

Four- to six-year-old children individually watched a televised film in which a male adult model demonstrated four different types of "novel" aggressive acts toward an adult-size Bobo doll. Toward the end of the film, one group of children observed the model being rewarded by a second adult ("You are a strong champion,") while the other group observed the model being punished ("Hey there, you big bully, if I catch you doing that again, I'll give you a hard spanking."). Following this phase of the experiment, the children were then taken to a playroom and were left alone with the same Bobo doll and other objects that had been used by the model. Bandura found that the different consequences that the film model experienced for his aggression were important determinants of the children's spontaneous imitative behavior. Those who saw the model being rewarded performed more aggressive behavior, both imitative and nonimitative, than those who watched the model being punished.

Does this finding mean that the children in the model-rewarded condition learned the model's aggression more than the children in the model-punished condition? To answer this question, Bandura offered the children candy rewards and asked them to recall and act out as many of the model's acts as they could. With this, the previously observed difference in the frequency of imitative aggression between the two conditions disappeared. The children in both conditions now accurately exhibited the sequence of modeled aggression equally well. The implication of these findings is that different consequences to the model influence the child's imitative *performance,* but these consequences have little effect on observational *learning,* since the children in the model-punished condition also learned the responses but did not perform them to the same extent.

As illustrated above, the basic components of the experimental paradigm in observational learning research generally are: (1) The research participant is exposed to a model engaging in some type of novel activity, and (2) the participant is tested some time later for the evidence of observational learning.

Novel Activity. The opportunity to observe a model behaving produces in the observer responses that have some resemblance to those of the model. This resemblance, however, cannot always be used as evidence for observational learning. In the experiment cited above, the children showed nonimitative aggressive acts that were not displayed by the model but presumably already existed in their response repertoires. This nonimitative aggression is the effect of either social facilitation or disinhibition in which the model's behavior serves as a cue to release the observer's already well-established responses. To attribute the behavior similarity between the model and observer to observational learning, it is important that a *novel* response pattern, one not already available, or an unusual combination of previously learned responses be used.

Assessment of Evidence. The second methodological issue concerns assessment. An observer may learn modeled responses quite well, but for some reason these behaviors may not be performed spontaneously. Learning *has* occurred, but it is not demonstrated. Such was found under the model-punished condition in Bandura (1965). Therefore, in order to assess the extent of observational learning, experimenters explicitly request the observer (as Bandura did) to emit the model's behavior sequence. However, even with this instruction young children may not conduct an exhaustive memory search, and, consequently, their recall scores may underestimate their observational learning. The younger children's retrieval deficiency may be overcome by providing more specific cues that may help them recall the observed events (e.g., "Tell me everything you have seen," vs. "What did he (the model) do with the *dart gun?* What did he do with the *Bobo doll?*")

While Bandura used a film-mediated model in the 1965 study, he used both real-life and cartoon models in other studies (Bandura, 1967). The modeled response may also be transmitted merely by using words to describe a correct sequence of responses. Typically the model is a confederate whose behaviors are prearranged by the experimenter, but this is not the basic requirement for a study of observational learning. Rosenbaum (1967), for example, used a naive model in the presence of an observer and subsequently compared the observer's degree of learning with the model's degree of learning.

Animal Studies

The question of whether animals have the ability to acquire a new response through observation of behavior is not new. Earlier researchers generally provided negative evidence for this question (e.g., Thorndike, 1911). Imitative learning in infrahuman subjects, however, has been documented by more recent researchers.

In a typical experiment, an observer rat placed in an observation chamber watches a model rat perform a visual discrimination task. The model rat may be required to approach one of two doors, differently painted, to obtain a reward. The observer rat is then transferred to the same discrimination task apparatus and is also trained to solve the discrimination learning problem. With

this method, several researchers (e.g., Groesbeck & Duerfeldt, 1971; Kohn, 1976; Kohn & Dennis, 1972) have shown that observers learn to choose the stimulus that had been positive for the model in fewer trials than control subjects not given observational experiences. The observer apparently learns, from watching the model's performance, that a particular stimulus (e.g., a door with vertical stripes) is associated with a certain outcome.

Roy John and others (John, Chesler, Bartlett, & Victor, 1968) conducted studies with cats. In their first study, an observer cat viewed a "student" cat receiving 20 training trials for a conditioned avoidance response. A buzzer was presented for 15 seconds, and shock to one foot was administered to the student cat unless a hurdle was jumped. Next, the observer cat watched a fully trained model perform the same task for 20 trials. The observer cat was then subjected to training trials until a criterion of 90% correct performances was reached. The investigators found that the observer cat learned the conditioned avoidance response much faster than the "student" cats that received a trial-and-error training method. Two of the six observer cats demonstrated almost errorless performance. In a second study, the cats were required to learn to respond to a light stimulus by pressing a lever to obtain food. Again, the observer cats learned this task with significantly fewer errors than conventionally trained cats. One of the six observer cats showed errorless performance after observing 30 demonstration trials. These impressive results led John et al. (1968) to conclude: "Observational learning may be the primary method of acquiring language, ideas, and social habits in man, and such learning may also play an important role in the adaptation and survival of lower organisms" (p. 1491). Certainly, the ability to learn to avoid aversive stimuli by viewing the avoidance behavior of the model animal, as was examined in the first study, is of survival importance.

Powerful capacity among primates to learn through observation has been documented by a number of researchers (see Hall, 1963). In one study (Darby & Riopelle, 1959), monkeys were given a long series of object discrimination problems to solve. On each problem, the monkeys had to choose one of the two objects that covered a food well containing a reward. Prior to the first trial on each problem, the monkeys observed another monkey (naive demonstrator) execute a single demonstrational trial. After approximately 150 problems, the observer monkeys became able to choose the correct object about 75% of the time on their first trial after a single opportunity to observe the demonstrator's performance. The most interesting finding of the study is that the observers' performance was more accurate when the demonstrator's performance was inaccurate. Thus, the observer monkeys were not merely mimicking the demonstrator's choice behavior in order to solve the problems; rather, as Aronfreed (1969) concluded, the observers must have used a cognitive representation of the contingencies between the model's acts and their outcomes.

In a different study (Warden, Fjeld, & Koch, 1940), an observer monkey watched a model monkey perform mechanical tasks, such as pulling a chain which hung down within easy reach of the front of a panel, raising a door, and exposing a raisin in a hole. The observer monkey then was allowed to perform the task. The experimenters reported that the observer reproduced the model's behaviors within 10 seconds on 40% of the test trials and within 60 seconds on 76% of them.

The occurrence of observational learning in natural settings has also been reported. Japanese field studies on the behaviors of monkeys not only show instances of observational learning of new behaviors but also give some idea how such new behaviors spread in a group. For example, one young female started a habit of washing sweet potatoes in a shallow stream before eating them. This habit was picked up first by siblings and other close members of the originator's family and then by other members of the group (Imanishi, 1957). On the basis of these studies, Aronfreed (1969) concluded that affective components of the observational situation are crucial determinants of the observer's attention, and the opportunity for learning is dependent on the observer's emotional attachment to the model.

Human Studies

Because it is not possible to present in this brief section a comprehensive review of existing studies on human observational learning, four topics will be selected for discussion and illustration with applicable studies. Two of the four processes hypothesized by Bandura, namely, attention and retention, will be taken up initially, followed by higher-order forms of observational learning. This is one of Bandura's unique contributions in that he has expanded the scope of imitative learning, showing that modeling effects are not restricted to mere mimicry. Bandura's observational learning theory has also stimulated applied research concerned with practical problems, as illustrated by studies concerning the influences of televised programs on children.

Determinants of Attentional Processes. A person does not attend to every event occurring in life. What are some factors that control selective attention? According to Bandura (1977b), there are at least two major variables, in addition to motivation, affecting this process. The first is associated with the model's characteristics and the second with the observer's characteristics. The illustrative studies are organized according to these two determining variables of attention.

Models who are attentive to observers' needs and who frequently reward observers will be selected, while those lacking such characteristics may be ignored. Consequently, observers should learn observationally from the former more than the latter type. In Rosenblith (1959), kindergarten children were initially given the Porteus Maze test. One half of the children then interacted with a nurturant attentive model for ten minutes, while the remaining half interacted with a model who maintained attentive behavior during the first five minutes and then withdrew attentiveness during the remaining five minutes. At the end of this period, a maze that a subject child previously failed was presented to the model, who traced it slowly and correctly. Then the child was given the same maze. This procedure was followed for several different mazes. Rosenblith also included a condition in which the children performed on the mazes without observing the model's performance. She reported that the children generally were more likely to attend to the behaviors of a model who was consistently nurturant than to a model who terminated nurturance during

the initial social interaction, and the children improved their performance on the maze tests to a greater extent under the former condition than the latter. Rosenblith also reported that children learned more efficiently through observation than through continued practice by themselves using trial and error.

In a related study, Yussen and Levy (1975) examined the hypothesis that children would attend to a nurturant model more than to a nonnurturant model. During the initial social interaction period, preschool and third-grade girls played a pegboard game with a pair of female models under one of the following three conditions: (1) a warm-neutral condition, in which one model displayed affection through physical contact and verbal exchange while the second (neutral) model avoided conversation, (b) a neutral-neutral condition, in which both models remained neutral, and (c) a warm-warm condition, in which both models displayed warm attitudes throughout the interaction period. Individual children were then asked to watch the models play a picture preference game and were invited to sit between the two models in such a way that only one model could be attended to at any one time.

Yussen and Levy found that during the picture preference test, a warm and nurturant model drew more attention than a neutral model for both age levels of children (warm-neutral condition). When both models were initially nurturant, the children were likely to divide their attention equally between them. The children were finally asked to recall each model's responses on the preference test. Attention scores and recall scores (observational learning scores) correlated +.53 for the preschoolers and +.47 for the third graders. This study, then, provided evidence for the link between attention and observational learning hypothesized by Bandura (1969, 1977b).

In this study, Yussen and Levy directly assessed the focus of their subjects' attention. Researchers sometimes use an incidental learning paradigm to infer a person's focus of attention. In reading, for example, detecting the main idea of each paragraph is a central task, but detecting different colors of printed words which compose the paragraph is irrelevant or incidental. If the person recalls more of the former than the latter, then we infer that the person attended more to the central than to the incidental features of the task, and vice versa.

Such an incidental learning paradigm was used in Ross (1966) to study observer characteristics. Ross hypothesized that high-dependent observers (assessed by their teachers) would recall incidental aspects of a model's behavior, while low-dependent observers would recall central aspects of a model's behavior. She taught preschool children how to run a post office (central task). The central task included seven responses such as giving stamps, collecting money, talking on the phone, and various regulations for processing letters. While teaching these central responses, the model displayed many irrelevant behaviors, such as taking an indirect route while walking to a mailbox and tapping a balloon while talking on the telephone. The children were then asked to teach the observationally learned behaviors to their peers. The findings showed that the low-dependent children reproduced many of those model's behaviors directly relevant to the operation of the post office but ignored incidental behaviors. In contrast, high-dependent children tended to pay equal attention to both task-relevant and task-irrelevant behaviors.

Another characteristic of the observer affecting the attention process is developmental level. Usually older children have a longer attention span than younger children. In addition, the older child may know when to attend and when not to attend to the model. This selectivity of attention is nicely illustrated in Yussen (1974). In this study, preschool and second-grade children watched a model choose a favorite object among a series of three common ones. The children were instructed to learn the model's favorite choices. Two types of attention for each child were used: One measure was based on the number of modeling trials in which the child paid attention to the modeling task at the moment when the model pointed to the child's favorite item (*frequency of attention*), and the second measure was based on the total amount of time the child spent on the modeling task (*duration of attention*). The study showed that the older children recalled the model's choices more than the younger children. Even though no age-related differences were found with the duration-of-attention measure, the older children had a significantly higher frequency of attention measure than the younger ones. The experimenter concluded from these findings:

> Apparently, the older children were capable of deploying attention in a more strategic fashion than the preschoolers. They looked more at the moments when looking had informational value but did not look for a significantly longer period of time during the entire modeling sequence. As a consequence, the older children also recalled significantly more items than the preschooler. (Yussen, 1974, p. 100)

These studies provide evidence suggesting that there is a link between attention and learning in observers, and that the attention is affected by models' characteristics as well as observers' characteristics. However, because a complete account of observational learning is assumed to depend on several interrelated processes, and because these additional processes, especially retention, were not well controlled in the studies reported, it is not entirely clear whether the findings can be explained solely by differences in attention variables. For example, a child may attend carefully to a nurturant model and at the same time rehearse the modeled behaviors, thus confounding the retentional process with attention. Enhanced observational learning in such cases cannot be attributed solely to attentional variations. Future studies should attempt to control for any effects of other processes which influence observational learning, if a direct and clear link between attention as such and observational learning is to be demonstrated.

Determinants of Retentional Processes. To account for the occurrence of observational learning in the absence of direct practice, it has been argued that the observer's symbolic representations are of major importance (Bandura, 1969). Typically, the significant role of symbolic representation in observational learning has been examined by asking the observer to describe verbally the modeled events. It is assumed that the observer's verbalizations would affect the representational process.

In an early experiment by Bandura (Bandura, Grusec, & Menlove, 1966), seven-year-old children watched a film-mediated model demonstrating a series of relatively novel patterns of behavior. The children were asked (1) to verbalize every action of the model during exposure (verbalization condition), or (2) to watch the film carefully (passive condition), or (3) to count while viewing the films (interference condition). Children who generated verbal equivalents of the

modeling stimuli subsequently recalled the model's behaviors more than children who passively watched the film. The children in the passive condition, in turn, showed higher levels of observational learning than children who engaged in interfering verbalization. This study, then, suggests that symbolization during observation enhances observational learning.

The ability to use symbolic representation should show age-related improvement. Coates and Hartup (1969) conducted a study similar to the one just described, using four- and seven-year-old children. They found that seven-year-old children spontaneously utilized symbolic mediators even under the passive condition and, consequently, the children at this age level did not benefit from further prompting by the experimenter to use symbolic activities (i.e., verbalization condition). In contrast, the verbalization condition improved the four-year-old children's performance only slightly, as compared with the passive condition. The younger children needed additional help from the experimenter in producing relevant verbalization to enhance their observational learning.

Verbal description of the observed events, utilized in the preceding two studies, is just one of several different coding operations which may be used, and which may not be the most efficient way to retain information. Evidence for differential effects of different coding operations on the retention of modeled responses is provided in Gerst (1971). In this study, college students observed a filmed model perform intricate motor responses drawn from the manual language of the deaf. After observing each of the modeled responses, the students engaged in one of the following symbolic activities: They were instructed to (1) develop summary labels that encompassed essential elements of the responses, (2) visualize the modeled responses in vivid imagery, (3) describe aloud the specific movements and positions of the modeled responses, or (4) perform arithmetic calculations designed to impede symbolic coding of the modeled responses.

In the immediate test of observational learning, students who used imaginal and summary label codes achieved higher matching scores than students who verbally described the modeled responses. In turn, the latter exceeded the level of observational learning shown by students who performed arithmetic calculations. In the delayed test, the students in the summary labeling condition were able to perform more modeled behaviors than those in the other three conditions. Thus, the Gerst study provides evidence for the hypothesis that symbolic coding operations play an important role in observational learning. At least during the immediate test, all three coding systems facilitated observational learning as compared with the control condition, in which the students did not have an opportunity to code the modeling events. The findings also support the notion that different coding systems vary in their relative efficacy in observational learning. Similar findings were reported in Bandura and Jeffrey (1973).

The findings summarized in this section may not be particularly surprising to the reader familiar with the experimental literature on verbal learning and memory. In typical verbal learning tasks, a person is exposed to a series of pictorial or verbal items during a study period and later is asked to recall what was seen. In these situations, young children do not engage in verbal rehearsal spontaneously to improve future recall (e.g., Coates & Hartup, 1969, already cited). If, however, they are instructed to rehearse

verbally recall items and then use this strategy, they are likely to improve recall performance (see Flavell, 1970). When children are told to relate learning items in a meaningful manner (as in Gerst, 1971), their recall performance will be greater than when they are instructed to rehearse (e.g., Rohwer, 1973). The studies reviewed in this section, therefore, appear to represent a direct extension of ordinary verbal learning studies to social learning situations. Perhaps what is needed is research in which the role of social factors in individuals' use of symbolic mediators is examined. A brief description of such a study may illustrate the point.

Grusec and Mischel (1966) were interested in the effect of a model's social characteristics on behaviors to be observationally learned by preschool children. The children interacted either with a highly rewarding and powerful model (the model described herself to the child as a future nursery school teacher) or with a nonrewarding and less powerful model. The model then displayed aversive behaviors (e.g., imposed delay of reward) and novel neutral behaviors. The children who initially had interacted with a rewarding and powerful model recalled her behaviors more than the children who had interacted with a nonrewarding and less powerful model. According to the investigators, these findings are consistent with the hypothesis (Bandura, 1969; Maccoby, 1959) that children pay more attention to, and engage in more rehearsal of, a powerful model because the model's behaviors are relevant to guide the plan about future actions. Studies such as this point to the importance of social factors which influence the retention process (see also Grusec & Brinker, 1972).

Higher-Order Form of Observational

Learning. In the studies reviewed thus far, the occurrence of observational learning was assessed by asking the observer to reproduce concrete patterns of modeled behavior. However, a person frequently detects a "rule" underlying such concrete behaviors of the model and subsequently generates similar patterns of behavior in different social contexts. In an experimental paradigm of this higher-order form of observational learning, an individual observes a model responding to diverse situations on the basis of a predetermined rule. Tests for the acquisition of the rule are determined later, in the absence of a model's performance, by using entirely new test items.

An early illustration of how a rule-governed behavior can be acquired through observation was provided in a study designed to modify the orientation for making moral judgments in school children (Bandura & McDonald, 1963). According to Jean Piaget (1932), there are two stages of moral orientations. In the first stage, or *objective orientation,* children judge "naughtiness" of behavior in terms of material damages rather than intentions. In the second stage, or *subjective orientation,* children judge the naughtiness of behavior in terms of its intent rather than its damage.

On the basis of pretests, Bandura and McDonald (1963) selected two groups of children: one showing predominantly objective moral judgments and the other showing predominantly subjective moral judgments. The children were then exposed to adult models who consistently made moral judgments contrary to the children's usual orientations. The modeling procedure was effective in modifying the children's judgments. Children with an objective orientation modified their moral judgments toward the subjective type, while those with the subjective orientation shifted toward the objective type. In addition, the children continued to express their revised moral orientations to new tasks in the absence of the models. Because they had not watched the model responding to the new moral judgment tasks, the findings cannot be explained in terms of mimicry of the specific responses. The children must have abstracted a general moral orientation on the basis of a series of diverse modeled responses and applied this observationally derived rule to the new tasks.

As they grow older, children are able to generate an infinite number of novel sentences that they have not heard before. This is possible because they abstract rules by which words are organized rather than memorizing specific sentences that adults produce. Bandura and Harris (1966) empirically demonstrated children's learning of linguistic rules by using the higher-order form of modeling technique. In this study, Grade 2 children were first presented with 20 familiar words, one at a time, and were told to generate a sentence for each word. This preliminary phase of the experiment was to obtain a base rate for the children's use of passive voice, one rarely used by them, such as "I am well treated by my teacher," instead of "My teacher treats me well." The model then constructed sentences with a set of new words, using the passive voice exclusively. Following this treatment phase, the children generated significantly more passives. Since different words were used for constructing sentences, the children rarely duplicated the models' verbal productions. In fact, some of the sentences reflected inventiveness. Examples would be "The tea was dranked," and "Ice are put in boxes sometimes." Bandura and Harris concluded that these findings "provide further evidence that people can acquire observationally principles exemplified in a model's behavior and use them for generating novel combinations of responses" (p. 351).

The two studies summarized in this section have been replicated by other investigators (e.g., Cowan, Langer, Heavenrich, & Nathanson, 1969; Odom, Liebert, & Hill, 1968). Furthermore, there are now many other studies in which experimenters have shown that children are able to acquire a wide variety of conceptual skills, such as Piagetian conservation (Rosenthal & Zimmerman, 1972), problem-solving strategies (Laughlin, Moss, & Miller, 1969), and creative behaviors (Arem & Zimmerman, 1976). Although a significant role of imitative processes in the development of social behavior was emphasized previously (Bandura & Walters, 1963), these studies (e.g., Rosenthal & Zimmerman, 1972) have shown that the modeling processes are also important for the development of intellectual skills. A comprehensive review of such studies is available in Zimmerman and Rosenthal (1974).

Observational Learning in Relation to TV. Do children learn aggression through exposure to aggressive models? This question has been one of primary concern in the experimental literature in this area, reflecting many people's reasonable concern about the influences of televised violence on human behavior. In typical experiments concerning this question (e.g., Bandura, 1967), preschool children were allowed to watch real-life, film-mediated, or cartoon models displaying aggressive verbal statements and novel aggressive acts toward an inflated plastic Bobo doll. The children were then left alone in a room with toys while their verbal and motor behaviors were observed. Since the film-mediated and cartoon models were as effective as real-life models in eliciting and transmitting aggressive responses in these studies, Bandura concluded that "televised models may serve as important sources of behavior" (1967, p. 47).

Many critics, however, have questioned the validity of generalizing experimental findings about television and violence, on the grounds that experimental procedures are far removed from real-life situations. First, hitting a Bobo doll represents playful activities rather than any real injury to a person or object. Second, the aggression in these studies does not have any aversive consequences for the child (e.g., punishment by teachers or parents). Third, the imitative aggression is assessed in a restricted setting, and consequently it is unclear whether or not the child will generalize the behavior to other situations.

To provide more direct answers to this question, a naturalistic study was conducted by Friedrich and Stein (1973) with preschool children. During the first three weeks, these investigators obtained a baseline measure of the children's patterns of social interactions. They were then exposed to a half-hour TV program each day for the next four weeks under one of three conditions. One group watched only films with aggressive episodes ("Batman" and "Superman"), the second group saw prosocial films ("Mister Rogers's Neighborhood"), and the third group viewed neutral films. The effects of the programs were assessed by changes that occurred from the baseline to the periods during and after exposure. The investigators found that those children who were already high in aggression became more so following exposure to the aggressive films. In addition, these children became less tolerant of minor frustrations and less obedient to rules. In contrast, children who were less aggressive prior to the exposure to the aggressive films were not particularly affected by them.

Friedrich and Stein studied preschool children, but what happens with older children? Feshbach and Singer (1971) conducted a study with preadolescent and adolescent boys attending several residential schools. One group was exposed to aggressive television programs (Western movies and crime shows) over a six-week period, while the second group was exposed to nonaggressive programs (comedies and talk shows). Contrary to usual predictions, it was found that the boys who watched aggressive films actually decreased aggressive behaviors. This trend was clearer in boys from the lower-class backgrounds than in boys from the upper-middle class. Also, viewing aggressive films appeared to reduce the expression of aggression among initially aggressive boys.

These two studies suggest that violence on television is likely to affect younger aggressive children but not older ones. There may be several reasons for this difference. Younger children perhaps cannot separate reality and fantasy as readily as the older ones. Also, they may be more prone to imitate than the older children (e.g., Kohlberg, 1969). At any rate, the studies suggest that televised violence may have different effects on different viewers, depending on their developmental stages. More research is obviously needed before conclusions can be drawn with anything but caution.

An additional comment on the effect of televised violence on children's behavior may be made. Several authors (e.g., Drabman & Thomas, 1974) have speculated that repeated exposure to violence on television may result in emotional habituation. For example, the emotional arousal of college students progressively declines while watching a victim receive a large number of painful electric shocks (Berger, 1962). The implication is that, even though an observer may not imitate aggressive acts of the model, repeated observation of televised violence may increase tolerance for violence that occurs in the real world.

While many people have focused their attention on negative aspects of television, there is evidence indicating that TV programs can be used as a constructive tool. In a study cited above, Friedrich and Stein (1973) reported that the preschool children who watched prosocial films over a four-week period became more likely to persist at tasks and more willing to obey rules than children who saw neutral films. The study also showed that exposure to prosocial films increased cooperative behaviors, especially among the lower-class children.

Ball and Bogartz (1972) studied the effects of "Sesame Street" on the acquisition by younger children of simple educational skills (e.g., letters, number, geometric forms, classification), which is the purpose of the program. According to these investigators, the viewing children showed an impressive improvement in a wide variety of cognitive skills, in contrast to children who did not watch. Furthermore the amount of improvement increased as the amount of viewing increased. Additional findings were: (1) Three-year-olds who watched the program acquired more basic skills than five-year-olds, who rarely watched the program, indicating that the three-year-olds are capable of learning many skills usually considered appropriate for five-year-old children. (2) Disadvantaged children who frequently watched "Sesame Street" performed better on the cognitive skills test than middle-class children who rarely watched the program. These findings suggest that young children can acquire many basic cognitive skills through observation and that television can be an important educational tool toward this end.

IMPLICATIONS

Theoretical

Bandura's social learning theory was at one time often identified among the S–R behavioristic positions (e.g., Baldwin, 1967). Although Bandura has always expressed some dissatisfaction with traditional behavioristic concepts derived from Hull and Skinner to explain the results of his research on observational learning, he included many of the principles of reinforcement in the earlier versions of his explanations of behavior changes (see Bandura & Walters, 1963). Now, however, it is becoming increasingly difficult to include the present broadened scope of his theory of social learning within strict S–R positions. To be sure, the principle of learning by the application of reinforcement contingencies to overt behavior continues to be a prominent feature of his theory and research works (Bandura, 1977b). However, the function of reward is emphasized as providing information about desirable responses and their probable outcomes, rather than inducing simple reinforcement linkages. This reconceptualization of behavior outcomes in terms of symbolic processes is more in agreement with current cognitive psychology (e.g., Lindsay & Norman, 1977).

Bandura's learning theory differs from the traditional behavioristic theories in that it emphasizes, in addition to observational learning, symbolic representational and self-regulatory processes. Many studies in the field of human learning and memory currently are being evolved around these two processes. Studies concerning how information is symbolically represented in memory and how human memory systems function have been flourishing (Lindsay & Norman, 1977). Furthermore, developmental psychologists recently have been investigating children's self-regulatory activities through the study of metamemory (see, for example, Flavell & Wellman, 1977). *Metamemory* refers to a person's active monitoring of memory processes and regulation of them. Thus, Bandura's theory is closely related to current research activities in human cognition.

The implications of Bandura's theory are not limited to the field of learning. In the field of personality development, for example, Kobasa and Maddi (1977) recently observed that ". . . the evidence favors approaches that employ concepts concerning the interaction between person and situation variables. The emphasis now is shifting to theories of personality that highlight cognitive processes, consciousness, planfulness, decision making, and the like" (p. 273).

Practical

The practical implications of Bandura's theory are far-reaching, and its heuristic potential in developing, for example, new child rearing or educational procedures is promising. This section, however, will be restricted to a discussion of the theory as it applies to the modification of problem behaviors in a clinical setting. The emphasis will be on vicarious learning.

Let us suppose, as an illustration, that a male college student is painfully shy and withdrawn. He experiences much interpersonal anxiety, especially with members of the opposite sex. Direct failures in social interactions in his early adolescence and restricted family modeling have resulted in his encoding these experiences in such a way that the thoughts and images operating are strongly negative, being dominated by anticipations of rejection or ridicule and by preoccupations with social inadequacy. These cognitive mediators not only control large areas of interpersonal patterns in the form of avoidance or escape but also result in reduced sensitivity and distorted interpretations of social experiences. For example, an acquaintance may pass him in a hall without acknowledging him because the other person is preoccupied with some personal matter. The possibility of this being considered an explanation for the slight is remote; instead the event is incorporated into the existing cognitive framework of self-inadequacy, and as a result he ruminates excessively about the event. After much hesitation, he seeks help from the counseling center at the university because another acquaintance had gone there and seemed to benefit a great deal. The move toward change was thus initiated, at least in part, by observing a model receive a positive outcome for a behavior which prior to the observation was inhibited.

Many procedures could be used to overcome the relatively common difficulty of this college student. Many counselors or therapists would use an eclectic approach employing a variety of techniques. Therapists influenced by Bandura's model would also be likely to use diverse procedures, but their selection and predicted effectiveness would be integrated by the unifying construct of self-efficacy (Bandura, 1977a). *Self-efficacy* is the set of expectations a person holds that a given course of behavior will meet with success. In the example, the self-efficacy of this student for attaining gratifying social experiences is low. The therapist therefore would use procedures known to alter the level and strength of his expectations and would provide experiences which base these expectations on firm, realistic grounds.

There are four principal sources of information which a therapist could manipulate to change the client's self-efficacy: (1) performance accomplishments, in which the expectancy information is based on the client's actual performance; (2) vicarious experiences or observational learning, in which the expectancy information is based on indirect experience of performance; (3) verbal persuasion, in which expectancy information is told to the client based on the therapist's experience; and (4) emotional arousal, in which expectancy information is based on the client's awareness of his emotional states.

The more dependable these sources of information, the greater will be the changes in the client's perception of his self as a person able to master the problem. Thus, information based on the client's actual social performance would be more influential for self-efficacy than information based on persuasion through such methods or rational interpretation of the difficulty or suggestion. The therapist's goal is to foster a belief that the client can succeed in now-threatening social situations, basing this belief on the most solid ground available, actual performance experiences.

To occasion performance experiences which would stably modify the self-efficacy expectation of the student in this example, the therapist must teach the client how to behave in new or different ways. This response information can be transmitted through physical demonstration, words, or film. An ideal way for the therapist to effect changes in expectancy information would be to have available an actual or filmed model similar in appearance and personality characteristics to the client and have the model behave in a prescribed fashion, receiving many social rewards from various threatening people. The client at first could mimic the model's behavior and then gradually experiment with new responses, all the while receiving the positive interpersonal experiences. Obviously such procedures are often not feasible. Therefore in most counseling situations, restricted as they are in media resources and confederate cooperation, response information is likely to be transmitted verbally.

The therapist may begin, with the cooperation of the client, to construct a realistically attainable verbal portrait of the type of person the client would like to or should become. This verbal model could be presented as a flexible device with which the client could experiment, adopting, modifying, or rejecting as he sees fit (Kelly, 1955). The sketch could also be read onto a cassette the client could play in private, as an aid to attenion and retention.

Concurrent with the development of the sketch the therapist could explain the learning experiences which led to the present debilitation, attributing the diffi-

culties to their likely origin and suggesting, especially in an indirect way (see Haley, 1974), the probability of success. The therapist could thus incorporate verbal persuasion into the construction of various experience procedures, so that both could contribute to the modification of expectancy information. However, it must be kept in mind that thus far no experience base through performance accomplishments has been laid, nor has any stable reduction in anxiety been attempted.

To effect a reduction in anxiety, the therapist may undertake a program of systematic desensitization. In this procedure, the client is put into a state of deep muscular relaxation and is asked to imagine systematically scenes that are increasingly fear-provoking. Under these conditions, the scenes often lose their power to elicit anxiety, and a transfer to the real world may take place. (According to Bandura, 1977a, the major effect of this procedure is a cognitive reevaluation of the effects of arousal on the client's social competencies, and interpretation at variance with other therapists. For example, see Wolpe, 1978.)

Up to this point, a symbolic model has been provided and some stabilization of arousal has been effected. The therapist could then use role-playing (Starr, 1977) to give the client an experience of enactment of the behaviors contained in the sketch, and more importantly, to encourage behavior toward the therapist during the counseling session in a manner similar to the modeled personality, such as an increased assertiveness. The actual incorporation into the counseling session of those behaviors called for in the sketch would give the client the opportunity for experimenting with new modes of behavior, the opportunity for corrective feedback information, and an experiential basis for successful execution.

The therapist could at this point try to bring the new or disinhibited modeled behavior into the social life of the client. The client could be asked to observe three diverse people who seem to be socially adept and who resemble somewhat the sketched personality, to see what kinds of behavioral amalgams he might wish to organize and try for himself. He may find that some socially relaxed people similar to the model exhibit social initiative, show generosity, pay verbal compliments, and touch others often. Perhaps some of these patterns would be too threatening or too dissimilar to the self-system of the client and would be rejected, but others could be incorporated for experimentation. The client could then be encouraged to enact the behaviors in settings outside the therapy situation to provide the performance experiences required.

This brief and overly simplified case example cannot and does not do justice to the work of Bandura (1977a) on the process and predictions of psychotherapy. Each of the four major sources of information, for example, contains many procedures other than those mentioned in this example. One of Bandura's major theoretical contributions to psychotherapy is to provide a theoretical framework, much of it supported by empirical research, for making differential predictions of the efficacy of the diverse forms of psychotherapy available today. It is recognized that much further research is needed. But it is likely that the empirically derived model developed by Bandura, based on his observational learning career, could become a major integrative theory for the assessment of psychotherapeutic procedures, as well as an impetus for the development of new and more powerful techniques.

SUMMARY

Observational learning, cognition, and self-regulatory processes are emphasized in Bandura's social learning theory. The present chapter is mainly concerned with the discussion of observational learning processes, namely how a person learns new responses through the observation of others. There are four major issues in the area of observational learning: (1) the acquisition of novel responses, (2) the mechanisms mediating observation and performance, (3) the factors affecting the selective nature of observational learning, and (4) the motivational factors determining the selective aspects of imitative performance. A comprehensive theory of observational learning must address itself to these matters.

One way to provide the contemporary context for Bandura's theory is to examine various conceptualizations of imitative learning. The human tendency to imitate was regarded as innate by early theorists. With the advent of learing theories, the classical or instrumental conditioning paradigm was applied to the study of this tendency. The classical conditioning theory is limited because it fails to explain selective aspects of imitation. Both classical and instrumental conditioning theories do not adequately account for the acquisition of novel responses through observation, in the absence of overt practice and external reward. Bandura advanced a multiprocess theory of observational learning which addresses itself to the four major issues described above.

According to Bandura's theory of observational learning, new responses are required as the stimulus input from the model is encoded, stored, and transformed by the observer. This acquisition through cognition takes place before the learned response is performed. For the learning to become overt, motor capacities must be available and incentive conditions must be favorable. In addition to external and vicarious rewards, self-reinforcement is emphasized in this theory as a determinant of behavior selection. One significant aspect of Bandura's theory of observational learning relates to a wide scope of modeling effects. The observer abstracts general principles from instances of modeled behaviors that permit a wide range of transfer to new situations.

Experimental studies are available concerning variables that control attentional and retentional processes of observational learning. For example, children pay more attention to the model who is nurturant, and consequently, they are likely to learn that model's behaviors. Children assimilate different aspects of the same model's behavior, depending on the children's personality characteristics. Regarding the retention process, it has been shown that observers who were instructed to transform complex motor responses into verbal codes reproduced the observed behavior well. In contrast, individuals who were deprived of such opportunities reproduced fewer imitative behaviors. Studies concerned with the observational acquisition of general principles also point to the importance of cognitive representational processes.

The broad scope of Bandura's social learning theory has much to say to many areas of contemporary psychology. Its synthetic potential promises to point the way to a comprehensive and integrated model of human functioning.

ANNOTATED BIBLIOGRAPHY

Bandura, A. *Principles of behavior modification.* New York: Holt, Rinehart & Winston, 1969.

This, one of Bandura's major works, is a difficult but valuable source book. Bandura applies the principles of social learning for effective behavioral change, especially in a clinical setting. The book emphasizes cognitive factors and contains important chapters on causal processes involved in deviant behavior and on symbolic controls of behavioral changes. Broad in scope and compact in style, it well repays efforts to master it.

Bandura, A. *Aggression: A social learning analysis.* Englewood Cliffs, N.J.: Prentice-Hall, 1973.

Bandura provides a comprehensive review of various theories and hypotheses of aggression and presents social learning views concerning (1) the acquisition of aggressive modes of responses, (2) events likely to evoke aggressive behaviors, and (3) conditions that maintain aggressive responses. He reviews experimental studies on aggression and also covers socially relevant topics such as highjacking, televised violence, and juvenile delinquency. A chapter describes programs and procedures by which various forms of aggressive behaviors may be controlled. Vicarious, cognitive, and self-regulatory processes are emphasized in the acquisition and control of aggressive behavior.

Bandura, A. *Social learning theory.* Englewood Cliffs, N.J.: Prentice-Hall, 1977.

This relatively short work is highly recommended as a brief, readable, and comprehensive statement of Bandura's current position with regard to the formation of human personality. Extended treatment is given to the antecedent and consequent determinants of behavior, as well as cognitive processes. The final chapter contains the most complete statement to date of the concept and implications of reciprocal determinism. This book was used as a resource for much of this chapter.

Bandura, A., & Walters, R. H. *Social learning and personality development.* New York: Holt, Rinehart & Winston, 1963.

As the title suggests, this brief book attempts to demonstrate that personality development can be explained in terms of social learning principles. A single distinctive feature lies in the authors' argument that imitation plays a significant role in the acquisition of all forms of social behaviors, both deviant and socially approved. The authors' early research projects on modeling are extensively reviewed.

REFERENCES

Arem, C. A., & Zimmerman, B. J. Vicarious effects on the creative behavior of retarded and nonretarded children. *American Journal of Mental Deficiency,* 1976, *81,* 289–296.

Aronfreed, J. The problem of imitation. In L. P. Lipsitt & H. W. Reese (Eds.), *Advances in child development and behavior* (Vol. 4). New York: Academic Press, 1969.

Baer, D. M., Peterson, R. F., & Sherman, J. A. The development of imitation by reinforcing behavioral similarity to a model. *Journal of the Experimental Analysis of Behavior,* 1967, *10,* 405–416.

Baer, D. M., & Sherman, J. A. Reinforcement control of generalized imitation in young children. *Journal of Experimental Child Psychology,* 1964, *1,* 37–49.

Bagehot, W. *Physics and politics.* New York: Appleton, 1873.

Baldwin, A. L. *Theories of child development.* New York: John Wiley & Sons, 1967.

Ball, S., & Bogartz, J. Summative research of Sesame Street: Implications for the study of preschool children. In A. D. Pick (Ed.), *Minnesota symposia on child psychology* (Vol. 6). Minneapolis: University of Minnesota Press, 1972.

Bandura, A. Social learning through imitation. In M. R. Jones (Ed.), *Nebraska Symposium on Motivation.* Lincoln: University of Nebraska Press, 1962.

Bandura, A. Influence of models' reinforcement contingencies on the acquisition of imitative responses. *Journal of Personality and Social Psychology,* 1965, *1,* 589–595.

Bandura, A. The role of modeling processes in personality development. In W. W. Hartup & N. L. Smothergill (Eds.), *The young child* (Vol. 1). Washington: National Association for the Education of Young Children, 1967.

Bandura, A. *Principles of behavior modification.* New York: Holt, Rinehart & Winston, 1969.

Bandura, A. (Ed.). *Psychological modeling: Conflicting theories.* Chicago: Aldine-Atherton, 1971.

Bandura, A. *Aggression: A social learning analysis.* Englewood Cliffs, N.J.: Prentice-Hall, 1973.

Bandura, A. Modeling theory. In W. S. Sahakian (Ed.), *Learning: Systems, models, and theories* (2nd ed.). Chicago: Rand McNally, 1976.

Bandura, A. Self-efficacy: Toward a unifying theory of behavioral change. *Psychological Review,* 1977, *84,* 191–215. (a)

Bandura, A. *Social learning theory.* Englewood Cliffs, N.J.: Prentice-Hall, 1977. (b)

Bandura, A. The self system in reciprocal determinism. *American Psychologist,* 1978, *33,* 344–358.

Bandura, A., & Barab, P. G. Conditions governing non-reinforced evaluation. *Developmental Psychology,* 1971, *3,* 244–255.

Bandura, A., Grusec, J. E., & Menlove, F. L. Observational learning as a function of symbolization and incentive set. *Child Development,* 1966, *37,* 499–506.

Bandura, A., Grusec, J. E., & Menlove, F. L. Vicarious extinction of avoidance behavior. *Journal of Personality and Social Psychology,* 1967, *5,* 16–23.

Bandura, A., & Harris, M. B. Modification of syntactic style. *Journal of Experimental Child Psychology,* 1966, *4,* 341–352.

Bandura, A., & Jeffery, R. W. Role of symbolic coding and rehearsal processes in observational learning. *Journal of Personality and Social Psychology,* 1973, *26,* 122–130.

Bandura, A., & Kupers, C. J. Transmission of patterns of self-reinforcement through modeling. *Journal of Abnormal and Social Psychology,* 1964, *69,* 1–9.

Bandura, A., & McDonald, F. J. The influence of social reinforcement and the behavior of models in shaping children's moral judgements. *Journal of Abnormal and Social Psychology,* 1963, *67,* 274–281.

Bandura, A., Ross, D., & Ross, S. A. Vicarious reinforcement and imitative learning. *Journal of Abnormal and Social Psychology,* 1963, *67,* 601–607.

Bandura, A., & Walters, R. H. *Social learning and personality development.* New York: Holt, Rinehart & Winston, 1963.

Berger, S. M. Conditioning through vicarious instigation. *Psychological Review,* 1962, *69,* 450–466.

Butcher, S. H. *The poetics of Aristotle.* London: MacMillan, 1922.

Coates, B., & Hartup, W. W. Age and verbalization in observational learning. *Developmental Psychology,* 1969, *1,* 556–562.

Cowan, P. A., Langer, J., Heavenrich, J., & Nathanson, M. Social learning theory and Piaget's cognitive theory of moral development. *Journal of Personality and Social Psychology,* 1969, *11,* 261–274.

Darby, C. L., & Riopelle, A. J. Observational learning in the Rhesus monkey. *Journal of Comparative and Physiological Psychology,* 1959, *52,* 94–98.

Drabman, R. S., & Thomas, M. H. Does media violence increase children's tolerance of real-life aggression? *Developmental Psychology,* 1974, *10,* 418–421.

Feshbach, S., & Singer, R. *Television and aggression.* San Francisco: Jossey-Bass, 1971.

Flavell, J. H. Developmental studies of mediated memory. In H. W. Reese & L. P. Lipsitt (Eds.), *Advances in child development and behavior* (Vol. 5). New York: Academic Press, 1970.

Flavell, J. H., & Wellman, H. M. Metamemory. In R. V. Kail, Jr., & J. W. Hagen, *Perspectives on the development of memory and cognition.* Hillsdale, N.J.: Lawrence Erlbaum Associates, 1977.

Friedrich, K. L., & Stein, A. H. Aggressive and prosocial television programs and the natural behavior of preschool children. *Monographs of the Society for Research in Child Development,* 1973, *38* (Serial No. 151).

Gerst, M. S. Symbolic coding processes in observational learning. *Journal of Personality and Social Psychology,* 1971, *19,* 7–17.

Gewirtz, J. L. Conditional responding as a paradigm for observational, imitative learning and vicarious reinforcement. In H. W. Reese (Ed.), *Advances in child development and behavior* (Vol. 6). New York: Academic Press, 1971.

Gewirtz, J. L., & Stingle, K. G. The learning of generalized imitation as the basis for identification. *Psychological Review,* 1968, *75,* 374–397.

Groesbeck, R. W., & Duerfeldt, P. H. Some relevant variables in observational learning on the rat. *Psychonomic Science,* 1971, *22,* 41–43.

Grusec, J. E., & Brinker, D. B. Reinforcement for imitation as a social learning determinant with implications for sex-role development. *Journal of Personality and Social Psychology,* 1972, *21,* 149–158.

Grusec, J., & Mischel, W. Model's characteristics as determinants of social learning. *Journal of Personality and Social Psychology,* 1966, *4,* 211–215.

Guthrie, E. R. *The psychology of learning* (Rev. ed.). New York: Harper & Row, 1952.

Haley, J. *Uncommon therapy.* New York: Ballantine, 1974.

Hall, K. R. L. Observational learning in monkeys and apes. *British Journal of Psychology,* 1963, *54,* 201–226.

Holt, E. B. *Animal drive and the learning process* (Vol. 1). New York: Holt, 1931.

Imanishi, K. Social behavior in Japanese monkeys: *Macaca fuscata. Psychologia,* 1957, *1,* 47–54.

John, E. R., Chesler, P., Bartlett, F., & Victor, I. Observation learning in cats. *Science,* 1968, *159,* 1489–1491.

Kaufman, A., Baron, A., & Kopp, R. E. Some effects of instructions on human operant behavior. *Psychonomic Monograph Supplements,* 1966, *1,* 243–250.

Kelly, G. A. *The psychology of personal constructs* (Vol. 1). New York: Norton, 1955.

Kobasa, S. C., & Maddi, S. R. Existential

personality theory. In R. J. Corsini (Ed.), *Current personality theories*. Itasca, Ill.: F. E. Peacock, 1977.

Kohlberg, L. Stage and sequence: The cognitive-developmental approach to socialization. In D. A. Goslin (Ed.), *Handbook of socialization theory and research*. Chicago: Rand McNally, 1969.

Kohn, B. Observation and discrimination learning in the rat: Effects of stimulus substitution. *Learning and Motivation*, 1976, *7*, 303–312.

Kohn, B., & Dennis, M. Observation and discrimination learning in the rat: Specific and nonspecific effects. *Journal of Comparative and Physiological Psychology*, 1972, *78*, 292–296.

Kuhn, D. Imitation theory and research from cognitive perspective. *Human Development*, 1973, *16*, 157–180.

Laughlin, P. R., Moss, I. L., & Miller, S. M. Information processing in children as a function of adult model, stimulus display, school grade, and sex. *Journal of Educational Psychology*, 1969, *60*, 188–193.

Lindsay, P. H., & Norman, D. A. *Human information processing: An introduction to psychology* (2nd ed.). New York: Academic Press, 1977.

Lumsdain, A. A. (Ed.). *Student response in programmed instruction: A symposium*. Washington, D.C.: National Academy of Science—National Research Council, 1961.

Maccoby, E. E. Role-taking in childhood and its consequences for social learning. *Child Development*, 1959, *30*, 239–252.

McCall, R. B., Parke, R. D., & Kavanaugh, R. D. Imitation of live and televised models by children one to three years of age. *Monographs of the Society for Research in Child Development*, 1977, *42* (Serial No. 172).

McDavid, J. W. Imitative behavior in preschool children. *Psychological Monographs*, 1959, *73* (Whole No. 486).

McDougall, W. *An introduction to social psychology*. London: Methuen, 1908.

McLaughlin, B. *Learning and social behavior*. New York: Free Press, 1971.

Miller, N. E., & Dollard, J. *Social learning and imitation*. New Haven: Yale University Press, 1941.

Odom, R. D., Liebert, R. M., & Hill, J. H. The effects of modeling cues, reward, and attentional set on the production of grammatical and ungrammatical syntactical construction. *Journal of Experimental Child Psychology*, 1968, *6*, 131–140.

Parton, D. A. Learning to imitate in infancy. *Child Development*, 1976, *47*, 14–31.

Piaget, J. *The moral judgment of the child*. New York: Harcourt, Brace, 1932.

Rohwer, W. D., Jr. Elaboration and learning in childhood and adolescence. In H. W. Reese (Ed.), *Advances in child development and behavior* (Vol. 8). New York: Academic Press, 1973.

Rosenbaum, M. E. The effect of verbalization of correct responses by performers and observers on retention. *Child Development*, 1967, *38*, 616–622.

Rosenbaum, M. E., & Arenson, S. J. Observational learning: Some theory, some variables, some findings. In E. C. Simmell, R. A. Hoppe, & G. A. Milton (Eds.), *Social facilitation and imitative behavior*. Boston: Allyn & Bacon, 1968.

Rosenblith, J. F. Learning by imitation in kindergarten children. *Child Development*, 1959, *30*, 69–80.

Rosenthal, T. L., & Zimmerman, B. J. Modeling by exemplification and instruction in training conservation. *Developmental Psychology*, 1972, *6*, 392–401.

Ross, D. Relationship between dependency, intentional learning, and incidental learning in preschool children. *Journal of Personality and Social Psychology*, 1966, *4*, 374–381.

Sheffield, F. D. Theoretical considerations in the learning of complex sequential tasks from demonstration and practice. In A. A. Lumsdaine (Ed.), *Student response in programmed instruction: A symposium*. Washington, D.C.: National Academy of Science—National Research Council, 1961.

Starr, A. *Psychodrama: Rehearsal for living*. Chicago: Nelson-Hall, 1977.

Steinman, W. M. Implicit instructions and social influence in "generalized imitation" and comparable nonimitative situations. *Merrill-Palmer Quarterly*, 1976, *22*, 85–92.

Tarde, G. *The laws of imitation*. New York: Holt, 1903.

Thorndike, E. L. *Animal intelligence*. New York, Macmillan, 1911.

Warden, C. J., Fjeld, H. A., & Koch, A. M. Imitative behavior in the Cebus and Rhesus monkeys. *Journal of Genetic Psychology,* 1940, *56,* 311–322.

Wilson, W. C. Imitation and the learning of incidental cues by preschool children. *Child Development,* 1958, *29,* 393–397.

Wolpe, J. Cognition and causation in human behavior and its therapy. *American Psychologist,* 1978, *33,* 437–446.

Yussen, S. R. Determinants of visual attention and recall in observational learning by preschoolers and second graders. *Developmental Psychology,* 1974, *10,* 93–100.

Yussen, S. R., & Levy, V. M., Jr. Effects of warm and neutral models on the attention of observational learners. *Journal of Experimental Child Psychology,* 1975, *20,* 66–72.

Zimmerman, B. J., & Rosenthal, T. L. Observational learning of rule governed behavior by children. *Psychological Bulletin,* 1974, *81,* 29–42.

12

Rotter's Social Learning Theory

E. JERRY PHARES

INTRODUCTION

Overview

There is hardly a more ubiquitous concept in all of psychology than that of learning. From the works of the Greek philosophers right up to the latest *Annual Review of Psychology,* learning concepts are both prominent and pervasive. Nor is a preoccupation with learning exclusive to psychologists; the lay person is equally concerned. Modern society has developed a huge bureaucracy, supported by billions of dollars, which is devoted to ensuring that our children learn properly. Learning is regarded as a very serious matter by nearly everyone.

While there is considerable agreement about the importance or value of learning, there is much less agreement about its nature. Of course, defining it as some kind of modification of behavior as a function of experience may not provoke a great deal of disagreement. However, such definitions are too general to be of much help in the systematic investigation of learning processes. Such definitions neither identify the important variables in the process, nor do they specify the kinds of changes in behavior that do

not qualify as learning (such as native responses).

Most theories of learning appear quite different from one another. Connectionism, operant conditioning, sign learning, mathematical models, and functionalism are but a sample of the heterogeneity in approaches. But learning theories have historically had at least one thing in common. They have, each in their own way, attempted to promulgate a series of principles by which people in general learn. Thus the emphasis has been on the common aspects of human behavior.

Personality theory, on the other hand, is traditionally concerned with individual differences. For example, given the same conditions of stimulation, why is it that people respond differently? Why do they seemingly learn different things? Or can we employ individual differences that appear to have some consistency across situations to better predict behavior?

The social learning theory of Julian B. Rotter (1954) arises from the broad traditions of both learning theory and personality theory. However, its focus is not on simple stimuli or stimuli complexes. Rather, in line with the interests of an increasing number of psychologists, it deals with the complex behavior of individuals in complex social situations. The theory subsumes and integrates three broad historical trends in psychology: behavior, cognition, and motivation. The emphasis is on learned behaviors that are determined simultaneously by the variables of expectancy (cognition) and reinforcement value (motivation). Furthermore, these variables are regarded by the theory as strongly influenced by the situational context in question. Therefore, social learning theory gathers the diverse strands of behaviorism, cognitive theory, motivational theory, and situationism into one systematic, coherent framework. One may question, as does Leon Levy (1970), whether psychology is yet ready to describe its conceptions of behavior or personality as theories. Nevertheless, be it theory or conception, it is clear that Rotter's way of looking at events provides a broad and utilitarian framework. For under its umbrella investigators with either learning orientations or personality-social inclinations, as well as clinical psychologists, can find something of value. While many theories in psychology are either behavioral or motivational or cognitive-phenomenological, social learning theory transcends these narrow confines and provides a viable, unifying approach that has already displayed considerable stamina.

Social learning theory was designed not only with an eye toward rigor and objectivity but also to have practical significance. Specifically, it was designed to be of use to the practicing clinical psychologist. The breadth and utility of the theory is illustrated in *Applications of a Social Learning Theory of Personality* (1972) by Julian Rotter, June Chance, and Jerry Phares. The book explores applications to learning, personality development, personality theory and measurement, social

psychology, psychopathology, and behavior change and therapy.

Major Issues

The Construct View. In describing his theory, Rotter adheres to a construct point of view. That is, he does not see the issue as whether a theory or its concepts are true or capture the essence of reality. Rather, his concern is with utility. The measure of a good theory is whether it is useful in understanding the events with which it seeks to deal. He argues that a theory does not provide a blueprint of truth or reality. Instead, it offers a way of looking at events, a method of construing the world. For each of us, our view of reality is colored by our own idiosyncratic past experiences and resultant biases, which prevent us from seeing events as they really are. This explains in part why there are so many competing theories and concepts in psychology. In the final analysis, theories will be judged in the arena of prediction and usefulness and not by strident claims or appeals.

Language of Description. Another issue for Rotter is the development of a language of description. As a clinician, he was ever conscious of the vagueness and ambiguities of so many clinical and personality terms. Therefore, he resolved to develop terms that would be free of these defects. First, he sought to define concepts in a manner such that scientists observing the same events from the same orientation would arrive at similar judgments of quantity. Second, he strove to develop a system of terms that would have minimum overlap. That is, confusion would be reduced by minimizing the number of behavioral referents for a single word and the number of words with the same behavioral referent. Third, Rotter attempted to employ the minimum number of terms necessary for an inclusive description of the relevant data. Finally, he included only the terms that were useful for prediction of the events in which he was interested. He argued, for example, that a term such as *anxiety* is not automatically required to be included in a theory. The lack of such a term is a handicap only if it can be shown that, by not including the term, prediction suffers. But if, to continue the example, Rotter chooses to describe certain events in terms of a low expectancy for attaining a valued goal (rather than anxiety) and is able to satisfactorily predict, then there is no problem.

Operationalism. To avoid the problems of loose terminology, social learning theory attempts to employ operational definitions that specify actual measurement operations. Because so many of our operational definitions do not come close enough to our ideal definitions, it is still necessary to settle for *working definitions,* definitions that represent a compromise between the occasional sterility of operational definitions and the imprecision of ideal definitions. To achieve this, social learning theory employs definitions that refer to observable behavior, specify the conditions of measurement, and describe the cultural setting of the behavioral referents. Social learning theory maintains the rigorous and systematic qualities identified with so many learning theories through objective, operational definitions. This is as true of the theory's cognitive constructs as it is of its motivational ones. Thus, while some cognitive theories are decried as lacking in measurements that are tied to observable, objective operations, this critique does not apply to Rotter's cognitive notions.

A Social Learning View. It is not accidental that Rotter's attempt to account for human behavior is described as a social learning theory. The words *social* and *learning* signify the essence of his theoretical posture. The emphasis on learning conveys the assumption that much of human behavior takes place in a meaningful environment and is acquired through social interactions with other people. One's environment takes on meaning or acquires significance as a result of past experience. Specifically, the individual develops the capacity to pursue rewards and to evade punishments in a broad context of social or interpersonal mediation. All of this is inherent in Rotter's (1954) comment: "It is a *social* learning theory because it stresses the fact that the major or basic modes of behaving are learned in social situations and are inextricably fused with needs requiring for their satisfaction the mediation of other persons" (p. 84).

Motivation and Cognition. Another major issue is whether either motivational or cognitive approaches are sufficient in themselves to account for the complexity of human behavior in social situations. There have long been difficulties with strictly motivational approaches, since drive reduction theorists have so many problems in measuring drives (especially secondary or acquired ones) and in demonstrating any actual physiological drive reduction following reinforcement.

But cognitive approaches have, historically speaking, been equally open to criticism. Expectancy measures, for example, have not always been models of objectivity or reliability. Furthermore, cognitive theories have often given short shrift to reinforcement notions. For many people, simply relegating reinforcement to a role of confirming expectancies has never been adequate for valid prediction. As a consequence, social learning theory has combined the concepts of reinforcement and expectancy into the framework of a single theory. Each concept alone quickly manifests severe predictive shortcomings. But combined into the same theory they become conjointly a powerful tool in the service of prediction.

Social learning theory is distinctive in that it extends older learning theories by adding an expectancy concept. But it has not lost its identity with reinforcement theories. Social learning theory utilizes an *empirical law of effect* to avoid the pitfalls encountered by reinforcement theories in their attempts to define reinforcement or drive reduction. The reinforcing properties of a goal are inferred from the direction of behavior. When the person moves toward a goal, that goal is thought to be positively reinforcing; when the person moves away from a goal, the inference is that the goal has negatively reinforcing properties. But the theory avoids being drawn into any debates about physiological or tissue changes that result from reinforcement. While some may regard this definition of reinforcement as circular, it is not necessarily so, as long as the reinforcements for a particular person or culture can be identified in advance of prediction. In any case, it is this empirical law of effect that gives the theory its motivational cast in addition to its cognitive-expectancy flavor.

Performance versus Acquisition. Rotter's social learning theory was not developed to provide a precise account of the specific manner in which bits of human behavior are acquired or learned. Rather, it is a broad, molar theory whose goal is the prediction of which behavior (once acquired) in the individual's repertoire will occur in a given situation. This emphasis on human performance in complex social situations leads the theory away from studies of animal behavior or physiological research. Social learning theory, in the beginning, did study a good deal of human behavior in circumscribed, controlled environments that involved simple stimuli and rather simple responses. This was necessary to demonstrate the utility of the theory's basic and relatively molecular concepts. But in recent years the thrust of the research has been toward prediction in the broader social context. Complex human beings typically function in uncontrolled, nonlaboratory settings. They use language, they make abstractions, and their past experience interacts in an ongoing fashion. This requires a broad, socially based theory to account for the subsequent occurrence of a behavior once it has been acquired. In summary, the emphasis is on the prediction of behaviors that have been acquired and not on principles of conditioning, contiguity, association, or primary stimulus generalization.

Basic Concepts

Behavior Potential (BP). This is a relative concept that refers to the likelihood that the person will respond in a certain way, compared to available alternative behaviors. The concept of behavior is quite broad and includes not only directly observable behavior but also implicit behavior. Behavior thus runs the gamut from smiling to swearing, from repressing to projecting, from thinking to planning. The concept is formally defined by Rotter (1954) as "the potentiality of any behavior occurring in any given situation or situations as calculated in relation to any single reinforcement or set of reinforcements" (p. 105).

Expectancy (E). This is a kind of subjective probability, denoting that it is not actuarially determined but is influenced by a variety of other factors such as the way people categorize events, the manner in which they generalize from past experience, attribute causality, and so on. Such factors imply that a person's subjective probability cannot be calculated solely by counting previous reinforcements. Rotter (1954) has formally defined an expectancy as "the probability held by the individual that a particular reinforcement will occur as a function of a specific behavior on his part in a specific situation or situations. Expectancy is independent of the value or importance of the reinforcement" (p. 107).

Reinforcement Value (RV). Reinforcement value is a relative term which indicates that one favors something over something else. Reinforcement value is never determined in an absolute sense but only in relation to some specified group of alternatives. Rotter (1954) states that reinforcement value is "the degree of the person's preference for that reinforcement to occur if the possibilities of occurrence of all alternatives were equal" (p. 107).

The Basic Determinants of Behavior. Putting the above terms together, we can say that the likelihood that a specific behavior in the individual's repertoire of behaviors will occur in a given situation is determined basically by two variables: expectancy and reinforcement value. Stated another way, the potential strength of a specific behavior in a given situation is determined by the E and RV variables. This is shown in the form of a predictive formula (No. 1) in the Appendix at the end of this chapter.

The Psychological Situation. Explicit in the foregoing is the role of the situation. This means that the context or setting of the behavior must be considered. The way in which the person construes or psychologically defines the situation will affect the values of both reinforcement and expectancy thereby influencing the potential for any given behavior to occur.

A Broader Approach. Very frequently, psychologists must deal not just with one discrete behavior but with a class of behaviors. For example, we may wish to predict the occurrence of violent behavior in general rather than a specific kick or left-handed blow. This is particularly so as we predict to broader, social situations. This means that we must consider multiple behavior potentials, expectancies, and reinforcement values. Formula 2 in the Appendix shows these relationships.

To simplify communication, the behavior potential term is replaced by need potential (NP), expectancy is referred to as freedom of movement (FM), and reinforcement value as need value (NV). The notion of the situation is implicit. For example, the likelihood that a person will behave in any of several violent ways (NP) is determined by the mean level of expectancy (FM) that these behaviors will lead to certain desirable outcomes and the mean value of the reinforcements (NV) in the situations involved. These relationships are shown in Formula 3 in the Appendix.

HISTORY

Beginnings

Social learning theory began to assume its present shape in the late 1940s and early 1950s. Julian B. Rotter depended heavily on his graduate students to provide a forum to try out, discard, and modify various aspects of his developing theory. Indeed, for many years Wednesday evenings for his Ohio State University students were devoted to team meetings with Rotter. In these sessions from

8 to 15 graduate students developed, criticized, and modified ideas in a free atmosphere of give and take. At first the intellectual ferment could be awesome and intimidating, but this was where the participants learned to think, and they recognized that the real essence of Ph.D. training was in these sessions. The meetings also provided a forum for students to present their thesis and dissertation ideas. When the meeting adjourned to a tavern across the river, the stimulation was polished in good conversation about everything from the place of clinical psychology in modern society to what should be done on the current sociopolitical scene.

No theory springs full-blown upon the scene. The ideas and influences of a number of people are certainly evident in Rotter's social learning theory. He has both formally (Rotter, 1954, p. 85) and informally acknowledged a number of such influences. Personal associations with Alfred Adler, Kurt Lewin, and J. R. Kantor were quite important. He attended a number of Adler's clinics, lectures, and society meetings at the Long Island College of Medicine. He worked with Lewin, and the intellectual influence stemming from contact with Kantor is apparent in his formal theorizing.

In particular, the field or environmental influence of Lewin is quite obvious in Rotter's first postulate (see Proposition 1 below). Kantor's influence shows up in the second postulate (Proposition 2), which describes an historical approach to the study of events, as well as in the third postulate (Proposition 3), which addresses problems in the description of events. Rotter's ideas in Postulate 5 (Proposition 5), which discusses the unity of personality, have a distinct Adlerian flavor. Lewin's influence is seen in Postulate 6 (Proposition 6), a motiva-

tional one which incorporates an empirical law of effect rather than drive reduction, as are the ideas of Sigmund Freud, Alfred Adler, Prescott Lecky, E. L. Thorndike and Clark Hull. Rotter's emphasis on an empirical law of effect also is not far removed from Skinnerian notions. The expectancy concept introduced in Postulate 7 (Proposition 7) has direct antecedents in the work of both Adler and Edward Tolman and his colleagues.

These individuals reflect a variegated intellectual heritage. But then social learning theory is a broad, yet systematic theory. It is a learning theory and a personality theory. It is both cognitive and motivational. It encompasses situational as well as personality variables. And through it all, this theory is designed to be useful for the clinician. No wonder, then, that it draws from sources as heterogeneous as Adler, Freud, Hull, Lewin, Kantor, Thorndike, and Tolman.

Major Theorists

The architect of social learning theory, Julian B. Rotter, was born in 1916 in Brooklyn, New York. His parents were immigrants, his father arriving in this country from Austria at age 13 and his mother from Lithuania at age 1. Julian was their third son.

As Rotter says, "Brooklyn was a tough place and you learned how to take care of yourself." He was a good student who generally received high marks, though he notes that his marks for conduct were considerably lower. His interest in psychology seems to have stemmed from books by Freud, Adler, and Karl Menninger which he obtained from the public library.

He majored in chemistry at Brooklyn College but was also interested in psychology and philosophy. He cites Solomon Asch and Austin B. Wood as having been particularly important teachers, and he was strongly impressed by his contacts with Alfred Adler.

Rotter decided to go into clinical psychology, he says, "Because I was interested in it." However, a cursory glance at his theory (and attendance at some of his lectures) would not lead us to accept this statement at face value, for it would be tantamount to a testimonial to the concept of functional autonomy. Rotter matured in an age concerned with social justice and economic deprivation. He undoubtedly both witnessed and experienced discrimination. It was a tough period in the social history of America; many youths spent time on the picket line, and Rotter was among them. Like many others he was idealistic and thought there must be a way to improve the lives of others. In this respect he was probably not different from many others who select clinical psychology as a career—they want to save the world. Furthermore, he did not want to go to medical school and become a physician just to gain the privilege of practicing psychology.

He attended graduate school at the University of Iowa (M.A., 1938) and Indiana University (Ph.D., 1941). His M.A. advisor was Lee Travis and his first published paper was on the psychology of stuttering. He worked with Kurt Lewin and was significantly influenced by him. He did an internship at Worcester State Hospital when Eliot Rodnick, Saul Rosenzweig, and David Shakow were on the staff. His Ph.D. advisor was C. M. Louttit who was both a good friend and a strong personal influence. It was also at Indiana that he came under the intellectual influence of J. R. Kantor.

He received his Ph.D. just before being drafted; Rotter says, "I was too young to get a commission in the Army and too color-blind to get one in the Navy." He went through Armored OCS but did mostly psychological work in the Army. Several of his publications of the mid–1940s are based on this work: military psychology, methods of officer candidate selection, and so on.

In 1946 Rotter joined the faculty of Ohio State University where, in collaboration with George A. Kelly, he helped build a clinical training program of national renown, one that became a model of the scientist-practitioner tradition of training. It was at Ohio State that Rotter developed his social learning theory. During his tenure at Ohio State he worked with extremely large numbers of graduate students; it was not at all unusual for Rotter to supervise five or six theses and four or five dissertations per year. Many of these projects provided empirical support for his developing theoretical notions. Interestingly, the prodigious program of research that Rotter and his theory stimulated was only rarely supported by research grants. The force of his ideas and personality, coupled with the enthusiasm of his students, was support enough.

In 1963 Rotter moved to the University of Connecticut, where he continues to serve as professor of psychology and director of the Clinical Training Program. Psychology has bestowed many honors and distinctions on Rotter which testify to the heuristic nature of his many articles, chapters, monographs, books, and test manuals published over the years.

But despite his prolific scientific career, Rotter has always maintained his identity as a clinician. He continues to see patients, to actively participate in the clinical training of students, and to serve on various boards and committees of the American Psychological Association that deal with clinical issues. As much as anyone, he has, by his own example and by his structuring of clinical training programs, demonstrated the viability of the scientist-practitioner model in psychology.

Clearly, Rotter has been and continues to be the dominating figure in social learning theory. While other researchers and theorists (especially his former students) continue to publish and contribute, these are essentially applications and demonstrations rather than substantive alterations in the theory. Most of these individuals are cited in the two major social learning theory volumes (Rotter, 1954; Rotter, Chance, & Phares, 1972) and in the two major recent applications of the theory, locus of control (Lefcourt, 1976; Phares, 1976) and interpersonal trust (Rotter, 1977).

Current Status

The current status of social learning theory can best be understood against a backdrop of the several stages through which it has passed. The late 1940s and early 1950s were periods of excitement in which the basic theory was developed and the research necessary to establish its point of view was executed. This period was capped in 1954 by the publication of Rotter's basic work, *Social Learning and Clinical Psychology*. The 1960s represented essentially a period devoted to exploring and demonstrating the applications of the theory to diverse areas such as personality development theory and measurement. Other applications included social psychology, psychopathology, and psychotherapy. This phase culminated in the publication in 1972 by Rotter, Chance, and Phares of *Applications of a Social Learning Theory of Personality*.

In the 1970s the significance of Rotter's 1966 monograph on internal-external control really took hold. Perhaps driven by the forces of alienation that were loosed upon the nation as the significance of the civil rights movement and the Vietnam War became apparent, the *locus of control* concept became probably the most widely investigated personality variable in the history of psychology. During this period Rotter introduced another social learning theory concept, *interpersonal trust* (Rotter, 1967b), which has been increasingly investigated of late. Thus the 1970s witnessed a social learning theory emphasis on generalized personality variables. But it should be noted that many of the people involved in research on such variables as locus of control are interested largely in those variables and show no special commitment to social learning theory itself.

Nevertheless, social learning theory has come to be recognized as a unifying theoretical force in psychology. Because of its broad theoretical base in motivation, cognition, and situationism, it has the capacity to subsume or integrate several current trends in applied psychology. This is indeed a key capacity, since in recent years many psychologists have not been interested in theory; their concerns have been with developing techniques, procedures, or even movements that have little articulation with theory. However, at some point these psychologists must explain why their procedures are effective, or they must justify their utilization. As they do so, they begin to cast about for a theoretical framework to anchor their work. Often, social learning theory becomes the choice. An example of this is the cognitive emphasis that has begun to envelop behavior therapy procedures (Phares, 1979). Social learning theory can readily integrate this cognitive-behavioral emphasis in therapy. Another example is in the growing area of community psychology. Social learning theory, especially with its locus of control concept, can make a significant contribution to theoretical integration in this area (Rappaport, 1977).

Many investigators throughout the country are actively involved in social learning theory research to one degree or another. Many of these are former students of Rotter's, while others are not. A glance at the references in either Rotter (1954) or Rotter et al. (1972) will reveal their principal research interests, and their current institutional affiliations can be found in the latest *American Psychological Association Directory*.

Social learning theory research appears in a variety of journals. Three of the most frequently used have been *Journal of Personality and Social Psychology, Journal of Consulting and Clinical Psychology,* and *Journal of Personality.* However, a wide range of journals have published both theoretical and applied social learning studies. The references at the end of this chapter will provide a good sampling of these outlets.

Other Theories

Two social learning theories along with Rotter's have largely dominated the scene. The first is the theory of John Dollard and Neal Miller (1950). This approach, a stimulus-response formulation, drew heavily from Hull and tended to view learning in terms of the physical or objective properties of stimuli. Reinforcement is seen as a function of drive reduction. Learning occurs when a habit or S–R connection is formed.

The significance of the work of Dollard and Miller is essentially historical rather than contemporary. However, learning theorists and clinicians alike owe a large debt to them. While some have dismissed their contribution as a mere translation of Freudian concepts into the language of learning, this was a significant accomplishment, because these two theorists demonstrated that social-personality phenomena could be described and explained with the more objective and reliable concepts of a learning theory. Thus they set the stage for subsequent social learning approaches.

The second approach, by Albert Bandura (1971), offers a social learning conceptualization that largely emphasizes the role of observation. He believes that while learning can be facilitated by reinforcement, it is not dependent upon it. What the individual knows or has observed can determine that person's performance. In addition to conditioning or direct reinforcement, attention to the task, a cognitive representation of it, and rehearsal are all important. In recent years, Bandura has relied increasingly on cognitive approaches, particularly in his work on methods of inducing behavioral change (Bandura, Adams, & Beyer, 1977). Such efforts are quite consonant with Rotter's pioneering approach.

Another recent contribution is by Walter Mischel (1973). Described as a "cognitive social learning reconceptualization," it borrows heavily from Rotter's theoretical notions. Mischel proposes several cognitive social learning variables: cognitive and behavioral construction competencies, encoding strategies and personal constructs, behavior-outcome and stimulus-outcome expectancies, subjective stimulus values, and self-regulatory systems and plans.

PROPOSITIONS

Social learning theory (Rotter, 1954; Rotter, et al., 1972) is presented in a series of seven postulates and attendant corollaries (the postulates are presented as propositions here). The postulate-corollary format helps convey with clarity exactly where the theory stands on various issues. But we should not regard these general principles as describing a finished theory; new concepts may be added and old emphases downgraded. For example, in Rotter's original exposition in 1954 no mention was made of the concept of internal versus external control of reinforcement, which has become so prominent in the research literature today that some people seem to confuse it with social learning theory generally.

1. *The unit of investigation is the interaction of the individual and his meaningful environment.*[1]

Rotter takes a *field theory* view of behavior. Other theories, particularly some personality theories, emphasize inner determinants (ego, id, traits, types, etc.) as the chief predictors of behavior. It is the contention here, however, that useful predictions of human behavior cannot be made without an adequate description of the environment or situation in which the behavior occurs. It cannot be emphasized enough that Rotter's is an interactionist theory which relies heavily on both personality and situational variables.

The term *meaningful environment* refers to the environment as perceived. That is, the significance of the environment lies not in its objective parameters but in the acquired meaning it takes on for the individual. Situations, then, are not just collections of physical stimuli. They are also collections of cues that (based upon past experience) arouse ex-

pectancies for the occurrence of certain events or stimulate expectancies regarding the probabilities that certain behaviors will lead to certain outcomes. This implies the importance of experience or learning, which are stated in a pair of corollaries of this first postulate.

Corollary 1: *The study of personality is the study of learned behavior. Learned behavior is behavior that is modifiable, that changes with experience.* The social learning theorist chooses to focus on learned behavior; to predict from one learned reaction to another. This is not to say that physiology, genetics, reflex actions, maturation, or related factors are unimportant. Indeed, such factors may be crucial in initially establishing the quantity and quality of learned behavior. But it is difficult if not impossible to trace learned behaviors back to such origins. It is equally difficult to measure instinctual, genetic, or biological factors. As a practical matter, then, it appears more profitable to focus on learned reactions and then to predict from one set of learned behaviors to another. As an example, how shall we predict excessive eating behavior and develop means of curbing it in an overweight person? We could take metabolic measurements and even attempt to compile a genetic history. In a few instances such a course would reveal a defect and possible medical solution, in which case social learning theory would be less useful than an alternative view. But in many cases, we would find that previous learning history, personality problems, or learned reactions in dealing with stress are the factors controlling excessive eating. Consequently, understanding the behavior and outlining a method to change it would depend more on knowledge of the person's learning history than a biological, instinctual, or medical history.

---

[1] These postulates (propositions) and corollaries are taken from Rotter (1954). In the interests of space limitations, some of Rotter's postulates have been shortened or paraphrased.

Corollary 2: *This theory requires the study of experience or sequences of events. Its method is historical, for an analysis of any behavior involves the investigation of the conditions preceding its appearance.* Basically, this corollary states Rotter's contention that people's behavior can only be understood or explained by recourse to prior events in their lives. Of course, the past does not cause the present. How can it? It is already gone. Perhaps eventually we will develop a descriptive technology so powerful that all we need do is describe people *now* in order to predict their future behavior. But we have not arrived at that point yet. Consequently, we must rely on a historical approach. We must, to some degree, reconstruct the person's past. How minutely we execute this reconstruction is determined by how precisely we wish to predict and over what range of situations. For example, should we wish only to predict a person's final grade in chemistry we might use just a chemistry aptitude test that deals exclusively with the person's present responses. But if we want to predict that person's reaction to any achieved grade, or the remedial steps to be taken, or whether the student will remain in school or change career plans, then some knowledge of that person's history of learned reactions will be necessary.

2.   *Constructs of this theory are not dependent for explanation upon constructs in any other field.*

In effect, Rotter argues here that constructs from one mode of description should be consistent with those from another. But no hierarchy exists. In this postulate Rotter rejects reductionistic modes of thought which suggest that all

psychological explanations must be reduced to, for example, neurological or physiological explanations. A construct point of view means that there is no true way of describing events—only alternative ways. An event may be described medically, economically, religiously, et cetera. Which description is employed depends on one's purposes. When investing, I employ an economic frame of reference. When ruminating about the meaning of life, I may seek a religious outlook. When I feel a sharp pain in the abdomen, I am likely to relinquish my religious set and move on to things medical. Each conceptual level contains a focus of convenience that defines its utility. Nor is it true that reducing explanations to ever-increasing molecular levels (for example, from religion to psychology to physiology to biochemistry) is always useful. For example, it is not at all clear what neurology has to offer in the case of many questions about human social behavior. Reductionism leads inevitably to an infinite regress. Therefore, the level one chooses to employ for explanation is a utilitarian decision and not a matter of which level is the "truly" basic one.

3.   *Behavior takes place in space and time; it may be described by psychological constructs but also by physical constructs.*

Thus, there may be psychological descriptions or constructions of behavior and personality. But there may be physical, chemical, or neurological ones as well. Any approach that views the events themselves, rather than the description of the events, as different is rejected as *dualistic.*

Corollary 1: *Any conception of behavior wherein "physiological behavior" is* conceived of as causing personality behavior or vice versa is rejected as dualistic.

Corollary 2: *Any conception of behavior wherein explanation is made on the basis of the interaction of body with mind is rejected as dualistic.*

As noted previously, an event may be described biochemically, medically, psychologically, or whatever. But description should not be confused with the event itself. To argue that a pain is caused by fear of failure is really to argue that one level of description causes another. However, we become so accustomed to saying such things as a headache is caused by frustration that dualism almost seems to become one of life's givens. While in the short run dualistic explanations such as those typified by the psychosomatic approach may be useful, over the longer theoretical-research haul they inevitably invite confusion and fuzzy thinking.

4. *Not all behavior may be usefully described with personality constructs; the level, complexity, and stage of development of the organism are crucial.*

Psychological concepts cannot explain why yeast makes dough rise any more than medical concepts can explain the decline of the dollar. Psychological concepts fail us with certain species as they do with newborn human infants. With which species they are useful or exactly at what stage of human development they achieve real utility is an issue that can only be settled in the research arena.

Corollary 1: *Physiological or other constructs may be used in describing some of the conditions present when personality characteristics are first acquired.*

This acknowledges that before we can deal with the organism from a psychological point of view we must depend on concepts from nonpsychological levels of description.

Corollary 2: *Physiological or other constructs may be used by psychologists for any practical purpose.* This may occur especially when there are known correlations between physiological and psychological descriptions and when the psychological description is, practically speaking, difficult to make.

Corollary 3: *The human organism may interact with itself using learned meanings (or symbols) to describe in physiological terms or in terms characteristic of other modes of description.* Thus, we learn to use, for example, physiological terms such as *hungry* or *thirsty*. But these reactions are often most usefully described psychologically. Experienced hunger may actually correlate poorly with tissue states, and sometimes thirst is not really related to body dehydration at all. Rather, the person may be expecting to fail, and the described physiological state may only reflect fear.

5. *A person's experiences influence each other; otherwise stated, personality has unity.*

A new experience is colored by acquired meanings, and old acquired meanings or learnings are influenced and changed by new experience. Ideally, perfect prediction of learned behavior would require total knowledge of previous experience.

This suggests that the behavior of individuals becomes increasingly stable as time goes on. Not only do individuals choose the situations or experiences they will undergo because of their previous experiences, they also interpret and attach meanings to these new experiences on the basis of past experience. This lends an increasing unity, coherence, and stability to the person's behavioral patterns over the years. Consequently, it is fair to say that one's personality becomes more and more recognizable as time passes. None of this, however, is meant to imply that we can ignore the contribution of specific situational factors in prompting a given behavior, nor does it suggest that new experiences never have a strong impact. As an example, social learning theory would decry the tendency of psychoanalytic explanations of adult behavior that give exclusive attention to childhood experiences at the expense of more recent ones. In essence, the social learning theory perspective is a dynamic one that accepts the interaction of personality and situation but also takes note that individuals tend to select behavioral situations that they regard as compatible.

Corollary 1: *One cannot truly speak of the "cause" or "etiology" of behavior as described by personality constructs but only of the conditions, present and antecedent, necessary for the occurrence of the behavior. Such descriptions are never "ultimate" or final.* To say that a behavior was caused by X has a basic or final ring to it. Actually, there is a chain of events that lead up to the one in which we are interested. A man is killed in an auto crash. What was the cause? An ongoing driver who crossed the median strip? But who or what prompted the victim to be on the highway in the first place? And who taught the other driver how to drive? The answers to all of these questions (and many more) could be considered as causes. The social learning approach is to give up the quest for causes and, instead, to identify past and current conditions that are sufficient to allow us to predict a given event with a satisfactory degree of efficiency. To search for basic causes is to become caught up in an infinite regress of causes; from a swerving oncoming driver, to poor driver training, to irresponsible parents, to Henry Ford, and so on.

6. *Behavior has a directional aspect; it may be said to be goal-directed, and the directional aspect is inferred from the effect of reinforcing conditions.*

This postulate acknowledges what is perhaps the most ubiquitous principle in psychology—that human behavior is motivated and goal-directed and that its acquisition can frequently (but not always) be understood to be determined by motivational factors. Human behavior, then, is directed toward or away from various aspects of the environment.

Rotter's orientation here, as noted in an earlier section, reflects what might be termed an *empirical law of effect*. This means that the reinforcing effects (positive or negative) of an event are inferred from the person's movement toward or away from the goal. Attempting to demonstrate actual drive reduction in the case of human behavior is exceedingly difficult and fraught with all kinds of logical and empirical problems. How, for example, are we to show that praise experienced by individuals really reduces their need for it? Human psychological needs seem particularly enduring and resistive to reduction—even temporarily, in many instances. To circumvent these problems social learning theory views any stimulus complex as possessing reinforcing properties to the extent that it produces movement in the person toward or away from it.

This view of reinforcement is sometimes regarded as circular. That is, no determination seems possible as to whether an event is reinforcing until the individual has moved toward or away from it. While it is true that individuals sometimes develop rather idiosyncratic goals (particularly so in psychopathological groups), it is also true that there are widespread agreements among people about what is reinforcing and what is not. Both at a broad cultural level and for specific groups it is possible to make this assertion. And so long as this is so, circularity is not a seriously limiting problem.

Social learning theory speaks of *goals* (or reinforcements) when the focus is on environmental conditions that produce behavioral movement. When our focus is on the person, then the term *need* is employed. But both needs and goals are inferred from the direction of the individual's behavior. For example, achieving high marks, being awarded a fellowship, or being praised by a professor are all goals which a given student may pursue. When the student does so we also refer to a need for achievement. Both the need and the reinforcing quality of the specific environmental events are inferred from the direction of behavior (pursuit of those goals).

Corollary 1: *The needs of a person as described by personality constructs are learned or acquired. Early goals (and some later ones) may be spoken of as arising owing to the association of new conditions with the reinforcement of physiological homeostatic movements, and most later goals or needs arise as means of satisfying earlier learned goals.*

Corollary 2: *Early acquired goals in humans (which play a great role in determining later goals) appear as the result of satisfactions and frustrations which, for the most part, are entirely controlled by other people.* This, then, is what is meant by a *social learning* theory. The ultimate development of social-personality behavior is heavily dependent on the child's relationships and interactions with other people. Biological or tissue needs motivate much early behavior. But the learning that stems from such needs leads to the development of new social, psychological needs involving those people who care for the child. Paradoxically, these social or psychological needs often subsequently become more powerful than the very biological needs which produced them.

Corollary 3: *For any behavior to occur regularly in a given situation or situations, it must have been made available to the person using it by leading to some reinforcement or reinforcements during previous learning experiences.* While availability may come about by various means, including observation and imitation, *regular occurrence* of a behavior will be determined by reinforcement.

Corollary 4: *A person's behaviors, needs, and goals are not independent but belong in functionally related systems. The nature of these relationships is determined by previous experience.* For example, a group of behaviors, all of which lead to the same or similar outcomes, will develop a kind of functional equivalence. That is, a positive reinforcement of one will increase the potential strength of all. They will thereby achieve a greater degree of intergroup similarity than a group of randomly selected behaviors. The same is true for a group of reinforcements. If mother, father, aunt, and wife all provide dependency satisfactions, they too will develop a greater degree of intergroup similarity than a randomly selected group of reinforcers. The point is that prediction need not involve just specific behavior-reinforcement sequences. Instead, we may make predictions that involve groups of functionally related behaviors or reinforcements.

7. *The occurrence of a behavior is determined not only by goals or reinforcements but also by the person's expectancy that these goals will occur.*

Where Proposition 6 introduced the motivational component of Rotter's theory, Proposition 7 introduces the cognitive, anticipatory element. This concept asserts that something besides reinforcement is necessary to account adequately for human behavior. While an expectancy concept may not be necessary to predict the behavior of lower organisms, it does appear to be a distinct aid in the case of humans. However, it seems that recently even animal behaviorists are increasingly finding a place for expectancy notions in their work with animals.

The foregoing postulates (propositions) and corollaries provide the basis for understanding how this social learning theory attempts to account for human behavior. We can now proceed to outline the concepts employed by Rotter's theory. This will include their characteristics, their determinants, and the manner in which they are measured.

Behavior Potential. Behavior conceptualized broadly includes direct, overt, physical acts as well as more implicit behaviors such as thinking or planning. The latter behavior would, of course, be inferred from other directly observable behaviors. The measurement of behavior potential (in the case of observable behavior) involves simply determining the presence, absence, or frequency of occurrence of a given behavior.

Presumably, when a behavior occurs this signifies that it was the one with the greatest potential for occurrence. The basic concepts presented earlier state that behavior potential is determined by both expectancies and reinforcement value. The exact mathematical relationship between expectancy and reinforcement value has yet to be determined (although it is probably multiplicative). But it can be demonstrated that behavior potential is higher when expectancy and reinforcement value are both high, or when one is high and the other moderate, than when both are low.

When we are dealing with groups of functionally related behaviors the concept of *need potential* is used. This refers to the mean potentiality of a group of functionally related behaviors directed toward obtaining the same (or a set of similar) reinforcements. To measure need potential it is possible to employ such means as direct observation over a period of time, paper and pencil techniques, rankings, or paired comparisons.

Reinforcement Value. It is true that social learning theory regards psychological needs or reinforcements as having arisen from their association with physiological need reduction. But what determines the present value of a reinforcement for a given individual? The value of a reinforcement does *not* depend on primary drive reduction. Psychological goals, needs, or reinforcements attain their value because of their association with other reinforcements.

For example, money has no intrinsic value. Its value resides in the subsequent reinforcements which the person expects that money will buy. The value of money, then, lies not in itself but in the reinforcements with which it is associated. Formula 4 in the Appendix expresses these determinants of reinforcement value.

In general, the values of reinforcements are rather stable. They have acquired their values under spaced conditions of learning and also under partial rather than 100% reinforcement conditions. Furthermore, relationships among reinforcements are often not verbalized. For example, the individual may never have verbalized the fact that achievement goals are really valued because they lead to parental acceptance.

But changes in reinforcement value do occur. *Persistent* nonoccurrence of parental praise for achievement (assuming the achievement is not also associated with other reinforcements) will reduce the value of achievement goals. The value of money or things material may decline as one acquires highly valued friends who denigrate their value. Psychotherapy may lead to insights about relationships among personal values that will prompt some changes. But in general, a reinforcement tends to maintain its value until new associations or pairings with other reinforcements are made on a stable basis.

The value of a reinforcement can also be understood by its membership in a group of functionally related reinforcements. Three versions of generalization help account for these functional relationships. First, there is *primary stimulus generalization.* A child, for example, may learn to attach a negative value to pudding because, on the basis of sheer physical similarity, it resembles strained foods which he or she does not like.

In the case of *mediated stimulus generalization,* the individual learns that several behaviors are functionally equivalent because they all lead to the same reinforcement. If, for example, a husband learns that feigning illness, complaining what a hard day he had at the office, and reciting the litany of his humble origins all lead to wifely concern, then a strong reinforcement (either positive or negative) of one of these behaviors will affect the potential occurrence of all of them.

Generalization of expectancy changes relates to the idea that a group of reinforcements is interrelated. When one of them occurs, this affects the individual's expectancy for the occurrence of the others. Thus, a child who is refused permission to go to the movies is not likely to expect to be allowed to attend the circus. But such a refusal will have little effect on the expectancy of being allowed to go to the library. Of course, in all these examples of generalization, the outcome may be quite different if specific differentiations have been learned.

Reinforcement value is defined as the degree of preference for any one of a group of reinforcements to occur, assuming the probabilities of all occurring are equal. Two methods of measuring reinforcement value have most frequently been used. The first method has been illustrated by Phares and Rotter (1956). They presented male junior high school students with a list of 18 reinforcements (e.g., Be praised by the teacher for writing a good book report; Win a wrestling match with a friend). They were first asked to imagine that all the reinforcements were equally likely to occur and then asked to rank them in order of their preferences. The second technique involves behavioral choices (Lotsof, 1956). Again, if expectancy is controlled, we can assume that when a person chooses one reinforcement over others this reflects the superior value of that reinforcement.

The broader conceptualization of reinforcement value is termed *need value.* Reinforcement value refers to a preference for *one* reinforcement over others. Need value describes a preference for a group of functionally related reinforcements. By functionally related is meant that what happens to any reinforcement in the group affects all the other members. To measure need value, techniques such as objective tests (Liverant, 1958), projective devices (Fitzgerald, 1958), and interview methods (Tyler, Tyler, & Rafferty, 1962) have been used.

Expectancy. This is a subjective probability held by the individual that any given reinforcement or set of reinforcements will occur in a specific situation. The determinants of expectancy are: (1) probability based on one's history of reinforcement (including factors of recency, patterning, and the person's perception of the nature of the casual link between behavior and reinforcement); and (2) the generalization of expectancies from other related behavior-reinforcement sequences. Therefore, it is clear that factors other than the objective counting of prior occurrences of a reinforcement are important in determining one's expectancies.

For example, a student's expectancy for achieving an A on a physics examination will be determined by the student's previous experience on similar tests in the same class. But he or she will probably also generalize expectancies based on similar situations in other science-related courses. Thus, an expectancy is determined both by specific previous experiences and by general ones as well. These relationships are shown in Formula 5 in the Appendix.

In relatively new or novel situations, an individual's expectancies will be largely based on generalizations from other related experiences. But as experience in a specific situation increases, then generalizations from related situations will decline in importance, and specific expectancies will "carry the freight." The role of amount of previous experience is expressed by Formula 6 in the Appendix.

Two general methods of measuring expectancies are commonly used. The first, a behavioral choice method, requires that we hold the value of a group of reinforcements constant and then observe which behavioral choice the person makes. Choosing alternative A over alternative B indicates a higher expectancy of achieving reinforcement by means of A.

The second general approach is verbal. For example, persons may be asked to state a probability of a particular outcome on a scale from perhaps zero to 10 or zero to 100 (e.g., Phares, 1964; Schwarz, 1966). Another task-oriented technique is to ask individuals which score in a series of possible scores they most expect to receive (e.g., Chance, 1959). A third technique employs betting on a behavioral outcome, which is thought to place a premium on accuracy and thus circumvent the tendency of persons to state inordinately high expectancies (wishful thinking, boasting) or very low expectancies (defensiveness). Ford (1963) has used the betting method of measuring expectancies.

The broader analogue of expectancy is *freedom of movement.* This is a mean expectancy for obtaining gratifications from a set of related behaviors directed toward the attainment of a group of functionally related reinforcements. If the individual has, overall, a high expectancy for being successful in the academic achievement need area, then we say that person has high freedom of movement in that area. A variety of direct methods of measurement can be used as above (verbal statements, behavioral techniques such as betting, and decision times). Indirect methods (e.g., projective methods) have been used as well.

Generalized Expectancies for Problem-Solving Skills. This version of generalized expectancies is different from those discussed earlier. It is a relatively recent addition to social learning theory (Rotter et al., 1972) that was stimulated by locus-of-control research (Phares, 1976; Rotter, 1966) and notions about the nature of interpersonal trust (Rotter 1967b, 1971). Both these topics will be taken up later. Generalized expectancies for problem-solving skills indicate that specific behaviors (such as looking for alternative solutions, trusting others, or viewing the locus of reinforcement as residing in fate) will help in the solution of certain kinds of problems. This is regardless of the probability that certain reinforcements will occur.

In short, we are all very much categorizing organisms. We develop ways of looking at situations, irrespective of whether they are achievement or dependency situations or whether we expect to succeed or fail in them. For example, we develop a generalized expectancy (much akin to attitudes) that people can be trusted or that our own efforts are really what determine the occurrence or non-occurrence of rewards. We categorize people or situations not just on the basis of whether reinforcements can be obtained in connection with them, but also on the basis that we expect certain strategies or methods of approach to enhance the likelihood of achieving the desired reward from them.

This variation of generalized expectancies has been expressed formally by Formula 7 in the Appendix.

Minimal Goal Level. This is another frequently encountered social learning concept. Rotter (1954) defines it as "the lowest goal in a continuum of potential reinforcements for some life situation or situations which will be perceived as a satisfaction" (p. 213). On a dimension of reinforcements ranging from positive to negative, the minimal goal level is the point where reinforcements change from positive to negative. This concept has a special application to questions of adjustment and psychotherapy. For example, when someone's minimal goal level in a given need area is high and that person is not achieving reinforcement, freedom of movement will be low and, by definition, the person will be maladjusted. High minimal goals can also lead a person to experience failure, even though others might be quite content with the same level of achievement.

The Situation. The importance of the situation is not an idle cliché in social learning theory. The formulas in the Appendix illustrate that situational influences are regarded as pervasive. Both the definition of concepts and their measurement require strict attention to situational factors.

Personality psychologists have long underemphasized the role of situational factors. But there is really no alternative to a careful analysis of situations so that the cues that affect reinforcement values and expectancies can be identified. Merely providing successively more "insightful" analyses of general personality characteristics will never be a substitute for a complementary situational analysis.

RESEARCH

Methodologies

Social learning theory research is greatly facilitated because it provides three definitions for each construct: (1) *ideal definitions* expressed in the general language of the culture, (2) *working* or *systematic definitions,* which state the relationship of the particular construct to others in the theory and also indicate the construct's antecedents and consequents, and (3) *operational definitions,* which provide a method for measuring the construct. Such a multilevel definitional approach offers a considerable advantage both in communication and in research. Let us illustrate how this approach relates to some typical methodologies employed by the theory.

Expectancy is defined as a subjectively held probability that a particular behavior will lead to a particular reinforcement. This is the ideal definition. At the systematic level, however, there are several definitions expressed by formulas. Each of these formulas expresses a relationship among several theoretical constructs and suggests that the value of an expectancy is a consequence of certain antecedents. For example, the formulas noted earlier define an expectancy as being determined by previous experience in a given situation, expectancies generalized from other situations, and the number of experiences in the situation. Expectancies also are defined operationally by their measurement. Rotter, Fitzgerald, and Joyce (1954) have compared several such measurement approaches. Three of these are: (1) verbal statements expressed by a quantitative scale (e.g., zero to 10 or zero to 100); (2) amount of money the individual is willing to bet on the likelihood of being correct on a given trial; or (3) scores assigned by judges to stories generated by persons in response to projective stimuli such as TAT cards.

There are many research illustrations of these measurement techniques. For example, in a study of the effects of reinforcement value on expectancy statements in skill and chance situations, Phares (1965) used a verbal method. Individuals were required before each trial to indicate their confidence in achieving a specific score on a motor skill by rating themselves along a scale from zero to 10. Rychlak (1958) used a variant of this procedure in which individuals reported the task score they were most confident of achieving. To place a premium on accuracy, Ford (1963) had people bet on task outcomes. However, it should be noted that betting procedures can be influenced by artifacts such as amount of money accumulated. Moreover, no method is totally free of factors that affect accurate measurement. In a study of frustration, V. J. Crandall (1951) employed a projective device (TAT) to measure generalized expectancies (freedom of movement) for success. His interest was not in a single expectancy for a given task outcome but in a broad, general confidence of being successful in a given need area. Trained judges examined the TAT stories for indicators of low freedom of movement such as: central character expresses feelings of self-doubt, the stories have unrealistic endings or the environment is described as threatening.

In the case of reinforcement value, there are the same three levels of definition. Ideally, reinforcement value is defined as a degree of preference for one reinforcement as compared to a specified group of reinforcements (assuming the expectancy of occurrence for all is equal). Systematically, we saw earlier that reinforcement value is determined by (1) the expectancies that the reinforcement in question will lead to other reinforcements, and (2) the value of these other reinforcements. There have been a number of operational approaches to the measurement of reinforcement value, as illustrated earlier (e.g., Lotsof, 1956; Phares & Rotter, 1956).

When one is interested in comparing the value of groups of functionally related reinforcements (need value), a variety of methods can be used. Liverant (1958) developed an objective test to measure the value of or need for recognition versus love and affection. He then presented statements in a forced-choice format and controlled persons' expectancies for attaining these reinforcements through instructions. Fitzgerald (1958) measured need for dependency through the TAT. Trained judges rated people's stories by paying attention to various elements or cues in those stories (e.g., feeling indebted to parental figures; difficulty in making decisions; close relationship with parents). Tyler, Tyler & Rafferty (1962) used an interview method to assess need value.

Social learning theory affords the "situation" considerable prominence, and its emphasis shows up throughout the theory. Consequently, descriptive categories for situations would be highly useful. Unfortunately, little research to develop such categories has been done. However, Rotter (1955) has made a preliminary effort in this direction by outlining four methods of categorizing situations. In the first method, it is suggested that situations be classed as similar for an individual if they arouse similar expectancies for reinforcement. A second method would be to sample the actual reinforcements in specific situations and determine similarity on that basis. Third, assuming we have already classified behaviors in terms of the goals toward which they are directed, those situations that generate similar behaviors would be regarded as similar. Fourth, we could utilize a generalization approach. That is, we could pretest a behavior (or a reinforcement or an expectancy) in several situations. Following this, we could increase or decrease this behavior potential in one situation and then test for a generalization of the increase or decrease in another situation. The greater the generalization between two situations, the greater their similarity.

The methodologies employed in social learning theory have two broad purposes. The first is to account for the manner in which individuals acquire and change their behavior patterns and also to specify the conditions under which they choose to behave one way rather than another when their behavioral repertoire includes both capabilities. This describes what Rotter (1967c) has called a *process theory*. Such a theory attempts to specify the relationships among prior events and later behavior. These prior events can be, of course, either inherited or experiential in character. This kind of theory will also specify the conditions necessary for behavior to change. In a sense, a process theory tries to specify the abstract relationships between variables. Most learning theories are, then, process theories, and Rotter's social learning theory is no exception.

To achieve these goals, the initial methods of social learning theory were heavily disposed toward accounting for the occurrence of specific behaviors. Much of the research was of a highly controlled variety and was concentrated in laboratory settings. Many of the master's theses and doctoral dissertations cited by Rotter in 1954 were devoted to laying out and demonstrating the basic relationships among theoretical variables and the utility of the methods employed to measure these variables. For some (Bandura & Walters, 1963) this seeming preoccupation with laboratory research signified the theory's lack of real-life applicability. Actually, however, this research was designed to study the basic utility of Rotter's view of behavior and to determine the usefulness of its measurement techniques.

The studies of this period tended to deal with specific behaviors (choosing a toy, pushing a button, stating an expectancy from zero to 10, etc.). Much emphasis was on how expectancies generalized in controlled situations. Questions about the relationship between expectancy and reinforcement value were asked. The conditions that affected a person's rank ordering of reinforcements were scrutinized. Relatively speaking, the methods were molecular and the conditions often far removed from the realities of everyday life. But from this basic research came an increased confidence that the constructs of social learning theory provided a potentially useful way of viewing complex social behavior.

But it is important to recall that social learning theory is not just a process theory. It is not just concerned with bits of behavior. As much as anything it is a personality-oriented theory. In addition to the constructs of behavior potential, expectancy, and reinforcement value, it also contains a parallel set of constructs— need potential, freedom of movement, and need value, respectively. These are the kinds of constructs, so necessary to the personality theorist or to the clinician, which provide for a description and account of the broader, more stable patterns of behavior typical of human adults.

These latter constructs are useful in explaining individual differences in behavior. This is what a *content theory* must do. Over the years, the methodology of social learning theory research has shifted more to the realm of individual differences. To achieve this purpose, social learning theory has increasingly looked to the parallel system of constructs. As Rotter (1967c) put it: "To satisfy the second purpose one needs a content theory or a theory which specifies what are the useful descriptive terms

which characterize the more general and consistent behavior of one individual versus another, allowing for prediction in what culturally would be considered a variety of important life situations" (p. 465). This concern with individual differences casts social learning research in the role of a content theory.

In many learning theories, their methods focus on how things are learned rather than on what is learned. But in the case of Rotter's system there is a tentative list of needs, and there are generalized expectancies both for success and in terms of problem-solving strategies (e.g., interpersonal trust, locus of control). As a process theory, social learning theory, as with most other learning theories, tells something about the acquisition and performance of a behavior as a function of reinforcement value and expectancy. But as a content theory it also views each of these variables in terms of functionally related members (Rotter et al., 1972). Consequently, it can also, for example, discuss aggression as a function of the need for love and affection and its associated freedom of movement.

Two studies contrast the process and content methodological aspects of the theory. Phares (1957) investigated the manner in which specific expectancies for success change as a function of the nature of the situation. The question was whether the role of reinforcement would be the same in skill situations as in those perceived by students as determined by chance factors. Female college students were asked to perform difficult perceptual judgments over a series of trials. In the first condition they were instructed that the task was so difficult that being correct was a matter of luck. In the second condition they were told that, although difficult, the task related to skill, and people varied in their ability to make correct responses. The basic result was that expectancy changes were greater and more frequent under skill than under chance conditions. Apparently, chance conditions provide less basis on which to generalize expectancies based on past success or failure, as compared to skill conditions. Such a study demonstrates that the way in which reinforcement (being right or wrong in this case) influences expectancies is not invariant but is significantly tied to the nature of the situation in which that reinforcement occurs. Notice that content was not the focus of this study. This was a laboratory study which established some additional relationships among constructs in the theory. Thus, the same results might be expected for all reinforcements, regardless of need area (approval, affection, achievement, etc.) and expectancy (for success or failure).

On the content side of the coin, Efran and Broughton (1966) set out to examine the effects on visual behavior of expectancies for social approval. Male college students took two paper-and-pencil measures of generalized expectancies for achieving social approval. Subsequently, each student was required to talk about himself for five minutes in front of two confederates. Previously, interaction with one of the confederates had led the students to expect approval from that confederate. During the five-minute period it was found that the students maintained more eye contact with the person from whom they had received approval than with the other confederate. Clearly, this study deals with personality content. It suggests that people high on the individual-differences continuum of social approval will behave differently from those low on the continuum. Furthermore, while these results can be generalized to a variety of behaviors that are functionally related to social approval, they *cannot* necessarily be generalized to areas such as achievement, aggression, or the like.

Rotter et al. (1972, pp. 328–331) catalogued a lengthy list of social learning studies that dealt with content in various need areas (recognition-status, love and affection, dominance, dependency, independence, academic recognition and achievement, social approval, aggression, and altruism) and in generalized expectancies (guilt, locus of control, cautiousness, and interpersonal trust). That list has now grown considerably longer, especially in the area of generalized expectancies.

Animal Studies

Almost without exception, social learning theory research has been carried out with humans. While there is no question that animal and physiological research has taught us much about the nature of the learning-behavioral processes, social learning theory was designed to predict the behavior of humans in complex social situations. Consequently, its constructs, particularly those of a cognitive nature, make the application of animal research tenuous at best. Animal research can sometimes be regarded as suggestive. But the dual purpose of social learning theory (both a learning theory and a theory of personality) limits the adequacy of animal research in handling the complex explanations required for human behavior.

Nevertheless, some may argue that the current popularity of research on learned helplessness (Seligman, 1975) proves that inattention to animal research leads social learning theory to overlook important issues. After all, our knowledge of learned helplessness in humans grew out of laboratory research with animals. But the social learning concept of locus of control (Lefcourt, 1976; Phares, 1976; Rotter, 1966) is a broader, more complex, and theoretically derived concept that can readily subsume notions of learned helplessness. The locus of control notion was developed prior to the animal research on learned helplessness. It was developed solely out of inferences from previous social learning research with humans.

Human Studies

Social learning theory is a multipurpose theory. As a result, the research associated with it deals with learning, personality development, personality and its measurement, social psychology, psychopathology, and psychotherapy. We will concentrate in this section on research that deals with learning and personality, and in the Implications section we will outline some of the theory's implications for other areas. In any case, the research based on the theory is so extensive that we can provide only a brief sampling.

Learning. A major contribution to our understanding of the learning process is research which explicates the ways in which expectancies generalize and change. Both expectancies and reinforcement value determine the occurrence of behavior. But reinforcement of one behavior does not affect every behavior in the person's repertoire. Neither does it always affect only the specific behavior reinforced. The effects of a reinforcement may be selective and specific, general, or nearly inconsequential. The crucial factor is the manner in which a reinforcement affects the expectancy for that behavior and others to lead to reinforcement in the future. How, then, do expectancies generalize?

Chance (1959) found that expectancies generalize to a greater extent when individuals see two behaviors as leading to the same goal, as opposed to when the behaviors lead to different goals. Thus, generalization may be said to occur along lines of need relatedness. In her study, some people were told that both tests employed in the study measured the same thing. Other people were instructed that they measured different things. All persons estimated their probable scores on both tests before taking either. After taking one test, they received a prearranged score below their previously stated expectancies. Next, they reestimated their probable scores on the second test before taking it. The generalization measure was the difference between the first and second estimate for the second test. That difference turned out to be a function of whether the two tasks were described as measuring similar or different things (even though physically they were quite similar). Dean (1960) reported similar results. At a broader level, V. J. Crandall (1951) measured expectancies for success on the basis of judges' ratings of thematic stories. He, too, observed that when persons were frustrated there was generalization such that expectancies for success decreased for behaviors related to the same need that was frustrated, but not when the needs were unrelated. In summary, then, the success or failure of given behaviors will have effects on subsequent behavior that are, in large measure, determined by whether the behaviors lead to the same or similar goals.

Many learning theories give the appearance of neglecting individual differences. Yet, the way in which generalization takes place is undoubtedly heavily influenced by such differences. For example, Rychlak and Lerner (1965) defined anxiety as a low generalized expectancy for success. They discovered that anxious people generalize expectancies from more recent experiences, while non-anxious people are more likely to resist the influence from recent experience and to evidence a greater stability in generalized expectancy. Phares and Davis (1966) showed that individuals who typically employ broad categories in construing their environment also tend to generalize expectancies from one task to another to a significantly greater extent than do narrow categorizers. Although some (Touhey, 1973) may consider generalization here to be really a measure of risk-taking, the fact remains that generalization of expectancies can be linked to individual differences and is not just a simple function of the situation at hand. At the very least, then, it is necessary to know something of the individual's learning history (individual differences) if we are to predict behavior with increasing accuracy.

Earlier we described a study (Phares, 1957) which suggested that the effects of reinforcement are not invariant. Instead, they vary depending on whether individuals perceive the reinforcement as contingent on their own behavior or on luck. This work has been confirmed in several studies, including Walls and Cox (1971). A considerable amount of social learning research demonstrates that learning under *skill* conditions is quite different from learning in chance situations. For example, James and Rotter (1958) instructed one group that a task was governed by chance factors while another was told that performance was determined by skill. Half of each group was reinforced on a 50% schedule; the other half on a 100% regimen. Of especial interest was the data on extinction of expectancies (three consecutive trials on which an expectancy of zero or 1 was

stated). Under skill conditions the trials to extinction were longer for the 100% reinforcement schedule than for the 50% schedule; under chance conditions the reverse was true. Both Stabler and Johnson (1970) and Holden and Rotter (1962) obtained similar results with somewhat different populations and expectancy measures. But these results were produced by manipulating the nature of tasks through experimental instructions. Will the same results be obtained when the skill and chance nature of tasks is determined by a person's prior experience with them? Rotter, Liverant & Crowne (1961) used an ESP task for the chance condition and a hand steadiness task in the skill condition. The results regarding extinction of expectancies were exactly the same as those reported above.

Basically, the results of these and related studies have two implications. First, when persons adopt the expectancy that they do not control the occurrence of reinforcement, they generalize less from the past and do not use increasing experience to gauge the future. Consequently, as Phares (1976) put it: "They learn a great deal less, and this decrement in learning seems directly attributable to the effects on expectancy of a belief that, in a given situation, they do not control the relationship between behavior and reinforcement" (p. 30, italics deleted).

The second implication of these skill-chance studies is that many conclusions about human learning could bear re-examination, since such learning data have so often been collected in laboratory settings that may have been construed by subjects as under experimenter control (Rotter, 1966). As we have seen, experimenter control can lead to some surprising outcomes, a reversal of the customary results on extinction as a function of reinforcement being the most handy example.

Another prominent contribution of social learning research involves our understanding of the effects of delay of reinforcement (and the bases of those effects). For example, why will human subjects sometimes forego a small, immediate gratification for a delayed larger one? And why do they sometimes reverse this preference? Much research has implicated the significant role of both reinforcement value and expectancy (Mischel, 1966).

A study by Mahrer (1956) illustrates some of the basic methodology in this research area. He ascertained the toy preferences of a group of second- and third-grade boys. These boys were led to develop either high, moderate, or low expectancies for the occurrence of delayed reinforcements (toys). Three days later these boys were given a choice between an immediate or a delayed reinforcement. The results led Mahrer to conclude that expectancy for the occurrence of delayed reinforcements can be developed and modified by previous experiences in which delayed reinforcements either do or do not occur.

Mischel and Staub (1965) studied eighth-grade boys who worked on a series of problems and were allowed to succeed, fail, or else were provided no feedback. Later, each boy chose between (1) less valuable but immediately obtainable rewards that were not dependent for their occurrence on a successful task performance, and (2) more valuable rewards whose attainment was contingent on achieving successful solutions to problems during a delay period. Contingent rewards were more often chosen after initial success than after failure. Even under no-feedback conditions, boys who possessed high generalized expectancies

for success more often chose the contingent rewards than did boys with low generalized expectancies. This study involved actual behavior and not just stated expectancies, and it also introduced instrumental activity into the delay period, thereby coming closer to what actually transpires in real-life situations.

Seeman and Schwarz (1974) studied the relationship between affective state and preference for immediate versus delayed reward. They noted that success and failure produce corresponding affective states which, in turn, mediate preferences for reinforcement. The children (nine-year-olds) who experienced success more often chose delayed rewards than did those who failed.

Still another factor that tempers the effects of reinforcement is a delay during a trial sequence. Research by Phares (1964) and by Schwarz (1966) illustrates this factor. In the latter study, predetermined success and failure were provided persons on a motor skills task. Several orders of success and duration of delay periods during the trial sequence were employed. Prior to each trial a verbal expectancy statement for success was taken. It was found that a long delay period tends to shift expectancies in the direction of those held earlier in the same situation and also in the direction of expectancies generalized from other related situations. Thus, the effects of recently administered reinforcements will be weakened if a delay period of some length follows them and if they are relatively inconsistent with previously obtained reinforcement.

A social learning theory analysis can also help bring order to the disarray in research that attempts to determine the relationship between expectancy and reinforcement value. There has long been a controversy over this relationship. Some (e.g., Atkinson, 1957) have stressed the inverse relationship between the two variables. Rotter (1954) and Edwards (1954) have argued, however, that they are independent. Specifically, the social learning construction here (Rotter et al., 1972) is that expectancy and reinforcement values are systematically independent. However, for given individuals in certain conditions they may be related because of prior learning experiences. For example, some individuals (especially children) may state higher expectancies for the occurrence of valued reinforcements. What this really suggests is an element of wishful thinking that can be controlled when incentives for accuracy are introduced (Crandall, Solomon, & Kellaway, 1958). Yet, Jessor and Readio (1957) could find no evidence that value influences expectancies in children, but with college students, as the value of an event increases, so does its expectancy of occurrence (especially when objective probabilities hover around .50). In another study Hess and Jessor (1960) observed that the rate of learning and asymptotic level of expectancies are independent of reinforcement value. Furthermore, Worell (1956) found that a valued event tended to depress expectancies for its occurrence. To account for such a finding, Worell suggested that achievement situations may sometimes challenge our sense of competency, with the result that defensive reactions (lowered expectancy statements) are provoked.

Basically, the foregoing investigations (and others like them) suggest that the kind of results produced are very much a function of the nature of the situation. Wishfulness, defensiveness, or accuracy of expectancy statements can all be elicited, depending on how individuals construe the cues in the situation. Likewise, studies by Phares and Rotter (1956) and by Henry and Rotter (1956) showed that situationally aroused expectancies can alter the value of reinforcement in the situation. Thus, regardless of what the abstract nature of the relationship between expectancy and reinforcement value ultimately turns out to be, one thing is clear. Accurate predictions in a specific situation will be achieved only by a careful analysis of relationships between situational cues and expectancy for behavior-reinforcement sequences.

Personality and Learning. The multifaceted nature of social learning theory has been noted; it is both a process and a content theory. Its basic concepts are relatively molecular, but its parallel broader conceptions give it a molar texture as well. The basic concepts in the theory are particularly appropriate when the focus is on single behaviors; the broader concepts are better able to handle predictions for functionally related categories of behaviors (need potential).

Because of this versatility, social learning theory has been able to study the role of individual differences variables in mediating the learning-behavior process. Consider, for example, the notion of internal versus external control of reinforcement (Lefcourt, 1976; Phares, 1976; Rotter, 1966, 1975). This is a generalized expectancy regarding the manner in which events may best be construed in order to solve the problems presented by these events. It is a continuum: Individuals toward the internal end (internals) tend to regard the occurrence of reinforcement as mediated by their own efforts, while individuals toward the external end (externals) attribute responsibility to luck, chance, fate, powerful others, or perhaps to the complexity of the world.

Three illustrations in the area of decision making are relevant here. Rotter and Mulry (1965) found that in a skill situation internals took significantly longer to make difficult discriminations than did externals. With chance instructions, however, there was a trend for externals to take longer to arrive at a decision than internals. Not only does this study suggest that decision time can be used as a measure of reinforcement value (importance of being correct in this situation), it also suggests that to account adequately for decision-making behavior we must consider generalized expectancies for internal-external control—an individual differences variable.

Liverant and Scodel (1960) determined that internals tended to prefer bets that were of intermediate probability or else very safe ones, and also that they bet more money on safe versus risky possibilities, as compared to externals. Lefcourt (1965) noted that black individuals behaved in an internal fashion in a gambling situation; for example, they chose fewer low probability bets, made fewer shifts in bets, and generally took fewer risks than whites. Both these studies imply that prediction of current behavior will be enhanced by knowledge of the person's relevant learning history or, stated otherwise, individual differences.

Verbal conditioning is another excellent example of how learning interacts with personality variables. Considerable research shows that internals are more resistant to subtle influence from another person than are externals (see Phares, 1976). Furthermore, neither sheer exposure to reinforcement nor the person's discovery of the reinforcing cue and its contingency to the critical response seem enough to explain verbal conditioning. This suggests some interesting possibilities. For example, there is the work of

H. Getter (1966). Based upon both acquisition and extinction trials, he established four groups: (1) *conditioners,* who reached a specific criterion during both conditioning and extinction trials; (2) *latent conditioners,* who did not condition during the acquisition trials but did so during extinction trials; (3) *nonconditioners,* who did not reach the criterion on either set of trials; and (4) *conditioner extinguishers,* who reached the criterion only during acquisition trials. Of particular interest is the fact that the conditioners were especially externally oriented. This suggests that the individuals who showed the best evidence of verbal conditioning were more suggestible. Equally important was the finding that latent conditioners (who showed no evidence of conditioning during training but did so during extinction trials) were quite internal in their orientation. The idea that internals are resistant to influence and externals are suggestible conforms to other findings by both Gore (1962) and Ritchie and Phares (1969).

Strickland (1970) also studied verbal operant conditioning as it relates to internal-external control expectancies. Following her conditioning procedures, she interviewed individuals regarding their awareness of the reinforcement contingencies. She also separated the individuals according to whether they had conditioned or not. She could find no evidence relating internal-external expectancies and ability to condition. She did, however, note that there were substantial differences between persons who were aware and did not condition and those who were aware and did condition. The former individuals were significantly more internal than the latter group.

Subsequent research by Jolley and Spielberger (1973) investigating relationships among internal-external control, anxiety, and awareness suggests the complexity of verbal conditioning processes. It emphasizes that such processes cannot be understood simply in terms of reinforcement contingencies or sequences but that some understanding of the individual differences variables operative in the persons being conditioned is required. Similarly, Doctor (1971) found that aware externals accounted for the conditioning effect, while aware internals, unaware persons, and a control group all performed basically alike in showing no change in rate of emission of reinforced responses.

Other research by Pines and Julian (1972) and Pines (1973) indicates that internals are especially responsive to the informational demands of a task, while externals respond to the social demand characteristics of tasks. Putting this together with the previous research suggests the conclusion that in verbal conditioning paradigms, internals resist complying with what they perceive to be the experimenter's wishes, while externals are only too willing to comply.

Continuing with the theme of the effects of internal-external control expectancies on the learning process, there is also considerable evidence for superior learning in internal subjects (Phares, 1976). Two studies will illustrate the general contours of this research area. DuCette and Wolk (1973) presented individuals with a simple problem-solving task in which a nonverbal cue from the experimenter would suggest the problem's solution. Internals, compared to externals, took significantly fewer trials to discover the solution. Even when experimenters had been instructed not to emit the cue, similar differences occurred (leading to the possible conclusion that internals were ferreting out highly covert cues from the experimenter). Davis and Phares

(1967) placed persons in a situation that required them to attempt to influence the attitudes of another person regarding the Vietnam conflict. For assistance, they could avail themselves of information about the person they were to influence. Davis and Phares reasoned that if internals believe that reinforcements are contingent upon their own behavior, they will more actively seek relevant information so as to influence the other person better. And this is exactly what happened. This and other research led Phares (1976) to conclude the following about the superior learning performances demonstrated by internals:

> The most basic characteristic of internal individuals appears to be their greater efforts at coping with or attaining mastery over their environments. . . . It is confirmed in the field as well as in the psychological laboratory. [This is] accomplished through their superior cognitive processing activities. They seem to acquire more information, make more attempts at acquiring it, are better at retaining it, are less satisfied with the amount of information they possess, are better at utilizing information and devising rules to process it, and generally pay more attention to relevant cues in the situation. (p. 78)

Ryckman (1979) has discussed in detail how the internal-external control continuum relates to a variety of research areas including (1) activity preference and choice behavior, (2) risk-taking strategies, (3) expectancy shifting, (4) achievement motivation and behavior, and (5) schedules of reinforcement.

The foregoing remarks reinforce the notion that the learning process is affected by attention to proper cues. Furthermore, in the case of humans especially, an enormous amount of learning is either mediated by other humans or else takes place in their presence. Recognizing this, Efran and Broughton (1966), in a study noted earlier, utilized social learning theory to formulate the hypothesis that the "looking behavior" subjects will be oriented toward whichever peer they expect to be more approving. Indeed, their results confirmed the idea that visual interaction between people (a prime basis for much learning) is heavily affected by differences in expectancy for approval. Efran (1968) also found that the reinforcement value associated with individuals (as well as the probability of their giving approval) determines visual focus in certain situations.

Another crucial factor in determining both quantity and quality of learning is persistence. Historically, learning psychologists have been largely preoccupied with motivation as a determinant of persistence. But expectancy for success can also be a prime determinant. For example, Lefcourt and Ladwig (1965) found that among black reformatory inmates, those who believed that a task involved skills they possessed were more likely to persist longer on the task than those who did not have such skills. Similarly, Battle (1965), in a study of junior high school students, observed that persistence on an academic task was positively associated with expectancy for success in that need area.

IMPLICATIONS

Theoretical

Many of the theoretical implications of social learning have already been touched on. Its cognitive emphasis particularly suits the theory to explain the individual's choice of behaviors already in the behavioral repertoire. Other theories, such as S–R approaches, seem better equipped to explain how behaviors

are acquired—behaviors not yet in the individual's repertoire (Levy, 1970). The more complex the behavior we wish to explain, the greater the capacity of the cognitively oriented social learning theory to outperform its S–R counterparts in predicting behavior. S–R theories tend to rely on correlations between behavior and the physical properties of stimuli. Social learning theory, with its notions of functional relatedness and generalization of expectancies, tends to be less bound to such physical properties and views stimuli as cues that arouse expectancies for the success or failure of particular behaviors.

Social learning theory (and the research it generates) suggests the artificiality in compartmentalizing learning and personality. Its notion of functional relatedness (needs, freedom of movement) and its emphasis on generalization of expectancies assume a degree of stability of behavior. This, in turn, suggests the necessity for developing instruments or tests for assessing these stable characteristics. Once measured, these characteristics can help explain the cross-situational properties of much human behavior. S–R theories, on the other hand, often stress reinforcement contingencies or stimulus generalization, and these concepts are not likely to encourage the development of personality tests that will capitalize on the stability element in human subjects.

Some people, however, seem to misinterpret the attention of social learning theory to such concepts as generalized expectancies and assume that the theory ignores situational specificity. Social learning theory does, in fact, emphasize both aspects. As Rotter (1977) put it: "Of course there is both situational specificity and cross-situational generality determining behavior, the relative importance of each depending upon the amount of previous experience with the particular situation being considered" (p. 2).

Thus far, our emphasis has been chiefly on the learning and personality aspects of social learning theory. These have been labeled *process* and *content* emphases, respectively. In addition, however, social learning theory has particular implications for social-psychological theory. The special implications here involve a social learning theory analysis of beliefs and social attitudes.

Rotter (1967a) introduced his analysis of beliefs and attitudes by stating: "I equate a *simple expectancy* regarding a property of an object or series of objects or events with the terms *belief* or *simple cognition*" (p. 114). He assumes that cognitions or beliefs do not have all-or-none qualities but may vary in magnitude between zero and 1. They are just like subjective probabilities, and they are capable of change. Thus, I may believe that politicians are chiefly interested in their own self-promotion. What I may really be asserting, however, is that I strongly expect that such persons are self-oriented, but my subjective probabilities are still less than 1. Furthermore, should I encounter a series of selfless politicians, my expectancy that they are self-oriented will decrease significantly.

As children grow and develop, they label their experience and the nature of the properties of the objects or events in that experience. They form concepts. When a series of objects or events have all been similarly labeled, experience with any one of them will affect or generalize to the others. Thus, again, we encounter the notion of functional relatedness. Based on our own direct experience as well as communications from other people, we form broad beliefs or expectancies. These cognitions-attitudes-expec-

tancies-beliefs play an important role in determining our expectancies for behavior-reinforcement sequences. Stated otherwise, they affect the kinds of behaviors we employ (particularly in novel situations). For example, suppose a person has a generalized attitude that others cannot be trusted. Therefore, when listening to a previously unknown salesman extol the virtues of a vacuum cleaner, one's attitude of distrust will probably encourage the person to leave the store without buying. If, however, that salesman had been someone the person had dealt with before and learned to trust (an exception to the person's generalized belief), then a generalized attitude of mistrust would not contribute much to behavior. Instead, the customary notions of need (how important it is that I have a vacuum cleaner) and freedom of movement (expectancies that buying the vacuum cleaner will satisfy the need) will carry most of the predictive freight.

Within social learning theory, two principal attitudes or generalized expectancies for classes of problem-solving situations have been investigated. The first is the previously discussed internal-external or locus of control concept. Another is interpersonal trust (Rotter, 1967b, 1971, 1977). It has been defined as a generalized expectancy (belief) held by an individual that the word, promise, and verbal or written communication of another person or group can be relied on (Rotter, 1967b). An objective scale (Rotter, 1967b) has been developed to measure this expectancy. A variety of investigations have revealed that high-trust persons are less likely themselves to lie or cheat and are more prone to respect the rights of others. They are also less likely to be unhappy, conflicted, or maladjusted and more likely to be sought as friends.

A variety of papers employing social

learning concepts have been reprinted in Rotter et al. (1972). They illustrate the manner in which social learning theory may be applied to social psychology and to the social sciences generally.

Practical

There are a number of practical implications of social learning theory, although at times the distinction between theoretical and practical becomes blurred.

Psychopathology. There have been several general treatments of the implications of social learning theory for psychopathology (Katkovsky, 1976; Phares, 1972). It should be noted, however, that social learning theory specifies no particular criteria for maladjustment, nor does it perceive any need to introduce special concepts to explain pathological behavior. Behavior is just behavior. When it is labeled as maladjusted this reflects someone's value judgment that it is undesirable or else needs to be altered. But this in no way exempts it from customary theoretical analyses (Phares, 1979).

As Katkovsky (1976) points out, everyone behaves in a maladjusted fashion at one time or another. What is really important is whether positive or negative reinforcements flow from this behavior. Maladjusted behavior will be maintained as long as positive reinforcements follow it, thus maintaining the expectancy that such behavior will, in the future, be reinforced. However, the corollary question involves the reasons for persisting in maladjusted behaviors when the consequences ultimately turn out to be negative (failure, disapproval, anxiety, etc.). There are several possible explanations.

First, maladjusted behaviors are often observed in individuals who possess a strong need for gratifications in a certain area but who also have very low expectancies (freedom of movement) for attaining them. From a social learning theory point of view, this is the prototypical maladjusted person. As a result such persons will often avoid a situation in which they expect to fail, or else they will pursue alternative means of gratification. But avoidance all too often prevents their learning skills or behaviors that could lead to satisfactions, while the alternative behaviors are often idiosyncratic or symbolic (obsessions, paranoid ideas, phobias, etc.) and eventually only generate further problems. Jessor, Carman, and Grossman (1968) showed how the discrepancy between need value and freedom of movement can culminate in drinking as a solution.

A second explanation for continued maladjusted behaviors involves the generalization of expectancies. When low expectancies for success become broadly generalized to many situations, the potential for maladjustment rises accordingly.

A third explanation for continued maladaptive behavior is shown by a person who attaches enormous value to the satisfaction of one need. Such an overriding passion often leads to a failure to discriminate among situations. For example, the bedroom, the classroom, the Monopoly game may all become major arenas for the satisfaction of achievement needs. Individuals who fail to make appropriate situational discriminations in satisfying a need are likely to create substantial personal problems for themselves. Jessor, Liverant, and Opochinsky (1963) demonstrated that a particularly strong need that preempts other need satisfactions is often associated with maladjustment.

In still other instances, the source of the individual's problems may stem from the direct or indirect reinforcement of maladjusted behavior (e.g., attention from friends, drinking to gain social approval from others, failure to perceive a personal success because of excessively high minimal goals). Furthermore, a number of cultural, social, or familial conditions may have conspired to prevent the person from ever learning adjusted behaviors in the first place. In the latter case, maladjusted behavior becomes the absence of adjusted behavior (Katkovsky, 1976).

Another interesting application of social learning theory concepts involves the study of deviant behavior in a tri-ethnic community. Jessor, Graves, Hanson, and Jessor (1968) observed that Anglo-Americans, Spanish-Americans, and Indians who all lived in the same western community displayed different rates of problem behavior. Of particular interest, in view of the importance of discrepancies between need values and expectancies, were these groups' scores on these values/expectancies. The differences in need values among the three groups were minor, but differences in expectations for the satisfaction of these needs were significant. Deviant behavior, and particularly drinking, was directly related to individuals' expected inability to satisfy their needs. This study is especially valuable in showing the operation of theoretical variables at both the cultural and individual levels.

The concept of learned helplessness advanced by Seligman (1975) has been the subject of widespread recent research. Growing out of animal research, the basic idea is that individuals who are subjected to inescapable pain or trauma (Task 1) develop a kind of attitude of helplessness (and depression) which then generalizes to subsequent situations (Task 2). As a consequence, even though the person may now, in reality, have potential control over the situation, the person will fail to exercise that control. This feeling of helplessness or lack of control can easily be discussed in terms of social learning concepts of specific expectancies, reinforcement values, generalization of expectancies, and internal-external control of reinforcement. That is, the generalized expectancies existing prior to Task 1 and the specific expectancies developed during that situation will generalize to Task 2 and result in the person's behaving in an apathetic fashion. All of this is highly related to work on internal-external control.

In a different area of psychopathology, Cromwell (1963, 1972) showed how social learning theory concepts may be applied to success-failure reactions in mentally retarded children. Relying on several expectancy notions from social learning theory, Cromwell argued that a large number of retarded children come to expect failure. From this assumption Cromwell was able to demonstrate that: (1) continued success will produce greater initial performance gains in retardates as compared to normals, (2) the magnitude of reaction to failure will be less in retardates than in normals, and (3) increased effort after failure will characterize normals more than retardates. This suggests that the reactions of retardates cannot be understood solely in terms of genetics or medical concepts, and that the application of social learning concepts is not restricted to normals or to those with "emotional problems."

Returning for a moment to a related theoretical point that has practical implications, some mention should be made of a paper by Liverant (1960). He points out that one of the clinical psychologist's most difficult tasks is the utilization of intelligence estimates or IQs to help predict behavior. We seem unable to place information on intellectual functioning into the larger context of a behavioral theory. Thus, behavior is determined by many variables—personality factors, IQ, socioeconomic status, education, and so on. According to Liverant, what is required is a theory of problem solving that will systematically incorporate all these variables. He would discard intelligence as a noun and treat it as an adjective (i.e., people exhibit intelligent behavior, but not intelligence). He would then look to social learning theory concepts such as needs, expectancies, and behavior potentials to provide a framework for the analysis of intelligent or unintelligent behavior.

Psychotherapy and Behavior Change. Perhaps the major assumption of social learning theory is that behavior and behavior change in therapy are not qualitatively different from behavior outside of therapy. The mechanisms and theoretical constructs necessary to account for such changes are the same. Rotter et al. (1972) presented some of the specific research and analysis associated with specific therapeutic procedures. Rotter (1970) also summarized the implications of social learning theory and research for this area.

In recent years, behavior therapy has become especially prominent. Social learning theory helped in this development in several ways. First, a number of clinicians were trained with a social learning background. These clinicians were ready to accept behavioral techniques, and they possessed a theoretical viewpoint capable of integrating strict behavioral approaches with cognitive notions. In addition, social learning theory, with its twofold approach of motivation and cognition, allowed for the fusion of older psychodynamic therapeutic approaches with the newer behavioral ones. Rotter's theory has not produced any new or attention-getting therapeutic methods. Consequently, it has not achieved the therapeutic prominence of certain other clinical approaches. Yet it has widespread relevance for therapeutic practices.

The following are a few of these implications (Rotter, 1970):

1. Psychotherapy is a learning situation in which the therapist helps the patient achieve planned changes in observable behavior and thinking.
2. It is useful to construe a patient's difficulties in problem-solving terms.
3. A common role of the therapist is guiding the learning process so that inadequate behaviors and attitudes are weakened and more constructive and satisfying behaviors are strengthened.
4. Attention must be devoted to how certain behaviors and expectancies arise in patients and how patients misapply or overgeneralize their prior experience.
5. New experiences in real life are often more effective in influencing the patient than those that occur during the therapy hour.
6. Therapy is a form of social interaction.

These implications suggest flexibility of technique from patient to patient, the need to increase problem-solving skills in patients, an active therapeutic role (incorporating interpretation, suggestion, and direct reinforcement), the frequent need for (but not the invariant necessity of) patient insight to bring about behavior change, the importance of guiding patients into real-life situations that will assist in promoting change, and a belief that the laws which account for behavior generally also apply to therapeutic encounters.

Rotter (1978) specifically discussed the role of generalized expectancies for problem solving as they relate to adjustment and psychotherapy. He provides a number of examples of how the following strategies or expectancies can be encouraged and increased in patients to enhance their level of adjustment: internal control, looking for alternatives, interpersonal trust, understanding the motives of others, long-term planning, and discriminating differences in psychological situations.

Health and Body Care.   It was observed earlier that internally oriented individuals, as compared to externals, are consistently more active in trying to cope with their world and attain some measure of mastery over it. A specific manifestation of this tendency lies in the area of health and body care. Strickland (1974) discussed the significant and even dramatic implications that locus of control offers for both physical and emotional well-being. Similarly, Phares (1978) observed that, based on available research evidence, internals more often seek and possess information about their physical condition, are likely to quit smoking, will undertake prophylactic dental behavior, use seatbelts in autos, take preventive medical inoculations, participate in physical fitness activities, exert self-control in weight reduction programs, and practice more effective birth control.

Obviously, the determinants of behavior in the health-care area are complex: Internal-external control is certainly not to be regarded as the sole contributing variable. Nevertheless, this general social learning theory personality variable has shown significant relationships with many behaviors. Indeed, the array of relationships goes quite beyond mastery efforts or health care and includes such things as conformity, social activism, achievement, and pathology and defensiveness. In fact, the volume of research on this social learning theory variable of inter-

nal-external control has been so great (Phares, 1978) that it has become the most heavily investigated personality variable.

Test Construction.   A particular problem in the measurement of personality is the frequent low levels of prediction achieved with assessment techniques. To a considerable extent, this may represent a failure to apply our theories of learning or behavior to methods of testing and to the situations in which testing takes place.

Rotter (1960) has commented on three aspects of these problems. The first aspect relates to the fact that so many test instruments are not derived from a specific theory. Often, tests are "adapted" to purposes for which they were never intended.

The second aspect relates to the failure to regard a person's test behavior as subject to the same behavioral laws as any other behavior. For example, suppose a test subject construes the testing procedure as a means of gaining social approval from the examiner. When these test results later fail to predict a criterion behavior, the examiner is likely to blame the person for faking or else blame the test for being saturated with social desirability. However, we could just as easily "blame" the examiner for failing to apply some theoretical frame of reference to the test situation so that the test taker's needs or expectancies in the situation are examined as they may or may not relate to the situation to which the test is predicting.

A third aspect involves the frequent failure of tests to provide a logical, theoretical basis for predicting from test responses to nontest behavior. For example, if a person expresses a predominant preference on a test for the social approval items, does this mean that he or she will predominantly seek social approval goals in real-life situations? Of course, we could simply say that after a test has been put together we can then empirically determine its correlates. But how much more efficient it would be to select items initially that relate directly to the theoretical constructs necessary for prediction.

From a social learning theory point of view, the implication is that we should develop tests that specifically measure such concepts as need potential, need value, and freedom of movement. Failure to differentiate among such constructs can lead to considerable confusion. For example, a person may express a preference for all the items that relate to need for achievement. Yet, if that person has low freedom of movement in the achievement area, he or she is not likely to behave in an achievement fashion in nontest situations. On another test, certain individuals may indicate that a given class of behaviors (say, sexual behaviors) is typical of them. But this does not tell us why. (Is it because of a strong need or because of a particularly favorable set of expectancies?) Consequently, we are limited in our understanding of how we might change such behavior should there be the need to do so. As Rotter (1960) put it: ". . . a satisfactory theory of goal directed behavior is a primary prerequisite for developing adequate tests. Knowledge of statistics and test construction procedures can be valuable but they cannot supplant an adequate theory of behavior which is applied to the test taking behavior itself" (pp. 314–315).

Personality Development. Social learning theory attempts to deal not merely with adult personality but also with the development of personality. In doing so, it emphasizes the role of the individual's experience and also the differences in situations encountered by individuals. While this gives social learning theory an advantage over maturational theories such as those of Sigmund Freud and Jean Piaget (whose emphasis is perhaps more on stages and less on experience), it also prevents the theory from giving much attention to physiological, biochemical, or even genetic factors that are partially involved in the maturational process. In this respect social learning theory is not much different from other learning theories whose chief focus is limited to the study of learned behavior.

In large measure, social learning theory views socialization as a process in which certain behaviors are acquired and expectancies and values are attached to the potential outcomes of these behaviors in specific situations. The theory also provides a framework which encompasses and describes both the child's and the parent's behavior. Of course, it is necessary to recognize that behavioral or test referents for such variables as need value or freedom of movement will differ depending on age, sex, socioeconomic status, and so on. For example, a behavioral referent for dependency needs in an 18-year-old might be a refusal to leave town to attend a distant college. In a three-year-old it may be crying when a baby sitter shows up. Rafferty, Tyler, and Tyler (1960) showed how observations of the free play of children can be reliably classified according to their implications for need value and expectancy.

The research programs of Vaughn and Virginia Crandall and their associates have been largely oriented toward the study of achievement behavior and its development. For example, work by V. J. Crandall, Dewey, Katkovsky, and Preston (1964) and by Katkovsky, Preston, and Crandall (1964a, 1964b) applied a conceptual scheme derived from social learning theory to both mothers and fathers, as well as to their children. Among other things, it was found that the achievement values parents hold for themselves are similar to those they apply to their children. This similarity shows up not only in the way in which they respond to the child's school achievement but also in the child's achievement behavior in school. These are examples of how social learning theory may be applied to the study of the socialization process.

Other social learning theory work has been oriented toward increasing our understanding of how certain generalized expectancies develop. Both Lefcourt (1976) and Phares (1976) discussed the developmental antecedents of locus of control expectancies. Work by Katkovsky, V. C. Crandall, and Good (1967) and by Davis and Phares (1969) is illustrative of research which suggests that parental nurturance, warmth, and acceptance are significantly related to the child's development of an internal locus of control. However, V. C. Crandall (1973) has also suggested that, in the long run, some degree of maternal "coolness" and criticality may be necessary for an internal orientation to maintain itself all the way to adulthood. Consistency of parental reinforcement has also received some support as a determinant of internal expectancies (Davis, 1969, Levenson, 1973, MacDonald, 1971). Other antecedents reviewed by both Phares and Lefcourt include social class variables, cultural factors, and even ordinal position in the family.

Rotter et al. (1972) discussed the versatility of social learning theory as being both a conceptual and a methodological tool for understanding the developmental process. A variety of behaviors, such as achievement, persistence, working for larger delayed rewards rather than smaller immediate ones, and observing, have been studied. The development of generalized expectancies for in-

ternal-external control and interpersonal trust have also been examined extensively.

Community Psychology. A major development in psychology in recent years has been the emergence of community psychology (Rappaport, 1977). This is a broad movement that has grown both from the seeds of political activism and the failure of the individual model of intervention (e.g., psychotherapy, behavior modification) to significantly reduce the nation's mental health problems. Often it seeks to shift the arena of intervention from the individual to the societal level. Thus, to better the human condition, the community psychologist will focus not so much on changing the individual but on altering social institutions or environments. There is an emphasis on cultural relativity, diversity, and ecology. And the goal is to increase the "fit between persons and environments" (Rappaport, 1977).

Social learning theory is especially compatible with community psychological approaches since it emphasizes situational-environmental variables, as well as active intervening strategies for behavior change. In their discussion of poverty, Gurin and Gurin (1970) point out the special importance of the concept of expectancy in two respects. First, the impoverished typically have a low expectancy of attaining valued goals. Second, they are often overcome by an expectancy of powerlessness. Both expectancies are created through an oppressive environment. But if such expectancies are created by the environment, they can also be changed by the environment. Another way of stating this is to say that we can increase expectancies for success and self-determination by providing an environment in which success occurs (e.g., employment) and where personal effort really influences outcomes (e.g., neighborhood group participations to influence city hall). The implication here is that changes in these kinds of expectancies are perhaps more efficiently brought about by environmental events than by some form of individual therapy that emphasizes insight or the analysis of past experience. Clearly, this notion of powerlessness is quite akin to the social learning theory concept of internal-external locus of control. The belief that one can influence outcomes will lead to a more active, controlling kind of behavior (Phares, 1978).

Rappaport (1977) has characterized the importance of the locus of control variable in this context as follows:

> What is important about this variable for community psychology is its connection to the sociological idea of power and its converse, alienation. Locus of control is one of the few variables in social science that may be shown to have a consistent relationship which ties research across levels of analysis. (p. 101)

SUMMARY

The social learning theory of Julian B. Rotter was developed in the late 1940s and early 1950s. More than 25 years after the publication of *Social Learning and Clinical Psychology* (Rotter, 1954), the theory shows all the signs of increasing popularity and utility. For example, two of his major contributions were determined as the second (Rotter, 1966) and tenth (Rotter, 1954) most frequently cited works (and he the most frequently cited author) in the *Journal of Consulting and Clinical Psychology* for the years 1970–1974 (Cox, 1978). In large measure, this reflects the widespread utility of an approach that is at once a learning theory, a theory of personality, and a framework in which the clinical psychologist can understand, assess, and plan treatment for patients.

Rotter's social learning theory is a grand attempt to combine simultaneously several separate phases in psychology, thus producing one of the broader theories of human behavior. In an age of molecular minitheories, this makes the theory even more serviceable. It provides a framework for handling overt human behavior, cognitive behavior, and personality, as well as changes in behavior and personality.

The major change in the theory since 1954 has been the addition of the concept of problem-solving expectancies. Most frequently, this has referred to the notions of interpersonal trust and internal-external control of reinforcement. Both concepts have led to significant research. In addition, each is a concept that is not only theoretically meaningful but also relates to human concerns that are especially relevant to the era in which we live. That is, trust and alienation are concerns that resonate strongly in society today.

The *internal-external* control concept especially has led to a veritable flood of research, making it the most heavily investigated personality variable in recent memory. Its relevance for areas such as social psychology, pathology, therapy, personality, learning, and community psychology have made it not only popular but heuristic as well.

Social learning theory is especially valuable because it integrates both process and content aspects of theories. For example, it not only provides principles and formulas to determine which behavior in a person's repertoire will occur in a given situation; it also addresses itself to the content of personality and behavior. Thus, it breathes the life of needs, such as recognition or dependency, and expectancies, such as trust or locus of control, into abstract theoretical principles.

Continuing the tradition of Dollard and Miller (1950), the theory emphasizes the essential continuity of learning and personality. In so doing it provides a vehicle as useful to the clinician as to the learning theorist or the personality investigator. Furthermore, its utilization of cognitive, motivational, behavioral, and situational variables has kept it in the mainstream of psychology and enabled it to serve an integrating theoretical function. Although the theory's personality constructs may have helped to preserve its popularity, its unique cognitive-motivational-situational qualities will allow it to continue its increasingly popular integrational functions in the future.

APPENDIX

Formulas in Rotter's Social Learning Theory

1. $BP_{x,s1,Ra} = f(E_{x,Ra,s1} \& RV_{a,s1})$

The potential for behavior x (BP_x) to occur in Situation 1 in relation to reinforcement a is a function of the expectancy (E_x) of the occurrence of reinforcement a following behavior x in Situation 1 and the value of reinforcement a (RV_a) in Situation 1 (Rotter, 1967c, p. 490).

2. $BP_{(x-n),s(1-a),R(a-n)} =$
$f(E_{(x-n),s(1-a),R(a-n)} \& RV_{(a-n),s(1-a)})$

The potentiality of the functionally related behaviors x to n (BP_{x-n}) to occur in the specified Situations 1 to n in relation to potential reinforcements a to n is a function of the expectancies (E) of these behaviors leading to these reinforcements in these situations and the values of these reinforcements (RV) in these situations (Rotter, 1967c, p. 491).

3. $NP = f(FM \& NV)$

Need potential (NP) is a function of freedom of movement (FM) and need value (NV).

4. $RV_{a,s1} = f(E_{R_a \to R_{(b-n)}, s1} \& RV_{(b-n), s1})$

The value of reinforcement a (RV_a) in Situation 1 is a function of the expectancies that this reinforcement (E_{R_a}) will lead to other reinforcements b to n in Situation 1 and the values of these reinforcements (RV) b to n in Situation 1 (Rotter, 1954, p. 152).

5. $E_{s_1} = f(E'_{s_1} \& GE)$

Expectancy (E_{s_1}) is a function of probability of occurrence as based on past experience in situations perceived as the same (E'_{s_1}) and the generalization of the expectancies for the same or similar reinforcements to occur in other situations for the same or functionally related behaviors (GE) (Rotter, 1954, p. 166).

6. $E_{s_1} = f(E'_{s_1} \& \frac{GE}{N_{s_1}})$

An expectancy (E_{s_1}) is a function of the expectancy for a given reinforcement to occur as a result of previous experience in the same situation (E'_{s_1}) and expectancies generalized from other situations (GE) divided by some function of the number of experiences in the specific situation (N_{s_1}) (Rotter, 1954, pp. 166–167).

7. $$E_{s_1} = \frac{f(E' \& GE_r \& GE_{ps_1} \& GE_{ps_2} \cdots G_{ps_n})}{f(N_{s_1})}$$

An expectancy (E_{s_1}) is a function of the expectancy for a given reinforcement to occur as a result of specific experience in the same situation (E'), expectancies generalized from other situations (GE_r), and problem-solving generalized expectancies 1 to n. The latter two variables $(GE_r$ and $GE_{p_s})$ are divided by some function of the number of experiences in the specific situation (N_{s_1}) (Rotter et al., 1972).

ANNOTATED BIBLIOGRAPHY

Lefcourt, H. M. *Locus of control: Current trends in theory and research*. Hillsdale, N.J.: Lawrence Erlbaum Associates, 1976.

This book provides an extensive description of research and theory pertaining to the concept of locus of control.

Phares, E. J. *Locus of control in personality*. Morristown, N.J.: General Learning Press, 1976.

The origins of locus of control and its place in social learning theory are described, and the I-E Scale and research related to locus of control are dealt with extensively.

Rotter, J. B. *Social learning and clinical psychology*. Englewood Cliffs, N.J.: Prentice-Hall, 1954.

This book, the basic and initial statement of Rotter's social learning theory, presents the theory and states its relationship to, and implications for, clinical psychology. One chapter deals with the theory's relationship to other theories. Separate chapters deal with the role of theory in clinical psychology, some major problems in clinical psychology, and problems of description. The application of social learning theory to personality measurement, therapy, and the environmental treatment of problem children is also explored.

Rotter, J. B. Generalized expectancies for internal versus external control of reinforcement. *Psychological Monographs*, 1966, *80* (Whole No. 609).

This paper is the basic presentation of the rationale for the locus of control con-

cept. The validation data of the highly popular I-E Scale are included, along with normative information.

Rotter, J. B. A new scale for the measurement of interpersonal trust. *Journal of Personality*, 1967, *35*, 651–655.

In this paper Rotter introduces the concept of interpersonal trust and presents a scale to measure it.

Rotter, J. B. Generalized expectancies for interpersonal trust. *American Psychologist*, 1971, *26*, 443–452.

This paper presents a further elaboration of the interpersonal trust notion.

Rotter, J. B. Generalized expectancies for problem solving and psychotherapy. *Cognitive Therapy and Research*, 1978, *2*, 1–10.

The place of generalized expectancies for problem solving within social learning theory is described.

Rotter, J. B., Chance, J. E., & Phares, E. J. *Applications of a social learning theory of personality*. New York: Holt, Rinehart & Winston, 1972.

Rotter's second major publication in social learning theory is composed of both original contributions and reprinted research reports, predominantly the latter. Part 1, a relatively concise statement of the theory, is followed by six sections of papers which illustrate the theory's application to learning theory, personality development, personality theory and measurement, social psychology and the social sciences, psychopathology, and psychotherapy and complex behavioral change. Each section consists of from 5 to 11 papers and an integrating summary and discussion.

REFERENCES

Atkinson, J. W. Motivational determinants of risk-taking behavior. *Psychological Review*, 1957, *64*, 359–372.

Bandura, A. *Social learning theory*. Morristown, N.J.: General Learning Press, 1971.

Bandura, A., Adams, N. E., & Beyer, J.

Cognitive processes mediating behavioral change. *Journal of Personality and Social Psychology,* 1977, *35,* 125–139.

Bandura, A., & Walters, R. *Social learning and personality development.* New York: Holt, Rinehart & Winston, 1963.

Battle, E. S. Motivational determinants of academic competence. *Journal of Personality and Social Psychology,* 1965, *2,* 209–218.

Chance, J. E. Generalization of expectancies among functionally related behaviors. *Journal of Personality,* 1959, *27,* 228–238.

Cox, M. W. Frequent citations in the *Journal of Consulting and Clinical Psychology* during the 1970s. *Journal of Consulting and Clinical Psychology,* 1978, *46,* 204–205.

Crandall, V. C. *Differences in parental antecedents of internal-external control in children and in young adulthood.* Paper presented at the American Psychological Association Convention, Montreal, 1973.

Crandall, V. J. Induced frustration and punishment-reward expectancy in thematic apperception stories. *Journal of Consulting Psychology,* 1951, *15,* 400–404.

Crandall, V. J., Dewey, R., Katkovsky, W., & Preston, A. Parents' attitudes and behaviors and grade-school children's academic achievement. *Journal of Genetic Psychology,* 1964, *104,* 53–66.

Crandall, V. J., Solomon, D., & Kellaway, R. The value of anticipated events as a determinant of probability learning and extinction. *Journal of Genetic Psychology,* 1958, *58,* 3–10.

Cromwell, R. L. A social learning approach to mental retardation. In N. Ellis (Ed.), *Handbook of mental deficiency.* New York: McGraw-Hill, 1963.

Cromwell, R. L. Success-failure reactions in mentally retarded children. In J. B. Rotter, J. E. Chance, & E. J. Phares (Eds.), *Applications of a social learning theory of personality.* New York: Holt, Rinehart & Winston, 1972.

Davis, W. L. *Parental antecedents of children's locus of control.* Unpublished doctoral dissertation, Kansas State University, 1969.

Davis, W. L., & Phares, E. J. Internal-external control as a determinant of information-seeking in a social influence situation. *Journal of Personality,* 1967, *35,* 547-561.

Davis, W. L., & Phares, E. J. Parental antecedents of internal-external control of reinforcement. *Psychological Reports,* 1969, *24,* 427–436.

Dean, S. J. The generality of expectancy statements as a function of situational definition. *Journal of Consulting Psychology,* 1960, *24,* 558.

Doctor, R. M. Locus of control of reinforcement and responsiveness to social influence. *Journal of Personality,* 1971, *39,* 542–551.

Dollard, J., & Miller, N. E. *Personality and psychotherapy: An analysis in terms of learning, thinking, and culture.* New York: McGraw-Hill, 1950.

DuCette, J., & Wolk, S. Cognitive and motivational correlates of generalized expectancies for control. *Journal of Personality and Social Psychology,* 1973, *26,* 420–426.

Edwards, W. The theory of decision making. *Psychological Bulletin,* 1954, *51,* 380–417.

Efran, J. S. Looking for approval: Effects on visual behavior of approbation from persons differing in importance. *Journal of Personality and Social Psychology,* 1968, *10,* 21–25.

Efran, J. S., & Broughton, A. Effects of expectancies for social approval on visual behavior. *Journal of Personality and Social Psychology,* 1966, *4,* 103–107.

Fitzgerald, B. J. Some relationships among projective test, interview, and sociometric measures of dependent behavior. *Journal of Abnormal and Social Psychology,* 1958, *56,* 199–204.

Ford, L. H., Jr. Reaction to failure as a function of expectancy for success. *Journal of Abnormal and Social Psychology,* 1963, *67,* 340–348.

Getter, H. A personality determinant of verbal conditioning. *Journal of Personality,* 1966, *34,* 397–405.

Gore, P. *Individual differences in the prediction of subject compliance to experimenter bias.* Unpublished doctoral dissertation, Ohio State University, 1962.

Gurin, G., & Gurin, P. Expectancy theory in the study of poverty. *Journal of Social Issues,* 1970, *26,* 83–104.

Henry, E. M., & Rotter, J. B. Situational influences on Rorschach responses. *Journal of Consulting Psychology*, 1956, *20*, 457–462.

Hess, H., & Jessor, R. The influence of reinforcement value on the rate of learning and asymptotic level of expectancies. *Journal of General Psychology*, 1960, *63*, 89–102.

Holden, K. B., & Rotter, J. B. A nonverbal measure of extinction in skill and chance situations. *Journal of Experimental Psychology*, 1962, *63*, 519–520.

James, W. H., & Rotter, J. B. Partial and 100% reinforcement under chance and skill conditions. *Journal of Experimental Psychology*, 1958, *55*, 397–403.

Jessor, R., Carman, R. S., & Grossman, P. H. Expectations of need satisfaction and drinking patterns of college students. *The Quarterly Journal of Studies in Alcohol*, 1968, *29*, 101–116.

Jessor, R., Graves, T. D., Hanson, R. C., & Jessor, S. L. *Society, personality, and deviant behavior: A study of a tri-ethnic community.* New York: Holt, Rinehart & Winston, 1968.

Jessor, R., Liverant, S., & Opochinsky, S. Imbalance in need structure and maladjustment. *Journal of Abnormal and Social Psychology*, 1963, *66*, 271–275.

Jessor, R., & Readio, J. The influence of value of an event upon the expectancy of its occurrence. *Journal of General Psychology*, 1957, *56*, 219–228.

Jolley, M. T., & Spielberger, C. D. The effects of locus of control and anxiety on verbal conditioning. *Journal of Personality*, 1973, *41*, 443–456.

Katkovsky, W. Social-learning theory analyses of maladjusted behavior. In W. Katkovsky & L. Gorlow (Eds.), *The psychology of adjustment: Current concepts and applications* (3rd ed.). New York: McGraw-Hill, 1976.

Katkovsky, W., Crandall, V. C., & Good, S. Parental antecedents of children's beliefs in internal-external control of reinforcements in intellectual achievement situations. *Child Development*, 1967, *38*, 765–776.

Katkovsky, W., Preston, A., & Crandall, V. J. Parents' achievement attitudes and their behavior with their children in achievement situations. *Journal of Ge-*

netic Psychology, 1964, *104*, 105–121. (a)

Katkovsky, W., Preston, A., & Crandall, V. J. Parents' attitudes toward their personal achievements and toward the achievement behaviors of their children. *Journal of Genetic Psychology*, 1964, *104*, 67–82. (b)

Lefcourt, H. M. Risk taking in Negro and white adults. *Journal of Personality and Social Psychology*, 1965, *2*, 765–770.

Lefcourt, H. M. *Locus of control: Current trends in theory and research.* Hillsdale, N.J.: Lawrence Erlbaum Associates, 1976.

Lefcourt, H. M., & Ladwig, G. W. The American Negro: A problem in expectancies. *Journal of Personality and Social Psychology*, 1965, *1*, 377–380.

Levenson, H. Perceived parental antecedents of internal, powerful others, and chance locus of control orientations. *Developmental Psychology*, 1973, *9*, 268–274.

Levy, L. H. *Conceptions of personality: Theories and research.* New York: Random House, 1970.

Liverant, S. The use of Rotter's social learning theory in developing a personality inventory. *Psychological Monographs*, 1958, *72* (Whole No. 455).

Liverant, S. Intelligence: A concept in need of re-examination. *Journal of Consulting Psychology*, 1960, *24*, 101–110.

Liverant, S., & Scodel, A. Internal and external control as determinants of decision making under conditions of risk. *Psychological Reports*, 1960, *7*, 59–67.

Lotsof, E. J. Reinforcement value as related to decision time. *Journal of Psychology*, 1956, *41*, 427–435.

MacDonald, A. P., Jr. Internal-external locus of control: Parental antecedents. *Journal of Consulting and Clinical Psychology*, 1971, *37*, 141–147.

Mahrer, A. R. The role of expectancy in delayed reinforcement. *Journal of Experimental Psychology*, 1956, *52*, 101–105.

Mischel, W. Theory and research on the antecedents of self-imposed delay of reward. In B. Maher (Ed.), *Progress in experimental personality research* (Vol. 3). New York: Academic Press, 1966.

Mischel, W. Toward a cognitive social

learning reconceptualization of personality. *Psychological Review*, 1973, *80*, 252–283.

Mischel, W., & Staub, E. Effects of expectancy on working and waiting for larger rewards. *Journal of Personality and Social Psychology*, 1965, *2*, 625–633.

Phares, E. J. Expectancy changes in skill and chance situations. *Journal of Abnormal and Social Psychology*, 1957, *54*, 339–342.

Phares, E. J. Additional effects of massing and spacing on expectancies. *Journal of General Psychology*, 1964, *70*, 215–223.

Phares, E. J. Effects of reinforcement value on expectancy statements in skill and chance situations. *Perceptual and Motor Skills*, 1965, *20*, 845–852.

Phares, E. J. A social learning theory approach to psychopathology. In J. B. Rotter, J. E. Chance, & E. J. Phares (Eds.), *Applications of a social learning theory of personality*. New York: Holt, Rinehart & Winston, 1972.

Phares, E. J. *Locus of control in personality*. Morristown, N.J.: General Learning Press, 1976.

Phares, E. J. Locus of control. In H. London & J. E. Exner (Eds.), *Dimensions of personality*. New York: Wiley-Interscience, 1978.

Phares, E. J. *Clinical psychology: Concepts, methods, and profession*. Homewood, Ill.: Dorsey Press, 1979.

Phares, E. J., & Davis, W. L. Breadth of categorization and the generalization of expectancies. *Journal of Personality and Social Psychology*, 1966, *4*, 461–464.

Phares, E. J., & Rotter, J. B. An effect of the situation on psychological testing. *Journal of Consulting Psychology*, 1956, *20*, 291–293.

Pines, H. A. An attributional analysis of locus of control orientation and source of informational dependence. *Journal of Personality and Social Psychology*, 1973, *26*, 262–272.

Pines, H. A., & Julian, J. W. Effects of task and social demands on locus of control differences in information processing. *Journal of Personality*, 1972, *40*, 407–416.

Rafferty, J. E., Tyler, B. B., & Tyler, F. B. Personality assessment from free play observations. *Child Development*, 1960, *31*, 691–702.

Rappaport, J. *Community psychology: Values, research, and action*. New York: Holt, Rinehart & Winston, 1977.

Ritchie, E., & Phares, E. J. Attitude change as a function of internal-external control and communicator status. *Journal of Personality*, 1969, *37*, 429–443.

Rotter, J. B. *Social learning and clinical psychology*. Englewood Cliffs, N.J.: Prentice-Hall, 1954.

Rotter, J. B. The role of the psychological situation in determining the direction of human behavior. In M. R. Jones (Ed.), *Nebraska Symposium on Motivation*. Lincoln: University of Nebraska Press, 1955.

Rotter, J. B. Some implications of a social learning theory for the prediction of goal directed behavior from testing procedures. *Psychological Review*, 1960, *67*, 301–316.

Rotter, J. B. Generalized expectancies for internal versus external control of reinforcement. *Psychological Monographs*, 1966, *80* (Whole No. 609).

Rotter, J. B. Beliefs, social attitudes, and behavior: A social learning analysis. In R. Jessor & S. Feshbach (Eds.), *Cognition, personality, and clinical psychology*. San Francisco: Jossey-Bass, 1967. (a)

Rotter, J. B. A new scale for the measurement of interpersonal trust. *Journal of Personality*, 1967, *35*, 651–655. (b)

Rotter, J. B. Personality theory. In H. Helson & W. Bevan (Eds.), *Contemporary approaches to psychology*. New York: D. Van Nostrand, 1967. (c)

Rotter, J. B. Some implications of a social learning theory for the practice of psychotherapy. In D. J. Levis (Ed.), *Learning approaches to therapeutic behavior change*. Chicago: Aldine, 1970.

Rotter, J. B. Generalized expectancies for interpersonal trust. *American Psychologist*, 1971, *26*, 443–452.

Rotter, J. G. Some problems and misconceptions related to the construct of internal versus external control of reinforcement. *Journal of Consulting and Clinical Psychology*, 1975, *48*, 56–67.

Rotter, J. B. *Interpersonal trust, trustworthiness, and gullibility*. Presidential address delivered at the annual meeting of the Eastern Psychological Association, Boston, April 1977.

Rotter, J. B. Generalized expectancies for problem solving and psychotherapy. *Cognitive Therapy and Research,* 1978, *2,* 1–10.

Rotter, J. B., Chance, J. E., & Phares, E. J. *Applications of a social learning theory of personality.* New York: Holt, Rinehart, & Winston, 1972.

Rotter, J. B., Fitzgerald, B. J., & Joyce, J. A comparison of some objective measures of expectancy. *Journal of Abnormal and Social Psychology,* 1954, *49,* 111–114.

Rotter, J. B., Liverant, S., & Crowne, D. P. The growth and extinction of expectancies in chance controlled and skilled tasks. *Journal of Psychology,* 1961, *52,* 161–177.

Rotter, J. B., & Mulry, R. C. Internal versus external control of reinforcement and decision time. *Journal of Personality and Social Psychology,* 1965, *2,* 598–604.

Rychlak, J. F. Task influence and the stability of generalized expectancies. *Journal of Experimental Psychology,* 1958, *55,* 459–462.

Rychlak, J. F., & Lerner, J. J. An expectancy interpretation of manifest anxiety. *Journal of Personality and Social Psychology,* 1965, *2,* 677–684.

Ryckman, R. M. Perceived locus of control and task performance. In L. C. Perlmuter & R. A. Monty (Eds.), *Choice and perceived control.* Hillsdale, N.J.: Lawrence Erlbaum Associates, 1979.

Schwarz, J. C. Influences upon expectancy during delay. *Journal of Experimental Research in Personality,* 1966, *1,* 211–220.

Seeman, G., & Schwarz, J. C. Affective state and preference for immediate versus delayed reward. *Journal of Research in Personality,* 1974, *7,* 384–394.

Seligman, M. E. P. *Helplessness: On depression, development, and death.* San Francisco: W. H. Freeman, 1975.

Stabler, J., & Johnson, E. E. Instrumental performance as a function of reinforcement schedule, luck versus skill instructions and set of child. *Journal of Experimental Child Psychology,* 1970, *9,* 330–335.

Strickland, B. R. Individual differences in verbal conditioning, extinction, and awareness. *Journal of Personality,* 1970, *38,* 364–378.

Strickland, B. R. *Locus of control and health related behaviors.* Paper presented at the XV Interamerican Congress of Psychology, Bogota, Colombia, December 1974.

Touhey, J. C. Category width and expectancies: Risk conservation or generalization? *Journal of Research in Personality,* 1973, *7,* 173–178.

Tyler, F. B., Tyler, B. B., & Rafferty, J. E. A threshold conception of need value. *Psychological Monographs,* 1962, *76* (Whole No. 530).

Walls, R. T., & Cox, J. Expectancy of reinforcement in chance and skill tasks under motor handicap. *Journal of Clinical Psychology,* 1971, *27,* 436–438.

Worell, L. The effect of goal value upon expectancy. *Journal of Abnormal and Social Psychology,* 1956, *53,* 48–53.

Glossary

Words italicized in these definitions are words that are defined in this glossary. For example, the definition of *limen* is: *threshold* of perception. The fact that the word *threshold* is italicized in this definition means that that word is also defined in the glossary. Consequently, if you don't understand a definition, follow up on other words that are italicized. Also, check the index of the book for the first citation of a particular word; you are likely to find that the author defines the term the first time it is mentioned.

Absolute threshold. The weakest intensity of any stimulus that can be detected.

Absorption. The *behavior* of an organism in a two-choice situation in which the organism chooses one of the two choices all of the time, even though neither choice is rewarded every time.

Accommodation. Piaget: A basic function of any organic system whereby information stored in the system is changed so that it is similar to information newly received from an external source.

Acetylocholine. A chemical which occurs at the *synapse* connecting the *neurons* and which when activated by the nervous impulse of an electric charge coming down the axon of neuron A, for example, causes neuron B to activate.

Acquisition. The process of gaining, obtaining, achieving, learning new responses, new information, et cetera.

Act. Guthrie: An integrated sequence of muscle movements; a complex behavior that appears purposive or goal directed.

Adaptation. (1) The successful capacity of an organism to adjust, to survive, and to reproduce. (2) The ability of a sensory modality to adjust to the outside environment, as for example when the sense of smell "adapts" to a bad odor so that we no longer smell it. (3) The adjustment of the sensory or receptor system to stimulation. Thus, the size of the iris adapts to the amount of light in the environment. (In *ethology,* any evolved characteristic of body or behavior by which an animal is better able to survive and reproduce in a particular environment.)

Afferent neuron. A single nerve cell that carries impulses from the receptors to the central nervous system (see *efferent neuron*).

Afferent trace impulse. The aftereffects of receptor stimulation which continue after termination of a *stimulus.*

Affordance. The capability of an object to permit an animal to react to it in some way, such as to walk on it or manipulate it.

Aggregate inhibitory potential (I). Hull: A concept denoting the total of all inferred organismic processes operating against performance of a response (*reactive inhibition, conditioned inhibition*).

"Aha!" The moment of *insight* in which a previously senseless, uncomprehended situation or problem becomes clear and understood.

All-or-none learning. The concept that *learning* consists essentially of associations which are either fully learned or not at all on any one trial. (cf. *incremental learning*).

Alpha behavior. A denial that two facts are contradictory when by objective standards the two facts are contradictory. The alpha behavior usually consists of treating the two facts as separate, without a sense that each has an implication for the other.

Amnesia. A loss of memory.

Amplifier elements. A theoretical device proposed by Estes in which it is assumed not only that elements that have been associated with a given behavior need to be sampled on any given trial, but also that elements that represent the motivation or drive state of the organism need to be in the sample. These latter probabilities combine in a multiplicative manner with the former elements so that in a sense they "amplify" the associations already in existence.

"Andsums." Wholes that equal the sum total of their component parts.

Anticipation method. A method generally used to measure verbal learning in which a series of terms, such as *nonsense syllables,* are presented one at a time. When you call off one item of the series, you are then shown what you anticipated, for feedback and new learning purposes, and this item now helps you to anticipate the next one.

Apparent motion. The perception of motion of stimuli that do not actually move. Lights on a theater marquee that turn on and off give the appearance of motion.

Approach-approach conflict. A conflict between two desired goals which results when there are two goals which cannot be achieved at the same time. An animal which is hungry and thirsty and has to decide whether to eat or drink is in an approach-approach conflict situation.

Assimilation. Piaget: A basic function of any organic system whereby information from an external source is changed so that it is similar to information already stored in the system.

Assimilatory schemes. Patterns of thinking that are repeatedly used to interpret new experiences. For example, a child might conclude that an object on the floor weighs more than that same object on the table because the child assimilates the former to the scheme of falling and greater impact.

Association value. The ability of a word to generate associations. For example, a nonsense syllable like GOL might have many associations, such as "gold, golf, ghoul, guilt, goal," while another nonsense syllable like JIS may have fewer associations and therefore a lower association value.

Associative inhibition. Guthrie: *Extinction* of a response is the learning through association of a new and incompatible (inhibitory) response. The old response is not unlearned; it is replaced by a different response that interferes with the original one.

Associative process. In Hull's system, any process which directly influences the development of *habit strength* (H).

Attention. The focused selection of one element of several or many in an environment with competing elements; the focusing of perception on one part of a complex situation. Guthrie: The concept of *stimulus* was redefined by Guthrie to include the act of "noticing" its presence. In this view, learning, or the formation of stimulus-response association, is not possible until the organism has first attended to the stimulus.

Attention, divided. Performance where attention must be split between different tasks or task components (see *time-sharing, dichotic listening*).

Autonomic nervous system. The nerve complex that connects the central nervous system to the smooth muscles and the glands of the body, leading to their automatic regulation.

Autoshaping. In *operant* theory, a respondent procedure which affects a skeletal response such as the pigeon's key peck. When key-light illumination reliably precedes food deliveries, the pigeon comes to peck the lighted key, even if key pecks do not affect food deliveries.

Aversive conditioning. Manipulating behavior through punishment.

Avoidance. The removal or prevention of a *negative reinforcer* which maintains responding because it prevents or delays the onset of an aversive stimulus (cf. *escape*).

Avoidance-avoidance conflict. A situation in which the organism does not want either of two unpleasant alternative goals. In Nevada, for example, a condemned murderer has the choice of being hanged or shot.

Axon. The part of the *neuron* that conveys electrical impulses from the cell body to the fine "branches" that end on the *dendrites* of another neuron.

Backward conditioning. The *unconditioned stimulus* is present first, and then the *conditioned stimulus* after the US is terminated. This form of conditioning, is the least effective method of training.

Bait shyness. Avoidance of contaminated bait, which sometimes occurs after a single incident of becoming sick from the bait. Since sickness and eating the bait do not occur close together in time, bait shyness appears to violate the principle of *contiguity.*

Behavior. A generic term for what an organism does. Thus, it is appropriate to speak of one response and two responses, but it is ordinarily inappropriate to speak of two behaviors; two kinds of behavior is preferred because behavior is implicitly plural.

Behavior potential. In a given situation, the likelihood of a specific behavior occurring in order to achieve a specific goal.

Beta behavior. A budding awareness that two facts are contradictory. The beta behavior usually consists of creating some incomplete explanation of the contradiction.

Biofeedback. Methods of allowing individuals to have knowledge of their own generally unknown physiological functions, such as brain wave patterns, to permit voluntary control of these ordinarily unknown and uncontrollable functions. Procedures which permit people to have instant feedback knowledge of what is happening in their physiological systems.

"Blind." A response to a situation that, instead of being insightful, is piecemeal, rote, automatic, or stupid.

Cerebellum. The lower rear part of the brain which controls body balance and body movements.

Cerebrum. The major part of the brain, divided into two hemispheres.

Chained schedules. A sequence of schedules in which each component schedule operates in the presence of a different stimulus and in which the completion of one component initiates the next component; completion of the final component produces the reinforcer. For example, in a three-component, chained, fixed-ratio schedule, completion of the first ratio produces the stimulus correlated with the third and final ratio, and completion of that ratio produces the reinforcer.

Chaining. The establishment or maintenance of sequential responding through the discriminative and reinforcing functions of the components of the sequence. The stimuli at any point in the sequence are reinforcers with respect to preceding responding, and discriminative stimuli with respect to subsequent responding. In lever pressing, for example, visual contact with the lever reinforces movement toward the seen lever and sets the occasion for pressing down on the lever, and so on.

Channel model. See *Limited-capacity channel.*

Chunking. A process in which units are organized into "chunks," or combined units.

Classical conditioning. Also known as Pavlovian conditioning, a process through which a *reflex* becomes associated with a previously *neutral stimulus,* so that the stimulus now produces the reflex.

Classical environmentalist. A person who claims that, given a healthy individual, he or she can train the person to become any type of specialist he or she selects.

Coding, encoding, symbolic coding. These terms refer to the processes by which events are transformed into the memory system. The processes may include selective attention, interpretation, naming, paraphrasing, and imagery.

Concept. A category which involves both *discrimination* and *generalization,* relative to two or more specific items.

Conditioned avoidance response. A learned response to avoid aversive stimuli.

Conditioned discrimination. The capacity of an organism to react to only one of two somewhat similar stimuli, thus discriminating between them. For example, pecking at a circle but not at an oval.

Conditioned inhibition ($S^I R$). Hull: A learned habit of not responding which acts in opposition to tendencies to make the response.

Conditioned reinforcer. A reinforcer which has acquired its reinforcing effectiveness usually by virtue of its relation to some other *reinforcer* which is already established. For example, a stimulus in the presence of which responding produces food may become a conditioned reinforcer.

Conditioned stimulus (CS). A formerly neutral stimulus which now can elicit a conditioned response.

Conditioned suppression. The reduction in *operant* responding produced by a stimulus that reliably precedes an aversive event.

Conditioning. A process whereby an originally neutral stimulus paired repeatedly with a *reinforcer* elicits a response on its own.

Configurationism. The name given by the structuralist Edward Bradford Titchener to Gestalt psychology.

Connecting neuron. An "in-between" *neuron* which receives an electrical impulse from one neuron and passes it on to another.

Conservation of quantity. Piaget: Quantity is conserved when an observer realizes that changes in the spatial arrangement of parts do not change the total quantity of those parts.

Conservation task. Piaget: Any one of a variety of tasks which ask an individual to reckon with the invariance of an aspect of the stimulus array, in spite of apparent changes in the stimulus array. For example, changing the shape of a ball of clay does not vary its weight, i.e., weight is conserved.

Constraints of learning. The biological predisposition of the organism to overrule or negate certain responses in that organism.

Construct. A concept representing relationships between inferred events or processes.

Consummatory response. Usually the terminal response in an act or integrated series of movements. The consummatory response may involve actual consumption of a physical substance, such as food or water. More broadly, it includes escape, as from a painful or aversive stimulus. In some theories, the consummatory response is equated with *drive reduction* or constitutes the reinforcing event.

Contiguity. The one principle of *learning* in Guthrie's theory. When a response occurs in the presence of a stimulus, an association is formed such that recurrence of the stimulus will evoke the response.

Contingencies. In operant theory, probability relations among responses and environmental events, as when a lever press produces food pellets according to some *reinforcement schedule,* or as when an avoidance response reduces the likelihood that an electric shock will be delivered.

Contingency-governed behavior. Behavior controlled by its consequences. (See *rule-governed behavior.*)

Counterconditioning. A behavioral therapy technique using conditioning procedures which are introduced for the specific purpose of counteracting or eliminating previously learned behavior; e.g., relaxation response is used as a counterconditioning procedure for excessive anxiety.

Creative thinking. The capacity to invent solutions to problems, to imagine new situations, or to find new relationships.

Criterion. In learning experiments, this word generally refers to the standard established for determining when to stop any training. For example, we may state that a rat has learned a maze if it goes through it twice without making a single error. So, the criterion of learning would be two errorless trials for this particular experimenter.

CS. A conditioned stimulus (see *conditioned stimulus*).

Cued recall test. A test in which people are given external cues intended to affect recall.

Cumulative record. A graph in which responses accumulate vertically while the passage of time is represented horizontally. In such a record, the slope of the line is proportional to the rate of responding. Used in recording *operant* behavior.

Cybernetics. The scientific study of mechanical and organic systems that have properties of self-regulation, particularly systems that contain feedback circuits for self-correction. Automatic control systems, in particular as applied to the operation of the nervous system and the brain.

Delayed conditioning. In this procedure the *CS* begins from a few seconds to a few minutes before the *US* and continues until the response begins.

Dendrites. The "branches" of a *neuron* which can receive impulses.

Dichotic listening. An experimental paradigm in which two independent messages are presented, one to each ear.

Didactic learning. An example of expository learning; learning from information provided by a teacher.

Differential reinforcement. The reinforcement of responses within a specified class. For example, if a pigeon's pecks are reinforced only if their force exceeds ten grams, these high-force pecks are said to be differentially reinforced.

Differential-reinforcement-of-rate schedules. Reinforcement schedules that arrange reinforcers based on the rate at which responding occurs. For example, in differential-reinforcement-of-low-rate, or *DRL schedules*, the reinforcer is produced only by slow responding; in differential-reinforcement-of-high-rate, or DRH schedules, the reinforcer is produced only by rapid responding.

Differentiation. The establishment of an operant class through differential *reinforcement.*

Directed thinking. Usually found in problem solving: a formalized, logical order of thinking intended to arrive at a desired conclusion.

Discovery learning. A kind of inductive thinking based on finding a concept through specific examples.

Discriminated operant. An *operant* class that includes among its defining properties the stimuli present when a response occurs. For example, *differential reinforcement* may establish a pigeon's pecks in the presence of a green light as a different response class from those in the presence of a red light. Pecking in the presence of green may therefore be called a discriminated operant.

Discrimination. The organism's ability to respond selectively to stimuli.

Discriminative stimulus. In *operant* theory, a stimulus that sets the occasion for different consequences of responding. For example, if a pigeon's key pecks produce food in the presence of green but not red, the green and red stimuli are discriminative stimuli with respect to key pecking.

Disturbance. Piaget: A cognitive event that results from the awareness of an inconsistency between what was expected and what was observed or between two facts that are logically contradictory.

Drive. Differential sensitivity to particular stimuli based on changes in physiological balances.

Drive reduction. A theory of *reinforcement* which states that the effectiveness of a reinforcer depends on the extent to which it reduces some physiological state of drive (e.g., hunger, thirst). According to Hull, learning occurs only when drives, corresponding to biological needs, are reduced (e.g., through consumption of a reinforcement).

Drive stimulus. The assumed internal stimulus accompaniments of any *drive* state.

DRH schedules. See *differential-reinforcement-of-rate schedules.*

DRL schedules. See *differential-reinforcement-of-rate schedules.*

Dynamic self-distribution. The tendency for any whole or system to restructure itself so as to yield optimal *Prägnanz.*

Eclectic learning. Learning through idea association.

Effective habit strength. The combined strengths of habits elicited by the original training stimulus and similar stimuli (see *generalized habit strength, stimulus generalization*).

Effector activity. Neural impulses directed toward muscles.

Efferent neuron. A neuron that carries impulses to the muscles or glands from the central nervous systems (See *afferent neuron.*)

Elicitation. The production of a response by a stimulus, as in a reflex relation.

Emission. The production of a response by a stimulus without an identifiable eliciting stimulus, as in *free-operant* responding. Responding in the presence of a discriminative stimulus is said to be emitted rather than elicited because the response depends not only on the stimulus but also on its consequences in the presence of that stimulus (see *elicitation*).

Empty organism. The organism seen only in terms of its overt behavior. To the extent that some behavioral treatments deny that internal events (e.g., neural functions, mental processes) are relevant to the analysis of behavior, these approaches are referred to as psychologies of the empty organism.

Encoding. The transformation of information into a mental code.

Encoding specificity principle. Retrieval of learned material is aided to the extent that retrieval conditions match the specific encoding operations performed when the material was originally learned.

Endogenous processes. Piaget: Basic laws of structuring experience that are not learned as such but rather are intrinsic to natural functioning of an organic system. For example, the regulations that are activated by a disturbance to the organic system are endogenous processes.

Engram. A hypothetical element in the brain as a result of some prior stimulation, a kind of memory trace. This can be considered a kind of *intervening variable* to explain retention of specific memories.

Epiphenomenalism. The doctrine which states that consciousness is a by-product of neural activities and that mental events such as cognitions or attitudes are not the causes of human behavior.

Epistemology. The branch of philosophy that deals with the process of knowing: how we obtain knowledge.

Equilibration. Piaget: Reestablishment of equilibrium after a disturbance. Equilibration is a set of dynamic laws that account for the development of the organism from one stage to the next. These laws consist of regulations activated when the organism experiences some disturbance to the functioning of the organic system. These regulations assure that the organic system is both maintained and developed.

Escape. Maintaining a response because it terminates an aversive stimulus which has already been presented (see *avoidance*). An instance of negative reinforcement.

Ethology. A study of animal behavior that emphasizes evolution.

Exogenous processes. Piaget: Basic laws of structuring experience that are learned as a direct consequence of experiencing certain regularities in the environment. For example, the expectation that large objects are heavy results from the exogen-ous coincidence of certain sizes with certain weights.

Expectancy. An organism's subjectively held probability that a certain reinforcement will occur if a specific behavior is directed toward its achievement.

Experimental neurosis. A neurosis created in animals through conditioning processes involving prolonged stress and/or conflicts.

External subjects. See *locus of control.* Those who believe that the occurrence of reinforcements is determined by luck, fate, chance, or powerful others.

Extinction. The decrease in responding that results from the discontinuing of reinforcement. Guthrie: A process of response interference (see *associative inhibition*).

Fading. A procedure for changing the stimulus control of a response by gradually changing the stimuli of a discrimination task.

Figurative knowledge. Knowledge that results from attention to and memory of static features of physical stimuli, such as the color and shape of a single object or the exact words of a particular person.

Filter theory. Broadbent's theory of attention in which information is believed to be held in parallel in a sensory system before it is attended to in a serial manner by the perceptual system.

First signal system. A term used by Pavlov for the connection found in lower animals between the *CS* and *US* which brings about the CR. It is compared to the more sophisticated second-signal system (language) found in humans.

Fixed-interval (FI) schedule. A reinforcement schedule which arranges a reinforcer for the first response occurring some constant time after some environmental event, such as an earlier reinforcer or the onset of a light. Responses that occur earlier in the interval have no effect. For example, in FI 30-sec. the first response after 30 seconds have elapsed is reinforced.

Fixed-ratio (FR) schedule. A reinforcement schedule in which the reinforcer is produced by some constant number of responses. For example, in FR 50 every 50th response is reinforced.

Fluctuation theory. A variant of stimulus sampling theory in which it is assumed that stimulus elements can be divided into two mutually exclusive categories, those that are available and those that are not available on a given experimental trial. Between trials, elements are assumed to flow from one set to another, with various probabilities.

Forced-choice recognition test. A multiple-choice test.

Forebrain. The frontal part of the brain containing cerebral hemispheres, olfactory lobes, the thalamus, and the hypothalamus.

Forgetting. Loss of a previous ability, such as no longer being able to recite a poem or to ride a bicycle.

Fractional anticipatory goal response (r_G). A component of the *consummatory* or goal *response* which can occur prior to the presentation of reinforcement.

Free operant. A response class consisting of responses that can be repeated without the experimenter's intervention (e.g., a rat's lever presses), as opposed to responding that is restricted to discrete trials (e.g., a rat's successive runs down a straight alley, in which the rat must be returned to the startbox to begin a new trial).

Free parameter. A component of a formula whose value must be determined from data in order to be able to plot a theoretical curve.

Free recall. A memory test in which people may recall the learned material in any order.

Freedom of movement. The expectancy of obtaining positive satisfactions as a result of a set of related behaviors that are directed toward achieving a specific group of reinforcements.

Functional analysis. In *ethology,* an analysis of behavior in terms of how it benefits the animal by helping to solve some life problems.

Functional relatedness. Several behaviors (or goals) are functionally related when something that occurs to one affects all the others.

Gamma behavior. A full awareness of contradiction between two facts, plus an understanding of how the contradiction can be resolved. The gamma behavior usually consists of creating a new system of relations that shows how the contradiction is only a result of using a more elementary and less complete system of relations.

Gap. Piaget: An inherent and unavoidable discontinuity in information that comes from the world external to ourselves. For example, the distinction between seeing one object twice and two identical objects once at different times can never be made by use of the senses alone. The gaps must be filled by mental inferences.

Generalization. Either a process or a result leading to a conclusion about a whole class of items from experience with a limited number of items. For example, if a girl child has been teased by her brother and some male cousins, she is likely to generalize that all boys are teasers.

Generalization decrement. The idea that responses to stimuli that were not specifically extinguished will also extinguish in proportion to the similarity of the stimulus. This is the reverse of *stimulus generalization.*

Generalized habit strength (H). In Hull's system, the strength of habit elicited by stimuli similar to the original training stimulus (see *stimulus generalization*).

Gestalt. An articulated whole, an integrated structure that is different from the mere sum of its component parts.

Gestalt therapy. Perls's name for his form of psychotherapy that concentrates on feelings in the here and now.

Group dynamics. The study of the relationships among individuals, and between group structures and group performance.

Habit strength (H). Hull: A formal term referring to the stimulus-response association produced in the organism by training. A theoretical measure of an association between a stimulus and a response.

Hierarchical association theory. A theoretical view of learning which assumes that the basic unit of learning, the association, is tied to the contextual conditions surrounding its occurrence in a hierarchical fashion, much as the branches of a tree are tied to the trunk. As a result, the "trunk" must be stimulated in order for the associations to become operative.

Higher order conditioning. A classical conditioning procedure whereby a previously established stimulus with a strong conditioned response is paired with a *neutral stimulus* resulting in the neutral stimulus eliciting the previously *conditioned response.*

Higher order reinforcement. Reinforcement of a reinforcer.

Holism (wholism). Belief that wholes are more than the mere sums of their component parts.

Hybrid processing. A flow of internal information in which some stages operate serially and others operate in parallel.

Hypermnesia. Improvement in memory through any of various means, such as by drugs, hypnosis, or traumatic situations.

Hypothalamus. Part of the forebrain, a connector between the brain as a whole and the body which contains and controls emotions as well as such body functions as sleep, temperature, hunger, and thirst.

Hypothetico-deductive method. In theory construction, coordination of a mathematical system with an empirical system to generate testable deductions.

Identity operator model. A mathematical model that incorporates the assumption that the probability of a choice response is unchanged when the organism goes unrewarded for its choice. Typically applied in a noncorrection situation.

Imitative learning. Learning by imitating.

Imprinting. Certain stereotyped species-specific behavior which occurs only during a certain period of development of the organism, such as the tendency of ducklings to follow any object in the ducklings' environment during their early development.

Incentive (K). In Hull's theory, the motivational system in the organism resulting from receiving *reinforcement.* The system is generally conceived as an anticipation of the reinforcement.

Incidental learning. In learning experiments this refers to material learned without intention on the part of the subject or the instructions of the experi-menter. Learning that occurs without apparent reinforcers; accidental learning; latent learning.

Incremental learning. Learning that increases in small increments, such as gaining greater ability to typewrite weekly over several months of training (see *one-trial learning*).

Information processing. An approach to studying cognitive functioning that emphasizes the transformation of information from the external world to information inside the organism as it is transformed by various processes that are assumed to occur in the nervous systems and the brain.

Inhibition. A hypothetical process to explain extinction; a mental blocking; the inability of the person to function even though no external agency prevents the functioning.

Inhibition response. A process whereby an organism suppresses or restrains activity.

Inhibitory/disinhibitory effect. Strengthening or weakening a previously learned *inhibition* tendency through exposure to a model. One of the three modeling influences suggested by Bandura.

Insight. Achieving a veridical understanding of the inherent structure of a situation or problem. An "aha!" experience such as occurs when we suddenly learn the answer to a problem, see the point of a joke, or have an understanding of ourselves or of others' behavior or thinking.

Instinct. Unlearned, patterned, goal-directed behavior which is species specific. An unlearned goal-directed behavior pattern characteristic of a species.

Instinctual drift. The tendency of an organism to exhibit an innate behavior overriding a behavior which was conditioned.

Instrumental conditioning. In this form of conditioning the reinforcement (reward) is contingent on some instrumental response by the subject. For example, pressing a lever (the operation) leads to a pellet of food (the reward), which now conditions the animal to repeat the instrumental act. Reinforcements can be positive (food) or negative (shock).

Intelligence. This term is practically undefinable, since there are so many meanings. One would be ability to learn quickly. Another would be capacity for higher-order thinking or learning. Another would be behavior that leads to success.

Intentional learning. Learning that occurs when there is an intention or a set of instructions to learn.

Interference. Disruptive influence of other learning on present learning.

Interference theory. The notion that forgetting is due to the interference of the memory by some new learnings which block the recall of the old memory.

Internal subjects. See *locus of control*. Those who believe that *reinforcements* occur because of their own efforts.

Interoceptive conditioning. Conditioning of physiological processes.

Interstimulus interval (ISI). The time elapsing between the presentation of two sequential stimuli.

Integrated curriculum. A curriculum philosophy that fuses several subject matter areas: for example, while teaching literature, principles of mathematics may be introduced and learned.

Intertrial interval. Refers to the amount of time between successive trials of a learning experiment.

Interval schedule. See *fixed-interval schedule, variable-interval schedule.*

Intervening variable. A construct signifying an unobserved organismic process; employed as a link between antecedent operations and the subsequent behavioral consequences.

Intraverbals. In operant theory, verbal responses that are generated through *chaining*. This class of responses constitutes only a small part of verbal behavior, and the treatment of sequential properties of verbal behavior in operant theory is not restricted to interpretations in terms of chaining.

Intrinsic motivation. Engaging in an activity for its own sake, rather than for the purpose of achieving some arbitrary, external reward.

Inverse. Piaget: The direct opposite of a given change. For example, taking ice cubes out of a glass of water is the direct opposite of adding ice cubes to the water. To be distinguished from the *reciprocal*, the indirect opposite to a given change.

Irradiation. Pavlov used this term to describe the spreading of inhibition or excitation through the cortex. It is the presumed physiological basis of *generalization*.

Isomorphism. The doctrine that the form of a perceptual experience is identical to the form of the corresponding and correlated brain events.

Just noticeable difference (jnd). The smallest change in a stimulus that can be detected.

Latency. The period between the onset of stimulation and the onset of the response.

Latent learning. Learning which is not exhibited, but which exists as a potential.

Law of Effect. A statement that an organism learns best those behaviors that result in satisfaction, but does not learn those behaviors the results of which are unpleasant. Trial-and-error learning probably occurs as a result of this law.

Law of Exercise. The basic concept of this law is that if an act is performed, a subsequent performance is more likely to occur, to be easier than the first time, and to be more perfect.

Law of Prägnanz. The tendency for the organization of any whole to be as "good" as the prevailing conditions allow.

Learned helplessness. Impaired instrumental responsiveness following exposure to inescapable aversive events. Often equated to depressive behavior.

Learning. This word has many definitions: (1) Any relatively enduring change as a result of some experience. (2) Associations between a stimulus and a response. (3) Associations between stimuli in a chain fashion, leading to a response.

Learning curve. A plot of learning on a graph. There are several general types of such curves, such as one that starts slowly and accelerates (increasing returns); or that starts rapidly and decelerates slowly (decreasing returns); or that continues in a straight line (equal returns).

Leveling. The tendency to disregard minor differences among objects, shapes, or structures.

Life space. An individual's internal and external environment, as seen by that individual.

Limen. *Threshold* of perception.

Limited-capacity channel. A theoretical

model of the human as an information processor which claims that people can transmit only a limited amount of information in a given time.

Linear learning operator. A mathematical rule that describes the change in the probability of a given response as a result of the response and reward sequence of a given trial. This change is linear with respect to trial number.

Locus of control. A concept referring to beliefs about the causal relationship between behavior and the susequent occurrence of a reinforcement. External control refers to a belief that fate, luck, chance, or powerful others mediate the relationship. Internal control refers to the belief that the occurrences of reinforcements are contingent upon one's own behavior.

Macro. A gross measure or approach to learning theory and phenomena.

Maintaining stimulus. Guthrie: Motivation consisting of a set of continuous internal stimuli that function in maintaining activity until an act is completed.

Management of learning. Making arrangements to achieve most economically a systematic way of learning; an educational system such as the Montessori system or Individual Education.

Markov model. A model that assumes discrete *stochastic model* processes in which the probabilities of future states depend only on the present state of the system.

Massed practice. Intensive and extensive practice; long-lasting, single learning session.

Matched-dependent behavior. One form of imitation in which a less knowledgeable observer matches (imitates) a more knowledgeable model's behavior by depending on the model's knowledge about how to respond and when to respond.

Matching law. A summary of the responding generated when *reinforcers* are produced by two or more different responses. The relative frequency of a given response (proportion of total responses) approximately matches the relative frequency of the reinforcers produced by that response.

Matching-to-sample. Discriminative responding based on a matching relation among stimuli. For example, in a three-key pigeon chamber, a sample stimulus is presented on the center key (e.g., red or green). Comparison stimuli are then presented on the two side keys. The pigeon's peck is reinforced if it occurs on the side key with the color that matches that of the sample center key.

Maturation. Changes that occur, physically and mentally, purely as a result of aging. This is change but not learning in the technical sense. A continuing normative process of change.

Meaning. The inherent nature, the genuine significance of a whole.

Mediated stimulus generalization. Behaviors leading to the same goal acquire a functional equivalence. For example, if both kicking and screaming lead to the same outcome, a negative reinforcement of one will affect the other.

Mediational unit. "Something in the brain" as a result of learning, a memory trace, *engram*, etc., which is available for use.

Mental chronometry. The study of the time course of information processing.

Mental hygiene. A healthy state of mind which is the result of thinking and practicing appropriate thoughts and behaviors.

Millisecond (msec). A unit of time equal to one thousandth of a second.

Minimal goal level. The lowest goal in a continuum of goals that will be perceived as satisfying.

Mixed model. A model for *discrimination* learning proposed by Estes in which it is assumed that the acquisition of a discrimination is controlled by the patterns of stimulation, while the generalization to untrained stimuli is controlled by the elements or components that comprise the stimuli.

Mnemonic system. A way of remembering through memorizing some symbols to which new symbols can be attached.

Modality effect. Refers to the usual advantage of auditory to visual presentation in immediate recall of the last few elements of a series.

Model. A person whose characteristics (behaviors, attitudes, feelings, thoughts) are imitated by an observer.

Modeled response. The response of the

subject imitated following observation of the model's behavior.

Modeling. The process which occurs when a person imitates the characteristics of another person.

Modeling learning. Learning based on imitating, copying, or modeling the behavior of others.

Molar. An adjective applied to methods, theories, or events that deal with relatively large units. For example, talking or interacting with others.

Molar behavior. Total, overall, comprehensive behavior, such as climbing, running, or talking, but made up of smaller (molecular) units.

Molecular behavior. The behavior of small units of the body, such as muscles or glands. The summation of these units leads to *molar behavior.*

Molecular. Adjective applied to methods, theories, or events that deal with relatively small units. For example, single responses such as an arm movement or a glance.

Motivation. A general term which refers to the arousal, maintenance, and channeling of a behavior toward a goal.

Motivational stimulus. Any stimulus which arouses or excites an organism.

Movement. Guthrie: The movement of a muscle is the response, as distinguished from the more molar or goal-directed "act" made up of individual responses.

Movement-produced stimulus. Guthrie: Each individual muscle movement generates a stimulus (proprioception). These stimuli are part of the complex of cues to which a response may be conditioned.

Multiple-cue probability learning. An experimental situation in which specific cues have associated with them a given probability of being correct, and the subject is exposed to a number of such cues.

Nature-nurture controversy. A historic debate whether human behavior is due to nature (biology) or nurture (culture).

Need potential. The mean likelihood that a group of functionally related behaviors will occur in a given period of the person's life in order to achieve a given class of goals.

Need value. The mean preference value of a set of functionally related *reinforcements.*

Negations. Piaget: A form of thinking whereby the individual considers the absence of something or its opposite. The consideration of the absent or the opposite gives meaning to the thing so compared.

Negative reinforcer. A stimulus, the removal or prevention of which is an effective reinforcing event for a response.

Negative transfer. Interference in learning something new because of something previously learned (see *positive transfer).*

Neomentalism. The study of mental events by using objective, behavioral methods.

Neoteny. A theory that humans, unlike animals, can keep on learning maximally throughout life.

Nerve. A fiber in which, usually, many neurons are found going in the same direction.

Neuron. A single nerve cell, which can range in length from a fraction of an inch to several feet.

Neutral stimulus. A stimulus which does not produce a particular response prior to conditioning.

Nonassociative construct. Hull: Any *construct* signifying organismic processes which affect performance, but not the formation of habit strength (H). Some examples are *incentive* (K), *drive* (D), and *inhibition* (I).

Nonconservers. Piaget: Individuals who fail to understand that changes in spatial distribution of parts do not change quantity. These individuals are usually misled by the way the stimulus array looks after the change in spatial distribution of parts. For example, a ball of clay might look like less when rolled in the form of a skinny sausage, even though the amount has not changed.

Nonsense syllable. Usually a three-letter, meaningless syllable such as RIK, FID, CUF, or DOB, used in memory experiments.

Novelty or novel response. In social learning theory, a response which has a low or zero probability of occurrence prior to the learning experience.

Object permanence. Piaget: Awareness that a hidden object still exists in time and space behind the shield that occludes the object from view. When the infant searches for the hidden object, Piaget assumes that the infant has discovered that objects exist in time and space independent of immediate contact with them.

Objectivism. A philosophy of science based on the assumption that all knowledge is derived solely from observations of publicly verifiable physical events. This philosophy provided the foundations of methodological behaviorism.

Observational learning effect. The acquisition of new response patterns through exposure to a model. One of the three modeling influences suggested by Bandura.

Observational learning technique. A method used in probability learning whereby the subject simply observes a sequence of trials in a probability learning study and is not required to respond.

One-trial learning. Learning that occurs as the result of one exposure; single-step learning; learning that occurs immediately.

Operant. Skinner: A class of responses sensitive to their consequences *(reinforcers)* and for which there is no specific eliciting stimulus.

Operant behavior. Behavior that operates on the environment.

Operant conditioning. See *instrumental conditioning.*

Operative knowledge. Knowledge that results from making inferences to fill in the gaps that exist when only static features of a stimulus array are observable. Operative knowledge is knowledge that is true by logical necessity, as opposed to empirical probability.

Operator. Refers to a mathematical rule that is applied to a specific situation, given that a specific response-reward sequence has just occurred. The rule (equation) is said to "operate" upon the response probability.

Organization. The internal structure or articulation of a whole; the segregation of a field into constituent structures, units, or component parts.

Orienting reflex. A reflex which changes the organism's position with respect to a source of stimulation. For example, a moth genetically programmed to orient

toward a light source would turn in the direction of the light.

Overlearning. Continued practice after learning has been achieved. For example, generally the alphabet is overlearned, since we tend to practice it periodically even after it is known. The same goes for some songs.

Overt behavior. Obvious or evident or observable behavior.

Paired-associate learning. A verbal learning and memory task wherein subjects are taught to associate one event (a stimulus) with another (a response). There is typically a list of such stimulus-response pairs.

Paradigm. A symbolic representation of procedures or of relations among events. For example, the paradigm $S^D (R — S^R)$, in which S^D is a *discriminative stimulus,* R is a *response,* and S^R is a *reinforcing stimulus,* represents the relations among the terms of a three-term contingency.

Parallel processing. A flow of internal information wherein each *stage* can simultaneously access incoming information.

Parasympathetic nervous system. Part of the *autonomic nervous system;* scattered ganglia that affect glands and muscles.

Partial reinforcement acquisition. That training condition wherein the organism is only occasionally reinforced for responding.

Pattern model. A variant of stimulus sampling theory proposed by Estes in which it is assumed that the organism perceives a situation in terms of patterns of stimulation, rather than in terms of the elements or components that comprise the stimulus population.

Perceptual salience. The extent to which a perceptual object stands out from its context.

Phenomenon. Some observed event or relation. For example, because they are observed properties of behavior, reinforcement, chaining, and stimulus control are all examples of behavioral phenomena.

Placebo. A condition in which subjects are treated identically to participants in an experimental condition, with the exception of one critical factor (e.g., a drug given to the participants) and sugar pills to the placebo group.

Plateau of learning. On a learning curve, what happens when for a while there is a leveling off, no change for a while, a period of no change or of no learning.

Pleasure principle. A psychoanalytic concept that the id operates in terms of immediate gratification of its wants.

Positive reinforcer. A stimulus, the presentation of which is an effective reinforcing event for a response.

Positive transfer. A process in which learning is made easier due to earlier learning.

Power function of time. Hull: How neural activity increases for a brief period following stimulation.

Prägnanz. The completeness, symmetry, simplicity or elegance of a structure or whole.

Primacy, Law of. A statement that one tends to learn best in a series those elements that come first, such as the first line in a poem, the first word in a series of nonsense syllables. (See *Recency, law of.*)

Primary negative drive. An inferred organismic state which operates in opposition to the tendency to make a response (see *reactive inhibition*).

Primary reinforcement. The effect of a *stimulus* that meets the primary needs of an organism, such as food for an animal.

Primary reinforcer. A biological satisfier; any event with innate satisfying qualities.

Primary stimulus generalization. Behaviors or goals become functionally related largely on the basis of physical similarity. For example, similar responses are made to all four-legged animals.

Proactive inhibition. Forgetting due to interference from prior learning.

Proactive interference. Forgetting of material produced by prior learning.

Probabilistic discrimination. A *discrimination* situation in which no element, component, or cue is perfectly correlated with reward. Rather, every element has some probability of being associated with reward.

Probabilistic model. A model which assumes that the behavioral universe can be described by the classical-urn model of probability theory, in contrast to a deterministic universe.

Probability learning. An experimental situation in which each choice has some probability of being correct, without the aid of any external cue to the organism.

Probability matching. In a two-choice situation, when the relative frequency with which a given choice is made equals the relative frequency with which that choice is rewarded.

Probe. An experimental paradigm wherein a reaction-time signal is inserted during some other primary task. The time required to respond to the probe signal is an index of the difficulty of the primary task.

Problem solving. A kind of directed thinking which aims at solving problems.

Process. To process information means to effect some transformation upon it, as in *encoding* a stimulus.

Programmed instruction. Learning which is facilitated by automatic self-instruction.

Protective inhibition. A condition wherein individuals begin to shut out information when flooded with excessive stimulation.

Pseudoreflex. Skinner: In early operant theory, the relation between a *discriminative stimulus* and the *response* it occasioned.

Psychological refractory period (PRP). An experimental *paradigm* wherein two stimuli are presented in close temporal succession, usually less than one-half second apart. Reaction time to the stimuli are increased, relative to a control condition wherein only a single stimulus is presented.

Punisher. A stimulus that is effective in reducing responding when it is a consequence of responding. (Some usages distinguish positive punishers, effective when presented, and negative punishers, effective when removed. For example, if a child's misbehavior is punished by the withholding of an allowance, it is appropriate to speak of negative punishment.)

Punishment. The delivery of a *punisher* when an undesired response occurs, or the reduction in responding produced by that procedure. Guthrie: The presentation of a stimulus following a response may evoke a movement incompatible with the punished response. Effective punishment involves the formation of an association between the incompatible response and the stimulus that originally evoked the punished response.

Purposive behaviorism. The behaviorism of Tolman, which attempted to provide a behavioral treatment of purposive or goal-directed responding.

Ratio schedule. See *fixed-ratio schedule, variable-ratio schedule.*

Ratio strain. See *strain.*

Reaction potential (E). Hull: Representation of the observed behavior of an organism.

Reaction threshold (L). Hull: Processes operating to produce performance must exceed some minimal value before behavior occurs.

Reactive inhibition (I_R). Hull: A process operating against responding which results from the effort involved in responding.

Recall. A means of measuring learning through evaluation of how much can be remembered.

Recency, law of. The tendency to learn quickly the last items in a series, such as the last line of a poem or the last word of a series of nonsense syllables. (See *primacy, law of.*)

Recency principle (principle of postremity). Guthrie: The last or most recent response associated with a stimulus will be the first response to occur when the stimulus is again presented.

Receptor activity. Activity resulting from stimulus energy impinging on a sense receptor of the organism.

Reciprocal. Piaget: The indirect opposite to a given change. For example, pouring water out of a glass of ice cubes is the indirect opposite to adding ice cubes to that water in the first place. Removing the ice cubes would be the *inverse.*

Reciprocal determinism. A theory of human functioning which states that personal factors (e.g., attitudes), behaviors, and environmental forces are the determinants of each other (i.e., they are reciprocally determining influences).

Reciprocal inhibition. The idea that if a response can be taught that is incompatible with an undesired response, the new response will inhibit the old response. For example, if an anxious client is taught relaxation, the relaxation is incompatible with being anxious and will come to inhibit the anxiety.

Recognition. A means of measuring learning through asking a person to recognize what he or she has learned. For example, suppose we show a person photographs of 10 people for 10 seconds; and then later show 50 photographs with these 10 scattered about; the number properly selected would be those correctly recognized.

Recruitment phase. Initial response of a receptor to stimulation.

Redintegration. A special kind of recall triggered by a single stimulus in which an entire complex memory is achieved.

Reflective abstraction. A general cognitive process of thinking about the procedures that produced an interesting event and thereby abstracting the general form of those procedures. To be distinguished from physical abstraction, defined as thinking about the physical features of objects that exist in the environment.

Reflex. An innate, automatic, unplanned-for, and generally uncontrollable response to a stimulus. Cowering when struck suddenly is a reflex action. Skinner: Neither stimulus nor response, but a reliable correlation between a stimulus and the response it elicits.

Reflex-circle. The tendency for muscle movements to activate reflex loops which, in turn, strengthen the muscle movements.

Refractory period. The period (usually very brief, in the nature of a millisecond) when the muscle or nerve is unresponsive to stimuli which occur immediately after stimulation and activation. During the absolute refractory period, no response at all occurs; during the relative refractory period, a much stronger than normal stimulus is necessary to get the nerve or muscle to respond.

Regulation. Piaget: Any procedure which the organism uses to reestablish the integrity or logical consistency of the organic system which has been temporarily disturbed.

Reinforcement. An increase in responding produced by the consequences of a response.

Reinforcement schedule. The arrangement of intermittent reinforcement, or reinforcement of only some of the responses within an operant class. Reinforcement may be scheduled on the basis of number of responses, passage of time, or rate of responding. See specific cases: *differential-reinforcement-of-rate schedules, fixed-interval schedule, fixed-ratio schedule, variable-interval schedule, variable-ratio schedule.*

Reinforcement value. From a specific list of reinforcements that are all equally likely to occur, the degree to which the person would prefer a given one to occur.

Reinforcer. A stimulus that is effective in increasing responding when its presentation or removal is a consequence of responding. Stimuli effective when presented (e.g., food produced by a rat's lever presses) are called *positive reinforcers.* Stimuli effective when removed (e.g., electric shock terminated by an escape response) are called *negative reinforcers.*

Reinforcing stimulus. Any *stimulus* that strengthens the *response.*

Relational determination. Attributes of related parts are affected by the nature of the relationships among them.

Relearning. The process of learning again what had been forgotten. The difference in time or energy of this second learning over the first learning represents the "saving" due to some memory still being in the brain.

Reorganization. A change in how a whole is articulated, usually resulting in greater *Prägnanz.*

Respondent. A class of responses defined by its eliciting stimulus. For example, one respondent class consists of the knee jerks elicited by taps on the patellar tendon.

Respondent behavior. Behavior elicited by a specific stimulus.

Respondent conditioning. In operant theory, the equivalent of classical or Pavlovian conditioning.

Response. Any instance of behavior whether emitted or elicited.

Response acquisition. The acquisition of a response through a learning procedure.

Response amplitude. A measure of response strength.

Response chaining. See *chaining.*

Response class. A category of behavior.

Response hierarchy. The family of response potentials possessed by an organism, ordered according to probability of occurrence.

Response latency. The time interval between presentation of a stimulus and the onset of the organism's response.

Response probability. The relative frequency of occurrence of a given response, or the theoretical relative frequency of a given response.

Response-reinforcement analysis. An analysis of behavior which bases the explanation of an observation on reinforcement principles. Such an analysis usually implies that the explanation need not appeal to mediating processes such as cognitions.

Retention interval. In a memory experiment, this refers to the time that has elapsed between the presentation of some material and the test of whether the subject has retained any of that material.

Retrieval. The processes by which encoded and stored information is brought from storage to use. These processes include recognition, reconstruction, and recall.

Retroactive inhibition. The disruptive effect of later learning by material learned earlier. *X* now learned negatively affects *Y,* learned before. (See *proactive inhibition.*)

Retroactive interference. Forgetting of material produced by the learning of subsequent material. (See *proactive interference.*)

Reversibility. Piaget: A general concept whereby the individual understands the relation between undoing and conservation. For example, say the individual sees water in a tall, skinny glass poured into a short, wide glass. The individual understands that, since this change can be reversed, the apparent change in quantity is not real.

Reward. Guthrie: A stimulus or, more properly, a change in stimulation. Since the last response to occur in the presence of a stimulus is learned, reward acts to preserve or maintain associations by changing the stimulus before a new response occurs.

Reaction time (RT). The time between the

onset of a stimulus and the response to that stimulus.

RTT. Refers to an experimental procedure using a *paired-associate learning* method, denoting three trials. A reinforced trial, *R*, in which the stimulus-response pair is presented together; a second trial that is a test trial, *T,* in which only the stimulus is presented; the third trial is another test trial, *T,* in which again only the stimulus is presented. On both test trials the subject is to give the appropriate response; however, the subject is not told if the response he or she gave is correct or not.

Rule-governed behavior. Behavior under the control of verbal instructions. Such behavior is usually contrasted with *contingency-governed behavior,* which is behavior under the control of its consequences.

Saltatory learning. Proceeding by leaps and bounds; learning that increases dramatically. This term is used generally in *Gestalt* learning theory and occurs when there is insight into a solution.

Satisfier. Any situation which leads to satisfaction.

Saving method. Experimental procedure to measure strength of retention through decrease in time/errors/trials, etc., for relearning forgotten material.

Schedule of reinforcement see reinforcement schedule.

Schizokinesis. A term used to describe the finding that physiological responses to conditioning may remain long after the overt conditioned responses have ceased to exist.

Second signal system. Pavlov's term for language. He believed lower animals were restricted to object thinking because they had only a primary signal system, whereas humans were capable of higher-order thinking because of their second signal system, or language.

Secondary reinforcement. A stimulus which derives its reinforcing qualities from association with a primary reinforcer.

Selection. This is a function of attention: picking some elements out of many in the environment.

Selection pressure. A challenge from the environment, such as the presence of predators or the shortage of food, to which some animals are better adapted than others and are thus better able to survive and reproduce.

Selectivity (selective attention). A term referring to a common observation in which some features of the environment are attended to, while other features are not.

Self-efficacy. A person's self-perceived or actual abilities to produce desired results.

Self-regulatory process. A person's tendency to regulate his or her own behavior by cognitive processes.

Semantic generalization. A response elicited not only by the conditioned word or sentence, but also by other stimuli not directly conditioned. These other stimuli usually have some logical connection with the CS. Generalization is assumed to occur through a mediational process.

Sensory preconditioning. A procedure wherein two stimuli are first presented to establish an association. A response is then conditioned to the first of these stimuli. The second stimulus is later presented to determine if it will also elicit the conditioned response, which it usually does.

Serial position. The place that an item occupies in a series.

Serial processing. A flow of internal information wherein each *stage* operates sequentially. Until a stage has completed its processing, there is no output for the next stage to use.

Shaping. Differential reinforcement of successive approximations to a response.

Sharpening. The tendency to exaggerate minor differences among objects, shapes, or structures.

Sigmoid relationship. A relationship between performance and some manipulated variable, where performance shows a rapid increase early in training, followed by a more gradual increase later in training.

Sign-Gestalt. Tolman: Articulated complex whole symbolized by a stimulus.

Sign-Gestalt-expectation. Tolman's term for the expectation built up within an organism that a particular action in a particular situation is likely to lead to a particular outcome.

Signaling. An informal term for the discriminative functions of a stimulus.

Skinner box. The experimental chamber developed by Skinner for the study of free-operant responding. The term is common outside of the experimental analysis of behavior but is infrequently used by researchers within that field.

Social facilitation effect. Elicitation of previously learned responses through exposure to a model. One of the three modeling influences suggested by Bandura.

Social learning theories. Any of several learning theories to the effect that personality is a function of learned responses to stimuli (usually other people) in the environment.

Spacing effect. Refers to a phenomenon in memory which indicates that memory performance improves as the time between presentations of the same material increases.

Specialization. Any distinctive adaptation of body or behavior.

Species-specific, species-typical. Species-characteristic behaviors. Adaptive behaviors showing various degrees of species specificity.

Spontaneous recovery. The return of a lost response following rest.

Spontaneous regression. A reduction in the strength of a conditioned response as a result of the passage of time from the end of one learning session to the beginning of the next session during the acquisition phase.

Stage. A hypothetical internal device which performs one mental transformation upon information flowing through it. Piaget: A general capability of cognitive functioning that is qualitatively different from general capabilities that define the preceding stage of development. The stages are sometimes called periods, such as the sensorimotor period, preoperational period, concrete operational period, and formal operational period.

Stage iv error. Piaget: An error that occurs during the later half of the sensorimotor period. The infant will search for an object behind the screen where he or she last found a toy instead of behind the screen where he or she most recently saw the toy hidden. For example, if the infant successfully finds the toy behind screen A on two occasions, he or she will return to screen A immediately after see-ing the toy hidden behind screen B. Sometimes called the AAB error.

State-dependent retrieval. Retrieval of material is often better when an organism is tested in the same state as when the material was learned, as opposed to an altered state.

Stimulus. Something that affects the organism outside of the organism, affecting one or more of the senses, such as light, sound, or touch. Any form of energy which impinges on receptor organs and stimulates them. Light is a stimulus for the retina, for example.

Stimulus afferent impulse. Neural activity resulting from stimulation of a sensory receptor.

Stimulus control. The control of responding by discriminative stimuli.

Stimulus evocation paradox. Although a stimulus-response bond (habit) may be formed, the exact stimulus is unlikely to ever reappear. Learning, however, will be manifest in performance, since all the habits elicited by various stimuli in a learning situation will summate.

Stimulus generalization. The fact that a response conditioned to one stimulus may also occur to other stimuli.

Stimulus generalization gradient. The relationship between stimulus similarity and the strength of a response. The more similar a stimulus is to the original conditioned stimuli, the greater the conditioned response will be.

Stimulus intensity dynamism (V). Hull: An *intervening variable* representing the fact that an intense stimulus will elicit an intense response.

Stimulus learning paradox. Some learning requires multiple presentations of stimuli, yet exactly the same stimuli do not repeat themselves from trial to trial. Since habits generalize, however, and generalized habits summate, the growth of habits can still be predicted to occur across trials (see *generalized habit strength*).

Stimulus sampling theory. Estes: The basic concept views the stimulus as a hypothetical population of entities called stimulus elements. On any one learning trial, an organism is assumed to be exposed to a subset of the population called a sample.

Stimulus situation. The external (or internal) events surrounding an organism that typically is related to the behavior of the organism.

Stochastic model. A model based upon a random or probabilistic process.

Storage. The process by which a person puts information into memory. The information persists during an interval of no practice.

Strain. The development of interruptions of responding as a result of increasing the response requirements of a reinforcement schedule. The term is most commonly applied to ratio strain; with increases in the number of responses required per reinforcer, the steady high-rate responding usually maintained by ratio schedules is likely to be broken up by frequent long pauses in responding.

Strategy, behavior. A pattern of behavior organized for long-term benefits rather than short-term effectiveness.

Structure. The internal articulation of a whole.

Subtractive method. A technique developed by Donders to calculate the time required for mental processes by subtracting the time taken to perform tasks with different components.

Successive approximations. What the individual goes through in *trial-and-error* learning, making small steps (which are rewarded) and small steps (which are not rewarded); repeating the rewarded small steps and giving up tne unrewarded small steps; moving gradually to the final goal or standard of performance.

Superstition. In *operant* theory, the maintenance of behavior by accidental relations between responses and reinforcers. If responding that happens incidentally to be followed by a reinforcer is affected in the same way as when the responding actually produces the reinforcer, the responding may be said to be superstitiously maintained. The concept of superstition is controversial.

Suprathreshold excitatory potential. Reaction potential (E) which exceeds the minimal threshold value needed to result in observable activity.

Sympathetic nervous system. Part of the *autonomic nervous system;* a chain of ganglia on either side of the spinal column.

Synapse. The point of junction between two neurons where *acetylcholine* is manufactured to convey electrical nerve impulses.

Tabula rasa. Term used by John Locke, meaning a "blank tablet" and referring to the human mind as free and uncluttered and as containing no innate ideas.

Test-trial technique. A procedure used in classical conditioning to evaluate the strength or weakness of a conditioned response. Specifically, test trials are given in which the CS alone is presented for longer duration than on training trials.

Temporal conditioning. A form of classical conditioning in which the time interval between repeated presentations of the US come to serve as a CS. That is, the time interval itself comes to be the CS.

Threshold. A place along a graded series of stimulus intensity at which the organism will respond 50 percent of the time; the *limen.*

Timesharing. An experimental *paradigm* wherein a person must perform two distinct tasks together at the same time.

Token economy. A system of reinforcement used for modifying behavior in groups, usually in institutional settings. For example, tokens may be used to maintain the self-care behavior (brushing teeth, washing, coming to meals) of patients on a psychiatric ward. In effect, the tokens are conditioned reinforcers, functioning much like money in the standard economy.

Topography. The form of a response. A rat's lever press with one paw is topographically different from a press with both paws, even if both are equally effective in depressing the lever.

Topological psychology. Lewin: Diagrams used to depict an individual's life span.

Topology. A nonmetric modern form of mathematics which describes relations among regions in space.

Trace conditioning. In this form of conditioning, the CS is first presented and then removed before the US is presented. Not as efficient as simultaneous conditioning.

Trace decay theory. Notion that some memory traces lose their strength simply because of the passage of time.

Trace field. The long-term memory, which

contains traces (continuing aftereffects) of particular experiences.

Transfer. Carrying over an activity (such as a problem-solving strategy) from one situation to a different but similar situation. The facilitating (positive transfer) or disruptive (negative transfer) effect of old learning on present learning. Learning to steer a car may have negative transfer value on learning to steer a boat. Usually called transfer of training.

Transfer of learning. The effect of prior learning on new learning.

Transitivity task. Any of a variety of tasks which requires the individual to deduce the relation of two terms, *A* and *C,* from information given about the relation between *A* and *B* as well as *B* and *C.* For example, given that *A* is larger than *B* and that *B* is larger than *C,* it is true by logical necessity that *A* is larger than *C.* An individual who solves the transitivity task realizes that the nature of the *AC* relation is contained in the information given about *AB* and *BC.*

"Transsums." Wholes that transcend the sum total of their component parts. (See *"Andsums."*)

Traumatic learning. Learning due to some previously neutral event being associated with some painful event.

Trial-and-error learning. The kind of learning that occurs when an organism successively tries various behaviors to achieve a particular end, and gives up on those behaviors that do not work and retains those that do. An example would be a cat in a cage learning how to operate a simple latch to escape.

Trials to criterion. The number of trials needed to reach a criterion set by the experimenter; for example, the number of trials taken to recall a list perfectly.

Two-factor theory. See *Interference theory.*

Two-process theory. Mowrer: **One of the** basic theoretical approaches in learning, wherein a phenomenon is explained by resorting to a theory that assumes two processes are operating to account for it. An example is to assume that the organism first learns to be fearful and then associates the reduction of fear with jumping over a barrier, as in a classical avoidance situation.

Unconditioned reflex or response (UR). The natural response or reflex to a particular stimulus, such as a hungry dog salivating at the sound and smell of food.

Unconditioned stimulus (US). A stimulus that is naturally capable of producing a reflex action or a particular response, such as food producing an unconditioned response of salivation. The stimulus that evokes an *unconditioned response* (UR) naturally and normally.

U-shaped function. A graph shaped like a U.

Variable-interval (VI) schedule. A reinforcement schedule which arranges a reinforcer for the first response occurring some time after an environmental event, and in which this time varies from one reinforcer to the next (see *fixed-interval schedule*).

Variable-ratio (VR) schedule. A reinforcement schedule in which each reinforcer is produced by some number of responses, and this number varies from one reinforcer to the next (see *fixed-ratio schedule*).

Wholism. See *Holism.*

Zeigarnik effect. The tension that results if a task is incomplete, which results in "unfinished business"; the tendency to remember or want to go on to something that is not finished, such as remembering a joke if the "point" has not been made. Recalling more incompleted than completed tasks.

Name Index

Subject Index

THE BOOK MANUFACTURE

Theories of Learning: A Comparative Approach was typeset at Fox Valley Typesetting, Menasha, Wis. Printing and binding was by Parthenon Press, Nashville. Cover design was by Mead Design, internal design by the F. E. Peacock Publishers art department. The typeface is Times Roman.